PHILOSOPHY

An Introduction
to the Art of Wondering

JAMES L. CHRISTIAN

CHAIRMAN, DEPARTMENT OF PHILOSOPHY
SANTA ANA COLLEGE, SANTA ANA, CALIFORNIA

PHILOS

AN INTRODUCTION TO THE

OPHY

ART OF WONDERING

RINEHART PRESS

SAN FRANCISCO

Uno itinere non potest perveniri ad tam grande secretum.

"The heart of so great a mystery can never be reached by following one road only."

Q. AURELIUS SYMMACHUS
Relatio Tertia

Philosophy: An Introduction to the Art of Wondering by James L. Christian

Acknowledgments for the use of quoted and copyrighted materials are given on pages 509–522.

© 1973 by Rinehart Press, 5643 Paradise Drive, Corte Madera, Calif. 94925
A division of Holt, Rinehart and Winston, Inc.

Library of Congress Catalog Card Number: 72-90221
ISBN: 0-03-080259-8

PRINTED IN THE UNITED STATES OF AMERICA
4 5 6 7   061   9 8 7 6 5 4

Prelude

The following pages
may cause you to wonder.
That's what philosophy is.
Wondering.

To philosophize
is to wonder about life—
about right and wrong,
love and loneliness,
war and death,
about freedom, truth, beauty, time . . .
and a thousand other things.

To philosophize
is to explore life.
It means breaking free
to ask questions.
It means resisting
easy answers.
To philosophize
is to seek in oneself
the courage to ask
painful questions.

But if, by chance,
you have already asked
all your questions
and found all the answers—
if you're sure you know
right from wrong,
and whether God exists,
and what justice means,
and why men fear and hate and pray—
if indeed you have done your wondering
about freedom and love and loneliness
and those thousand other things,
then the following pages
will waste your time.

Philosophy is for those
who are willing to be disturbed
with a creative disturbance.

Philosophy is for those
who still have the capacity
for wonder.

CONTENTS

PART 3: THE REAL WORLD: KNOWING AND UNKNOWING

PART 5: COEXISTENCE: MAN'S LOVE/HATE CONDITION

PART 6: THE PROTOPLASMIC VENTURE

PART 7: MICROCOSM/MACROCOSM/COSMOS

PART 8: OF ULTIMATE CONCERN

CREDIT/BLAME/ ACKNOWLEDGMENTS

I have written this book for my philosophy students . . . and for all who are caught up in the wonderment of life—its mystery, its enormity, its diversity.

All of us wonder, sometime or often, about our place within the existential ecosystem. What we are asking is how we can relate most happily to ourselves, to others close about us, to fellow creatures with whom we share our delicate planet, and to our mind-boggling, pulsating, multibubble universe. We burn with an urgency to know all that can be known, but we search for a *method* to help us assimilate that knowledge with insight.

A philosophy text should offer cautious counsel to all who would seek intelligent, nonpartisan guidance on the life-and-death questions of human existence; but many textbooks are found wanting in the face of life's final questions.

Eliot Aronson notes that so many of our students ask us what time it is, and we respond by presenting to them the history of time-keeping from waterclocks to wristwatches. By the time we finish, they have turned elsewhere to ask their questions.

And J. B. Priestley hurts when he reminds us that the man who shouts "My house is on fire!" may not be able to define precisely what he means by *my* and *house* and *is* and *on* and *fire*, but he may still be saying something very, very important.

That's why this book has been written.

* * * * * * *

One gratifying—though quite unexpected—discovery has been the potential use of this book in interdisciplinary studies. During development, a typescript of this text was used with five semesters of classes. When it came time in the schedule to discuss topics closely related to specialized disciplines, colleagues from those fields were invited to lecture to our philosophy classes. They did so . . . and gave us far more than we could have anticipated; for what they shared with us was not at all their own specialized knowledge, but rather their larger reflections upon the meaning of their own areas of inquiry. That is, they *philosophized* about their fields and shared their insights and broader concerns with us, reflections of great value which many of the teachers probably never get around to sharing with their own classes. I found colleagues always willing to share, and our classes were invariably richer for it.

* * * * * * *

For an author to attempt to pay his debts is sheer folly . . . but I must try. I owe so much to so many who have understood and lent me strength. As I scribbled out my ideas, it was a continual surprise to discover that so many of the notions I assumed to be my own turned out to have developed from seeds planted by others, and really belong to them. Such insights spread through my being like colored dye, their sources too easily forgotten.

To several generations of philosophy students: Thank you for a myriad of ideas, wrestlings, ponderings; for gathering volumes of materials; for critical suggestions for the book in its developmental phase (you were not always gentle, but you *were* always helpful).

To colleagues: Thank you for your encouragement; for taking time to read portions of the typescript; for your assistance in developing illustrations. A special thank you to Dave Hartman and Ron Smith.

To the men at Rinehart Press—Dick Raihall, Greg Hubit, and Emmett Dingley: Your professionalism never wavered and your warmth as men was never compromised by the pragmatics of production. As Managing Editor, Greg Hubit has handled the book's complexities in a way which insured that the final product would be faithful to the original dream. A special word of appreciation to Alden Paine: Your perceptive guidance at the inception of this project meant more than we can say.

To some special people who, in a variety of ways, are part of this book, thank you . . . many times over: Terry Allen, Bob Baker, Carol Friesen, Marge Hennen, Court Holdgrafer, Nancy Jones, Don Meyer, Bob Moore (photographer par excellence), Jill Olson, Bob Putman, Doris Sauter, Dorothy Symms, John Velasquez, Larry West.

To all who granted permission to use materials, our sincere appreciation. Due credit has been noted at the back of this book, and we earnestly hope there have been no oversights. Many individuals have given us more than perfunctory responses, and, in extra ways, gave us their time, help, and, in some cases, friendship. We would like to acknowledge those extra courtesies: Ray Bradbury, John Buechler, Abner Dean, Houston Harte, Jay W. Klug, Kelly Lange, Stanley Miller, Cyril Ponnamperuma, Maarten Schmidt, Ralph Solecki, Joseph Stacey, Harry Torczyner, Helmut Wimmer.

To the publishers and institutions who granted us permission to reproduce materials, thank you. Again, we found that many of you went beyond the routine requirements of business protocol, and we would like to acknowledge those who went the extra mile: *Audubon, Esquire,* Fairchild Stamp Co., Harvard College Observatory, International Society for General Semantics, *Life,* National Accelerator Laboratory, National Aeronautics and Space Administration, National Geographic Society, *Playboy, Psychology Today, The Smithsonian,* Edith Tolkin of MGM, Charles E. Tuttle.

To some other people—perplexing innocents all, but wise—who are very special: Cathy, Dane, Carla, Marcia, Sherrie, Reinar, Laurie, Shawna, Shannon, Linda. Somehow, there were those of you who understood. *Thank you.*

J.L.C.

Dedications

EDWIN PRINCE BOOTH

Though it comes too late, thank you for showing me why we must tirelessly seek out the profoundly human element in all events since only therein can their meaning be found. . . .

ARNOLD TOYNBEE

Thank you for the passion to see all existence as a single phenomenon without losing sight of the most minute details—this cave painting, this footnote, this flower in this crannied wall. . . .

HERMAN and ANNE

Thank you each for a parent's love, and more; for faith, hope, strength, phone calls, and countless instances of critically-timed support. There are no words to express my appreciation of you both. . . .

BARBARA, my wife

Thank you for your faith in, and unwavering dedication to, the completion of our book; for an incisive intellect which can clarify even the muddiest of philosophical problems; for a rare creative brilliance in the understanding of psychodynamic processes; for the relentless reminders to relate helium-filled abstractions to real people; . . . for loving me.

What do you mean philosophy???

1   Sometime, at your leisure—if you want to know what philosophy is—go into a large bookstore and browse. Check a variety of books in psychology, anthropology, physics, chemistry, archeology, astronomy, and other nonfiction fields. Look at the last chapter in each book. In a surprising number of cases, you will find that the author has chosen to round out his work with a final summation of what the book is all about. That is, having written a whole book on a specialized subject in which he is probably an authority, he finds that he *also* has ideas about the larger meaning of the facts that he has written about. The final chapter may be called "Conclusions," "Epilogue," "Postscript," "My Personal View," "Implications," "Comments," "Speculations," or (as in one case) "So What?" But in every instance, the author is trying to elucidate the larger implications of his subject matter and to clarify how he thinks it relates to other fields or to life. He has an urge to tell us *the meaning* of all his facts *taken together*. He wants to share with us the *philosophic implications* of what he has written.

When he does this, the author has moved beyond the role of a field specialist. He is a philosopher.

2   This is a textbook in synoptic° philosophy. It is an invitation to ponder, in the largest possible perspective, the weightier, more stubborn problems of human existence. It is an invitation to think—to wonder, to question, to speculate, to reason, even to fantasize—in the eternal search for wisdom. In a word, synoptic philosophy is an attempt to weave interconnecting lines of illumination between all the disparate

For man, the unexamined life is not worth living.
SOCRATES

° *Synoptic.* **From the Greek** *sunoptikos,* **"seeing the whole together" or "taking a comprehensive view." The attempt to achieve an all-inclusive overview of one's subject matter. See glossary.**

realms of human thought in the hope that, like a thousand dawnings, new insights will burst through.

By its very nature, philosophy is a do-it-yourself enterprise. There is a common misunderstanding that philosophy—like chemistry or history—has a content to offer, a content which a teacher is to teach and a student is to learn. This is not the case. There are no facts, no theories, certainly no final truths which go by the name of "philosophy" and which one is supposed to accept and believe. Rather, philosophy is a skill—more akin to mathematics and music; it is something that one *learns to do*.

Philosophy, that is, is a *method*. It is *learning how* to ask and re-ask questions until meaningful answers begin to appear. It is *learning how* to relate materials. It is *learning where* to go for the most dependable, up-to-date information that might shed light on some problem. It is *learning how* to double check fact-claims in order to verify or falsify them. It is *learning how* to reject fallacious fact-claims—to reject them no matter how prestigious the authority who holds them or how deeply one would personally like to believe them.

3   The student should be aware that philosophy has never been just one kind of activity with a single approach to a single task. Rather, there have been many kinds of philosophy: the quiet philosophy of the

Understanding man and his place in the universe is perhaps the central problem of all science.

DUNN AND DOBZHANSKY

The meaning of life is arrived at . . . by dark gropings, by feelings not wholly understood, by catching at hints and fumbling for explanations.

ALFRED ADLER

What Do You Mean Philosophy???

sage who sees much but speaks little because language cannot hold life; the articulate, noisy dialectics of Socrates; the calm, logical apologetics of Aquinas; the mystical philosophy of Plotinus and Chuang-tzu; the mathematical philosophy of Russell and Wittgenstein.

Each school of philosophy has concentrated upon some aspect of man's knowledge. Logical/analytical philosophy has worked long and hard on the confusion which vitiates so much of our thinking and communicating. Pragmatism has concentrated on finding solutions to problems of man's social existence. Existential philosophy has been concerned with making life meaningful to each, unique individual. Activist schools argue that philosophers spend too much time trying to make sense of the world and too little time trying to change it. Several schools of philosophy, Eastern and Western, challenge the individual to turn away from an alienating society and to seek harmony with Nature or Ultimate Reality.

Each kind of philosophy has made an immense contribution to its area of concern. Each was doubtless a part of the *Zeitgeist*—"the spirit of the age"—which gave it birth and to which it spoke.

The present unhappy condition of human knowledge calls for the application of a synoptic methodology. We now possess vast accumulations of specialized knowledge in countless fields, but these fields remain isolated from one another. Yet it is increasingly clear that many of our urgent problems can be understood only when the specialized information from a variety of these separate fields is integrated and "seen together"—synoptically. It is only then that we can develop realistic solutions to these complex problems.

What all the schools of philosophy have in common is a concern for the condition of human knowledge and our knowledge of the human condition.

There's a cartoon strip with a picture of a little girl who sets up a psychiatric booth which says "Psychotherapy 5¢." In Los Angeles a chaplain at a college has set up a booth which says "Spiritual Counseling 5¢," and he says that one of his most frequent questions is "What is the meaning of life?" The answer to that ought to be worth at least 5¢.

DAVID BRINKLEY
"NBC Nightly News"

4   It is often said that philosophers engage in two basic tasks: "taking apart"—*analyzing* ideas to discover if we truly know what we think we know (and we don't)—and "putting together"—*synthesizing* all our knowledge to find if we can attain a larger and better view of life (we can).

But in practice philosophers do a lot more than this. They talk a lot. They carry on dialogues with anyone who comes within range. And they argue a great deal. Not the usual kinds of argument in which egos fight to win, but philosophical arguments in which they attempt to clarify the reasoning that lies behind their statements; and no one cares about winning since, in philosophical arguments, everyone wins.

They also ask one another for definitions to be sure they're thinking clearly; and they push one another to pursue the implications of their ideas and statements. They prod themselves and others to examine the basic assumptions upon which their beliefs and arguments rest.

Philosophers are persistent explorers in the nooks and crannies of human knowledge which are commonly overlooked or deliberately ignored. It is an exciting but restless adventure of the mind.

5   Philosophers, however, do not engage in this critical task just to make nuisances of themselves. Indeed, the central aim of philosophers has always been . . . to construct a picture of the whole of reality, in which every element of man's knowledge and every aspect of man's experience will find its proper place. Philosophy, in short, is man's quest for the unity of knowledge: it consists in a perpetual struggle to create the concepts in which the universe can be conceived as a *uni*verse and not a *multi*verse. The history of philosophy is the history of this attempt. The problems of philosophy are the problems that arise when the attempt is made to grasp this total unity. . . .

It cannot be denied that this attempt stands without rival as the most audacious enterprise in which the mind of man has ever engaged. Just reflect for a moment: Here is man, surrounded by the vastness of a universe in which he is only a tiny and perhaps insignificant part—and he wants to *understand* it. . . .

WILLIAM HALVERSON

6   In one respect, philosophic material can be deceptive. Since it deals with life by examining the sort of questions we ask every day, some of the subject matter will have an easy, familiar ring.

The fact is that synoptic philosophy must be as diligently studied as any other subject, not to remember data, but to set the mind in motion toward developing larger concepts, connecting ideas, and seeing through and beyond mere words and facts.

In a sense, intellectual growth *happens to us;* it is not really something that we do. But it happens to us only when our minds are given a chance to operate on their terms. They take their own time to process information and to begin developing a web of interconnecting lines of illumination among their materials. This undertaking is partly conscious, of course; but largely it is an unconscious process. This is why much philosophic insight just happens, as though the light moves from the depths upward and not from the rational conscious downward.

Only disciplined study with an open mind will produce philosophic awareness. Insight and consciousness still come only with relentless labor. In this age of instant everything, there is still no instant wisdom, unfortunately.

7   No two of us possess precisely the same information, or see things from the same viewpoint, or share the same values. Therefore, each of us must do synoptic philosophy in his own unique and personal way. A student entering upon the activity of philosophizing may need to be on guard against developing a world-view which resembles, a bit too closely, the prepackaged philosophy of life belonging to someone else or to some institution. Most of us are philosophically lazy, and it is easy to appropriate another's thoughts and rationalize our theft. The British logician Wittgenstein warned us that "a thought which is not independent is a thought only half understood." Similarly, a philosophy of life that is not the authentic product of one's own experience is a philosophy only half understood.

Nor will any of us succeed in developing a finished philosophy; for as one changes with life, so does one's thinking. A philosophy *of life* must change *with life.* Doing philosophy is an endless activity.

For this reason, this textbook is merely an example of synoptic philosophy. This is the way I have had to do it because of *my* perspectives, *my* interests, *my* areas of knowledge, *my* personal concerns, and *my* limitations. But *your* world-view will be different because it will be *yours,* and *yours alone.*

This is why my attempt to do synoptic philosophy is, at most, a guideline showing how it might be done; at least, the expression of a hope that, someday, in your own way, you will resolve the contradictions of your own existence—both of knowing and of being—and proceed to see life in a larger, more fulfilling way.

"There is an old saying that philosophy bakes no bread. It is perhaps equally true that no bread would ever have been baked without philosophy. For the act of baking implies a decision on the philosophical issue of whether life is worthwhile at all. Bakers may not have often asked themselves the question in so many words. But philosophy traditionally has been nothing less than the attempt to ask and answer, in a formal and disciplined way, the great questions of life that ordinary men put to themselves in reflective moments."
Time, *January 7, 1966*

As soon as man does not take his existence for granted, but beholds it as something unfathomably mysterious, thought begins.
ALBERT SCHWEITZER

One can tell for oneself whether the water is warm or cold.
I Ching

1

THE FINE ART
OF WONDERING

1-1

THE

WORLD-RIDDLE

1   Shortly before a solar eclipse was to occur in central India, an Indian physicist—who was also a member of the Brahmin caste—was lecturing to his students at the university. He told them precisely when the event would begin and described in detail how the moon's orbit would take it between the sun and the earth. In their city there would be only a partial eclipse, but on a wall map he pointed out the path of totality as it moved across the terrestrial globe to the north of them. They discussed such things as the corona, solar flares, the beauty of annular rings, and the appearance of Bailey's beads during that rare total eclipse. Some of the students from the rural villages had heard stories about a Giant Dragon that swallowed the sun, but their teacher's lucid presentation of celestial mechanics had dispelled any fears they might have felt.

Having dismissed his class, the professor returned to his village and, since he was a Brahmin, assumed his duties as a priest. Around his shoulders he draped the vestments of his office and began counting through his string of beads, calling aloud the names of the gods. A goat was beheaded in sacrifice to Kali, the Black Goddess, the cause and controller of earthquakes, storms, and other evil things, and the archenemy of demons. Prayers were offered to her that she might frighten away the Dragon. "Glory to Mother Kali," the priest and people chanted.

While in the classroom there was nothing illogical about describing the solar eclipse in terms of celestial mechanics; neither was there anything wrong in offering a gift to the Black Goddess—*just in case . . .*

2   To sensitive spirits of all ages, life is filled with cruel contradictions and bitter ironies. Human experience is capricious and our finite

The most important thing . . . we can know about a man is what he takes for granted, and the most elemental and important facts about a society are those that are seldom debated and generally regarded as settled.

LOUIS WIRTH

minds are not able to see enough of life *at one time* for us to know for sure what is going on. We see only fragments of life, and never the whole. We are not unlike children struggling with a jigsaw puzzle handed to us as a cosmic joke.

Just under the surface of the entire human enterprise, implicit in all we think and do, there lies the eternal question: *What is the meaning of existence?* It is the ultimate question of all Mankind, yet it must be reopened by each of us in our turn. If we refuse to take the contradictions of life for granted; if we can't accept prepackaged solutions; if we can't persuade ourselves to accept a mere fragment of life as the whole of life—then for all of us, the question persists. While we may have great difficulty finding satisfactory answers to it, we also know that there is no escape from it.

Philosophy is the eternal search for truth, a search which inevitably fails and yet is never defeated; which continually eludes us, but which always guides us. This free, intellectual life of the mind is the noblest inheritance of the Western world; it is also the hope of our future.

W. T. JONES

Information on illustrations, along with sources and credits, will be found on pages 516ff.

3   On the real-life scene where the human tragicomedy plays itself out, our question splits into two further practical questions. Stated positively: How can we make life worth living? Stated negatively: How can we prevent life from turning into tragedy?

Through the ages, man has sought clues to life's meaning through his religions and philosophies. To date they have given us immense help, but a contemporary overview of Mankind's quest supplies us with a superabundance of answers, so many answers in fact that we can't decide among them. Some would attempt to evade the problem by a "leap of faith" into a garden of plastic flowers, while others play a sort of religious roulette. But such arbitrary shortcuts fail to face the essential complexity of human existence.

Furthermore, after a more critical reexamination, we discover that most of man's religions and many of his philosophies have concluded that, in the final analysis, life-in-this-world is *not* worth living. At best it's but a time of troubles to be endured until we can reach something better.

Today, that's a conclusion we find difficult to live with.

4   In Panshin's *Rite of Passage* the heroine, a young girl, states candidly: "If you want to accept life, you have to accept the whole bloody universe." She may be right. But how can we really "accept" a universe of wild and destructive contradictions? After all, we seem to be as ambivalent about ultimate realities as the Indian physicist/priest.

The natural world is not the contradiction today that it was some four centuries ago with the birth of the New Science. We are fairly secure in our general mathematical descriptions of the physical universe. Our "scientific laws" will undergo continued refinement, of course, and there is little doubt that we will discover new realms, or new dimensions, of realities. But there is such a high degree of consistency to our experience of nature's operations that we have arrived at the point of accepting a naturalistic world-view *for nature*. With this physical universe—from galaxies and gravity fields to television and laser beams—we have made our peace. Though our comprehension of nature is far from complete, we can live with the foundations of understanding so far secured. The unintegrated cosmos which challenged the existence of ancient men and eluded their understanding is no longer a bewildering problem to us.

Our serious problems, therefore, lie buried somewhere within the protoplasmic venture which we call "life." To borrow a phrase from Buckminster Fuller, the puzzlement seems to be that this protoplasmic experiment came without an instruction manual.

5   Long before the birth of modern psychology, there were perceptive individuals who felt stirrings from the depths of the human organism, but it was left to Sigmund Freud to launch the fantastic journey into the inner world. As the Viennese doctor shook loose the secrets of the

Every man, whether he is religiously inclined or not, has his own ultimate presuppositions. He finds he cannot live his life without them, and for him they are true. Such presuppositions, whether they be called ideologies, philosophies, notions, or merely hunches about life, exert creative pressure upon all conduct . . .

GORDON ALLPORT

"This is all there is."

human psyche, it was no longer deniable that the subconscious mind, quite without our conscious permission, pushes us headlong into all forms of irrational behavior. The subconscious mind is a vast depository for emotionally charged experience which, for one reason or another, we cannot face; and these repressed elements determine to a large extent how we feel, think, and behave.

But, to realize that we do countless things without understanding why—this can be a soul-jarring discovery. We are manipulated, like puppets on a string, by inner forces over which we have little control. We scurry about in frenzied activity, accomplishing little else than satisfying the whims of the shadowy slavedriver. Not knowing our motivations, we don't understand what we do; and much of the time our striving brings little fulfillment.

Perhaps here is one source of the meaninglessness of our lives. We have no clear notion of what we are after, but we plunge blindly ahead in search of something.

6   "Good morning," said the little prince.
"Good morning," said the railway switchman.
"What do you do here?" the little prince asked.
"I sort out travelers, in bundles of a thousand," said the switchman. "I send off the trains that carry them: now to the right, now to the left."

And a brilliantly lighted express train shook the switchman's cabin as it rushed by with a roar like thunder.

"They are in a great hurry," said the little prince. "What are they looking for?"

"Not even the locomotive engineer knows that," said the switchman.

And a second brilliantly lighted express thundered by, in the opposite direction.

"Are they coming back already?" demanded the little prince.

"These are not the same ones," said the switchman. "It is an exchange."

"Were they not satisfied where they were?" asked the little prince.

"No one is ever satisfied where he is," said the switchman.

And they heard the roaring thunder of a third brilliantly lighted express.

"Are they pursuing the first travelers?" demanded the little prince.

"They are pursuing nothing at all," said the switchman. "They are asleep in there, or if they are not asleep they are yawning. Only the children are flattening their noses against the windowpanes."

"Only the children know what they are looking for," said the little prince. "They waste their time over a rag doll and it becomes very important to them; and if anybody takes it away from them they cry . . ."

"They are lucky," the switchman said.

SAINT-EXUPÉRY
The Little Prince

7   In Freud's world, life is at once a blessing and a curse, for *eros* (the life-force) is pitted in mortal combat against *thanatos* (the death-wish).

On the one hand, we possess drives toward self-preservation which countermand almost all other impulses. We fear the cessation of breath and sense. "Let me not see the death which I ever dread!" cried the hero of the Gilgamesh Epic three thousand years ago. While alive, we dream our dreams, work toward our goals, and feel the joyous pain of activity and growth. All this indicates the depth of our hunger for life; we will fight to the death in order to live. *Eros.*

On the other hand, "To exist is to suffer," taught the Buddha, and we have devised ingenious ways of escaping existence. We sense a futility in our dreams; an inner voice chides us for yearning for goals we can't achieve. We often have an empty feeling when we hold in our hands something we have fought for, wondering why we wanted it. All around us we see loneliness, surd hatreds, and pointless sadisms. Mephistophilis speaks for many: Hell is no fable, for *this life IS* hell. Away from all this, we are pulled toward death, as though it would be a blessing to have done with it. *Thanatos.*

Out of frustration, perhaps we ought to ask whether the essential implication of so many of man's religions and philosophies might be correct after all—the implication that the human condition is uninhabitable. Perhaps it really is possible that there is something inherently wrong. Perhaps Norman Brown is close when he calls man a "disease." It's not inconceivable that self-destruction, in some sense, is already an accomplished fact.

"Realistic people" who pursue "practical aims" are rarely as realistic or practical, in the long run of life, as the dreamers who pursue their dreams.

HANS SELYE

To lose one's life is a little thing and I shall have the courage to do so if it is necessary; but to see the meaning of this life dissipated, to see our reason for existing disappear, that is what is unbearable. One cannot live without meaning.

ALBERT CAMUS

Albert Schweitzer once wrote that he remained optimistic because hope is an indispensable ingredient of daily life, but that when he took a long look at human history he could not escape the gloom of pessimism.

When asked if he were "optimistic these days about the state of the world," Alan Watts replied: "I have to be. There is no alternative. For if I were to bet, I would bet that the human race will destroy itself by 2000. But there's nowhere to place the bet."

8 Modern men are caught in an "existential vacuum," writes Viktor Frankl, a feeling of

> the total and ultimate meaninglessness of their lives. They lack the awareness of a meaning worth living for. They are haunted by the experience of their inner emptiness, a void within themselves. . . .

The idea that so much suffering can be in vain is intolerable to me, it kept me awake all night: I'm awake now. . . .

ANDRÉ GIDE

The existential vacuum is a widespread phenomenon of the twentieth century. This is understandable; it may be due to a twofold loss that man had to undergo since he became a truly human being. At the beginning of human history, man lost some of the basic animal instincts in which an animal's behavior is embedded and by which it is secured. Such security, like Paradise, is closed to man forever; man has to make choices. In addition to this, however, man has suffered another loss in his more recent development: the traditions that had buttressed his behavior are now rapidly diminishing. No instinct tells him what he has to do, and no tradition tells him what he ought to do; soon he will not know what he wants to do. . . .

9 The search for life, if it is to succeed, must be an individual odyssey. Each of us is caught in the philosophical enterprise. There is not one of us who is not trying to make sense of his existence, and at some level of our being each is seeking fulfillment. Our experiences come pouring into us in endless variety and they do not come neatly packaged and labeled. Each one of us must select and assimilate, organize and arrange, value and apply. So we are all philosophers by default, not by choice.

To be sure, we must seek the guidance of others who have searched; we can listen to those who have found answers that work *for them.* But in the last analysis, no one else can donate an insight to us. It has to be indigenous, grown from native soil.

Nor is our quest for meaning a quixotic tilting after windmills. There are many who find, to some degree, what they are seeking; they find the clues that set them in the right direction. When we listen to their recounting of what has happened in their lives, we cannot doubt the depth of meaning to which their insights have led them.

Each of the following men, at some point in his search, found an answer or a perspective which affected the quality of his entire existence.

10 After working through the long hot days with his patients at the Lambaréné hospital, Albert Schweitzer would retire to his cluttered study in the evening and take up again the problem from which he could not escape. He was attempting to discover a positive ethical principle upon which civilization could be securely grounded.

For months on end I lived in a continual state of mental excitement. Without the least success I let my thought be concentrated, even all through my daily work at the hospital, on the real nature of world- and life-affirmation and of ethics, and on the question of what they have in common. I was wandering about in a thicket in which no path was to be found.

The story of Eden is a greater allegory than man has ever guessed. For it was truly man who, walking memoryless through paths of sunlight and shade in the morning of the world, sat down and passed a wondering hand across his heavy forehead. Time and darkness, knowledge of good and evil, have walked with him ever since . . .
LOREN EISELEY

I was leaning with all my might against an iron door which would not yield.

While in this mental condition I had to undertake a longish journey on the river. . . . Slowly we crept upstream, laboriously feeling—it was the dry season—for the channels between the sandbanks. Lost in thought I sat on the deck of the barge, struggling to find the elementary and universal conception of the ethical which I had not discovered in any philosophy. Sheet after sheet I covered with disconnected sentences, merely to keep myself concentrated on the problem. Late on the third day, at the very moment when, at sunset, we were making our way through a herd of hippopotamuses, there flashed upon my mind, unforeseen and unsought, the phrase, "Reverence for Life." The iron door had yielded: the path in the thicket had become visible. Now I had found my way to the idea in which world- and life-affirmation and ethics are contained side by side! . . .

The world-view of Reverence for Life follows from taking the world as it is. And the world means the horrible in the glorious, the meaningless in the meaningful, the sorrowful in the joyful. However it is looked at it remains to many a riddle.

But that does not mean that we need stand before the problem of life at our wits' end because we have to renounce all hope of comprehending the course of world-events as having a meaning. Reverence for Life brings us into a spiritual relation with the world which is independent of all knowledge of the universe. . . . It renews itself in us every time we look thoughtfully at ourselves and the life around us.

Reverence for Life. "In that principle my life has found a firm footing and a clear path to follow."

11   The editors of *Psychology Today* wrote a brief note after the death of Dr. Abraham Maslow. In it they remarked that he had "a joyful affirmation of life that surged through the long tapes he often dictated for us, encouraging *Psychology Today* to explore questions that have no easy answers. Much as we loved this beautiful man, we did not understand the source of his courage—until the last cassette came in."

On that tape, they say, Dr. Maslow

talked with intense introspection about an earlier heart attack that had come right after he completed an important piece of work. "I had really spent myself. This was the best I could do, and here was not only a good time to die but I was even willing to die. . . . It was what David M. Levy called the 'completion of the act.' It was like a good ending, a good close. I think actors and dramatists have that sense of the right moment for a good ending, with a phenomenological sense of good completion—that there was nothing more you could add. . . .

"My attitude toward life changed. The word I used for it now is the post-mortem life. I could just as easily have died so that my living constitutes a kind of an extra, a bonus. It's all gravy. Therefore I might just as well live as if I had already died.

"One very important aspect of the post-mortem life is that everything gets doubly precious, gets piercingly important. You get stabbed by things, by flowers and by babies and by beautiful things—just the very act of living, of walking and breathing and eating and having friends and chatting. Everything seems to look more beautiful rather than less, and one gets the much-intensified sense of miracles.

"I guess you could say that post-mortem life permits a kind of spontaneity that's greater than anything else could make possible.

"If you're reconciled with death or even if you are pretty well assured that you will have a good death, a dignified one, then every single moment of every single day is transformed because the pervasive undercurrent—the fear of death—is removed. . . . I am living an end-life where everything ought to be an end in itself, where I shouldn't waste any time preparing for the future, or occupying myself with means to later ends. . . ."

Abe's message ended there.—The Editors.

12   Dr. Gordon Allport has written, in the preface to Viktor Frankl's book *Man's Search for Meaning:*

As a longtime prisoner in bestial concentration camps, [Viktor Frankl] found himself stripped to naked existence. His father, mother, brother, and his wife died in camps or were sent to the gas ovens, so that, excepting for his sister, his entire family perished in these camps. How could he—every possession lost, every value destroyed, suffering from hunger, cold and brutality, hourly expecting extermination—how could he find life worth preserving? . . .

From [Frankl's] autobiographical fragment the reader learns much. He learns what a human being does when he suddenly realizes he has "nothing to lose except his so ridiculously naked life." Frankl's description of the mixed flow of emotion and apathy is arresting. First to the rescue comes a cold detached curiosity concerning one's fate. Swiftly, too, come strategies to preserve the remnants of one's life, though the chances of surviving are slight. Hunger, humiliation, fear and deep anger at injustice are rendered tolerable by closely guarded images of beloved persons, by religion, by a grim sense of humor, and even by glimpses of the healing beauties of nature—a tree or a sunset.

But these moments of comfort do not establish the will to live unless they help the prisoner make larger sense out of his apparently senseless suffering. It is here that we encounter the central theme of existentialism: to live is to suffer, to survive is to find meaning in the suffering. If there is a purpose in life at all, there must be a purpose in suffering and in dying. But no man can tell another what this purpose is. Each must find out for himself, and must accept the responsibility that his answer prescribes. If he succeeds he will continue to grow in spite of all indignities. Frankl is fond of quoting Nietzsche, "He who has a *why* to live can bear with almost any how."

13   Our urge to ask "Why?" seems irresistible. If, for example, an avalanche plunges down the mountainside burying sixty schoolchildren in a few seconds, is it humanly possible for the families of the children not to ask *why* it happened?

Nor is a naturalistic answer satisfying, even though a scientifically adequate one may be quite possible: "The avalanche was produced by a week of especially warm days alternating with cold nights. Much snow melted during those days, and when the water refroze at night the expanding ice gradually loosened the snowbank. The slide occurred during the daytime because melting snow finally produced enough water to weaken the last friction spots holding the snowbank to the mountainside. The snow gave way and cascaded down the slope."

Such an explanation is scientifically sound. However, at the mass funeral service for the children, imagine in your mind the presiding clergyman presenting the scientific/naturalistic explanation for the tragedy—and stopping there.

Does this not prove Frankl's thesis that, above all else, man must find meaning in his living and, finally, in his dying?

ZORBA. Why do the young die? Why does anybody die, tell me?

SCHOLAR. I don't know.

ZORBA. What's the use of all your damn books? If they don't tell you that, what the hell do they tell you?

SCHOLAR. They tell me about the agony of men who can't answer questions like yours.

Zorba the Greek

---

14   It would be comforting to know that life has meaning; it would feel good to know that "nothing happens without a purpose." But our need for meaning leads us to find easy and absurd answers to our why-questions.

In the year A.D. 410 when the city of Rome fell to Alaric the Goth, the "pagans" blamed the Christians for having abandoned the true gods of Rome; but Saint Augustine spent a dozen years writing *The City of God* to show that the fall of Rome was a part of God's plan to vanquish paganism and establish the Reign of God.

In November of 1755 one of the world's worst earthquakes struck Lisbon. In a few minutes, more than thirty thousand people were killed. The event occurred on All Saints' Day when churches throughout the land were filled with worshippers. French clergymen interpreted the disaster as punishment for the sins of the Portuguese. Protestants blamed the event upon the tyranny of the Catholics, while the Roman clergy laid the event to the fact that there were so many Protestant heretics in Catholic Portugal.

In April 1970, after the near-tragic *Apollo XIII* lunar mission was aborted, an American political leader stated on national television that mission failure was a warning from God that man is not to attempt further ventures into space. "A warning," he said; man's next attempt would result in tragic consequences.

15   In a hotel in East Africa, weary hunters relax from their safaris into the veld. In the hotel lounge one finds a comfortable set of sofas covered with zebra skins, and on one wall hang several lion skins separated by a dozen or so Masai spears spread out as a fan. Higher up, on all four walls of the lounging area, are mounted heads of game animals. One looks up at the heads of the great African antelopes: elands with long, straight horns; kudus with screw-twisted spires; dainty gazelles; stately sables with long, back-curving horns; and wildebeests with short upturned hooks. Other sentinels which look down upon visitors include the legendary African buffalo whose horns cover its forehead and spread widely on either side; a rhinoceros with double-horns rising from its snout; and a warthog with ivory tusks coming out of either side of its lower jaw and curling over its nose. Various smaller game animals are mounted between the larger heads.

Down through evolutionary time, each animal had developed a means of defense and/or killing. The overwhelming and singular thrust of evolution seems to have been to produce some mechanism of survival against attackers: horns to hold predators at bay; spiked tusks to rip apart and kill; fangs, claws, sharp hooves; thick skins, powerful jaws; sleek, strong legs for running and jumping.

Each animal must exist in unending competition with other creatures that would kill it. Species prey upon species. Nature is, after all, "red in tooth and claw."

No single animal had anything to say about it. It possessed no "freedom" to choose a "life-style." Its place in the scheme of nature is entirely determined for it. What a strange, impertinent thought—that any single, individual animal *could* have had freedom to *choose* its own life-style or to determine its "role" in life.

What forces would design creatures to prey upon one another and, at the same time, instill into each creature the capacity for intense pain and suffering?

And what an unbelievable, ironic condition: in this "deadly feast of life," each of us, in order to exist, must *eat* living things which harbor the same life-drive we possess. *Life feeds upon itself!*

16   Desmond Morris is quite sure that our problems are genetic in origin. In *The Naked Ape* he refers to the "deep-seated biological characteristics of our species" and contends that certain patterns of social behavior "will always be with us, at least until there has been some new and major change in our makeup."

"Species that have evolved special killing techniques for dealing with their prey seldom employ these when dealing with their own kind." But man's trouble, writes Konrad Lorenz, "arises from his being a basically harmless omnivorous creature, lacking in natural weapons with which to kill big prey, and, therefore, also devoid of the built-in safety devices which prevent 'professional' carnivores from abusing their killing power to destroy fellow members of their own species. . . ."

The "Law of the Jungle," writes Morris, is that you don't kill your own kind. "Those species that failed to obey this law have long since become extinct."

17   It was in early spring when Captain Jacques Cousteau's oceano-graphic vessel *Calypso* anchored off the shore of a southern California island. One night his crewmen noticed a churning of the waters and the ship's lights were turned on. In the water were millions of squid, six to ten inches long. Cousteau and his men had accidentally discovered the breeding ground of the sea arrows. The small squid returned here in cycles of two or three years to mate, lay their eggs, and die. Arriving on the scene by the millions, they milled around, waiting.

Then a frenzy of mating began. The females had developed their eggs in tubular egg-cases. Now as the sea arrows darted about, males would grab females and hold them fast in their arms. A special tentacle was used to insert a capsule of sperm under the mantle of the female. The mating continued for days.

Then the females extracted the elongated egg-cases from their bodies and attached them in clusters to the rocks below, where the cases slowly swayed, like fingers covering the bottom of the ocean. Each female would carefully place six to eight egg-cases in position. With the last case attached, her time was finished; she went limp and died. The males, fertilization completed, had already died.

A few days later Cousteau's divers scoured the bottom for signs of life. Of the millions of squid that had made the waters alive, nothing survived. As though covered with snow, the ocean bottom was white with the bodies of the squid. They had fulfilled their purpose, and it was all over. All that the divers found were acres of egg-cases, now covered with a leathery skin to protect them. Inside each egg-case another generation of sea arrows waited to be born. They would come singly out of their eggs, begin to grow, move out to sea and continue the cycle of life. Then, at their appointed time, they would return to the breeding ground as their parents had done to meet their destiny and die.

In the last days of the squid's life, two of the *Calypso*'s crewmen, swimming the bottom, came upon a female trying to push the last egg-case from her body. Gently they helped her by pulling out the case and attaching it to a rock. Then, joining the rest of her sea arrow family, she too died.

18   The instinct to fulfill the breeding cycle is so deep that no single sea arrow could thwart or change it. The "meaning of existence" for the squid is species-wide; it is provided by its instinctual makeup.

Is it conceivable that man has been totally separated from that evolutionary past when the instincts determined all significant behavior? If our problems are species-wide (as Morris and others believe), is it not possible that there also exist impulses-to-meaning—goal-directed instincts—which are species-wide? Might there not be such leftover urges moving in us, pulsing in the dimmest reaches of our being so that we are unaware of them, yet determining still our most basic behavioral patterns?

The world's a failure, you know. Someone, somewhere, made a terrible mistake.

Mission Impossible
CBS–TV

The world has always been ruled by Lucifer. The world is evil. Call his name, my love. Call the name of Lucifer.

Ritual of Evil
NBC–TV

"From what is presently known, Homo sapiens—the modern form of man—has existed on earth for approximately a hundred thousand years in numbers large enough to constitute a population. Barring catastrophic accidents, it can be expected that man will continue living on earth for many millions of years. Using a somewhat fanciful kind of arithmetic, it can be calculated from these figures that the present age of humanity corresponds to very early childhood in the life of a human being. Pursuing still further the same farfetched comparison, reading and writing were invented a year ago; Plato, the Parthenon, Christ, date from but a few months; experimental science is just a few weeks old, and electricity a few days; mankind will not reach puberty for another hundred thousand years. In this perspective, it is natural that so far mankind should have been chiefly concerned with becoming aware of the world of matter, listening to fairy tales, and fighting for pleasure or out of anger. The meaning of life, the problems of man and of society, become dominant preoccupations only later during development. As mankind outgrows childhood, the proper use of science may come to be not only to store food, build mechanical toys, and record allegories, myths, and fairy tales, but to understand, as well as possible, the nature of life and of man in order to give more meaning and value to human existence."

RENÉ DUBOS
The Torch of Life

As a psychologist, Abraham Maslow believed he had discerned such drives. He was convinced that

the human being has within him a pressure (among other pressures) toward unity of personality, toward spontaneous expressiveness, toward full individuality and identity, toward seeing the truth rather than being blind, toward being creative, toward being good, and a lot else. That is, the human being is so constructed that he presses toward fuller and fuller being. . . .

[There is] a single ultimate value for mankind, a far goal toward which all men strive. This is called variously by different authors self-actualization, self-realization, integration, psychological health, individuation, autonomy, creativity, productivity, but they all agree that this amounts to realizing the potentialities of the person, that is to say, becoming fully human, everything that the person *can* become. . . .

19   It is still not out of the question that man, unique among living things, lies free and lost. Perhaps Sartre is right in saying we are "condemned to be free." Perhaps there is no God, no Goddess, no Spirit, no Fate, no Moral Law, no phylogenetic urge-to-life, no instinct—and no meaning.

Perhaps Kierkegaard was right: "There is no truth, except truth *for me.*" The nihilistic existentialists have consistently held that the cosmos is depressingly meaningless and human society absurd. Our lives can achieve meaning only if we boldly grasp the choices before us and make whatever meaningful responses we can.

To be sure, many of us wake up each morning—and wonder why.

20   Richard Strauss composed the great tone poem *Also Sprach Zarathustra* in the spring and summer of 1896 and based it on passages from Nietzsche's book of the same title, written a dozen years earlier. Strauss himself wrote:

> I meant to convey by means of music an idea of the development of the human race from its origin, through various phases of its development, religious and scientific, up to Nietzsche's idea of the Superman. The whole symphonic poem is intended as an homage to Nietzsche's genius. . . .

Life's but a walking shadow, a
  poor player
That struts and frets his hour
  upon the stage,
And then is heard no more. It is a
  tale
Told by an idiot, full of sound and
  fury,
Signifying nothing.

SHAKESPEARE
Macbeth

Nil desperandum.
There's no cause for despair.

HORACE

Will the mind of man ever solve the riddle of the world? A few calm introductory bars, and already the trumpet sounds, *pp,* their solemn motto C–G–C, the so-called World-Riddle theme which, in various rhythmic guises, will pervade the whole symphonic poem through its very end. The simple but expressive introduction grows quickly in intensity and ends majestically on the climactic C major chord of the organ and full orchestra. . . .

And then comes the mystical conclusion which, ending in two different keys, aroused much controversy when the work was first performed. While the trombones stubbornly hold the unresolved chord C–E–F-sharp, the violins and upper woodwinds carry upward the Theme of the Ideal to higher register in B major . . . the pizzicati of the basses all the while sounding repeatedly the C–G–C of the World-Riddle. *Evidently the great problem remains unsolved.*

Wise men come ever promising
The riddle of life to know.
Wise men come. . . .
Ah, but over the sands,
The silent sands of time
They go. . . .

Kismet

From "The Sands of Time" by Robert Wright and George Forrest. © 1953 by Frank Music Corp. Used by permission.

1-2

THE SPIRIT OF PHILOSOPHY

1   The word *philosophy* comes from two Greek words: *philein* ("to love") and *sophia* ("wisdom"), implying that a philosopher is (or should be) a "lover of wisdom." Among countless definitions of "philosophy" this is still one of the simplest and best.

2   And so, the would-be philosopher unabashedly admits that he wants to become wise. The wisdom he seeks, however, is not merely the acquisition of facts to dispel ignorance. Rather "wisdom" is the antonym of (and antidote for) "foolishness." It is indeed the "fool" who may aquire volumes of information yet not know how to use it. To be "wise" is to possess the understanding and skill to make mature judgments about the use of human knowledge in the context of daily life.

When Empedocles remarked to him that it is impossible to find a wise man, Xenophanes replied: "Naturally, for it takes a wise man to recognize a wise man."

DIOGENES LAERTIUS

But this sort of wisdom is elusive. It dissolves when desired too desperately, and in times of need it can become paralyzed. Wisdom is not unlike the Tao: if defined too precisely, it will lose its essence; if sought too diligently, it will be missed.

Nevertheless, the philosopher at least knows what he is looking for: *wisdom.*

3   "Wisdom! What wisdom? . . . I certainly have no knowledge of such wisdom, and anyone who says that I have is a liar and wilful slanderer." Thus Socrates begins his defense when brought to trial in Athens in 399 B.C.

You know Chaerephon, of course. . . . Well, one day he actually went to Delphi and asked this question of the god [Apollo]. . . . He asked

whether there was anyone wiser than myself. The priestess replied that there was no one. . . .

When I heard about the oracle's answer, I said to myself "What does the god mean? Why does he not use plain language? I am only too conscious that I have no claim to wisdom, great or small; so what can he mean by asserting that I am the wisest man in the world?" . . .

After puzzling about it for some time, I set myself at last with considerable reluctance to check the truth of it in the following way. I went to interview a man with a high reputation for wisdom. . . . Well, I gave a thorough examination to this person—I need not mention his name, but it was one of our politicians that I was studying when I had this experience—and in conversation with him I formed the impression that although in many people's opinion, and especially in his own, he appeared to be wise, in fact he was not. . . . I reflected as I walked away: "Well, I am certainly wiser than this man. It is only too likely that neither of us has any knowledge to boast of; but he thinks that he knows something which he does not know, whereas I am quite conscious of my ignorance. At any rate it seems that I am wiser than he is to this small extent, that I do not think that I know what I do not know."

From that time on I interviewed one person after another. I realized with distress and alarm that I was making myself unpopular. . . . After I had finished with the politicians I turned to the poets, dramatic, lyric, and all the rest. . . . It seemed clear to me that the poets were in much the same case; and I also observed that the very fact that they were poets made them think that they had a perfect understanding of all other subjects, of which they were totally ignorant. So I left that line of inquiry too with the same sense of advantage that I had felt in the case of the politicians.

Last of all I turned to the skilled craftsmen. I knew quite well that I had practically no technical qualifications myself, and I was sure that I should find them full of impressive knowledge. . . . But, gentlemen, these professional experts seemed to share the same failing which I had noticed in the poets; I mean that on the strength of their technical proficiency they claimed a perfect understanding of every other subject, however important. . . .

The effect of these investigations of mine, gentlemen, has been to arouse against me a great deal of hostility. . . . This is due to the fact that whenever I succeed in disproving another person's claim to wisdom in a given subject, the bystanders assume that I know everything about that subject myself. But the truth of the matter, gentlemen, is pretty certainly this: that real wisdom is the property of [Apollo], and this oracle is his way of telling us that human wisdom has little or no value. It seems to me that he is not referring literally to Socrates, but has merely taken my name as an example, as if he would say to us "The wisest of you men is he who has realized, like Socrates, that in respect of wisdom he is really worthless."

PLATO
The Apology

4   The birth date of philosophy and science is usually taken to be 585 B.C., for about that time a philosopher named Thales made an assumption which broke with the world-view of his day. He assumed that all things were made of a single substance (Thales thought it might be water) and that the processes of change come from within the substance itself. Thales seems to have thought that the principle of motion and change was inherent in the basic material of which the universe is made.

Now why is this assumption significant? Before Thales, physical events were explained by supernatural causes. Since the cosmos was inhabited by all sorts of gods and goddesses, godlets, demigods, demons, ancestral ghosts, and a host of other spirits good and bad, it was reasonable to conlude that all events of human experience occurred *because they had been willed.*

If lightning struck, Zeus had hurled another thunderbolt. When the sun moved through the heavens, all knew that Apollo was driving it in his fiery chariot. If the Greeks lost the battle of Troy, or if Jason's ship slipped safely between the rocks of Scylla and the whirlpool of Charybdis, then the Olympians were playing games again.

And so, before the time of these first philosophers, all *natural* events were attributed to *supernatural* causes. G. K. Chesterton once remarked that for those holding the ancient world-view, the sun moved across the sky each day only because God got up before the sun and said to the sun, "Sun, get up and do it again."

The first philosophers were not quite satisfied with all this. Perhaps they realized that if, to every question you can ask, you get but a single answer ("The gods willed it"), then in fact you know nothing meaningful or useful. So the Milesian philosophers (Thales and his pupils Anaximander and Anaximenes) sought a different *kind* of explanation: when they asked about the cause of events, *they made the assumption* that the answer might be found in "nature" or within the matter itself. In other words, they deliberately ignored the unpredictable wills of the anthropomorphic Greek deities.

This assumption marks the beginning of knowledge in the West. This is the breakthrough that has been called "the Greek miracle."

5   Only two centuries passed between the Milesians and philosophy's zenith under Plato and Aristotle; yet in that time, using new instruments of inquiry, vast amounts of knowledge had been acquired.

Mathematics in the Greek world had its nebulous beginnings with earlier philosophers, notably the Eleatics (Parmenides and Zeno) and Pythagoras; but it was at Plato's Academy that mathematics flourished, for this "exact science" was Plato's first love and became the model for his metaphysics. Over the entrance to the Academy was the inscription: "Let no one without geometry enter here."

Through applied mathematics, Plato's friend Archytas, we are told, made three monumental discoveries: the pulley, the screw, and the rattle. The first two led to the development of engineering, while the third, wrote Aristotle, "gave children something to occupy them, and so prevented them from breaking things around the house."

Although Aristotle (385–322 B.C.) approached philosophy through the empirical sciences (especially biology), he was still enthralled with every aspect of learning. He founded the Lyceum in 334 B.C. and initiated the first coordinated research into the history of the sciences. His pupil (and later successor) Theophrastus worked on the history of the natural philosophers (the *physici*), while Menon studied the history of medicine and Eudemus recorded the history of arithmetic, geometry, and astronomy.

Within a half-century after the death of Aristotle, this synoptic approach to learning came to an end. By the beginning of the third century B.C. almost every branch of learning had been freed from philosophy to go its own way.

Scientific inquiry, being incompatible with religious dogmatism, died out in the West during the "Dark Ages" (c. A.D. 500–1000), and

the entire corpus of Greek philosophic and scientific knowledge passed into the hands of the Arabs. After their considerable contribution, this body of knowledge, still essentially Greek, made its way back to the Latin West, eventually giving birth to the Renaissance and the New Science.

From the great period of Greek science (roughly 300–100 B.C.) until the present day, various branches of inquiry have split off from philosophy and established themselves as independent disciplines. The natural sciences, mathematics and geometry, and astronomy have continued to individualize themselves (although the latter—astronomy—has had a promiscuous affair with astrology since Greek days, and even now not a few devotees are still trying to promote a marriage). With the rise of the universities and the development of science, new fields proliferated (such as physiology, anatomy, medicine); but the most recent offspring of philosophy (the "baby sciences," which, significantly, are the *human* sciences) have been psychology, anthropology, sociology, and political science. Today, philosophy just may be in the process of divesting itself of its last specializations: logic (associated more with mathematics and the computer sciences) and epistemology (frequently considered a new branch of psychology).

6　　　Thus, with history as a guide, we can assume that all the fields of knowledge heretofore classified as branches of philosophy will become specialized sciences.

How, then, can we continue to speak of "philosophical problems"? Clearly, any problem which can be subjected to empirical° investigation can no longer be thought of as "philosophy." This does not mean that the problem has been solved. But if, in theory, specialized research could produce dependable data about it, then the problem can no longer be classified as the property of the philosopher.

A *philosophical problem* is one whose solution depends upon insights arrived at by synthesizing the most secure facts and best hypotheses from many branches of learning. Note the three key points of that definition: The philosopher *brings together and synthesizes* (the activity of establishing meaningful relationships within his materials) *the most secure facts and best hypotheses* (that is, the carefully chosen fact-claims and conclusions of specialists) *from many fields* (that is, he wants to "cross-fertilize" all relevant

Faith can move mountains, or lead a man endlessly down a blind path. . . .

JAMES E. GUNN

Chances are . . . that philosophy will learn to coexist with science and (in Mortimer Adler's phrase) reach its delayed maturity, provided it resolutely insists on being a separate discipline dealing publicly and intelligibly in first-order questions.

Time, January 7, 1966

°**Empirical, empiricism.** In philosophy the word "empiricism" is defined in two distinct ways. (1) It refers to knowledge acquired by our senses only. (2) "Empirical" is often used to refer to *any* knowledge gained by human experience (not merely sense experience). This wider definition would include dreams, emotions, religious experiences, and so on.

In these pages, unless otherwise noted, these terms will be used only in the narrow sense, as in (1) above: "empirical" knowledge is gained alone through the senses. See glossary.

knowledge) in order to gain a deeper understanding into the problem and to enable him to project possible solutions to it.

The perennial, inescapable "stubborn questions"—for instance, questions about "purpose" in evolution, freedom and responsibility, ethical criteria for deciding "right" from "wrong"—are rendered intelligible only by means of a synoptic approach. It is very doubtful that such questions could ever be "solved" by specialized scientific research.

7   Francis Bacon (1561–1626) once wrote that he intended to take "all knowledge to be his province." He planned to sample all existing branches of knowledge in order to reorganize it, since he had concluded (rightly) that it was in great need of repair. Bacon launched a massive attack on the whole world-view of his day. This he called his *Magna Instauratio*—the "Great Reconstruction"—and in it he was remarkably successful.

The philosopher does essentially what Bacon did. It should be clear now that he is not a specialist in competition with the specialists. As a synthesizer, he depends upon the specialists. But like Socrates, he knows that he is not an expert in anything and that he is in debt to all.

As a result of his dependent role, however, the philosopher must face the problem of ascertaining who the "experts" are and whom he can safely turn to. He sometimes feels a gnawing anxiety that he may have listened to the wrong authorities.

As we move further into the seventies, our accumulation of knowledge will become staggering, and we will be subjected to more fact-claims than any generation in human history. It will not be easy, but it will be imperative, that all of us learn effective methods for distinguishing facts from fictions.

8 Men of Athens, I know and love you, but I shall obey God rather than you, and while I have life and strength I shall never cease from the practice and teaching of Philosophy. . . . I am that gadfly which God has attached to the state, and all day long and in all places am always fastening upon you, arousing and persuading and reproaching you. . . . I tell you that to do as you say would be a disobedience to God, and therefore I cannot hold my tongue. Daily to discourse about virtue, and about those other things about which you hear me examining myself and others is the greatest good of man. The unexamined life is not worth living. . . . In another world I shall be able to continue my search into true and false knowledge. . . . In another world they do not put a man to death for asking questions: assuredly not.

PLATO
The Apology

9 Philosophy and freedom were born together. Neither have ever existed without the other. If we possess freedom, we inquire. But if our freedom to inquire is too limited, then freedom, which is rightly a condition, becomes itself the goal for which we are willing to fight and die.

10 Throughout Western history, of course, religious sentiment has resisted critical inquiry into certain questions the final answers to which were allegedly known. The question of God's existence, for example, was not considered debatable. In more recent times there has been opposition to investigation into the nature of man, especially his evolutionary origin and the operations of his inner world. The possibility of synthesizing life in the laboratory has also been feared and fought. In such areas scientists have long since probed where others feared to search and have reduced the *mysterium* to quantitative analysis.

For the philosopher, as for the scientist, there is no holy ground—unless indeed *all* is Holy Ground.

Love is a strong word, but not, I think too strong for a passion which scorns the harlotry of fantasy and demands that those dedicated to an austere beauty should be faithful even unto death. The love of truth—which must not be confused with love of certainty—has seldom made much appeal to religious minds.

HECTOR HAWTON

11 Despite our background of Greek rationalism, reason in the Western world has had a difficult time. In the Judeo-Christian tradition it is made clear that we are saved by faith and not by our rational intellects or academic credentials.

The epitome of the righteous man was Abraham, who was willing to go so far as to kill his son Isaac *in order to obey* the word of his God, Yahweh. He assumed no right (according to the story in Genesis 22) to question the command; there was no chance of his debating with Yahweh the morality of the order. (However, read Genesis 18:20-33 where Abraham—yes, Abraham—carried on a running argument with God about a similar moral issue—and won!) In sacrificing Isaac, absolute obedience was required, and because of his submission Abraham has been held up as the ideal "Man of Uprightness" for more than three thousand years. Salvation is a reward for faith and obedience.

I do not seek to understand in order that I may believe, but I believe in order that I may understand, for of this I feel sure, that, if I did not believe, I would not understand.

ST. ANSELM

12   In the gospel tradition, Thomas is the example of what we are not to be, if we can help it. Thomas doubted. He wanted better evidence than he had before believing something reported to him by others, that is, before he *could* believe emotional second-hand reports of an event which, at first glance, seemed extremely improbable. Eventually "doubting Thomas" was told to place his hands in the wound in Jesus' side so that then he too might believe. But this skepticism is not commendable, for Jesus is reported to have said, "Blessed be those who have not seen me and yet believe!" (John 20:29).

Similarly, Saint Paul had grave misgivings about human wisdom and those who seek it. It appears that he had a rather sour experience with some Stoic and Epicurean philosophers in Athens. "Where now is your philosopher? Your scribe? Your reasoner of today?" he wrote to the Corinthian Christians. "Has not God made a fool of the world's wisdom?" A similar word of caution was sent to his friends in the Lycus Valley: "Take care that nobody exploits you through pretensions of philosophy. . . ."

Time and again, Paul found that philosophers were the hardest minds to sway, and, despairing of their lack of understanding, he moved on to the towns where he could find people who had the capacity for faith.

13   Reason and knowledge are of little value in achieving salvation, according to orthodox Western theology. On the contrary, they can be a positive hindrance. We are saved by *faith*. Redemption is for the illiterate as much as for the educated. For in Christ, Paul reminds us, there is neither Jew nor Gentile, male nor female, slave nor free. "In union with Christ, all men are one." In matters of salvation, that is, all men of faith are equal.

The Church Fathers and Scholastic philosophers, of course, followed Paul's lead. Saint Augustine (A.D. 354–430) always asserted the primacy of faith: *Fides proecedit intellectum,* "Faith must exist before one can understand." Augustine "never abandoned or depreciated reason," writes a church historian; "he only subordinated it to faith and made it subservient to the defence of revealed truth. Faith is the pioneer of reason, and discovers the territory which reason explores."

Saint Anselm of Canterbury (1033–1109) took the same position. *Credo ut intelligam,* "I believe in order to understand." Revealed truth must first be accepted, and in the light of that certainty one can then know how to interpret all else. The revealed truth cannot itself be subject to doubt.

Peter Abelard (1079–1142) disagreed and stoutly declared it was the other way around. Understanding comes first, and only then can one decide what to believe. Abelard was not afraid of questions and doubts: "For by doubting we come to inquiry, by inquiry we discover the truth."

Needless to say, Augustine and Anselm won, and Abelard lost. We speak of *Saint* Augustine and *Saint* Anselm, but we do not say "Saint" Abelard.

14 In a postscript to *A Study of History,* Arnold Toynbee conjures an imaginary Hindu who scolds Christianity for its rational self-immolation.

> "I feel little respect for the Christian application of thought to Christianity because your Christian thinkers do not dare to have the courage of their convictions. The characteristic virtue of thought is to follow the argument whithersoever it may lead; if thought flinches from fulfilling this first commandment of intellectual honesty, it commits a stultifying sin against its own nature; and this is the moral infirmity by which your Christian thinking is invalidated. Your imposing *Summa Theologiae* is confined within the prison-walls of a mythology which your hearts have dictated to your heads; and in matters of religion Christianity allows the Intellect to operate only under a perpetual edict serving notice 'Thus far and no farther.' What is the World to think of a Christian intelligence that consents to work under conditions that make nonsense of the Intellect's essential function? . . . I am proud—however high your Christian judgement may rate the moral price—that my Hinduism does not sacrifice honest thinking to prejudiced sentiment."

15 "My trade is to say what I think," said Voltaire. We might add that the philosopher's vocation is to think what he pleases, and then to speak and write what he thinks. He cannot in good faith accept any restraint upon his professional calling. For economy and efficiency, of course, he will choose how he limits himself and how he articulates his questions, but he will resist any external threat to his freedom of inquiry.

In this spirit, he will grant to all others the same freedom he insists upon for himself. To turn again to Voltaire, a well-known, but little-heeded, line is attributed to the French philosopher: "I do not agree with a word that you say, but I will defend to the death your right to say it."

16 Time and again, when we want to understand ourselves, we find that we must return to the two great traditions which together make up our Western heritage. Like intellectual archeologists, we have to chip at the clay and brush away the dust from the remains of our buried past.

Countless ideas inherited from our two ancestral worlds—Greco-Roman and the Judaic—have been harmonized into a coherent world-view, and Western life has been richer for it. But like a dissonant undercurrent, a few Greek and Judeo-Christian beliefs have remained stubbornly incompatible, and thinkers have tried in vain to work out some sort of coexistence.

The most ordinary misinterpretation of faith is to consider it an act of knowledge that has a low degree of evidence. . . . If this is meant, one is speaking of belief rather than of faith. . . . Almost all the struggles between faith and knowledge are rooted in the wrong understanding of faith as a type of knowledge which has a low degree of evidence but is supported by religious authority. One of the worst errors of theology and popular religion is to make statements which intentionally or unintentionally contradict the structure of reality. Such an attitude is an expression not of faith but of the confusion of faith with belief.

PAUL TILLICH

We have now, in this chapter, encountered basic assumptions about life, involving ultimate commitments, which are logically and psychologically incompatible. For almost two millennia we have been torn by the conflict. Despite all healing attempts by some of the West's greatest minds, we are still intellectually dichotomized.

The Greek commitment is to reasoned inquiry into the nature of existence. This commitment has enabled us to understand the natural world we live in and to lay the foundations for an understanding of man.

On the other hand, the Judeo-Christian commitment has been to religious beliefs which lie beyond human understanding. What has been revealed by the Infinite Mind cannot be comprehended by finite minds; the "mysteries of faith" will remain beyond our grasp, for "we see through a glass, darkly." Our purpose in life should not be to analyze the Infinite or synthesize life's fragments. Rather, our goal should be "to get into a right relationship with God," to do his will through faith, and to look forward to an eternity which will transcend this mortal existence.

And so, for many, it is either/or. Here the road forks and one may be forced to choose the road he will travel. Many have tried to blaze a way between them, but no clear path has yet been found.

17 In this dichotomy, the philosopher generally chooses to travel with Socrates. The philosopher has no doubt about the transforming power and the pragmatic virtue of faith, but he believes that courageous inquiry, and growth from the knowledge thereby gained, hold out greater hope for both personal fulfillment and the future of Mankind.

"I have said some things," Socrates once remarked, "of which I am not altogether confident. But that we shall be better and braver and less helpless if we think that we ought to inquire, than we should have been if we indulged in the idle fancy that there was no knowing and no use in seeking to know what we do not know—that is a theme upon which I am ready to fight, in word and deed, to the utmost of my power."

18 The philosopher engages in doubt as a *modus operandi.* He insists upon doubting a fact-claim to force it to defend itself. For example, René Descartes (1596–1650) used "methodical doubt" as the foundation of his philosophical system. He doubted everything he could in the hope of arriving at some "fact" that he could not further doubt. When he discovered such a "fact" (*Cogito, ergo sum,* "I think, therefore I exist"), he began to build deductively upon that certified first principle. This brand of doubt has played a significant role in all the knowledge-gathering sciences. A historian once said that the beginning of *all* knowledge is a "good healthy doubt."

Beyond such methodological doubt, it seems clear now that no religious faith can escape the pain of doubt. It is questionable whether undiluted faith (*credentia,* "blind faith") is a psychological possibility; it appears more to be mythic or wishful thinking than a true function of the human personality.

Furthermore, "existential doubt" appears to be the flip-side of religious experience itself. Existential doubt is more ultimate than any other kind of doubt and is implied in human existence as such. It is the unconditioned doubt felt in direct proportion to the depth of one's involvement in life's ultimate problems *to which there can be no definitive and final answers.*

19   Every act of faith, writes Paul Tillich, involves risk, and all risk is accompanied by doubt. Authentic doubt

> is always present as an element in the structure of faith. . . . There is no faith without an intrinsic 'in spite of' and the courageous affirmation of oneself in the state of ultimate concern. This intrinsic element of doubt breaks into the open under special individual and social conditions. If doubt appears, it should not be considered as the negation of faith, but as an element which was always and will always be present in the act of faith. Existential doubt and faith are poles of the same reality, the state of ultimate concern.

20   In his investigations of what he termed the "self-actualizing" personality, Abraham Maslow wrote:

> Our healthy subjects are uniformly unthreatened and unfrightened by the unknown, being therein quite different from average men. They accept the unknown, they are comfortable with it, and often are even attracted by it. To use Frenkel-Brunswick's phrase, "they can tolerate the ambiguous." . . . Since for healthy people, the unknown is not frightening, they do not have to spend any time laying the ghost, whistling past the cemetery, or otherwise protecting themselves against danger. They do not neglect the unknown, or deny it, or run away from it, or try to make believe it really is known, nor do they organize, dichotomize, or rubricize it prematurely. They do not cling to the familiar, nor is their quest for truth a catastrophic need for certainty, for safety, for definiteness, and order. The fully functioning personality can be, when the objective situation calls for it, comfortably disorderly, anarchic, vague, doubtful, uncertain, indefinite, approximate, inexact, or inaccurate.

21   To my way of thinking, a college is a community of seekers—a community of those devoted not solely to the appreciation and preservation of the past, but dedicated to the discovery of greater truth. It is a community of those who do not believe that *all* truth has been found in *any* area—who refuse to invest any particular statement, book, creed, institution, or person with finality or infallibility. It should be a community of those who are completely dedicated to the best that they know but believe

The real tragedy that may occur in any of our lives is not the losing of our faith. . . . The real tragedy is not to lose our faith . . . to be satisfied, to be smug and content, to have arrived . . .

BERT C. WILLIAMS

Almost all the spiritual traditions recognize that there is a stage in man's development when belief— in contrast to faith—and its securities have to be left behind.

ALAN WATTS

Flight from insecurity is catastrophic to any kind of human growth. To flee from insecurity is to miss the whole point of being human. It is to miss, at any rate, the whole point of religion.

PETER BERTOCCI

I do not agree with a word that you say, but I will defend to the death your right to say it.

Attributed to VOLTAIRE

It is only charlatans who are certain. . . . Doubt is not a very agreeable state, but certainty is a ridiculous one.

VOLTAIRE

Conviction is something that can be discussed without anger.

FRANK MC GEE

that there is a better-to-be-known in all areas. Persons in such a community should be doubters and sceptics in the sense that they suspend judgment and question all assumptions and conclusions, so that each one will be forced to justify itself before the bar of critical analysis. Such attitudes are never apt to win friends or to influence people among that segment of society that believes that it has the truth.

BERT C. WILLIAMS

1-3

THE WAYS OF

PHILOSOPHY

1   The definition of philosophy, with a clear statement of its task, has long been made difficult by the baffling complexity of life itself. Since life's problems can be tackled in various ways, philosophers choose their angle of attack and, from that vantage point, cut as deeply as they can.

Therefore, one finds—to no one's surprise—a variety of ideas of what philosophy should be. After all, how could philosophy be expected to perform the same function for a Scholastic theologian, an atheistic existentialist, a Taoist sage, and a symbolic logician?

Philosophers sometimes make the claim that *their* brand of philosophizing is the only "right" one and all other endeavors called "philosophy" are misconceived or misnamed. A philosopher, like anyone else, can make aristocentric° claims; but humility would seem more appropriate for those who, by definition, are "lovers of wisdom." William James stated a fact which philosophers above all should know: our knowledge is a drop, our ignorance an ocean.

If we overcome the temptation to take up partisan positions, we find that the various concepts of philosophy complement one another. In concentrating on a particular aspect of the World-Riddle, each approach has sharpened our skills and enriched our understanding. The Roman senator Symmachus said it well: "The heart of so great a mystery can never be reached by following one road only." The simple fact is that we are indebted to the whole range of man's philosophic inquiries.

2   There have been four general ideas of what philosophers are supposed to be doing. They can be classified as (1) synoptics, (2) activists, (3) antinomians, and (4) analytics.

Dulce est desipere in loco. Woe to philosophers who cannot laugh away their wrinkles. I look upon solemnity as a disease.

VOLTAIRE

It makes all the difference whether one sees darkness through the light or brightness through the shadows.

DAVID LINDSAY

°*Aristocentric, aristocentrism.* **An inordinate claim to superiority for oneself or one's group. From the Greek** *aristos* **(superlative of** *agathos,* **"good") meaning "the best of its kind" or "the most to be valued," and** *kentrikos,* **from** *kentron,* **"the center of a circle."**

The word philosophy means the love of wisdom. And the love of wisdom, I suppose, is like any other sort of love—the professionals are the ones who know least about it.

ABRAHAM KAPLAN

The synoptic philosophers have in common the desire "to see life steadily and to see it whole" (Whitehead) or, at least, to understand every event in the largest possible way (James). Commonly we find the synoptic philosophers having a very wide range of interests and concerns. They are usually fascinated by almost all areas of human knowledge. They will have special interests, of course, but they will delve into all sorts of knowledge to better obtain an overview of life and the problems they wish to work on.

3 In the spring of the year 334 B.C., as Alexander the Great was setting off across Asia to conquer the world and bring the gift of Greek civilization to all Mankind, Aristotle left his home town in Thrace and returned to Athens to establish his own school of learning. In a green grove just outside the city, near a temple dedicated to Apollo Lyceus, he founded the Lyceum. It had a campus, classrooms, a chapel, covered walkways, and shaded gardens. In time it also contained the Western world's first great library, a museum of natural history, and a zoological garden.

During morning hours Aristotle lectured to his students in technical subjects as they strolled along the pathways. (For this they came to be nicknamed Peripatetics or "the Strollers.") In the afternoons he lectured on popular subjects to crowds from outside the school. At dinner teacher and students dined together and often held symposia. Aristotle reserved his evening hours for his own research and writing.

Out of this atmosphere emerged our first empirically grounded synoptic philosophy.

In the work of Einstein, for instance, the layman—however far he may fall short of understanding the great man's thought—can at least perceive that he is thinking about the Physical Universe as a whole and not just about this or that slice of physical reality. Perhaps the layman may even venture further and conjecture that this broad attitude of mind—this comprehensive way of thinking—has been an essential condition of Einstein's achievement.

ARNOLD TOYNBEE

4 Aristotle was the first great *synoptic* philosopher. His mind ranged over every known realm of human knowledge, and he produced brilliant, creative writing in every field. Drawing upon the immense amount of empirical data collected by his students and sent to him by Alexander from foreign countries (one report has it that Alexander set a thousand men collecting specimens of flora and fauna for Aristotle's laboratories and museums), Aristotle was also the West's first true scientist.

While hundreds of Aristotle's writings have been lost, some forty works survive. He wrote extensively in what we would call the *natural sciences* (physics, astronomy and cosmology, geology, meteorology), the *life sciences* (biology, anatomy, physiology, genetics), the *social sciences* (psychology, politics, ethics), the *practical arts* (oratory and rhetoric), and "*philosophy*" (logic and epistemology, esthetics, theology, metaphysics).

His synoptic mind was continually at work weaving these vast areas of knowledge into a coherent philosophical system that served as the framework for man's thinking until the beginning of the scientific revolution. "He is probably the only human intellect that has ever compassed at first hand and assimilated the whole body of existing knowledge

Part 1   The Fine Art of Wondering

WHERE ARE THE WOMEN?

A mere glance through the history of philosophy shows a glaring absence. *Where are the women?* Didn't women become philosophers? Weren't they just as concerned as men with problems of human existence?

Most civilizations have been men's worlds, and those professions likely to bring fame have been closed to the female of the species. Few women became military heroines, for instance; and on the rare occasions when they did (Joan of Arc comes to mind) they did so along paths quite outside society's *modus operandi.*

And so it was with philosophy. There was but one profession which encouraged women to make the most of their intellectual capacities and cultural interests. Since the classical Greeks fostered intellectual attainments in its male citizenry to a degree previously unknown in the Western world, it is not surprising that there arose a class of women trained to be the intellectual companions of such men of culture and ability. They comprised history's highest class of courtesans and were appropriately called *hetairai,* "companions." They alone, it seems, enjoyed the requisites for philosophizing: adequate leisure time, professional incentive, and freedom from the traditional child-bearing role expected of women. A few of these courtesans transcended whatever social stigmata they encountered and became renowned intellectuals in the highest philosophical and literary circles of their times.

Aspasia (c. 470–410 B.C.) was one of the most effective women's liberationists of all time. She opened a school of philosophy and rhetoric for women in Athens and did much to advance their education and encourage their emergence into public life. The great men of her era, including Pericles and Socrates, attended her lectures. She became the mistress of Pericles and their home became a center of Athenian culture.

Of *Diotima* we know very little, but in Plato's *Symposium* Socrates states that he was her pupil and says: "There is a speech about Love which I heard once from Diotima of Mantineia, who was wise in this matter and many others."

Leontium became the concubine of Epicurus and through her voluminous writing established herself as an articulate philosopher and, when necessary, a defender of womanhood. *Arete,* daughter of the famous hedonist philosopher Aristippus, was apparently not a courtesan. She succeeded her father as head of the Cyrenaic school of philosophy, wrote some 40 books, and achieved such distinction that she became known as "The Light of Hellas."

The supremely brilliant and beautiful *Hypatia* (A.D. 370–415) became head of the famed school of Neoplatonism in Alexandria. Her fame spread through her lectures, teaching and erudite writing. She was murdered by an outraged mob of Christians—ostensibly because of her liaison with Orestes, the prefect of Alexandria—and thus became the first woman philosopher to die for her beliefs.

Through the centuries other women became the intellectual lights of their times, though most of them moved merely on the periphery of philosophy per se. Among them: the Empress Theodora, wife of Justinian; Eleanor of Aquitaine; Marguerite d'Angoulême, Queen of Navarre; and Queen Christina of Sweden (who dispatched a warship to persuade René Descartes to come to Stockholm to establish an academy for her). In our century, for whatever reasons, the names are only slightly on the increase: Susanne Langer, L. Susan Stebbing, Simone de Beauvoir, Ayn Rand.

Now that lifestyles are changing and women are breaking free of the cultural traditions which have heretofore predetermined their roles, it will be interesting to see if history begins to record a greater equality among those who professionally confess to being "lovers of wisdom."

on all subjects, and brought it within a single focus—and a focus, at that, which after more than two thousand years still stands as one of the supreme achievements of the mind of man."

5　　One goal of synoptic philosophy is the development of an empirically sound and rationally coherent world-view to serve as an operational model for the interpretation and valuation of all our experience. Such a world-view provides unity and consistency to the whole of life.

　　A common result of synoptic activity is what Dr. Robert Fischer has called "an ecology of understanding": the discovery that all knowledge is related and that any rigid compartmentalization of data ("chemistry," "biology," "psychology," etc.) is artificial and eventually self-defeating. Knowledge is seen to be a unity, an "ecological system" in which all parts must be understood in relation to one another.

Niccolò Machiavelli turned to philosophy when he lost all hope of political advancement and found himself exiled to his country home outside Florence. He wrote about his manner of life in a letter to his friend Vettori, then Florentine ambassador to Rome (December 10, 1513).

　　"Since my last misfortunes I have led a quiet country life. I rise with the sun, and go into one of the woods for a few hours to inspect yesterday's work; I pass some time with the woodcutters, who have always some troubles to tell me, either of their own or their neighbors'. On leaving the wood I go to a spring, and thence up to my bird-snaring enclosure, with a book under my arm—Dante, Petrarch, or one of the minor poets, such as Tibullus or Ovid. I read their amorous transports and the history of their loves, recalling my own to my mind, and time passes pleasantly in these meditations. . . .

　　"At nightfall I return home and seek my writing room; and divesting myself on its threshold of my rustic garments, stained with mud and mire, I assume courtly attire; and thus suitably clothed, I enter within the ancient courts of ancient men, by whom, being cordially welcomed, I am fed with the food that alone is mine, and for which I was born, and am not ashamed to hold discourse with them and inquire the motives of their actions; and these men in their humanity reply to me; and for the space of four hours I feel no weariness, remember no trouble, no longer fear poverty, no longer dread death; my whole being is absorbed in them."

6   The *activist* philosophers believe that the philosophic enterprise must be a part of life itself and that the philosopher cannot be a mere spectator of life's tragicomic drama. He may not have auditioned for a role in the drama, but he has been cast nevertheless. He can no more resign from the cast than he can resign from the human race.

There are at least three distinct varieties of activist philosophers: (1) the prophetic activists, (2) the pragmatists, and (3) the existentialists. Each, however, insists on participation in the human drama for quite different reasons.

7   The *prophetic° activists* contend that the task of philosophy is to bring about drastic reforms in social conditions; human suffering in all its forms must be dealt with *now*. Karl Marx, for example, became disillusioned with the ivory-tower philosophy in vogue in nineteenth-century Germany, a grandiose metaphysics of human history which was blind to the concrete realities of day-to-day human experience. Indeed, much German philosophy (and especially Hegelian idealism) hardly acknowledged the existence of the individual per se.

Against such dehumanizing theories, there arose numerous reactions, Marx's among them. Marx wrote that "philosophers have only *interpreted* the world differently: the point is, however, to *change* it." He therefore developed a philosophy of history in which change (and the doctrine of "inevitable progress") was the central idea. "Marx's aim," writes Erich Fromm,

> was that of the spiritual emancipation of man, of his liberation from the chains of economic determination, of restituting him in his human wholeness, of enabling him to find unity and harmony with his fellow man and with nature. Marx's philosophy was, in secular, nontheistic language, a new and radical step forward in the tradition of prophetic Messianism; it was aimed at the full realization of individualism, the very aim which has guided Western thinking from the Renaissance and the Reformation far into the nineteenth century.

Since our main concern here is to describe what philosophers are supposed to be doing, it is of interest to note that Marx the man was more philosopher than revolutionary. "A man whose whole creed was one of action," notes Untermeyer, "he spent practically all his time in libraries." To be sure, he had himself engaged in social action in Paris and Brussels, but the last thirty years of his life were spent writing in the British Museum and in a dingy two-room London apartment. Instead of taking action he philosophized about it.

This is not to be taken as an indictment. On the contrary, it suggests that philosophy and social activism may be competing preoccupations. One can do one or the other, or one can alternate from one to the other, but it appears doubtful that both activities can be carried on effectively at the same time.

Heretofore philosophers have only interpreted *the world differently: the point is, however, to* change *it.*

KARL MARX

°The word "prophetic" is used here in its original sense as referring to those who, with a passion for justice, advocate a crash program of social reform. This is precisely the position of the prototypical prophets of the Old Testament such as Amos, Isaiah and Jeremiah. By definition a "prophet" was a "spokesman of God," but his social function was to initiate social change by courageously exposing the corruption and the corruptors. While the scriptural prophets were not philosophers in any precise sense, their social concerns and actions were the same as those of the activist philosophers dealt with here.

° *Pragmatism.* From the Greek *pragma,* "deed" or "action." An American philosophical movement associated with Peirce, James, and John Dewey. The basic theme of pragmatism is that ideas have meaning only in relation to the practical results which they effect.

A page from Kierkegaard's *Journals.*

8 The American *pragmatists*° represent a second reaction against the prevailing German idealism. "Damn the Absolute!" was William James's response to Hegel's idea that history is the manifestation of the "Absolute Mind" of God. James believed that philosophers should get down to the task of solving the problems of life. Too long have they been playing around with metaphysical speculations. An idea is to be judged by its "cash value," wrote James; and philosophical concepts should be evaluated in terms of their practical consequences.

It has often been noted that pragmatism could only have been born on American soil, since it reflects the spirit of the nineteenth century, the frontier spirit of individualism, self-reliance, and practicality. Americans had traditionally been castigated by European thinkers as "long on action but short on thought." William James successfully argued that it was time for a carefully thought-out philosophy of action which would deal candidly with real issues.

James's down-to-earth attitude sometimes shocked staid academicians. "This universe will never be completely good as long as one being is unhappy," he said, and added, "or as long as one poor cockroach suffers the pangs of unrequited love."

1835

Gilleleie, August 1, 1835

What I really lack is to be clear in my mind *what I am to do,* not what I am to know, except in so far as a certain understanding must precede every action. The thing is to understand myself, to see what God really wishes *me* to do; the thing is to find a truth which is true *for me,* to find *the idea for which I can live and die.* What would be the use of discovering so-called objective truth, of working through all the systems of philosophy and of being able, if required, to review them all and show up the inconsistencies within each system;—what good would it do me to be able to develop a theory of the state and combine all the details into a single whole, and so construct a world in which I did not live, but only held up to the view of others;—what good would it do me to be able to explain the meaning of Christianity if it had *no* deeper significance *for me and for my life;*—what good would it do me if truth stood before me, cold and naked, not caring whether I recognised her or not, and producing in me a shudder of fear rather than a trusting devotion? I certainly do not deny that I still recognise an *imperative of understanding* and that through it one can work upon men, *but it must be taken up into my life,* and *that is* what I now recognise as the most important thing. That is what my soul longs after, as the African desert thirsts for water. That is what I lack, and that is why I am left standing like a man who has rented a house and gathered all the furniture and household things together, but has not yet found the beloved with whom to share the joys and sorrows of his life. But in order to find that idea, or better still, in order to find myself, it is no use throwing myself still further into life. And that is just what I have done hitherto. That is why I thought it would be a good thing to throw myself into the study of the law so as to develop my

---

9   The *existentialists*° have all shared the basic belief that life has meaning only when it is fully experienced. Life is not a thing to be thought, but an existence to be lived. To think and to exist are quite different things, and most philosophers have sold their existence for a handful of thoughts. To watch someone else enjoy a sunset or experience love may not be without value; but it's a world away from enjoying the sunset and feeling love within and for oneself.

The existentialist becomes involved in life, therefore, not primarily to change the world or even to solve its problems, but in order to discover, for himself, the meaning of existence.

Søren Kierkegaard, the "father of existentialism," and all subsequent existentialists have criticized traditional philosophy as a collection of astute observations by "spectators." It therefore has a hollow ring, for it has missed life.

The existentialists believe that the only "reality" that is worthwhile is experience—what takes place personally and uniquely in the inner world of each of us. Moreover, since neither past nor future exist, the concrete present is where the full intensity of life is to be found. The advice of the existentialist, therefore, is to live life and not let it pass by while meditating on it.

°**Existentialism.** A school of philosophy arising during World War II, but drawing heavily from the long-neglected writings of Kierkegaard (1813–1855). One central theme of existentialism is that the only realistic understanding of life comes from focusing upon the moment-by-moment, concrete existence of individual persons, especially their inner worlds. All intellectual speculation is secondary to the experiencing organism involved in living.

He alone is aware of a chance which raises him to the rank of the adjutores Dei *who are passive in their relation to God but active in their relation to Mankind.*

HENRI BERGSON

SØREN KIERKEGAARD
1813   1855

30

KGL. POST

DANMARK

It was intelligence and nothing else that had to be opposed. Presumably that is why I, who had the job, was armed with an immense intelligence.

KIERKEGAARD

Somewhere in the Journals *Kierkegaard remarks that the skipper of a fishing-smack knows his whole cruise before sailing, but a man-of-war gets its orders only on the high seas.*

ALEXANDER DRU

°Antinomian. From the Greek *anti*,
"against," and *nomos*, "law"; hence,
"against the law." In the widest
sense (as used here), it refers to
those who deliberately choose to
exist outside the accepted norms of
society.

10   Not all philosophers would agree that social action is the noblest of human activities. The *antinomian*° philosophers have held that a realistic assessment of the human condition necessarily leads anyone concerned with the quality of his existence to withdraw from the world. Western monastics, of course, have disengaged themselves from the world since at least the second century before Christ. Hindus revere the *sannyasin* who enter the forests to meditate, their ultimate goal being total withdrawal into the trance-state of *nirvana*. Zen and Theravada Buddhists share similar attitudes toward life-in-this-world.

The best known Western critics of society are perhaps Jean-Jacques Rousseau and Henry David Thoreau. Both contended that a return to nature and the simple life is necessary to preserve one's self and sanity. Both, however, were sensitive to social ills and neither managed to withdraw from the world for very long.

The true antinomian philosophers are such men as Diogenes the Cynic and Chuang-tzu the Taoist.

"I can't decide whether to go to the orgy or listen to Socrates."

11   *Antinomianism—Western Style.* After Athens's Golden Age was over, many diverse philosophical schools were born. One such school, the Cynics, was founded by Antisthenes. He held his classes in a gymnasium outside Athens and catered to the poor, the illegitimate, and the foreign-born. He taught without fees, lived simply, and dressed shabbily. Socrates once said to him, "Antisthenes, I can see your vanity through the holes of your cloak."

His most famous pupil was Diogenes, who had tried banking in Asia Minor, failed, and came to Athens. He was forced to beg, and Antisthenes helped him rationalize his condition into a philosophy. He gathered the accouterments of a beggar—old clothes, a bowl, and a staff—and lived in a large tub in the courtyard of an Athenian temple. His only companions were dogs.

The Cynics disdained culture and ridiculed sophistic learning. They rebelled against the customs and codes of society. They wandered from place to place, evangelically denouncing the absurdities and corruptions of society and preaching a simple, back-to-nature existence in which all Mankind could be one family.

Diogenes tried to practice what he preached. He slept on the ground or in his tub, eating whatever he could beg. He tried never to

Western history seems to imply that the best thing that can happen to a philosopher is to be excommunicated or exiled; that the best thing that can happen to his writing is that it be banned, burned, or placed on the Index.

Every man of greatness discovers, finally, that he cannot live in the world; but this is a discovery of no great moment. What is important is where he decides to go from there.

hurt anyone. Above all he wanted to be free—free of material possessions, relationships, traditions, laws. In fact, he recognized no laws, so he could neither obey nor disobey them. Freedom of speech was most important to him and he made much use of it, coarsely and wittily. He never thought of himself as a Greek (he wasn't) and considered himself as belonging to Mankind alone.

There is a legend to the effect that Diogenes often walked the streets of Athens with a lantern in his hand, looking—in vain—for an honest man.

12 *Antinomianism—Eastern Style.* The Taoist philosopher Chuang-tzu is considered by many to be the greatest sage that China has produced. We know little about his life, but as we listen to his thoughts we can feel the working of a wise and subtle mind.

Chuang-tzu lived in the state of Meng about 300 B.C. He became famous and could have held high office, but he disdained society, power, and wealth. He was irreverent toward pompous authorities and ridiculed all schools of philosophy (he never dreamed that his philosophy would become a "school"). He was especially critical of Confucian teachings because they produced obedient, cultured, "virtuous" men who were empty inside. Such men could play to perfection the artificial games of social custom, but they had lost the freedom for authentic, spontaneous behavior. They were imprisoned by arbitrary rules and social niceties.

Chuang-tzu wanted none of this. He preferred to watch the merry go-around from a distance. "The life of things passes by like a rushing, galloping horse, changing at every turn, at every hour. What should one do, or what should one not do? Let the changes go on by themselves!"

. . . The effect of life in society is to complicate and confuse our existence, making us to forget who we really are by causing us to become obsessed with what we are not.

CHUANG-TZU

13 Chuang-tzu with his bamboo pole was fishing in the river. The prince of Chu sent two officials to offer him formally the post of Prime Minister.

Chuang-tzu held his bamboo pole. Still looking into the river, he said, "I am told there is a sacred tortoise which has been dead now some three thousand years. Wrapped in silk, in a shrine on an altar in the temple. What do you think: Is it better to give up one's life and leave a sacred shell as an object of veneration in a cloud of incense three thousand years, or is it better to live as a plain turtle wagging its tail in the mud?"

"For the turtle," replied one of the officials, "it is better to live and wag its tail in the mud!"

"Then, begone!" ordered Chuang-tzu. "I too will stay here and wag my tail in the mud!"

14 Thomas Merton, an interpreter of the writings of Chuang-tzu, was a Trappist monk. Reflecting upon the philosophy of Chuang-tzu he sensed a familiar way of life. Father Merton wrote:

> I have been a Christian monk for nearly twenty-five years, and inevitably one comes in time to see life from a viewpoint that has been common to solitaries and recluses in all ages and in all cultures. . . . There is a monastic outlook which is common to all those who have elected to question the value of life submitted entirely to arbitrary secular presuppositions, dictated by social conventions, and dedicated to the pursuit of temporal satisfactions which are perhaps only a mirage. Whatever may be the value of "life in the world" there have been, in all cultures, men who have claimed to find something they vastly prefer in solitude.

Some of the most profound things that one must philosophize about, he must face in silence. To speak about them would be sacrilege.

15 From its beginning, one of the central concerns of Western philosophy has been the *analysis* of ideas. The origins of logic° are presocratic, but the special preoccupation with problems of clear thinking dates from Socrates himself. Much of his time was spent in asking questions about words, ideas, and beliefs and discovering the fallacies which mar a large part of our thinking.

Aristotle, however, is considered the founder of formal logic. He invented the syllogism and wrote the first textbook in logic. Since his time new systems of logic have been devised, including systems of symbolic logic which have had practical application in business fields and computer science.

Twentieth-century philosophical logic has had an ambiguous career. One name, however—Wittgenstein—has dominated the field for nearly a half-century.

°**Logic.** From the Greek *logike,* "the art of reasoning." In philosophy the word "logic" is a technical term referring to the study of valid inference. It is the disciplined study of the techniques of clear thinking. (Furthermore, the word *valid* is a technical term, used in logic, to refer to any idea which has been correctly inferred from other given statements.)

16 There were two creative periods in the life of Ludwig Wittgenstein, each of which culminated in a complex system of philosophy. His first period began in 1912 when he became a student of Bertrand Russell at Cambridge University; it ended in 1921 with the publication of an epoch-making (but remarkably brief) treatise entitled *Tractatus Logico-Philosophicus.* Subsequently he published almost nothing, as though his philosophic search had reached its end.

Then a second period of creative philosophizing began in 1929 when he returned to Cambridge, first as a student, then as a teacher. Out of his teaching a new philosophy was born, which resulted in his *Philosophical Investigations,* published posthumously in 1953.

His first period was devoted primarily to logic and logical systems, while his second period dealt entirely with the analysis of everyday language. The testimony to his genius is that each of his systems—esoteric, technical, and demanding—has strongly influenced the course of twentieth-century philosophical thought.

For this reason Wittgenstein occupies a singular place in the history of philosophy, having first at an early age written a work which exercised

SECTION E

PRODUCTS AND SUMS OF CLASSES

Summary of Section E.

In the present section, we make an extension of $\alpha \cap \beta, \alpha \cup \beta, R \cap S, R \cup S$. Given a class of classes, say κ, the *product* of κ (which is denoted by $p'\kappa$) is the common part of all the members of κ, *i.e.* the class consisting of those terms which belong to every member of κ. The definition is

$$p'\kappa = \hat{x}(\alpha \epsilon \kappa . \supset_\alpha . x \epsilon \alpha) \quad \text{Df.}$$

If κ has only two members, α and β say, $p'\kappa = \alpha \cap \beta$. If κ has three members, α, β, γ, then $p'\kappa = \alpha \cap \beta \cap \gamma$; and so on. But this process can only be continued to a finite number of terms, whereas the definition of $p'\kappa$ does not require that κ should be finite. This notion is chiefly important in connection with the lower limits of series. For example, let λ be the class of rational numbers whose square is greater than 2, and let "xMy" mean "$x < y$, where x and y are rationals." Then if $x \epsilon \lambda$, $\overrightarrow{M}'x$ will be the class of rationals less than x. Thus $\overrightarrow{M}''\lambda$ will be the class of such classes as $\overrightarrow{M}'x$, where $x \epsilon \lambda$. Thus the product of $\overrightarrow{M}''\lambda$, which we call $p'\overrightarrow{M}''\lambda$, will be the class of rationals which are less than every member of λ, *i.e.* the class of rationals whose squares are less than 2. Each member of $\overrightarrow{M}''\lambda$ is a segment of the series of rationals, and $p'\overrightarrow{M}''\lambda$ is the lower limit of these segments. It is thus that we prove the existence of lower limits of series of segments.

Similarly the *sum* of a class of classes κ is defined as the class consisting of all terms belonging to *some* member of κ; *i.e.*

$$s'\kappa = \hat{x}\{(\exists \alpha) . \alpha \epsilon \kappa . x \epsilon \alpha\} \quad \text{Df,}$$

i.e. x belongs to the sum of κ if x belongs to some κ. This notion plays the same part for upper limits of series of segments as $p'\kappa$ plays for lower limits. It has, however, many more other uses than $p'\kappa$, and is altogether a more important conception. Thus in cardinal arithmetic, if no two members of κ have any term in common, the arithmetical sum of the numbers of members possessed by the various members of κ is the number of members possessed by $s'\kappa$.

The product of a class of relations (λ say) is the relation which holds between x and y when x and y have every relation of the class λ. The definition is

$$\dot{p}'\lambda = \hat{x}\hat{y}(R \epsilon \lambda . \supset_R . xRy) \quad \text{Df.}$$

The properties of $\dot{p}'\lambda$ are analogous to those of $p'\kappa$, but its uses are fewer.

A page from the *Principia Mathematica* by Bertrand Russell and Alfred North Whitehead.

a decisive influence on the philosophical thought of his time, and then, in his mature years, rejecting his early theory and producing a second theory which, for sheer originality, stature and influence, is even more important than the first.

Wittgenstein and subsequent language analysts have been con-

The philosophical self is not the human being, not the human body, or the human soul, with which psychology deals, but rather the metaphysical subject, the limit of the world—not a part of it.

6   The general form of a truth-function is $[\bar{p}, \bar{\xi}, N(\bar{\xi})]$.
This is the general form of a proposition.

6.001   What this says is just that every proposition is a result of successive applications to elementary propositions of the operation $N(\bar{\xi})$.

6.002   If we are given the general form according to which propositions are constructed, then with it we are also given the general form according to which one proposition can be generated out of another by means of an operation.

6.01   Therefore the general form of an operation $\Omega'(\bar{\eta})$ is

$$[\bar{\xi}, N(\bar{\xi})]'(\bar{\eta}) \ (= [\bar{\eta}, \bar{\xi}, N(\bar{\xi})]).$$

This is the most general form of transition from one proposition to another.

6.02   And *this* is how we arrive at numbers. I give the following definitions

$$x = \Omega^{0}{}'x \text{ Def.},$$

$$\Omega'\Omega^{\nu}{}'x = \Omega^{\nu+1}{}'x \text{ Def.}$$

So, in accordance with these rules, which deal with signs, we write the series

$$x, \ \Omega'x, \ \Omega'\Omega'x, \ \Omega'\Omega'\Omega'x, \ldots,$$

in the following way

$$\Omega^{0}{}'x, \ \Omega^{0+1}{}'x, \ \Omega^{0+1+1}{}'x, \ \Omega^{0+1+1+1}{}'x, \ldots.$$

Therefore, instead of '$[x, \xi, \Omega'\xi]$',

I write   '$[\Omega^{0}{}'x, \Omega^{\nu}{}'x, \Omega^{\nu+1}{}'x]$'.

And I give the following definitions

$$0+1 = 1 \text{ Def.,}$$
$$0+1+1 = 2 \text{ Def.,}$$
$$0+1+1+1 = 3 \text{ Def.,}$$
(and so on).

119

A page from Wittgenstein's *Tractatus.*

vinced that most philosophical puzzlements are the result of sloppy use of language. Their task, therefore, is to analyze the function of language so that questions can be precisely constructed to which exact answers can be given. Only then can we know clearly what we are thinking and saying.

As Wittgenstein saw it, philosophy should not engage in synoptic or speculative tasks. Rather, its goal should be to help us think more clearly and precisely about anything and everything. Philosophy is therapy for our linguistic neuroses.

17 Because his whole being was so consumed with passionate thought, Wittgenstein could not give lectures as other university teachers do. To lecture in the ordinary way is to expound, or repeat what has already been thought; and to repeat a thought is not to think it, at any rate, not to think it with Wittgenstein's kind of intensity. So instead of giving conventional lectures, Wittgenstein *thought* what he said as he spoke. He did not reproduce what he had prepared before. And it was precisely because he went through this process of thinking in such a fresh, powerful and concentrated way, in the presence of his students, that he earned their respect, and even something approaching veneration.

Of course his lectures were not elegant in style or form; they were a kind of research, which really serious students—and only such attended Wittgenstein's lectures—found strangely inspiring. For them it was like being in the workshop of a great master where they could witness, and perhaps even participate in, the creation of new and often exhilarating thoughts.

A professor has his students and, if he is the founder of a school, his followers. Wittgenstein had both, but he also had disciples. It was perhaps not difficult to become his disciple because of his magnetic and compelling personality and because of the originality and depth and fervor of his thought. Wittgenstein was conscious of this, and regretted it. A disciple's spiritual dependence on his master at best hinders independent thought, and, at worst, prevents it. And a thought which is not independent is a thought only half understood. . . .

My propositions are elucidatory in this way: he who understands me finally recognizes them as senseless, when he has climbed out through them, on them, over them. (He must so to speak throw away the ladder after he has climbed up on it.) He must surmount these propositions; then he sees the world rightly. Whereof one cannot speak, thereof one must be silent.

WITTGENSTEIN

Three passions, simple but overwhelmingly strong, have governed my life: the longing for love, the search for knowledge, and the unbearable pity for the suffering of mankind.

BERTRAND RUSSELL

Keep me from the wisdom that does not weep, and the philosophy that does not laugh . . .

KAHLIL GIBRAN

18 There seems to be a motif, a pattern, which runs through the lives of almost all the great philosophers; it is a thread so fine that it might be overlooked. With few exceptions, their lives exhibit an alternation: a *withdrawal* from life-in-the-world, then a *return* to the world of men to apply in some way the insights they have gained. It is the ebb and flow of both psychic and physical energy, the alternation of the active and the passive—the Yin and the Yang.

On the one hand, the existentialist is very close to the truth. If one is merely a "spectator" of life, then his observations cannot be very meaningful; they are only second-hand. Apart from a full participation in life where "he laughs all his laughter and cries all his tears," one's philosophizing will not have the mark of life on it.

At the same time, the antinomians must be heard. Unless one can withdraw from life sufficiently to keep his experience in perspective, his insights cannot be trusted. To be sure, this is not easy, for when one has become involved in the human drama, reestablishing an overview may require considerable courage.

Yet a Yin-Yang alternation might be a very workable solution if one can manage it. Life is to be lived; but without the solitude which one finds in the desert, the forest, the mountains, by the seashore or in the study, the meaning of life will almost inevitably be missed. Wrestling with the Ultimate often seems to be preeminently a private affair.

19   In this tribal world, someone must still keep watch. He must stand apart, as best he can, to try to keep life in perspective. The party members won't do it, nor will the fearful, the brainwashed, the prejudiced, or the bigoted. But there must be someone.

There must be someone who remains sensitively aware of the essential humanness in every position that human beings take.

There must be someone who tries to stay as close to *all* the realities as possible, someone who tries, keeps on trying, and who will not give up.

And there is some value in knowing just that—that in this world of partisan proliferation there is someone who will struggle against being manipulated and polarized.

He will only partially succeed. He may reach moments of greater clarity and then fall back into a one-sided point of view, but then he will (like Kant) arouse himself from his "dogmatic slumbers" and start to work again fitting together the pieces of the jigsaw puzzle.

Truly, philosophers play a strange game. They know very well that one thing alone counts, and that all their medley of subtle discussions relates to one single question: why are we born on this earth? And they also know that they will never be able to answer it. Nevertheless, they continue sedately to amuse themselves. Do they not see that people come to them from all points of the compass, not with a desire to partake of their subtlety, but because they hope to receive from them one word of life? If they have such words, why do they not cry them from the housetops, asking their disciples to give, if necessary, their very blood for them? If they have no such words, why do they allow people to believe they will receive from them something which they cannot give?

JACQUES MARITAIN

2

THE CONDITION
AND THE
ODYSSEY

2-1

PREDICAMENT/
ILLUSION

1   Each of us has a world-view—merely because we're human. A world-view is a more or less coherent, all-inclusive frame of reference through which one sees the world; it is a subjective attempt to provide unity and consistency to the totality of one's experience. Since we cannot tolerate excess fragmentation, we must attempt to find an inclusive structure which will harmonize as much of our experience as possible.

For most human beings, a world-view is a given. We are born into it and live within it; we rarely break out of it or even realize that it exists. By and large this inherited framework contains all the essential ingredients for a meaningful existence: social structures which act as guidelines for relating to others; clear-cut value systems of right and wrong; codes indicating acceptable and unacceptable behavior; language, legends, and hero stories which provide group identity; myths which answer a multitude of ultimate questions about the world we live in. Any world-view that can provide all these life-giving elements must be considered a successful world-view.

2   It is one of the purposes of philosophy to help the individual build a world-view that is functional. We each possess what we might call a naive world-view in which many elements remain unsynthesized. The threads of experience have yet to be woven together into a harmonious picture; loose ends remain. Our "collection" of experiences is a hodge-podge of contradictions in values and beliefs.

The ideal world-view will be internally consistent, pragmatically realistic, and personally fulfilling. Philosophy can suggest guidelines and provide materials toward achieving this goal.

Every man takes the limits of his own field of vision for the limits of the world.

SCHOPENHAUER

The last creature in the world to discover water would be the fish, precisely because he is always immersed in it!

RALPH LINTON

There is no implication here that there can be but a single viable world-view. Such a claim would be patently false, for many exist for our examination. While individuals within the same culture tend to share similar world-views, every world-view is in fact unique, personal, and (hopefully) the product of one's own labors.

3   In the year 1910 an American philosopher, Ralph Barton Perry, published in a philosophical journal an article entitled "The Ego-Centric Predicament." Perry wanted to make a specific point about our knowledge of real° objects/events. Western philosophers have long debated whether such external realities in some way depend upon, or are changed by, our perception of them. As a philosopher might ask: What is the meta-physical° status of real objects/events? What is the real world like apart from our perception of it? Or can we ever know for sure what such objects/events really are as things-in-themselves?

Using very lucid logic, Perry made what seems an obvious point: to know what any real object/event is, we have to perceive it. We can never observe things in their "original" state as they might exist apart from our perception of them. How then can we know whether our perception of them changes them? In our knowledge of the real world, therefore, we are in a logical predicament, and a "predicament" by definition is a problem situation to which there is no solution.

As we shall see when we move into epistemology° and examine carefully the nature of human knowledge, these questions about our understanding of the real world are not as far out as they might seem.

4   Let's reexamine the "egocentric predicament" from another standpoint and proceed quite beyond the point Perry was making.

From birth till death each of us is locked into a physical organism from which there is no escape. We are caught in a body which contains all our perceptual and information-processing equipment. Each of us, for as long as we live, is confined within a particular system and we will be able to experience life only in terms of that singular system. This is an obvious limitation, but it's one we fight: who wants to be imprisoned in a narrow cell only six feet high for the duration of one's existence, with no hope of escape?

Yet apparently we must resign ourselves to this condition. No matter how much we would like to jump out of our skins, enter into another person's perceptual shell, and peer out at the world from his center, we can't. We are always reminded that we shall have but a single vantage-point from which we can assess existence.

It therefore appears to be an immutable fact that we can never know how existence is experienced by any other living creature.

5   This egocentric predicament entails an illusion. For the duration of our mortal existence we must occupy a physical organism; we must

2   The Condition and the Odyssey

°Refer to the Glossary for an explanation of *real, reality,* and *realism.*

°*Metaphysics.* The study of the nature of ultimate reality and the dynamic principles (natural, supernatural or other) by which reality exists.

°*Epistemology, epistemological* (often shortened to *epistemic*). The branch of philosophy specializing in the study of knowledge and the acquisition of knowledge.

St. Augustine looked at history from the point of view of the early Christian; Tillemont, from that of a seventeenth-century Frenchman; Gibbon, from that of an eighteenth-century Englishman; Mommsen, from that of a nineteenth-century German. There is no point in asking which was the right point of view. Each was the only one possible for the man who adopted it.

R. G. COLLINGWOOD

"occupy" a *point* in space and time. And herein lies *the egocentric illusion*, for it appears to each of us that our center is the hub of the whole universe; or conversely, it appears to each of us that the entire cosmos revolves around that point in space/time which we occupy.

This egocentric illusion continues to follow us no matter where in space/time we move our center. If I should move my center to Tokyo or the South Pole, it would appear *to me* as though the universe had shifted its center to accommodate me. If I should travel to a planet in the Andromeda galaxy, some 2 million light-years distant from our Milky Way galaxy, it would still appear to me that the cosmos revolved around my ego-center.

Perceptually, of course, *I am* the center of *my* universe, but not of *the* universe. Yet I *perceive* myself as *its* center. This illusion is not limited to human beings. Every living organism with conscious perception would share in the egocentric illusion because it would occupy *its* point in space/time. Every such creature would be enclosed within its physical organism, and so the universe would appear to revolve around it.

If any living creature really thinks of itself as the point-center of the cosmos, there is an illusion in that consciousness. No one of us is the center of the universe any more than a billion other creatures are in fact cosmic centers.

In a word: every living, conscious creature experiences itself to be the true center of the cosmos, but in truth the cosmos has no center. Rather, the cosmos is filled with creatures which share the illusion that they are cosmic centers.

6   At this point almost all men take a further step which our nonhuman fellow creatures probably do not. Taking the egocentric illusion seriously, we proceed to make *aristocentric claims.*° Whenever any creature fails to correct for his egocentric illusion and begins to feel that he really is the center of the universe, and further, if he feels that he *should* be treated by others *as though he were the center,* then he has taken a giant step beyond the illusion itself. He is making an aristocentric claim, an unjustified claim to superiority. In various ways he may conclude that he is special, and insist that the cosmos has favored him. He may claim that in some way his existence has special meaning, that he has a special knowledge or message, or is endowed with special grace or powers. In every case we can suspect that he has failed to make allowance for the illusion that all of us share.

We rarely make such aristocentric claims in the singular, for if any one of us should say, "I am the center of the cosmos" we would probably be laughed out of our illusion. So we make the aristocentric claim in the first person plural that "*We* are special," that "*We* are the Favored Ones of the cosmos," and we can reinforce one another's claim so that it's believable. It feels good to be special and belong to a special group, and if our numbers are large we might even persuade the world

"Faites qu'il pleuve demain et toujours."

The Prayer of the Little Ducks
Dear God,
give us a flood of water.
Let it rain tomorrow and always.
Give us plenty of little slugs
and other luscious things to eat.
Protect all folk who quack
and everyone who knows how to
swim. Amen.

CARMEN DE GASZTOLD

°*Aristocentric claim.* **An inordinate claim to superiority. See page 31.**

Much of what has been written in English-speaking countries in the last ten years about the Soviet Union, and in the Soviet Union about the English-speaking countries, has been vitiated by this inability to achieve even the most elementary measure of imaginative understanding of what goes on in the mind of the other party, so that the words and actions of the other are always made to appear malign, senseless, or hypocritical.

EDWARD HALLETT CARR

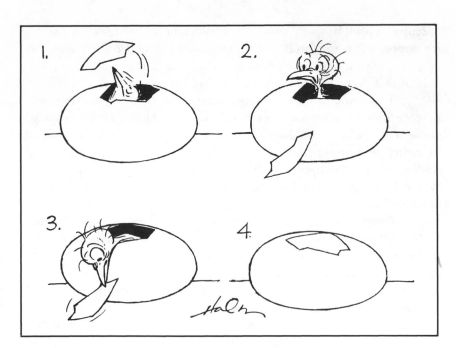

Just as it is possible to have any number of geometries other than the Euclidian which give an equally perfect account of space configurations, so it is possible to have descriptions of the universe, all equally valid, that do not contain our familiar contrasts of time and space.

BENJAMIN WHORF

Man can either remain within his "accidental" reference frame and unquestioningly accept the meaning it has to offer, or he can boldly emerge from his psycho–epistemological cocoon and broaden his reality image. The need for man to break out of his capsule is crucial, for encapsulation may well be the essence of contemporary man's spiritual emptiness.

JOSEPH R. ROYCE

to take us seriously. When the claim is made collectively, we can avoid the absurdity of standing naked and alone with an indefensible "I AM."

7   As sociologists, Paul Horton and Chester Hunt use the term "ethnocentric" when referring to any form of aristocentricism. They write:

> All societies and all groups assume the superiority of their own culture. . . . We are ethnocentric because (1) we are so habituated to our culture's patterns that other patterns fail to please us; (2) we do not understand what an unfamiliar trait means to its user and therefore impute our reactions to him; (3) we are trained to be ethnocentric; (4) we find ethnocentrism a comforting defense against our own inadequacies. Ethnocentrism (1) promotes group unity, loyalty, and morale, and thereby reinforces nationalism and patriotism; (2) protects a culture from changes, including those needed to preserve the culture; (3) reinforces bigotry and blinds a group to the true facts about themselves and other groups, sometimes preventing their successful adjustment to other groups and cultures.

8   The ultimate in aristocentric claims was recorded by a psychiatrist in the case of three men each of whom claimed to be Christ and God. All three were institutionalized as paranoid schizophrenics whose "delusions of grandeur" had taken the form of messianic fantasies.

Dr. Milton Rokeach wanted to know what adjustments these three men would make if placed together. After all, each was making the final exclusive claim: "I alone am God." The agony of their encounter was recorded by Rokeach in his book *The Three Christs of Ypsilanti.*

WORLD-VIEW I   *The Primitive*

I live in a capricious world, unpredictable and dangerous. Evil spirits hide in caves, ponds, woods, and sometimes in animals and people. I must be careful not to offend the evil spirits. I try to make them stay away from my fire and the door of my hut. The spirits of my ancestors will help me. All that happens—the storm and the rains, the green maize, a good hunt, my success in battle, the getting of many cattle, wives and children—all these are mine because I perform the rites of our ancestors and keep favor with the good spirits. The witchdoctor also helps.

WORLD-VIEW II   *The Hindu*

At last I am born a Brahmin and I therefore know that I lived a good life in my last incarnation. Perhaps now I can achieve moksha so that I shall not return again in mortal flesh. I shall therefore practice diligently, spending many hours daily in meditation. The world of maya around me will vanish and my soul will know the joy and peace of nirvana. Vishnu will aid me. Glory to thee, god of the lotus-eye! Have compassion upon me!

WORLD-VIEW III   *Early Christian*

I live on the brink of Eternity. The long cosmic struggle between the forces of Light—who dwell in the Heavens above—and the forces of Darkness—who dwell below—is nearly finished. God's plan for the ages is about to be fulfilled with the destruction of Satan. In Christ there will be no more death. We have been chosen to be the Children of Light and we will dwell with Him in His Kingdom. His only Son, Yeshua the Messiah, was the herald of God's Reign, and we must finish our earthly tasks quickly for His Reign is about to begin. Ἀμήν, ἔρχου κύριε Ἰησοῦ. Amen, return quickly, Lord Jesus.

WORLD-VIEW IV   *The Taoist*

I weary of the ways of men and I seek serenity by the waterfall and in the forest. Wherever men gather together, there are too many. The forces of yang and yin thrust them about and society is roiled as a muddy torrent. Let them begone! In the quietness of my solitude I shall seek the Tao, or rather the Tao shall seek me. Wu-wei—quiet now; no striving, no longing, no fear. Let me be filled with the tranquillity of silence and inaction; let me be immersed in Tao. Why should existence be like a drawn bow?

WORLD-VIEW V   *Western Scientific*

I live in a universe of matter in motion. The universe seems to follow consistent patterns which we can formulate into workable "laws" and describe with mathematical and geometrical terms. We now believe that life originated through natural processes and developed according to the principles of evolution. We exist in an "open" universe, containing billions of galaxies and, most likely, millions of planets sustaining intelligent life-forms. Man is unique, but he is also an integral part of nature and of natural processes which operate throughout the universe. With further scientific understanding man will be able to control his own destiny and mold his future.

At their first meeting each man was asked to introduce himself. Joseph obliged: "Yes, I'm God." Clyde admitted that "God" and "Jesus" were two of his six names. Leon stated that he was Lord of Lords and King of Kings, and added: "It also states on my birth certificate that I am the reincarnation of Jesus Christ of Nazareth. . . ."

Rokeach notes that "the confrontations were obviously upsetting."

Clearly, all of them felt threatened. The profound contradiction posed by others' claims had somehow penetrated deeply, to become transformed into an inner conflict between two primitive beliefs: each man's delusional belief in his own identity and his realistic belief that only one person can have any given identity. Many times Joseph said: "There is only one God"; and Clyde said: "I'm the only one"; and Leon said: "I won't deny that you gentlemen are instrumental gods—small 'g.' But I'm the one who was created before time began."

Each of the Christs of Ypsilanti ultimately made similar adjustments. Each decided that his godly qualities of compassion and magnanimity allowed him to accept the fact that the other two men were mentally disturbed. Each came around to a "compassionate acceptance" of the other deluded mortals.

> *Dense, unenlightened people are notoriously confident that they have the monopoly on truth.*
>
> JOSHUA LOTH LIEBMAN

> *Each individual is his own center, and the world centers in him.*
>
> KIERKEGAARD

ARISTOCENTRISM: *Religion*

"Thereupon Abram fell on his face; and God said to him, 'This is my covenant with you: . . . I am establishing my covenant between myself and you and your descendants after you throughout their generations as a perpetual covenant, to be God to you and your descendants." [Gen. 17:3–4, 7]

"If we wish to compare our people with foreigners, we find that although we are only their equals or even their inferiors in other matters, in religion—that is, in the cult of the gods—we are far superior." [Cicero]

"Do Jehovah's Witnesses believe theirs is the only true faith?"

"Certainly. If they thought someone else had the true faith, they would preach that. There is only 'one faith,' said Paul." [Milton G. Henschel, a Witness]

"The Catholic religion claims to be a supernaturally revealed religion. What is more important, it claims to be the one and only true religion in the world, intended for all men, alone acceptable to God." [*Toward the Eternal Commencement*, 1958]

"Japan is the divine country. . . . This is true only of our country, and nothing similar may be found in foreign lands. That is why it is called the divine country." [Kitabatake, a Shinto]

"Crinkled hills freckled with kraals plunge to the Nsuze River. In this region lies the legendary birthplace of a man called Zulu—which means 'heaven.' In the early 1600's he founded a clan that bears his name, and thus became progenitor of the Zulus, the 'People of Heaven.'" [*National Geographic*]

9   Dr. Rokeach writes:

Clyde and Joseph and Leon are really unhappy caricatures of human beings; in them we can see with terrible clarity some of the factors that can lead any man to give up realistic beliefs and adopt instead a more grandiose identity.

And they are caricatures of all men in another sense too. I believe it was the German philosopher Fichte who pointed out years ago that to some extent all of us strive to be like God or Christ. One or another facet of this theme is to be found in a good deal of Western literature—for example, in the writings of Sherwood Anderson, William Faulkner, and Dostoevsky. Bertrand Russell said it best of all: "Every man would like to be God, if it were possible; some find it difficult to admit the impossibility."

Man is encapsulated. By encapsulated I mean claiming to have the whole of truth when one has only part of it. By encapsulated I mean looking at life partially and proceeding to make statements concerning the whole of life. And by encapsulated I mean living partially because one's daily activities are based on a world-view of philosophy of life which is meager next to the larger meaning of existence.

JOSEPH R. ROYCE

A human self cannot be brought into harmony with Absolute Reality unless it can get rid of its innate self-centredness. This is the hardest task that Man can set himself; but, if he accomplishes it, his reward will be far more than proportionate to the toil and pain of the spiritual struggle. In giving up self-centredness he will have felt as if he were losing his life; but in achieving this act of self-sacrifice he will find that he has really saved his life, because he will have given his life a new centre, and this new centre will be the Absolute Reality that is the spiritual presence behind the phenomena.

ARNOLD TOYNBEE

10   This egocentric illusion which we all share produces within us distorted perspectives. Consider, for instance, the *egocentric illusion in time.* Our life-*times* are short in the perspective of geological time or human history, yet we tend to think of all existence in terms of our allotted span.

Time overpowers our minds. Are we really convinced that the fossil trilobite from Cambrian eras darted about on the ocean sand, alive and well, running from enemies and seeking food? Holding in one's hand the fossil animal, 500 million years old, staggers our time sense. And what of our australopithecine ancestors only 5 million years ago or the Sumerian clay-writers of five thousand years ago? Were they really flesh and blood like us, laboring, getting angry, telling lies, making love, laughing at tall stories, getting stoned, and fearing death? Most of us are almost—but not quite —convinced that their existence was real.

It is very easy to fall into the belief that things happening during our lifetimes have never happened before. *Our* times we take to be the norm, or the culmination of history, or the best times, or the worst times, or whatever. We may forget, or not care to know, that the same beliefs have been shared by all who breathe.

11   We are equally prone to a distorted perspective because of the *egocentric illusion in space.* Wherever we locate our space-occupying organism, the space around us takes on vividness and clarity and contains all things of significance for us; our life-space becomes the center of all things good, and more distant regions somehow lack the reality of our vicinity.

The most important shrine in the Greek world was at Delphi with its temple where the god Apollo revealed himself. Emissaries and pilgrims came from all around the Middle Sea to discover his will. When

---

ARISTOCENTRISM: *Race*

"Of old the Hellenic race was marked off from the barbarian as more keen-witted and more free from nonsense." [Herodotus]

A gray-bearded Kirghiz patriarch stated that the heart of a Kirghizian is superior to that of any other race of people, and, he added, "the heart is what really matters in men."

A modern Mexican painter inscribed a beautiful work with the words: "Through *my* race will speak the Spirit."

"True history begins from the moment when the German with mighty hand seizes the inheritance of antiquity." [H. S. Chamberlain]

"We the Black Nation of the Earth are the NUMBER ONE owners of it, the best of all human beings. You are the Most Powerful, the Most Beautiful and the Wisest." [Elijah Muhammad, referring to Black Muslims]

"Everything great, noble, or fruitful in the works of man on this planet, in science, art, and civilization . . . belongs to one family alone. . . . History shows that all civilization derives from the white race, that none can exist without its help, and that a society is great and brilliant only so far as it preserves the blood of the noble group that created it." [Le Comte de Gobineau]

"You have to leave something."

prophesying, the young priestess of the temple sat on a bronze tripod over an opening in the rock floor. This opening was the *omphalos,* the "navel" or center of the universe. From this "navel" arose a narcotic incense which induced an ecstatic trance in the priestess. While the young lady was out of her mind, Apollo could speak his.

This spatial predicament gives rise to various claims of sacred ground or holy lands. The Shintos, for instance, believed that the Japanese islands are "The phenomenal center of the universe," created by the primeval gods Izanagi and Izanami. "From the central truth that the Mikado is the direct descendant of the gods, the tenet that Japan ranks far above all other countries is a natural consequence. No other nation is entitled to equality with her. . . ." The Chinese made a similar claim: China was "the Middle Kingdom," that is, the center of the flat disc-

If the doors of perception were cleansed, everything would appear to man as it is, infinite. For man has closed himself up till he sees all things through the narrow chinks of his cavern.

WILLIAM BLAKE

shaped earth. Everything praiseworthy was found at that center; the farther one traveled from China the less civilized and respectable all things became.

The egocentric illusion in space contributes to various forms of tribalism and nationalism. We tend to devalue the lands and people which remain at a distance geographically and, therefore, psychologically. On the maps of human experience, distant space is still inscribed *terra incognita*.

Indeed, I do not forget that my voice is but one voice, my experience a mere drop in the sea, my knowledge no greater than the visual field in a microscope, my mind's eye a mirror that reflects a small corner of the world, and my ideas—a subjective confession.

CARL G. JUNG

12   At the prehuman level it seems very unlikely that any animal could have sufficient self-awareness to assess its own existential condition. Without the capacity for abstract reflection on experience, no creature could hope to rise above or out of its egocentric world-view.

Man, however, can develop such self-awareness. He can comprehend and transcend. "To understand our ethnocentrism will help us to avoid being so gravely misled by it. We cannot avoid *feeling* ethnocentric, but with understanding, we need not *act* upon these irrational feelings."

Human growth requires the transcendence of our egocentric illusions and, by an act of moral courage, the reconditioning of our aristocentric feelings and beliefs.

The spiritual struggle in the more exclusive-minded [Western] half of the world to cure ourselves of our family infirmity seems likely to be the most crucial episode in the next chapter of the history of Mankind.

ARNOLD TOYNBEE

13   To achieve an efficient balance between a useful pride in our own culture and subcultures and a realization of the real qualities of other groups is a difficult task. It requires both an emotional maturity which enables the individual to face his world without the armor of exaggerated self-esteem and an intellectual realization of the complexity of cultural processes. There is no guaranteed way to achieve this maturity. . . . But unless we can understand and control our ethnocentric impulses, we shall simply go on repeating the blunders of our predecessors.

HORTON AND HUNT

2-2

SELF/AUTONOMY

1   At this moment in space/time, I *think* I know *who* I am and where *I am.* As I (the Greek word for "I" is *ego*) write these lines, I am attached to a large desk in my study. The time is 11:40 p.m., and a fireplace blazes in the background.

But as *you* read these lines, where in space/time are you? *Who* are *you*? And what are *you* experiencing? We think it takes a "who" to experience—we can assume so for now—but it might not be too absurd to inquire later if *you* and *I* are whos at all.

2   Philosophers who have attempted serious thinking about the nature of the "self" have encountered formidable ambiguities. Normally, one would turn to the field specialists for some hard facts, but in this case psychiatric and psychological literature is of little help. The word "self" seems to be given an endless variety of meanings. Sometimes it is used to mean the whole of one's being, including all mental and physical operations. Sometimes it refers only to mental activity (conscious and unconscious) and excludes the body. Sometimes "self" refers to an organizing psyche which determines how one thinks, feels, and behaves. And sometimes "the self" is only a mental construct used to describe observable behavioral patterns.

So, what is a "self"? Or, perhaps more to the point, when I ask who I am, am I (!) asking a meaningful question at all?

3   *From the movie "Cleopatra."* At the end of a glorious career, Mark Antony, lying mortally wounded in the arms of Cleopatra, speaks of his impending death as "the ultimate separation of my self from myself." Apparently he means that his "genius"-self is about to separate from his physical-self, since it was current Roman belief that each man possesses

The accurate, realistic assessment of self resulting from acceptance makes possible the use of self as a dependable, trustworthy instrument for achieving one's purpose.

ARTHUR W. COMBS

"How much of me is me?"

a *genius* (and that each woman possesses a *juno*), a sort of individual spiritlike essence, distinct from the physical body, which gives him identity and has the power to protect him. But we can't be sure what he is saying.

News item. A man is indicted for embezzlement, but he is never caught and lives under an assumed name in another state for twenty-six years. Then, by a freak move, a relative turns him in. "Yes," he confesses, "I did it."

But did he? After twenty-six years, in what sense is he the same "self"? He does not have the same name; having lived for a quarter-century under a different name, he has developed a new identity. Nor does he have the same body; we are told the human body completely renews itself every seven to ten years. The "person" (that is, personality, self-image, behavioral style) has changed; with the passing of so many years he *feels* like a different person.

How much of the original person—"self" or "body"—still exists at all? To be sure, he does possess a memory of a past event. Does that make him guilty? But what if, through repression, he has blocked the painful event from his mind and has no memory of the crime? Is *he* guilty, despite his (?) confession?

From "The Sixth Sense" (*ABC-TV*). The doctor hypnotizes the young lady on the witness stand and regresses her (?) to a time on the afternoon of the previous Thursday and asks her (?) where she (?) is. "I (?) am sitting on a rock by the lake." "What do you (?) see?" "I (?) am not really at the lake. I (?) am in the large mansion looking at the man I (?) am about to kill." "But you (?) were not in the mansion, were you (?)?", he (?) persists. "No, I (?) was sitting at the lake." "Yes," he (?) answers, "I (?) know, because I (?) was sitting beside you (?)."

Would you care to try to figure out who is speaking to whom about whom and who is doing what when and where?

4   What each of us can become during our life/time is determined by two fundamental conditions: (1) the degree to which we experience a more or less consistent sense of self or identity, and (2) whether the feelings we have developed about that self are predominantly good.

These conditions are of crucial importance during our earlier years. If the environment in which we are nurtured inhibits the development of an integrated self and/or instills negative feelings about that self—self-hate in its many forms—then the quality of our existence can be permanently damaged. It is quite possible at a later time to face our inner problems and develop belatedly a sense of self and a feeling of self-worth; but the therapeutic path is often prolonged and painful.

5   The identity question—"Who am I?"—must be persistently asked by each of us during our separation years. We all go through an "identity

An almost unshakable tradition has it that the man who has not sought out his own nature and come to terms with his findings will, in his actions, commit himself to conflicting goals and bring about his own undoing. . . . The theme has a corollary: the self that is sought must not give up too easily. It takes a full lifetime to be human. Thus, the task of hunting for one's true nature cannot be ignored, and it cannot be quickly finished, except on pain of an early eclipse of the self.

BERTRAND P. HELM

One of the best known Western statements that there is no such entity as a self is from the philosopher David Hume (1711–1776). The more he meditated on the problem, the more he became convinced that the "mind" or "self" is nothing other than a "bundle of perceptions," that is, the totality of perception. He wrote: "There are some philosophers who imagine we are every moment intimately conscious of what we call our *self*; that we feel its existence and its continuance is existence; and we are certain, beyond the evidence of a demonstration, both of its perfect identity and simplicity. . . . For my part, when I enter most intimately into what I call *myself*, I always stumble on some particular perception or other of heat or cold, light or shade, love or hatred, pain or pleasure. I never can catch myself at any time without a perception, and never can observe anything but the perception. When my perceptions are removed for any time, as by sound sleep, so long am I insensible of *myself*, and, may truly be said not to exist."

crisis" beginning near the onset of puberty. In the early teen years no adolescent has a consistent feeling of being a self. Besides the fact that he still identifies with authorities, it is also during these years that dramatic physiological and emotional changes are taking place, and there is a correlated upheaval in the psyche. Body and self are both changing and developing.

During these years, separation from the decision-making, behavior-setting authorities normally takes place. Each developing self begins to discover his own feelings and thoughts; he must explore his own "style" of doing things. As he experiences more and more spontaneous and authentic expressions of his own being, he begins to feel a sense of identity. He finds that there is a consistency and a distinctiveness in the way he behaves, thinks, and feels. This is a gradual process, not to be accomplished overnight. Throughout these years of separation, it is essential that the question "Who am I?" be continually asked, not explicitly in words, but implicitly in all that the self-in-process-of-becoming does.

6   Selfhood develops, or is allowed to develop, as one perceives his "self" in action, as one thinks his own thoughts and feels his own feelings. The commonest problem most of us face lies in the fact that conflicting elements have been "programmed" into us by various authorities. Few if any of us have been guided by consistent authority. Most of us have grown up under the guidance of two or more "significant others" whose

2 *The Condition and the Odyssey*

beliefs and values differed. What they demanded of us varied. Since we were dependent upon them, we had to take their standards seriously and accede to them.

So, as separation takes place and freedom is experienced, these diverse elements must be integrated into a "self." Gradually it must become a harmonious, smoothly operating system. After some years of practice in experiencing one's self in action, he should feel a sense of identity. Then he can say meaningfully, "I know who I am."

To borrow an analogy from space technology, the self becomes an "onboard guidance system." The system cuts the umbilical cord and goes on internal power. It functions automatically, runs smoothly, and operates on schedule.

7 The second major condition which determines the quality of existence is the feeling one develops about his self. In general, if things go right for us, then we develop positive feelings: self-worth, self-esteem, self-love. Whatever the terms, we are referring to a cluster of constructive feelings which we develop about the self and the things the self does.

One who has these positive feelings feels privileged at being who he is and what he is; he enjoys living with himself.

How we feel about our selves strongly reflects how others felt

"What do you recommend for someone going through the agony of soul-searching and inner criticism?"

about us during our earliest years. If we were loved, then we feel lovable; we can love our selves. If we were accepted, then we feel acceptable; we can accept our selves. If we were trusted, then we feel trustworthy; we can trust our selves. If our very existence was valued, then we feel valuable; we value our selves.

It is impossible to escape the severe fact that we are wholly dependent upon the feeling-reflections of others during these early stages of development.

8 The self concept, we know, is learned. People learn who they are and what they are from the ways in which they have been treated by those who surround them in the process of their growing up. This is what Sullivan called learning about self from the mirror of other people. People discover their self concepts from the kinds of experiences they have had with life—not from telling, but from experience. People develop feelings that they are liked, wanted, acceptable and able from having been liked, wanted, accepted and from having been successful. One learns that he is these things, not from being told so but only through the experience of being treated as though he were so.

ARTHUR W. COMBS

The member of a primitive clan might express his identity in the formula "I am we"; he cannot yet conceive of himself as an "individual," existing apart from his group. . . . When the feudal system broke down, this sense of identity was shaken and the acute question "who am I?" arose.

ERICH FROMM

9 One who has been loved during his formative years develops a love of self. There is a common confusion between "self-love" and "selfishness." Self-love is neither a narcissistic obsession with one's physical or intellectual qualities nor egotism, the inordinate desire to look out for one's own interests at the expense of others.

Erich Fromm writes:

If it is a virtue to love my neighbor as a human being, it must be a virtue—and not a vice—to love myself, since I am a human being too. There is no concept of man in which I myself am not included. A doctrine which proclaims such an exclusion proves itself to be intrinsically contradictory. The idea expressed in the Biblical "Love thy neighbor as thyself!" implies that respect for one's own integrity and uniqueness, love for and understanding of one's self, cannot be separated from respect and love and understanding for another individual. The love for my own self is inseparably connected with the love for any other being. . . . Love of others and love of ourselves are not alternatives. On the contrary, an attitude of love toward themselves will be found in all those who are capable of loving others.

10 In summary, if we are among the fortunate ones for whom things have gone right on both scores—in our sense of identity and self-esteem—then we can be sure that some of the following things have happened to us.

We were loved and not rejected; therefore, we are lovable.
We were given consistent guidelines for learning social behavior.

According to Zen, awareness of oneself dawns gradually, step by step. A Zen master of the twelfth century, Kakuan, drew the "ten oxherding pictures" to represent this progression toward enlightenment. The bull symbolizes the dynamic principles of life and truth; the ten bulls suggest the sequence of steps in "the realization of one's true nature." [Paul Reps]

1. The Search for the Bull

In the pasture of this world, I endlessly push aside the tall grasses in search of the bull.
Following unnamed rivers, lost upon the interpenetrating paths of distant mountains,
My strength failing and my vitality exhausted, I cannot find the bull.
I only hear the locusts chirring through the forest at night.

Comment: The bull never has been lost. What need is there to search? Only because of separation from my true nature, I fail to find him. In the confusion of the senses I lose even his tracks. Far from home, I see many crossroads, but which way is the right one I know not. Greed and fear, good and bad, entangle me.

2. Discovering the Footprints

Along the riverbank under the trees, I discover footprints!
Even under the fragrant grass I see his prints.
Deep in remote mountains they are found.
These traces no more can be hidden than one's nose, looking heavenward.

Comment: Understanding the teaching, I see the footprints of the bull. Then I learn that, just as many utensils are made from one metal, so too are myriad entities made of the fabric of self. Unless I discriminate, how will I perceive the true from the untrue? Not yet having entered the gate, nevertheless I have discerned the path.

We say "I think so-and-so" and this word "I" suggests that thinking is the act of a person. . . . It is supposed that thoughts cannot just come and go, but need a person to think them. Now, of course, it is true that thoughts can be collected into bundles, so that one bundle is my thoughts, another is your thoughts, and a third is the thoughts of Mr. Jones. But I think the person is not an ingredient in the single thought: he is rather constituted by relations of the thoughts to each other and to the body. . . . The grammatical forms "I think," "you think," and "Mr. Jones thinks," are misleading if regarded as indicating an analysis of a single thought. It would be better to say "it thinks in me," like "it rains here", or better still, "there is a thought in me."

BERTRAND RUSSELL
Analysis of Mind

We learned that we were of value for what we *were,* and not for what we *did.* Unacceptable behavior was not confused with *being* unacceptable as selves.

As we were ready to cope with new experiences, we were allowed the freedom to explore life, on schedule, a little at a time.

We were provided with the support which enabled us to handle hurt and failure without loss of self-esteem.

We were allowed to express our feelings honestly, even verbally, without fear of punishment for having such feelings.

We tested boundaries—within and without—and developed realistic estimates of their limits.

We were encouraged to integrate periods of instability and change as a natural part of our growth.

We gradually found that we could exist independently and apart from our parents' protection.

Eventually we came to terms with a separate identity and felt comfortable with our own value systems and beliefs.

The person who "knows what he believes" can be one of the most dangerous individuals in our society. He has not only cut himself off from life in order to preserve his defenses; he would bring all his resources to bear upon us to do the same.

11   Most of us never move beyond *self*-consciousness. During the Who-am-I? stage we are never quite sure how we are going to respond to people, symbols, or situations. We have been accustomed to reacting as others have conditioned us, but now the question becomes: "How would I really respond to it in *my* way?" So, we try out new forms of behaving and explore new experiences. "Do *I* like liver and onions?" "How do *I* feel about him?" "Do *I* really *believe* that?"

3. Perceiving the Bull

I hear the song of the nightingale.
The sun is warm, the wind is mild, willows are green
*   along the shore,*
Here no bull can hide!
What artist can draw that massive head, those majestic
*   horns?*

Comment: When one hears the voice, one can sense its source. As soon as the six senses merge, the gate is entered. Wherever one enters one sees the head of the bull! This unity is like salt in water, like color in dyestuff. The slightest thing is not apart from self.

4. Catching the Bull

I seize him with a terrific struggle.
His great will and power are inexhaustible.
He charges to the high plateau far above the cloud-mists,
Or in an impenetrable ravine he stands.

Comment: He dwelt in the forest a long time, but I caught him today! Infatuation for scenery interferes with his direction. Longing for sweeter grass, he wanders away. His mind still is stubborn and unbridled. If I wish him to submit, I must raise my whip.

While working through the identity problem, we are forced, therefore, into self-consciousness. But after one has developed a congenial style of behavior, then he no longer wonders how he will respond, nor does he plan his responses: he merely responds. He asks himself less and less how he thinks and feels about things: he simply thinks and feels. So the self-consciousness that was a necessary part of the developmental phase begins to fade away.

12　　Buddhism is explicitly committed to the doctrine of *anatta*, "no self." The "self" is an illusion. The Buddhist believes that the feeling of individuality is an acculturated condition. The "ego" is the unfortunate result of a bit of social programming which has persuaded us that we are separate and distinct identities.

The egoless state is one of pure spontaneous experience. Ideally, the good Buddhist, through years of disciplined practice, attempts to banish any culturally conditioned "self" that says "This is good" or "This is the proper way to behave" or "This is my way of doing things." Rather, spontaneous behavior is above and beyond acculturation; it is impersonal because it is not culturally produced or ego-defined. It is a way of experiencing everything in an unmediated way. One can look at a candle and experience the pure flame, not as subject-object, but as direct unmediated experience, as though the experiencer were impinging directly upon the flame.

We in the West are habituated to putting a name to everything so we can store it away, call it back, talk about it, or reexperience it dimly at a later time. The Easterner values more the quality of the original experience without any sort of conceptual or verbal intervention.

The Buddhist point of view, therefore, is that the ego interferes with pure experience, and once one begins to know pure experience, he no longer has a need for ego to mediate it.

The Buddhist has a strong self behind the no-self. That is, with careful definition, we can say that the very strong self (Western) that has passed beyond self-consciousness to spontaneous experience has reached a state very similar to the Buddhist no-self state. If one has succeeded in developing a self-system that works smoothly and harmoniously, then the identity question has become meaningless. Enjoying the strong feeling of unity pervading all his experience, he has forgotten that he "has" a self.

13　　The word "autonomy" refers to one's ability to function independently in terms of an authentic self. The measure of one's autonomy is his capacity to determine his own behavior and make decisions consonant with what he truly is, in contrast to behavior which conforms to norms set by others which may be discordant with his own existential needs.

Here Phaethon lies: in Phoebus' car he fared and though he greatly failed, more greatly dared.

OVID

A farmer went out to sow, and as he sowed some seed fell along the path and the birds ate it. Other seed fell on rocky ground and was scorched by the heat of the sun. Some seed fell among thorns which outgrew the grain and choked it. But still other seeds fell on fertile soil and grew. . .

Mark 4:1–9 (paraphrase)

And some seeds fell upon a conveyor-belt and were carried into a factory, where they were processed, refrigerated, and sterilized.

ARNOLD TOYNBEE

2　The Condition and the Odyssey

5. Taming the Bull

The whip and rope are necessary,
Else he might stray off down some dusty road.
Being well trained, he becomes naturally gentle.
Then, unfettered, he obeys his master.

Comment: When one thought arises, another thought follows. When the first thought springs from enlightenment, all subsequent thoughts are true. Through delusion, one makes everything untrue. Delusion is not caused by objectivity; it is the result of subjectivity. Hold the nose-ring tight and do not allow even a doubt.

6. Riding the Bull Home

Mounting the bull, slowly I return homeward.
The voice of my flute intones through the evening.
Measuring with hand-beats the pulsating harmony, I
*   direct the endless rhythm.*
Whoever hears this melody will join me.

Comment: This struggle is over; gain and loss are assimilated. I sing the song of the village woodsman, and play the tunes of the children. Astride the bull, I observe the clouds above. Onward I go, no matter who may wish to call me back.

The ability to make autonomous decisions presupposes several things. First, it requires an awareness of one's needs, and this comes only from experience. It means being able to recognize one's own feelings and to sort out authentic needs from acculturated needs, or acculturated beliefs *about* needs.

Another requisite is the courage of self-affirmation. To accept all that one is, and especially those aspects of one's self which are objectionable (to authorities or peers), imperfect (to perfectionist parents), and unacceptable (to society), takes courage. Self-acceptance always contains an implied "in spite of": "I affirm my existence in spite of my bad habits, short temper, dependence needs," or whatever. This courage grows as we experience self-affirmation in concrete situations.

A third requisite is an understanding of the culture-patterns within which one has lived his existence. Without recognition of the beliefs and values which one has unknowingly followed, it is difficult to separate autonomous behavior from conformity.

14   How does one experience his existence if he has achieved autonomy?

For one thing, in terms of identity, he knows who he is and who he isn't. He feels like a whole self, and there is no felt need to engage in competitive behavior to preserve his identity. It feels genuine. He doesn't feel like an empty shell having to pretend that there is something inside. A self—someone—dwells inside. This is the feeling of being integrated.

One with a clear sense of self knows his likes and dislikes. He has a distinct personal feeling of right and wrong; he does not operate on borrowed guidelines labeled "moral" by others. Nor does he experience a sense of panic that he might be easily persuaded to do what he does not want to do or, more important, to be what he is not. In occasional situations, of course, he will choose or even be forced *to do* things which he does not want or like to do; but he knows that—short of brainwashing—he can never be forced *to be* what he is not.

15   When one feels like a whole self, he also has a feeling of authenticity. He feels genuine rather than phony. His behavior doesn't feel like playacting, as though all his social interactions were merely speaking lines from an endless drama.

Out of an authentic self, authenticity comes, and therefore he can be honest with others, freely and by choice and not from a compulsion to obey formalistic rules. In normal relationships he finds no need to be manipulative or indirect. Nor will he use his honesty to hurt others.

For the authentic person the game-playing patterns of social relationships take on a different meaning. He may decide that he will play games—social roles, rank roles, political strategies, good-manners

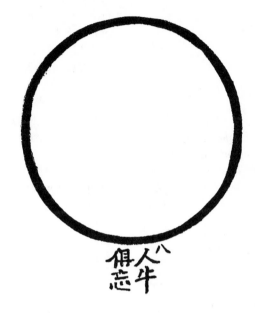

7. The Bull Transcended

Astride the bull, I reach home.
I am serene. The bull too can rest.
The dawn has come. In blissful repose,
Within my thatched dwelling I have abandoned the
*   whip and rope.*

Comment: All is one law, not two. We only make the bull a temporary subject. It is as the relation of rabbit and trap, of fish and net. It is as gold and dross, or the moon emerging from a cloud. One path of clear light travels on throughout endless time.

8. Both Bull and Self Transcended

Whip, rope, person, and bull—all merge in No-Thing.
This heaven is so vast no message can stain it.
How may a snowflake exist in a raging fire?
Here are the footprints of the patriarchs.

Comment: Mediocrity is gone. Mind is clear of limitation. I seek no state of enlightenment. Neither do I remain where no enlightenment exists. Since I linger in neither condition, eyes cannot see me. If hundreds of birds strew my path with flowers, such praise would be meaningless.

The self has to be achieved; it is not given. All that is given is the equipment and at least the minimal (mother and child) social environment. Since the self is achieved through social contact, it has to be understood in terms of others. "Self and other" is not a duality because they go so together that separation is quite impossible.

EARL C. KELLEY

Hell is—other people.

NIETZSCHE

Happiness is the emotional state that accompanies need satisfaction.

GAIL AND SNELL PUTNEY

games, and so on; but his playing will not be infused with a seriousness or compulsiveness ("uptightness"). They are not panic-plays since there is no inner need to play them; there is no do-or-die emotional investment in them. He plays games deliberately as situations demand, plays them with an awareness of the game-structure and the prevailing rules. He can accept the games and follow the rules, but he doesn't use rules, policies, laws, or legalisms to meet neurotic needs: to avoid taking responsibility, making decisions, or relating honestly with others.

An important result of the authentic feeling is that he is not afraid to "look inside himself" or to allow others to see and know him. He has no need to use formalities to prevent others from knowing him. He can remove his masks if he so wishes, as if to say, "This is what I am." If he should be rejected, his life is not shattered. The integrity of his self remains intact and his self-worth is not seriously affected.

16   A clear sense of identity often results in a relaxed existence. All of life loses some of its anxiety and tension. In knowing who one is, he does not have to fight the inner battles of an identity crisis. There is no compulsion to prove to others what he is or what he can do. (This does not mean that he can't be effectively competitive when the situation calls for it.) He does not need to prove to others his worth; that's already firmly established within himself.

This feeling of security creates an openness to new ideas. He is the opposite of the self that has undergone closure, has an answer to every question, and has finalized all his ideas. Paradoxically, a strong sense of identity enables one to experiment with new ideas, experiences, and lifestyles. He is not threatened by them. He will try on new ways of life and new ideas to see if they fit. If they don't, he is free to discard them; if they do, he has become richer for it. If they are not for him, then he is left with a better understanding of others' ideas and ways.

17   In an article entitled "The Fully Functioning Personality," Dr. S. I. Hayakawa summarized the studies of two well-known humanistic psychologists—Abraham Maslow and Carl Rogers—on the subject of the human potential. The two scientists had attempted independently to find out what qualities those people had in common who were actually using an unusually high degree of their capabilities. Maslow called them "self-actualizing" individuals; Rogers used the terms "fully functioning person" and "creative person"; Hayakawa settled on the term "genuinely sane person." In any case, there were six distinct characteristics shared by all such people:

(1) Actualized individuals are not "well-adjusted" in the sense that they conform to social norms; but neither are they rebellious against society. They can conform or not conform, as the situation calls for it,

2   *The Condition and the Odyssey*

返本還源
九

入鄽垂手
十

昭和辛卯夏
寶吾郎
画並刻擂

9. Reaching the Source

Too many steps have been taken returning to the root
    and the source.
Better to have been blind and deaf from the beginning!
Dwelling in one's true abode, unconcerned with that
    without—
The river flows tranquilly on and the flowers are red.

Comment: From the beginning, truth is clear. Poised
in silence, I observe the forms of integration and
disintegration. One who is not attached to "form"
need not be "reformed." The water *is* emerald, the
mountain *is* indigo, and I see that which *is* creating
and that which *is* destroying.

10. In the World

Barefooted and naked of breast, I mingle with the people
    of the world.
My clothes are ragged and dust-laden, and I am ever
    blissful.
I use no magic to extend my life;
Now, before me, the dead trees become alive.

Comment: Inside my gate, a thousand sages do not
know me. The beauty of my garden is invisible.
Why should one search for the footprints of the patriarchs? I go to the market place with my wine bot-
tle and return home with my staff. I visit the wine-
shop and the market, and everyone I look upon
becomes enlightened.

because neither is important in itself. What is important is that they possess their own well-developed behavioral norms.

(2) They are unusually open to what is going on inside themselves. They experience fully their own thoughts and feelings. Self-awareness is great; self-deception is minimal. They are realistic about themselves and resort to few myths about themselves or life.

(3) They are not bothered by the unknown. They can be comfortable with disorder, indefiniteness, doubt, and uncertainty. They don't have to know all the answers. They can accept "what is" without trying to organize and label neatly all of life's contents.

(4) They are remarkably existential: they enjoy the present moments of life more fully, not as means to future ends, but as ends in themselves. Their lives are not a perpetual preparation for the future; they enjoy living now.

(5) They are creative individuals, not merely in customary roles such as painters or musicians, but in all that they do. The commonest things—from conversing to washing dishes—are all performed in a slightly different, more creative way. Their own distinctive style touches everything they do.

(6) Actualized persons are "ethical in the deepest sense." They rarely follow the superficial, conventional norms of moral behavior. They consider the majority of so-called moral issues to be trivial. Their ethical concern is expressed in a positive, constructive attitude toward all people and all things. Since they easily identify with the conditions of others, they care, and their caring is the wellspring of their ethical nature.

2-3

SELF/ALIENATION

1   Dr. and Mrs. Harry F. Harlow have for years studied the growth patterns of rhesus monkeys. In the Primate Laboratory of the University of Wisconsin, the Harlows discovered that their monkeys have a developmental sequence which, under normal conditions, produces mutually beneficial social behavior. The young monkeys' emotional development must proceed in this order: (1) affection and security, (2) fear and adjustment, and (3) social-sexual interaction. If this growth sequence is disrupted, then tragic results, in varying degrees, take place in the inner worlds of the young monkeys.

The unforgivable sin is not to become all that you can as a human being, given the circumstances of life that we have to accept.

R. D. LAING

2   Affection and security are basic to the monkey's earliest stages of growth. Normally he first knows these feelings in relation to his mother. She is the prime source of comforting reassurance as he begins to experience the world about him.

     The Harlows found that if a monkey is separated from its mother at birth, but is given the chance to live and develop with age-mates, then affectional ties can grow between them. Emotional bonds are established as they play together.

> Young monkeys that have not been permitted to establish relationships with other infants are wary of their playmates when finally allowed to be with them, and these deprived monkeys often fail to develop strong bonds of affection. Yet monkeys that have been deprived of mother love but provided with early contacts *can* develop ties with their peers which seem comparable to the bonds formed by mother-reared infants.

3   The worst thing that can happen is for a young monkey to be deprived of both his mother and his playmates. If this happens, no bonds of affection and trust can develop.

Fear is the overwhelming response in all monkeys raised in isolation. Although the animals are physically healthy, they crouch and appear terror-stricken by their new environment. . . . They cringe when approached and fail at first to join in any of the play. During six months of play sessions, they never progress beyond minimal play behavior, such as playing by themselves with toys. What little social activity they do have is exclusively with the other isolate in the group. When the other animals become aggressive, the isolates accept their abuse without making any effort to defend themselves. For these animals, social opportunities have come too late. Fear prevents them from engaging in social interaction and consequently from developing ties of affection.

If young monkeys are reared in isolation for a long period of time—for up to twelve months—then their lifetime behavior is seriously affected, and it appears that little or nothing can undo the damage.

As one goes through it
one sees that the gate one
went through
was the self that went through it. . .
R. D. LAING

4   We continued the testing of the same six- and twelve-month isolates for a period of several years. The results were startling. The monkeys raised in isolation now began to attack the other monkeys viciously, whereas before they had cowered in fright. . . . The monkeys which had been raised in the steel isolation cages for their first six months now were three years old. They were still terrified by all strangers, even the physically helpless juveniles. But in spite of their terror, they engaged in uncontrolled aggression, often launching suicidal attacks upon the large adult males and even

attacking the juveniles—an act almost never seen in normal monkeys of their age. The passage of time had only exaggerated their asocial and antisocial behavior.

In those monkeys, positive social action was not initiated, play was nonexistent, grooming did not occur, and sexual behavior was not present at all or was totally inadequate. In human terms, these monkeys which had lived unloved and in isolation were totally unloving, distressed, disturbed and delinquent.

Throughout our studies, we have been increasingly impressed by the alternative routes monkeys may take to reach adequate social behavior, which by our criteria includes affection toward peers, controlled fear and aggression, and normal sexual behavior. In protected laboratory conditions, social interaction between peers and between mother and child appears to be in large part interchangeable in their effect on the infant's development. A rhesus can surmount the absence of its mother if it can associate with its peers, and it can surmount a lack of socialization with peers if its mother provides affection. Being raised with several age mates appears to compensate adequately for a lack of a mother. . . .

After numerous and varied studies at the University of Wisconsin, we have concluded that unless peer affection precedes social aggression, monkeys do not adjust; either they become unreasonably aggressive or they develop into passive scapegoats for their group.

5   The Harlows are writing of rhesus monkeys, not man; and all careful scientists are wary of extrapolating their findings from experiments with one species to any different species. However, there is evidence that human developmental patterns are quite similar.°

For human beings, as with the Harlows' monkeys, normal psychosocial development appears to follow a sequential order: (1) reassurance/security/trust → (2) courage/aggression/exploration → (3) self/autonomy/maturity.

If this growth sequence is interrupted or the requisites not provided at any stage, we too become disturbed creatures cringing in the corner of life with our hands over our faces.

When things go wrong, one wonders whether the young monkey is more fortunate than human young. The monkey's behavior is a spontaneous expression of need-deprivation; it is doubtful that he *wonders* why

Why are Americans so hungry for the approval of others?

The adjusted American lacks self-approval; that is to say, he has not developed a self-image that he can believe is both accurate and acceptable. To do so he would require successful techniques for creating an accurate and acceptable self-image through honest introspection, candid association, and meaningful activity. The patterns to which he has adjusted do not include such techniques. Instead, the culture abounds with misdirections, which the adjusted American acquires. . . . Perhaps above all he learns to seek self-acceptance indirectly, by seeking to substitute the good opinions of others for self-approval. It is thus that he becomes "other-directed."

GAIL AND SNELL PUTNEY

°See Chapter 2–5, sections 4 through 6.

"You've made me very happy."

*All children paint like geniuses.
What do we do to them that so
quickly dulls this ability?*

PICASSO

he is "disturbed." He simply is. But our *self*-consciousness becomes acutely painful; *we know* (most of us) that something has gone wrong, and *we* wonder why.

6   When things have gone very wrong for us and need-deprivation has been acute, the image we develop of ourselves is distorted, confused, inaccurate. Having developed without reassurance and support, we remain vulnerable to the varied, inconsistent responses of others. Nor do we move through the normal stages of growth. There is no period of separation from authority during which we evolve a healthy reliance on our own thoughts and feelings. We are held at a level where the tenuous "mirror-images"—what others think and feel about us—continue to reinforce a fragmented self. We become alienated from the potentially authentic self, the remnants of which still cry out from deep inside.

7   If, very early, we do not receive love, we quickly know that we are unlovable.

If we are rejected, by word or deed, we learn to reject ourselves.

2   The Condition and the Odyssey

If we find that what we *do* is more important than what we *are,* then doing the "right thing" becomes all important; in fact, we strive desperately *to be* what *we do.*

If our parents are permissive so that we see them as "not caring," we will feel unwanted and worthless.

If our parents "care" too much, especially when they call it "love," then we may never establish self-reliance.

If we are given behavioral ultimatums that demand repression of authentic feelings, we will develop inauthentic selves which comply to required specifications.

If we have been denied the warmth we crave, we will carry with us the ache of an insatiable emptiness.

8   Most of our parents cared, and they gave us the most suitable environment which *their* maturity permitted. The majority of us can place ourselves somewhere between the extreme poles where things go very wrong or very right. And at different times, conditions may have altered the emotional climate of our homes so that we experienced gratification or deprivation accordingly. A life-affirming mother may go through a period of depression, during which she is unable to give "nurturance." She may recognize her problem, seek counsel, change environmental conditions, or otherwise adjust; she may handle the causes of her melancholy and be able to return to her formerly affectionate role. When such changes occur, a child often turns out to be hardier than we expect, and no permanent alienation results from temporary rejection.

9   Economic conditions can also influence how we feel about ourselves, particularly as one moves out into the community. It is difficult to develop a positive self-image when one is born into a cultural subgroup that deviates from the "acceptable" middle-class norms. In more isolated minority communities, the stress of meeting physical needs—food, shelter, and safety—may take precedence over concern with "adequate emotional nurturance." Still, it is not the socioeconomic variables as such that determine a child's earliest evaluation of himself. Rather, it is whether he is wanted and worthwhile. It is the *quality* of the relationship—and not even the quantity of time spent with the child—that determines his primal feelings about himself.

10   Few of us are fortunate enough to have had parents who appreciated our early spontaneous expressions of life and self and, at the same time, taught us to "play the games" of adjustment to other norms outside the home. How many mothers prefaced a lecture on cleanliness with a word or two about the social realities we would face—for instance, when preparing us to attend a friend's party—without instilling in us the idea that "dirty" itself is bad and "clean" is inherently good?

That hatred springs more from self-contempt than from a legitimate grievance is seen in the intimate connection between hatred and a guilty conscience.

ERIC HOFFER

My mother does not love me. . .
I am bad because she does not love me
She does not love me because I am bad

R. D. LAING

The concept of the superego is quite ambiguous. On the one hand, it is the basis of all cultural life because it restricts the uninhibited actualization of the always-driving libido; on the other hand, it cuts off man's vital forces, and produces disgust about the whole system of cultural restrictions, and brings about a neurotic state of mind.

PAUL TILLICH

The growing self must feel that it
is involved, that it is really part of
what is going on, that in some
degree it is helping shape its own
destiny, together with the destiny of
all. . . . When the fearful person
withdraws within his psychological
shell, the self becomes less adequate
and the whole person loses its ability to do, to venture, to create.

EARL C. KELLEY

Yet it's an idea which children can grasp at a remarkably early age. "If you want to go to Suzy's party, then Suzy's mother will want you to look clean. I want you to look clean too. I'm happy you enjoy playing in the mud, but this is the way of the world, so let's wash up."

This is a reality-perspective that permits the child to enjoy playing in the mud and at the same time choose to "play the games" required in order to attain a goal, in this case attending Suzy's party.

11   Far more than other creatures, man has the capacity to be "many things to many people." As the situations call for it, we can be different "persons" or wear different masks (the word *person* is from the Greek *persona*, meaning "mask"). Some of us become quite adept at putting on masks or switching masks; thus we can insure that we always have ready a *persona* that is acceptable. It effects minimal rejection by any other person or group.

But the price we pay is very dear. In the process of switching masks, we may discover that there are *nothing but* masks; indeed they may begin to feel familiar and genuine, all of them. And if someone should demand, "Will the *real* self please stand up?" we find to our horror that there is no one there. It is not uncommon to make the discovery during some personal crisis that an authentic self never developed. If we glimpse this may be the case, in panic we may seize our masks and fit them more tightly, reluctant to remove them ever again.

The feeling that one does not know "who he is" may be intuited by ourselves and inferred by others, but it is perhaps that last thing that we will confess to ourselves or others. The pain which our masks cover is too great for anyone to see. We can't risk being open. We are ever fearful that someone might see beneath our masks and discover . . . *nothing.*

12   Our resourcefulness helps us compensate for basic need-deprivation. The "games" we can play in order to survive (physically and emotionally) are subtle and intricate.

If we should reach a stage in our psychological development similar to that of the uncontrollable aggression which characterizes the isolate monkeys, then the ways we humans find of expressing our hostilities are devious and imaginative. Children act out their misdirected angers and frustrations in their dealings with each other, belittling someone weaker in an effort to ease the ache of being treated insignificantly at home. They conform to group norms so that the pain of alienation hurts a little less; they ostracize the deviant to gain a few moments of ambivalent potency within the peer power structure.

As we grow into adults we continue to employ the same techniques.

13   Self-hate has many sources. Perhaps the commonest are early conditions in which we were disliked by parents or other authority-figures, and their feelings toward us have been internalized into our feelings about our selves.

There are other sources of self-hate. If one has been given a set of behavioral dos and don'ts, and they have the moral force of a conditioned conscience behind them, then violation of such codes can generate self-hate: hatred of a self that cannot or will not do what is "right." This is the problem of the will which agonized some of the saintliest personalities in Western religion: they *knew* what was "right," but they could not *will* it into action. From a more objective point of view, the behavioral codes may have been arbitrary, culturally local, parochial, self-destructive, or morally questionable; but all this is irrelevant. If the individual considered them to be binding upon him, and if, through internal conflict, he is prevented from behaving according to their mandates, then hatred for the "sinful self" is inescapable.

If one has succeeded in aligning his neuroses with his goals so that his neuroses are working for *him, it is next to impossible for him to empathize with the person whose neuroses are still working* against *him.*

It is only in emotional and spiritual crises of suffering that people will endure the pain and anxiety involved in digging out the deep roots of their problems.

Psychology Today

I do not understand my own actions.

ST. PAUL

14   Self-hate can also be engendered by a "perfectionism" programmed into us early in our lives. If, during those formative years we
can never "do anything right" in the eyes of those whom we depend
upon; if we feel we must be perfect before we are acceptable; then, since
we are never perfect, nothing we do is acceptable. This attitude, too, we
internalize so that nothing we do is acceptable to ourselves. We have
internalized a set of impossibilities. We reject ourselves, therefore, not
for our actions as much as for what we *are not*. Nothing we are or do
quite measures up, and we hate ourselves for it.

Another source of self-hate is related to the physical organism
we inherit or develop. It may be "abnormal": "ugly," obese, chemically
imbalanced, or the like. Whatever the "abnormality" may be, it is evaluated in terms of some set of criteria, and those criteria usually derive
from the society one belongs to—peers, subcultures, culture, or institu-
tional groups. The standards of judgment are cultural and relative, but
if one is so strongly conditioned with the values that he buys them, then
self-hate is a frequent result.

15   Some individuals must adjust to far greater limitations than others,
such as physical deformities, chemical imbalances, congenital problems,
organ malfunction, and so on. It may be considerably more difficult to
come to terms with these conditions which, one assumes, cannot be
changed.

A large part of the problem, however, lies in the fact that these
features have been rejected by others; and if we have been repeatedly
rejected because of specific "abnormalities," then it becomes difficult
indeed for us to accept them.

This is where moral courage becomes crucial: the courage to
accept ourselves when others don't. Whether self-rejection be mild or
severe, the therapeutic path is the same: getting in touch with oneself
and challenging, with all the strength one can find, the rejecting values
of society.

This is the fundamental premise of growth: that we come to terms
with all that we are, including whatever is labeled "good" and "bad."
How? By letting ourselves experience the pain of unmasking. The degree
to which we can overcome all forms of alienation depends upon the degree
to which we let ourselves honestly experience what we are. One can
experience—purely—the pain of what one is, or one can develop a mask
to protect oneself from it.

On the surface, it would seem more difficult for some individuals—those with physical "abnormalities," for instance—to accept themselves. But in real life, it doesn't seem to work this way. The fact of
the matter is that most self-hating individuals are perfectly normal physically, sometimes even "beautiful." Public figures come to mind—TV and
movie stars, for instance—people of whom we would quickly say, "They

have everything." But the known behavioral problems, as well as the number of suicide attempts, indicate that their problems, including at the center the problem of self-acceptance, are deeper than those of most of the rest of us who don't have nearly so much going for us.

16   Perhaps the most tragic turn that alienation can take is the "double bind." All double binds share the same "vicious circle" pattern: the harder we think we are trying to break them, the tighter their hold on us becomes.

For instance, if during our earliest years we are not loved, we quickly conclude that we are not lovable. If we are told, by word and deed, that we are not wanted, we get the message: it is our existence that is not valued; it is clear that our *non*existence would be preferred. From this it follows that we reject ourselves, for we too cannot accept the unacceptable.

But our psychophysical organism fights back. We will *force* from others the recognition of our existence. But the more we force, the more we are rejected; the more we are rejected the more unlovable we feel; the more unlovable we feel, the more we force. The double-bind has taken control. The years pass and much of our behavior will be unconsciously designed to elicit the attention, acceptance, and love which we desperately need. But *we* now know that we are not lovable, so when others offer us love, even genuine love, we know *they* are being deceived; for since we are not lovable, they cannot truly love us. The double-bind has become our personal tragedy. No love can permeate the boundaries of our alienation, and that which our whole being longs for, we can no longer receive.

The philosopher Friedrich Nietzsche was himself caught in a double-bind of self-hate, and was aware of it. He once wrote: "It is so seldom that a friendly voice reaches me. I am now alone, absurdly alone . . . and for years no refreshment, not a drop of humanness, not a breath of love has reached me." Again, with great insight, he wrote: "At an absurdly early period—at the age of seven—I already knew that no human word would ever reach me." Nietzsche gives us the cause of his tragedy: the depth of his self-hate was almost beyond endurance. "What I am not," he wrote, "that for me is God and virtue."

Aggression and hostility are so clearly defensive and protective drives. However, in humans hostility can readily turn against the self and become self-destructive, even as it can fuse with sexual impulses to become sadism.

THEODORE LIDZ

Once a man has become self-conscious. . . he is morally obliged to act in no way that will deaden his preoccupation with his integrity. He is obliged to impregnate all his actions with some sense of their relevance to him, as a man and as a person.

JEAN-PAUL SARTRE

2-4

CHANGE/GROWTH

1   Oedipus is the prototype of the man who gains knowledge about himself and pays the ultimate price. The issue in the drama is: Shall Oedipus know what he has done? Shall Oedipus know who he is and what his origins are? . . .

Oedipus is a hero precisely because he will let no one stand in the way of his knowledge about himself. He is the hero because he faces his own reality. He cries out with pain again and again, but he repeats, "I will not stop till I have known the whole."

ROLLO MAY
Love and Will

2   Deep within the unconscious mind of man, there moves a longing to recover the innocence of childhood, a condition that he nostalgically (mis)interprets as a state of blissful happiness. Intuitively, we sense that with knowledge comes insight, and with insight comes pain. Most of man's religions have in their mythologies some place or state where he may reenter into that paradise of unknowing where suffering will cease. The Garden of Eden was a paradise only as long as the fruit of *knowledge* remained untouched. It would have been better to be innocent, the story seems to say, than to know the pain of understanding. Once innocence has been lost, however, there is no return.

Once we possess knowledge we must leave the Garden of Eden, and we leave it forever.

3   *To be innocent is not to know.* To be innocent is to be childlike, and to be childlike is to be unaware of certain facts or experiences. A child does not have certain information at his disposal which he can use, information which others do have; and all decisions related to those areas have to be made by others.

Therefore, to be innocent is to be dependent. If one cannot make his

Every time you teach a child something you keep him from reinventing it.

JEAN PIAGET

own decisions, others must. This is a normal condition for a child, and he accepts it. This vulnerability puts him at the mercy of those he depends upon; if his basic self-needs are met, however, this is a happy dependency.

Dependence requires trust and faith. For the innocent child there is no alternative. He must trust the decisions others make for him, that those decisions are right and good; and he must accept on faith information given to him, that it is right and true.

Dependence requires obedience. Wherever there is dependency, obedience is demanded, but if trust is not a part of that dependency relationship, then obedience is given grudgingly. With trust, however, obedience is given willingly, even joyfully. There is no need to question the authority to whom one submits.

Innocence is an instrument of control. Knowledge and know-how are potentially dangerous assets—dangerous to all who possess them but lack maturity to use them for good, and dangerous to any who wish to maintain a state of control. Parents guard their children against certain kinds of knowledge and experiences until they are "old enough" (that is, until they are aware and responsible) to make constructive use of it. A child may be told to do things he does not understand, or that he does not want to do; but obedience to authority is necessary since authorities (that is, those *with* knowledge) can make more realistic judgments. Obviously, in matters of destiny, it could be tragic if a child were forced to make critical decisions he is not yet equipped to make.

So, while we are children, we think like children—innocently: without information and awareness. We order our experience along simple lines and our behavior is guided by those we depend upon.

4 Desmond Morris employs two helpful concepts to describe the innate alternating feelings of fear and curiosity: neophobia and neophilia.

By *neophobia* he means that we are afraid of new objects, unfamiliar behavioral patterns in others, strange feelings in ourselves, or any other new and threatening elements of life that we do not understand. It is completely natural to be afraid of the unknown. To experience fear in the presence of potential danger has obvious survival value. Life may be likened to our moving forever on the edge of darkness, not knowing what exists just beyond the immediate circle of experience.

We can understand, too painfully, the first experiences of the infant monkeys described by the Harlows. When placed in a room cluttered with unfamiliar objects and without any mother or comforting "home base" to return to, the young monkey was unable to explore the room with its formidable array of unknowns. His fear was too great, and he could only huddle in the corner of the room with his hands over his eyes.

But when given the security of a mother, or even the comfort of a soft blanket or surrogate mother, to which he could periodically

We pay a heavy price for our fear of failure. It is a powerful obstacle to growth. It assures the progressive narrowing of the personality and prevents exploration and experimentation.

JOHN GARDNER

Individuals are able to trust their total organismic reaction to a new situation because they discover to an ever-increasing degree that if they are open to their experience, doing what "feels right" proves to be a competent and trustworthy guide to behavior which is truly satisfying.

When a person is open to experience there is a maximum of adaptability, a discovery of structure in experience, a flowing, changing organism of self and personality. It means discovering the structure of experience in the process of living the experience.

And as he lives and accepts these widely varied feelings, in all their degrees of intensity, he discovers that he has experienced *himself*, that he is *all* these feelings.

CARL ROGERS

Open people are free to devote their energies to what is positive and constructive. They can and do set more realistic goals for themselves. Their levels of aspiration are more likely to be in line with their capacities. They are more likely to achieve their goals because those goals are more realistic.

Openness to experience and acceptance refer not only to acceptance of events outside the person's self but equally to the individual's perceptions of self. The adequate person is less defensive and does not bar from perceptual organization what is true about self.

The accurate, realistic assessment of self resulting from acceptance makes possible the use of self as a dependable, trustworthy instrument for achieving one's purposes.

ARTHUR W. COMBS

I contradict myself. I am large. I contain multitudes.

WALT WHITMAN

return for reassurance and security, then step by step the monkey would explore the room's contents. An object would be touched, handled, played with; then the monkey would return to the mother (or blanket) for a security "rest period," then explore another object, and so on until all objects were familiar. Little by little, he would reduce his fear of all the objects in the room.

When he knew, from his own experience, that nothing in the room held any danger for him, he could then move about the room without fear. He had succeeded in making all the unknowns a part of his world.

The strongest principle of growth lies in human choice.

GEORGE ELIOT

Collection, The Museum of Modern Art, New York. Gift of Mrs. Simon Guggenheim.

2   The Condition and the Odyssey

5   *Neophilia* is a strong counterimpulse to neophobia. We are fascinated by the new and the unknown; we are drawn to new objects, new experiences, new ways of living—drawn by "curiosity" and by a sense of adventure and excitement. It is the neophilic impulse that provides us the possibility of growth. If our desire to explore the unknown is overwhelmed by fear, then we withdraw. We return to our corner. But if we have enough security when we need it, then we can explore more and more of the unknowns, assimilate them, explore some more, widen our horizons, and grow.

This kind of growth is open; it has no limits. There are always new worlds to be explored, new adventures to become excited about, new ways of living to be experienced, new ideas to be discovered, new problems to be solved.

"Are you happy? Why did you do all this, why did you struggle so hard to become a telepathist?"

"Why! For what!" Nikolaiev leaned forward and one sensed a sort of heraldic thunder rumbling in him. "Why, to be more. What else is life for? To develop all your possibilities. That is happiness, to love what you're doing, to keep expanding, to keep turning into something more."

OSTRANDER AND SCHROEDER

6   The *static concept of security* may be pictured by thinking of the oyster inside its shell, the frightened person behind his neurotic defenses, or prewar France behind the Maginot Line. The main idea in the static concept of security is to build up enough protective walls and to sit still inside them. The "search for security" for many people still is the task of building and mending walls around themselves.

The *dynamic concept of security* can be pictured by thinking of a skillful and self-confident driver speeding home in the traffic stream along Bayshore Highway. He knows that the highway is dangerous; he knows that he may encounter drunken drivers or cars with faulty brakes, and he knows that a slight error in judgment at sixty miles an hour may result in his not getting home at all. Nevertheless, he is not insecure, he is not frightened; in fact, this daily confrontation of danger doesn't worry him at all, because his security in this dynamic and dangerous situation depends not on walls to protect him from danger, but on internal resources—skill, knowledge, experience, flexibility—with which he knows he can cope with danger.

S. I. HAYAKAWA

7   With a positive view of self, one can risk taking chances; one does not have to be afraid of what is new and different. A sturdy ship can venture farther from port. Just so, an adequate person can launch himself without fear into the new, the untried and the unknown. A positive view of self permits the individual to be creative, original and spontaneous. What is more, he can afford to be generous, to give of himself freely or to become personally involved in events. With so much more at his command, he has so much more to give.

Truly adequate people possess perceptual fields maximally open to experience. That is to say, their perceptual fields are capable of change and adjustment in such fashion as to make fullest possible use of their experience.

ARTHUR W. COMBS

My own belief is that man has the capacity as well as the desire to develop his potentialities and become a decent human being, and that these deteriorate if his relationship to others and hence to himself is, and continues to be, disturbed. I believe that man can change and keep on changing as long as he lives.

KAREN HORNEY

TON ΠΑΘΕΙ
ΜΑΘΟΣ ΘΕΝ
ΤΑ ΚΥΡΙΩΣ
ΕΧΕΙΝ

THE LAW OF PATHEI MATHOS

Zeus, who taught men to think, has laid it down that wisdom comes alone through suffering.

AESCHYLUS

8   A variety of institutions and individuals specialize in providing us with the answers before we have asked the questions. The rationale for doing this is always altruistic: they want to protect us from dangerous ideas or bad influences; they must prevent our doing the wrong things; they wish to guide us into the right paths of feeling, thinking, and behaving. They give us answers because, they say, we have a "need to know."

The actual fact is that answer-givers have a need to persuade. One of their goals is to contain us within a state of innocence and thereby establish control over us. Their true motivation is disguised by perhaps the commonest of human rationalizations: that they are really helping us. Indeed, the claim that we need the answers can become so widely accepted that, without raising further questions, we too assume the claim to be true.

The price of such answer-giving is very high.

It prevents the individual from having to wrestle personally with life's problems and to ask the questions that lead to emotional and intellectual growth. Once trained to accept given answers, one may never learn how to formulate meaningful questions in terms of who he is or what life means to him.

Moreover, one who has been conditioned to accept answers tends to develop a rigid conceptual framework which undergoes early closure to new ideas and experiences. He knows if he lacks an answer, the authority can supply it. All he must do is ask for the answer instead of asking the question. Nor can he question the answer. It is common to find individuals who can repeat verbatim the "correct" answers, but when questioned about their meaning, they reveal little understanding; and if pressed, their only recourse is to fall back on other "remembered" answers.

One who has been protected in this way has been prevented from knowing both the "agony of insight" and the "ecstasy of growth." He has been preassured that no painful questions will have to be faced.

9   The date: A.D. 2198. The speaker: Mia, a young girl who has just survived "The Trial," a rite-of-passage which prepares youth to face themselves and their world.

It was only after I came back from Trial that I came to a notion of my own as to what maturity consists of. Maturity is the ability to sort the portions of truth from the accepted lies and self-deceptions that you have grown up with. It is easy now to see the irrelevance of the religious wars of the past, to see that capitalism in itself is not evil, to see that honor is most often a silly thing to kill a man for, to see that national patriotism should have meant nothing in the twenty-first century, to see that a correctly-arranged tie has very little to do with true social worth. It is harder to assess as critically the insanities of your own time, especially if you have accepted them unquestioningly for as long as you can remember,

2 The Condition and the Odyssey

for as long as you have been alive. If you never make the attempt, whatever else you are, you are not mature.

ALEXEI PANSHIN

10   One of the major roadblocks to autonomy is failure to achieve separation from authority. This is the failure to outgrow our dependence upon those who have nourished us; we prolong our need of them and rely upon them to make our decisions and provide directives for our behavior. Long past separation-time we continue to operate in terms of their values. Dependence, of course, means security; in a dependent state there is much of life we need not face and many responsibilities we need not assume. It is comfortable to maintain dependence and conform to BTF-patterns° that are not ours.

The longer dependence lasts, the more difficult separation becomes. Unless, sometime, we experience the feeling of being a separate self, the very idea of autonomy may remain meaningless.

11   The self that longs for autonomy—the self that longs for a life of its own—will not easily be put down. If the authorities are reluctant to relinquish control and/or if the separating self cannot outgrow its dependency, then the separation process is often prolonged and may reach crisis proportions. But paradoxically, as long as there is pain, there is hope; the separation process has not been abandoned.

This "crisis of authority" is felt on both sides. For the self that is fighting for autonomy, the severance of the umbilical cord brings fear and guilt. He is doing the very thing the authorities find unacceptable. He is behaving "badly" or "wrong." One commonly feels like a traitor in abandoning the values and beliefs of the authority-figures; and, unavoidably, the authorities will be hurt. They may experience a sense of failure, perhaps of betrayal. The crisis of separation is often as painful for the authorities as it is for the separating self, for authorities have as difficult a time letting go as the self has in cutting loose. An authority-figure, after all, must *be* an authority or his role—the role he has defined for himself and identified with—vanishes. He often feels (unconsciously) that his purpose in life will be lost if he is not needed by others; and if others do not *need* him then there will be no basis for a relationship with him. He will be alone. Therefore, authorities frequently bind us to them in an effort to give their own lives meaning. If seen from this perspective, it becomes clear that the dependency-ties go in *both* directions.

12   If the recovery of the whole self is to be one's goal, then the development of self-awareness is a prerequisite. If we sense that things have not gone right either in the development of identity or self-worth, and we genuinely want growth to take place, then self-knowledge is essential and some very deliberate choices will have to be made in terms of that knowledge.

°*BTF-patterns* is a convenient abbreviation which will be used to refer to all the elements which are interwoven to create selves and societies. *Behavior, thought,* and *feeling*—these are the three elements of human experience which are judged to be acceptable or unacceptable, right or wrong. Also, the single symbol "BTF" implies the important fact that behavior, thought, and feeling are ultimately inseparable and operate together.

The ultimate goal of the educational system is to shift to the individual the burden of pursuing his own education.

JOHN GARDNER

There seems to be a sort of progress in awareness, through the stages of which every man—and especially every psychiatrist and every patient—must move, some persons progressing further through these stages than others. One starts by blaming the identified patient for his idiosyncrasies and symptoms. Then one discovers that these symptoms are a response to—or an effect of—what others have done; and the blame shifts from the identified patient to the etiological figure. Then, one discovers perhaps that these figures feel a guilt for the pain which they have caused, and one realizes that when they claim this guilt they are identifying themselves with god. After all, they did not, in general, know what they were doing, and to claim guilt for their acts would be to claim omniscience. At this point one reaches a more general anger, that what happens to people should not happen to dogs, and that what people do to each other the lower animals could never devise. Beyond this, there is, I think, a stage which I can only dimly envisage, where pessimism and anger are replaced by something else—perhaps humility. And from this stage onward to whatever other stages there may be, there is loneliness.

GREGORY BATESON
"Language and Psychotherapy"

What's to say? I have the feeling that everybody knows everything so far as human interaction goes, and that we only choose to ignore or to forget. That's why social science is so hard to teach. The people I love best are the ones who dig daffodils as well as ancient history. . . .

JOHN M. SHLEIN

It is not uncommon to find ourselves experiencing repeatedly the same dominant negative emotions as we live through a variety of activities in time: anxiety, fear, anger, frustration, depression. We may engage in sundry projects and numerous relationships, expecting (or perhaps just hoping) that something will happen to change how we feel. But it doesn't happen. In our honest moments we can confess to a hunger for life, but something inside holds us where we are. At the deepest emotional level, it is always the same.

13 Where does one begin? A deceptively simple answer: We begin here and now. We begin with the sum of all that we are.

When we are open to experiencing our selves precisely as they are—rather than expending energy feeling anxious or guilty over what they are not—a change in feeling can take place. An awareness of all that we can contact inside must be brought into our consciousness. Whatever our shortcomings (on whatever criteria they are judged to be "shortcomings"), these too must be accepted as part of one's self. Here deliberate choice comes in. There are unpleasant things stored in the inner worlds of all of us, and we may be tempted to ignore them; but with self-awareness, we can deliberately choose to stay a moment, recognize heretofore repressed events, and begin the process of "de-charging" them.

A fact about emotion is that it changes when it is permitted expression and can run its course. When one allows himself to feel a feeling, and no longer permits himself the dangerous luxuries of repression and rationalization, then genuine change can follow.

For example, the monologue might heretofore have gone like this: "I feel sad. I don't want to feel sad, so I will pretend I don't feel sad. Others won't notice and I can fool myself as well." If we play this kind of game with our emotions, the sadness in this case is repressed and has little chance to change. It will remain stored as a charged energy-system within the psyche. This is true, of course, for all the bitter emotions—anger, hatred, frustration, fear, and so on.

On the other hand, the monologue might proceed: "I feel sad. I don't want to feel sad, but I'll not deny what exists. Rather I will feel the full force of the feeling and let it run its course. It will fade away by itself." This way, when we *choose* not to repress an emotion, we find that it will diminish and we can move on to better feelings. Nothing is repressed which can return later and wreak vengeance for not having been dealt with honestly.

In just this way, with self-awareness and deliberate choice, one can begin to integrate all that he is. These are first steps in the recovery of a wholeness which most of us, living in a fragmenting world, have to some degree lost and forgotten.

14   Men have long been aware that growth never comes without a price: pain. The Greek tragedian Aeschylus thought of man as subject to an "epistemic law" decreed by the god Zeus "who has laid it down that wisdom comes alone through suffering." Charlie Brown put it more succinctly after he lost his faith in the Great Pumpkin: "In all this world there is nothing more upsetting than the clobbering of a cherished belief."

> The agonies of insight are not strangers to any of us.
> The agony of discovering you are not one but many people, created in the images of those who have mattered most to you.
> The agony of having your childhood's faith crumble at the very moment when you needed it most to sustain you.
> The agony of doubting what you knew was right, and wondering if what you knew was wrong just could be right.
> The agony of watching your children enter new worlds you cannot enter, and cannot accept, yet cannot completely condemn.
> The agony of listening to your children condemn all that you believe in and tried to teach them.

Mary had a little lamb,
One and one made two.
Candles on a birthday cake,
Blow them out and your wish comes true.
Does she love me, does she not?
Tell me, daisy, do.
Oh, to be a child again!
Oaks from acorns grew,
One and one made two.
I believed it all, didn't you? [©]
ANTHONY NEWLEY
AND LESLIE BRICUSSE

> The agony of feeling like a traitor to your parents when you find you must abandon their cherished beliefs because, for you, they are not true.
>
> The agony of having to unlearn and relearn what you learned because what you were taught is no longer true.
>
> The agony of hating others for making you what you are, yet knowing in your honest moments that they could not have done otherwise.
>
> The agony of being concerned, when others are not.

[Speaking of "Longstreet" (ABC-TV), author Stirling Silliphant said that the series is] an existentialist statement based on the conviction that people who cannot suffer can never grow up, never discover who they really are.

TV Times

15   It is a painful insight to discover that one holds a belief because he needs the belief, and not because the belief is true. This is the sort of insight one would like to make go away, like a bad dream or clouds on a rainy day.

But this sort of insight, which comes with self-awareness, is the most difficult to dispel. When the process has begun by which one begins to examine the nature of the need which the belief fulfills, it follows that he asks whether the belief is *also* true—and often finds that it is not. The insight into the nature of the need has, for all pragmatic purposes, destroyed the efficacy of the belief.

Our pain can be especially sharp when the insight has destroyed the belief while our need for it is still alive. The head has said, "You can no longer believe it, for now you see through it." But the rest of one's being cries out in emptiness for what it has lost.

This is the cry of the soul that still needs healing but has discovered that the healers have lost their power. This is a Saint Paul, torn with conflict, realizing that the Law of Moses only increased his guilt. This is a Luther, still yearning for peace of soul, but finding that his faith in the sacraments has failed him and they cannot bring him peace.

This is the agony of alienated selves who have found themselves cut off from their roots, still longing for something *worth* believing in, but discovering that the old gods are gone and there is nothing to take their place.

16   You ask me how I became a madman. It happened thus: One day, long before many gods were born, I woke from a deep sleep and found all my

2 The Condition and the Odyssey

masks were stolen,—the seven masks I have fashioned and worn in seven lives,—I ran maskless through the crowded streets shouting, "Thieves, thieves, the cursèd thieves."

Men and women laughed at me and some ran to their houses in fear of me.

And when I reached the market place, a youth standing on a house-top cried, "He is a madman." I looked up to behold him; the sun kissed my own naked face for the first time. For the first time the sun kissed my own naked face and my soul was inflamed with love for the sun, and I wanted my masks no more. And as if in a trance I cried, "Blessed, blessed are the thieves who stole my masks."

Thus I became a madman.

KAHLIL GIBRAN

I will not let you (or me) make me dishonest, insincere, emotionally tied up or constricted, or artificially nice and social, if I can help it.

EUGENE T. GENDLIN

2-5

LIFE/TIME

1   To see life whole is to experience life in a very special way, but this is a difficult vision to attain.

Each single life/time is a living drama played out in space and time against the backdrop of eternity.

> All the world's a stage
> And all the men and women merely players,
> They have their exits and their entrances;
> And one man in his time plays many parts.

In each life, the curtain has arisen and the play is in progress. But not having read the script, the plot of the drama remains unknown. We can't foresee the acts that lie ahead—or when the play will end—because, as in living theater, the plot is developed extempore as line follows line and scene follows scene.

2   On rare occasions, however, we are able to see and feel, in a single sweep of comprehension, the whole of a life/time. Such a vision may flash through our minds after reading a biography or after watching a drama. Ofttimes at a funeral we are left in a reflective mood as we stand, for a short moment, at the end of a life just completed.

When the biography is closed—when the third-act curtain has been rung down—only then can the play be seen in its entirety. Every part relates to, and sheds light upon, every other part. For life *is* an unfolding drama. Scene follows scene, each illuminating what has gone before and pointing toward developments that lie ahead. We can trace the major motifs of later life back to their beginnings. We can see the

The curiosity of the human race is most evident in children. A child's innocent question will often give the adult to pause, and ponder carefully the answer. But there are other things than answers to be careful of when dealing with a child. . . .

JACK WILLIAMSON

inception of strengths that are to bring fulfillment and flaws that are to bring failure. We can point to the decisions that made all the difference.

To see life whole allows us to ponder the mystery of human existence with a special kind of awareness. The feeling of absolute finality forces upon us a reordering of values. We frequently feel that, in effect, "it has put things in perspective."

What would it be like if each of us could stretch our conceptual limits to reflect upon our life/time as a completed biography?

3 It is quite within the realm of possibility for us to view *the basic groundplan* which our lives follow. The capricious details of daily existence are unpredictable, to be sure; but we have within us a psychophysiological timetable which provides the plot of the human drama. Quite apart from contingencies and variables, we *can* see our own lives as a whole.

Current thinking in the human sciences tends to avoid dividing the life-cycle into neat, clearly defined "stages." Rather, life is phasic in nature; it is a continuum, with each phase emerging out of the previous phase. Distinct events occur more or less at scheduled times. There does in fact exist a clear psychophysiological growth-progression that is universal and constitutes the groundplan for the entire human life-cycle.

Erikson and others have emphasized the fact that life unfolds in

a sequence of challenges which must be resolved. Each challenge is a genetically programmed, psychophysiological readiness to incorporate *specific experiences* into our developing selves. As each challenge is successfully met, growth takes place and we can move ahead, on schedule, to face the next readiness period. Each phase of our lives literally grows out of the successful completion of the previous challenge. The precise schedule of these challenges is unique to each individual and determines the phasic nature of life.

The following sections should be read in a special way with a specific goal in mind. That goal is to feel the whole of a life-cycle, to see the human enterprise, from birth till death, in a single vision, as One. Perhaps reading rapidly through all the sections several times would accomplish this better than studying details which, in this case, are of secondary importance.

4   *Infancy.* During the first twelve to fifteen months of life, we awaken to the world about us. We are wholly dependent; our needs must be met by others. Therefore, the crucial challenge of this phase is the development of a feeling of trust, and the depth of our trust depends upon how well we are cared for. Whether we develop this capacity at all is out of our hands; we are pawns of our environment.

If these months are pleasant times, then we begin to open ourselves to life. We can feel hunger, pain, loneliness—whatever is authentic—and know that there will be someone to fulfill our needs. There is someone who cares. Thus we learn in a very natural way to be ourselves and to remain open to the actions of others. We trust them. By contrast, if the environment is capricious or hostile, we become fearful; we remain on guard; we cannot afford to open ourselves to others. Quite realistically, we have no grounds for trusting.

This phase is critical. If we don't develop trust and openness during this period, then severe conflicts lie ahead. Some personality theorists go much further and believe that if we don't experience love during this early period, then love is lost from our lives forever. We will never love—or be loved.

5   *Early Childhood.* A new phase begins when we learn to stand, walk about, and get into things. Better motor control brings whole new worlds within range of our curious hands. We venture into new rooms, play with new toys (*everything* is a toy), and find drawers and cupboards to explore.

The essential challenge of early childhood is striking a balance between an unbounded freedom to do anything (which *we* want) and the necessary limits and controls (which *others* want)—parameters within which we must exist. Guidelines must be consistent and firm. Our neophilic impulse to explore must not be dampened, but we must learn to accept limits; we must learn to live with the frustrations of not being able to do everything we want. If we can find a satisfactory balance between freedom and restriction, then we can continue, safely and happily, to explore the world about us. But if there is too much freedom, we will learn to resist all authority that would impose any limitations upon us; or if there is too much restraint, then we gradually lose the urge to explore life and give in to a neophobic passivity. Either extreme sets us up for problems which will return to bother us at a later time.

6 *Middle Childhood.* The next challenge is a different kind: it is the discovery that other people come in two varieties—and that we do too. We awaken to the fact that, physiologically, we are different from others in our family and from friends.

The psychological challenge of this phase is the successful acceptance of ourselves as boy or girl within the context of all our relationships. That is, we proceed to clarify and understand our sex-role identity. With positive guidance from authorities, our sex-role is accepted without undue stress or guilt. We begin to feel that being a girl or a boy is natural and good, that it was not a mistake or terrible accident that we were not born of the other sex.°

Those who employ Freudian concepts hold that there is also an Oedipal conflict to be resolved at this stage. The daughter finds herself in profound competition with her mother as she comes to realize they are of the same sex; similarly, the son feels a competitiveness toward his father—each for the love and sex-role approval of the other parent. The resolution of these conflicts leads to a new set of relationships all around, based upon the realities of sex-identity.

7 *Late Childhood.* About the age of six there begins a longer, smoother period of growth that lasts until the beginning of adolescence, a duration of five or six years. It is a time for consolidation of the growth-gains we have made so far. It is a sort of rest period from the ordeals of rapid change. However, if earlier growth-challenges haven't been effectively resolved, this "rest period" may be a sort of catch-up time for further resolution of these conflicts.

During this calmer time, if all goes well, there is a deepening sense of identity as the distinctive elements of our personalities become more coherent. Personality is still developing, to be sure; it is still shaky and tender. Our selves are not yet firmly grounded. Therefore, if our environment is especially hostile and rejecting at this time, painful feelings of inadequacy can result. Acceptance by our peers at this point is important; we seek it aggressively, though not often directly. We want to feel that we are like others, and that others approve of us.

If all goes well during this stabilizing phase, then the stage is set for the next critical ordeal of our life-cycle: adolescence.

Immortal God! What a world I see dawning! Why cannot I grow young again?

ERASMUS

°I hesitate (but only briefly) to mention that this was precisely the view of Aristotle and Saint Thomas Aquinas. Both believed that women are mistakes. According to the latter, nature always tries to produce a male, but a female results when something goes wrong (*mas occasionatum*); more than that, she is a defective and accidental creature (*deficiens et occasionatum*). No philosopher, as far as I know, has suggested that men are also mistakes, though I'm sure a very interesting argument could be constructed to support the notion.

Children don't believe what adults say, but they are ready to believe what adults do.

BRUNO BETTELHEIM

To pretend to satisfy one's desires by possessions is like putting out a fire with straw.

CHINESE PROVERB

Self and personality emerge from experience. If they are open to their experience, doing what "feels right" proves to be a competent and trustworthy guide to behavior which is truly satisfying.

CARL ROGERS

8   *Early Adolescence.* With the sudden physiological growth that initiates adolescence, we enter a time of "storm and stress," an upheaval that affects not only us but the lives of all who are within range.

Adolescence is transition. Heretofore, each of us has been a child. We have been treated as children, and our thoughts and emotions have been those of a child. We have been passing through the conflicts characteristic of childhood.

All this rapidly changes as the transition to adulthood begins. We identify increasingly with adults, and others treat us more and more as young adults. We are being thrust into adulthood. The allurement of freedom and independence beckon, but self-doubt and fear of responsibility draw us back. Adolescence is marked by spurts of growth and regression. All the while, the lingering little-boy or little-girl feelings haunt us; we are pulled and torn, not knowing from day to day which—and who—we are.

The prime challenge of early adolescence is the acceptance of the physiological and obviously sexual changes which our body undergoes. For a time we may feel like spirits inhabiting an alien organism. It changes almost daily; it is erratic and unpredictable. Alterations in body chemistry intensify our emotions, and many of them are new to us. Hormonal changes bring on dramatic, uncontrollable mood-swings.

As if all this weren't enough, we are hit by an excruciating realization that society has *norms* for our sexual characteristics and behavior. Society, we discover, expects us to grow in a specific way, and we

2 The Condition and the Odyssey

anxiously wonder whether we will ever measure up to its standards. Underlying all this is a diffuse, undefined, all-pervasive sexual uneasiness.

But eventually, with encouragement, we adjust to these drastic changes and accept this new body. We find—with mixed feelings—that others begin to respond differently to this body. A young woman faces the fact of her sexual attractiveness with embarrassment, self-consciousness, and delight; a young man begins to have exhilarating sexual feelings, but they may be compromised by anxiety, guilt, and bewilderment.

In summary, the central challenge of early adolescence is to be able to hold on tight while our bodies and emotions undergo dramatic alterations, carrying us through the transition into adulthood, and getting us ready for mating and parenting.

9   *Mid-adolescence.* During mid-adolescence physical and psychological turmoil continues, but as we feel more like adults our preoccupation shifts to the problem of independence from authority—that is, independence from other adults. This is the challenge of separation. Feeling increasingly like separate persons, we set out on our own. In the language of space technology, it is time to go on internal power. We venture further in our exploration of life, experimenting with a variety of new experiences. It is a time of trial and error, savoring successes but learning to accept failure when we don't achieve our goals. Independence means learning to set goals for ourselves, and inevitably some will be unrealistic. The challenge is learning to accept failure without feeling like failures—that is, without loss of self-esteem. Gradually we learn how to set more realistic goals.

Separation often involves a painful and prolonged revolt against authority, against parents and other immediate "controllers" (real or imagined) and also *symbols* of control. But while seeking independence we commonly displace our feelings toward all authorities who, we think, might keep us from gaining the desired separation. It is perhaps a hackneyed phrase, but "the crisis of authority" still describes accurately the experience of mid-adolescence. The more we have been restricted and repressed, the louder our protests and the sharper our attacks against the restraints and the restrainers; or if not permitted direct attack, then the greater will be our use of scapegoats.

The separation process produces great ambivalence. We feel loyalty to those who have cared for us, and separation is painful for everyone. And when others are hurt (we usually say that *"we* hurt *them,"* though in fact this is not the case at all), then we feel guilt. To ease our guilt-feelings we seek the approval of those we hurt; that is, we want to be forgiven. But we cry out for the very thing that can't be given. Parents and authorities feel rejected, too; they usually don't understand, and can't accept, our "separating behavior." A part of the individuating process, therefore, is learning to accept without excess remorse and guilt the fact

It is quite possible, Octavian, that when you die, you will die without ever having been alive.

MARK ANTONY

So many people die before they really begin to live.

AARON UNGERSMA

When I put on roller skates, I was as tall as Betty and everyone looked shorter. Then I realized that's how we look to Betty all the time.

SHANNON CHRISTIAN

Be patient . . . because it wasn't your parents who made the world.
ARNOLD TOYNBEE

Youth is the age of extremes: "if the young commit a fault it is always on the side of excess and exaggeration." The great difficulty of youth (and of many of youth's elders) is to get out of one extreme without falling into its opposite. For one extreme easily passes into the other. . . .

ARISTOTLE
(Summary by Durant)

that we have to proceed with the separation *without the approval* of the significant-others involved in the process. Depending upon the maturity of our parents, it is easy to see how manipulative games and bitter conflicts can complicate the mid-adolescent years and often thwart altogether the successful establishment of separate identities. Indeed, for years to come, our parents can linger on in us, and we in them, in a perpetual, agonizing entanglement.

During these troublesome times, we seek the support and understanding of our peers; and an important feature of the mid-adolescent years is "peer-conformity." The more we are misunderstood and rejected by our parents, the more we need the support of our peers who are themselves having similar experiences. They can understand.

10 *Late adolescence.* If these challenges have been met with continued self-esteem, then late adolescence will be characterized by a strong sense of self. We feel more like distinct, whole persons.

With a smoothly functioning self, we can successfully take on ever-greater responsibilities. Indeed, we enjoy responsibility and the satisfactions it brings. Underlying all of life's sundry experiences is a developing strength which carries us through.

If we are on schedule, and our feelings about both body and self are positive, then we will have developed, smoothly and naturally, the

capacity for intimacy, not merely sexual intimacy, but a sense of honesty and openness in all our relationships. The capacity for sexual intimacy is but a single—though often a central—manifestation of the comprehensive capacity for trusting, empathizing, and sharing. The better we feel about ourselves the more we long for intimacy with others.

Therefore, the challenge of late adolescence is the consolidation of a sense of self in relating to other persons, in developing a capacity for intimacy, and in gradually laying to rest our doubts and fears about what we can accomplish as unique selves, newly emerged on the scene and ready for life.

No task is more difficult for youth than allowing their elders to live with their myths; nor any task more difficult for adults than allowing youth their quest for myths.

11   *Developmental Psychology Today* makes a disquieting observation about the most critical aspect of adolescence: separation.

> Several recent, extensive studies suggest that the number of adolescents who achieve a decisive articulation of the self is diminishing. Elizabeth Douvan and Joseph Adelson found that a serious testing of values and ideology occurs only in a minority of adolescents. It appears that real independence is accomplished in lower-class and some upper-middle-class youngsters because these two extremes are so different from the core adolescent culture. But in studying the "silent majority" of adolescents, they found only token parent-child conflict and therefore token maturity and autonomy. They found that the peer group for many adolescents is only used to learn and display social skills—a kind of playpen designed to keep the children out of harm's way. Although for many, the peer group is an arena for confrontation of self, for many more it acts to hinder differentiation and growth.

12   *Young Adulthood.* The young-adult stage is primarily a time of mating and parenting, and from this it follows that the basic challenge of the period is learning to accept responsibility and feeling satisfaction in doing so. Both physiologically and psychologically we are prepared for intimacy, sexual activity, and rearing of offspring. It is probably the case (although research has yet to verify it) that if we are "on schedule" then we will find fulfillment in the responsibilities of parenting.

However, it appears that in most advanced cultures a large number of young adults have not resolved earlier conflicts and, while physically mature, are psychologically unprepared for the parenting role. For many of us reaching the young-adult stage, the wisest decision might be not to become a parent, for any number of reasons: genetic, financial, overpopulation, or because we value more highly other life-goals. Or, after a realistic assessment of our psychological schedule, we may decide not to victimize others with our own unresolved conflicts. We might decide to resolve more adequately the lingering misfortunes of the past before taking on mating and parenting roles.

Some theorists characterize the young-adult phase as a time of creation and productivity, a time to channel one's creative energies into a variety of activities, of which parenting may be only one. Many of us choose our vocation at this time, as well as various long-lasting avocations. All are ways of expressing the essence of our own personalities. Our creative urges can be realized in the art forms, in the professions, in roles which serve others, in competitive business ventures, in sports, and so on. Whether these should be interpreted as compensations for the parenting role is debatable.

During these years we may achieve for the first time a clear picture of the capacities and limitations that we will have to live with

"I have an important appointment."

for the rest of our lives. We may find that we must accept some basic limitations. At the same time we can develop a feeling for our growth potential and begin to set realistic goals in terms of what we truly are.

13   *Adulthood.* If the challenges of responsibility have been met, then the important foundations have been laid for the accomplishment of our goals. There now follows a period lasting fifteen to twenty years—until we approach our middle years, or roughly till the time when our children have separated from us and begun their young-adult years—a period during which our lives can flow more smoothly and stably, a growth-consolidation period. No drastic psychophysical changes occur during this time.

The challenge of this phase is one of growth and accomplishment. If we can assume responsibilities with assurance and skill, then the attainment of goals can bring deep satisfaction. We can enjoy the fruits of our labors. Autonomy and self-esteem can deepen. Our children grow. Social and material gains are made. With increased knowledge and skill in living, we can experience an ever-widening expansion of awareness. These can indeed be fulfilling years.

They can also be dangerous years. If we make unrealistic demands upon ourselves, set unattainable goals, and slide into a pattern of failure, then life, to some degree, can become hellish, and trouble lies ahead. Furthermore, if we become so absorbed in attaining social and material goals that we neglect to set goals that would promote the full growth of ourselves as persons, then the stage is set for us to approach the up-coming challenge of the middle years unprepared and empty.

For looming just ahead is a crucial challenge which will largely determine whether the rest of our life/time will be worth living at all.

14 *The Middle Years.* The challenge of the middle years can be the most crucial and precarious time of life since the turmoil of the adolescent transition, for this also is a time of transition. Life now calls upon all the resources we have been able to develop.

The middle years are a time of taking stock. One arrives at a point where he no longer *assumes* youthfulness; he no longer takes it for granted. He realizes that the youthful phase is passing and that there is nothing he can do about it. The essential challenge might be stated: "I have lived up the first half of my life/time, and I realize there is only so much time left and my life will end. I *experience* that I am mortal. I will die. Now, what do I really want to do with the rest of the time I have left?"

Several events may coalesce and contribute to the onset of this stock-taking period. (1) Our children may have achieved separation and we are no longer needed as parents. We have been freed of long-term responsibilities which have been taken for granted. Not to be needed in this familiar role can initiate an "agonized reappraisal" of our purpose in living. (2) With this change of roles, husband and wife often encounter one another for the first time in many years. They find that they are not the same selves. Without knowing it, both have changed, and rather suddenly their relationship also undergoes an "agonized reappraisal." Often a new relationship must develop. We may also find that we have moved in different directions, and the reestablishment of the intimacy essential to carry us through later years without profound loneliness may be difficult. It may be doubly difficult if such intimacy was never accomplished in the young-adult years.

To some extent, men and women differ in their experience of this middle-years challenge. Menopause may force upon a woman a self-image crisis which a man is spared. If a woman's primary feelings of worth have long been associated with her role as a mother, then the loss of her childbearing capacity—which frequently coincides with the time when her children reach young adulthood, leave home, and no longer need her as a mother—may create severe readjustment problems.

Physical appearance is also a common cause of self-image problems. If a girl's feelings of self-esteem derive primarily from her physical/sexual attractiveness, then as she sees these qualities fade, her self-esteem

Nel mezzo del cammin di
  nostra vita
Mi ritrovai per una selva
  oscura,
Che la deritta via era smarrita.

In the middle of the journey of our life I came to myself in a dark wood where the straight way was lost.

DANTE

Here I am, fifty years old and I don't know what I want to be when I grow up.

PETER DRUCKER

SUNRISE, SUNSET . . .

Is this the little girl I carried?
Is this the little boy at play?
I don't remember growing older.
When did they?
When did she get to be a beauty?
When did he grow to be this tall?
Wasn't it yesterday when they were small?

Sunrise, sunset,
Sunrise, sunset,
Swiftly flow the days.
Seedlings turn overnight to sunflowers,
Blossoming even as we gaze.
Sunrise, sunset,
Sunrise, sunset,
Swiftly fly the years,
One season following another,
Laden with happiness and tears.

What words of wisdom can I give them?
How can I help to ease their way?
Now they must learn from one another,
Day by day.
They look so natural together,
Just like two newlyweds should be.
Is there a canopy in store for me?

Sunrise, sunset,
Sunrise, sunset,
Swiftly flow the days.
Seedlings turn overnight to sunflowers,
Blossoming even as we gaze.
Sunrise, sunset,
Sunrise, sunset,
Swiftly fly the years,
One season following another,
Laden with happiness and tears.

SHELDON HARNICK
Fiddler on the Roof

The biologist looks at the worst aspects of aging, which tends to trouble people.

F. MAROTT SINEX

Treasure each other in the recognition that we do not know how long we shall have each other. . . .
JOSHUA LOTH LIEBMAN

may also fade. She may feel that she possesses no other qualities which could be a realistic basis for any continued self-esteem. She may feel an irreparable, tragic loss. She may spend her later years trying to recapture the attractiveness which she (and, she believes, others) so valued during the mating years. She may try to perpetuate the image of physical/sexual attractiveness which others can see has vanished. Coquettishness at twenty-two may be quite in order; at fifty-five it indicates a confusion of roles and may appear to others as a painful anachronism.

At forty or forty-five a man may note that some gray hair is showing and that younger people are calling him "sir." He may smile to himself and recognize that others' responses toward him are changing. (He may also misinterpret the "sir" and think it has something to do with respect.) There are numerous reminders that he has entered the middle years. Just as a woman may attempt to perpetuate the myth of youthful beauty, a man may try to recapture the image of a youthfulness which is passing away.

Failure to deepen the sense of autonomy and authenticity during the middle years is a sign that trouble is ahead. The foundations of integrity upon which the deeper experiences of our later years must build are shaky in the extreme. This is a crucial matter in the inevitable aging process which we all experience.

Autonomous men and women who have practiced authenticity will be more realistic. They had never attempted to be anything but what they are, and they accept change just as it comes, without myth. The autonomous individual values himself; others' responses to him may change, but his self-esteem remains intact. The later years can arrive more smoothly without our problems reaching crisis proportions.

Therefore, the central challenge of the middle years is the cluster of decisions regarding how we want to live the rest of our lives. The resolution of the middle-years challenge depends largely upon our capacity to reset meaningful goals for ourselves *in terms of who we are and the remaining life/time that we have.*

15 *The Later Years.* If the middle-years challenge has been successfully met, then the later years can be fulfilling. We will continue to grow, to actualize our goals, and simply to enjoy life. It often happens that our physiological processes begin to decline; we may be afflicted with a variety of somatic ailments. But today we know that in most instances our intellectual and emotional responses can remain viable. These faculties, which are the very substance of our existence, need not fade away. To be sure, faculties that were never developed may dim completely, but if our essential faculties have been used optimally, then there is no necessary decline of the quality of our existence with the decline of the somatic organism.

Indeed, the later years can usher us into a *quality of experience* which can rarely come at an earlier time. This can be a new sense of ultimacy in all that we are and do. We may feel a yearning, aching, profound beauty in our experience of simple things, and see previously unnoticed patterns of meaning in nature, and find new perspectives on, and a belated appreciation of, other people. The very fact of existence itself—not merely

Do not go gentle into that good night,
Old age should burn and rave at close of day;
Rage, rage against the dying of the light.

DYLAN THOMAS

IF I WERE EPITAPH

What would I say of me,
If I were Epitaph?
That there were silly bones in him?
The grim but made him laugh?
The jolly made him serious?
The glum made him delirious?
That lawyers talked him sleepy,
And made him snooze at noon,
But bed was his by nine o'clock
So he could rise with moon?
And roll upon the meadows
While other people dreamed,
With windows up and chilly
He smiled and only steamed?
They sealed him in a coffin
But could not make him stay.
His laugh too large, his smile too wide
For any Death to lay?
No matter what the moulder,
The maggot in his bin,
No measuringworm could inch and cir-
Cumnavigate his grin?
If Universe should claim me
And keep me with a sleep
I'd open up my laughter
And drop the Abyss deep;
There we would lie all friendly,
The empty stars and I
And speak upon Creation
And with God occupy
The time that's left for burning,
A billion years to sup,
Then open wide God's laughter
And let Him eat me up.

RAY BRADBURY

human life, but all life, and all existence—can become a glorious mystery that one feels privileged to participate in—"a cosmic drama, and I am actually a part of it!" If life has been a truly expansive adventure, then in these later years there can be an unspeakable love of life—measured by awareness, sagacity, and calm—which we would not exchange, if we could, for the physical vitality of the early years.

These later years may also bring a feeling of resolution, a time for wrapping up some of life's enterprises, a sort of tying up of loose ends. But at the same time, we may well feel the urge to savor all that life can offer. If we have been truly existential throughout our life/time, we will enjoy the warmth and intimacy of human relationships as much, or perhaps more, than ever before.

Admittedly, the other side of this coin is common. When conflicts from the middle years continue unresolved, then these later years may be filled with despair and disillusionment. If intimacy was never reestablished during the middle years, a shallowness and distance will characterize all our later relationships, resulting in an all-pervasive loneliness which is one of life's true tragedies: *the unrelated person.*

16 The adult who lacks integrity in this sense may wish that he could live life again. He feels that if at one time he had made a different decision he could have been a different person and his ventures would have been successful. He fears death and cannot accept his one and only life cycle as the ultimate of life. In the extreme, he experiences disgust and despair. Despair expresses the feeling that time is too short to try out new roads to integrity. Disgust is a means of hiding the despair, a chronic, contemptuous displeasure with the way life is run. As with the dangers and the solutions of previous periods, doubt and despair are not difficulties that are overcome once and for all, nor is integrity so achieved. Most people fluctuate between the two extremes. Most, also, at no point, either attain to the heights of unalloyed integrity or fall to the depths of complete disgust and despair.

Even in adulthood a reasonably healthy personality is sometimes secured in spite of previous misfortunes in the developmental sequence. New sources of trust may be found. Fortunate events and circumstances may aid the individual in his struggle to feel autonomous. Imagination and initiative may be spurred by new responsibilities, and feelings of inferiority be overcome by successful achievement. Even later in life an individual may arrive at a true sense of who he is and what he has to do and may be able to win through to a feeling of intimacy with others and to joy in producing and giving.

ERIK ERIKSON

17 It is not uncommon in our later years for us to return to some form of religion which we may have forgotten or neglected during our earlier years. Cynics will accuse us of trying to "play it safe" or to get comforted because of our fear of death. There is some truth in this, of course, but there is far more. It is an expression of our longing for ultimacy in our later time of life. Many of us enter the later years without profound "spiritual" (that is, ultimate) resources. Life has absorbed our energies in other concerns. We are limited in the ways we know of probing the ultimacy, the depth, the meaning of existence which is intuited as somehow essential to the successful completion of life. For very many of us, the only practical solution may be to return to the religion we knew at an earlier time. A great deal of the late return to

Here lies Dion, a pious man; he lived 80 years and planted 4000 trees.

LATIN EPITAPH

The life so short, the craft so long to learn.

HIPPOCRATES

religion is precisely that: returning to an earlier stage of life. However, a more resourceful resolution of the challenge of the middle years ("What do I really want out of life?") can lead on to far more effective and meaningful forms of ultimacy. It could make possible the flowering of one's own unique and profoundly personal existence. In any case, this religious emphasis should be seen as an attempt to explore the meaning of life and to achieve, in the short time left, an ultimacy which life has heretofore not attained.

18   *The Final Phase.* For many of us—though not all—there is a final phase to our life-cycle. It begins when we must face the fact that our own death is imminent. This is not merely the realization that one is mortal. Rather, this is the acceptance of the absolute fact that our own life/time has almost run out. Now the feeling may become very strong that we must take care of unfinished business and come to terms with the fact that our own cessation of consciousness is near. Dying is much in our thoughts and death-symbols pervade our dreams—a clock without hands, perhaps, as in Ingmar Bergman's *Wild Strawberries.*

If we have lived a long life, we are prepared for our own momentous death-event by having lived closely with death for some years. Others around us have died, more and more of those we have known: loved ones, friends, colleagues, acquaintances, notable contemporaries. This living with death is an essential time of preparation for our own death-event. It serves to diminish feelings of fear and dread.

There may also be a reliving of past events, a replaying of our memories. We are frequently critical of the person who begins "to live in the past," and, of course, if we develop such a habit long before the final phase, then it is probably a sign of premature withdrawal from life. During the final phase, however, it is natural and normal. Partly it is an attempt to see the life/time drama in perspective, and to write a good completion. But partly it is a final preparation for the death-event. It is a recapitulation, a sort of browsing through the storehouse of a lifetime of activities, a savoring of one's accomplishments, a final inventory of life's experiences—and taking mental note of what we will leave behind.

19   In a scene from Tolstoy's *Death of Ivan Ilytch,* the man is ill and dying. As he reflects upon the meaninglessness of his death, what now hits him so forcefully is the meaninglessness of his *life.* He had lived a conventional kind of existence, having achieved the material and social successes expected of him. But on his deathbed, these so-called successes appear in a different light.

"What do I want? . . . To live? How? . . . Why, to live as I used to—well and pleasantly." . . . And in imagination he began to recall the best moments of his pleasant life. But strange to say none of those best moments

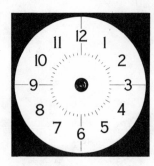

When a man is made to retire after a lifetime of good work, he'd better take his gold watch and hurry to the undertaker. There'll just be time for a down payment.

L. L. TAYLOR

°You may wish to proceed to Chapter 8–4 (Death/Immortality) from this point.

of his pleasant life now seemed at all what they had then seemed. . . . And the further he departed from childhood and the nearer he came to the present the more worthless and doubtful were the joys. . . . "It is as if I had been going downhill while I imagined I was going up. And that is really what it was. I was going up in public opinion, but to the same extent life was ebbing away from me. And now it is all done and there is only death." . . . "Maybe I did not live as I ought to have done." "But how could that be, when I did everything properly?" . . . And whenever the thought occurred to him, as it often did, that it all resulted from his not having lived as he ought to have done, he at once recalled the correctness of his whole life and dismissed so strange an idea.°

3

THE REAL WORLD: KNOWING AND UNKNOWING

3-1

KNOWLEDGE

1   All of us begin our philosophizing from a state of *epistemic naivety,* a condition in which we have not yet begun to question the origins, structure, and dependability of our information. To be sure, some of us may have discovered we were wrong about some things, or we may have "outgrown" certain beliefs; but few of us have peered deeply into the fundamental operations of the "information-processing system" we call "the mind."

Epistemology is the branch of philosophy defined as "the study of human knowledge." In exploring this field we are touching one of evolution's fundamental mechanisms of survival, for it is by knowledge that we orient ourselves in the world. Accurate knowledge of our two worlds—the real° world and the inner world—correctly informs us of the conditions we must cope with. To know true facts is to survive; not to know, or to assess one's environment wrongly, is to lose the fight for survival.

With the examination of the sources, nature, and accuracy of our knowledge, we begin to develop *epistemic awareness,* a more informed understanding of what we know and don't know.

2   We face two serious epistemological problems. (1) How can we determine which facts are true? (2) How can we determine which facts are important?°

Since we are victimized by fragmented, pressurized information, we must find a way to double check fact-claims. We must learn somehow to screen out the fictions but let in the facts. *On what criteria can we decide what are facts and what are false claims?*

Secondly, among the billions of bits of information at our fingertips, we can't distinguish high-priority data. There *are* facts that are

We have to live today by what truth we can get today, and be ready tomorrow to call it falsehood.
WILLIAM JAMES

°*Real, realism.* Recall that the word "real" is a technical term in philosophy. See glossary.

°This latter problem will be dealt with in Chapters 5-4 (Values/Priorities) and 5-5 (Ethics/Choices). In the present chapters we will work on the first question only: How can we decide what is true?

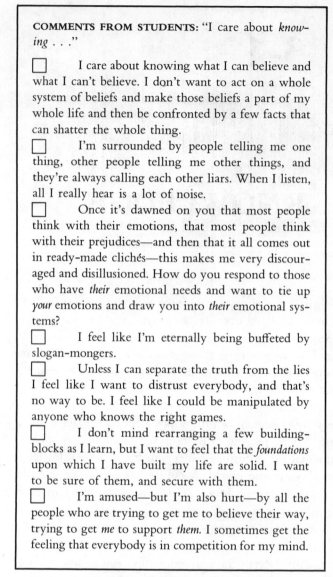

COMMENTS FROM STUDENTS: "I care about *knowing* . . ."

☐   I care about knowing what I can believe and what I can't believe. I don't want to act on a whole system of beliefs and make those beliefs a part of my whole life and then be confronted by a few facts that can shatter the whole thing.

☐   I'm surrounded by people telling me one thing, other people telling me other things, and they're always calling each other liars. When I listen, all I really hear is a lot of noise.

☐   Once it's dawned on you that most people think with their emotions, that most people think with their prejudices—and then that it all comes out in ready-made clichés—this makes me very discouraged and disillusioned. How do you respond to those who have *their* emotional needs and want to tie up *your* emotions and draw you into *their* emotional systems?

☐   I feel like I'm eternally being buffeted by slogan-mongers.

☐   Unless I can separate the truth from the lies I feel like I want to distrust everybody, and that's no way to be. I feel like I could be manipulated by anyone who knows the right games.

☐   I don't mind rearranging a few building-blocks as I learn, but I want to feel that the *foundations* upon which I have built my life are solid. I want to be sure of them, and secure with them.

☐   I'm amused—but I'm also hurt—by all the people who are trying to get me to believe their way, trying to get *me* to support *them.* I sometimes get the feeling that everybody is in competition for my mind.

important; there *are* causes that are crucial; there *are* ideas that work. But which? Since not all facts are of equal importance at a given time, we are forced to make value-judgments. *What criteria can we use for deciding what is more important, what less?*

3   Each of us has stored away in his repertoire hundreds of thousands of bits of knowledge, most of which, needless to say, we can't remember when we want to. What is the source of all these facts? How do they get into our heads and into our memory-banks?

Almost everything that we know originates from four basic sources. The first, *our senses,* can be considered our primary source of information. Two other sources, *reason* and *intuition,* are derivative in the sense that they produce new facts from data already supplied to our minds. The fourth source, *authority,* is by nature secondary, and second-hand facts prove to be the most difficult to handle. Beyond these four sources there may well be others; but if so, knowledge derived from them remains, at present, extremely problematic, and many of the sources are seriously to be doubted.

4   *The Senses.* The fundamental source of all knowledge is our own senses. Throughout our earlier years, this remains our dominant source of information about ourselves and our environment. As beginners in life we "learn by doing," and doing in large part means to see, to hear, to taste, to feel, and so on. Our senses are exploratory organs; we use them all to become acquainted with the world we live in.

We learn that candy is sweet, and so are sugar, jam, and maple syrup. Lemons are not, and onions are not. The sun is bright and blinding. Glowing coals in the fireplace are beautiful if you don't touch them. Sounds soothe, warn, or frighten us. Through millions of single sense-events we build a fabric of empirical° information which helps us interpret, survive in, and control the world about us.

Three of our senses—sight, sound, and smell—give us information about events and objects which lie at a distance, while two of the classical

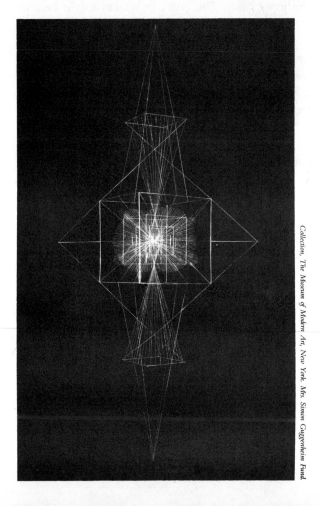

Collection, The Museum of Modern Art, New York, Mrs. Simon Guggenheim Fund

Think? Why think! We have computers to do that for us.
    JEAN ROSTAND
    (describing the computer age of the future)

°Empirical, empiricism. See definitions on page 23 and in the glossary.

If you cannot convince me that there is some kind of knowable ultimate reality, or if you cannot convince me that there are certain absolute values by which I can live my life, I shall commit psychological suicide. That is, either convince me that there is "one truth" or one right way of doing things, or I shall conclude that everything is meaningless and I will not try any more.

    JOSEPH ROYCE
    (describing the reality-image of contemporary man)

"five senses"—taste and touch—inform us about happenings in the immediate vicinity of our sensors. In the perspective of evolutionary survival, this arrangement has obvious benefits.

We have developed specialized sense receptors to perform four of these functions: eyes, ears, taste buds, and olfactory cells. By contrast, the sense of touch does not involve any specialized, strategically positioned organ; touching sensations take place all over our bodies. These "cutaneous sensors" are specialized, however; different types of nerve endings respond to different stimuli. Separate sensors are activated by heat, cold, touch, pressure, and cell damage (which we experience as pain). Nerve endings which react to one of these stimuli generally do not respond to the others. Taken together, all these "touching senses" give us a great deal of data which we put to immediate use in our assessment of real objects/events going on at close range.

These can be called *objective senses* since they tell us about the external world.

5   We also possess numerous *subjective senses* which inform us about our inner world. "Visceral senses" line the inner surfaces of our bodies. They are found in the mouth, along the digestive tract, and on the surfaces of some organs. Without such senses we would not experience a variety of sensations ("feelings"°) which we take for granted, such as headaches, stomachaches, or appendicitis pains. The latter nuisances might be considered minor losses if we didn't have them, but however much they hurt, the warning signals they send us are requisite to adjustment and survival.

Another group of subjective senses have nerve endings in our muscles, tendons, and joints. These are the "proprioceptive sensors" which tell us when our muscles are stretched or contracted; through them we sense if a hand is open or closed, which way our head is turned, and whether our knees are bent. Physical coordination is determined to some extent by these senses.

Another subjective sense is equilibrium. Located in the inner ear, it enables us to maintain our balance within a gravity field and tells us if we are moving or are at rest. We utilize the same principle in a carpenter's level.

This by no means exhausts the list of senses, subjective or objective. We human beings, along with all other living creatures, develop senses whenever conditions make it possible in order to enable us to acquire a bit more information about our two worlds, thus refining our operations and improving our adjustments.

6   Our senses present us with a serious credibility problem. Is there any way we can be sure that they are "telling us the truth" about the two worlds they represent? Can we *believe* what our senses seem to tell us?

Philosophy begins when one learns to doubt—particularly to doubt one's cherished beliefs, one's dogmas and one's axioms.

WILL DURANT

°The word "feeling" does double duty, of course, by referring to sense responses (specifically to touching: "I can feel his pulse") and to emotions ("I feel sad"). The unfortunate fact is that confusion reigns through much technical material (especially in psychological, psychiatric and physiological literature) on the usage of "sensation" and "feeling." In these pages the term "sensation" will always refer to "sense-responses" and never to emotions or to sense-responses with emotional resonances. The word "feeling" will generally refer to emotional feelings; but on rare occasions it will refer to touch-sensing. Context will make clear which meaning is intended.

3   The Real World; Knowing and Unknowing

At this point in our inquiry, the answer must be a reluctant no. Our senses do not give us a "true picture" of the real world; they give us an "operational picture." In fact, we can begin to construct an accurate picture of objective reality only after meticulous correction of the sense data which our senses transmit to us (to "us"—that is, to our minds). We now know that there are numerous inherent "deceptions" and "translations" in the data-transmission processes of the senses. Unfortunately, most of us never get around to making adequate corrections. We remain *naive realists.*°

°*Naive realism.* The uncritical acceptance of one's sense data as representing accurately the real world; a sort of "blind faith" in what one's senses seem to tell him.

7   *Authority.* Other people are continual sources of information. Such information, however, is always second-hand knowledge—or third-, fourth-, or *n*th-hand knowledge. The farther it is removed from our own personal experience, the more caution we must exercise before accepting a fact-claim.

Certain specific classes of knowledge necessarily come to us from the testimony of others. All our historical knowledge we acquire this way. Since the "past" doesn't exist in reality, it isn't subject to empirical observation. We must rely upon those who personally witnessed the living episodes and have recorded, orally or in graphic form, accounts of the events which they believed important. Historical knowledge begins for us when we attempt to re-create in our minds images of, and ideas about, those events. Our reliance upon others for *all* the input about those events is an inescapable dependency.

Most of our knowledge of the sciences also comes to us by authority. We can't personally repeat every experiment, so we must trust the specialists and accept, though sometimes provisionally, the discoveries

THEATER OF THE ABSURD?

What a brain! And you know how to prove things, like the big shots?

   Yeah, I have a special method for that. Ask me to prove something for you, something real hard.

   All right, prove me that giraffes go up in elevators.

   Let's see. Giraffes go up in elevators . . . because they go up in elevators.

   God, that was great! . . . Suppose I asked you to prove giraffes *don't* go up in elevators.

   That's easy. I just prove the same thing, but the other way around.

FERNANDO ARRABAL
The Automobile Graveyard

Yes, reason is an imperfect instrument, like medical science, or the human eye; we do the best we can with it within the limits which fate and nature set. We do not doubt that some things are better done by instinct than by thought: perhaps it is wiser, in the presence of Cleopatra, to thirst like Antony rather than to think like Caesar; it is better to have loved and lost than to have reasoned well. But why is it better?

WILL DURANT

Most of our assumptions have outlived their uselessness.

MARSHALL MC LUHAN

they record for us. Careful workers in the sciences document their researches in such manner that if we wish to double check the fact-claims ourselves we can obtain the necessary information to do so. Knowing that a fact can be double checked gives one better reason to trust the scientists' work.

By authority also we receive a good deal of knowledge from the society in which we live, but it can't be accepted uncritically. Every culture is a carrier of traditions, folklore, "common knowledge," and "common sense" which must be carefully screened before one can feel assured that he possesses dependable information.

8 How can we be sure that the "facts" others give us are true? In the face of conflicting fact-claims, how can we decide which authorities to follow? In a word, whom can we trust?

There is no simple answer. We *must* accept large amounts of knowledge which have been accumulated over the centuries; we would be personally impoverished without it. The solution lies in knowing how to apply checkout criteria to fact-claims and in maintaining an ever-vigilant, critical spirit. If one possesses the skill to check at will any fact-claim, and if one has learned when to be wary of those who would seduce him into accepting *their* "facts" without supplying evidence or sound reason—if one commands this equipment, he will feel far more confident in handling the knowledge which comes his way.

There is another, and perhaps more insidious, danger involved in relying upon others for knowledge. Most of us are prone to the development of dependencies. We commonly select one or two authorities, invest our trust in them, and indulge our laziness to the absurd point of accepting all they tell us. Despite the fact that developing one's critical skills is hard work, those who wish to feel more secure in their knowledge will avoid dependencies which inhibit personal inquiry and growth.

9   *Reason.* Our reasoning faculties can be a source of true facts. "Reason" might be defined as the process of using known facts to arrive at new facts. Hence, if we start with data which we are sure of, we can apply deductive or inductive procedures and arrive at new information which we did not have before.

The universe is not to be narrowed down to the limits of the Understanding,—but the Understanding must be stretched and enlarged to take in the image of the Universe as it is discovered.

FRANCIS BACON

If you are traveling in Mexico City and your travel guide reads, "One peso is equal to about 8¢ in U.S. money," you can readily find out how much your breakfast is going to cost if the menu reads, "Huevos Rancheros—35 pesos." It doesn't take much reasoning to discover that your eggs will cost you $2.80. Note merely that your conclusion—that you are considering a $2.80 breakfast—is new knowledge, making possible a new understanding. Reasoning itself, therefore, can produce new facts.

There are common abuses involved in both deductive and inductive reasoning.° Deductive procedure applies primarily in mathematics, geometry, and in systems of logic with clearly defined terms. Yet we often try to apply deduction to our familiar, ill-defined symbols and arrive at convenient conclusions which in no way follow from the premises.

The weakness of induction results mainly from our failing to realize that it always gives us *probable* knowledge and never *certain* knowledge. For example, if one should witness five auto accidents in the period of an afternoon, all involving the same make and model of car, most of us would be tempted to conclude that something is mechanically wrong with this particular make and model. This conclusion would be an inductive hypothesis, with apparent validity. But it is not a *certain* conclusion; it is only a possible and probable explanation. Add five more accidents with the same make and model. Is one more certain? Yes, but only *more,* not absolutely. Now what happens to the hypothesis when you discover that all ten drivers were driving on the wrong side of the freeway?

The induction problem forever haunts us. How many instances of a class must be studied before one can be "sure"? Are there other hypotheses which might better explain the data? In controlled investigations with a large sampling, one can often eliminate competing hypotheses and run up the probability factor for the correct explanation.

°*Deduction* is the process of drawing out (making explicit) the implications of one or more premises or statements of fact. If one *infers* correctly what the premises *imply,* then his inference (conclusion) is said to be "valid." *Induction* is the procedure of developing general explanatory hypotheses to account for a set of facts. In scientific induction one projects universal principles—for instance, concluding that *all* planetary orbits are parabolic—after having actually examined only a few cases. Notice that in deduction, the conclusion *necessarily* follows from the premises. (All cats are blue. Tom is a cat. Therefore, Tom is *necessarily* blue.) In induction, one's working hypothesis is always tentative; it is subject to change whenever further facts are obtained. ("I have seen only six cats, and they were all blue. I must conclude, tentatively, that all cats must be blue." All it takes in this case is one yellow cat to strike a fatal blow to a viable hypothesis. Inductive conclusions, therefore, are always subject to change.)

Nevertheless, the hypothesis shall always remain a *probable explanation*, and nothing more.°

°For further explanation of inductive reasoning, note the problem of the robins' eggs on pages 364ff. See also the case of the dead TV set on pages 165f.

10 *Intuition.* Although the word *intuition* calls up varied connotations, when carefully defined it can be considered a source of knowledge. Intuition refers to insights or bits of knowledge which emerge into the light of consciousness from the deeper subconscious. It is not uncommon to have sought-for ideas pop into our minds while consciously thinking about quite different things. We know that the subconscious mind can perform complex operations which the conscious mind, burdened with the task of mediating sense data, cannot handle.

An American theologian, Francis McConnell, recalls an instance of intuition when he was about fifteen and in high school. He had been assigned several algebra problems for homework and was having no trouble with them until the last problem became obstinate. He wrestled with it in prolonged frustration, but it would not give in, and finally, very late, he gave up and went to bed. Upon awaking the next morning the solution popped immediately into his mind. It dawned on him that his subconscious mind had continued to work on the problem while his conscious mind slept.

Why is a single instance, in some cases, sufficient for a complete induction, while in others myriads of concurring instances, without a single exception known or presumed, go such a very little way toward establishing a universal proposition? Whoever can answer this question knows more of the philosophy of logic than the wisest of the ancients, and has solved the problem of Induction.

JOHN STUART MILL

Man is a credulous animal and tends to believe what he is told. Historically, philosophers . . . have taken great pains to point out that authority is at least as important a source of error as it is of knowledge.

JOSEPH BRENNAN

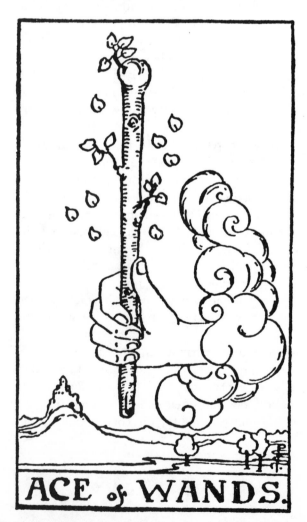

ACE of WANDS.

Having discovered such a helpful faculty, he decided to take full advantage of it. The next evening he glanced briefly over his algebra assignment, promptly forgot it, and went to sleep. Needless to say, when the morning came there were no solutions. McConnell recalls the lesson he learned: the subconscious mind can do creative work, but it must be treated fairly. It must be given adequate data to work with and also, perhaps, more than a little coaxing.

11 Sometimes intuition is experienced as an emotional feeling. We often say something like, "I have the feeling he's not telling the truth," and it may be just that: a feeling, but a feeling in the process of informing us of a true fact.

"I have a feeling it's going to rain." Perhaps such a statement rests on subliminally collected sense data subconsciously synthesized, giving us a "feeling" about a real condition we could not consciously recognize.

Occasionally we hear someone say, "I have a feeling something bad is going to happen." It's a presentiment, a foreboding. Jung suggested that the unconscious can correlate data in such a way that it can "foresee" events which the conscious mind, being preoccupied with perception and immediate concerns, cannot "feel." Strictly speaking, such feelings would not be precognitive insights, but rather premonitions derived from current data; but such premonitions, when accurate, would become genuine sources of knowledge.

The principal weakness of intuition and feeling as sources of knowledge is that the insights they produce are as likely to be wrong as right. If left to intuition, most algebra problems would remain unsolved. Intuitive fact-claims must be carefully double checked before credentials are issued.

12 Fact-claims have been made against other possible sources. For various reasons all of them are problematic, not the least because, in theory, most of them cannot be double checked at all.

(1) *Instinct.* There was a time when "instinct" was used to account for an "inherited pattern of behavior" in both animals and humans. Its existence in man is very doubtful, however, and the term is little used today. Even if it should prove to exist, it would not be a knowledge of facts, but a know-how system of survival behavior.

(2) *Racial Memory.* Evidence in support of racial memory is meager, though the concept has been developed by Dr. Carl Jung in his theory of the "collective unconscious." Granting that such memories might exist, and that they could be inherited, the archetypal images described by Jung are diffuse and seem to be devoid of any specific fact-claims.

(3) *Extrasensory Perception.* ESP in its several forms is commonly

The more extensive a man's knowledge of what has been done, the greater will be his power of knowing what to do.

DISRAELI

If a thing moves, then it must move either in the place where it is or in a place where it is not. But it cannot move where it is nor can it move where it is not; therefore it cannot move.

ZENO THE ELEATIC
(Formulated by William and Mabel Sahakian)

claimed to be a source of knowledge. About 20 percent of Americans relate experiences of telepathy, clairvoyance, or precognition. There is accumulating scientific evidence that some forms of ESP may exist, but at present we know very little about them. No viable unifying hypothesis seems to be developing which would account for all the varied ESP phenomena. Although it might eventually turn out to be a source of verifiable fact-claims, our present understanding of ESP is so incomplete that we must consider the source with great caution.

(4) *Anamnesis* ("recollection") refers to remembrance of things from a previous existence. The notion was held by several Greek philosophers, notably Pythagoras and Plato; and the "transmigration of souls" (*samsara*) is a basic Hindu doctrine. There are many recorded cases of people "remembering" people and places from previous lifetimes. If indeed anamnesis does exist, however, it is safe to say that for most of us it is inconsequential; our knowledge of any previous existence has long since faded away.

(5) *Supernatural revelation* has been a universal source-claim; every variety of human knowledge has been attributed to God or the gods. As a source of verifiable information, the supernatural in any form raises enormous problems. Time and again we are blocked when we try to make our way back to the primary personal experience where the facts would have originated. Historical documentation invariably presents a credibility barrier. All this aside, however, *if* there is a supernatural order of reality, and *if* facts truly derive from such a source, they would be subject to the same checkout criteria which we apply to all other fact-claims. Their source would not exempt them from having to prove their truth-value.

Knowledge means survival.
Whether we are speaking of a bass
darting under a rock away from an
approaching shadow, a fawn lying
motionless in the grass when it
hears a rustling of leaves, or a
man learning to swim or studying
the slide-rule—knowledge and
know-how mean survival.

(6) *Spiritualism.* Many books have been written allegedly containing information from discarnate spirits, communicated by mediums, fortune tellers, ouija boards, and the like. When such fact-claims can be checked they frequently turn out to be untrue. There are few "facts" from a discarnate world which cannot be better accounted for on known psychological principles, and most of those few remaining "facts" can be explained in terms of some form of telepathic phenomena. While it cannot be ruled out as a source of knowledge, it is difficult at present to feel much confidence in any known form of spiritualism.

(7) *Occultic Sources.* Astrology, Tarot, and other occultic sources are commonly believed to give us certain kinds of information. According to present knowledge, it is doubtful that there are any objective phenomena operating to reveal "facts" to us. This does not rule out the possibility of subliminal influences which may indeed exist, but any fact-claims deriving from the whole range of the occult are at present quite precarious.

Americans run an idea up the flag-
pole to see if anyone salutes, but
the British let an idea get broody
to see if anything will hatch.

PAUL A. KOLERS

3-2

SENSES/REALITY

1   Our senses constitute our interface with reality. The word *interface* is a modern term used to describe the boundary of contact between adjacent realms; it is the common surface where two areas of activity meet. Thinking in these terms, it is our senses which make up the surface-contact between our subjective world of experience and the objective world of reality. The phenomena that take place along these two surfaces are what concern us here, for now we face directly the problem of the nature of our interface with reality.

     What is going on where these two worlds meet?

2   Our senses are *transducers.* A transducer is any substance or device which converts one form of energy into another. A lightbulb, for instance, converts electricity into light. (You and I know that *light* does not run through the cord which is plugged into the wall outlet, but a primitive tribesman might arrive at the belief—with excellent reason—that if he cut the cord, light would spill out.)

     In our technological world we are surrounded by transducers. A hotplate changes electrical energy into heat, but eggbeaters, blenders, and power-mowers convert that same electrical energy into mechanical motion. Conversely, heat is used in nuclear power plants to produce electricity. Geiger counters convert radiation into sound—audible warning clicks. Tape recorders convert air waves into electrical impulses which are converted into magnetic lines of force which are stored in the oxides on the tape. Batteries change chemical energy into electrical energy, and solar cells convert light into electrical energy. An electroencephalograph converts brain waves (electrical) into squiggly lines on paper or dancing curves on an oscilloscope. Finally, there is chlorophyll, one of nature's grand transducers, which converts light into chemicals used in living processes.

A philosopher riding through the countryside on a train once leaned over to peer long and hard out the window. When asked what he saw, he replied that he was looking at a half of twenty sheep, and that he was wondering how he could find out about the other half.

And then there are fireflies, who spend a large percentage of their waking time (our sleeping time) converting biochemical energy into light.

3 A transducer, then, converts *one kind of energy* into a *different kind of energy*.

Each of our senses is a living transducer. So our question becomes: What kind of energy goes into the sense/transducer, and what kind of energy comes out? Or, to put it differently: (1) What is the energy input? (2) What is the energy output? and (3) How does the sense-converter do it?

If we can answer these questions, we can discover what actually is taking place along that boundary-surface which constitutes our interface with reality.

3 The Real World: Knowing and Unknowing

Let's answer question (2) immediately and return to the others later. From all our known senses, the output is the same: it is electrochemical energy which propagates along the neural pathways. So far as we know at present, the impulses which leave our senses and move toward the central nervous system and into the brain are in every case the same. What then makes the difference in our experience if the impulses are all the same? Only the location in the brain to which the message-impulses are carried. Visual sensors, for example, send impulses to the back tip of the occipital lobe; sound sensors send their messages to another area of the brain located on the top inner fold of the temporal lobe; and so on, for every sense we have. Each sensory area of the cortex "knows how" to convert the electrochemical impulses into the "right experiences."

Now, what if we should "get our wires crossed"? That is, what if we should have nerve fibers ending in the wrong area of the brain? If that should happen, the brain would *misinterpret* the impulses. If touch receptors sent their messages to the "cold center" in the cortex, the lightest touch would be felt as cold. In one laboratory experiment, scientists crossed the nerve fibers of the right and left rear feet of a white rat; when the pain sensors in the right foot were stimulated, the rat would jerk away the left foot, and vice versa.

If the nerve fibers from our eyes could be crossed with the nerve fibers from our ears, then undoubtedly we would "hear" colors and "see" sounds.

4   It is apparent that the gathering of information by our senses is a complex process, with many a possible slip twixt the energy input and the final experience. To clarify the problem, let's use one sense as an analogue.

A round, contented, bright yellow grapefruit lies in the fruit bowl on the table. Now, no matter how hard you try, it is a fact that you can never see the grapefruit—or touch, smell, or taste it.

What you *see,* of course, are light quanta which strike the grapefruit and are reflected back to your eyes. "White" light (that is, light of all wavelengths together) from some source such as the sun or a lightbulb strikes the surface of the grapefruit which, because of the molecular structure of its surface material, absorbs all the wavelengths of the spectrum *except* the "yellow" wavelengths (in the vicinity of 5600 to 5800 angstrom units), which are reflected back and reach your eyes. So, what do we *see?* Only the reflected light from the object, never the object itself.

5   Now, what are "light waves"? The best we can say is that they are electromagnetic waves of different lengths which travel at a speed of about 186,000 miles per second. *The waves themselves are colorless,* but the cones embedded in the retinas of our eyes are stimulated by the various wavelengths of radiation and send impulses to the visual centers of the

It's funny how the colors of the real world only seem really real when you viddy them on the screen.
ALEX
A Clockwork Orange

These sensory limitations, and the resulting failure to comprehend fully much of Nature, may be only a local deficiency. On the basis of the new estimates of the great abundance of stars and the high probability of millions of planets with highly developed life, we are made aware—embarrassingly aware—that we may be intellectual minims in the life of the universe. I could develop further this uncomfortable idea by pointing out that sense receptors, in quality quite unknown to us and in fact hardly imaginable, which record phenomena of which we are totally ignorant, may easily exist among the higher sentient organisms of other planets.

HARLOW SHAPLEY

cortex, *where they are interpreted as colors.* Human retinas possess three kinds of cones, which are sensitive, respectively, to three basic wavelengths, the wavelengths we interpret as red, blue, and green—the three primary colors for light (notice the three colors of phosphor dots on a color TV screen).°

°Textbooks occasionally define certain wavelengths with a certain color. This is an expediency for the sake of simplicity, but it is a conceptual fallacy. Modern physical theory consistently shows that physical entities—atoms, molecules, electromagnetic waves, etc.—cannot possess the qualities which we experience.

6   From these facts, two conclusions must be drawn which are of great significance for understanding the nature of our knowledge.

(1) *Color is an experience in our minds.* It is the experiential finale to a long and complicated process of transduction. The energy input to our visual transducers is uncolored electromagnetic radiation which enters our eyes with wavelengths (in the visual spectrum) of about 3800 to 7200 angstroms. Our transducer/cones identify the various wavelengths and send electrical messages along the neural pathways to the visual center of the brain. There and then *only* we see color.

(2) A corollary: *There is no color whatever in the external world of things.* Look around you. That grapefruit only *appears* to be yellow. All the colors you "see"—however beautiful, enchanting, stimulating they seem to you—are only experiences in your mind. The ocean is not deep blue, the pine forest is not green, and the aurora borealis does not scintillate with cosmic colors.

And there is no color in the rainbow.

7   This transduction pattern holds true for all our senses, and for all possible senses which we can imagine.

Sound. Once there was a famous tree in a forest, a tree that decided to fall when no one was around. It did its very best to make a noise; it wanted to be heard. But it went down to defeat. It did indeed set up quite a vigorous series of waves in the summer air, waves that alternately rarefied and compressed the air as they moved outward. But there was no sound in the land.°

°It is reported that a chipmunk, sunning on a rock at the top of the hill, had his transducers going, and that he *heard* the *sound* of a crash in the valley below. One transducer can make all the difference between sound and eternal silence.

Taste. Chemical substances penetrate the surface cells of our tastebuds, which apparently respond to only four basic "tastes": sweet, sour, salty, and bitter. All the flavors of our gastronomic spectrum are merely combinations of these four. But note: there is no taste to the chemical substances; they are only molecular structures. There is no "sweetness" in the peppermint candy, no "saltiness" in the sodium chloride, and no "sourness" in a lemon.

Smell. Gaseous molecules permeate the linings of the olfactory membranes in the upper nasal passageway. Precisely how the molecules manage to stimulate such a variety of "odor messages" is not understood, but our conclusion is again clear: there is no scent in the rose nor salty odors from the spray of the breakers on the beach. All the sweet fragrances of Samarkand are merely experiences in the mind.

Touch. Whether the stimulus is pressure or pain, heat or cold, the only things we "know" are the *experiences* which occur in various

areas of the cerebral cortex. But this is probably the sense which we most readily believe. After all, who ever claimed that "pain" was located in the red-hot coal?

In a word, before the development of sentient creatures on the planet earth, there were no colors, no sounds, no odors. There were no experiences because there were no experiencers.

8   As a result of such analysis, we may have the uneasy feeling that we are being deceived. We are being led, by our own senses, into believing things which are untrue. The grapefruit may not be yellow, but it surely *looks* yellow; it seems undeniable that the yellowness is in the rind of the fruit itself. Likewise, we would be willing to wager that the sweetness is in the peppermint candy and that the sound of a tree falling came from the bottom of the hill. These are only appearances, however. They are indeed "deceptions."

Furthermore, our *language* is a part of the conspiracy. For I look at the grapefruit and say, "The grapefruit is yellow." The subject of my statement is the noun "grapefruit" and the adjective "yellow" modifies the noun; and the "is" clearly attaches the quality of yellowness to the subject "grapefruit."

It is to be expected that our language would reflect the deception of our senses. Language crystallizes the deception, as it were, and reflects

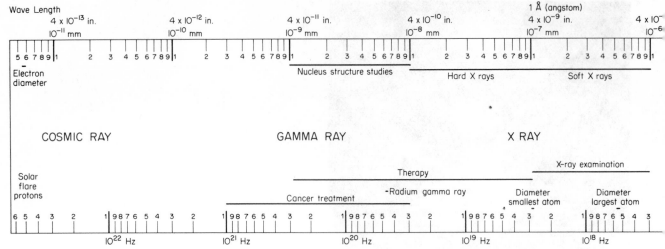

Wave Length

| 4 x 10⁻¹³ in. | 4 x 10⁻¹² in. | 4 x 10⁻¹¹ in. | 4 x 10⁻¹⁰ in. | 1 Å (angstom) 4 x 10⁻⁹ in. | 4 x 10⁻ |

Electron diameter

Nucleus structure studies   Hard X rays   Soft X rays

COSMIC RAY   GAMMA RAY   X RAY

Solar
flare
protons

X-ray examination

Therapy

Cancer treatment   -Radium gamma ray   Diameter smallest atom   Diameter largest atom

10²² Hz   10²¹ Hz   10²⁰ Hz   10¹⁹ Hz   10¹⁸ Hz

Frequency

WINDOWS ONTO THE UNIVERSE

A continuous frequency spectrum including both sonic and electromagnetic wavelengths is plotted here on a logarithmic scale. Placed together, the frequency ranges from 6×10^{22} Hz to 5×10^{-4} Hz. This is a range in wavelength from the diameter of an electron to a wave almost two hundred million miles long. Near the long end of the spectrum the "world resonance" (like the vibration of a giant bell) is a single cycle lasting about 20 seconds.

If this frequency spectrum represents two kinds of reality—sonic and electromagnetic—then we have two "windows" open to us onto the universe.

One is the audio window which, with our natural sense, is limited to a range of 20 to 20,000 Hz. The other is the visual window in the electromagnetic spectrum, a very small window ranging from about 3800 to 7200 Å. These windows set the limits to what we can hear and see in the real world.

All the other sonic and electromagnetic realities are there, moving about us; but we are deaf and blind to them, and they are meaningless to us.

When were these windows opened to us? Shall we say, for the audio and visual windows, perhaps a billion years ago? Whenever sentient creatures first began to sense vibrations in the atmosphere and respond to light.

When were the other windows opened to us? Only during the last one hundred years. They were all flung open with breath-taking rapidity.

What reason is there to believe that all the realities have now been discovered, all the spectra plotted, and all the windows opened?

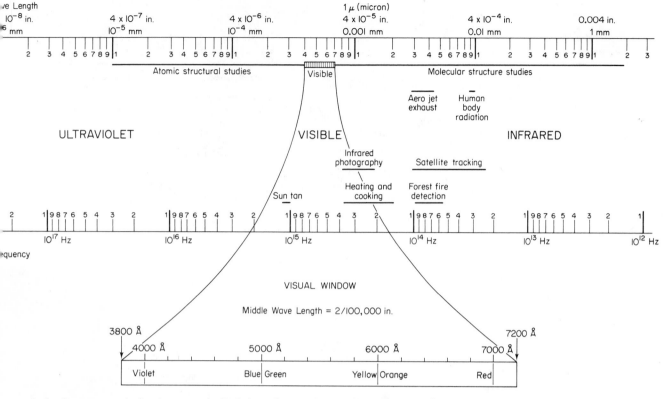

it back to us, reinforcing our belief that the quality yellow does in fact belong to the object.

9   To say that we are being "deceived" seems like a suspicious way of looking at it. After all, none of our senses "intend" to deceive us.

Perhaps the transduction process can be interpreted more positively. For the fact is that all our senses have developed in such a way that they can translate meaningless physical phenomena into meaningful experiences. To use an analogy, at this moment there are probably several television stations transmitting electromagnetic waves through the atmosphere where you are, but if your TV set is not turned on, the waves are meaningless. Turning your TV set on would convert useless phenomena into meaningful information.

This is precisely what our senses do: They turn on to the physical phenomena of the real world and render our environment meaningful. They translate the events going on around us into useful information.

They have given us the kind of information we need in order to survive. What more can we ask of them?

Knowledge, if it be taken without the true corrective, hath in it some nature of venom or malignity.

FRANCIS BACON

10   Let's look once again at the drastic sensory limitations we operate under. The electromagnetic spectrum is a good example. If we arbitrarily divide the range of all electromagnetic waves into sixty "octaves," then

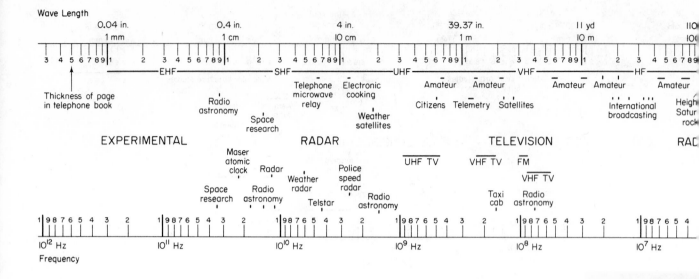

visually we can perceive only a single octave, from about 3800 to 7200 angstrom units. But the waves extend away to great distances on either side of that visual octave.

Below the blue end of the visual spectrum the waves grow shorter into the ultraviolet rays, X rays, and gamma rays. Above the red end of the spectrum the wavelengths grow longer into the infrared, the microwaves, short radio and long radio waves. We have developed instruments, of course, which are extensions of our senses and can reach out on either side of the visual octave.

Still, without the aid of our instruments, we are limited in perception to that single octave. It is a bit unnerving to realize how little physical reality we perceive, and how much more there really is.

11　　No creature ever has enough senses; it could always use more. Why, then, in the long course of evolution, did we not develop other senses? We believe the answer is fairly simple: given the time we had to evolve and the conditions our ancestors had to cope with, they developed the particular sensors needed most. But if other conditions had prevailed, our sense-systems would have been different in countless ways.

12　　We share existence on our planet with millions of species of sentient creatures, many of which have senses we might well envy. (In

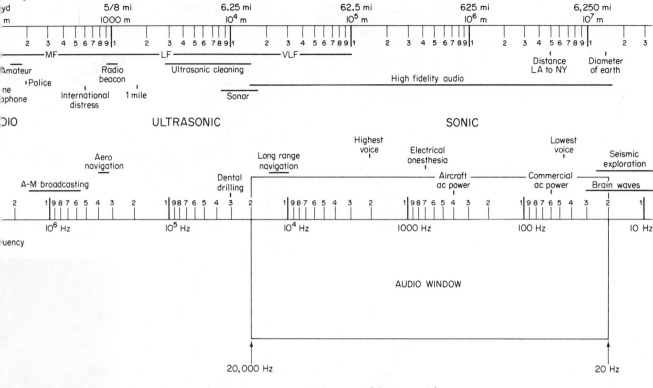

fact, we do envy them, for we duplicate every sense we possibly can with scientific instruments.)

Many animals, of course, possess the same senses we have, but they have intensified their sensitivity beyond our range of sensory pickup. Many animals can hear high-pitched sounds beyond our range. Bats emit high-pitched sounds and then listen to their echo to locate objects ("echolocation," the principle used in radar). Porpoises and fish have an underwater counterpart of the bat's "radar"—a "sonar" system. The

"There has been a complete changeover in human affairs. Where man has always been after *things,* after *reality*—reality being everything you can see, touch, taste, smell and hear—suddenly we're in a completely new kind of reality. The reality of the great electromagnetic spectrum which is part of this communications revolution. And we now know that what man can hear, smell, touch, taste and see is less than a millionth of reality."

BUCKMINSTER FULLER

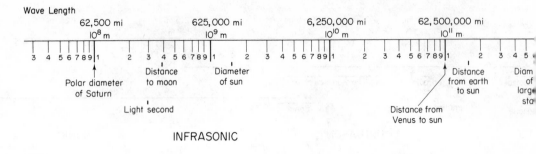

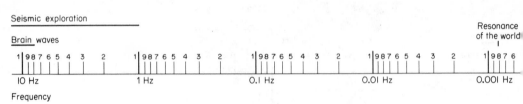

"lateral-line" sense in fishes is what we might think of as a combined touch-hear sense, for in the water these senses merge. Fishes living at great depths where no light can penetrate have developed hypersensitive lateral-lines; a preying fish can "take a fix" on its quarry and zero in with pinpoint accuracy.

Ants and other insects have delicate chemical senses (combining touch, taste, and smell?) by which they communicate and establish food trails. Moths both smell and hear with their antennae. Bees navigate to their honey sources by reckoning the sun's position.

Then there are still other senses which remain mysteries. At this point we can only admire and wonder about them: the senses by which birds migrate (perhaps partly by star navigation), the "homing sense" of dogs and cats and many wild animals, the senses which enable the Sargasso eels to return to the St. Lawrence and European rivers which their ancestors knew, but which they themselves have never seen.

And then there are fireflies. Hundreds of tiny sparks in the night: one wonders how they perceive their flashing world.

13 "Tell me," says Micromegas, an inhabitant of one of the planets of the Dog Star, to the secretary of the Academy of Sciences in the planet Saturn, at which he had recently arrived in a journey through the heavens—"Tell me, how many senses have the men on your globe?" . . .

It is impossible to explain . . . qualities of matter except by tracing these back to the behavior of entities which themselves no longer possess these qualities. If atoms are really to explain the origin of color and smell of visible material bodies, then they cannot possess properties like color and smell. . . . Atomic theory consistently denies the atom any such perceptible qualities.

WERNER HEISENBERG

"We have seventy-two senses," answered the academician, "and we are every day complaining of the smallness of the number. . . ."

"I can very well believe," says Micromegas, "for, in our globe, we have very near one thousand senses, and yet, with all these, we feel continually a sort of listless inquietude and vague desire, which are forever telling us that we are nothing, and that there are beings infinitely nearer perfection."

VOLTAIRE

14   Dr. Willard Geer, the inventor of the three-gun color television picture-tube, had an accident in the kitchen of his home in the early 1940s when a glass pane he was incising for an experiment shattered and a glass splinter embedded itself in his right eye. The injury altered his perception. Dr. Geer can now see, with that eye, a considerable way into the ultraviolet range of the spectrum. When asked to describe what he sees, he cannot. He only replies, "I just see things occasionally which other people can't."

15   Our sensory perception of reality turns out to be so limited that we must make careful allowance for what we can't perceive. In the sphere of sense experience, there is no place for dogmatism or final facts. It is only too easy to build towering knowledge-systems upon shaky empirical foundations.

To be sure, we are in the fortunate position of having much dependable empirical knowledge to use in constructing a more accurate picture of the world we live in, but we must be very careful.

There are undoubtedly worlds we know not of, even now.

The disputants I ween
Rail on in utter ignorance
Of what each other mean,
And prate about an Elephant
Not one of them has seen.
JOHN G. SAXE

3-3

KNOWING/ UNKNOWING

(An Historical Sidetrip)

1   At about this point, a feeling of loneliness may begin to overtake us—an "epistemic loneliness." For the egocentric predicament is really an epistemological condition: isolation within a world of our own making. We live in a shell, so to speak, a private, personal shell inside which takes place an immense variety of experiences, *all ours.* And when we try to break out of our shells to make contact with the world and other creatures, we only rediscover the depth of our predicament. We live in an epistemological shell with no doors. None may enter and none may share.

2   Since certain aspects of our epistemological condition appear to be inescapable, we must learn to live with them.

(1) *The fallacy of objectification is an ever-present danger.* Our experiencing system conspires to make us think that a variety of private experiences are in some way real, that they are events occurring in the real world of objects/events. (The tragic consequences of this fallacy will be felt especially when we try to untangle our value-experiences.)

(2) *Accordingly, we have all lived (unwittingly) in a state of confusion regarding the location of the occurrence of events.* Our subjective and objective worlds are interwoven: events we thought to be private may turn out to be objective, while many supposedly objective events often prove to be experiences only.

Occasionally an epistemolog is found who is capable of smiling, like Bradley or William James; occasionally one is found who understands that his 'ology is only a game, and, therefore, plays it with a worldly twinkle in his eye, like David Hume.

WILL DURANT

THE ENGLISH EPISTEMOLOGIST: *John Locke* (1632–1704)

John Locke is best known for his political philosophy, but he deserves equal praise for his work in the psychology of perception.

His father was a middle-class country lawyer and a Puritan, living near Bristol, England; and as a father he had enviable qualities. A friend later wrote that he provided a firm guiding hand for his son during his early years but that he relaxed "by degrees" his sternness as his son "grew up to be a man, till, he being capable of it, he lived perfectly with him as a friend."

Young Locke got an excellent education at Westminster and Oxford, but he considered his first college years a waste of time: his courses were irrelevant, too oriented toward scholastic tradition. After graduation and a Master's degree, he remained at Oxford tutoring and lecturing. He and some friends belonged to what they called an "Invisible College" made up of free thinkers who met together for lively discussions.

Locke never married. Among his unpublished papers, however, were letters indicating that during his college days he was not without close companions of the opposite sex. One such friendship, he tells us, "robbed me of the use of my reason." All his written records are an epitome of discretion, and wisely so, since one of his companions was the local pastor's daughter.

Locke was a physician by profession, but his concerns were so extensive that he was involved in all the problems of his day. Intolerance of one another, he believed, was our greatest sin. Throughout his life he boldly condemned persecution, argued for civil and religious freedom; this was his passion and for it he spent almost a decade in exile. He began writing his *Letters on Toleration* as early as 1666 and was working on a fourth such letter when he laid down his pen in 1704.

Despite his delicate health, Locke managed an active life. From about 1691, however, the London climate became too much for a chronic bronchial ailment, so he retired to the Essex country home of his old friends Lord and Lady Masham. (He paid one pound a week for board, plus one shilling for board for his horse.) There he had two rooms, one of them large enough for his library of some five thousand volumes. In their red-brick Tudor house, overlooking a garden, he continued to study, write, doctor his friends and entertain guests. Though he suffered much, his gentle spirit, courtesy and kindness toward everyone never failed. His had been the voice of sanity and tolerance in an age of bloodshed.

One evening in 1704, as he was sitting quietly listening to Lady Masham read from the Psalms, his heart stopped. He was 72.

(3) *We are restless with our evolutionary limitations and deceptions.* While we can be grateful that our sensory and information-processing systems have rendered our physical environment meaningful, we have reached a point in our quest for reality when we want to go beyond our limitations and to know what the world is really like. We want to make whatever corrections are necessary in our perception, so we can move out of our shells and come to know our universe and its principles of operation.

3   From this vantage point, the central problem of Western epistemology may be more intelligible. *If we know only our experiences, how can we be sure that we know anything about the real world?* More precisely, if objective physical phenomena are all converted *before we can experience them* into different kinds of energy, how can we know anything about the original phenomena? Can we even know what those phenomena are?

If we experience only the subjective side of our interface with reality, can we ever know anything about the objective side of that interface-boundary?

It will be helpful at this point to take time for a historical sidetrip. Almost four centuries of epistemological analysis has engaged some of the greatest minds the West has produced. Without feeling any obligation to believe all they say, let's listen to three philosophers, briefly.

4   John Locke published his *Essay Concerning Human Understanding* in 1690, and it became a turning point in Western thought.

Locke made a distinction between primary and secondary qualities. *Primary qualities,* he held, are to be considered as belonging to physical objects themselves; they inhere in the real object. Primary qualities are such things as solidity, extension (that is, volume, the occupation of space), shape, motion/rest, and number. (Today, still thinking in Locke's terms, we might wish to add such qualities as mass, atomic structure, radioactivity, magnetism, etc.) If we couldn't perceive objects—or if we perceivers didn't exist—these qualities would still exist in objects.

Secondary qualities are experiences only, stimulated in us by the powers residing in real objects, and these qualities are: colors, sounds, tastes, odors, weight, warmth, etc. Secondary qualities are our subjective human responses to the objective primary qualities. Clearly, we could not have our perceptions unless they are caused by real objects.

But those primary qualities—what do they really *belong* to? What is this "object" that has shape or is in motion or is solid? Locke had to answer "substance." But what is "substance"? Well, "substance" is what has shape, is in motion, and is solid!

That didn't get us very far, so let's put the question differently: How can we *know* "substance"? The only way we can know substance, Locke answered, is to observe the primary qualities: shape, motion,

For the sceptic to bewail the fact that we can know nothing but appearance is as silly as it would be to bewail the fact that we have nothing to wear but clothes and nothing to eat but food.

W. P. MONTAGUE

solidity, etc. But that's where we were before. Locke therefore concludes that "substance" cannot be known directly at all, but is rather an assumption which we are forced to make. After all, how can "shape" exist without a "substance" which is "shaped"?

Locke had to admit, therefore, that "substance" is merely a concept on which we "hang" the primary and secondary qualities, which we can indeed experience. "So that if any one will examine himself concerning his notion of substances in general, he will find he has no other idea of it at all, but only a supposition of he knows not what support of such qualities . . ."

This was not a satisfying conclusion, but Locke felt it was both good logic and common sense. After all, who in his right mind could possibly conclude that solidity and motion and shape might exist but that "substance" might not?

The answer to that question is: George Berkeley.

5   By the time he was twenty-five years old, George Berkeley had published his *Principles of Human Knowledge,* had stirred up international controversy in philosophical and theological circles (he was an Anglican clergyman, later a bishop), and was regarded as one of the most logical, eloquent, and charming philosophers the English-speaking world had produced.

As early as the age of twenty, Berkeley developed the habit of jotting down ideas, arguments, and reflections in notebooks. These autobiographical notes were unknown until they were discovered and published in 1871 and given the title of *Commonplace Book.* In 1706, when Berkeley was twenty-one, he wrote a paragraph in his notebook which pointed the direction his philosophy would take.

He wrote that the concept of materialism or "substance" had always been "the main pillar and support of skepticism" on which have been founded

> all the impious schemes of atheism and irreligion. . . . How great a friend material substance hath been to atheists in all ages were needless to relate. . . . When this cornerstone is once removed, the whole fabric cannot choose but fall to the ground. . . ."

Berkeley began with Locke's conclusions and went on to prove that substance really doesn't exist!

6   How did the Irish philosopher manage it?

He began by agreeing with Locke that the idea of substance (or matter) is merely an assumption on our part; we can never perceive substance directly. What we experience—and the *only* things we experience—are colors, tastes, odors, etc., that is, the secondary qualities.

Wherein, he resembled my Right Reverend friend, Bishop Berkeley [who was] extremely matter-of-fact in all matters touching matter itself. Besides being pervious to the points of pins, and possessing a palate capable of appreciating plum-puddings.
HERMAN MELVILLE
Mardi

THE IRISH IMMATERIALIST: *George Berkeley (1685–1753)*

George Berkeley (rhymes with "darkly") was born in a farmhouse on the grounds of ancient Dysert Castle in Ireland. His parents, while not wealthy, were able to provide him with an excellent education, first at Kilkenny School, later at Trinity College in Dublin (he entered March, 1700). Trinity College was a center for intellectual growth, justly praised for its freedom of inquiry and academic excellence; there was a spirit of revolt against outdated thinking in philosophy and science. Here Berkeley was at home. He was precocious, showed little respect for orthodox ideas. He and some friends organized a philosophy club to study "the new philosophy," which meant Locke.

Berkeley wrote continuously and travelled widely. He was much concerned with the social conditions in Ireland and agitated for social reform. In 1721 he wrote (but published anonymously, perhaps wisely) an *Essay Toward Preventing the Ruin of Great Britain.* His fame, however, rests on his *Principles of Human Knowledge,* Part I (he lost the manuscript to Part II on a trip to Sicily and could never bring himself to rewrite it). This work, along with his dialogues between Hylas and Philonous, contains the logical arguments for his "philosophy of immaterialism."

Berkeley was the first great philosopher to visit America. He had long dreamed of establishing a college in Bermuda, and to this end he had collected considerable funds from private donors and a promise of £20,000 from the House of Commons. So he and his bride (Anne Forster, married in August) sailed for America in September of 1728. They spent three relatively happy years in Rhode Island waiting for the money to arrive. It never came. Prime Minister Walpole refused the appropriation, so the Berkeleys, now saddened in 1731 by the death of a baby daughter, returned to Dublin. His dream of a college was never realized.

While in America Berkeley had penned a poem containing the line "Westward the course of empire takes its way." Because of that line, a California town was named for him.

The rest of his life was divided between his clerical responsibilities, social concerns, occasional writing, and his family. They lived in County Cork after he became a bishop in 1734.

He died painlessly and peacefully at his episcopal home in Cloyne after a trip to Oxford where he had enrolled his son in college. He was 68 years old.

Man is thus his own greatest mystery. He does not understand the vast veiled universe into which he has been cast for the reason that he does not understand himself. He comprehends but little of his organic processes and even less of his unique capacity to perceive the world about him, to reason and to dream. Least of all does he understand his noblest and most mysterious faculty: the ability to transcend himself and perceive himself in the act of perception.

LINCOLN BARNETT

But what about the primary qualities—shape, solidity, motion/rest, etc.—how do we know about these? We only infer those too, said Berkeley. How do you know the shape of a seashell? You run your fingers over the surface and feel it. Not exactly, Berkeley reminds us; we don't feel *it*. We only feel our sensations and proceed to *assume* that matter exists in "seashell" form and that the matter is the cause of our sensations. We further *assume* that the matter possesses certain (primary) qualities which we cannot experience directly.

So far, Berkeley seems to agree with Locke. But where Locke never doubts the *existence* of matter (he merely says we can never know it), Berkeley asks: If substance is merely an assumption, then could that assumption be wrong? Suppose the world of material objects doesn't really exist. How could we account for the supposed objects which cause our perceptions? Berkeley concluded that there is an alternative assumption, just as logical as "substance," and far more preferable.

Assume that God exists, and that he places in our minds all the perceptions which we experience. If we are making assumptions about reality to account for our perceptions, why is the assumption of matter a more reasonable assumption than the existence of God? And if one is a Christian philosopher, doesn't the assumption of a God-source become a more likely assumption than a matter-source?

This is Berkeley's "immaterialism"—matter does not exist. It is merely a fiction we thought we needed. The universe is composed of interacting minds only, and God is the source of all our perceptions. All the world is merely an interplay of mental images and ideas, grandly provided and coordinated by God.

Therefore, reasoned Berkeley, "to be is to be perceived"—*esse est percipi.* There are no "real" clouds, rocks, oceans, stars, penguins, or seashells. Such items are but mind-images derived from God. Nothing exists, therefore, except when it is being perceived.

How can we be sure the persistent objects of experience—our homes, friends, the familiar belongings—will "be there" when we want to perceive them? Does the seashell-image flicker off and on, in and out of existence every time we look at it or turn away from it. No, says Berkeley. God is the eternal perceiver, and all images continue to exist in the mind of God. They are always available to us for the asking, to be experienced as we would.

Indeed, comments Will Durant, "no one since Plato had written nonsense so charmingly."

7 Everyone discussed Berkeley's logical attempt to annihilate matter. Among others, the lexicographer Samuel Johnson rejected the system, as Boswell reports:

> After we came out of church, we stood talking for some time together of Bishop Berkeley's ingenious sophistry to prove the non-existence of

matter, and that everything in the universe is merely ideal. I observed that though we are satisfied his doctrine is not true, it is impossible to refute it. I shall never forget the alacrity with which Johnson answered, striking his foot with a mighty force against a large stone, till he rebounded from it, "I refute it thus!"

But what had Johnson really proved by kicking the rock? He had merely illustrated and confirmed Berkeley's argument. For all Johnson "knew" was the sharp pain in his toe, perhaps a numb feeling in his foot, and the sensation of a sudden stop which gave his leg a jar. All he had proven by kicking the rock was that he was capable of feeling a variety of subjective sensations. All he knew was his own experience, and that, after all, was the point Berkeley was making.

So Samuel Johnson had merely added his considerable support to the "philosophy of immaterialism."

8   What else is this, however, but "charming nonsense"? Most of us are convinced (we think) that physical matter exists. It seems to us that Berkeley made a simple mistake, a non sequitur: just because we cannot experience physical matter directly, it does not necessarily follow that matter doesn't exist.

But did Berkeley really go wrong? (1) Berkeley emphasizes the fact that we are limited *absolutely* to our own perceptions and cannot directly experience any "real" world. On this point he seems to be correct. (2) He is therefore repeating Locke's point that physical matter (or substance) is *only* a mental assumption which we *think* to be a logical necessity. On this point also, he is correct.

Whether you will go further with Berkeley and accept that his alternative assumption—God as the source of experience—is a better one will depend somewhat on personal preference and theological belief. Most of us remain convinced that the reality of matter is a better assumption, but perhaps that's only because we have lived uncritically with it most of our lives.

We must face honestly, however, Berkeley's singular challenge: Prove, if you can, that any material object exists apart from your perception of it. If you can, then Berkeley is wrong. If you can't, then you will have to concede (Berkeley would insist) that the world is merely your idea.°

9   If you enjoy science fiction, speculate on the following scene (which may or may not be from the realm of SF).

We are alone, each of us, in a small white cubicle, floating restfully in curvolounges fashioned to fit from heliostyrene. Over each of our heads is fitted a tantalum-crystal helmet, finely wired with thousands of micro-electrodes which have been surgically embedded in the sensory centers of our brain's outer layer, the cortex.

Things which we see are not by themselves what we see. . . . It remains completely unknown to us what the objects may be by themselves and apart from the receptivity of our senses. We know nothing but our manner of perceiving them. . . .

IMMANUEL KANT

°These words—"the world is my idea"—are from a later philosopher, Arthur Schopenhauer (1788–1861). Berkeley, of course, would say that the world is God's idea.

THE SCOTTISH SKEPTIC

David Hume (1711–1776)

A typical Scot in all but his philosophy, David Hume was born and raised on the family estate of Ninewells near Edinburgh. His father died when David was but a year old, so his mother, a woman of force and conviction, brought him up in the rigid Calvinism of the Scotch Presbyterian Church. Four hours of church services each Sunday, plus morning prayers and table grace.

Hume entered the University of Edinburgh at twelve, but dropped out three years later without getting a degree. At about sixteen, on his own, he plunged headlong into philosophy and literature and read voraciously. He confides in us: "I found a certain boldness of temper growing in me, which was not inclined to submit to any authority in these subjects." He was in love with learning, but he loved too seriously, became saturated, and suffered a mild breakdown at nineteen.

Wisely, he attempted to change his life-style, first by getting a job in business, then by avoiding his books for a while and traveling. But he could not stay away very long. In 1734 we find him hard at work again in the library of the Jesuit College of La Flèche in France. After three years of intense labor he completed his first masterpiece, *A Treatise of Human Nature* (he is 26). He returns to England with his manuscripts, confident and excited. His publisher, however, insists that numerous "offensive" passages (one on miracles, for instance) be excised before he will print it, so two years pass before it is published.

Brilliant works flow from his pen, and everywhere he offends the offensible. He is vilified as an atheist (he wasn't) and attacked by clerics for casting doubt on immortality. His analysis of causality and induction raises the wrath of scientists and rationalists. His multi-volume *History of England* irritates all political parties yet stands today as a superb example of objectivity and impartiality. For unpopular opinions and "shocking ideas" he was twice denied professorships at Edinburgh.

Hume calmly went his own way through all this, friendly to everyone, tolerant of opinions that differed with his. His open mind saw much. He possessed a keen sensitivity to hypocrisy, paradox and irony; he had a sense of the ridiculous in human affairs. But all his insights were tempered with gentleness, humor, and cheerful optimism.

By 1750 Hume was famous, much admired, even loved by a few who could love; he was fêted in salons, visited by celebrities, wined by kings. He loved Paris. His versatile intellect was more at home in the atmosphere of the Enlightenment than in an England that took itself too seriously or a Scotland where a Calvin *redivivus* still longed to light fires under heretics like Hume. Yet even in his home in Edinburgh, he lived happily within his circle of loyal friends.

When a friend scolded Hume for not being the gentle spirit he once was, Hume corrected him: "I am still a mild and temperate man. A sober, discreet, virtuous, frugal, regular, quiet, good-natured man with a bad character."

In the spring of 1775 Hume's health quickly failed. With calm spirit and clear mind he wrote an eight-page autobiography, *My Own Life.* Death came on August 25, 1776.

"He was an atheist," someone remarked at his funeral.

"No matter," another replied. "He was an honest man."

All senseq ("sensory-sequence") programs originate from, and are coordinated by, PROSELEC (Program Central for Sensory-sequence Selection). The electrical impulses which the electrodes generate in the cortex provide a variety of real-life experiences. Selection keys on the curvolounge's arm allow one to select from millions of stored program/experiences.

There are five categories of senseq programs available to the average customer. Real-time senseqs (R) are identical to living space-time experiences, like strolling along the beach. Special senseqs (S) are plot-programs, like old-fashioned movies or TriV dramas (these are mostly for old-timers and sentimentalists). Extra senseqs (E) are specific experiences, like visiting a friend or eating abalone almondine. Cosmic senseqs (C) are ecstasy-meditations during which one can experience a joyful union with Cosmic Reality. And lastly, dream senseqs (D) provide REM-sleep and are to be used for rest periods a minimum of four hours during any twenty-hour period of senseq experience.

There is one other kind of senseq. Occasionally PROSELEC preempts private time to channel what are considered especially beneficial programs. Some educational experience is essential; after all, if left to themselves almost everyone would choose only fun-and-games senseqs (except for a masochistic 6 percent who persist in selecting self-destructive senseqs). It is also to be noted that many senseqs in the R, S, and E classes are rated "X"; if a prohibited senseq is selected by a nonqualified customer, a mild impulse is channeled to the gland-control centers which in turn release chemicals which induce (for a seven-minute period only) strong guilt feelings.

The senseq impulses sent to the brain centers are identical in every way to the electrochemical impulses which the (now-vestigial) body-senses used to send to the cortex. The resulting sense-experiences, therefore, are identical (but superior, of course, in quality and variety) to real-life experiences of the kind known before the advent of PROSELEC.

Question: For anyone tuned in to PROSELEC, does the real world exist? *How could he possibly know whether or not it exists?* Would this PROSELEC world differ significantly from Berkeley's immaterial cosmos (with the possible exception of the "X" ratings; Berkeley's Eternal Perceiver seemed little concerned with censorship)?

Question: What would constitute reality for a PROSELEC customer?

Question: What constitutes reality for you and me?

10   His logic is brilliant and he almost succeeds. "His arguments are, strictly speaking, unanswerable," wrote Lord Chesterfield, and Boswell duly noted that although we are convinced that his doctrine is false, "it is impossible to refute it." David Hume agreed: Berkeley's arguments "admit of no answer and produce no conviction."

There remains the final reflection, how shallow, puny, and imperfect are efforts to sound the depths in the nature of things. In philosophical discussion, the merest hint of dogmatic certainty as to finality of statement is an exhibition of folly.
ALFRED NORTH WHITEHEAD

Truth is a property of beliefs, and derivatively of sentences which express beliefs.
BERTRAND RUSSELL

Because of George Berkeley, writes Durant, "European philosophy has not quite made up its mind that the external world exists. Until it reconciles itself to the extreme probability of it, and faces the problems of life and death, the world will pass it by."

11   Berkeley's system is the most extreme philosophical idealism° the Western world has produced. There is but one epistemological position—*solipsism*—which is more extreme.

If it is a fact that we know nothing of the external world, and if Berkeley could conclude from this that the external world of matter doesn't exist, then the solipsist will take the next step and conclude that only he himself exists. "I know only myself," he might say (to himself, of course). "The world is the fabrication of my imagination. Therefore, only I exist." Such a solipsistic position has been held by few thinkers and by no major philosophers.

°. . . for the solipsist.

(It was a solipsist, we are told, who, in deep anger, once said to a companion, "I'm going to kill you!" Whereupon he thrust a dagger into his own heart, and the other man ceased to exist. . . .°)

12   "To be is to be perceived"—*esse est percipi*—Berkeley contended. How can we know anything exists if we can't perceive it? The world of real objects is beyond perception; they exist only as images in our minds, and these images might just as well derive from a Divine Mind as from some hypothetical "substance" we conjure up in our fantasy.

That's where we stood with Berkeley. Now David Hume sets his incisive intellect to work.

First, Hume pointed out the obvious: the idea of God, like "matter," is merely assumption. The one is no more known to us than the other. We know only our experiences, and it follows that we know nothing of God *or* matter. If matter is "make-believe" then so is God. Berkeley never escaped Hume's net. God was the preferable assumption for the Irish cleric, but philosophers, Hume would contend, cannot live by assumptions alone.

He accords with Locke and Berkeley that we do not experience matter directly. Therefore, Hume—with a passion for accuracy—never denies the existence of the real world (how *could* you deny the existence of something you can't know?). He remains in a suspended state of agnosticism. We can't know the real world, and there's no more to be said about it.

Lord Russell tells us that he once received a letter from a well-known logician, a Mrs. Franklin, admitting that she was herself a solipsist and was surprised that no one else was. Russell comments: "Coming from a logician, this surprise surprised me."

Next, Hume takes the heart out of science by undermining our belief in causality. We never observe "causes." Our concept of causality results from a habit of association. When events occur together repeatedly, we learn to associate them; then we fabricate the "belief" that there is a necessary connection between events. But, Hume points out, we *observe* neither cause nor necessity. "All our reasonings concerning cause and effect are derived from nothing but custom." Causality has no objective status, so far as we know; it is only a mental habit without logical support.

Then Hume wonders about "mind." What we call the "mind" is merely "a bundle or collection of different perceptions." It is a movie screen on which the senses, our image-projectors, project their pictures. But there is no entity such as "mind"; for when the projections are turned off there is nothing. (This does seem to happen when we turn off all our sense-projectors and sleep; during periods of deep, dreamless sleep our sense of "self" or "identity" ceases to exist.)

In his quest for logical consistency, Hume becomes our most extreme skeptic.

Where, then, do our sense experiences come from? In truth, we cannot know.

> Their ultimate cause is perfectly inexplicable by human reason, and 'twill be impossible to decide with certainty whether they exist immediately from the object, or are produced by the creative power of the mind, or are deriv'd from the author of our being.

What can we know for sure? Nothing. David Hume makes mincemeat of our every attempt to convince ourselves that certainty is possible. No one in two thousand years of Western philosophy—no one since Gorgias the Sophist°—has made it quite so difficult for us.

°Gorgias and Hume are epistemological twins. Gorgias' famed remark set the tone for Western skepticism: Nothing exists; but if it did, we couldn't know it; and if we could know it, we couldn't communicate it. Hume almost proved Gorgias right.

RSVP

George Berkeley's philosophy of immaterialism has been happily summarized in a limerick:

> There was a young man who said, "God
> Must think it exceedingly odd
> If he finds that this tree
> Continues to be
> When there's no one about in the Quad."

> *Reply*

> Dear Sir:
> Your astonishment's odd.
> *I* am always about in the Quad.
> And that's why the tree
> Will continue to be,
> Since observed by
> Yours faithfully,
> God.
> Attributed to RONALD KNOX

---

13   In a moment of honesty, David Hume composed a confession which speaks for many great thinkers, from Socrates to the seventies, whose lifeblood is spent wrestling with abstract and unobservable entities, but who still possess the great gift of keeping their philosophical reflections in perspective. Hume wrote:

> Should it be asked me whether I sincerely assent to this argument which I have been to such pains to inculcate, and whether I be really one of those skeptics who hold that all is uncertain, . . . I should reply . . . that neither I nor any other person was ever sincerely and constantly of that opinion. . . . I dine, I play backgammon, I converse and am merry with my friends; and when, after three or four hours' amusement, I would return to these speculations, they appear so cold and strained and ridiculous that I cannot find in my heart to enter into them any further. . . . Thus the skeptic still continues to reason and believe, though he asserts that he cannot defend his reason by reason; and by the same rule he must assent to the principle concerning the existence of body, though he cannot pretend, by any arguments of philosophy, to maintain its veracity.

14   Let's take seriously what David Hume implies in this moment of truth. Here is our Scottish skeptic whose reason tells him one set of facts (we know nothing certain of the real world), but whose experience seems to contradict his reason ("I dine, I play backgammon, I converse. . . ."). When such conflict exists between theory and experience, then a solution must be sought. (Remember that infamous bumblebee which, according to aerodynamics, can't fly—but does?)

What Hume implies is: (1) it is very impracticable *not* to assume that the real world exists, and (2) day-to-day living is very difficult if one tries to operate on the assumption that he knows *nothing* about the real world.

There are few philosophers of the modern world who would *not* question, to some extent, the conclusions of Berkeley and Hume. After more than two centuries of debate, we now have adequate reason *to assume* (1) that the real world exists and (2) that we have at least a working knowledge of that world. It is the *nature* of that working knowledge which is still cause for concern.

15   If these conclusions are comforting, our philosophers have made three points which may seem less so. The following arguments seem basically sound and still stand today as starting points for an understanding of the nature of knowledge.

(1) We know only our subjective experience, which begins with sensory reaction and ends with the fabrication of knowledge. This appears to be an inescapable limitation.

(2) Accordingly, we cannot experience directly the real world of objects/events. Neither matter nor the principles of motion are directly perceivable.

(3) Our knowledge of the real world consists solely, therefore, of inferences which we make on the basis of our experience.

16   In summary, what is the nature of our knowledge about the real world of objects/events?

Our knowledge of reality is composed of ideas our minds have *created* on the basis of our sensory experience. It is a fabric of knowledge woven by the mind. Knowledge is not given to the mind; nothing is "poured" into it. Rather, the mind manufactures perceptions, concepts, ideas, beliefs, etc., and holds them as *working hypotheses* about external reality. Every idea is a (subjective) working model which enables us to handle real objects/events with some degree of efficiency.°

But ideas in our heads are not realities; they are but tools which enable us to deal with reality.

It is as though we drew nondimensional maps to help us understand four-dimensional territory. The semanticists have long reminded us to beware about confusing any sort of map with the real landscape. "The map is not the territory."

°Although for the moment we shall attempt to live with solutions which are essentially pragmatic, there may indeed exist another *kind* of knowledge which is not pragmatic: the "universal knowledge" of the sort found in mathematics, geometry and some logic systems. The question of "a priori" knowledge will be discussed on pages 366ff.

3-4

DATA PROCESSING

1   In its attempt to make sense of the energy-environment in which we live, the mind proves to be a versatile, creative instrument. It translates events of the real world into experiences we can use in living. The mind is not at all the "blank tablet," the *tabula rasa,* which some earlier thinkers thought it to be.

We have a fairly clear understanding now of the general nature of knowledge. Human knowledge is a collection of constructs created by the mind from the raw materials of sensation; it is a series of scaled-down maps which we use to find our way in the full-scale territory of the real world.

Concepts without percepts are empty. Percepts without concepts are blind.

IMMANUEL KANT

2   One of the basic functions of the human mind is to create *abstractions.*

What if we had to have a separate name for every object we ever knew: for each candle, coin, animal, bell, seashell, cloud, and penguin? and a separate word for every single event we ever experienced: the strumming of a guitar, the meteor trail through the sky, the smell of a summer rain? If we were forced to have a different symbol for each object and each event, clearly we would be in trouble. In no time we would run out of words and our minds could not handle the clutter of separate items.

What do we do then? We place such singular items in groups. All the objects/events which have common qualities we group together into a single package with a single label. Once we have so packaged them, we no longer have to deal with the individual objects; we deal only with the whole package.

This is why we create abstractions. Abstractions *are* packages.

3   An abstraction, by definition, is an idea created by the mind to refer to all objects which, possessing certain characteristics in common, are thought of in the same class. The number of objects in the class can range from two to infinity. We can refer to *all* men, *all* hurricanes, *all* books, *all* energy-forms . . . *all* everything.

     Abstractions are formed at various levels of generalization. For instance, if we begin with an orange—a particular object as yet unclassified and unlabeled—then the first level of abstraction might be "Valencia orange," grouping together the qualities shared by all Valencia oranges. A next level might include all oranges (Valencia, the navels, sour oranges, etc.); next might come all "citrus fruit" (including oranges, grapefruit, lemons, kumquats, etc.). Still higher would come the whole basket of fruit (citrus fruit, figs, apples, apricots, breadfruit, etc.). Above this level we might class together all "edible things," and more general still, a very-high-level abstraction, "material objects."

     Notice how far we have come in the breadth of generalization: from a single orange to an all-inclusive class labeled "material objects." At each higher level of abstraction the objects have less and less in common. Yet such broad, general abstractions dominate our thinking and communicating. We think of fruits and vegetables, or food; we class together medicines, drugs, pollutants; we speak of nations, races of people, Hindus, Easterners, Eskimos, and so on.

     While abstraction-building is an inescapable mental process—in fact it is the first step in the organization of our knowledge of objects/events—a serious problem is inherent in the process. At high levels of abstraction we tend to group together objects which have but a few qualities in common, and our abstractions may be almost meaningless, without our knowing it. We fall into the habit of using familiar abstractions and fail to realize how empty they are. For example, what do the objects in the following abstractions have in common? All atheists, all Western imperialists, all blacks or all whites (and if you think it's skin color, think twice), all conservatives, all trees, all Frenchmen, all Christians. When we think with such high-level abstractions, it is often the case that we are communicating nothing meaningful at all.

4   The mind has another technique to enable it to assimilate information. *It classifies abstractions and labels them.* This is our mental filing system.

     In *Language in Thought and Action,* Dr. S. I. Hayakawa imagines a primitive village—your village—in which a variety of animals scamper about. Some of the animals have small bodies, some large. Some have round heads, while others have square heads. Some have curly tails, others straight tails. And such distinguishing marks are very important.

     For you have discovered through experience that the animals with

Jean Piaget tells of a little girl who was asked whether one might call the sun the moon and the moon the sun. She explained impatiently that no one could confuse the sun and the moon because the sun shines so brightly.

small bodies eat your grain, while those with large bodies don't. The small-bodied animals you have labeled "gogo" and you shoo them away; and when you call to a neighbor, "Quick, chase the gogo out of your garden!" he knows what you means. The large-bodied animals (labeled "gigi") are harmless, so you allow them to wander where they will.

However, a visitor from another village has had a different experience. He has found that animals with square heads bite, while those with round heads don't. Since he has no gardens, their biting is a more noticeable characteristic than their habit of eating grain. The square-heads that bite he calls "daba" and he scares them away. He generally ignores the round-headed "dobos."

Still another man, a relative from a distant village, has found that the animals with curly tails kill snakes. Such animals are valuable; he calls them "busa" and breeds them for protection. But those with straight tails (which he calls "busana") are merely a nuisance, and he's quite indifferent to them.

Observers are not led by the same physical evidence to the same picture of the universe unless their linguistic backgrounds are similar or can in some way be calibrated.

BENJAMIN LEE WHORF

3 *The Real World; Knowing and Unknowing*

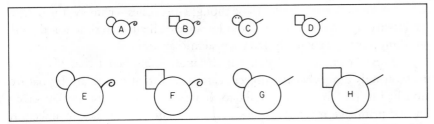

Now, one day villagers from far and near meet to trade and talk. You are sitting in on a barter-session when one of the animals runs by (let's say the animal marked "C" in the diagram). You spot the animal headed for your garden, so you call down the path for someone to chase the "gogo" away. A visitor, however, looks at you with disdain, for he knows that the animal is a "dobo." It has a round head. It doesn't bite, and he is surprised that you don't know this. A third visitor scornfully tells the both of you that the animal is clearly a "busana," as everyone knows; it doesn't kill snakes or have any other redeeming qualities.

A heated discussion ensues as to what the animal really is. Is it a "gogo," a "dobo," or a "busana"? A quarrel is brewing as to what the animal *really is.*

It hardly helps when another tribesman, asking what the talk is all about, declares with finality that the animal (still "C") is a "muglock" because it is edible and they feast on it every full moon. All the inedible animals in his village he labels "uglocks".

This discussion finally ends where all such discussions finally end.

5   What is the animal *really*? What is *any* object, *really*? In the last analysis, all one can do is point to the object as if to say, "It is what it is." As Hayakawa puts it, "The individual object or event we are naming, of course, has no name and belongs to no class until we put it in one."

All the objects/events of our experience are classified in this manner: in terms of our experience of them. In the English language, for instance, we have two words that originated in the Middle Ages for the animal *Sus scrofa.* The word "swine" was the term used by the serfs and swineherds who had to tend them; the word "pork" was always employed by those who ate their succulent flesh at the banquet table.

Systems of classification, therefore, are *reflexive.* They inform us about the person who is doing the classifying—they tell us about *his* experience—and they tell us relatively little or nothing about the object classified. Classification never tells us what the classified object *really is.*

Classification systems are *pragmatic.* They are guidelines for operation. They tell us how to think about the object, how to treat it, use it, or relate to it. We classify objects and utilize the classification as long as the system is convenient; the moment it ceases to work, then we reclassify.

Geological eras, periods, and epochs are human inventions; they are man's attempt to put huge stretches of time in their place and make them seem reasonably comprehensible. Nature was indifferent to such fine distinctions. Time flowed on continuously with one phase changing imperceptibly into another without dividing itself neatly into segments.

PHILIP VAN DOREN STERN

6   An understanding of these thought-processes—namely, the nature of classifying and labeling—provides an excellent criterion for distinguishing epistemic naivety from epistemic awareness.

A prescientific thinker has the unshakable belief that his classification tells him what the object really is and that names are by nature attached to the objects they refer to. It was a universal assumption made by the primitive mind that there is an intimate and *necessary* connection between the symbol and the object symbolized. Indeed, a mystical power resides in the symbol itself, and words are to be feared or desired in the same way the object/event referred to is to be feared or desired.

To attempt to persuade a primitive thinker that his classifications and labels are merely his mental tools, relative and arbitrary, would be a hopeless task. His own name is "Marika," he will inform you, and it could not be otherwise. His god's name is "Mbwenu" and the deity can be called upon only by using his "right name." And, as everyone knows, a horse is a "horse" and a man is a "man." How could it possibly be otherwise?

7   People are "objects" from the standpoint of classification. If we lived in a small community and knew only a few people, we might find it possible to give each a separate name and deal with him as a singular personality. Our thinking might remain relatively concrete.

But in our modern world where we contact millions of people (personally and via various media) the temptation to move at high-level abstractions is enormous. As stated earlier, we do this because it simplifies our handling of vast amounts of data (or people). The bigger the bundles the better.

Therefore, we move very far from the individual person, just as we moved very far from the single orange we held in our hand. We package people into ever larger groups with fewer characteristics in common and refer to them under a single label: Arabs, liberals, dopers, doctors, rightists, Catholics, Jews, Germans, Japanese, Gooks, Republicans,

The human brain craves understanding. It cannot understand without simplifying, that is, without reducing things to a common element. However, all simplifications are arbitrary and lead us to drift insensibly away from reality.

LECOMTE DU NOÜY

"Everyone must have a label."

politicians, capitalists, Chicanos, Latins, jetsetters, Bantu, managers and workers, teachers, teamsters, police, astronauts. . . .

Not a single label listed above tells us about the object/person classified. It merely serves as a means of organizing our information about them and clues us in on how we should think about and relate to the individual so classified.

8   Do we need to be reminded that classification alone—arbitrary, unscientific classification—often means the difference between life and death?

Villagers from southeastern Laos were burned out of their homes as the war moved into their area; they escaped over the border into Vietnam. There they became a serious classification problem for Vietnamese officials: Were they "escapees" or "refugees"? The difference? "Refugees" were permitted to remain in Vietnam, while "escapees" were forced to return. Which were they *really*?

In Nazi Germany, to be *classified* a "Jew" meant extermination. The classification was a fallacy: In Hitler's mind "Jewish" meant "Jewish race." There is no "Jewish race," of course. To be a "Jew" is to belong to a religion—Judaism. Hitler, however is not the first or the last classifier to make such a mistake.

Ashley Montagu, among other anthropologists and ethnologists, has long reminded us that the concept of race is a fallacious myth—"our most dangerous myth." Physiological characteristics which we classify as "racial" are merely the result of environmental adaptation which took place as our presapient ancestors migrated in search of food and hospitable living conditions. If we could trace our genetic history, each and every one of us would find that we possess various blends of gene stock. A careful historical look will show only an ever-changing series of gene pools.

Still, race remains one of our most pragmatic classifications, although it completely lacks scientific support. While it says nothing of the person classified, it makes quite clear how we are to think about him, treat him, deal with him, and use him. Could one expect a myth to be more useful than that?

9   It might be argued that some classification systems, such as scientific taxonomy, tell us much more precisely what the classified object really is. Such a claim would probably not be made, however, by either (1) a knowledgeable scientist, or (2) the object classified.

Scientists are quite aware that they have merely agreed on the criteria they will use for their system, namely, evolutionary kinship. When sufficient data are available, lines of evolutionary development can be traced, and the common characteristics of species, genera, families, orders, etc. serve as workable criteria for ordering our knowledge. Scientific systems sometimes reveal facts about the classified objects: they tell

A big wild animal of the antelope family and known as the "Nehil Gae" was causing extensive damage to crops in the field. But the farmers would not harm it because "Nehil Gae" means "Blue Cow," and the cow is sacred to the Hindu. So the Indian Government has changed the name to "Nehil Goa"—which means "Blue Horse." Horses are not sacred, and so now the beast can be killed to protect the crops.

Associated Press

The subtlest and most pervasive of all influences are those which create and maintain the repertory of stereotypes. We are told *about the world before we see it. We imagine most things before we experience them.*

WALTER LIPPMAN

We request that every hen lay 130 to 140 eggs a year. The increase can not be achieved by the bastard hens (non-Aryan) which now populate German farm yards. Slaughter these undesirables and replace them. . . .

Nazi Party News Agency
April 3, 1937

us how they may relate (those of the same species can mate, those of different species can't—except that this is not always the case); it tells us who might have been the ancestor of some animal or plant; it sometimes tells us (in the words themselves) about the physiology of the object ("vertebrate," "bony fishes," "mammals"). But such information lies in the labels we have chosen to use for the common characteristics we have selected for classifying. Again, as Hayakawa has said, no animal is a "vertebrate" until we put it in that "vertebrate" class.

It might be worth noting that for the animal classified, the scientific system probably means very little. If a queen conch is gliding through the sand at dusk in search of a meal, the classification "edible" holds more significance for a clam than its proper taxonomic status as "Chione undatella (Sowerby)."

10   The French philosopher Henri Bergson (1859–1941) describes another way in which the mind handles its knowledge of reality.

The human intellect, notes Bergson, has one habit which stands in the way of its perceiving reality accurately: its propensity for chopping reality into fragments.

For example, the mind takes "time" and cuts it into discrete units: seconds, minutes, hours, days, weeks, seasons, years, decades, centuries, cosmic years, and so on. But time is a continuum, with no breaks, rhythms, or cycles. Our minds create *units of measurement* for the time-continuum so that we can conceive it in usuable "lengths"; then we label these units and proceed to think in "units of time"; we may also begin

to believe that such "units of time" are real. But where do "hours" exist? or "days"? or "years"? We have *defined* a year as the time it takes the earth to revolve once around the sun; but the earth would have gone on swinging in orbit for millions of "years" without being affected by our definition of its motion—as though the earth ripped off its December sheet as it passed a certain point in space.

11   And what about space and objects in space? We measure them. We have devised units without end to quantify distance and volume. For spatial distances: millimeters, inches, yards, meters, fathoms, miles, parsecs, light-years, and so on. Mass or volume we measure with grams, ounces, pounds, tons, tablespoons, cubic centimeters, acre-feet, a "pinch" of salt and a "dash" of pepper.

Such units are created by our minds to help us reduce the environment to usable proportions; they enable us to conceive small bits of reality at a time (the mind can't possibly think of *all* matter at once).

But after reflection, could any of us believe that such "units of measurement" exist as part of the real world? Just ask: "Please give me eighteen millimeters." Eighteen millimeters of what? "I need five minutes. Can you get it for me?" Five minutes of what? "Time," of course, but once measured, what exactly do you have?

One must conclude that such units exist in the mind, and only in the mind. Such mental units serve to parcel out our environment into practicable quantities.

12   Look at a globe of the earth and note the lines that criss-cross it. There are pole-to-pole lines we *call* meridians, and lines parallel to the "equator" which we *call* latitudinal lines; then there are anomalous lines dividing colored areas. Thus, with a marked globe we have *organized* the earth so that our minds can think about it. ("Where is Bolivia?" "Point out the Arctic circle." "Locate the magnetic pole.") How else could the intellect deal with the earth except in pieces?

In a planetarium, it is of great help to have a celestial grid overlaying the stars on the dome, or to have a projected image linking together the stars in a constellation. When such grids are not used, the thousands of patternless points of light are scattered at random and we cannot remember or make sense of them. Since the mind must organize the points of light, it "draws" connecting lines. So a small square is seen in Hercules, a triangle in Aquarius; or we see several stars whose pattern reminds us of some known object (Aquila the Eagle, Delphinus the Dolphin). In just this way the ancient skywatchers organized the random bits of light which they saw nightly.

In the planetarium, the grid lights can be turned off, reminding us that the grid is only a mental tool for organizing our experience. In no way could one mistake the grid as a part of the real sky.

ohm	millimeter
ampere	kilometer
watt	millisecond
erg	second
gauss	minute
oersted	hour
coulomb	day
volt	year
lumen	cosmic year
hertz	percent
acre	cycles per second
section	miles per hour
grain	parts per million
gram	Richter scale
pound	equator
ton	radian
kilogram	cubic inch
angstrom	flux units
horsepower	farad
bar	rod
decibel	peck
magnitude	dram
psi	acre feet
carat	caliber
degree F	jigger
degree C	mach number
degree K	barrell
degree	furlong
micron	knot
meter	joule
inch	atmosphere
foot	century
cubit	millennium
yard	octave
mile	homer
fathom	ephah
parsec	mina
light-year	cord
ounce	darwin
pint	rpm
fifth	megaton
quart	frames per second
liter	week
gallon	dyne
bushel	newton
electronvolt	decade
BTU	hands
calorie	smidgen

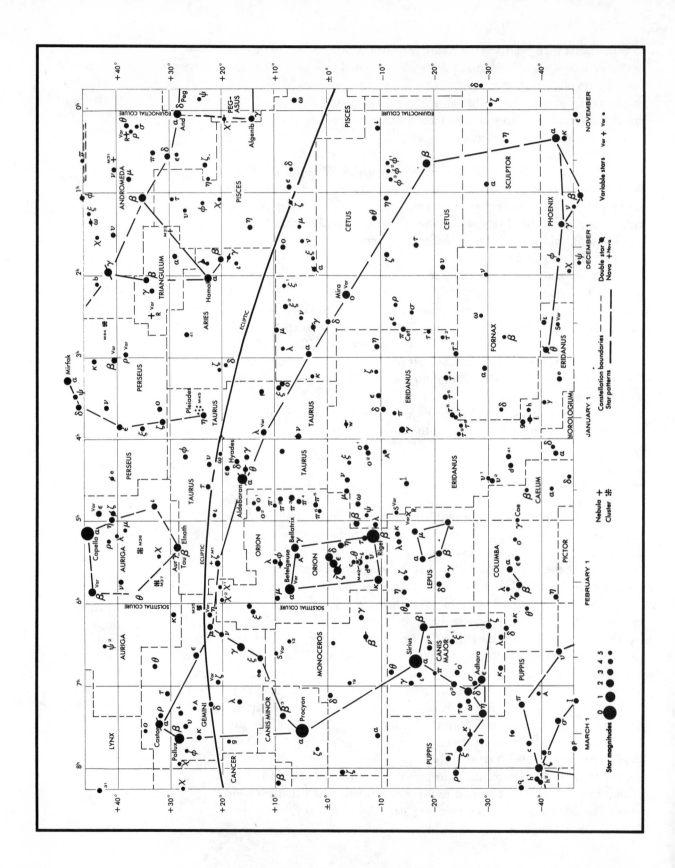

3   *The Real World: Knowing and Unknowing*

In this manner, however, the mind places grids on all that it perceives.

13   What remains when all the mind's "grids" are turned off? Reality—unmeasured, undivided. A continuum of matter in motion and a consciousness of time undisturbed. No days or weeks; no miles or parsecs. To be sure, there do exist in the real world a multitude of rhythms and cycles, and we attempt to coordinate our mental "units of measurement" with these natural rhythms.

Our minds, says Bergson, can indeed "move through" all the pragmatic grids and intuit the nature of reality itself. By a sort of "intellectual empathy" we can come to know the ever-changing, endlessly moving continuum which *is* reality. But to do this we almost have to tell the intellect to cease and desist in its persistent habit of reducing the universe to discrete, manageable units.

To know what the real world is like, therefore, we must turn off the grid lights and let the stars shine. Reality *is,* and that is all.

It seems that the human mind has first to construct forms independently before we can find them in things . . . knowledge cannot spring from experience alone but only from the comparison of the inventions of the intellect with observed fact.

ALBERT EINSTEIN

3-5

TRUTH

1   The word *truth* is a delicate and thoughtful symbol, to be used sparingly. But few words are more desecrated. We like its sound: it has that authoritative, virtuous ring, like "freedom" and "rights"; and it serves our aristocentric purposes so well.

Truth-tests are used for checking and double checking the things people say so that we can decide if their statements are true or false. With such tests we can verify or falsify the fact-claims which they make.

There are three truth-tests, and only three, so far as we know.

What is Truth but to live for an idea? . . . It is a question of discovering a truth which is truth for me, of finding the idea for which I am willing to live and die.

KIERKEGAARD

2   One method of checking fact-claims is by *the correspondence-test.* This test requires one to check a mental concept against a real object/event, and if the subjective concept "corresponds to" the real object/event, then the concept is considered to be true.

Quite simply, if someone tells you there is a solar eclipse in progress in your area, you can look at the sun; and he is either right or wrong. If you can observe a crescent sun, then his statement can be accepted; if you cannot, his statement is false. You have checked it personally and established to your satisfaction the accuracy of the statement. If there was indeed a correspondence between the mental concept of an eclipse and an actual event taking place, then the fact-claim has become a fact.

A whole class of fact-claims are easily checked this way. "The book you are after is in Section B-16 in the bookstore." *Go look.* "On this side of the tape are selections from Puccini's *Madame Butterfly.*" *Play the tape and listen.* "Some prankster mixed salt and sugar in the sugarbowl." *Taste and find out.* "His pulse is very slow." *Feel it and count.* "The coals are ready for the steak." *Look at them glow red and feel the heat.* "This watermelon is ripe and ready." *Feel it, thump it and listen to the thump, plug it, smell it, and taste it.* All the senses can't be wrong—can they?

3   In order to apply the correspondence-test, two things are involved: (1) a subjective mental concept, and (2) a real object/event to which the mental concept corresponds. The following precautions must be taken seriously when checking fact-claims with the correspondence-test.

    (1) We have already noted some of the mind's imaginative operations and the way it creates concepts. No created concept is ever an exact replica of any external object/event. The mind selects a few elements of any object/event to assimilate into the model which it will use for thinking. Furthermore, we have seen that all the physical events which exist in the real world are translated by our transducers into quite different experiential phenomena.

    Remembering all this, we must conclude that no mental concept can ever correspond 100 percent with objects/events. Rather, we have only a degree of correspondence between the two. If the degree of correspondence is high, we hold the fact-claim to be true; if it is not, we decide it is false. Where the breakoff point is along that scale of correspondence would be the subject of endless debate.

    (2) Since, in the last analysis, we are limited to our own subjective experiencing world, how is it possible for us to harmonize a subjective concept (which we can experience) with a real object/event (which we cannot directly experience)? The answer, of course: we can't. What then does the correspondence-test really do? It compares a concept with a set of sensations—the sensations we use when we go about inferring what exists in the real world. Therefore, we are checking a subjective concept with a subjective set of sensations. If they match to some tolerable degree, then we call the concept true; if they don't, we call it false.

    This is really not a happy condition to live with, but given our present knowledge of cognitive processes, the predicament seems inescapable. It looks as though—on this test at least—we can never be completely certain of anything.

4   There is an obvious limitation to the use of the correspondence-test. The real world has to be directly accessible for observation, otherwise there is nothing real against which one can check his concept. In such cases a second checkout method—the coherence-test—might be applicable.

    According to *the coherence-test,* a fact-claim can be accepted as true if it harmonizes (coheres) with other facts which one has *already* accepted as true. Like the previous test, this is a routine kind of test we use every day.

    "There are sharks in Lake Mead." No, that can't be, and I don't

No one is so wrong as the man who knows all the answers.

THOMAS MERTON

When all else fails, follow the directions.

American Proverb

have to go to Lake Mead to check the fact-claim with the correspondence-test; for I already know that sharks can't live in fresh water, and Lake Mead is a fresh-water lake. The fact-claim just can't be made to harmonize with other known facts.°

"When I looked into the mirror, I couldn't see myself. I have lost my reflection!" We would reject such a statement with hardly a second thought. We have read of such fantasies in *Tales of Hoffmann,* and Alice just might be able to manage it. But in the real world of human experience such a fact-claim doesn't harmonize with any experience I know. We will happily keep such "facts" in the world of make-believe.

"Alexander the Great never returned to Rome because he fell in love with Cleopatra and spent the rest of his life in Egypt." No, these fact-claims can't be made to cohere with other previously known data. Alexander died in 323 B.C. and he was certainly no Roman; and Cleopatra died about 30 B.C. Now, it might be possible to substitute Antony for Alexander (with Cleopatra's permission), and the fact-claims would then cohere with one another.

The coherence-test is applicable to large areas of knowledge which are not accessible to personal observation. Two such areas are (1) fact-claims relating to the past ("history"), which is never available for observation, and (2) all contemporary events which we cannot personally witness. This applies to practically all the information we get via television, newspapers, and magazines. A very large percentage of the events which "make news" take place too far away for us to observe, so we test them by making them cohere with the facts we already know.

5   The coherence-test has one serious weakness. A new fact-claim may fit coherently with a large number of previously accepted "facts" *all of which are untrue;* or, similarly, a new fact which is *true* may be rejected because it can't be made to harmonize with one's set of previously accepted false fact-claims.

In other words, it is about as easy to build an elaborate coherent system that is false as an elaborate coherent system that is true. Unless previously accepted data are well supported by evidence, the truth-status of that new "fact" remains in doubt, no matter how well it fits in.

This point has historical significance. System-building has been the stock-in-trade of philosophers, theologians, political theorists, et al. It has been a common practice to rewrite history from the point of view of some ideology; facts can be selected, interpreted, and squeezed into almost any framework. Resulting systems may be highly coherent, therefore, yet bear little resemblance to anything in the real world.

6   There is a third test which, like the coherent test, is wholly subjective in that it requires nothing immediately accessible in the real

---

°I have now been informed that fresh-water sharks do indeed exist. So, what does this do to my use of coherence as a truth-test? I am warned, first, that a fact-claim may nicely cohere with a set of firmly-held fictions, and that I could easily become dogmatic in my belief in, and defense of, ideas that are dead wrong. I am also alerted to the fact that the coherence truth-test is useful only to the degree that my previously accepted "facts" are supported by a broad base of empirical evidence. Thirdly, I am struck by the fact that I can never be 100% sure of *any* fact-claim.

Any judgment is true if it is both self-consistent and coherently connected with our system of judgments as a whole.

EDGAR S. BRIGHTMAN

Assume coherence as the test, and you will be driven by the incoherence of your alternatives to the conclusion that it is also the nature of truth.

BRAND BLANSHARD

Begin by believing with all your heart that your belief is true, so that it will work for you; but then face the probability that it is really false, so that you can accept the consequences of the belief.

JOHN RESECK

world to serve as validating criteria for the mental concept. This is *the pragmatic-test,* and in some ways it is the most complex of the three.

This test was developed by the American philosopher-psychologist William James, but the seminal idea came from Charles S. Peirce. In an article published in 1878, Peirce (pronounced like "purse") attempted to answer the question, "What makes ideas meaningful?" He was interested in clarifying the source and nature of meaning. In his article he concluded that ideas are meaningful if they make some difference in our experience. As Peirce put it, "our idea of anything *is* our idea of its sensible effects. . . ." If we say ice is cold or a match flame is hot, those *ideas* are meaningful only because they relate in a predictive way to what we would experience if we touched the ice or the flame. The ideas have meaning in relation to effects. If we could not touch the ice or the flame, the ideas would be meaningless.

This was a *theory of meaning* only, but William James saw deeper implications in the theory and developed it into a *test of truth.* In 1898, in an address delivered at the University of California at Berkeley, James presented his theory of pragmatism. The truth-value of any idea is to be determined by its results; a "true" idea brings about desired effects. In short—and somewhat more ambiguously—"if an idea works, then it's true."

Peirce had labeled his "theory of meaning" pragmatism, but when he heard what James had done to his theory by changing it into a test of truth, Peirce was upset. He rechristened his theory of meaning with such an "ugly name," as he said, that no one would ever kidnap his theory again. He called it "pragmaticism." We now associate "pragma*tism*" with William James and John Dewey, and "pragmati*cism*" with Peirce.

7   The pragmatic-test can be used to check out fact-claims in several different areas of knowledge, and we find that the *function* of the test is different in each. This is why the test presents serious problems.

First, let's note our routine use of the pragmatic-test. We use it to check the workability of our ideas and hypotheses, even our guesses and hunches. It is an integral part of our trial-and-error way of solving daily problems.

If, for instance, you turn on your TV set and nothing happens, then you are forced into creating a hypothesis to find out what is wrong. Your first hypothesis may be that the cord is not plugged in. So you check it. It is plugged in, so your hypothesis is wrong. So, since that hypothesis didn't work, you proceed to another one. Perhaps something is wrong inside the TV set. You check the warmup tube and find it cold, so you conclude that electricity is not getting into the set. Now the problem begins to look serious (that is, a solution may cost you time and/or money). You are on your way to the telephone to call a TV repairman when you notice that the nightlight by the telephone is off. You check and find other lights off. So, new hypothesis: a fuse must be tripped. You check. All fuses are in the "ON" position except one. You flip this one to "ON" and power is restored.

By empirical means, you gradually developed a hypothesis which accounted for all the facts. You were forced to collect more and more data before you could develop a workable hypothesis—that is, a hypothesis on the basis of which the TV problem could be corrected. Happily, the hypothesis that finally worked will probably cost you little time and no money.

This illustrates the essential claim of pragmatism: the idea that *works* is the *true* one.

8 Our ideas have a profound effect on how we feel and behave. This fact is fundamental to all of man's religions, and here we discover the rationale for "faith" and "belief."

William James knew from personal experience this pragmatic process he was attempting to formulate into a philosophy. Having been reared in a family distraught with emotional instability, James developed psychophysical illnesses which plagued him most of his life. He suffered from sleeplessness, digestive disorders, headaches, and depression. He came to believe that there was no escape from his misery, that his suffering had been fatalistically determined for him so that he could do nothing to change his condition. He could easily use his illness as a rationalization for not facing the buffeting which is a part of life.

The crisis for James came in 1869–70 when he thought again of ending his life. After a period of deep depression he forcefully rejected suicide as a solution to his problem. He made a commitment which

> marked a decisive break in his attitude toward death and signalized his new belief in the creative dimensions of personal existence. While it cannot be said that the resolution of this crisis ended the pervasiveness of what Perry calls his "morbid traits," it did symbolize for James a new set of possibilities.

About this time he read an essay by Renouvier which convinced him of the reality of personal freedom. His life was not determined irrevocably for him; he really could change the course of his life. *An idea—the idea of personal freedom—had taken hold of him.* On April 30, 1870, James wrote in his notebook: "I think that yesterday was a crisis in my life. . . . My first act of free will shall be to believe in free will." He had committed himself to the affirmation of life; he would not escape from it.

> Having rejected suicide in favor of the possibility of a creative life un-supported by certitude, James developed a doctrine to sustain such a

Doubt is an uneasy and dissatisfied state from which we struggle to free ourselves and pass into the state of belief; while the latter is a calm and satisfactory state which we do not wish to avoid, or to change to a belief in anything else. On the contrary, we cling tenaciously, not merely to believing, but to believing just what we do believe.

C. S. PEIRCE

3 The Real World: Knowing and Unknowing

belief. . . . If it can be said that James assented to "The Will to Believe" until the end, we must caution that it was a belief always shot through with irresolution and doubt. Behind the consistent cadences of a rich and future-oriented prose, there lurked a well-controlled but omnipresent sense of despair. James was neither an optimist nor a cynic; he was a man of moral courage, who knew, all too well, the ambiguity and precariousness of the human condition.

9   What about the "truth-value" of a belief powerful enough to prevent one from opting for suicide? Whatever the *rationale* within the belief—that one's time has not yet come, that one has not yet accomplished his purpose in life, that one should not cause others to suffer, or that taking one's life is morally wrong—whatever the rationale, isn't this belief true? Isn't the truth of ideas to be found in the results they effect? Or, as James so pungently put it, don't we judge the worth of ideas by their "cash value"?

Pragmatism's only test of truth is what works best, wrote James.

If theological ideas should do this, if the notion of God, in particular, should prove to do it, how could pragmatism possibly deny God's existence? It could see no meaning in treating as "not true" a notion that was pragmatically so successful.

10   The *pragmatic paradox* may be stated thus: In order for an idea to work pragmatically, one must believe that it is true on other than pragmatic criteria. Now, if we *define* "truth" as an idea that works (that is, that brings about desired results), then we have no serious problem. If an idea works, then it's true; and conversely, if an idea is true, then it works.

But this is not yet the heart of the matter. In order for an idea or belief to work *pragmatically,* we must believe it in terms of *correspondence*. This kind of insight can become a blessing or a bad dream.

For instance, in order for the belief in immortality to become a sustaining belief (that is, *to work*), one must accept that immortality exists in reality; one must believe that there is an objective event which corresponds to the concept. Even though we may not be able to check out the belief with the correspondence-test, if it is not believed on a *correspondence* basis then the belief can have no *pragmatic* results.

What if you should say to yourself: "I have no evidence that souls survive death, but I want to experience the benefits of the belief in immortality (strength, courage, comfort), so I will accept the belief on a pragmatic basis. I will *believe* in immortality and make the idea work for me." What are the chances of making the idea "work"? For most of us, very poor indeed. (Incidentally, we see clearly here the role of the authority in our lives, the charismatic figure who can persuade us to believe *on his authority* that an idea is objectively true; this way we can

In the whole New Testament, there appears but a solitary figure worthy of honor: Pilate, the Roman Viceroy. . . . The noble scorn of a Roman, before whom the word "truth" was shamelessly mishandled, enriched the New Testament with the only saying in it that has any value—"What is truth?"

NIETZSCHE

Grant an idea or belief to be true, what concrete difference will its being true make in any one's actual life? How will the truth be realized? What experiences will be different from those which would obtain if the belief were false? What, in short, is the truth's cash-value in experiential terms?

WILLIAM JAMES

manage to believe, without empirical evidence, what we wanted and needed to believe to begin with but couldn't accomplish on our own.)

One must believe in immortality "with all his heart." With equal conviction one must "know" that a loving Father-God does in fact exist (that is, that God is real); then the belief can be true pragmatically. Likewise, if the devout Muslim knows that Allah endows him with courage in battle, then he will not falter as the Holy War is waged. And the kamikaze pilot could look forward with patriotic fervor to the moment when he could dive his Suisei bomber onto the deck of an aircraft carrier, since he knew beyond doubt that he would return in spirit directly to the Yasukuni Shrine and be visited by family and friends.°

Believing these ideas to be objectively true, they become pragmatically true.

°See the letter written by the kamikaze pilot on page 474.

To say that Newton's law of gravitation is true is to say that it can be applied successfully; so long as that could be done, it was true. There is no inconsistency in saying that Newton's law was true and that Einstein's law is at present true.

HECTOR HAWTON
(describing Pragmatism)

11   A "fact" which is true on one truth-test may be false on another.

For instance, a Muslim would say, "There is no God but Allah" (this fact-claim is a part of the Islamic Creed). Is such a statement true? Check it with the three truth-tests. You can be sure of three things: (1) The Muslim accepts his belief on a pragmatic basis; that is, his faith in Allah works for him. Therefore, *for him,* the statement is true on the pragmatic-test. (2) He also accepts his belief in Allah on the coherence-test; that is, the belief undoubtedly coheres with numerous other accepted data from the Quran and Islamic tradition (the Hadith). Therefore, *for him,* the statement is true on the coherence-test. (3) While it would be extremely difficult or impossible to discover the real object/event referred to as "Allah" so that the correspondence-test could be applied, you can be quite sure that the Muslim *believes* that such a real object/event exists.

So, is the fact-claim true or false?

Now, if you should reply, "I don't believe your statement is true," what exactly are you saying? (1) Using the pragmatic-test, you are stating that the concept of Allah is not meaningful to you, hence not true *for you.* (2) Using the coherence-test, belief in Allah does not harmonize with facts you have accepted as true. Where can you fit such a fact-claim into the Jewish, Christian, atheistic, or scientific world-view? It is false, therefore, *for you.* (3) Using the correspondence-test, you are stating that you don't think "Allah" is real. If the Muslim claims that Allah is real, we often respond with the challenge, "Prove it"—meaning show us *by the correspondence-test* that there is a real object/event called "Allah." Of course, he cannot.

Therefore, we think we have won our case. Using only the correspondence-test, you retort that the Muslim's fact-claim is untrue. His statement about "Allah" is false. *And yet, on the other two criteria—the pragmatic and coherence—the fact-claim is undeniably true . . . for the Muslim.*

So again we ask: Is the fact-claim true or false?

CAN TRUTH BE RELATIVE?

In pondering the relativity of truth, Plato pointed out in the *Theaetetus* that the relativistic position is a paradox: "The best of the joke is, that Protagoras acknowledges the truth of their opinion who believe his opinion to be false; for in admitting that the opinions of all men are true, in effect he grants that the opinion of his opponents is true."

In their book *Realms of Philosophy,* the Drs. Sahakian summarize the dilemma in the following composed dialogue:

> PROTAGORAS. Plato, what is true for you, is true for you, and what is true for me, is true for me.
>
> PLATO. Do you mean to say that my personal opinion is true?
>
> PROTAGORAS. Indeed, that is precisely what I mean.
>
> PLATO. But, my dear Protagoras, my opinion is that truth is not relative; truth is not a matter of opinion, but objective and absolute. Furthermore, my opinion is that your belief in the relativity of truth is absolutely false and should be abandoned. Do you still hold that my opinion is true?
>
> PROTAGORAS. Yes, you are quite correct.

The NBC television program *My World and Welcome To It* updated the dilemma in a dialogue between the cartoonist (Monroe, based on Thurber) and the newspaper editor who publishes his cartoons:

> EDITOR. I understand your cartoon this time, and it's not funny.
>
> MONROE. You're entitled to your opinion.
>
> EDITOR. It's not an opinion. It's a fact.
>
> MONROE. You can't say that.
>
> EDITOR. Why not? You said I was entitled to my opinion. And in my opinion, it's a fact.

In either case, who is logically correct? Would it be meaningful to ask who is *psychologically* correct?

At ebb tide I wrote
A line upon the sand
And gave it all my heart
And all my soul.
At flood tide I returned
To read what I had inscribed
And found my ignorance upon the
* shore.*

KAHLIL GIBRAN

Truth is the approximation of
thought to reality. It is thought on
its way home. Its measure is the
distance thought has travelled,
under guidance of its inner com-
pass, toward that intelligible system
which unites its ultimate object
with its ultimate end.

BRAND BLANSHARD

12   We frequently find ourselves caught in interminable arguments where no meeting of minds takes place—as would undoubtedly happen in the case of the Muslim's claims about Allah. If we can cease to argue long enough to clarify our thinking, we would often find that different truth-tests are being used to support fact-claims.

It is good advice, therefore, to examine carefully the truth-tests being used (or merely assumed). If indeed one individual is using the correspondence-test as the only acceptable criterion for verifying "facts" while another is relying on pragmatic criteria or is caught in the pragmatic paradox, it is no wonder that such discussions end in fruitless stalemates. We are left with frustration because the other person can't accept what is so obviously true to us.

13   Examination of the truth-tests will disclose three points worth noting. (1) All three tests are constantly used by all of us and are indispensable to thinking and communicating. Each has its sphere of legitimate operation.

(2) Each truth-test has intrinsic problems. We cannot be absolutely sure of any "fact" on any test. We are forced to conclude that "truth" is a probability item, with greater or lesser degrees of likelihood attached to various specific fact-claims.

And (3), this being the case, all truth is tentative. It is always subject to further modification and refinement as new fact-claims are verified and become facts.

4

THE INNER WORLD: THE FANTASTIC JOURNEY

4-1

PSYCHE/SOMA

1   As adults, we have forgotten most of our childhood, not only its contents but its flavor; as men of the world, we hardly know of the existence of the inner world: we barely remember our dreams, and make little sense of them when we do; as for our bodies, we retain just sufficient proprioceptive sensations to coordinate our movements and to ensure the minimal requirements for biosocial survival—to register fatigue, signals for food, sex, defecation, sleep; beyond that, little or nothing. Our capacity to think, except in the service of what we are dangerously deluded in supposing is our self-interest and in conformity with common sense, is pitifully limited: our capacity even to see, hear, touch, taste and smell is so shrouded in veils of mystification that an intensive discipline of unlearning is necessary for anyone before one can begin to experience the world afresh, with innocence, truth and love.

R. D. LAING

2   Man's ignorance of his inner world has been an abysmal "darkness of unknowing." Is there, as a matter of fact, anything that we understand less than we understand ourselves? And when we begin to see the facts, how quickly we turn away and refuse to face the truth about our own being. The history of man's exploration of human nature is marked by a singular lack of courage.

In a way, all this is surprising, for there is probably no human adventure more exciting than the exploration of "inner space." To be sure, it can lead us into uncharted country. It can evoke sacred fears and involve unscheduled risks, and not a few may fear that they have strayed into forbidden territory.

And too, it can be a lonely odyssey. No one else can travel with us; they can only call to us, as from a distance.

Yet there can be a feeling of joyous ultimacy in the unique adventure of coming to know one's inner world. Most of us have sensed

The exploration of the interior of the human brain will be as dangerous as that of the Antarctic continent or the depths of the oceans, and far more rewarding.

J. B. S. HALDANE

Freud described the therapeutic process as one in which layers of consciousness were gradually removed until the unconscious was reached. [But Allen Wheelis] found that after the layers were peeled, there was often—nothing—a great void that the analyst, though called upon to do so, could not possibly fill.

BERNARD ROSENBERG

the mysterious forces—more errant than the winds—that drive and direct our lives. Who among us has not wondered what he would find if he began in earnest to probe the depths of his own being?

3   "Dare I explore my inner world?" The question is rarely stated this directly, but in some form the implicit decision "to explore or not to explore" is forced upon us each day.

And, because human history is in a critical state of change in our understanding of man, the answer, assuredly, must be "yes." The fact is that man has always cast furtive glances inward, but heretofore he has sojourned in his psychic hinterlands without adequate roadmaps. He has groped haphazardly, not knowing where he was going, how to get there, or what he would find. This is no way to begin a journey.

All this is changing. Modern cartographers have begun to do their work and today we have rudimentary but helpful maps to guide us.

4   There is no obvious reason why one should spend his lifetime solely in the two traditional mind-states: the problem-solving conscious state and the "recovery" sleep state. Most of us, in fact, wander off the narrow path and spend time in free-association (woolgathering), browsing through our memories, and enjoying flights of fantasy; we might even tune in a few alpha rhythms. So our reduction of human existence into an alternation of consciousness and unconsciousness—waking and sleeping—is a local (Western) oversimplification.

There are other modes of conscious and subconscious experience which can enrich our lives; and on the condition that they do not rob us of our sanity° or endanger others, there is no valid reason why they should not be known.

°The words "sane" and "insane" are much-abused layman's terms which cover a multitude of neurotic and psychotic conditions. Don't be disturbed by their general use here; they will be given more precise definition—or rather various possible definitions will be explored—in Chapter 4-4.

Ful wys is he that can himselven knowe!
(*Very wise is he that can know himself.*)

CHAUCER

5   In the Eastern tradition other modes of consciousness such as focused concentration (*samadhi,* leading to *nirvana*), ecstatic trances, and Zen meditation (*zazen,* leading to *satori*) have been considered, for thousands of years, to be higher, more desirable mind-states, valued far above the reality-mode of consciousness. Such outlooks contrast greatly with our Western single-track commitment to just one form of waking experience.

This is not entirely true, however, for even in our Western tradition revered mystics have seen visions and known the rapture of religious ecstasy; and such experiences were invested with ultimate value. They were experiences devoutly to be sought. In these Western cases the *interpretation* of the experience has given them their value. They were understood to be instances of spirit-possession (by the Holy Spirit) and not merely altered psychological states.

It appears that the West has used a "double standard" in assessing the value of various modes of psychic experience.

6   There is a fundamental condition to the deliberate exploration of human consciousness, a condition which Eastern religions have scrupulously observed. That condition is that the conscious mind not be impaired in its basic functions, which are to mediate reality and to solve problems. Whatever realms of the inner world we decide to explore, we know that we must shortly return to the reality-mode of consciousness and reestablish relations with the real world. The conscious mind must be adequate to the performance of numerous pragmatic functions: it must be able to organize perception, to remember pertinent information, to make operational value-judgments, to engage in rational thinking as needed, and so on.

In some Eastern religions we find acceptable ways of annihilating one's physical organism as well as the "self." Such practices rest on the obvious assumption that the individual will not be required to reenter the reality-mode of consciousness. He may have decided to withdraw into the forest and proceed into the eternal nirvana from which there is no return. But such instances, while permissible, are rare; and the fact of the matter is that, without exception, Eastern religions emphasize the *quality* of the reality-mode of consciousness and look with concern upon Western ("amateur") experiments which endanger conscious functioning. This is precisely the reason why Eastern spiritual leaders are critical of Western use of mind-altering chemicals.

7   The most important aspect of the new worldview is close to the consciousness idea. It is simply that people today, young persons especially, are willing to accept new levels of reality as part of their ordinary experience.

In this, of course, the drug phenomenon has been central. It has made it clear that the spectrum of human experience need not be limited to the ordinary waking state and to a few peripheral ones such as dreaming.

IS CONSCIOUSNESS RELATIVE?

The relativity of our reference point can be demonstrated by taking a moving picture of a plant at one frame a minute and then speeding it up to thirty frames a second. The plant will appear to behave like an animal, clearly perceiving stimuli and reacting to them. Why, then, do we call it unconscious? To organisms which react 1800 times as quickly as we react, we might appear to be unconscious. They would in fact be justified in calling us unconscious, since we would not normally be conscious of their behavior.

ROLAND FISCHER, "Biological Time,"
J. T. Fraser (ed.), *Voices of Time*

In the province of the mind, what one believes to be true either is true or becomes true within limits to be found experientially and experimentally. These limits are beliefs to be transcended.

JOHN C. LILLY

It has dramatized that the mind is far richer than most of us ever thought and that the ninety per cent of the mental iceberg that has remained under the water for all but a few great mystics is something that we can all tap.

Drugs were only a catalyst and a raiser of expectations, though, and in a real sense we have entered a post-drug era. I remember picking up a hitchhiker along the California coast some time ago who said that he had dropped acid a hundred and fifty times but now wouldn't even touch aspirin. His search for "natural" highs had led him into some sort of yoga. Others may prefer brain-wave feedback, or transcendental meditation, or encounter, but the quest for life along a wider emotional and mental spectrum underlies them all.

EDWARD B. FISKE

8   Our normal waking consciousness . . . is but one special type of consciousness, whilst all about it, parted from it by the filmiest of screens, there lie potential forms of conscious entirely different. We may go through life without suspecting their existence; but apply the requisite stimulus, and at a touch they are all there in all their completeness, definite types of mentality which probably somewhere have their field of application and adaptation. No account of the universe in its totality can be final which leaves these other forms of consciousness quite disregarded. How to regard them is the question—for they are so discontinuous with ordinary consciousness. Yet they may determine attitudes though they cannot furnish formulas, and open a region though they fail to give a map. At any rate, they forbid a premature closing of our accounts with reality.

WILLIAM JAMES

9   Aldous Huxley was one of the greatest minds of our century. He had developed, through discipline, a technique for utilizing a high degree of his considerable mental power. At will, Huxley could withdraw into what he called his state of "Deep Reflection" (DR state), a mind-state

marked by physical relaxation with bowed head and closed eyes, a profound progressive psychological withdrawal from externalities but without any actual loss of physical realities nor any amnesias or loss of orientation, a "setting aside" of everything not pertinent, and then a state of complete mental absorption in matters of interest to him.

When Huxley was in such a meditative state it was possible for him to engage in physical activity to some extent—jotting down notes or exchanging pencils—without remembering afterward anything that he had done. As he said, these physical events did not "impinge" on his mental processes. Loud noises could not reach him. He would emerge from his reflective state only when he had finished his self-set creative goals; his emergence was inner-willed.

Frequently Huxley began his day's work by entering into his DR state. He would organize his ideas and sort his tasks for that day. One

P – O₁

Ơ₁ – O₂

T – O₂

T – O₁

P – O₂

afternoon he was working with total absorption on a particular manuscript when his wife returned from shopping. She inquired whether he had taken down the note she had phoned in to him. Somewhat bewildered, he helped her look for the note, which they found near the phone. He had been in his DR working state when she called, had answered the phone as usual—"I say there, hello!"—listened to the message, jotted it down—all this without remembering a word of the episode. His mind had apparently proceeded to carry on its work without interruption.

The essential point is that this was Huxley's way of working efficiently. His friend Milton Erickson experimented with him in the DR state, and Huxley frequently found himself prepared for work but with nothing to do. He would emerge from his DR state rather puzzled. "There I found myself without anything to do so I came out of it."

His wife commented that when in the state of Deep Reflection, he seemed

like a machine moving precisely and accurately. It is a delightful pleasure to see him get a book out of the bookcase, sit down again, open the book slowly, pick up his reading glass, read a little, and then lay the book and glass aside. Then some time later, maybe a few days, he will notice the book and ask about it. The man just never remembers what he does nor what he thinks about when he sits in that chair. All of a sudden, you just find him in his study working very hard.

The last letter of the Tibetan alphabet symbolizes for the Buddhist the fully-awakened state of consciousness (*Maha Ati*).

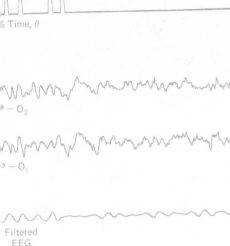

*It seems to me that the greatest les-
son of adult life is that one's own
consciousness is not enough. What
one of us would not like to share
the consciousness of half a dozen
chosen individuals? What writer
would not like to share the consciousness of Shakespeare? What
musician that of Beethoven or
Mozart? What mathematician that
of Gauss? What I would choose
would be an evolution of life
whereby the essence of each of us
becomes welded together into some
vastly larger and more potent
structure.*

FRED HOYLE

10   Religious mystics the world over make a common assertion: no one can understand a profound religious experience until he has himself experienced it. No amount of description with mere symbols can touch its true meaning.

Western mystics—Plotinus, Groot, Eckhart, Tauler, et al.—have consistently stated that there is no experience in daily life that can help one to understand the meaning of the mystical experience, for it is not a mundane experience which is different in degree; rather it is a different *kind* of experience.

The same observation comes from the Eastern mystics: if you think you have achieved an intellectual understanding of nirvana, then you've missed it. Similarly from the Taoist: "The Tao that can be expressed in words is not the true Tao."

11   One of the most valued but ineffable mystical experiences in both East and West is the experience of unity. So profound is it that the mystics thereafter remain silent concerning it. They may indeed write volumes around the periphery of the experience, but they avow that they could not possibly describe what they have seen.

It is an event in which all experience is somehow seen together. The outer world and the inner merge into one; no distinction is made between subject and object. All knowledge is interwoven; everything is seen in the light of everything else, as though every fragment of knowledge and understanding illuminated every other fragment of knowledge and understanding. There is a coalescence; everything is related; all the contents of the mind become unified. It is all One, and this One may be felt as in some way merging with the cosmos itself; it may be conceived as the uniting of one's essence with Ultimate Reality or Godhead.

By analogy, suppose that you have spent a dozen years devouring knowledge. Imagine that you have carefully read hundreds of books in psychology, history, biology, chemistry, physics; you have studied all the textbooks in higher mathematics, geometry, astronomy, and philosophy; you have memorized the great outpouring of human feeling in music, poetry, literature, and art. . . .

But how do we store and recover such information? Ordinarily our minds move with a pokey, linear motion. They plod along, thinking of one thing at a time. We never read a book at a time, nor even a page at a time: we read only a few words or perhaps a line.

But suppose some psychophysical happening suddenly opened the doors to all your stored information and this vast accumulation of knowledge could flow together into one sustained flash of understanding. Suppose every fact related to every other fact. Suppose that all you had ever learned had somehow bonded into a harmonious whole. In your mind, All was One. Such an experience would indeed be ineffable, so far beyond words that one could never hope to describe what he had seen.

Saint Thomas Aquinas may have had this kind of experience. After producing scores of volumes of systematic theology—the crowning achievement of Western religious thought—Thomas had a vision near the end of his life after which, he said, everything he had previously written was straw. He never attempted to put into mere human words what, at last, he had seen.

12   The state of consciousness sought by the Zen Buddhist is called *satori,* usually translated as "flash of enlightenment." It is a mind-state quite different from a trance or hypnotic condition. It is a state of sharp alertness and wide awareness accompanied, at the same time, by a deep sense of inner calm. We know now that those who practice Zen meditation (*zazen*) are in a specific mental state with a characteristic EEG (electroencephalographic) pattern of brainwaves. Studies show that EEG patterns of experienced Zen meditators are quite different from those of beginners. In advanced patterns the alpha waves begin to diminish and a rhythmic "theta train" appears. The typical "advanced" Zen meditation moves through four stages. It begins with initial alpha waves with eyes open (I); then a sharp increase of the alpha (II) followed by a gradual decrease of the alpha (III); and finally there is a sustained period of rhythmic theta waves (IV).

How does zazen feel from the standpoint of the meditator? For Western students, Erich Fromm has described the indescribable as well as anyone can.

> If we would try to express enlightenment in psychological terms, I would say that it is a state in which the person is completely tuned to the reality outside and inside of him, a state in which he is fully aware of it and fully grasps it. *He* is aware of it—that is, not his brain, nor any other part of his organism, but *he,* the whole man. He is aware of *it;* not as of an object over there which he grasps with his thought, but *it,* the flower, the dog, the man, in its or his full reality. He who awakes is open and responsive to the world, and he can be open and responsive because he has given up holding on to himself as a thing, and thus has become empty and ready to receive. To be enlightened means "the full awakening of the total personality to reality."

The great cause of much psychological illness is the fear of knowledge of oneself—of one's emotions, impulses, memories, capacities, potentialities, of one's destiny.
ABRAHAM MASLOW

13   A state of consciousness which a Western religious minority has highly prized is a form of religious ecstasy. Those belonging to the "Pentecostal" tradition—or other traditions which value "spirit possession" (in Christianity, possession by the Holy Spirit)—have sometimes made the ecstatic experience a condition of membership. Within their circles they cultivate an attitude of expectancy in which members may anticipate for years the glorious soul-filling experience.

In religious ecstasy several things occur. The word *ecstasy* derives from the Greek *ek* ("out of") and *stasis* ("standing"), implying that the

Le coeur a ses raisons que la raison ne connaît point.
(*The heart has its reasons which reason knows nothing of.*)
PASCAL

4   The Inner World: The Fantastic Journey

true person is "standing outside" his body, the assumption being that a "spirit" has taken his place. Thus an "ecstatic" individual is no longer in possession of his own body, and the original "self" is no longer in a reality-mode. An ecstatic individual no longer responds to the realities about him; his behavior has "switched to automatic." Some deeper level of the psyche has taken control while the normal controlling ego has suspended operations.

A typical ecstatic experience is known as *glossolalia,* "speaking in tongues." In this state, one feels he has gradually been overcome or "possessed." He may begin to speak unintelligible words ("babble") to himself or to bystanders. His voice may sound quite different from his own; he may sing beautifully when ordinarily he sings not at all. To the ecstatic individual it feels as though the words and songs are uttered by someone else deep within, and are quite beyond his control. As in cases of hypnosis, some aspect of the personality other than the ego has taken control, and any content originates from the deeper levels of consciousness.

In "Pentecostal" experiences where the ecstatic state is considered to be possession by the Holy Spirit, it not infrequently brings about a fundamental reorientation in the individual's life—a "conversion" or "born again" experience. It is difficult to imagine any experience more meaningful than being possessed by God.

14   I was in the desert, in a very beautiful place I visited frequently last year. Involved in the experience were: the beauty of nature, a strong feeling of my relationship with that Mother Nature, some very loving, very close people putting me physically and mentally in a very comfortable, relaxed physical and emotional setting.

The experience physically was brought on by a cold river and hot springs. Imagine: cold river, hot springs: water of 120 degrees, air of 110, river water somewhere in the 60s.

I began by sitting in the 120-degree water until sweat poured from my face and I could no longer stand the physical feeling of that heat. I jumped out of the hot water, climbed a rock and dove fifteen feet into a three-foot pool of very, very cold water. Now this does quite a number to your body and your mind. I swam across the river to where there was a shaded area and sat in the cold water in the shade until I began shivering and began getting extremely uncomfortable from the shivering, swam back across the river and jumped back into the hot water, feeling absolutely nothing immediately and then an extreme rush. And back and forth nine times.

At the completion of the ninth time I climbed back up on top of the rock to dive back into the cold water, and as I looked down I experienced something that I will call the "white light," the clear light, and as I looked down to see the pool into which I was to dive, my vision was of naught—a complete nothing, of the void. And I can remember

As I see it, such a man, the man who is engaged in a lifetime quest away from encapsulation, moving in the direction of the broadest and deepest possible reality image, has the key to what it means to be and to see. He is thereby representative of man in his deepest and most significant sense. For such an orientation would mean that he was very much alive in the best meaning of the term "existential" and very much aware in the best meaning of the term "philosophical." Such a man would be a man of great compassion, great sensitivity, and great thought. He would, in short, be reaching for ultimate consciousness. And while it is true that such an open approach to life is very risky for the individual man in the short view, it is clearly more creative and productive, and therefore, more viable for all men in the long run.

JOSEPH ROYCE

OLD MAN (sarcastically). *Being spiritual, the mind cannot be affected by physical influences?*

YOUNG MAN. *No.*

OLD MAN. *Does the mind remain sober when the body is drunk?*

MARK TWAIN

It is constantly being borne in upon me that we have made far too little use in our theory of the indubitable fact that the repressed remains unaltered by the passage of time—this seems to offer us the possibility of an approach to some really profound truths.

SIGMUND FREUD

thinking, feeling, reacting, something . . . so that the next thing I knew I was sitting down on this large flat rock. And this is very difficult to relate to you because it didn't happen with words—there were no words in my mind then. But I sat down in a position like this, with my heels against my bottom, went back, flat on my back with my arms flat out, feet still touching here, soles of my feet together—and by the way I've never done this before and could never hope to repeat it again—this physical position—still touching here, flat on my back, arms straight out, and allowed myself for the first time in my life to let go of my body. My knees went down and touched the rock, so that I was lying like this, completely flat, released my self from my body. And the next thing I knew I was looking down at that body lying on the rock from a point a little bit higher than the peak of a mountaintop next to the hot springs.

It scared me, and it scared me very much. Part of that fright was because at the time I was into a very heavy "me-man, you-earth" state of mind, and I wasn't really willing or ready to relate to "me-essence, you-universe." And I snapped real quick, and I was back in my body, and I was hearing my name being called. And I stood up and the experience was gone. And it lasted a total of—from the time I climbed the rock until I was back down—maybe thirty seconds. And yet that experience of only thirty seconds was one of such purity and one of such truth and one of such extreme pure emotion, that I could never possibly hope to forget it. . . .

TERRY ALLEN

15   In the Indian religions, the state of nirvana is a trance-state outwardly resembling a deep sleep. It is marked by a progressive deepening of the trance through religious disciplines that are similar to techniques of self-hypnosis. Gradually, as *samadhi* ("concentration") is practiced, the devotee learns to block out all sensory stimuli from the external world; simultaneously, sensory and emotional input from the inner world are reduced and finally stopped; no bodily sensations or emotions—hunger, pain, fear, loneliness—are registered. Further, however, the mystic enters into a mind-state of zero cognition—no ideas, memories, or rational activity. It is a "contentless" state of consciousness.

This Eastern trance resembles Huxley's "Deep Reflection" in one respect: loud noises or other stimuli are not perceived. But in its central nature, it contrasts with Huxley's DR state. In the latter's mind a high pitch of intellectual activity raced through its plan of operations, while in nirvana there is no mental *content* of any sort. It is *pure consciousness,* a seemingly discarnate, free-floating experience of nothingness.

This is the ultimate achievement of human existence for the Hindu and Buddhist. It is said to be experienced as an indescribable state of tranquillity, inner peace, and joy, a timeless state of union with the cosmos itself. In Hindu terms, the self-essence (*atman*) has become one with Ultimate Reality (*Brahman*).

17   The individual who lacks awareness of the depths and facets of his psyche is something less than a whole man, and considerably less than he could be. He is living a single-dimensioned existence in a multidimensional psychic universe. There is no reason not to explore other worlds and—like the Zen monk or religious ecstatic—spend some time living there. The qualifying condition, as emphasized, is that he preserve his autonomy and the integrity of his reality-mode of consciousness.

Of course, our Western methods for accomplishing anything are distinctive: we employ chemistry and physics in everything. It is quite in character that we approach psychic/somatic functions with pills and gadgets, milligrams and voltages. And, typically, we will find faster ways of "getting there" and run the risks so characteristic of our rapid conquest of all known worlds.

In the seventies we are in process of breaking through archaic traditions regarding the human psyche. We have already come so far that there is now little doubt that we will continue to loosen the confines and, hopefully, move ahead to positive controls and enriching experiences.

But we must take care, for *this* is the "fantastic journey" into the delicate nuclear center of human existence itself—the Mind of Man.

Nirvana is not the blowing out of the candle. It is the extinguishing of the flame because day is come.
RABINDRANATH TAGORE

4-2

PAST/PRESENT/
FUTURE

1   Time affects us in so many ways. We use it; we abuse it; we enjoy it; we fear it.

The way we respond to the challenges of time is a test of what we are, of what we are becoming. We grow older day by day, older in the calendar. Does that fact disturb us greatly, little, sometimes, often? How else are we growing in the same time? How much of our time do we enjoy doing what? Do we frequently or seldom feel that the time was really well spent? The answers we would give to these questions reveal our *philosophy of time*. We all acquire one, though we rarely, if ever, venture to spell it out.

R. M. MAC IVER

What is time? If no one asks me, I know. If I try to explain it to someone asking me, I don't know.
ST. AUGUSTINE

The Moving Finger writes; and, having writ, Moves on. . . .
OMAR KHAYYAM
The Rubaiyat

2   A "philosophy of *time*." Time possesses at once, for us all, the *fascinosum* and the *mysterium;* it is intimately familiar *and* ultimately formidable. Time *is* life, and life *is* time; and somehow we know this in the marrow of our bones. But in all of human experience, is there anything which more befuddles our understanding? Is there any concept which, when we try to force open its secrets, betrays the frailty of our thought and the ineptness of our language? Whitehead said it all: "It is impossible to meditate on time and the mystery of the creative passage of nature without overwhelming emotion at the limitations of human intelligence."

3   "Time is like an ever-flowing stream." (The *stream* of consciousness, the *flow* of an electric current, the *flow* of words of a great orator?) "Time unrolls like a carpet." (*Unrolls* in the sense of uncovering something which was previously hidden but now lies exposed to view; and will it continue to be displayed or will the carpet begin to re-roll from the other end and thus hide something again?) "Clocks *keep* time." (As we *keep* our possessions, *keep* our moral principles, *keep* a house?) "Time passes." (As we *pass* an automobile on the road, *pass* a course in a university, *pass* from life to the hereafter?) "Time is ever coming into being and passing out of being." (Where was it before it *came into being* and where does it go when it *passes out of being?*) "Time is all-embracing." (If it is all-embracing does it also *embrace time?*) "We tell time." (To whom, in what language, and *what* do we tell about time?) "We expect the future, experience the present, and remember the past." (Is time then merely a subjective image created by our mind, and having no counterpart in the world?) "Time is the relation of before and after." (But *before* and *after* refer *only* to time; hence we are saying literally time is time.) Does this not show that what I have called the straightforward descriptions of time contain metaphors and analogies, ambiguous words, subjective terms, hidden contradictions, and definitions which are purely verbal?

CORNELIUS BENJAMIN

AWARENESS

Awareness means the capacity to see a coffeepot and hear the birds sing in one's own way, and not the way one was taught. It may be assumed on good grounds that seeing and hearing have a different quality for infants than for grownups, and that they are more esthetic and less intellectual in the first years of life. A little boy sees and hears birds with delight. Then the "good father" comes along and feels he should "share" the experience and help his son "develop." He says: "That's a jay, and this is a sparrow." The moment the little boy is concerned with which is a jay and which is a sparrow, he can no longer see the birds or hear them sing. He has to see and hear them the way his father wants him to. Father has good reasons on his side, since few people can afford to go through life listening to the birds sing, and the sooner the little boy starts his "education" the better. Maybe he will be an ornithologist when he grows up. A few people, however, can still see and hear in the old way. But most of the members of the human race have lost the capacity to be painters, poets or musicians, and are not left the option of seeing and hearing directly even if they can afford to; they must get it secondhand. The recovery of this ability is called here "awareness."

ERIC BERNE
Games People Play

[*Time*] *brings to mind the ideas of corrosion and decay, the knowledge of inexorable and irreversible aging and death. Hence man's efforts to arrest time, to cast off his chronological chains, and to build cities and monuments, pyramids and empires which can resist the teeth of time. Hence, too, his pursuit of a mirage of love which does not wither or fade with time, and his dream of a glory which is outside time. The more man reflects on time, the more his mortality weighs upon him, and the more he realizes that "all our yesterdays have lighted fools the way to dusty death."*

JOHN COHEN

One encouraging note can be heard above all our confusion. It has been noted by Friedrich Waismann that, although most of us haven't the foggiest notion what time *is,* our time-language seems to keep on *working.* We understand the meaning of the *word* "time" in various contexts ("What time is it?" "He arrived just in the nick of time." "We all had a great time." Etc.) and thus we continue to function pragmatically without ever knowing what we're talking about.°

Three philosophical questions about time will come into focus here. (1) What is time? How do we experience it? Can we understand it? (2) What is meant exactly by "past," "present," and "future"? In what sense can each of them be said to exist? (3) Where in time do we live? What does time have to do with personal existence?

4   We use the word "time" to refer to at least three different phenomena, all quite distinct, though usually confused in our minds.

One is clock time or chronological time (the latter deriving from the Greek *chronos,* meaning "time"—which doesn't help matters in the least.) Clock time probably has nothing whatever to do with time. Clocks measure space. One hour of chronological time is the apparent movement of the sun from, say, its zenith point (12 o'clock noon) to a point 15° westward along its orbital path. The clock on the wall is set to correlate with the sun's motion. While the sun moves 15° in space, one clock hand moves 360° while the other smaller hand moves 30° in space. Both events (sun and clock) are cases of matter-in-motion which we have correlated for practical purposes. We usually say we have "syn*chron*ized" sun and clock, implying our belief that real time is involved in the operation. But this is doubtful. We are correlating events and not synchronizing time.

5   A second kind of time is subjective time—psychological or experiential time. This is the only temporal phenomenon of which we have any clear conception, and many philosophers are of the conviction that experiential time is the only true time. Psychological time is our individual experience of the continuum of our consciousness. Consciousness *is* time. When we are asleep or unconscious, time is nonexistent for each of us, but it begins again the moment we regain consciousness.

In this context, we can properly speak of the speeding up and slowing down of time, for the metabolic processes which determine our time-consciousness do just that. They vary. To speak of time variability is to describe accurately an experience of consciousness which is a function of the rate of oxygen consumption by the brain.

Henri Bergson preferred the term "duration" when speaking of conscious time. Pure duration is our ongoing experience of the continuum of consciousness. Bergson insisted that our purest intuition of the true nature of all reality is our experience of this duration of our own consciousness.

°The use of the word "time" in this chapter is sufficient evidence of this point. I count at least 30 *different* definitions of the word in the text of this chapter, most of which, in context, succeed in communicating ideas with some degree of adequacy, but do not necessitate an understanding of what time truly is. What could better illustrate the astounding fact that we can and do communicate with one another continually *without* knowing *what* we are talking about?!

The relativity of our reference point can be demonstrated by taking a moving picture of a plant at one frame a minute and then speeding it up to thirty frames a second. The plant will appear to behave like an animal, clearly perceiving stimuli and reacting to them. Why, then, do we call it unconscious? To organisms which react 1800 times as quickly as we react, we might appear to be unconscious. They would in fact be justified in calling us unconscious, since we would not normally be conscious of their behavior.

ROLAND FISCHER

4   The Inner World: The Fantastic Journey

What does it mean then to enjoy this sense of fulfillment, of time that is really lived, nor merely passed through? The problem we have been viewing from the angle of time is the universal problem that men have approached from various other angles: What makes life worth while? What gives us the sense that life is for us, for you or for me, really worth while? The answers offered have been themselves various and conflicting. But whatever they are, whether they find salvation through a way of believing, a way of doing or a way of feeling, they have all had at their base a common element. The way they prescribe must enlist the personality in wholehearted unison with some reality that absorbs and fulfills the being. The fulfillment of personality is thus a form of communion, whether it be with the God a man worships; or with nature under some aspect; or through intimate communication with ideal things, the inexhaustible quality of beauty or truth that pervades the universe; or with some cause that calls into action all one's power; or even with things of lesser significance so long as they suffice to satisfy the human craving for union. As I muse over my own hours of fullest experience, I realize that it was always in the active presence of what for me was precious and intrinsic reality.

R. M. MAC IVER
The Challenge of the Passing Years

To say that time is consciousness may be misleading since we (in the Western world) tend to think of consciousness as consciousness *of something*. Here is one source of confusion about the nature of time. We objectify time and think of it as a sort of fluid medium in which objects/events occur. Just as we find it difficult to conceive of consciousness apart from consciousness of something, so also for time: we have difficulty thinking of time as "pure time" (Bergson's "pure duration") apart from real objects/events. But time and matter-in-motion must be separated in thought. Our ordinary waking consciousness is the time-continuum upon which external objects/events impinge. The telephone rings or someone speaks, and these external stimuli activate sensations which enter directly into consciousness (time) as content. But time and the content are not the same. Time might more easily be conceived as the continuum of consciousness without content.

One important implication of this understanding of time is that if there were no experiencers (no conscious minds), there could be no time. Therefore, there was a time (!), perhaps 4.5 billion years ago, before

The delicious melodies of Purcell or Cimarosa might be disjointed stammerings to a hearer whose partition of time should be a thousand times subtler than ours.

SAMUEL TAYLOR COLERIDGE

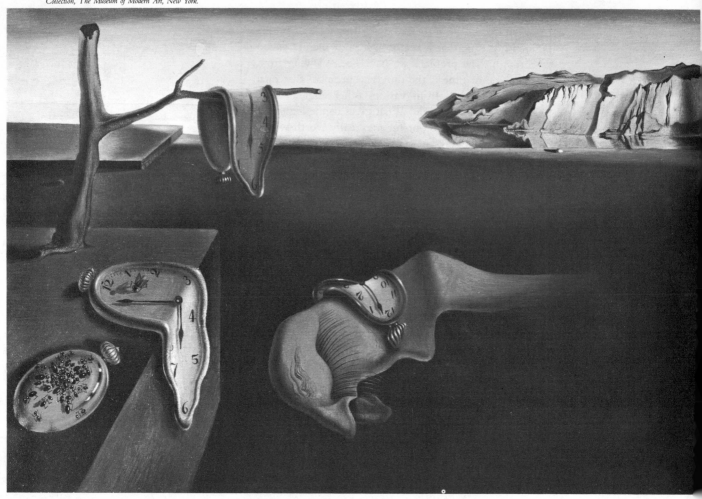

conscious creatures had evolved, when there was no time. Likewise, if all life on earth should cease to exist in the future, time would be no more.

6   As early as 1860 the Austrian physicist Ernst Mach, the first Western thinker to treat time scientifically, concluded that "the time of the physicist does not coincide with the system of time sensations." The physicist can assume an "even flow" of time or, when very great speeds are involved, describe temporal variations ("time dilation") with Einstein's relativistic formulas. His kind of time still behaves with congenial consistency.

The psychologist is not so fortunate: his time is wildly capricious. Psychological time varies with body temperature: if temperature is raised, time passes slower; if lowered, it passes faster. If our metabolic rate is increased, time passes slower; if decreased, it passes faster. Time plods at half a snail's pace in the eager experience of a child; it accelerates like a speed-demon as the adult years pass by.° All these variations are determined by the rate of oxygen consumption by the brain.

°On the variations of time-experience with age, see box on page 102.

Illness and disease can also produce variations in time experience. Among these are Parkinson's disease, some forms of mental/emotional illness, and certain disorders produced by alcoholism.

Almost all hallucinogens, euphoric drugs such as opium and marijuana, and even some common nonprescription drugs can induce extreme alterations in time experience. Under many conditions, clock time seems to pass incredibly slow.

We say that time "slows down" and "speeds up." But in relation to what? In relation to chronological time—to the ticks of the clock—as well as in relation to our memory of what is for oneself a "normal" experience of time. We are surrounded by clocks by which we constantly gage our experience of time: clocks and watches proper, the sun in motion, cars going by, traffic signals, jet planes flying overhead, our own heart-

---

The experimenter has striven to identify the properties of the inner clock, and to trace the parallelism, such as it is, between private and public timekeeping. But the thought of time goes beyond this. It brings to mind the ideas of corrosion and decay, the knowledge of inexorable and irreversible aging and death. Hence man's efforts to arrest time, to cast off his chronological chains, and to build cities and monuments, pyramids and empires which can resist the teeth of time. Hence, too, his pursuit of a mirage of love which does not wither or fade with time, and his dream of a glory which is outside time. The more man reflects on time, the more his mortality weighs upon him, and the more he realizes that "all our yesterdays have lighted fools the way to dusty death."

A theory of time adequate to a "world picture" must encompass human experience as an integral part of nature. And in this experience is the bitter foreknowledge of one's own death, a confrontation with the certainty of dissolution. Death is a biological event which comes at the end of one's days, but the thought of death is our lifelong companion. This thought must find its place in the psychology of time which, as Proust affirmed, is as surely needed as a geometry of space.

JOHN COHEN, "Subjective Time"
in J. T. Fraser (ed.)
The Voices of Time

Man's short-term subjective time scale may depend upon the constancy of his internal temperature. For so-called cold-blooded animals this would not hold. For them time would presumably pass slowly on warm days and rapidly on cold days. . . . Time would not appear to flow steadily in the linear sort of way familiar to us mammals.

HUDSON HOAGLAND

beats, the duration required for us to move from one place to another along a familiar route, the time it takes our eggs to fry or toast to burn. These and a thousand other daily events are clocks against which variations in our time experience would be noticed and measured.

7 A third kind of phenomena which we think of as "time" is matter-in-motion, that is, sequences of events occurring in the real world. The sun rises, dandelion seeds float through the air, clouds gather, rain falls, waves break upon the shore. The majority of time-theorists would hold that all these are *only* sequences of events and do not involve any kind of time per se. However, nothing prevents our using the word "time" to refer to such real events while we measure such events against our calibrated clocks and/or experiential time.

If we ask how long it takes a cannon ball dropped from the top of the Tower of Pisa to hit the ground, then we can time the event with our clocks, in which case we are doing what we did with our clocks and the sun (correlating spatial events); or we can time the event experientially with conscious time as we watch the cannon ball fall.

8 At some point in his life, almost every philosopher has become preoccupied with the nature of time. Several developed noteworthy models to explain time and its mysterious operations.

Saint Augustine's concept of time is conditioned by his theological presuppositions. God *created* time, Augustine reasoned, when he created everything else. Since God created time, he existed *before* time, he will exist *after* time, and therefore he exists *outside* time. There was no time before he created it. Judeo-Christian doctrine has consistently held that God created *all* that exists—including time and presumably space—*ex nihilo*, "out of nothing."

In the mind of God, there is no "before" or "after"; there is only a "now." In "God's experience" all events occur simultaneously. To put it another way, all the past and all the future (that is, *our* past and future) exist together in God's present. Thus, when Augustine elaborates on the doctrine that God foresaw the Fall of Man, God really didn't *foresee* anything, as though he were peering ahead through time (as we would have to) and saw what had not yet transpired. In God's all-inclusive present, "future" events are taking place now. God didn't *foresee*; he merely saw. Likewise, he doesn't foreordain an event; he merely ordains (causes) what he sees happening. This, to Augustine, is what it meant for God to be omniscient and omnipotent.

We humans experience the present, remember the past, and anticipate the future; but God is not limited by our human time. It is not correct to say, as some theologians do, that there are really two times, God's and ours. Rather, we are *in* time; God is timeless.

All the vital problems of philosophy depend for their solutions on the solution of the problem what Space and Time are and more particularly how they are related to each other.

SAMUEL ALEXANDER

4 *The Inner World: The Fantastic Journey*

9   Sir Isaac Newton appears to have assumed, somewhat uncritically, that time is real, being an integral part of the operations of nature. But this objective time is not to be *equated with* matter-in-motion, or with objects per se which endure in time. Real time is separate from real objects/events. Newton's oft-repeated description of time—and his critics have had a field day with it—is as follows:

> Absolute, true, and mathematical time, of itself, and from its own nature, flows equably without relation to anything external, and by another name is called duration: relative, apparent, and common time, is some sensible and external (whether accurate or unequable) measure of duration by means of motion, which is commonly used instead of true time; such as an hour, a day, a month, a year.

It was Newton who first introduced into Western thought the notion of an absolute time. This absolute time (whatever it is) is a universal medium which flows smoothly and evenly, unaffected by all the events which occur *inside* it.

Newton's assumption of absolute time dominated the thinking of physicists until the unorthodox reflections of Einstein at the beginning of our century proved it to be an unworkable assumption and rendered it obsolete.

10   Immanuel Kant considered our sense of time to be inherent in the structure of the mind. Our time-sense is not developed through experience; it is rather "a priori," prior to experience. It is a mode of perception, a subjective mental form which the mind employs in its organization of perception. Dr. Cornelius Benjamin has made a succinct summary of the logical arguments which Kant developed to defend his a priori view of time.

> First, time cannot be an empirical conception since its essential characteristics (coexistence and succession) cannot be perceived by us unless we have some prior notion of time in our minds. In other words, sensations cannot be observed as temporal if we do not already know what is meant by "coexistence" and "succession." Second, we cannot think of phenomena as outside of time, yet we can readily think of empty time. Objects, therefore, can be annihilated from thought, but time cannot. This makes time logically prior to phenomena. Third, only on the supposition that time is a form of intuition can we explain why it is impossible to think of a two-dimensional time or of two coexistent times. This incapacity of our minds is due not to the fact that experience reveals no such notions but to the unthinkable character of the notions. Fourth, time is not a generalization from different times, for different times are merely parts of one and the same time; hence time is an a priori form which interrelates phenomena into a temporal manifold. Fifth, conceptions of time-segments,

In te, anime meus, tempora metior.
(*It is in you, O my mind, that I measure time.*)

ST. AUGUSTINE

i.e., limited durations, are possible only on the assumption of an unlimited or infinite time; but this cannot be an empirically derived notion and must consequently be given as a prior form of intuition under which phenomena are perceived.

11   Many of us find that our ideas about the past, present, and future run together, overlap, or are otherwise blurred.

Ivar Lissner once wrote a book which he entitled *The Living Past.* It's not difficult to infer what he wishes to say with this title, but, for openers, we might logically ask whether, in any sense, the past could be "living" (present tense). Isn't the past dead? And isn't the past, by definition, placed outside the boundary of the present? This is not to say that influences from "past presents" don't linger on and influence us. They do, but their existence is felt only in our living present.

Yet to say the past is "dead" is surely incorrect. To call something "dead" implies that it was once alive, but the past is never "alive." We could just as well speak of a "living future"—which seems to make little sense. Only the present is "alive"—isn't it? Apparently we are having language troubles again.

The nature of the past is of primary concern to the historian since "the past" is his sole subject matter. From his standpoint, the past exists only as it is recreated in the historian's mind. The concrete events of the past are forever gone, and they can be recreated again in the historian's imagination only to the extent that records of some kind have survived from those who witnessed the events. The telltale signs left by events are many: words of eyewitnesses who selected what aspects of any event were significant to them, plus their interpretation and valuation; fossil tracks, leaves, bones; geological records in rocks, volcanic layers, seamounts, oceanic trenches, and so on. If an event leaves no record, then it is forever irretrievable; no historian can reconstruct it nor, for that matter, would he have reason to guess that it had ever occurred.

12   What about the future? Unless we hold to some such theory as Augustine's notion of time, then questions about the existence of the future leave our intellects bewildered.

Can we experience the future? If we can answer "no," then the future can be defined as our expectation that events will continue to occur or that, experientially, we will continue to experience "presents." Our personal future is merely the expectation that our consciousness will continue.

But if, in any way, we can say "yes" to the question "Can we experience the future?", then we must face the most difficult of all philosophical problems and the one with the most far-reaching implications. There is at present ample unexplained time phenomena to prevent our closing the question. Arthur C. Clarke, who, even in his fiction, tries to remain a sound scientist, gives in to the possibility of precognition.

It is worth remembering that we never see or experience anything but the past. The sounds you are hearing now come from a thousandth of a second back in time for every foot they have had to travel to reach your ears. This is best demonstrated during a thunderstorm, when the peal from a flash twelve miles away will not be heard for a full minute. If you ever see a flash and hear the thunder simultaneously, you will be lucky to be alive. I have done it once and do not recommend the experience.

ARTHUR C. CLARKE

It's a poor sort of memory that only works backward.

LEWIS CARROLL
Through the Looking-Glass

Whether the future can be known, even in principle, is one of the subtlest of all philosophical questions.

ARTHUR C. CLARKE

4   The Inner World: The Fantastic Journey

Soils equus, Lunæque, mucetum quattuor Horis,   Proripiunt Tempus: curru quod præpete secum   Pone subit, cuncta rebus Fama vna superstes,
Signa per extenti duodena volubilis Anni,   Cuncta rapit comiti Morti non rapta relinquens   Gætulo boue vecta, implens clangoribus orbem

"I would be willing to state that seeing into the future . . . [is] impossible, were it not for the impressive amount of evidence to the contrary."

If we can experience the future, then under any theory of time we have now, we must conclude that the future has *already* taken place or is *now* taking place. (Recall that Augustine, in order to allow God fore-knowledge of the future, was compelled to theorize that our past, present, and future are all taking place concurrently in God's mind.)

If the future has happened or is happening, then the very structure of our normal waking experience is destroyed. Gone also are numerous axiomatic assumptions such as cause-and-effect and before-and-after. Causal relations become meaningless: that the seed must be planted before the organism can grow, that the song must be sung before it can be heard, that the fire must be lit before the wood can burn—all such statements are wrong. Experience is shot through with contradictions and illusions.

13   Whether we do experience the future has not been established, but experiences which are difficult to explain on any other basis are not uncommon. J. B. Priestley correctly notes that "if one, just one, precognitive dream could be accepted as something more than a coincidence—bang goes our conventional idea of Time!"

Not only is precognition the most stubborn of all philosophical problems, but (if it exists) it often presents itself as a puzzle within a puzzle. Many instances of precognition, especially of tragic episodes, appear as warnings which make it possible for the person having the experience to take evasive action and prevent the tragedy which was foreseen. But this is a contradiction: to be perceived, the future already exists; but when perceived, it can be altered. Therefore, what has already happened can subsequently be changed. Which makes no sense at all.

Priestley—who accepts precognition as fact—says it best.

> Let me put it briefly and brutally. The future can be seen, and because it can be seen, it can be changed. But if it can be seen and yet be changed, it is neither solidly there, laid out for us to experience moment after moment, nor is it non-existent, something we are helping to create, moment after moment. If it does not exist, it cannot be seen; if it is solidly set and fixed, then it cannot be changed. What is this future that is sufficiently established to be observed and perhaps experienced, and yet can allow itself to be altered?

(This problem, too, has an interesting theological parallel. A centuries-old controversy turns on whether God's foreknowledge of events necessarily implies predestination. That is, if God "foresees" an event, does that event *have to occur* or can it be altered? In other words, can God be wrong in what he foresees? It would seem that he can be wrong if the hint of human precognition is applicable: prevision does *not* mean predestination.)

At present we have no time-theories which can explain such occurrences. We must either deny that the future can be experienced now, or develop new models regarding the nature of time. Philosophers and scientists have avoided the time problem, partly because of its association with the occult. But those who professionally wonder about the nature of existence should, like foolish angels, rush in—albeit with fear and trembling—and attempt to create comprehension where chaos now reigns.

14   Since Zeno the Eleatic (fl. c. 450 B.C.), analytical thinkers have been bothered by the nature of the present—the "now" of experience. A long-standing tradition has held that the present is a durationless point. This is the theory of the "punctiform present." It seems that the moment we experience the present, it has already become the past, while the very near future keeps rushing across this knife-edge present into the past. The "now" has no duration; it seems like only a timeless boundary between future and past. If this present has any "width," then it must be composed of a series of (durationless) instants. Louise Heath nicely states this line of logic (although she does not herself accept it):

> The nature of time is such that when the present is, the past has been and *is no* longer, the future will be, but *is not* yet, while the present which *is,* turns out on analysis to be not a part of time but only the boundary between past and future.

Precognition is key to the mysteries of psi [in the opinion of Dr. Milan Ryzl, a Russian parapsychologist]: "I believe the answer lies in a new understanding of space and time. And I think it is very deep."

OSTRANDER AND SCHROEDER

4   *The Inner World: The Fantastic Journey*

This leaves us in a quandary. If, on either side, the past and the future sort of squeeze the present into a durationless boundary line, then where does human experience take place? Or might experience be an illusion, after all, as Zeno believed?

Something must be wrong with our reasoning. We don't live in the past or future, so we must live in the present. Is the "now" of our experience really a point? or does it have width? If so, how wide is it? Perhaps our "now" extends a little bit into the future and past, as William James believed:

> The only fact of our immediate experience is what has been called the "specious" present, a sort of saddle-back of time with a certain length of its own, on which we sit perched, and from which we look in two directions into time. The unit of composition of our perception of time is a duration, with a bow and a stern as it were—a rearward- and a forward-looking end. It is only as parts of this duration-block that the relation of succession of one end to the other is perceived. We do not feel first one end and then the other after it, and from the perception of the succession infer an interval of time between, but we seem to feel the interval of time as a whole, with its two ends embedded in it.

15   James, at last, is on the right path. What we call the "present" is by its very nature a *psychological* event, rather than a mathematical or physical (real) event.° As a psychological event involving perception and consciousness, it therefore possesses duration. The notion of time as a timeless instant is fallacious. Experiencing takes time; it has width. An experience involving intricate psychophysiological processes "stretches out" and lasts a while and could never occur in a "timeless instant." A French psychologist, Paul Fraisse, describes the present from a modern point of view:

> My present is one "tick-tock" of a clock, the three beats of the rhythm of a waltz, the idea suggested to me, the chirp of a bird flying by. . . . All the rest is already past or still belongs to the future. There is order in this present, there are intervals between its constituent elements, but there is also a form of simultaneity resulting from the very unity of my act of perception. Thus the perceived present is not the paradox which logical analysis would make it seem by splitting time into atoms and reducing the present to the simple passage of time without psychological reality. Even to perceive this passage of time requires an act of apprehension which has an appreciable duration.

Therefore, we can define *time* as the experience of the duration of our consciousness, and *the present* as the perceptual time-span of that duration.

But what is the span of that duration? How long does it last? Its duration is not a constant, but depends rather upon the nature of perceptual events which constitute the perceived present. It depends partly

Until the coming of the missionaries in the 17th century, and the introduction of mechanical clocks, the Chinese and Japanese had for thousands of years measured time by graduations of incense. Not only the hours and days, but the seasons and zodiacal signs were simultaneously indicated by a succession of carefully ordered scents.

MARSHALL MC LUHAN

°**This would seem to be a fairly obvious conclusion since (1) mathematicians make no claim that mathematical time-points ("instants") are anything other than mental constructs which are useful in solving certain problems; (2) in physics, Einstein's theories have annihilated the notion of simultaneity, that is, that there exists a "universal now"; what is present for one experiencer may be past or future for another experiencer. See the box on page 388.**

on the number of sense stimuli which are perceived as a unitary event. Any event lasting for more than about two seconds "spills over" into the past, and part of the event is remembered. A series of stimuli (the notes of a melody or the number of spoken sounds) is usually perceived as a unitary event when they last for about one-half to one second. It has been observed that when a clock strikes three or four, we can usually identify the hour without counting the number of consecutive chimes; but beyond four, we have to start counting the number of strikes to identify the hour.

No perception of the present is independent of its content. The duration of the present depends upon the number and nature of the stimuli perceived, the intervals between stimuli, and the organization of the stimuli. The duration of the present also depends upon the state of consciousness of the perceiver and the familiarity and meaningfulness of the organized stimuli. The duration of meaningful sounds in our own language differs from the duration of meaningless sounds in a foreign language. The same is true for a familiar melody in contrast to one never heard before.

In summary, therefore, while in a normal waking mode of consciousness, our perceived present rarely lasts longer than five seconds, and frequently it lasts less than a second. On the average the time-span of our perceived present persists for two to three seconds.

16   Time and personality are fundamentally related. There is nothing unhealthy about reliving in one's memory the happy moments of one's past or anticipating in imagination the possible happy events of the future. But such movements into past or future can become unhealthy if one is "pushed out of the present" by unbearable conditions and develops the habit, involuntarily, of existing in past or future. In such cases the past becomes not merely a memory of experienced events, but a fabricated blend of actual and imagined events; and likewise the future becomes a confused mélange of possible events and impossible "castles in air." When such intensities prevail, one's temporal horizon has been distorted.

Before such extreme conditions set in, however, "where we live" has already been integrated into our character-structure. In a word, if past experiences have been mostly unpleasant we may be oriented toward the future and change. On the other hand, if past experiences have been generally more pleasant and we come to dread future and change, having no grounds for the anticipation of happy events, we may well tend toward the conservation of the conditions of the past which provided the happier experiences.

In a word, those who experience a profound dissatisfaction with the present want change. But whether one seeks better conditions through a future-orientation or a past-orientation will depend upon a fundamental temporal character-structure long since determined by personal experience.

17   The philosophical world-view which goes by the name of existentialism has been immensely popular since World War II. While no two existential philosophers hold quite the same ideas, all share the same attitude toward how we exist in the living present.

Jean-Paul Sartre coined the most famous catch-phrase of modern philosophy: *existence before essence.* To existentialists the word "existence" refers to the concrete "human reality" of experience. Existence is what is—not what should be or might be. By contrast, the word "essence" refers to whatever qualities we deem "essential" to man: "human nature," "original sin," "innate aggression," "rationality," or whatever; but all these are abstractions created after the concrete fact. Minds fabricate essences, and Sartre denies that such notions have any significance for understanding the uniqueness of the individual person.

Sartre is thinking only of *human* existence, for objects possess a different *kind* of existence. To see this difference, contrast man's existence with the existence, say, of the *Saturn V* rocket which launched America's lunar missions. Everything about the *Saturn* rocket—its three stages, engine systems, telemetry, payload capacity, engine-out capability, etc.—was conceived *in the minds* of scientists and engineers and elaborated on the design boards long before any single rocket was constructed. The rocket's purpose, conceived in men's minds, determined every element of its design. Once the design had been completed (still in men's minds), then an infinite number of single rockets, produced to perform in a specific way, could be constructed from those master specifications. All the rockets would be identical.

We can speak meaningfully, therefore, of the *essence* of the *Saturn V* rocket: its essence *is* all the elements of structure and function, conceived by its designers, which enables it to accomplish its purpose. For the *Saturn V,* this rocket essence preceded the existence of any single rocket which eventually stood majestically on the launch pad. For created objects, therefore, *essence* precedes *existence.*

Not so for man, argues Sartre. For man *existence* precedes *essence.* Man was not planned out on a drawing board, nor was he preconceived in any mind (divine or otherwise) for a *purpose* and *then* designed to fulfill such a purpose. Man is not created as objects are created. *Man creates himself.* Man even designs himself—*from within.* Each single person is unique since there is no master template which stamps out identical copies of persons, like minted coins. Therefore man has no essence, as does the rocket, which *predetermines* what he shall be and do. For man, and man alone, existence precedes essence.

18   Existentialism is a philosophy of time and consciousness. To emphasize existence is to place supreme value upon the quality of one's immediate consciousness. As a philosophy of time, existentialism counsels us to exist as fully as possible in the living "now," to accept and actualize the intense "human reality" of the spontaneous present. For the existen-

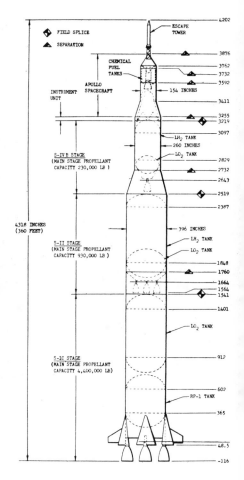

*All animals, large or small, homeo-
thermic or poikilothermic, burn the
light of their lives with relative
equality. Life, at least on the organismic level, is a democratic process: all of us must die, and the duration of our existence is the
same. . . .*

ROLAND FISCHER

tialist, the past is only a repertory of recordings to be used in the service
of the present, and the future is but a set of dreams to give the present
direction and purpose.

Existentialism asks that we reexamine the way in which we live
out our existence within that duration we call the present. Sartre reiterates
that the choice is ours as to how we create consciousness. We can hand
it over to conditioned responses from our past; we can allow feelings,
memories, or habits to impinge upon our present and determine its content
and quality. Similarly, we can allow anxieties about future events to
impinge upon our present and rob it of its spontaneity and intensity. Thus
we can allow our "now" to be deadened.

As a philosophy of time, therefore, existentialism is a way of
reevaluating how we use and abuse consciousness. But more than that,
it contends that we *can* do something about how time is lived. Within
the parameters of our unique personal existence, we can make decisions
as to how we shall live the only thing which, in the final analysis, each
of us actually possesses—namely, consciousness of time–present.

4   *The Inner World: The Fantastic Journey*

19 The creative person, instead of perceiving in predetermined categories ("trees are green," "college education is a good thing," "modern art is silly") is aware of this existential moment as it *is,* and therefore he is alive to many experiences which fall outside the usual categories (in *this* light this tree is lavender; *this* college education is damaging; *this* modern sculpture has a powerful effect on me).

      The creative person is in this way open to his own experiences. It means a lack of rigidity and the permeability of boundaries in concepts, beliefs, perceptions and hypotheses. It means a tolerance of ambiguity where ambiguity exists. It means the ability to receive much conflicting information without forcing closure on the situation.

CARL ROGERS

20 At the end of the spring semester, I packed a few articles and began a four-day trip through the mountains. It was the end of an especially trying school year, and I wanted to make the most of a short vacation before returning to teach summer school.

      The countryside was still green and wildflowers gathered in

nodding communities along the roadside. I drove alone in my small car, and in a small car one can feel very close to things about him. As I drove, or when I stopped to absorb the landscape, I could almost touch the reddish earth, the striated rocks, the weeds and flowers and grasses. I was one among them.

So I travelled. I saw the trees, the flowers, the animals. The broken clouds sometimes painted blue-green patches on the hillsides. I looked up at tall pines and they looked down at me. I smelled pine fragrance and listened to bird calls.

I began to feel alive again. I was *experiencing* things instead of *doing* things. I was feeling and seeing and hearing rather than thinking about . . . and trying to remember . . . and planning ahead.

Or so I thought.

As I watched cloud-shadows shaping their way across the valleys I caught myself deciding if I should reach for my camera. Would they show up just right in color? And was that lightning-split pine silhouetted in black-and-white against the sky "artistic" enough for a picture? I saw purple flowers and found myself wondering if they were lupins, wild larkspurs, or what.

I had the right names for few of the beautiful things I beheld: golden poppies, lavender verbenas, sprays of yellow mustard. Also for the pines (I could remember "ponderosa") and cedars (all I could recall was "juniper"). How little I knew! My new-found ignorance bothered me.

But somewhere—and I don't know when or why—I began to realize what I was doing. I was seeing things just to stuff them into my memory *for later use.* I was building a storehouse of pretty details to impress upon others *after I returned.* The mental habits which dominated my days during the year still controlled my brain. I was organizing the events of my journey as though it were another classroom preparation!

I was insane! Quite literally, I was insane! I was allowing myself to pass my hours out of touch with the realities around me. Here I was in the midst of life, and I wasn't seeing it, wasn't hearing it, wasn't feeling it. Rather than experiencing, I was expending my time *processing* experiences!

I became determined, then, to stop my processing habits. When the next cluster of wildflowers appeared beside the road, I didn't say to myself, as to an audience: "I see a cluster of golden poppies. . . ." Rather, I experienced them—saw them, felt them, moved among them, savored them. I refused to let my mind tag them with names or tie them into bundles.

As I tell it now, I find words sufficient to describe my memory of the undulating flight of the mockingbird and the gliding turn of the swallow. I can recount my memories of the smell of pines and fresh rains.

These are things I can do now. But before my short journey ended, I had proved to myself that I could recover the capacity to experience afresh the world about me. I had succeeded in touching reality again.

JUNE HILLMAN

4-3

FREEDOM/
CHOICE

1   I would like to describe for you a pattern of experience which I have observed, and in which I have participated. . . . It is an experience on which I have placed various labels as I have tried to think about it—becoming a person, freedom to be, courage to be, learning to be free—yet the experience is something broader than, and deeper than, any of its labels. It is quite possible that the words I use in regard to it may miscommunicate. The speculations and ideas I present, based on this experience, may be erroneous, or partly erroneous. But the experience itself *exists*. It is a deeply compelling phenomenon for any one who has observed it, or who has lived it.

CARL ROGERS

2   But does the experience of freedom, in fact, exist? Or does the *feeling* of freedom mask an illusion?

In one experiment with hypnosis, a man was led into a deep trance and given a simple posthypnotic suggestion. About a month from that date, he was told, after lunch on a certain day, he would sing "America the Beautiful." During the next week following this first suggestion, it was reinforced twice during similar deep trances. But at no time was the man informed that any posthypnotic instructions had been given.

When the day for singing arrived, he recalls having the feeling in the morning that he wanted to sing; he did in fact hum or sing a few bars of various tunes. As noontime neared, the impulse to sing unexplainably grew stronger.

Immediately after lunch, he sauntered over to the piano, let his

If a man referred to his brother or to his cat as "an ingenious mechanism," we should know that he was either a fool or a physiologist. No one in practice treats himself or his fellow-man or his pet animals as machines; but scientists who have never made a study of Speculative Philosophy seem often to think it their duty to hold in theory what no one outside a lunatic asylum would accept in practice.

C. D. BROAD

fingers move over the keyboard, and then, on schedule, proceeded to sing "America the Beautiful."

This sort of experiment is common enough in hypnosis. The significant point has to do with *cause:* What *caused* him to sing this specific song at this appointed time. He *felt* free. He felt that it was a *choice* that he had made, and that he could have made other choices. But paradoxically, he also *felt* determined. The impulse to sing the song grew to such proportions that it was difficult or impossible *not* to act it out.

3   This dramatic experiment symbolizes one of our deepest human dilemmas. On the one hand, we feel free; our social lives are founded on the assumption that we and others make genuine choices and should be responsible for them. We blame others for mistakes (that is, they were free *not* to have made them), and we feel guilt at our own mistakes (that is, we ourselves could, and should, have acted differently).

On the other hand, we feel determined. As Saint Paul eloquently put it, "I do not understand what I am doing, for I do not do what I want to do; I do the things that I hate. . . . I do not do the good things that I want to do; I do the wrong things that I do not want to do. But if I do the things that I do not want to do, it is not I that am acting. . . ." Paul's lament rises to a painful crescendo: "What a wretched human being I am!"

Based on experience, we are forced into the conclusion that there are capricious causal forces inside us, directing us to do countless acts against our wills. It was only natural that premodern man interpreted these forces as good/evil spirits thrashing around inside him—"possessing" him—and acting as causal agents behind the thoughts, feelings, and actions over which he felt little control. Today we can better account for the causes of our behavior in empirical terms—in terms of conditioning or with physiological or chemical explanations. Still, the result is the same: we have a dual experience of both freedom and determinism. Both experiences *feel* authentic, and we have never quite understood how to reconcile the apparent contradiction.

4   Western Christian theology has symbolized this experiential dilemma with remarkable accuracy. There is abundant biblical support for two basic beliefs: (1) God is omnipotent and he therefore determines every event in our lives; (2) Man possesses free will and is therefore responsible for his sins; he can justly be condemned to hell for wrong decisions.

In their extreme forms, these two doctrines are logically contradictory; they can't both be true. But Western theology had no alternative but to accept both as absolutely true; they were both given (hence, not debatable) by biblical authority and ecclesiastical tradition. For almost two

SAINT THOMAS AQUINAS: THE PARADOX OF DETERMINISM

Man is predestined . . .

It is fitting that God should predestine men. For all things are subject to His Providence. . . . As men are ordained to eternal life through the Providence of God, it likewise is part of that Providence to permit some to fall away from that end; this is called reprobation. . . . As predestination includes the will to confer grace and glory, so also reprobation includes the will to permit a person to fall into sin, and so impose the punishment of damnation on account of that sin.

Summa Theologica, I, 23, 1, 3
Summa contra Gentiles, III, 163

Man is free . . .

Man has free choice, or otherwise counsels, exhortations, commands, prohibitions, rewards and punishments would be in vain.

If the will were deprived of freedom . . . no praise would be given to human virtue; since virtue would be of no account if man acted not freely: there would be no justice in rewarding or punishing, if man were not free in acting well or ill: and there would be no prudence in taking advice, which would be of no use if things occurred of necessity . . .

Summa Theologica, I, 83, 1
Summa contra Gentiles, III, 73

Can man be both predestined and free?

The predestined must necessarily be saved, yet by a conditional necessity, which does not do away with the liberty of choice. . . .

Man's turning to God is by free choice; and thus man is bidden to turn himself to God. But free choice can be turned to God only when God turns it. . . . It is the part of man to prepare his soul, since he does this by his free choice. And yet he does not do this without the help of God moving him. . . . And thus even the good movement of free choice, whereby anyone is prepared for receiving the gift of grace, is an act of free choice moved by God. . . . Man's preparation for grace is from God, as mover, and from free choice, as moved.

Summa Theologica, I, 23, 3; I–II, 109, 6; I–II, 112, 2, 3.

We are forced to fall back on fatalism as an explanation of irrational events, that is to say, of events the rationality of which we do not understand.

TOLSTOY

thousand years now, Christian theologians have wrestled valiantly with these two doctrines, trying to harmonize them so that men could believe both and maintain their intellectual honesty. No two theologians have resolved the problem in exactly the same way—in fact no solution is wholly free of logical difficulties—but there are several general approaches toward a solution. If either doctrine is softened, then they can be reconciled. If God does not predetermine every event of our lives, then we can claim to have some free will; or, if we admit that we are not wholly free, then some predestination can be accepted.

Whatever the solution, however, the striking point is that the theological formulation is an accurate doctrinization of the very real human dilemma. We are *both* determined *and* free; and somehow we must work at the contradiction until we achieve a realistic understanding of how both can be true.

5 Without prejudging at this point the relative degrees of human freedom and determinism which we experience, we can speak meaningfully of the limiting factors which diminish our freedom. The point to note is that we confuse primal limitations with secondary limitations: it follows that we also confuse primal freedoms with secondary freedoms. Distinguishing between them is crucial.

Primal freedom is inner freedom, and primal limitations come from within. These limitations may be genetic (sickle-cell anemia, thalidomide deformities), physiological (paralysis from polio or accident), ontological° (fear of death and nonbeing), or conditioned (inability to trust or love). Such limitations are causal; they inhibit us from thinking, feeling, or doing specific things; and as causes, they arise from inside our own psychophysiological organism. Primal freedom, therefore, is freedom *from* such limitations: from conflicts and frustrations, unfounded fears, nail-biting anxieties, lingering hatreds, debilitating habits, and life-negating bitterness. Primal freedom is freedom *for* the full utilization of our abilities, the freedom for each person—considering all the givens of his own unique existence—to be all that he can be.

Primal limitations burden us all. We may want to enjoy a day at the beach but find, while there, that we are reliving the emotional battles of the day; and try as we will, we can only act at having fun. Or we try to concentrate on reading a book, but in vain, because relentless worries intrude and disturb our will-to-thought. And how often do we undertake a task, knowing full well we have the capabilities to accomplish it, only to find that primal limitations—fears of inadequacy, fears of others' opinions, even fear of success itself—keep us from attaining our goal? Freedom from all these inner limitations is primal freedom.

By contrast, *secondary limitations* originate in our environment. Therefore, we can speak of secondary freedoms as freedom from external limitations. Secondary limitations are placed upon us by nature itself (we

°*Ontological.* An inherent and inescapable aspect of our being. *Ontology* is the branch of philosophy which delves into the nature of being. See glossary.

There is no doubt that Sartre finds it impossible to make a distinction between freedom and free acts. The free man is not distinguished by his beliefs, but by the quality of his actions.

NORMAN N. GREENE

4   The Inner World: The Fantastic Journey

can't move backward in time), and by other persons and by our society. We are limited by the customs, common-sense traditions, sociological structures, moral suasions, and civil laws of the society in which we live. We are also limited by the immediate needs and desires of other people. Such secondary limiters impose upon us injunctions *not* to think, feel, and do specific things.

6   We cause ourselves endless troubles by confusing primal freedom with various secondary freedoms. We often think we are being subjected to external limitations when in fact we are suffering from inner restraints, and vice versa. Primal limitations are undoubtedly more difficult for us to admit and face; recognition of them presupposes some degree of self-knowledge, the ability to empathize with others, and some capacity for abstract thinking. Since secondary limitations appear more concrete, and since we share them with others and can deal with them collectively ("Fight Gun Control," "Legalize Marijuana"), we often expend great amounts of energy in crusades against particular "encroachments upon our freedoms."

   We may never realize that such crusades are in fact a struggle against primal limitations. We may accuse others of not liking us when the source of our agony is that we don't like ourselves. We may accuse others of conspiring to harm us when our problem is that we never developed the capacity to trust. In such cases, our desire for freedom is authentic, but we have mislocated the source of the limitation.

   This is why it is common for us to spend our lives fighting for causes, only to find later that (to parody a cliché) the causes were won but our freedoms were lost. We may indeed achieve specific freedoms ("The bill finally passed!"), only to find that we are bound with the same primal fetters as before. We do not *experience* an increase of freedom. But having a row of (secondary) freedom awards to point to, we can't quite understand why we don't experience more freedom.

   Other things being equal, the greater one's experience of primal freedom, the less he is concerned with secondary freedoms; and conversely, those who are deeply driven to crusade for secondary freedoms are often suffering from excruciating primal limitations.

7   Few philosophical problems have greater practical implications than the question of freedom versus determinism.

   For one thing, if there is no freedom, then there can be no moral, legal, or any other kind of responsibility. Yet the fact of personal responsibility is one of our most cherished assumptions. We blame others for their mistakes and give them credit for their achievements. We hold ourselves responsible and feel guilt for our misdoings. We indict alleged lawbreakers, hold trials, and convict or free them. We operate on the assumption that human beings can be morally and legally respon-

This is one of man's oldest riddles. How can the independence of human volition be harmonized with the fact that we are integral parts of a universe which is subject to the rigid order of Nature's laws?
SIR ARTHUR EDDINGTON

One's ability to move his hand at will is more directly and certainly known than are Newton's laws. If these laws deny one's ability to move his hand at will, the preferable conclusion is that Newton's laws require modification.
ARTHUR COMPTON

sible—that is, free. But if our assumption of freedom is false, then life as we live it is a cruel joke founded upon a tragic illusion. We are playing the game all wrong.

Secondly, we struggle from day to day and year to year, in desperation or joy, and always with hope, to attain our life-goals. But if we are not free, then all our striving is meaningless. We only think we set our own goals whereas in fact they are set for us; and whether or not we attain them is apparently already determined, or at least out of our hands. Life itself, as struggle, is an illusion.

Thirdly, and most deeply, the question of freedom has to do with what we are—or aren't. What can life mean if we have no freedom to make choices, choose lifestyles, set goals? Since we labor under the deepest conviction that, to some extent at least, we are free, then existence itself is a hoax. We think we're free, feel like we're free, act like we're free; we treat ourselves and others as though we were free; we develop monumental moral and legal systems based upon the assumption that we're free—all this fantasized by blind puppets dangling helplessly on black nylon strings?

We are not what we think we are; life is not what we think it is; the rules of the game are not what we thought. In fact, we discover that we're not playing the game at all: *we are the chessmen and something or someone else is playing the game.*

8   For almost fifteen years, Dr. Bruno Bettelheim has followed the case of Joey—"the mechanical boy." Joey's loss of freedom was clearly psychogenic rather than genetic or physiological. From birth he had been almost completely ignored; to his mother he hardly existed. Since all that he was as a budding human was bothersome and unacceptable, he quickly got the message; his humanness must be eliminated—repressed. So Joey literally became a machine. He acquainted himself very early with machines and could dismantle and reassemble them with some skill. He also envied the machines and identified with them; they were liked, used, toyed with; they gave no trouble, were never punished. Gradually he came to think of himself as a machine.

Before he could eat, for instance, he would unroll his imaginary cord and plug it into the outlet, set his switches, and check his bulbs. He could perform routine actions only after he had monitored his circuits, checked his dials, flipped the right switches. He made sure his machine-self was working properly.

All this was more than merely a game of playing like a machine; this "game" was deadly serious. He was playing the machine-game to escape the unbearable anguish of further rejection of any of his human qualities.

Bettelheim noted that "Joey's pathological behavior seemed the external expression of an overwhelming effort to remain almost nonexistent as a person." Joey had created a world of his own that he could live in, a world that was preferable to the hostile real world. In his fantasy-world he had found a way of life which was at least tolerable. Since he did not need to be human, his human qualities atrophied; more and more Joey *became* a machine.

Machines are not free. Indeed, the word doesn't apply. Machines operate on principles of cause and effect—total determinism. Joey "the mechanical boy" knew no freedom.

9　One of the strongest contemporary cases for determinism has been made by a psychologist-novelist who recently—in *Beyond Freedom and Dignity*—has become a philosopher: Dr. B. F. Skinner of Harvard.

According to Skinner's way of thinking, freedom is a myth, and a dangerous myth because we have invested the myth and its symbol ("freedom") with something close to sacred qualities. It is a fact that many of those who think they disagree with Skinner are eager to make his observations the object of religious and patriotic causes.°

Freedom, Skinner argues, is not a fact of human experience. *All* of our responses—the impulses that lie behind so-called free choices—are the result of unique past contingencies of conditioning and reinforcement that have shaped us into what we are. Skinner's famed laboratory experiments with pigeons and rats have shown that animal behavior can be predicted and controlled, and even produced according to specification. By selecting specific causes (stimuli), desired effects (responses) will result. This is merely the application to the field of animal behavior the scientific assumption of causality. The assumption that every cause produces an effect and every effect is preceded by a cause is the foundation of all science. Whatever made us think that it would *not* apply to the behavioral sciences as well as to the natural sciences?

What we *call* freedom is merely the successful avoidance on the part of any organism of some aversive feature in its environment. All organisms are manipulated and controlled, therefore, by the dynamic features of their environments.

To be sure, when Skinner writes that freedom is an illusion, he is not denying our experience of a rather pleasant *emotion* which we commonly call freedom; but he is saying unequivocally that this emotion is itself a *conditioned* (caused) response. We may label this feeling "freedom" or something else; but whatever we call it, it has been produced by past experience; it was conditioned into us at some prior time and now becomes, in turn, the causal agent of present behavior.

10　Among the illustrations used by Skinner are the accounts of the falling leaf and the buzzing fly.

Picture a leaf, yellowed from the first frosts, fluttering and suddenly beginning to fall from the top of a tall, red-gold maple tree. In

Give me a dozen healthy infants and I'll guarantee to take any one at random and train him to become any type of specialist I might select—doctor, lawyer, even beggarman and thief, regardless of his talents, penchants, tendencies, abilities.

JOHN B. WATSON (1925)

°Skinner's book was still warm from the press when one congressman, in a speech before the House, denounced him for "advancing ideas which threaten the future of our system of government by denigrating the American traditions of individualism, human dignity and self-reliance." As is so often the case, further comments revealed a fundamental misunderstanding of what Skinner is saying.

zigzag motions, hovering on the currents of air, it picks a poetic path downward and settles eventually upon a cushion of leaves on the ground.

Now, there isn't a physicist alive who would argue that the leaf is "free." We esthetic onlookers may be mesmerized by the leaf's timeless descent, and even envy the "freedom" of the floating maple leaf wafting to earth. But we have confused our poetic idealism with our physics. The fact is that the leaf follows precisely known laws of physics, laws which can easily be found in any physics textbook.

Yet as the leaf starts its historic fall from the top of the maple tree, what physicist, by applying his formulas, could predict the leaf's trajectory or the spot where it will finally come to rest? The journey is too complex; there are too many variables: air currents, atmospheric density (in terms of elevation above sea level and barometric pressure), humidity, minute photon forces, the mass and volume of the leaf, its configuration, and so on. The number of possible combinations of variables is so great that, although knowing all the applicable laws, predicting the leaf's path or destination is a feat quite beyond the ability of any physicist (or computer) alive today.

So, is the leaf "free" in any proper sense of the word? Not at all. It follows inexorable causal laws.

11   Elsewhere, Skinner ponders a housefly buzzing around a room. In describing the motions of the maple leaf, we were applying physical laws to a passive object. The trajectory of the buzzing fly is infinitely more complex since we are dealing with the active nervous system of a living thing. Our causal factors, to some extent, become internal.

If man has once become aware that in his forlornness he imposes values, he can no longer want but one thing, and that is freedom, as the basis of all values. That doesn't mean that he wants it in the abstract. It means simply that the ultimate meaning of the acts of honest men is the quest for freedom as such.

JEAN-PAUL SARTRE

PUPPET THEATER?

We see the puppets dancing on their miniature stage, moving up and down as the strings pull them around, following the prescribed course of their various little parts. We learn to understand the logic of this theater and we find ourselves in its motions. We locate ourselves in society and thus recognize our own position as we hang from its subtle strings. For a moment we see ourselves as puppets indeed. But then we grasp a decisive difference between the puppet theater and our own drama. Unlike the puppets, we have the possibility of stopping in our movements, looking up and perceiving the machinery by which we have been moved. In this act lies the first step towards freedom.

PETER L. BERGER
Invitation to Sociology

If we knew *everything* about the buzzing fly—its previous conditioning, its present chemical states, its "needs," "drives," "goals," or whatever, and all the aerodynamics of a fly's flight—then, according to Skinner, we could predict exactly where the fly will buzz, where it will land, what it will eat, and so on.

But we are facing the same paradox with the fly as with the leaf. We might feel that the fly is free as it flies about; it looks free; it even seems to make choices. But such freedom is myth, Skinner contends. There is no more freedom in any buzz of the fly than there was in any flutter of the leaf. Every motion could be predicted if the causal forces were precisely known. More simply, all matter-in-motion obeys the laws of physics, and a fly is matter-in-motion.

These same principles apply to human action, and our complexity, apparently, is no argument against determinism, since the same causal laws apply in every case. Our behavior is more complex than the fly's, just as the fly's behavior is more complex than the leaf's. But freedom is just as much a fallacy for us as it is for the leaf or fly.

12   Rogers says freedom exists. Skinner says it doesn't. Rogers records the following brief exchange between them at a conference at which Skinner had read a paper.

> From what I understood Dr. Skinner to say, it is his understanding that though he might have thought *he chose* to come to this meeting, might have thought he had a purpose in giving this speech, such thoughts are really illusory. He actually made certain marks on paper and emitted certain sounds here simply because his genetic makeup and his past environment had operantly conditioned his behavior in such a way that it was rewarding to make these sounds, and that he as a person doesn't enter into this. In fact if I get his thinking correctly, from his strictly scientific point of view, he, as a person, doesn't exist.

In his reply to Rogers, "Dr. Skinner said that he would not go into the question of whether he had any choice in the matter (presumably because the whole issue is illusory) but stated, 'I do accept your characterization of my own presence here.'"

13   Human freedom has been stoutly defended by a distinguished line of thinkers in various traditions, East and West. No voice in its defense has been more persuasive than that of the existentialist philosopher Jean-Paul Sartre, whose vehement pronouncements for freedom arise from his own intense experience of human struggle during the Nazi occupation of France in World War II.

The fashionable notion that we are predetermined in our behavior by past experiences—by "operant conditioning"—to the point of losing our free will—this, for Sartre, is an outrageous fallacy. On the contrary,

Existentialism's first move is to make every man aware of what he is and to make the full responsibility of his existence rest on him.

JEAN-PAUL SARTRE

man is not merely responsible for what he does, but he is even responsible for all that he is.

Sartre is convinced that there is no determinism of any kind. *Nothing* tells me what to do. I myself decide. I cannot blame God, or others, or my past environment. I am—now—what I make myself to be. I have to accept the consequences of my own freedom, take the responsibility for my decisions and face the consequences thereof. For human freedom, as Sartre sees it, is not always a blessing; it is more often a tragedy. Whether we like it or not, man is *condemned to be free.*

But why does Sartre speak of our being "condemned" to freedom? Why such a gloomy term? Shouldn't freedom be a joyous thing? Sartre's position is that freedom carries with it an unavoidable anguish when we fully realize how overwhelming the implications of our freedom can be. It entails tragic choices with formidable consequences. Out of our freedom we do not make decisions for ourselves alone, but for others, and sometimes for all mankind. To realize completely what this means can be a nightmarish insight into the very nature of human existence.

To be free means to be caught in a paradox. We are forever dissatisfied with existence as we know it. But to live means to dream a million dreams and forge ahead to catch the fullness of our being. Indeed, each mortal man wants to be God, but the truer fact is that we are finite and our limitations are crushing. Still, they are unacceptable. So we continue to compete and strive, dreaming our dreams, even though they are futile dreams, and even though we know it.

Why? Why do we do all this? Simply because we cannot do otherwise. For to exist is to be free, and to be free is to act, to take initiative, to make choices and decisions, to dream impossible dreams—however unreachable they are—and to fail. In a word, we *must try to do* what we already know we *cannot* do.

14 Sartre is attempting to get us to see that we exist in an antinomian world without guidelines. Cultural norms are relative, and societies are humorlessly absurd. There is no God and therefore no absolute mandates to give life order. There is no meaning to human life as such. Nor is there any past conditioning which we can blame for making us what we are. There is not even a "human nature" which might help us to define ourselves.

There is nothing to help us—because the moment we become conscious of what we are, then we become responsible for everything we are and do. Of course, we can join the mob and let our passions collectively carry us along, but *we make the decision* to do so, and we are responsible for that decision. We can conform to society's whims, or follow an irrelevant, legalistic ethical code, or accede to peer pressures; but in each instance *we make the decision* to do so, and we must accept the responsibility for that decision.

What is an obstacle for me may not be so for another. There is no obstacle in an absolute sense. . . . Human-reality everywhere encounters resistance and obstacles which it has not created, but these resistances and obstacles have meaning only in and through the free choice which human-reality is.

JEAN-PAUL SARTRE

4 The Inner World: The Fantastic Journey

Whenever we are conscious, therefore, we are responsible. For at the cutting edge of consciousness, we are truly free. At each moment of the living present, we have an infinite number of choices before us, ways of thinking, feeling, and behaving—the options are numberless, so many that to feel them fully is to become overwhelmed by them. It's at this moment of revelation that we frequently retreat into the myths of determinism. We convince ourselves that we move within carefully defined and unbreakable limits, and that we are not really free. Yet, from behind our safe parameters we will *claim* to be free. We are "not supposed" to think, feel, or do certain things, or so we are told by society, church, friends, laws, conscience. But all these excuses are retreats from freedom; and the true fact is that we can do all of them. But since experience of such freedom is fraught with fear, we eagerly accept all the fashionable limitations.

15   Jean-Paul Sartre penned a now-famous passage about the experiences of the French Resistance movement against the Nazis in France.

> We were never more free than during the German occupation. We had lost all our rights, beginning with the right to talk. Every day we were insulted to our faces and had to take it in silence. Under one pretext or another, as workers, Jews, or political prisoners, we were deported *en masse.* Everywhere, on billboards, in the newspapers, on the screen, we encountered the revolting and insipid picture of ourselves that our suppressors wanted us to accept. And because of all this we were free. Because the Nazi venom seeped into our thoughts, every accurate thought was a conquest. Because an all-powerful police tried to force us to hold our tongues, every word took on the value of a declaration of principles. Because we were hunted down, every one of our gestures had the weight of a solemn commitment. . . .
>
> Exile, captivity, and especially death (which we usually shrink from facing at all in happier days) became for us the habitual objects of our concern. We learned that they were neither inevitable accidents, nor even constant and inevitable dangers, but they must be considered as our lot itself, our destiny, the profound source of our reality as men. At every instant we lived up to the full sense of this commonplace little phrase: "Man is mortal!" And the choice that each of us made of his life was an authentic choice because it was made face to face with death, because it could always have been expressed in these terms: "Rather death than . . ." And here I am not speaking of the elite among us who were real Resistants, but of all Frenchmen who, at every hour of the night and day throughout four years, answered *No.*

16   The essential freedom, the ultimate and final freedom that cannot be taken from a man, is to say No. This is the basic premise in Sartre's view of human freedom: freedom is in its very essence negative, though this negativity is also creative. At a certain moment, perhaps, the drug or the pain

Let [the child] believe that he is always in control, though it is always you [the teacher] who really controls. There is no subjugation so perfect as that which keeps the appearance of freedom, for in that way one captures volition itself. . . .

ROUSSEAU

inflicted by the torturer may make the victim lose consciousness, and he will confess. But so long as he retains the lucidity of consciousness, however tiny the area of action possible for him, he can still say in his own mind: No. Consciousness and freedom are thus given together. Only if consciousness is blotted out can man be deprived of this residual freedom. Where all the avenues of action are blocked for a man, this freedom may seem a tiny and unimportant thing; but it is in fact total and absolute, and Sartre is right to insist upon it as such, for it affords man his final dignity, that of being man.

WILLIAM BARRETT

4-4

SANITY/REALITY

1   Once there ruled in the distant city of Wirani a king who was both mighty and wise. And he was feared for his might and loved for his wisdom.

Now, in the heart of that city was a well, whose water was cool and crystalline, from which all the inhabitants drank, even the king and his courtiers; for there was no other well.

One night when all were asleep, a witch entered the city, and poured seven drops of strange liquid into the well, and said, "From this hour he who drinks this water shall become mad."

Next morning all the inhabitants, save the king and his lord chamberlain, drank from the well and became mad, even as the witch had foretold.

And during that day the people in the narrow streets and in the market places did naught but whisper to one another, "The king is mad. Our king and his lord chamberlain have lost their reason. Surely we cannot be ruled by a mad king. We must dethrone him."

That evening the king ordered a golden goblet to be filled from the well. And when it was brought to him he drank deeply, and gave it to his lord chamberlain to drink.

And there was great rejoicing in that distant city of Wirani, because its king and its lord chamberlain had regained their reason.

KAHLIL GIBRAN

The usual distinction between sanity and insanity is a false one. We are all insane; the difference between Napoleon and a madman who believes he is Napoleon is a difference in degree, not in kind; both are acting on a limited set of assumptions.

COLIN WILSON

2   There are several reasons why the question of the nature of sanity/insanity could become a major issue in the near future:

1. Political use of psychopathological labels may be frequently used to silence critics and remove nonconformists from the action scene. Those so charged may not be insane by any meaningful definition of the term, but name calling with scientific-sounding diagnoses could continue to accomplish partisan or totalitarian ends.

Men in masses are gripped by personal troubles, but they are not aware of their true meaning and source.

C. WRIGHT MILLS

2. In the light of our growing understanding of various modes of consciousness, mind-states heretofore considered "sane" and "insane" should be revaluated. It could be that some forms of consciousness labeled "insane" may not be so; and some states of mind considered "sane" (and hence "normal") might be better classified as forms of "insanity."

3. Many psychotherapists are presently taking a second look at the function of "insanity" processes. It has long been held by some theorists that psychoses should be thought of as healing processes taking place along with, or subsequent to, the disintegrating processes. To attempt to change psychotic behavior, they say, is merely symptom relief which doesn't touch the root-causes of the malady. If given a chance, or treated effectively, the psyche can reestablish, on its own terms, a "sane" mode of consciousness.

4. From a philosophical standpoint, the most significant question has to do with the nature of reality. Any meaningful definitions of "sane" and "insane" must be developed in relation to what is considered to be "real." But if all we ever know of reality is a mental construct, and if this mental "reality" is not merely a private construct but a social fabric, then any and all psychic states may need redefinition in relation to this "subjective reality."

3   For most of the twentieth century we have viewed mental health as being closely related to accepted behavioral norms. The idea of "normal" has been based on values derived from the culture viewed as a whole, and the bell-shaped curve applied to all BTF-patterns. "Well adjusted" has been a term given to all those individuals who fall within the 68.26% or "average" part of the curve.

Deviation from the norm has been regarded as "abnormal," and psychotherapy has generally concentrated on helping people learn how to function within the boundaries of the "normal"; relatively little attention has been paid to individuals considered to be "successfully adjusted."

Our educational systems have been designed to aid in the acculturation process toward the middle of the curve. Those whose behavior was obviously different soon learned that they were excluded from the privileges of class membership and that they had better "shape up" or face the consequences.

4   Once "normal" and "sane" become synonymous, the door is open to various problems. Henceforth, by definition, the person who is abnormal is also in-sane. Societies are so structured that there is an innate pressure upon the individual to conform to the "norm," the BTF-patterns of the majority. The infinitely varied demands of society are directed against one's designing a life outside the 68.26% of the curve.

Societies always assume the prerogative of demanding a certain amount of conformity, and within limits, of course, this is necessary. "In

Psychoadaptation, or How to Handle Dissenters

Official methods of dealing with dissident intellectuals in the Soviet Union have always been harsh and arbitrary. They are no longer, as in Stalin's day, summarily shot. Now, with the authorities anxious to preserve legal forms, an increasingly common punishment for dissenters is confinement to mental hospitals that are often jails in disguise. Technically, Soviet courts cannot sentence a man to prison or labor camp unless he has violated the criminal code. Health officers, however, can commit anyone to "emergency psychiatric hospitalization" if his behavior is simply deemed abnormal. "Why bother with political trials," a leading Soviet forensic psychiatrist reportedly has said, "when we have psychiatric clinics?"

One Soviet citizen who has suffered such treatment is the prominent geneticist and gerontologist Zhores Medvedev, 46, a leading spokesman for the "loyal opposition" within the Russian intelligentsia. In 1970 he was forced to spend 19 days in a madhouse for a condition diagnosed as "split personality, expressed in the need to combine the scientific work in his field with publicist activities; an overestimation of his own personality; a deterioration in recent years of the quality of his scientific work; an exaggerated attention to detail in his publicist writing; lack of a sense of reality; poor adaptation to the social environment."

Medvedev irritated Soviet authorities when two of his works reached the West. In 1969 the Columbia University Press printed *The Rise and Fall of T. D. Lysenko,* a devastating history of how the crackpot genetic theories of Stalin's pet scientist were established as unassailable dogma until the fall of Khrushchev in 1964.

After that book was published, Medvedev was fired from his job as head of the Obninsk radiological institute, 35 miles southwest of Moscow. Unable to find another job, he set about writing a calm, straightforward survey of the restrictions, censorship, and surveillance that oppress many Soviet intellectuals. This work too found its way to the West via *samizdat* (literally "self-publishing"), the literary underground. It was his authorship of that book, published in the U.S. . . . by St. Martin's Press as *The Medvedev Papers,* which led directly to Medvedev's forced hospitalization in 1970.

Medvedev was released only after his twin brother, Roy, an eminent historian, mobilized a protest by a group of internationally renowned writers and scientists, including Alexander Solzhenitsyn, physicists Andrei Sakharov and Pyotr Kapitsa, and Mstislav Keldysh, president of the Academy of Sciences. In the summer of 1970, in an attempt to hush up the embarrassing affair, the KGB (Soviet secret police) promised the Medvedevs that they would "close the case" and asked for assurances that the brothers would not write about what had happened. Roy Medvedev agreed, on the condition that there be no more "psychiatric blackmail."

Shortly afterward Zhores Medvedev was notified to report for "a routine checkup" at the local psychiatric clinic at Obninsk, where he discovered that he was registered as an outpatient with a record of "incipient schizophrenia" accompanied by "paranoid delusions of reforming society." Since the authorities had broken their part of the bargain, Medvedev wrote an account of his ordeal; Roy added his own diary of the affair. This document was brought

out in Russian . . . by Macmillan, Ltd. of London. An English translation will be published in the U.S. by Alfred A. Knopf . . . under the title *A Question of Madness.*

One of Zhores Medvedev's foremost fears is that the Soviet government may be experimenting with a sinister new form of repression, which he calls "psychoadaptation," as a means of controlling dissent. In *A Question of Madness* he writes:

"Totalitarian centralization of the medical service, while introducing the progressive principle of free health care for all, has also made it possible to use medicine as a means of government control and political regulation. Medical 'dossiers' in clinics and hospitals are available to government officials, and a growing number of institutions and agencies ask for reports about a person's state of health with details of his past medical history and symptoms. Psychiatrists are playing an increasingly important role in all this; they may secretly veto a young person's entry to an academic institution, or a trip abroad—even only as a tourist—or pronounce on his suitability for many categories of employment. The medical record kept in a clinic or outpatient department may cause a man as much trouble as a court conviction or Jewish origin."

The Medvedev book is an articulate, dispassionate argument that such practices violate Soviet legality, and that "the inhumane use of medicine for political purposes" threatens to undermine the ethics of doctors and the morale of patients. "People are beginning to be afraid of psychiatric hospitals, resorting to them only in cases of extreme necessity," writes Zhores. "If things go on like this, it will end with healthy, sane people sitting in madhouses while dangerous mental cases will walk about freely, denied the treatment they need."

A Question of Madness ends with an appeal on behalf of dissidents who are still locked up in prison asylums and in many cases undergoing brutal pseudomedical treatment with debilitating drugs. One dissenter who has fared far worse than Medvedev is the philologist Vladimir Bukovsky, 28. Since 1963 he has suffered a number of what Medvedev calls "psychiatric reprisals" as well as imprisonment for his activities in the Soviet civil rights movement.

Not that Zhores Medvedev is off the hook. Thanks to the intervention of some of the most illustrious members of the Soviet Union's scientific elite, Medvedev was allowed in October 1970 to take a relatively minor job as a senior research fellow in a laboratory at an institute of the Lenin Agricultural Academy near Obninsk. But he was given that job on a probationary basis. As a psychiatric outpatient registered with the local clinic, he is subject to a summons for another "checkup" at any time.

Time, September 27, 1971

Ruth Benedict's book Patterns of Culture *is a well written account of the importance of these cultural differences in the determination of the "normal" personality of three very different peoples, the Pueblo Indians of New Mexico, the Kwakiutls of the Northwest, and the Dobuans of New Guinea. The Pueblos are described as being essentially self-effacing, the Kwakiutls as being concerned with glorification to the point of megalomania, and the Dobuans as being a treacherous, and even murderous, lot.*

JOSEPH ROYCE

this society we don't kill each other; neither do we lie, cheat, or swindle." But in the broadest historical perspective, societies don't limit their enforcement to a few general principles; in practice they have coerced a narrow range of values and beliefs upon all their members.

In previous ages the threatening deviants of a society were labeled "heretics" or "infidels" and racked or staked. In the Dark Ages unusual behavior was thought to be witchcraft or the Devil's work and was often rewarded by the stake, either through the heart or being burned at.

But since our age is psychologically oriented, it works best to find psychopathological labels to separate the conformist from the nonconformist, the "sane" from the "insane." Historically, society's critics have been charged with about everything; to charge them with "insanity" to accomplish this end would be a typical modern method of doing things. Indeed "psychoadaptation" has already been widely practiced in the twentieth century in most advanced countries of the world.

5   What, then, is "sanity?" What is the person like who is genuinely "sane"? And how does the individual who is "insane" behave? Can these words be given clear definition? Is the person who is "insane" fundamentally different from "the rest of us"? And on what criteria can we decide that *we* are "sane" or that *others* are "insane"?

Among field specialists the words "sane" and "insane" have been discarded as ambiguous and useless. Those engaging in careful thought usually speak specifically of the various forms of neuroses and psychoses; or if they need a general term they may refer to "mental or emotional disturbances." The words *insane* and *crazy* have become a part of our smear vocabulary, and their connotations have become intolerable. "War is insane." "Smoking is crazy." Such symbols are used to express emotion and not to communicate ideas.

However, the terms *sane, insane,* and *unsane* will be used here with consistent and specific definition.

6   "Sanity" may be defined as the ability on the part of an individual to enter into an efficient reality-mode of consciousness and to remain there as long as he wishes to or conditions require it.

Let's ponder (and wander) for a moment. If defined this way, then any mind-state other than the reality-mode is not a sane state, and none of the following individuals would be sane: one who is sleeping and dreaming; one who has downed sufficient vodka or smoked cannabis or is under the influence of acid; one engaged in samadhi meditation or dervish ecstasy; one who experiences the orgasmic white light of sexual union; one who momentarily experiences blinding anger or gripping fear.

These and many other experiences occur wholly outside the reality-mode, yet we surely can't label them "insane." Since the problem is merely semantic and we need symbols in order to think and communicate, let's call these mind-states "unsane," and rest the matter there. Most of the modes of consciousness listed above can be positive, life-affirming experiences, and to call them "insane" would imply, by innuendo, what is untrue.

Such unsane modes of consciousness have a common characteristic: the individual is not expected to move effectively in the world of realities—to perform routine activities or make judgments—*while* he is experiencing such mind-states. This is merely pointing out the obvious: a sleeping person is hardly expected to behave rationally; and after four martinis we caution a person not to try to behave as though he were in a reality-mode. In all the above-mentioned unsane states, should realistic activity be suddenly demanded of the individual, others would be forced into making decisions for the person. But despite the fact that the individual cannot be "responsible for his own behavior," we don't label him insane for the simple reason that these are considered to be temporary modes of consciousness, and we expect the individual to return to the reality-mode shortly, at will, or as the martinis wear off.

These unsane modes of consciousness become social problems only if the individual attempts to engage in activities which demand the reality-mode, or if he pretends to be in a reality-mode when he isn't.

It is hard to avoid the conclusion that we are accepting a definition of sanity which is insane, and that as a result our common human problems are so persistently insoluble that they add up to the perennial and universal "predicament of man," which is attributed to nature, to the Devil, or to God himself.

ALAN WATTS

"Escape into reality"

THE UNIVERSAL NEUROSIS OF MANKIND

Thus Freud's first paradox, the existence of a repressed unconscious, necessarily implies the second and even more significant paradox, the universal neurosis of mankind. Here is the *pons asinorum* of psychoanalysis. Neurosis is not an occasional aberration; it is not just in other people; it is in us, and in us all the time. . . . The doctrine of the universal neurosis of mankind is the psychoanalytical analogue of the theological doctrine of original sin. . . .

. . . Man the social animal is by the same token the neurotic animal. Or, as Freud puts it, man's superiority over the other animals is his capacity for neurosis, and his capacity for neurosis is merely the obverse of his capacity for cultural development.

Freud therefore arrives at the same conclusion as Nietzsche. . . . Neurosis is an essential consequence of civilization or culture. . . .

NORMAN O. BROWN
Life Against Death

---

7   This definition of "sanity"—the ability to enter into an efficient reality-mode as desired or needed—contains two significant implications.

First, it implies that the individual has control of his experience so that, when he so wishes, he can enter into the reality-mode; he has maintained control so that he can deliberately make a choice should the situation require it. This does not mean, of course, that he will not enjoy a martini or practice samadhi; but these temporary states he would enter only when he is fairly sure that the reality-mode will not be expected of him.

It is interesting to note that some psychoses may be related to conditions in body chemistry. If this is the case, such states would not differ *in kind* from the body-states chemically induced by alcohol or acid. In all such cases, a chemical condition underlies a particular mode of consciousness. The crucial difference, however, is obvious: in the former cases the chemical condition is not within our control and is long-acting; in the latter, the chemical conditions are under control and are short-term alterations.

8   The second implication of this definition of "sanity" is that the individual has the ability to construct efficient concepts of the real world. The only way of knowing reality is by means of representations we construct in our minds, and the "genuinely sane individual" has the ability to construct highly efficient concepts. He will be able to construct workable ideas about matter-in-motion (distances, relationships, speeds, etc.); he will be able to make functional value-judgments about the importance of specific objects/events; he will be able to infer with some degree of accuracy the experience of other people by observing their behavior; and he will be able to interpret symbols meaningfully in the immediate context in which he experiences them. These and other functions are necessary for survival. Quite simply, an "insane" person—that is, one who cannot perform these reality functions—has little chance of surviving on his own.

9   It's simple enough to define "sanity" as the ability to conceptualize reality efficiently, but the problem can become stubborn when we press for further clarity about "reality."

We have defined "reality" before as the sum of everything that exists apart from our perception; but this definition is useless when attempting to understand sanity/insanity, since we saw that we cannot know reality as such. The only "reality" we know is a mentally manufactured system of pragmatic constructs about the real world.

In a book entitled *The Social Construction of Reality,* Berger and Luckmann show that "reality" must be thought of, not merely as an individual construct, but as a social construct produced collectively by the members of the same culture. It is a fabric woven from objects/events which have been valued, selected, conceptualized, and articulated by the group. We are individually acculturated into a society and into *its* reality.

Therefore, when each of us "constructs reality" we create it not merely by following ontological processes of the mind, but also according to the guidelines of society. Such realities will differ from one society to another. These are the various world-views (see Chapter 2-1), each equally workable in the society in which it is held.

Paranoid thinking is characterized by the fact that it can be completely logical, yet lack any guidance by concern of concrete inquiry into reality; in other words, logic does not exclude madness.

ERICH FROMM

10   A psychiatrist trying to diagnose an individual whose psychological status is in doubt asks him questions to determine the degree of his "reality-orientedness." This is quite logical; from a psychiatric viewpoint there is obviously something problematic about an individual who does not know what day of the week it is or who readily admits he has talked with departed spirits. Indeed, the term "reality-oriented" itself can be useful in such a context. The sociologist, however, has to ask the additional question, "*Which* reality?" Incidentally, this addition is not irrelevant psychiatrically. The psychiatrist will certainly take it into account, when an individual does not know the day of the week, if he has just arrived by jet plane from another continent. He may not know the day of the week simply because he is still "on another time"—Calcutta time, say, instead of Eastern Standard Time. If the psychiatrist has any sensitivity to the sociocultural context of psychological conditions he will also arrive

Insanity in individuals is something rare—but in groups, parties, nations, and epochs, it is the rule.

NIETZSCHE

at different diagnoses of the individual who converses with the dead, depending on whether such an individual comes from, say, New York City or from rural Haiti. The individual could be "on another reality" in the same socially objective sense that the previous one was "on another time." In other words, questions of psychological status cannot be decided without recognizing the reality-definitions that are taken for granted in the social situation of the individual. To put it more sharply, *psychological status is relative to the social definitions of reality in general and is itself socially defined.*

BERGER AND LUCKMANN

However romantic it seemed to be a beachcomber, I learned I had to get back to the neurotic society I need in order to function.

ALBERT FINNEY

At present, the gap between the sane man and the maniac is very small indeed. As William James rightly understood, the "hour" can strike for any of us. Remove a few of the walls of illusion, and the sane man becomes insane.

COLIN WILSON

11 Schizophrenia, like any other psychotic state, must be defined not only in psychiatric terms but also in social terms. Schizophrenic experience *beyond* a certain threshold would be considered a sickness in any society, since those suffering from it would be unable to function under any social circumstances (unless the schizophrenic is elevated into the status of a god, shaman, saint, priest, etc.). But there are low-grade chronic forms of psychoses which can be shared by millions of people and which—precisely because they do not go beyond a certain threshold—do not prevent these people from functioning socially. As long as they share their sickness with millions of others, they have the satisfactory feeling of not being alone; in other words, they avoid that sense of complete isolation which is so characteristic of full-fledged psychosis. On the contrary, they look at themselves as normal and at those who have not lost the link between heart and mind as being "crazy." In all low-grade forms of psychoses, the definition of sickness depends on the question as to whether the pathology is shared or not. Just as there is low-grade chronic schizophrenia, so there exist also low-grade chronic paranoia and depression. And there is plenty of evidence that among certain strata of the population, particularly on occasions where a war threatens, the paranoid elements increase but are not felt as pathological as long as they are common.

ERICH FROMM

12 There are occasional philosophers and psychologists who, on their gloomier days, would suggest that insanity is ontological. The psychologist might prefer to say it is endemic to the human species. In any case, they mean that insanity—"misreading reality"—is somehow built into the very structure of human experience. In most of us these "misreading" patterns are relatively weak, but these are the same patterns of experience which, during times of trouble, can be escalated into full-fledged psychoses.

Advocates of this point of view are saying that *all of us* are slightly insane *all the time;* and that we are all potentially more insane if tragic conditions should drive our present incipient states into full-scale conflict.

The age-old belief that those who are classified "insane" are somehow different in kind from the rest of us is a myth that has had its day. "The insane," as someone put it, "are just like us in every way—only more so."

4 The Inner World: The Fantastic Journey

KRENWINKEL SAYS SHE HAD "KILLED MYSELF"

LOS ANGELES (UPI)—Patricia Krenwinkel said Friday she was willing to face her own death because she already had "killed myself" the night she fatally stabbed coffee heiress Abigail Folger.

The dark-haired Miss Krenwinkel put on an eerie display of the power Charles Manson wields over her as she sat in the witness stand at the Tate trial going over in a monotone two nights of murder for which she said she felt no sorrow.

Manson, sitting at the counsel table, suddenly raised his left arm and pointed his index finger straight upwards toward the ceiling.

The 23-year-old defendant stared at him, halting her testimony. Then slowly, seemingly almost against her will, she raised her left arm and index finger in the same gesture, occasionally letting it fall to her head and then raising it again.

Also at the counsel table, Susan Atkins and Leslie Van Houten pointed upward in a similar gesture. Manson kept his arm extended for 35 straight minutes before dropping it at a recess and the girls copied him, occasionally lowering their arms when the strain became too much.

The "Manson Family" followers have told the jury the 36-year-old ex-convict never gave them orders or influenced them to commit murders, but their zombie-like action spoke for itself.

Defense lawyer Irving Kanarek asked Miss Krenwinkel if there was some reason she felt no remorse.

"I am satisfied with myself," she said. "I am willing to face my own death because that night [in the Tate home] was my death. I killed myself. I know that everything that was done was done."

"What do you mean by saying you killed yourself?" Kanarek asked.

"To kill someone is to kill yourself. We are all one. We all run on the same thoughts, God's thoughts."

"It's you who voted for Nixon that are killing every young boy you send to Vietnam . . . Children stand starving on the streets and you go to the moon."

Kanarek asked her about taking LSD more than 100 times.

"I have taken so much acid [LSD] that I am acid," she said. "I've never come down. It opens you up to what you are and then you are that."

Kanarek asked her why she used her knife on Miss Folger.

"I don't understand what reason is. Everything is done because it is done. I don't know the why, wherefore or reason for anything. It just was."

4-5

SYMBOLS/
COMMUNICATION

"When I *use a word,"*
Humpty-Dumpty said in a rather
scornful tone, "it means just what
I choose it to mean—neither more
nor less."

"The question is," said Alice,
"whether you can *make words*
mean different things."

"The question is," said
Humpty-Dumpty, "which is to be
master—that's all!"

LEWIS CARROLL

1 —Lift envelope gently from package do not use force—indicate choice with a cross (✕) or check (✓) mark—make check or money order payable to the Book-of-the-Month Club—do not write in this space—do not moisten envelope—place stamp here—list checks separately—remove carbon and tear on dotted line—

"Dear, why sit at your desk all day? Why don't you go for a drive in the country?"

—See inside you may have won $200 a month for life—pull tab—do not throw away, see valuable coupons inside—

"O.K. I will. See you later."

—Keep off the grass—beware of the dog—drive carefully—children at play—begin construction—wait for flag—slow—form one lane—caution, men at work—end construction—resume safe speed—

—Yield—one way do not enter—enter here–caution, merging traffic—do not pass on right—quiet, hospital zone—impeach Earl Warren—support the college of your choice—be safe in the arms of the Lord—fight inflation—fight communism—fight cancer—fight fear—love one another—use indicator signals when changing lanes—get more satisfying flavor with nifty, thrifty First for Thirst—

—Slow—pay toll ahead—keep left for exact change lane—if coins miss basket stay in your car, sound horn and wait for attendant—fasten seat belts—go to church Sunday—win with Wallace—fly now, pay later—resolve to save—vote for Grabowski—spend a pleasant night at Ziggy's Motel, magic fingers, ezee rest mattresses, adjoining restaurant and color TV—vote Row A all the way—support our boys in Vietnam—turn back you just passed Ziggy's—. . .

—Think—post no bills—commit no nuisance—stay on Route 50, topless ahead (after 8 p.m.)—vote as you please but vote—learn to fly—keep awake—take Sominex and sleep, sleep, sleep—give her an emerald—think Florida—

—Exit—begin construction—wait for flag—form one lane—caution, men at work—drive carefully, children at play—resume safe speed—beware of the dog—keep off the grass—leave messages here—

"Hello, dear, have a nice drive?"

CHARLES J. MC DERMOTT

2   One wonders whether the invention of words was man's greatest step toward civilization after all. If there is an accurate characterization of our times, it might be: "Words, words, words!" We are inundated with symbols to the point of having to desensitize ourselves to them.

We might envy the Macaca monkeys of Japan who are limited to a meaningful vocabulary of some thirty-seven words. To be sure, they can say less, but we might find that they *communicate* more.

The tragedy of our age is the awful incommunicability of souls.

W. O. MARTIN

3   The fundamental goal of all communication is to transcend our egocentric predicament. As described earlier (Chapter 2-1), we are located from birth till death in a space/time predicament which subjects us to limitations we can't accept. Communication between living creatures is a means of transcending this condition. We create symbolic media for transmitting to other beings something of the experience-world going on inside us.

We invent symbols, therefore, which can stimulate the sensors of another person. From this we would like to persuade ourselves that, because we can activate the senses of another organism, we can transfer living experience from one person to another. We want to believe in—and we profoundly long for—a transfer of *content* rather than symbolic transmittals between closed systems.

Man is therefore a symbolic creature *because of* his egocentric predicament. If direct transfer of living experience could somehow be arranged, he would hasten to dispense with all his symbols.

Note that we humans share this condition with all living creatures. The common statement that man is a symbolic creature, while other animals are not, is false. They too must resort to symbolic means of bursting through their egocentric predicaments: the courtship rituals and territorial warnings of birds, the danger barks of baboons, the scent which the female gypsy moth disperses through the night air—these are analogous to man's symbolic communication, and for the same reasons.

Man's ability to use highly abstracted and complex symbols is not to be denigrated, of course. But with all our symbolic sophistication, is our transmittal of *experience* all that great? Are we, as a matter of fact, less lonely?

I know that you believe
you understand
what you think I said,
but
I am not sure
you realize that
what you heard
is not
what I
meant.

ANONYMOUS

I fall far short of achieving real communication—person-to-person —all the time, but moving in this direction makes life for me a warm, exciting, upsetting, troubling, satisfying, enriching, and above all a worthwhile venture.

CARL ROGERS

4　It's a curious fact that most of us tacitly assume that the primary function of language is the rational communication of ideas, whereas our everyday experience shows that this isn't so. Happily, our linguistic equipment is designed to serve numerous functions.

In the following list of ten common uses of language, note that usage falls into two categories: whether the primary purpose is to change conditions in ourselves (the subject—S) or in another (the object—O). Equally significant is whether the specific usage is designed to promote emotional results (E) or rational/intellectual results (R). A glance at the list indicates that the primary functions of language are emotional rather than rational and that much use of language is reflexive—designed to alter conditions within ourselves.

5　Language is used to accomplish the following goals.

S　(1)　*To express emotion* (E). "I love you." "Younger than springtime am I" (from *South Pacific*). "Ouch!" "Damn!" Found here also are the interminable arguments we get into which take the form of idea-exchange but which in fact are prolonged venting of accumulated emotional charges. One of the prime functions of taboo words (obscenities, "four-letter words," etc.) and name calling is to let off emotional steam.

S　(2)　*To drown out silence* (E). In countless ordinary situations we find silence intolerable: waiting along with others in a doctor's office, sitting beside someone on a bus or plane, passing time with a casual acquaintance. Polite social conversation generally lessens our anxiety. When alone we often turn on TV or radio to ease our loneliness; lacking these, some of us talk with our selves.

S　(3)　*To enjoy the sounds of language* (E). Language produces esthetic pleasure, especially familiar phrases with happy associations. This is one purpose of much poetry—"word music." Also, just as there is "mood music" there is "mood language," a fact well known to preachers, hypnotists, playwrights—indeed, to anyone wishing to "set the tone" for an ensuing event. [Incidentally, Littlechap's plaint—"My wife's voice is a symphony"—should probably be classified under (1) above: to express agony!]

S　(4)　*To establish a feeling of belonging* (E). Religious ceremonies in which words are repeated together—unison prayers, litanies, chants; protest chants; cheers led by cheer leaders; war dances. "We shall overcome." Especially effective are hymns, national anthems, and songs recalling a past togetherness—the singing of the alma mater or fraternity/sorority songs.

SO　(5)　*To establish relationships* (E). "Aloha." "Good morning." "How do you do?" Buenos dias, señor." How've you been?" "Bonjour, monsieur." "Shalom aleichem." "Hyambo." And polite exploratory conversation: "Looks like it's going to be a nice day." "I'm sure I've seen you somewhere before." Included here also would be ritualized language for severing relationships: "Goodnight." "Adios." "Hasta la vista." "Auf Wiedersehen." "Have a nice day."

O (6) *To affect others' emotions* (E). Sermons, patriotic speeches, rallies for causes, TV commercials. "Smile, God loves you." "Oh, I didn't realize you could wear a size sixteen." Popular therapy would be included here: "Don't cry. It's going to be all right." "Don't worry about tomorrow." "The Lord giveth and the Lord taketh away." "You can stand the pain." More professionally: "What are you really feeling—guilt or anger?"

O (7) *To affect others' behavior* (E-R). "Don't do that!" "Speed Limit 35." "Vote for Smith." Here must be placed the TV commercials which are designed to make us convince ourselves that we need a specific product and to go right out and buy it. Also: "Get hooked." "Think." "THINK BIG." "think small." This is termed "directive language."

O (8) *To suggest insights* (R). This is a philosophic and literary usage especially employed by Chinese sages and Indian philosophers. "When a man is in turmoil how shall he find peace / Save by staying patient till the stream clears?" (Lao-tzu). "Does the grass bend when the wind blows upon it?" (Confucius). This is commonly the purpose of parables, anecdotes, proverbs, logia or "sayings" ("Jesus said . . . ," "Confucius said . . ."), and maxims of folk-wisdom ("A rolling stone gathers no moss").

O (9) *To communicate ideas and facts* (R). "You're overdrawn." "I'd like a hamburger and coffee." "I'm happy to report that it's not malignant." "I regret to inform you. . . ." Here we can classify all media for the transmittal of knowledge: TV newscasts, magazines, books, and technical journals of all sorts, and all our routine daily transfer of information for coping and surviving.

O (10) *To effect word-magic* (E-R-?). "Open Sesame!" "Be thou healed in the Name of Isis." "Om" or "Om mani padme hum!" Our language still contains numerous quasi-magical formulas, often disguised: "Well, here goes." "Good luck!" "Gesundheit!" "God bless you." "God damn you." Akin to primitive word-magic are such phrases as "You're stupid!" and "Go on, you can do it" where the words themselves are designed to help bring about the results alluded to. Closely related to word-magic is the "placebo effect": "Two capsules after meals and you'll feel like a new person."

6 At the human stage of sophistication, language (that is, sounds and printed symbols) is our primary symbolic equipment. But our need to communicate is so great that we expect far more of words than they can deliver; we deceive ourselves into believing that our words are accomplishing what is inherently impossible. We are caught in the predicament of having to reduce the fullness of our experience to a few words

Whenever two or more human beings can communicate with each other, they can, by agreement, make anything stand for anything.
S. I. HAYAKAWA

We can never achieve a satisfactory definition of language, for there is no factor common to all our uses of language—describing, joking, praying, commanding, singing, asking, and so on. Wittgenstein asks us to think of the tools in a toolbox: hammer, pliers, a saw, a screwdriver, a ruler, a gluepot, glue, nails and screws. What we do with words is as different as what we do with these objects.
JOSEPH BRENNAN

We have been given two ears and but a single mouth, in order that we may hear more and talk less.
ZENO OF CITIUM

ESP AND THE DREAMER

Most scientists put mental telepathy in the same category as the Ouija board—an entertaining parlor game, but hardly a subject for serious investigation. Yet some, such as Dr. Montague Ullman, remain open-minded about this form of extrasensory perception. The claims about knowledge of tragic events and other messages "transmitted" over long distances, they hold, can't be explained on the basis of coincidence alone. Taking their cue in part from Sigmund Freud—who speculated that such messages might be picked up by the unconscious but distorted by the conscious, waking, mind—

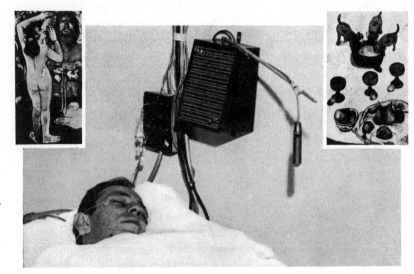

Testing telepathy: Gauguin paintings and wired-up subject.

they have searched for telepathic evidence in the dreaming mind. Ullman, director of psychiatry at Brooklyn's Maimonides Hospital, and psychologist Stanley Krippner have set up a "dream laboratory" at Maimonides, and have carried out studies using the classic techniques of dream investigation devised by Dr. Nathaniel Kleitman at the University of Chicago.

When a person dreams, Kleitman found, his eyes move rapidly from side to side. By watching for these telltale rapid eye movements (REM's) and rousing his subjects during the REM's, Kleitman could elicit dream descriptions in unprecedented detail. In a manner similar to Kleitman's experiments, Ullman put volunteers to bed in an isolated room and attached electroencephalograph electrodes to their heads and sensors to the corner of the eyes to pick up REM's. Aroused at the end of each dream by a researcher watching the EEG and REM tracings in a room nearby, they dictated their dreams into a recorder.

In the Ullman experiment, an "agent" in a third room—usually Ullman or an assistant—fixed his attention on a "target object," such as a painting, and attempted to transmit recognizable impressions to the sleeper.

In one experiment, the target object was "Zapatistas" by José Clemente Orozco, showing followers of the Mexican revolutionary, Zapata, marching along a road with a range of mountains in the background. In a series of separate dream episodes, the volunteer reported dreaming about New Mexico, where he once lived, specifically noting the mountains, the coloring of the landscape, and Indians trooping into Santa Fe at fiesta time.

Gauguin's paintings were used as target objects twice. One was "The Moon and the Earth," portraying a nude, deeply tanned Tahitian girl. The target dreamer, a young secretary, reported dreaming about wearing a bathing suit. In subsequent episodes, she dreamed of a girl with fair skin who wanted to get a tan. The other Gauguin was "Still Life With Three Puppies." The volunteer dreamed of "a couple of dogs making a noise" and saw "dark blue bottles." The Gauguin goblets are blue.

Ullman will claim only that the "striking correlations" between the dream material and the target objects are significant enough to warrant more study and experiments by serious scientists. "The important thing," he says, "is to take the mysticism out of telepathy and study it on a rational basis."

Newsweek, May 24, 1965

and gestures. We try, as it were, to encapsulate life in symbolic containers that are hopelessly inadequate for the task.

But we don't want others to hear our symbols: we want them to hear our experience. And others want the same from us.

Success in communication depends not upon the speaker, but upon the hearer. One wishing to communicate his experience to another can try forever, but quite in vain, if the hearer refuses to hear. If for any reason a listener has undergone closure—he may be preoccupied with other problems, he may have developed an ego-defense system to block out pain, or he may have been conditioned against the immediate words or events before him—then his hearing will be symbol-centered, fragmented, incomplete.

Commonly, we are threatened by new or different ideas, and we set up roadblocks so they can't get through. Or if one has developed a rigid conceptual structure, when he listens to another's experience he translates it (and distorts it) to fit it into his own inflexible system.

Bertrand Russell once wrote that the stupid person always reduces brilliant concepts to his own level of stupidity since he must oversimplify them to understand them. Something like this takes place in our communicating with one another. Because of our own preestablished conceptual points of view, we "translate" what another is saying into the familiar experiences of our own world. In doing this, we miss the living experience which the other person is in fact attempting to convey.

7   Listening has aptly been called "a stillborn art form." How difficult it is for most of us to remain silent in the presence of different or "wrong" ideas. The urge to clobber an alien idea swells within us like a self-righteous demon, and a speaker rarely gets halfway through his sentence before we give way to an impulse to cut him down.

We all know the experience of wanting to be heard by others (or by some one) and not being able to get through. One of our persistent human frustrations is to discover that another person is hearing only words rather than the living experience we feel so deeply and are aching to convey.

Few insights leave one with such a sense of loneliness. To realize suddenly that, no matter how earnestly you try, you can't be heard—this is why there are so many lonely people who belong to the lonely crowd.

The number of individuals who are *word-oriented* rather than *experience-oriented* indicates the existence of a widespread "normal" neurosis in our society.

8   When my child was a three-year-old—that's the little girl—I was pounding away at my typewriter in my study and she was drawing pictures on the floor, and she suddenly said, "I want to go see the popentole."

I kept typing.

Then I stopped and said, "What?!"

The individual who can hear another's experience requires very few words. He is not listening for words; he is not word-oriented. He takes symbols for what they are: road-signs pointing to a destination. If one came upon a sign reading "Pine Valley – 10 miles," who in his right mind would stop beside the signpost and declare "We've arrived!"?

"What must I do, to tame you?" asked the little prince.

"You must be very patient," replied the fox. "First you will sit down at a little distance from me—like this—in the grass. I shall look at you out of the corner of my eye, and you will say nothing. Words are the source of misunderstandings. But you will sit a little closer to me, every day. . . ."

ANTOINE DE SAINT-EXUPÉRY

The trouble with speakers who never leave the higher levels of abstraction is not only that they fail to notice when they are saying something and when they are not; they also produce a similar lack of discrimination in their audiences. Never coming down to earth, they frequently chase themselves around in verbal circles, unaware that they are making meaningless noises.

S. I. HAYAKAWA

She said, "I want to see the popentole."

"Did you say popentole?"

Yes, she said popentole.

I just stopped. It was a puzzle to figure out, and I did. In a few seconds I said, "You mean like last Sunday, you want to go to Lincoln Park and see the totem-pole?"

She said, "Yes."

And what was so warm about this, so wonderful about it, was that having got her point across she played for another twenty minutes singing to herself, very very happy that she had communicated. And I felt very proud of myself at the time for having understood. I didn't say to her, "Okay, I'll take you next Sunday to see the popentole." The mere fact that she'd made her point and got it registered was a source of intense satisfaction to her.

S. I. HAYAKAWA

9   Semanticists remind us that symbols can be understood intelligibly only within the context of actual usage. The semantic axiom that no word ever has the same meaning twice would appear to be an overstatement, since in practice we seem to use words repeatedly with about the same meaning. But in fact their observation is accurate. *Definitions are predictions of possible meanings which a term may be given in concrete situations.* The precise meaning of any term cannot be known until it occurs in a living context, and then its meaning is inextricably interwoven with the total event and cannot be understood apart from it.

There is a strand of Western tradition going back at least as far as Aristotle that would attempt to give all words exact definitions and insist that they be employed only in this unambiguous way. Within certain academic fields this precise approach has yielded valuable results. But this sort of operation has little relation to our richly varied use of language in daily life.

The individual who is rigidly literal in his use of definitions often fails in the communication of experience. If he has the habit of bringing prefabricated definitions into fluid, living situations, he is apt to miss entirely the nuances and connotations which terms take on in a specific context. Words are "containers" into which we pour the meanings and feelings of the moment, and this personal investment of ourselves in our symbols is intimately tied to the immediate experiences of life.

10   No two persons ever react to any word or symbol in exactly the same manner. How could they? In order to do so, they would have to have the same past experience, the same present environment, the same prospect of the future, the same pattern of thought, the same flow of feelings, the same bodily habits, and the same electro-chemical metabolism. The chances that such multidimensional patterns coincide are practically nil. The surprising thing is not that we often disagree; it is that we ever succeed in achieving some sort of agreement.

SAMUEL BOIS

11   "Taboo words"—profanities, obscenities, "four-letter words," etc.—are truly universal and are similar in all languages. The use of taboo symbols to express emotion is obvious, and the abundance of such terms, as well as their surrogates, indicates our need for such means of expression. In our English tradition recognizable surrogates are "cripes" and "criminy" (for Christ); "jeez" and "gee whiz" (for Jesus); "jimminy crickets" (for Jesus Christ); "darn" (for damn); "gol darn," "dad gum," and "gosh darn" (for god damn). There is in fact a surrogate for almost every taboo word.

    Taboo words serve many other purposes. They possess shock power; they "get a reaction," which is very often our purpose in using them. They are also effective weapons for directing hostilities against those who are sensitive to the connotations of such words. Not infrequently we use them in order to become accepted into peer groups in which they are commonly used. It's an interesting fact that an immigrant from another culture often begins to be accepted into his new environment when he becomes capable of using the vernacular taboo words of that culture.

12   It is surprising how often people still speak of "dirty words" or "obscene language" and believe that *symbols* are *inherently* dirty or obscene. Semanticists keep reminding us that words mean nothing at all until we give meanings to them. There simply is no such thing as a "dirty word"; there are only symbols which individuals and groups have invested with certain (negative) meanings and feelings.

    Nevertheless, the fact that large numbers of individuals are offended by *symbols—quite apart from the experience symbolized—*is a social reality. If one sincerely desires to communicate experience, there is good pragmatic justification for not making unnecessary use of *any* symbols which are apt to produce symbol-centered reactions in others—which can be done with erudite phrases and technical terminology as well as by the use of taboo language. As a general rule, any sort of language that causes us to focus on the symbols rather than the experience symbolized serves to break down the process of communication.

13   Does telepathic communication exist? There is some evidence that it does, and the widespread popular belief in telepathy is based on actual experiences for which a telepathic hypothesis seems at present the best explanation.

    The more plausible fact-claims about telepathy hint at some interesting possibilities. One is that telepathic experiences are less common in cerebral individuals, in "intellectual" and rational people. A domineering intellect stands in the way of nonrational experience in general, including telepathy. Similarly, individuals from less cerebral cultures seem to be more capable of having telepathic experiences. Members of societies which express emotion openly—those that still dance and experience

A man of true science uses but a few hard words . . . whereas the smatterer in science . . . thinks that by mouthing hard words he understands hard things.

    HERMAN MELVILLE

Let us not forget that a word hasn't got a meaning given to it, as it were, by a power independent of us, so that there could be a kind of scientific investigation in what the word really *means. A word has the meaning someone has given to it.*

    LUDWIG WITTGENSTEIN

Words have no meaning. Only people have meaning.

    American Red Cross
    (Radio Commercial)

> **empathize** (em′pȧ-thīz) To diagnose, that is to recognize and identify the feelings, emotions, passions, sufferings, torments through their symptoms is to *realize intellectually,* to *understand* them, in a remote way to identify oneself with the patient, without ever having personally experienced those feelings,—to *empathize,* as it is known in psychiatry.
>
> On the other hand, to place oneself in the position of the patient, to get into his skin, so to speak, to be able to duplicate, live through, *experience* those feelings in a vicarious way, is closely to identify oneself with another, to *share his feelings with him,* to *sympathize,* from the Greek *sýn,* together with, and *páthos,* suffering, passion.
>
> **empathy** (em′pȧ-thē) . . .   Empathy is thus a form of identification; it may be called intellectual identification in contrast to affective identification.
>
> HINSIE AND CAMPBELL
> *Psychiatric Dictionary*

Not higher sensitivity, not longer memory or even quicker association sets man so far above other animals that he can regard them as denizens of a lower world; no, it is the power of using symbols that makes him lord of the earth.

SUZANNE LANGER

ecstasy, in a word, those who are in touch with the Dionysian side of life—these are more open to supersensory experiences than individuals driven by the Apollonian pursuit of intellect and order.

Another fact is that telepathic experiences appear to have some correlation with physical or psychical abnormalities. They occur more frequently after brain damage, or during alterations of endocrine chemistry, extreme emotional states, or recovery from an illness or accident.

In considering the future capabilities of communication, there is an interesting hint that when we receive telepathic messages from others, the event is not at all a pure transfer of experience. Rather, the content is immediately assimilated into our own fabric of understanding and feeling. That is, we still interpret the telepathic communication in terms of *our* experience, just as we do with all other forms of knowledge which we receive by symbolic means.

Lastly—if telepathy exists—it seems that its base of operation is somewhere deep in the unconscious regions of the psyche. Telepathic channels appear to operate outside the conscious mind and then break in uninvited.

14   In my dream I was driving my car along a road near my home, and quite suddenly, out of nowhere, it seemed to me, a little girl about three years of age appeared right in front of the car. I did all I could but found it impossible to avoid hitting her. On getting out, I was told that she was dead. I looked at her as she lay in the road, and felt completely shattered,

4   The Inner World: The Fantastic Journey

though I had never had a chance to save her from what seemed to me to be her inevitable fate. I must stress that feeling I had of inevitability.

When I awoke, I realized with horror that I had to drive down that road that very morning, on my way to lunch with my youngest daughter, and I decided to be more than usually careful. On approaching the spot, I looked round most carefully for any sign of children, and there were none in sight, only about five women standing at a bus stop. Relieved beyond words, I glanced down at my speedometer to check, and on lifting my eyes, was completely horrified to see, standing still in the middle of the road, the little girl of my dream, correct in every detail, even to the dark curly hair and the bright blue cardigan she was wearing. I was afraid to use my horn, in case I startled her and precipitated what I felt was going to be a fatal accident, so I slowly brought the car to a halt, just beside her. She never moved, but stood staring at me.

Meanwhile, the women in the bus queue made no sign of interest, and no one tried to get such a young child off the busy road. In fact, they seemed more interested in the fact that I had stopped. Feeling very shaky, I continued on my way, and looking in the mirror, I saw that the child was still standing there, and nobody was bothering about her. By the time I got to my daughter's flat, I was over half an hour late. When she opened the door, she was looking very worried and upset, and said how glad she was to see me safe and sound.

I asked why she had been so worried, as I have been driving for over thirty years, and she looked at me and said, "I know that, Mummie, but you see, last night I had a terribly vivid dream. In this dream you ran over and killed a lovely little girl, dressed in a bright blue cardigan and with lovely dark curly hair!"

15   This dream, which is representative of a very common experience, is recounted by the British author J. B. Priestley. He double checked the facts of the episode with the mother, her husband, and the daughter (but not the little girl!). Priestley comments:

> Telepathy, and not any Time effect, was at work here. Whether the daughter took the tragic little-girl-episode from the mother, or the mother from the daughter, we cannot tell. . . . What is certain is that this fascinating double dream is well worth the attention of ESP experts and researchers.

A Soviet parapsychologist, Dr. Pavel Naumov, has concluded that "biological ties between mother and child are incontestable."

> In the clinic, mothers are in a distant section, separate from their babies. They cannot possibly hear them. Yet, when her baby cries, a mother exhibits nervousness. Or when an infant is in pain, for instance as a doctor takes a blood specimen, the mother shows signs of anxiety. She has no way of knowing the doctor is at that moment with her child. . . . We found communication in 65 percent of our cases.

Staggering as it may be to contemplate, a life signal may connect all creation. . . .
CLEVE BACKSTER

Many similar events are noted by Sheila Ostrander and Lynn Schroeder in their book *Psychic Discoveries Behind the Iron Curtain*. They comment that

such cases open up philosophical, ethical, personal and scientific questions. Across a distance, is mind influencing body? Is body influencing body? Is body influencing mind? As psi° moves into the picture, the iron edges of biology and psychology begin to dissolve and mix, pointing to a whole new dynamism underlying both.

16   Dr. Naumov tells of another experiment in telepathy which was conducted aboard a Russian submarine at sea. In this case the subjects were not human beings, but a mother rabbit and her litter of newborn bunnies.

Naumov relates:

As you know, there's no known way for a submerged submarine to communicate with anyone on land. Radio doesn't work. Scientists placed the baby rabbits aboard the submarine. They kept the mother rabbit in a laboratory on shore where they implanted electrodes deep in her brain. When the sub was deep below the surface of the ocean, assistants killed the young rabbits one by one.

  The mother rabbit obviously didn't know what was happening. Even if she could have understood the test, she had no way of knowing at what moment her children died. Yet, at each synchronized instant of death, her brain *reacted. There was communication.* . . . And, our instruments clearly registered these moments of ESP.

Tens of thousands of years have elapsed since we shed our tails, but we are still communicating with a medium developed to meet the needs of arboreal man. . . . We may smile at the linguistic illusions of primitive man, but may we forget that the verbal machinery on which we so readily rely, and with which our metaphysicians still profess to probe the Nature of Existence, was set up by him, and may be responsible for other illusions hardly less gross and not more easily eradicable?

OGDEN AND RICHARDS

17   The claims of an extrasensory tie between all creatures doesn't sound as unbelievable as it once did, thanks to the unusual and well tested work of Cleve Backster, . . . [who] has good evidence to show that there is a sort of "primary perception" inherent in all living things. For instance, when tiny shrimp are killed there is a reaction in other living things—such as plants—in the surrounding areas. "Nothing seems to be able to stop this communication," says Backster, "not even lead shields."

  . . . This discovery of a mind-link, body-link between all living things has vast implications for our philosophy, for our own view of the world. . . .

  Everyone knows that mystics and gurus always insist we are all somehow connected. All is one, the paradox goes, and within the one there is individuality. Dr. Gardner Murphy, President of the American Society of Psychical Research, often compares individuals to volcanic islands projecting above the sea. Underneath, they slope to the ground from which they came, in which they all connect.

  If the early Soviet results are correct, currents of communication are crisscrossing beneath the wavery surface of things.

OSTRANDER AND SCHROEDER

5

COEXISTENCE:
MAN'S LOVE/HATE
CONDITION

5-1

CIVILIZATION/
FUTURE

1   Arnold Toynbee is considered by many to be the greatest of
contemporary philosophers of history. His massive twelve-volume *Study
of History* stands today as the supreme effort of the human mind to
disentangle the complexities of human history in order to see whether
there is any large-scale meaning to the whole human enterprise.

Late in 1911 Toynbee left Oxford for a nine-month tour of the
Mediterranean lands where he saw for himself the remains of the great
civilizations he knew so well from history books. He spent much time
walking over the countryside surveying the legacies of these long-dead
worlds. He chatted with monks on Mount Athos, examined Etruscan
tombs at Cerveteri and Corneto, and mused on the past glory of the
Minoan palaces on Crete. Before this visit, the Acropolis had been a page
in a book; now its panorama sprawled before him in all its breathtaking
reality.

At the same time, he listened to the sounds of the living world.
He spent his evenings in Greek cafes and heard talk of world affairs; he

*Until philosophers are kings, or the
kings and princes of this world
have the spirit and power of philosophy, and political greatness and
wisdom meet in one, and those com-
moner natures who pursue either to
the exclusion of the other are compelled to stand aside, cities will
never have rest from their evils—
no, nor the human race. . . .*

PLATO

visited Greek villages and caught apprehensive conversations among peasants and shepherds about the possibility of war.

He reflected on these two worlds. One was dead, it seemed, the other very much alive. The contrast was a shattering reminder of life, death, and time. Toynbee pondered: What does man's past tell us about the present or future? How dead, really, are past civilizations? If they are dead, what caused them to die? What is their relationship to our own busy world? *Is our civilization also doomed to die like the rest?* If so, why? Could it perhaps be saved? If so, what could save it?

2   This contrast between the dead dreams and the living realities disturbed Toynbee for a decade.

In September of 1921 he was aboard a miserably slow train traveling across Thrace. The rumbling of his train crossing a bridge near Adrianople awakened him before dawn, and during the next few hours, as a countryside haunted with history glided past, his mind began to call up the epochal events of history and legend that had been set in this great theater.

He knew that he was now crossing the westernmost boundaries of the vast empire of the Persian Achaemenids and that when that kingdom had run its course, these rolling hills and lazy pasturelands came under the shield of the young Alexander of Macedon. Three centuries later the astute plans of a Caesar for the conquest of central Europe were shattered when Varus and his legions were lured into the nearby Teutoberg Forest and annihilated by the Germans. Through here the Goths and the Huns passed, followed in turn by the Crusaders with red crosses flashing on their white tunics and the fire of holy war flashing in their eyes; after encountering the gaily clad Saracens those that returned crept homeward in bloodsoaked rags, and not a few laid their embattled bones beside the little streams in the Thracian woodlands. Much later this countryside, then Rumelia, was drawn into the Ottoman Empire and the Muslims settled the land and made it theirs. Thus it had remained until modern times.

Hour after hour Toynbee stood by the window watching the scenes of history pass by. That night, as the train sped along in the light of the full moon, he jotted down on a half-sheet of notepaper a plan for a comparative study of the civilizations of mankind. He had decided to embark on a research program which would take him on a prolonged journey through all known civilizations in order to determine whether meaningful patterns were discernible in the lifetimes of these civilizations. His primary interest was to discover where we stand today in Western civilization and to glimpse where we are going. He figured that his project would require decades of work, and it did. He completed the last page of his lifelong study on June 15, 1951—thirty years of labor to discover where we are.

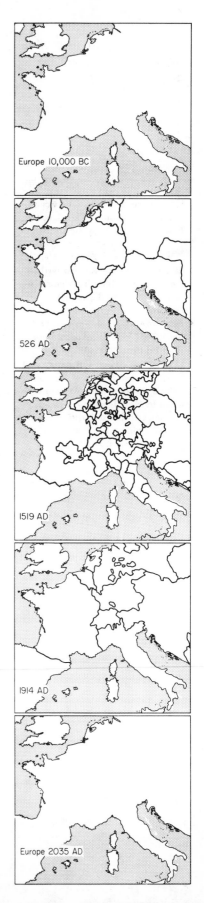

°The abortive civilizations: Scandinavian, Far Western Christian, Far Eastern Christian, Syriac.

°Those still alive: Western, Near Eastern Christian, Russian Orthodox Christian, Islamic, Hindu, Chinese Far Eastern, Japanese Far Eastern.

°The arrested dead: Spartan, Ottoman. The arrested living: Polynesian, Eskimo, Nomadic.

°Those now dying: Polynesian and Nomadic.

°Those threatened by Western civilization: Near Eastern Christian, Russian Orthodox Christian, Islamic, Hindu, Chinese Far Eastern, Japanese Far Eastern, and Eskimo.

3   Toynbee thinks in terms of civilizations, not nations. The latter are but ephemeral and illusory fragments of civilizations. In the wider perspective of man's civilizations, nations are merely ethnocentric tribes which come and go so rapidly that they are quite secondary in importance, though in their short lifetimes they are the source of much narrow internecine bickering within the larger cultural body.

The subject matter of Toynbee's study of history are all the civilizations known to man. He lists twenty-seven civilizations which have been born to date (that includes five arrested civilizations). There were also four abortive civilizations which started out normally but could not make the grade.°

Subtracting the arrested civilizations from the total, we have twenty-two that reached maturity. Of those twenty-two civilizations, fifteen are now dead and buried, while only seven are still alive.° Of the five arrested civilizations, two are dead and three are still living.°

There are, then, a total of seventeen dead and ten living civilizations.

But two of these ten living civilizations are now in their death throes.° That leaves only eight, and six of these "bear marks of having already broken down and gone into disintegration," and seven of the eight are presently seriously threatened with annihilation and/or assimilation by Western civilization.°

As of the twentieth century, therefore, our own Western civilization stands at the top of the list. From appearances, we are still relatively healthy, and our general prognosis, according to Toynbee, can be one of guarded optimism.

4   From this Promethean comparison, what else had Toynbee found?

Western civilization is probably on the threshold of what Toynbee calls a "universal state," and the appearance of this state in the developmental pattern of a civilization is the unmistakable sign of disintegration. The breakdown of our civilization began in the fifteenth or sixteenth century, probably with the religious wars, and since that time there have been innumerable symptoms of disintegration in the arts, philosophy, religion, and material culture. We recognize these signs from their appearance in corresponding stages in past societies. Since there are only two or three great powers left in the world today serving as rallying points for all the other nations, the universal state cannot be far away.

But at this point a new element has entered the picture: the actual fact of One World. When we ask what sort of universal state we shall see, Toynbee suggests two possibilities. The first kind would have all the characteristics of the universal states of the past. It would be ushered onto the stage of history by the same self-inflicted knockout blow in which one member-state succeeds in a coup of all the other member-states and itself becomes the universal state. No society has ever been able to recover

5   *Coexistence: Man's Love/Hate Condition*

THE DÉCOR OF TOMORROW'S HELL

Some movies are so inventive and powerful that they can be viewed again and again and each time yield up fresh illuminations. Stanley Kubrick's A Clockwork Orange *is such a movie. Based on Anthony Burgess's 1963 novel of the same title, it is a merciless, demoniac satire of a near future terrorized by pathological teen-age toughs. When it opened last week,* TIME *Movie Critic Jay Cocks hailed it as "chillingly and often hilariously believable." Below,* TIME's *art critic takes a further look at some of its aesthetic implications:*

Stanley Kubrick's biting and dandyish vision of subtopia is not simply a social satire but a brilliant cultural one. No movie in the last decade (perhaps in the history of film) has made such exquisitely chilling predictions about the future role of cultural artifacts—paintings, buildings, sculpture, music—in society, or extrapolated them from so undeceived a view of our present culture.

The time is somewhere in the next ten years; the police still wear Queen Elizabeth II's monogram on their caps and the politicians seem to be dressed by Blades and Mr. Fish. The settings have the glittery, spaced-out look of a Milanese design fair—all stamped Mylar and womb-form chairs, thick glass tables, brushed aluminum and chrome, sterile perspectives of unshuttered concrete and white molded plastic. The designed artifact is to *Orange* what technological gadgetry was to Kubrick's *2001:* a character in the drama, a mute and unblinking witness.

This alienating décor is full of works of art. Fiber-glass nudes, crouched like *Playboy* femlins in the Korova milk bar, serve as tables or dispense mescalinelaced milk from their nipples. They are, in fact, close parodies of the fetishistic furniture-sculpture of Allen Jones. The living room of the Cat Lady, whom Protagonist Alex (Malcolm McDowell) murders with an immense Arp-like sculpture of a phallus, is decked with the kind of garish, routinely erotic paintings that have infested Pop-art consciousness in recent years.

The impression, a very deliberate one, is of culture objects cut loose from any power to communicate, or even to be noticed. There is no reality to which they connect. Their owners possess them as so much paraphernalia, like the derby hats, codpieces and bleeding-eye emblems that Alex and his mates wear so defiantly on their bully-boy costumes. When Alex swats at the Cat Lady's sculptured *schlong,* she screams: "Leave that alone, don't touch it! It's a very important work of art!" This pathetic burst of connoisseur's jargon echoes in a vast cultural emptiness. In worlds like this, no work of art can be important.

The geography of Kubrick's bleak landscape becomes explicit in his use of music. Whenever the woodwinds and brass turn up on the sound track, one may be fairly sure that something atrocious will appear on the screen—and be distanced by the irony of juxtaposition. Thus to the strains of Rossini's *Thieving Magpie,* a girl is gang-raped in a deserted casino. In a sequence of exquisite *comédie noire,* Alex cripples a writer and rapes his wife while tripping through a Gene Kelly number: "Singin' in the rain" (*bash*), "Just singin' in the rain" (*kick*).

What might seem gratuitous is very pointed indeed. At issue is the popular 19th century idea, still held today, that Art is Good for You, that the purpose of the fine arts is to provide moral uplift. Kubrick's message, amplified from Burgess's novel, is the opposite: art has no ethical purpose. There is no religion of beauty. Art serves, instead, to promote ecstatic consciousness. The kind of ecstasy depends on the person who is having it. Without the slightest contradiction, Nazis could weep over Wagner before stoking the crematoriums. Alex grooves on the music of "Ludwig van," especially the *Ninth Symphony,* which fills him with fantasies of sex and slaughter.

When he is drug-cured of belligerence, strapped into a straitjacket with eyes clamped open to watch films of violence, the conditioning also works on his love of music: Beethoven makes him suicidal. Then, when the government returns him to his state of innocent viciousness, the love of Ludwig comes back: "I was really cured at last," he says over the last fantasy shot, in which he is swiving a blonde amidst clapping Establishment figures in Ascot costume, while the mighty setting of Schiller's *Ode to Joy* peals on the sound track.

•

Kubrick delivers these insights with something of Alex's pure, consistent aggression. His visual style is swift and cold—appropriately, even necessarily so. Moreover, his direction has the rarest of qualities, bravura morality—ironic, precise and ferocious. "It's funny," muses Alex, "how the colors of the real world only seem really real when you viddy them on the screen." It is a good epigraph to *A Clockwork Orange.* No futures are inevitable, but little Alex, glaring through the false eyelashes that he affects while on his bashing rampages, rises from the joint imaginations of Kubrick and Burgess like a portent: he is the future Candide, not of innocence, but of excessive and frightful experience.

■ *Robert Hughes*

McDowell rests between bashings in "Clockwork Orange"

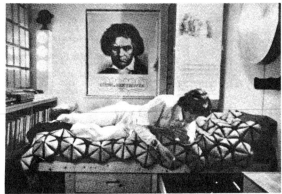

Time, December 27, 1971

from this suicidal act, and nothing can turn back the process of dissolution which now sets in. Thoughtfully, Toynbee asks, "Must we, too, purchase our *Pax Oecumenica* at this deadly price?"

The second alternative would be something new in human history: the creation of a new kind of universal state by peaceful means. The entire world is now moving toward homogeneity with unbelievable speed. Momentarily it is dominated by the technology of a materialistic West, but it is clearly, and increasingly, influenced by the nonmaterialistic values and concepts of the non-Western world. If it does prove to be true that we are on the verge of becoming *one* civilization with *one* culture, this may mean that a new type of political organization could manifest itself. This would be a genuine mutation of the laws of history. If it is possible for Western man to meet the challenge of One World by outgrowing his egocentric illusion—especially as it expresses itself in the nationalism of his parochial states—the doom of Western civilization may be avoided. There could be a new lease on life, and there could be a new world order.

There is the possibility, of course, that man may destroy himself through some nuclear holocaust, but Toynbee does not believe this to be the most probable alternative. But there is always the possibility that man might require a challenge as horrifying as the sufferings of mass destruction before he could learn how to live in peaceful existence with himself.

5   Whichever type of universal state may come, Toynbee is sure that in less than half a century "the whole face of the planet will have been unified politically through the concentration of irresistible military power in some single set of hands." At the present, we don't yet know whose hands these will be, but there is a growing possibility that they will be the hands of the West. Communism may seem to have an advantage from a short-range viewpoint, but in the long view Toynbee does not give communism much hope because, in insisting on shortcuts, it does not answer many of man's deepest needs. "There seems to be in human nature an intractable vein—akin to the temperament of Man's yoke-fellows the camel, mule, and goat—which insists on being allowed a modicum of freedom and which knows how to impose its will when it is goaded beyond endurance. . . . Even the most long-suffering peoples revolt at some point."

Within this coming universal state there will be less physical and material freedom than the peoples of the West have been used to, even in such "sacred" realms as family planning. As he sees it, "in a powerful, healthy, overpopulated world, even the proletarian's freedom to beget children will no longer be his private affair, but will be regulated by the state." He believes, in fact, that the problems of population control and food production will be the critical problems of the near future.

The world revolution, Arnold Toynbee has suggested, has begun. But who will eventually be fighting whom is still not clear.

R. D. LAING

The strongest political force of the day—nationalism—is driving nations to increase their populations rather than to moderate them. This is why I doubt whether action will be taken until the problem has developed from a threat to a disaster.

FRED HOYLE

> So the continuity of history reasserts itself: despite earthquakes, epidemics, famines, eruptive migrations, and catastrophic wars, the essential processes of civilization are not lost; some younger culture takes them up, snatches them from the conflagration, carries them on imitatively, then creatively, until fresh youth and spirit can enter the race. As men are members of one another, and generations are moments in a family line, so civilizations are units in a larger whole whose name is history; they are stages in the life of man. Civilization is polygenetic—it is the co-operative product of many peoples, ranks, and faiths; and no one who studies its history can be a bigot of race or creed. Therefore the scholar, though he belongs to his country through affectionate kinship, feels himself also a citizen of that Country of the Mind which knows no hatreds and no frontiers; he hardly deserves his name if he carries into his study political prejudices, or racial discriminations, or religious animosities; and he accords his grateful homage to any people that has borne the torch and enriched his heritage.
>
> WILL DURANT
> *The Story of Civilization*

What's it to me that nobody's guilty and that I know it—I need revenge or I'd kill myself. And revenge not in some far off eternity, somewhere, sometime, but here and now, on earth, so that I can see it myself.

DOSTOEVSKY
The Brothers Karamazov

Man cannot live without freedom, however, and "if freedom is suppressed on the material plane, it will break out on the spiritual plane." So in this new world there will be a spiritual freedom superior to that now known by Western man, and this gain will be more than worth the price that man will have to pay for it. "True spiritual freedom is attained when each member of Society has learnt to reconcile a sincere conviction of the truth of his own religious beliefs and practices with a voluntary toleration of the different beliefs and practices of his neighbors."

There will also be an equality among human beings and a respect for human dignity. There will be neither colonialism nor communism to deny these qualities to mankind. The idea of "democracy" as understood by the West to mean self-government will be considerably weakened, and "democracy" as employed by the non-Western peoples to mean social equality will predominate.

And what will be the role of religion? Toynbee clearly sees a resurgence of religion. Just as the nineteenth and the first half of the twentieth century have seen a steady movement away from religion, the twenty-first century will witness a countermovement in which mankind will turn from materialism and technology back to religion and spiritual values. What will this religion be like? A continuing interaction between

What experience and history teach us is this—that people and governments never have learned anything from history, or acted on principles deduced from it.

HEGEL

Violent revolutions do not so much redistribute wealth as destroy it. . . . The only real revolution is in the enlightenment of the mind and the improvement of character. The only real emancipation is individual . . . .

WILL DURANT

THE MIGHTY EMPIRES OF LILLIPUT AND BLEFUSCU

Which two mighty powers have . . . been engaged in a most obstinate war for six and thirty moons past. It began upon the following occasion. It is allowed on all hands, that the primitive way of breaking eggs before we eat them, was upon the larger end: but his present Majesty's grandfather, while he was a boy, going to eat an egg, and breaking it according to the ancient practice, happened to cut one of his fingers. Whereupon the Emperor his father published an edict, commanding all his subjects, upon great penalties, to break the smaller end of their eggs. The people so highly resented this law, that our Histories tell us there have been six rebellions raised on that account; wherein one Emperor lost his life, and another his crown. These civil commotions were constantly fomented by the monarchs of Blefuscu; and when they were quelled, the exiles always fled for refuge to that Empire. It is computed, that eleven thousand persons have, at several times, suffered death, rather than submit to break their eggs at the smaller end. Many hundred large volumes have been published upon this controversy: but the books of the Big-Endians have been long forbidden, and the whole party rendered incapable by law of holding employments. During the course of these troubles, the Emperors of Blefuscu did frequently expostulate by their ambassadors, accusing us of making a schism in religion, by offending against a fundamental doctrine of our great prophet Lustrog, in the fifty-fourth chapter of the *Brundecral* (which is their Alcoran). This, however, is thought to be a mere strain upon the text: for the words are these; *That all true believers shall break their eggs at the convenient end:* and which is the convenient end, seems, in my humble opinion, to be left to every man's conscience, or at least in the power of the chief magistrate to determine. Now the Big-Endian exiles have found so much credit in the Emperor of Blefuscu's Court, and so much private assistance and encouragement from their party here at home, that a bloody war hath been carried on between the two Empires for six and thirty moons with various success. . . .

JONATHAN SWIFT
Gulliver's Travels

all existing religions is certain, but for some time to come each of the living religions will maintain its identity and minister to its own adherents. However, there is a strong possibility that, as these great religions find themselves face to face in a shrinking world, a positive tolerance will replace their traditional fanaticism. They will find that all their fellowseekers are engaged in the same quest. In the long run, only a true monotheistic devotion to one Ultimate Reality accepted by all could meet the requirements of men who viewed their world as One World, and who looked upon all other men as brothers.

Can Western civilization survive all this? *Perhaps.* So many new factors have appeared in the modern world that our civilization, if it can come alive and face the challenge of change, can be infused with new vigor and win a reprieve, perhaps even a new chance at growth. If our response includes great leaders—an authentic "creative minority"—who can lead the way by facing realistically the problems of a new era, there is still hope.

Western civilization is not yet dead and buried, not quite.

6 Toynbee is representative of all those who have labored diligently to discover if there is any meaning to human history. There have been other great minds long before Toynbee—Saint Augustine and Ibn Khaldun, for instance—who sought history's secrets; but before modern times they tended to approach their subject matter with assumptions which largely determined the patterns they found. For example, many began with the assumption that God *uses* historical events such as the fall of Rome or Jerusalem to convey a message; and *the message,* therefore, would be *the meaning* of the event. Modern philosophers attempt to be as empirical as they possibly can, arriving at hypotheses ("patterns" perhaps) only after a careful study of the historical facts.

Other notable names in the philosophy of history are Oswald Spengler (*Decline of the West*), Pitirim Sorokin (*Social and Cultural Dynamics*), Karl Marx (*Das Kapital*), and Albert Schweitzer (*Philosophy of Civilization*). These philosophers, of course, don't always find the same patterns. Toynbee has been criticized (whether justly or not) for doing what ancient philosophers did: placing his own preconceived subjective constructs (in his case, patterns derived from Greek civilization) upon each society he studied.

Nevertheless, there are some significant points of agreement among most of these thinkers.

7 Most philosophers agree that when a civilization becomes materialistic and "sensate" (Sorokin's term) in its values, then it is in trouble. In this stage there is usually a universally held belief that this is the "golden age"—a bounteous time of unprecedented prosperity. In reality

WESTERN DEFENSE COMMAND AND FOURTH ARMY
WARTIME CIVIL CONTROL ADMINISTRATION

Presidio of San Francisco, California
April 24, 1942

INSTRUCTIONS
TO ALL PERSONS OF
JAPANESE
ANCESTRY

Living in the Following Area:

All of that portion of the City and County of San Francisco, State of California, bounded on the north by California Street, bounded on the east by Van Ness Avenue, bounded on the south by Sutter Street, and bounded on the west by Presidio Avenue.

Pursuant to the provisions of Civilian Exclusion Order No. 20, this Headquarters, dated April 24, 1942, all persons of Japanese ancestry, both alien and non-alien, will be evacuated from the above area by 12 o'clock noon, P. W. T., Friday, May 1, 1942.

No Japanese person living in the above area will be permitted to change residence after 12 o'clock noon, P. W. T., Friday, April 24, 1942, without obtaining special permission from the representative of the Commanding General, Northern California Sector, at the Civil Control Station located at:

> Japanese American Citizens' League Auditorium,
> 2031 Bush Street,
> San Francisco, California.

Such permits will only be granted for the purpose of uniting members of a family, or in cases of grave emergency.

The Civil Control Station is equipped to assist the Japanese population affected by this evacuation in the following ways:

1. Give advice and instructions on the evacuation.

2. Provide services with respect to the management, leasing, sale, storage or other disposition of most kinds of property, such as real estate, business and professional equipment, household goods, boats, automobiles and livestock.

3. Provide temporary residence elsewhere for all Japanese in family groups.

4. Transport persons and a limited amount of clothing and equipment to their new residence.

The Following Instructions Must Be Observed:

1. A responsible member of each family, preferably the head of the family, or the person in whose name most of the property is held, and each individual living alone, will report to the Civil Control Station to receive further instructions. This must be done between 8:00 A. M. and 5:00 P. M. on Saturday, April 25, 1942, or between 8:00 A. M. and 5:00 P. M. on Sunday, April 26, 1942.

2. Evacuees must carry with them on departure for the Assembly Center, the following property:

(a) Bedding and linens (no mattress) for each member of the family;
(b) Toilet articles for each member of the family;
(c) Extra clothing for each member of the family;
(d) Sufficient knives, forks, spoons, plates, bowls and cups for each member of the family;
(e) Essential personal effects for each member of the family.

All items carried will be securely packaged, tied and plainly marked with the name of the owner and numbered in accordance with instructions obtained at the Civil Control Station.

The size and number of packages is limited to that which can be carried by the individual or family group.

3. No pets of any kind will be permitted.

4. The United States Government through its agencies will provide for the storage at the sole risk of the owner of the more substantial household items, such as iceboxes, washing machines, pianos and other heavy furniture. Cooking utensils and other small items will be accepted for storage if crated, packed and plainly marked with the name and address of the owner. Only one name and address will be used by a given family.

5. Each family, and individual living alone, will be furnished transportation to the Assembly Center or will be authorized to travel by private automobile in a supervised group. All instructions pertaining to the movement will be obtained at the Civil Control Station.

Go to the Civil Control Station between the hours of 8:00 A. M. and 5:00 P. M., Saturday, April 25, 1942, or between the hours of 8:00 A. M. and 5:00 P. M., Sunday, April 26, 1942, to receive further instructions.

J. L. DeWITT
Lieutenant General, U. S. Army

> **OZYMANDIAS**
>
> I met a traveller from an antique land
> Who said: Two vast and trunkless legs of stone
> Stand in the desert . . . Near them, on the sand,
> Half sunk, a shattered visage lies, whose frown,
> And wrinkled lip, and sneer of cold command,
> Tell that its sculptor well those passions read
> Which yet survive, stamped on these lifeless things,
> The hand that mocked them, and the heart that fed:
> And on the pedestal these words appear:
> "My name is Ozymandias, king of kings:
> Look on my works, ye Mighty, and despair!"
> Nothing beside remains. Round the decay
> Of that colossal wreck, boundless and bare
> The lone and level sands stretch far away.
>
> PERCY BYSSHE SHELLEY

it is the onset of disintegration. Unless the culture can rediscover its creativity by successfully facing new challenges and recovering its "ethereal" values, it is doomed. What they are saying is that unless a fundamental change takes place in the priority of values of large numbers of people, but above all in the "creative minority" who are the true leaders of men, then the civilization has gone into irrevocable decline.

Another point of agreement among philosophers of history is that nationalism is a necessary but passing phenomenon. Those holding "organismic" theories of history usually liken man's present politico-cultural condition to adolescence, the time when the individual human self is laboring for separation and identity. But once the integrated self has been developed, there is no longer a preoccupation with identity or identity-labels. They suggest that mankind will move collectively through the ethnocentric stage, just as individually we pass (or should pass) through the egocentric stage. While quite normal in the adolescent phase, over-concern with self is hardly becoming to mature adults who have more important things to do than concentrating perpetually on the problem of *who* they are. What philosophers of history agree on is that conditions in the modern world are creating a single world-culture which will, with shattering speed, break down the boundaries of nationalistic consciousness. Indeed, within another thirty years or so, man's survival will be in serious jeopardy if large-scale ethnocentric consciousness still prevails.

A third point on which most philosophers of history agree is that the disintegration of a civilization is not the ultimate tragedy we may think it to be. Durant makes this point frequently in his *Story of Civilization.* "We should not be greatly disturbed by the probability that our civilization will die like any other. As Frederick asked his retreating troops

As for wars, well, there's only been 268 years out of the last 3421 in which there was no war. So war, too, is in the normal course of events.

WILL DURANT

at Kolin, 'Would you live forever?' Perhaps it is desirable that life should take fresh forms, that new civilizations and centers should have their turn." Toynbee has similarly noted that the most precious elements of any civilization do not die but become the seeds of a subsequent new civilization. Great inventions, advancements in science, philosophy, art and music, the profoundest insights into nature, and our knowledge of man—these are never lost though the culture that produced them may crumble. "These are the elements of civilization," writes Durant, "and they have been tenaciously maintained through the perilous passage from one civilization to the next. They are the connective tissue of human history."

8   What possible futures might we imagine if we peer ahead with the long-range vision of the philosopher of history?

To face the negative possibilities first, it would seem that there are only two world-tragedies that have any likelihood of actually occurring: (1) war and mass annihilation; (2) a totalitarian state and "an age of darkness." Both are extensions of the present.

Prophets of doom have long warned that World War III is inevitable. It may or may not be. It does seem that man frequently muddles through powder-keg conditions so that the worst, miraculously, doesn't happen. Yet we can hear the shocked expletive of the unbelieving astronaut in *Planet of the Apes:* "God damn you! You did it! You actually did it!" We know in our minds that nuclear devastation *could* happen, but we feel that it *won't* happen because, somehow, it *can't!*

It is intriguing to note that a Great War has been commonly written about (predicted?) in twentieth-century science fiction. Sometime in the last quarter of the twentieth century—in the '80s or '90s—a holocaust "occurred." On other counts the success score of SF predictions has been very high; countless elements of SF worlds have already become hard realities within a few decades of the authors' original visions. If they are on target this time, then we are coming up on the Great War very soon now. But after all, this is science *fiction,* isn't it?

9   Should nuclear war occur, there are several probable foreseeable results. Detonation of only a few nuclear warheads would break down world-civilization for a long time to come, but it is almost certain that sufficient numbers of people would survive to propagate the species. Only a deliberate, calculated dispersal of lethal fallout over the entire globe could exterminate every living human being, and this is unlikely. Survivors would be able to repopulate the earth, or at least significantly large patches of it. Their offspring, however, would carry so many mutant genes that the populations that followed would rapidly diversify and regroup into what might be classified as subspecies.

Such mass annihilation would result in a breakdown of all health services, distribution of essential medicines, food production and supply, and all forms of communication. The lifestyles of survivors would probably be primitive, simple, and—for those who remember—very difficult. A "rugged individualism" would probably develop in due time as small groups banded together to survive. Chances of survival would depend on the number of animals left alive, how severely food-chains were disrupted, and the degree to which ecological balances had been altered. Even if the worst took place, however, a few groups would certainly adapt and survive.

Nevil Chute's *On the Beach* depicts a possibility, but (we think) not a probability.

10   A projection of the next five thousand years based on the assumption of nuclear war has been developed by Professor Fred Hoyle in his *Encounter with the Future.* Hoyle's model is planned around mathematical probabilities regarding population expansions and depletions of various raw materials. He considers it nearly impossible at this late date for us to harness our reproductive energies and reduce birthrates to the level of deathrates. On the contrary, he believes, birthrates will continue almost exponentially and deathrates will diminish. But a point will be reached at which the world population will have neither living room nor adequate food; the world's organizational systems will suddenly disintegrate, followed by a sharp decrease in populations. Famines and plagues might play a part in this process, but Hoyle is fairly sure that nuclear wars will be the primary instrument of depopulation.

After all, when one tries to change institutions without having changed the nature of men, that unchanged nature will soon resurrect those institutions.

WILL DURANT

The ultimate outcome of this series of population growths and collapses will be the emergence of superior qualities in man, including an average I.Q. of perhaps 150. He will in fact be a new species of man wise enough, finally, to stop the oscillations and stabilize human existence at a more mature level. But only through a continuing experience of consummate tragedies can man prepare his fundamental nature for a more civilized phase of human (or posthuman) existence.°

°Time and again we come across the "Law of Pathei Mathos" in the thinking of some philosopher as he ponders a specific subject. Here we encounter it again as Hoyle applies it to future man: only further suffering, it seems, can produce sufficient maturity for man to live in peace with other men. See pages 90, 93.

Incidentally, there is a remarkably similar (and equally horrifying) projection of a future "dark ages" in the SF classic by Walter M. Miller Jr., *A Canticle for Leibowitz.*

11   Let me then outline in a few words, by way of conclusion, what the broad history of our species is going to be over the next five thousand years, give or take a millennium.

I think that at present we are in the first big expansion phase. This first phase is specially important. It possesses assets—coal, oil, etc—that will not be repeated again. In return for the consumption of these assets it must establish a body of knowledge around which future civilizations will be able to build themselves. Without the establishment of this body of knowledge I do not believe our species will have more than a few centuries of existence ahead of it.

"We need just one more war monument."

Copyright © by Abner Dean—1949. From *And on the Eighth Day.*

I think there will be a series of organizational breakdowns, or catastrophes, occasioned by overpopulation. This will lead to the saw-tooth-shaped population curve [in the diagram]. During the beginnings of the reexpansion phases there will be selection for greater sociability and for higher intelligence. The degree of selection in any one cycle need not be dramatically large because the effects of the repeated cycles are cumulative. Indeed, I expect the number of cycles—the number that occurs before they are damped away—to be determined by how much selection occurs per cycle. If this is large, the number of cycles will be small—and vice versa, the net effect being the same.

The ultimate outcome I believe will be a highly sociable, highly intelligent creature. With this, I would consider a new species to have arrived. It will have its own problems, no doubt, but they will not be as elementary as those with which we are faced today.

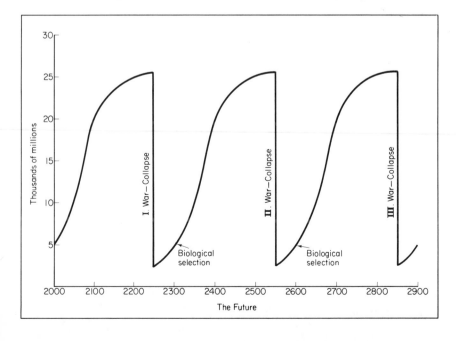

Special Guest Seer: Nostradamus. How seriously precognitive fact-claims should be taken is surely debatable since they open point-blank the question of the nature of time, a problem wholly unresolved at present.° However, it would seem arbitrary to ignore completely the fascinating predictions of the seer Nostradamus about *the events of our near future.* So, let's lend a cautious ear to Michel de Notredame (Latin: Nostradamus), who lived in France from 1503 to 1566 and whose detailed predictions are couched in brilliantly written quatrains. He became renowned during his own lifetime because some of his predictions seemed to come true.°

According to Nostradamus, a worldwide war will begin in 1973 and last some twenty-seven years, ending in the year 2000; this will inaugurate a prolonged period of world peace—the "millennial dawn"—which will begin in 2001. Before this great war begins there will be a time of confusion, debate and accusation, charge and counter-charge, at "fever pitch." This condition will apparently continue from the end of the last (World War II?) until the beginning of the great war.

°See pages 192ff. It may be that pre-cognition is not a true experience but only a working hypothesis which, lacking sufficient data, we can temporarily use to explain some other phenomenon.

°Since Nostradamus wrote in cryptic and allegorical quatrains, his allusions must be interpreted by experts in history and literature. All comments here rest upon the English translation *and interpretation* by Stewart Robb: *Prophecies on World Events by Nostradamus* (1961).

The world's biggest problems today are really infinitesimal: the atom, the ovum, and a bit of pigment.
HERB CAEN

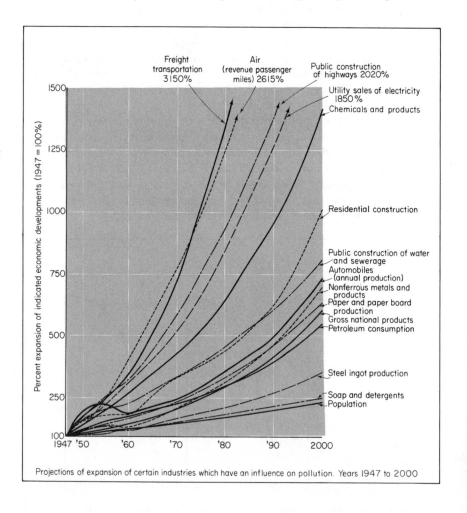

Projections of expansion of certain industries which have an influence on pollution. Years 1947 to 2000

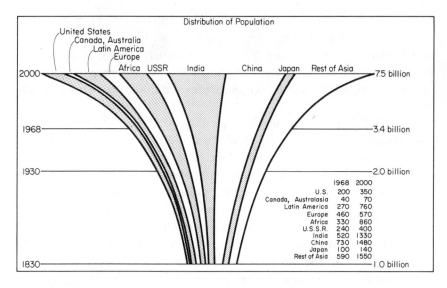

	1968	2000
U.S.	200	350
Canada, Australasia	40	70
Latin America	270	760
Europe	460	570
Africa	330	860
U.S.S.R.	240	400
India	520	1330
China	730	1480
Japan	100	140
Rest of Asia	590	1550

During this time a "great union" will take place between England and America (note that no American nation existed in Nostradamus's time, yet his reference to America—*l'Americh*—seems precise). England will play a secondary role in the union, partly because she will undergo severe internal problems. Great changes will occur in nature. (Earthquakes, climate changes, defoliation, pollution, or what? We can read countless events into such a general statement.) He also makes reference to some momentous journey which is apparently made by an American leader.

These are rather vague allusions, and the far-out interpretations often given them makes one wary. Nevertheless, Nostradamus's more specific statements can be philosophically disturbing—for instance, that in "the year 1999, seventh month" the end of the great war is in sight because the right—the side that stands "for the good cause"—will be heading toward victory.

13   A second world-tragedy might be a totalitarian state and "an age of darkness." All societies have their share of "authoritarian personalities." In any given number of individuals who will become the leaders of men, a large percentage, provided with the right circumstances, possess the character-traits to develop into dictators. They assume power "in times of emergency" and act "for the common good of the people." Severe measures are necessary, in their minds, to maintain law and order and to prevent rampant crime and immorality.

Fearful visions of future totalitarian societies have been woven into the fabric of our thinking by Huxley, Orwell, Bradbury, Rand, and others—*Brave New World, 1984, Fahrenheit 451, Anthem.* We are justly suspicious of Big Brother watching us, and we hardly need Huxley's *Brave New World Revisited* to remind us how rapidly some of the characteristics of the totalitarian state are descending upon us.

The military mind will be the curse of the race so long as there is a military . . . . or will it be the salvation?

CHRISTOPHER ANVIL

The beginning of this world-path could well be an initial stage of chaos and disintegration. This would be more likely to happen in the near future, probably during the next few generations. Chaos could be precipitated by food crises due to overpopulation and, perhaps, destruction of the natural environment from numerous simultaneous forms of pollution.

Two other events might contribute to chaos and disintegration. One could be the breakdown of systems—political, social, economic—because of increasing population alone. The human race could produce too many people to be controlled by any political system, and individuals would gravitate into subunits—gangs, cults, communities, "families"—which would exist as "laws unto themselves" outside the larger systems which are rendered powerless to enforce order.

Even before this, another event contributing to chaos might be a rapid increase in the amount of leisure time, an increase which arrives before we have developed the resources for living it creatively and constructively.

Hard-line authoritarians often arise by meeting the challenge of social chaos and, with the sincerest motives, assume dictatorial powers, declare martial law, and impose "strict security measures"—all to bring order out of truly chaotic conditions. But having found their niche in the system, they surround themselves (as we all do) with congenial coworkers; in their case this means other authoritarian personalities. History seems to indicate that such leaders rapidly change from "creative minorities" to "dominant minorities" (Toynbee's terms), and in so doing they lose the ability to distinguish between beneficial uses of power and actions designed to consolidate and perpetuate their position of power.

14   The most important question we would ask about the future is simple: *Will life be worth living?* The answer is equally simple: Yes, of course. Life in any age will be just as "worth living" as now.

If the worst should happen—if either world-tragedy should actually transpire—then (1) some who have known happier circumstances might find life practically unendurable; but (2) such conditions will be within tolerable limits to those who know no other way. If war and mass annihilation should occur, then for those still living life would probably not differ greatly from that of ancient men who had but a few simple tools and weapons and hunted for a living. Doubtless life was just as precious to primitive man as to us; he fought just as hard to stay alive. So, our ancestors survived, and life for them was "worth living."

For those who know but a single world-view, life is almost always worthwhile, precisely because no one is aware of alternative modes of existence. Living hell is reserved for the person confined to prison after experiencing freedom, for the person frustrated by perpetual danger after experiencing peace and security, for the person forced to the lowest level of physical survival after experiencing a lifestyle of personal fulfillment.

The *contrast* is the hell of it, and thus it would be in the future, whatever conditions prevail. Defeat would be less likely from life's realities as from the contrasts which we might remember or which we conjure in our imaginations.

However, if man succeeds in muddling through and avoids the tragic world-paths, then the advances which must come should provide him with promising conditions *within which* he can *pursue* fulfillment. In the goods and services which society will offer, life will be unimaginably richer.

But there's the splinter. After all is said, it's what happens in man's inner world that determines whether life is "worth living," and life is always in the singular, never the plural. Men are frequently tormented to the point of insanity or suicide in the midst of plenty.

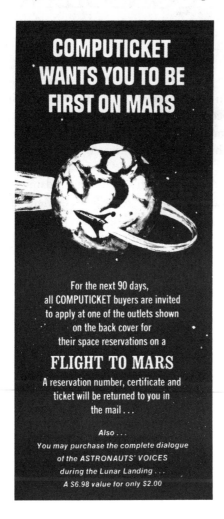

5-2

LAWS/

CONSCIENCE

1 All human societies possessing a modicum of individual freedom develop a wide spectrum of strongly held convictions about the structure and power of human society—"strongly held" because it is the human state, after all, which exercises ultimate temporal control over human destiny.

There exists also in such societies a fundamental tension between those who would obey different sets of laws. Men without freedom are spared this condition; those belonging to primitive tribes or rigidly authoritarian states are subject to but a single set of laws. But in freer societies numerous systems of laws burden the individual by claiming to have jurisdiction over him: he *should* obey them *all!*

This predicament is analogous to what we find in ethics. If one is subject to only a single moral code, then he is spared the complex decisions of free men who must make decisions among sundry codes demanding his loyalty.

Our Western experience has been an ongoing conflict of loyalties. Western society derives its deepest commitment from the scriptural concept of covenant which binds the community of the faithful to the laws of God. For well over a thousand years before Christ—indeed, from the time when Moses defied Egyptian law to lead the Children of Israel into a covenant relationship with Yahweh—man has struggled with the tension between obedience to the "laws of God" and the "laws of man." For all those who live under the divine mandate, their final loyalty has been to God; and man's mundane systems of law have, by comparison, only a weak, secondary claim upon their loyalty.

As for adopting the ways which the State has provided for remedying the evil, I know not of such ways. They take too much time, and a man's life will be gone. I have other affairs to attend to. I came into this world, not chiefly to make this a good place to live in, but to live in it, be it good or bad.

HENRY DAVID THOREAU

2   This tension between loyalties can be felt in the following passages. First, the case (often implicit) for a higher law.

Martin Luther King, Jr.:

I think we all have moral obligations to obey just laws. On the other hand, I think that we have moral obligations to disobey unjust laws because non-cooperation with evil is just as much a moral obligation as cooperation with good.

Henry David Thoreau:

[If the law] is of such a nature that it requires you to be the agent of injustice to another, then, I say, break the law.

Martin Luther:

When the law impels one against love, it ceases and should *no longer be a law* . . . You have need of the law, that love may be manifested; but if it cannot be kept without injury to the neighbor, God wants us to suspend and ignore the law.

We must be entirely clear that law is not God. It has always been a basic Christian conviction that there are times when a Christian ought to break the law.
EUGENE CARSON BLAKE

Mark 2:23–24, 27–28 (paraphrased):

One sabbath while he was walking through the grainfields, his disciples plucked some of the ears of grain and, milling the grain in their hands—which was against the Law of Moses—they ate them.

Some of the Pharisees said to him, "Look at them! Why are they doing what is illegal on the sabbath?"

He replied simply, "The sabbath was made for man, not man for the sabbath."

But those who knew the Law went away angry.

3   The practical—and pragmatic—side of the dilemma is stated with great clarity in the following passages.

Lewis F. Powell, Jr.:

An ordered society cannot exist if every man may determine which laws he will obey, . . . that only "just" laws need be obeyed and that every man is free to determine for himself the question of "justness."

Saint Paul (Romans 13:1–2, 5):

Everyone must obey the authorities that are over him, for no authority can exist without the permission of God; the existing authorities have been established by him, so that anyone who resists the authorities sets himself in opposition to what God has ordained, and those who oppose him will bring down judgment upon themselves. The man who does right has nothing to fear from the magistrates. . . . You must obey them, therefore, not only to escape God's wrath, but as a matter of principle, just as you pay your taxes. . . . Pay them all that is due them.

Immanuel Kant:

Resistance on the part of the people to the supreme legislative power of The State is in no case legitimate; for it is only by submission to the universal legislative will, that a condition of law and order is possible. . . . It is the duty of the people to bear any abuse of the supreme power, even though it should be considered to be unbearable. And the reason is that any resistance of the highest legislative authority can never but be contrary to the law, and must even be regarded as tending to destroy the whole legal constitution.

Saint Peter (1 Peter 2:13–15):

Submit to all human authority, for the Master's sake; to the emperor, as supreme, and to governors, as sent by him to punish evil-doers, and to encourage those who do right.°

°It is the consensus among biblical scholars that the letter called "The First Letter of Peter" was not written by the Apostle Simon bar Jonah. For some, this will detract from its authority.

4   Since this tension is rooted in religion, we would like to be able to turn to a founder of Western religion—to Jesus himself—for guidance; but we do so in vain. When forced into comment upon the dilemma, he merely mystifies the question!

Teacher, we know that you are honest and are not swayed by men; for you do not defer to the worldly positions of men, but truly teach the way of God. Tell us then, what you think. Is it lawful to pay taxes to the state, or not?

But sensing their hypocritical intent, he merely said, "Bring me a coin, and let me look at it."

So they brought him a silver denarius.

Then he asked: "Whose picture and inscription is this?"

They said, "Caesar's."

So Jesus replied: "Then render to Caesar what is Caesar's since Caesar's picture is on the coin; and render to God the things that are God's."

Having failed to entrap him as they planned, they went away angry.

Mark 12:14–17 (paraphrased)

5   The case for making a distinction between good and bad laws is well stated by King, Thoreau, Luther, and others. No matter how strongly one advocates lawful obedience to the state and its laws, it is inevitable that some laws will turn out to be bad ones. Lawmakers are not only human—which is sufficient cause for having a few bad laws—but a percentage of them will always be parochial in their interests, short-sighted or dead wrong in their opinion of what constitutes justice, mentally out of touch with reality, and woefully uninformed on the nature of values and value-judgments (and after all, laws are the legislation of human values). These statements can be made with some certainty simply because the leaders of men are not immune to the neurotic problems shared by the populace as a whole.

Therefore, *in any legal system,* it would be possible to point to laws ranging from mildly unjust to callously inhuman, and such laws *should* produce a feeling of outrage in individuals who are victimized by them, or see others hurt by them. More important, perhaps, is the fact that unless laws are periodically challenged—as the authors of the American system recognized°—then they don't get improved. Among mature men criticism is cherished; it is through the assessment of wise criticism that more just laws can be formulated and antiquated laws updated. Also, it is through open criticism that the selfish interests of those in power can be rapidly brought to the attention of enough citizens who can object and, if necessary, dissent before a deeper tyranny sets in.

°In 1787 Thomas Jefferson said, "God forbid, we should ever be twenty years without such a rebellion." Elsewhere he elaborated: "What country can preserve its liberties, if its rulers are not warned from time to time, that this people preserve the spirit of resistance? Let them take arms. . . . The tree of liberty must be refreshed from time to time, with the blood of patriots and tyrants."

6   I was talking about a vanishing ritual when we were interrupted. . . . We have another tradition in this country which is in danger of passing away: dissent. The responsibility to object. We might all do well to remember in these days of national distemper the comment of Pastor Niemoeller a quarter of a century ago in Nazi Germany. "They came after the Jews, and I was not a Jew, so I did not object. Then they came after the Catholics, and I was not a Catholic, so I did not object. Then they came after the trade-unionists, and I was not a trade-unionist, so I did not object. And then they came after me, and there was no one left to object."

Address by SENATOR STOWE
"The Bold Ones" (NBC-TV)

7   Unjust laws exist: shall we be content to obey them, or shall we endeavor to amend them, and obey them until we have succeeded, or shall we transgress them at once? Men generally, under such a government as this, think that they ought to wait until they have persuaded the majority to alter them. They think that, if they should resist, the remedy would be worse than the evil. But it is the fault of the government itself that the remedy *is* worse than the evil. *It* makes it worse. Why is it not more apt to anticipate and provide for reform? Why does it not cherish its wise minority? Why does it cry and resist before it is hurt? Why does it not encourage its citizens to be on the alert to point out its faults, and *do* better than it would have them? Why does it always crucify Christ, and excommunicate Copernicus and Luther, and pronounce Washington and Franklin rebels?

HENRY DAVID THOREAU

I, HENRY THOREAU, DID NOT JOIN . . .

Some years ago, the State met me in behalf of the
Church, and commanded me to pay a certain sum
toward the support of a clergyman whose preaching
my father attended, but never I myself. "Pay," it said,
"or be locked up in the jail." I declined to pay. But,
unfortunately, another man saw fit to pay it. I did
not see why the schoolmaster should be taxed to
support the priest, and not the priest the schoolmaster;
for I was not the State's schoolmaster, but I supported
myself by voluntary subscription. I did not see why
the lyceum should not present its tax bill, and have
the State to back its demand, as well as the Church.
However, at the request of the selectmen, I con-
descended to make some such statement as this in
writing: "Know all men by these presents, that I,
Henry Thoreau, do not wish to be regarded as a
member of any incorporated society which I have not
joined." This I gave to the town clerk; and he has
it. The State, having thus learned that I did not wish
to be regarded as a member of that Church, has never
made a like demand on me since; though it said that
it must adhere to its original presumption that time.
If I had known how to name them, I should then
have signed off in detail from all the societies which
I never signed onto; but I did not know where to
find a complete list.

HENRY DAVID THOREAU
On Civil Disobedience

8   Our Western (Judeo-Christian) legal tradition takes the form of
a hierarchy of laws—a sort of jurisdictional totem pole—with a clear order
of precedence.

Local laws must defer to higher and wider laws. Thus, in case
of conflict, the laws of a village or city must give way to state laws. State
laws are "higher"; they take precedent. It can be validly argued that in
specific areas of concern, only local laws can be truly relevant to local
conditions. But populations are mobile; individuals are travelers. If there
existed only local laws serving the self-interests of innumerable small
jurisdictions, it just wouldn't work. In matters which affect larger populations over larger areas, wider laws must prevail.

By the same principle, federal laws take precedent over state laws.
Neither cities nor states can be allowed to enact laws which would nourish
their limited interests at the expense of the larger society of which they

are but a part. Wider law must prevail if there is to be equal application of law—that is, if there is to be justice.

At this point the covenant principle upon which Western civilization is grounded must come in: that there is a higher and more universal law than that of any sovereign state. For some twenty-seven hundred years now, the Jews of the Dispersion who were carried off from their homeland have considered the Law of Moses to be higher than the laws of any state in which they lived. In the Roman Empire the fierce loyalty of Jews to their monotheistic faith won them exemption from the worship of Caesar; they alone were officially free of obligations to pour libations to the emperor's *genius* and make offerings to him as divine head of state. As Christianity grew in the early empire, some argued that Christians were Jews and should therefore share the exemption; but the majority of Christians declared emphatically that Christianity was not a branch of Judaism. As Christians established themselves to be a separate sect, they were then obliged to pay respects to the divine Caesar.

But like the Jews, they could not in good conscience do so. The Christians were therefore "disloyal"; they were considered dangerous subversives—"bad citizens." During the years of persecution which followed, the Christians became the main body of conscientious objectors against paying unjust allegiance to Caesar and his state; their highest loyalty was reserved for their God and his laws. For this stand Christians were accused officially of atheism and anarchy: atheism because they refused to worship the state-approved gods, and anarchy because they were "outlaws" who refused to take an oath of allegiance to their government.

It was this refusal to accept "man's laws" that sent Christians into the arena and put them to the sword.

It hasn't been done yet, so they haven't got around to prohibiting it.

Destination Moon

9   In broad terms, the allegiance to a "higher authority" has taken two forms: (1) loyalty to an institution considered to have divine authority over the state; and (2) loyalty to "God's law" as personally understood—by revelation, by "spiritual knowledge" (*gnosis*), or by conscience.

As the Roman Catholic Church developed and became the universal authority in Europe, the papacy pressed its claim to be the supreme power over all temporal authority; for the pope was the "Vicar of Christ" on earth and the Church was "the City of God."

Since the Emperor Constantine established Christianity as the state religion in A.D. 312, this dual claim upon their loyalty has plagued Western citizens. Continuing through the Middle Ages, the Renaissance and the Reformation, and into the modern world, there has been a tug-of-war between temporal authorities—who would diminish the Church's power ("God's laws") and increase their own—and the papacy—which would extend its authority and limit wordly governments ("man's laws"). Individuals found themselves caught in this power struggle.

The supreme confrontation between the claimants occurred on January 28, 1077. Pope Gregory VII had stripped all power from Henry IV of Germany with a decree of excommunication. To regain his kingdom Henry crossed the Alps in winter and knelt in the snow before the gate of the castle of Canossa into which the pope had retreated. Henry repented and after waiting penitently for three days, the pope released him from excommunication and restored him to power.

The second form of allegiance to a higher power is allegiance to the word of God as known personally, to one's own conscience, or to a set of ethical ideals or norms by which one judges the quality of actual laws. Such a position can be theistic and/or ethical, but in any case it commands the highest commitment of the individual. Whatever the path by which one arrives at his position, it often *feels* hypocritical to him to obey bad (unjust) laws when he has seen clearly in his ethical reflections the just laws which should prevail.

This stand was epitomized by Martin Luther in 1521 at the Council of Worms where, passionately and sincerely, he cried out, "My conscience is captive to the Word of God. . . . To go against conscience is neither right nor safe. God help me. Amen."

10   Pope Boniface VIII issued the papal bull *Unan sanctum* in 1302 to define clearly the superiority of God's laws—as embodied here in the Roman papacy—over man's laws—which in this case were represented by the royal heads of England and France. This bull still stands as the most extreme claim of the Church to stand in judgment over the state.

> We are obliged by the faith to believe and hold—and we do firmly believe and sincerely confess—that there is one Holy Catholic and Apostolic Church, and that outside this Church there is neither salvation nor remission of sins. . . .

And we learn from the words of the Gospel that in this Church and in her power are two swords, the spiritual and the temporal. . . . Both are in the power of the Church, the spiritual sword and the material. But the latter is to be used for the Church, the former by her; the former by the priest, the latter by kings and captains but at the will and by the permission of the priest. The one sword, then, should be under the other, and temporal authority subject to spiritual. . . .

Thus, concerning the Church and her power, is the prophecy of Jeremiah fulfilled, "See, I have this day set thee over the nations and over the kingdoms," etc. If, therefore, the earthly power err, it shall be judged by a greater. . . . Furthermore we declare, state, define and pronounce that it is altogether necessary to salvation for every human creature to be subject to the Roman pontiff.

11   At a Chicago meeting of businessmen working to end the war in Vietnam, awards were presented to individuals who had contributed most to the movement. The following episode took place during the ceremony.

In observing my colleagues, and in taking some part in policy decisions on a minor scale, I have been astonished by the way in which the tug of war between left and right is conducted. What seems to happen is this: the left, the ideas-men, the liberals, propose a new idea involving change. The conservatives oppose all change on principle. An argument now develops in which I find myself unable to take any real part. I know that without new ideas, without change, even the most modest enterprise soon congeals and dies. But I also know that most new ideas, like mutations, turn out very badly. Hence from the beginning I am aware of the basic dilemma. But not so the liberals or the conservatives. The liberals, for their part, are quite convinced that the new idea is an excellent one, but when pressed for proof they merely follow the dictum of Robert Owen, "never argue, repeat your assertion." So far as the liberals are concerned I feel as if I were in the presence of divine revelation. The conservatives on the other hand are blockers, stone wallers, Verdun-types with a "they shall not pass" expression written all over their faces. On the whole, because I know that most new ideas are dubious, I end by voting with the conservatives.

FRED HOYLE
Encounter with the Future

One of the big purposes of the Bill of Rights is to keep the government off our backs.

ARTHUR MILLER

THE SUN AND THE MOON
Pope Innocent III: Church and State

The Creator of the universe set up two great luminaries in the firmament of heaven; the greater light to rule the day, the lesser light to rule the night. In the same way for the firmament of the universal Church, which is spoken of as heaven, he appointed two great dignities; the greater to bear rule over souls (these being, as it were, days), the lesser to bear rule over bodies (these being, as it were, nights). These dignities are the pontifical authority and the royal power. Furthermore, the moon derives her light from the sun, and is in truth inferior to the sun in both size and quality, in position as well as effect. In the same way the royal power derives its dignity from the pontifical authority: and the more closely it cleaves to the sphere of that authority the less is the light with which it is adorned; the further it is removed, the more it increases in splendor.

Sicut universitatis conditort
Ep. i. 401, October, 1198

The true patriot is one who gives his highest loyalty not to his country as it is but to his own best conceptions of what it can and ought to be.

ALBERT · CAMUS

Wise men will never do battle over mere symbols, but they may fight to the death for what the symbols stand for.

Joan Baez, when given her award, asked "those who will not understand what I am about to do" to please stop and think. She walked to where the flags on their stanchions flanked the stage . . . and ever so gently laid them down along the raised ledge. It was an electric moment. Jolting—mind tingling. There were boos, . . . There was applause, . . . but above all there was a shared seismic shockwave at the audacity of the act.

Back at the rostrum she implored the 2500 of us assembled there to remember that man has killed for such "pieces of cloth" since the dawn of recorded history. Anguished, she sought to remind us indelibly that "no piece of cloth is sacred . . . ," that "only human life is sacred." But symbols come in time to have a life of their own. And despite Ramsey Clark's gentle reminder that we who believe in the principle of freedom of expression must tolerate its manifestation, there was enough mixed feelings to send two emissaries from the wings to stand the flags upright once more. Again the expressions of approval and disapproval from those gathered . . . and the scalp prickle sensation of impending confrontation.

Miss Baez stopped in the middle of her song . . . sensing from the audience reaction what was happening on stage behind her. Once more she crossed and gently laid the flags down, . . . this time helped by one of the young veterans on the program. The room pressed together in tense expectancy. Fearful that the differences between us could rend the fragile web that bound us to the common cause, . . . we waited. The flags stayed down, . . . spilling like blood over the ledges where they lay.

And so they lay until Cong. Pete McCloskey in presenting the special award of the evening to Daniel Ellsberg for his act of true patriotism . . . called for the flags to be raised and looked at anew in the meaning of their original symbolism—a tangible reflection of resistance to illegitimate authority. To the birth of our nation, the greatest dream of mankind. He and Ramsey Clark raised the standards again.

12   Associate Justice Lewis Powell presents persuasively the case for absolute obedience to duly constituted authority: laws must be obeyed, for if each person were permitted to decide which laws were good and which were bad, social chaos would necessarily result. For who is there among us who is able to determine just from unjust laws? And on what criteria could such judgments be made? Wouldn't it be inevitable that every political crank and religious fanatic—not to mention emotionally immature rebels of all ages—would decide that all the laws were "unjust" which didn't cater to his own self-centered interests?

This is precisely the position taken by Socrates when his old and dear friend Crito urged him to escape from prison the day before his execution. Socrates awoke before dawn to find Crito sitting silently beside him in his cell; he has apparently made all necessary arrangements for an escape.

But Socrates has already made up his mind and refuses to flee. He patiently attempts to make Crito understand his reasoning.

The surest way to corrupt a young man is to teach him to esteem more highly those who think alike than those who think differently.
NIETZSCHE

Look at it in this way. Suppose that while we were preparing to run away from here (or however one should describe it) the Laws and Constitution of Athens were to come and confront us and ask this question: "Now, Socrates, what are you proposing to do? Can you deny that by this act which you are contemplating you intend, so far as you have the power, to destroy us, the Laws, and the whole State as well? Do you imagine that a city can continue to exist and not be turned upside down, if the legal judgements which are pronounced in it have no force but are nullified and destroyed by private persons?"—how shall we answer this question, Crito, and others of the same kind? . . . Shall we say "Yes, I do intend to destroy the laws, because the State wronged me by passing a faulty judgement at my trial"? Is this to be our answer, or what? . . .

Supposing the Laws say "Was there provision for this in the agreement between you and us, Socrates? Or did you undertake to abide by whatever judgements the State pronounced?" . . . Do you not realize . . . that if you cannot persuade your country you must do whatever it orders, and patiently submit to any punishment that it imposes, whether it be flogging or imprisonment? And if it leads you out to war, to be wounded or killed, you must comply, and it is right that you should do so; you must not give way or retreat or abandon your position. Both in war and in the law-courts and everywhere else you must do whatever your city and your country commands, or else persuade it in accordance with universal justice. . . . "—What shall we say to this, Crito?— that what the Laws say is true, or not?

PLATO,
Crito

13   The problem of obedience to law might be visualized as an ellipse with two foci. Near one end of the ellipse is the question of human freedom. All of us want freedom, and we want *more* freedom; but as the number of problematic persons in our society increases, the more regulation is required and the less freedom we can enjoy.

The other focus in the ellipse is one's assessment of human nature. If one is basically optimistic about natural man and believes him to be trustworthy, then he will assume we humans can use freedom constructively and will not need punctilious systems of laws to tell us what to do and not to do. But if one distrusts human nature, convinced that it is fundamentally evil, then he must conclude that a complex system of laws is necessary to keep this selfish nature in line and coerce a semblance of order.

Around these two foci—and they *are* inside a single ellipse—turns the question of obedience to all law: to obey or not to obey. The mature, fully actualized person wants to guide his life solely by a few basic principles; he becomes restive and may chafe bitterly under irrelevant restraints upon his existence. For him they are not needed: he would do what is right anyway! By contrast, however, most human beings appear unable to experience very much freedom without harming others; we are unable to live with one another peacefully without having our behavior guided and restrained by specific regulations touching all aspects of our lives.

14   The dilemma between principles and law has tormented many great souls. Saint Paul, for instance: he tried diligently to follow the 613 precepts of the Jewish Law but only felt more guilty because he could not measure up to its numerous demands. In the end, he found peace only by abandoning the *Law* of Moses and accepting the *principle* of "justification by faith" in Jesus as the Christ.

Similarly, Martin Luther tried to make legalistic Roman Catholic laws work to his benefit, but he found himself caught, like Paul, on a wheel of guilt and ultimately found peace only by following Paul's lead and committing his life to a single principle: "salvation by faith alone."

It is worth noting that Hinduism has provided, within the parameters of acceptable religion, several systems to meet different needs. The "Ways of Liberation" are designed to accomplish this. The "Way of Works" (*Karma Marga*) specifies innumerable rites and duties which the worshiper has only to perform to gain good karma. It makes few intellectual demands. It's a matter of *doing;* one must meticulously perform

The American advocacy system is a wretched way to determine the innocence or guilt of a man. But no one has yet proposed a better way.

"The Bold Ones"
NBC-TV

the actions prescribed by the laws. This is the path chosen by a large majority of Hindus. By contrast, there is the "Way of Knowledge" (*Jnana Marga*). This is philosophical Hinduism, the way of study and meditation which will lead the mind out of the errors which produce human misery. This is the way of liberation for only a few who have the capacity for discipline and abstract reflection.

15   The dilemma between a few guiding principles and numerous laws was carefully explored by Joseph Klausner, an Orthodox Jewish historian, in a scholarly study entitled *Jesus of Nazareth* (1907, English translation 1925). In the squabble between the Pharisees who held firmly to the letter of the Mosaic Law and Jesus who deliberately disregarded Jewish law, Klausner concludes that, in the final analysis, the Pharisees were right. Judaism could never accept such a contemptuous attitude toward the Law.

> For the Jews their religion was more than simple belief and more than simple moral guidance: it was a *way of life*—all life was embraced in their religion. A people does not endure on a foundation of general human faith and morality; it needs a "practical religiousness," a ceremonial form of religion which shall embody religious ideas and also crown every-day life with a halo of sanctity.

By undermining the Law of Moses, Klausner is saying, Jesus would have destroyed the Jewish nation. Jesus' intentions are not to be inpugned, "but it is unquestionable that throughout his entire teaching there is nothing that can serve to the upkeep of the state or serve towards the maintenance of order in the existing world."

There were Jewish scholars long before Jesus who were capable of formulating the *essence* of the Law of Moses in one or two general principles. Hillel, an elder contemporary of Jesus, said: "What is hateful to thyself do not to thy neighbor: this is the whole Law, the rest is commentary: go and learn it." But such rabbis who *saw* the essence never dispensed with the literal requirements of the Law itself: for law regulates collective life and gives it order. People being what they are, Klausner writes that "the nation as a whole could only see in such public ideals as those of Jesus, an abnormal and even dangerous phantasy; the majority, who followed the Pharisees and Scribes (*Tannaim*), the leaders of the popular party in the nation, could *on no account* accept Jesus' teaching."

These illustrations seem to indicate that without firm law, and a sense of obedience to law, a society disintegrates.

16   Socrates sought truth with a rare courage. But he came too close; he was too relevant to be a security risk to Athens. For this he was handed a cup of hemlock in the spring or early summer of 399 B.C. Thus ended

When a legal distinction is determined . . . between night and day, childhood and maturity, or any other extremes, a point has to be fixed or a line has to be drawn, or gradually picked out by successive decisions, to mark where the change takes place. Looked at by itself without regard to the necessity behind it, the line or point seems arbitrary. It might as well be a little more to the one side or the other. But when it is seen that a line or point there must be, and that there is no mathematical or logical way of fixing it precisely, the decision of the legislature must be accepted unless we can say that it is very wide of any reasonable mark.

OLIVER WENDELL HOLMES

the career of one of the greatest minds the world has ever known, and the young men who followed Socrates knew then that something deep and terrible was wrong in men, individually and collectively. "This was the end of our comrade," wrote Plato, "a man, as we would say, of all then living we had ever met, the noblest and the wisest and the most just."

These men knew from their own bitter experience that societies persecute and/or execute their *best men* as well as their worst. This fact alone was enough to tell them that something tragic seems built into the human condition; and it was this insight that caused the first philosophers to begin to think deeply about life's problems and to search for solutions.

5-3

LIFESTYLES

1   Somewhere (and once upon a time) there was a small green valley lying quietly within the steep walls of surrounding mountains, and a village slept on the floor of the valley. No one from the village had ever ascended the mountain walls to travel beyond. Whatever lay beyond the rim of their valley, for them, did not exist. "Outside" had no meaning; nor did "beyond" or "stranger" or "distant lands" or "enemy tribes." No one else existed, or could possibly exist . . . until that day when someone found a path through a mountain pass, and came back to tell his kin that they were not alone.

2   The life history of the individual is first and foremost an accommodation to the patterns and standards traditionally handed down in his community. From the moment of his birth the customs into which he is born shape his experience and behavior. By the time he can talk, he is the little creature of his culture, and by the time he is grown and able to take part in its activities, its habits are his habits, its beliefs his beliefs, its impossibilities his impossibilities.

RUTH BENEDICT

The age of cultural innocence is passing; the American is beginning to recognize the patterns to which he conforms.

SNELL AND GAIL PUTNEY

3   Acculturation is one aspect of the human condition. Throughout recorded time, each individual has been born into, then blended into, a single, ongoing culture. It was given; no alternative to system-acculturation existed. His culture's world-view became his, including its values, myths, history, customs, traditions, and—deepest of all—the unexamined assumptions upon which his culture's world-view is grounded. All these became a part of his existence.

     The result has been universally the same, as Ruth Benedict has aptly phrased it: ". . . its habits are his habits, its beliefs his beliefs, *its impossibilities his impossibilities.*"

They are playing a game. They are playing at not playing a game. If I show them I see they are, I shall break the rules and they will punish me. I must play their game, of not seeing I see the game.

R. D. LAING

4   This condition no longer prevails for increasing numbers of people. In our time, a new alternative has been opened to us. We now have the genuine option of breaking free of the bonds of culture-systems. This can be either a blessing or a curse. The loss of roots which a culture provides can be agonizing, yet the opportunities offered by this new freedom are momentous.

For good or ill, therefore, the freedom is ours. For what is probably the first time in human history, we can pass judgment on our culture and make a more objective assessment of the ways in which it meets or fails to meet our basic needs.

What is asked of us—or *demanded* of us—is no easy path. We are at a crossroads requiring considerable moral courage: the courage to face freedom and seek autonomy *without* the roots and *without* the security which culture has heretofore guaranteed to each of us.

5   The sources of this new freedom are many; three are fairly obvious.

First, from the vast researches of the social scientists, we have come to recognize the cultural patterns which have shaped our existence. From the anthropologists' patient examination of other cultural patterns, we can see more dispassionately the patterns which others have unconsciously followed. After comparing the patterns of numerous societies we have come to understand the function and operation of a culture-system. We find that each culture is an internally coherent structure with its compo-

"What am I doing here?"

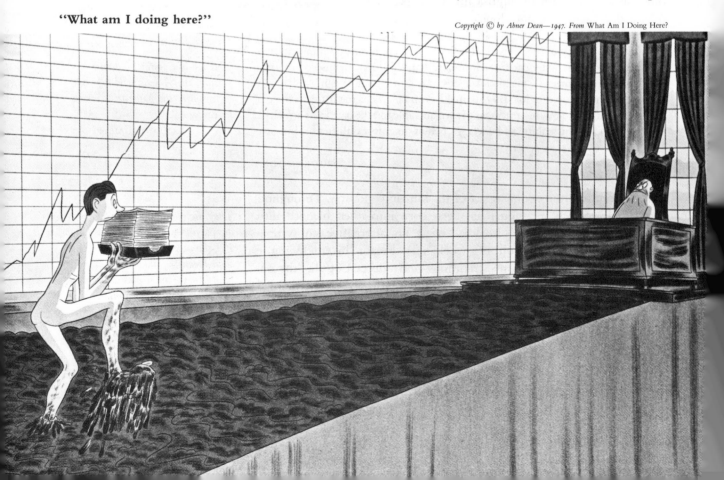

nent parts harmonizing into an interdependent working system. Each culture provides a world-view, so that life for each individual in the system has coherence and meaning.

When we apply this knowledge to our own culture, we begin to understand its function and our roles in it. We see how relative some of the patterns and values are. Previously—while living in that small green valley—we took them for granted; we may even have believed them to be universal or absolute. Now we find that they were merely functional. We have discovered that individuals immersed in their cultures, from the primitive to the most civilized, endow their respective patterns with the same ultimacy and finality which we felt. For each, his culture has worked pragmatically for him, and therefore no other culture existed, or could exist. We can now recognize ethnocentrism, wherever it occurs.

The result is that we see ourselves in a larger context, and having seen, we can no longer follow a tacit ethnocentrism. We see through it; we understand its root causes. The egocentric illusion has been found out!

Secondly, in the decade of the seventies we are involved in a cataclysmic increase in cultural interaction. No single major culture stands today as a monolithic, isolated system, as they all once did. Few places exist in the world today where one could be born and remain culturally naive. Arnold Toynbee has pointed out that a cultural map of the earth a few centuries ago showed large pure-color patches, distinct from one another and with fairly sharp edges; but by the end of our century the patches will have vanished and the cultural colors will everywhere be woven together—like "shot silk"—with only faint blushes of color remaining in a few isolated enclaves.

Probably the most significant world-fact of our time is the disintegration of cultures as distinct and separate functional systems. This is the fundamental fact that has given us our freedom—and our pain.

A third source of our freedom is new insight into the dynamics of our inner world. We know a great deal now about the processes of psychological conditioning and reinforcement. We know that individuals can be acculturated into any set of customs, beliefs, and values; they can be made to believe, value, and even worship almost anything. If societies can condition us, then we know that we can be *unconditioned* and *reconditioned*.

And so, as we gain a clearer picture of our basic human needs—*which may or may not be fulfilled by the particular culture in which we live*—we feel a new freedom to pursue their fulfillment. *We* can take the initiative. We no longer submit to the doctrine that we *must* remain, unquestioningly, within a particular system; indeed, with our awareness of alternatives, external coercion for us to do so might be interpreted as enslavement. Various cultures, subcultures, and segments of culture are readily accessible to us. We are free to experiment with them, identify with them; some can even find a home in several systems simultaneously or sequentially.

He who is his own servant cannot be his own master. A mere matter of space in our minds. He will think *kitchen, bathroom, laundry, garbage, instead of thinking living room and library, conversation and paintings, beautiful clothes and flowers. After a very short time he will become the servant of that servant: earn a living for him.*

NICCOLO TUCCI

About then I made a horrible discovery. I didn't want to go back to school, win, lose, or draw. I no longer gave a damn about three-car garages and swimming pools, nor any other status symbol or "security." There was no *security in this world and only damn fools and mice thought there could be.*

ROBERT HEINLEIN
The Glory Road

I do my thing, and you do your thing.
I am not in this world to live up to your expectations
And you are not in this world to live up to mine.
You are you and I am I,
And if by chance we find each other, it's beautiful.
If not, it can't be helped.

Fritz Perls.

6 In any society, specific BTF-patterns are considered "normal" not merely because the majority adheres to them, but also because they are meaningful and functional. They enable us to predict the behavior of others, and they ours. They create consistency in our experiencing of life together; they provide us with a unifying world-view. "Normal" behavior supports and enhances that unity; "abnormal" behavior does not cohere with the system and tends to destroy it.

As we move from culture to culture we find the same principles. Normal BTF-patterns will differ, but within each society these elements will cohere and interact. The system will provide guidelines for living and a high degree of conformity and security. Therefore, within each culture, these accepted BTF-patterns are normal and right.

The fact of cultural relativism was first recognized, so far as we know, by the Greek Sophist Protagoras. Denying that any belief or custom was absolute, Protagoras declared that "man is the measure of all things" (that is, customs are man-made, not divinely given); and he held that we have an obligation to conform to the cultural patterns of any society we might visit. After all, what right have we, flaunting our ethnocentric arrogance, to subvert a workable system by introducing our alien BTF-patterns?

The natural tendency to form social in-groups could never be eradicated without a major genetical change in our make-up, and one which would automatically cause our complex social structure to disintegrate.

DESMOND MORRIS

The central point in cultural relativism is that in a particular cultural setting, certain traits are right because they work well in that setting, while other traits are wrong because they would clash painfully with parts of that culture. This is but another way of saying that a culture is integrated, and that its various elements must harmonize passably if the culture is to function efficiently in serving human purposes.

HORTON AND HUNT

7   A phenomenon found in every culture is what we sometimes call the "double standard." There are, first, the acceptable BTF-patterns; these are the publicly professed, ideal patterns that everyone is "supposed to" follow. But along with these acceptable norms also exist clearly established, socially sanctioned ways of breaking the ideal norms. That is, *there are acceptable ways of misbehaving.*

Man, it would appear, finds it difficult to live with a single set of BTF-patterns; he must have at least two sets of rules. The first set represents his ideals, the way he believes his society should be. These are projections of what he would like others to think of him and the way he would like to think of himself and others. Many convince themselves that all or most people truly follow such ideal standards of behavior.

The unacceptable patterns are just as much a part of a cultural process as the acceptable patterns, and perhaps just as vital. Man seems to need these unacceptable BTF-patterns to express a side of his nature which he is reluctant to admit. They are outlets for taboo feelings—fears, sexual urges, hostilities, prejudices—feelings which he would prefer to repress and not worry about. But since he can't escape the fact that they exist, they are expressed in various cultures in "acceptable unacceptable" ways.

Every known society has a double standard, and the "unacceptable" patterns must be considered an integral part of that culture.

8   Tension is necessarily involved where individuals are forced to function in line with several BTF-patterns, as in the case of a double standard. After all, we can't be fully open about the repressed patterns no matter how widely they are practiced, for one of the rules is that they not be *openly* accepted. Some amount of deception with others—and perhaps with ourselves—is inevitable.

Such tensions, however, are not usually very destructive. Most individuals learn to accept the fact that conflicting sets of rules are a part of the culture. They proceed to live with them, or by them. Still, one must be most cautious about when and where he admits the existence of the "unacceptable" patterns of behavior.

9   Is there any quality of "American" thought which distinguishes it from that developed elsewhere?

The American divorce rate has been variously attributed to teen-age marriage, delayed marriage, pre-marital sexual experience, lack of sexual experience, decline of religious influence, residual Puritanism, glamorization of divorce, and even the automobile. But our analysis suggests a different, perhaps a shocking answer: American marriages are unstable because Americans marry for love.

SNELL AND GAIL PUTNEY

We cannot return to a simpler world. Much of contemporary social criticism is made irrelevant by its refusal to face that fact.

JOHN GARDNER

5 Coexistence: Man's Love/Hate Condition

One peculiar and all-pervasive characteristic is its pluralism. . . . Thought in America has developed in response to external influences and to internal problems and challenges. America has been receptive to many cultures and to a variety of intellectual themes. There is, for example, both a liberal and a conservative tradition throughout American history. There is the America of radical democratic individualism and equalitarianism of Thomas Jefferson, Thomas Paine, Ethan Allen, Benjamin Rush, Henry Thoreau, Abraham Lincoln and John Dewey—an America in which liberal causes are espoused or in which a dominant secular and naturalistic outlook prevails. But there is also a conservative stream in American history, represented in the religious interests of the Puritans, Jonathan Edwards, and Samuel Johnson, in the defense of orthodoxy by the Scottish realists and speculative idealists, and in

"I don't understand it. Why didn't he marry both of them?"

the conservative politics of Cadwallader Colden, Alexander Hamilton, John C. Calhoun, and even George Santayana. America is thus the meeting place of divergent ideas and movements: Puritanism, deism, materialism, Unitarianism, transcendentalism, idealism, realism, and pragmatism—and most recently of naturalism, positivism, analytic philosophy, Marxism, Thomism, phenomenology, Zen Buddhism, and existentialism. Any simple formulas designed to reduce these diverse elements into a uniform tradition are bound to be distorted.

PAUL KURTZ

10   Much current anxiety and alienation is the result of the interaction of cultures and their breakdown as functional systems. Since different systems have conflicting BTF-patterns, what happens when they collide and interact? Each system loses its coherence, integrity, and workability. We discover that various BTF-patterns are right *and* wrong, acceptable *and* unacceptable *at the same time,* depending upon which strand of culture one uses as the criterion of valuation.

"Shave it off! I'm changing my whole philosophy of life!"

What happens to you and me as we try to adjust to a cultural eclecticism? We *internalize* that eclecticism. The outer world is a hodge-podge, so our inner worlds become hodge-podges. Our culture is fragmented, so we too become fragmented. We don't know which values to follow, so we attempt to hold conflicting values which reflect our culture. We don't know what behavior is acceptable, so we behave differently in different settings.

Consistent behavior is no longer possible, and the integrity so essential to the harmonious operation of our inner world becomes ever more elusive. Self and sanity are at stake, and, by degrees, both can be lost.

11　When one is in this condition—when his inner world reflects the fragmentation of the outer world—he will feel from within a pressure to find a solution. Several easy and attractive alternatives are at hand; at least momentarily they can provide security and relieve anxiety.

One alternative is to identify with but a single isolated strand of culture where one can feel more at home. In such a group one's BTF-patterns will be shared by others and tensions can therefore diminish. One can feel more at ease with those who share his values. Feelings of alienation and fragmentation may subside. Surrounded by those who are congenial, one can usually ignore the uncongenial patterns which heretofore caused trouble.

The difficulty with this alternative is that it doesn't solve the problem. To be sure, changing the environment can be a step in the right direction, but one must recognize that the *vulnerability* to fragmentation is an inner problem, and it may remain. The wound is in the inner world, not in the environment. Finding congenial surroundings may ease the pain only temporarily unless healing can proceed within.

A similar alternative is to join a truth-group. One can plunge into a subcultural unit which devalues all other BTF-patterns; once devalued, they tend to lose their power over us. Relegating them to an inferior status brings more satisfaction than ignoring or repressing them. One doesn't have to take seriously the experience of any other person or group which differs, since he knows that their BTF-patterns are erroneous or wrong. Truth-groups usually make aristocentrism a condition of membership, and the sense of identity and security they offer is therefore especially rewarding.

This alternative prevents one from discovering effective channels of growth. Genuine identification with a truth-group is possible only while one remains unaware of the implications of the egocentric predicament. Nevertheless, when our cultural confusion becomes too great, such a refuge, for many, may be the only viable alternative.

For others, there is a third path, but it is anything but a choice. This is psychosis. If the real world appears too hellish, it is quite possible

The general thrust of the cultural trend throughout both the Western and Communist world is to say that man is not free, that there is no such thing as a free man. We are formed and moved by forces—cultural forces without, and unconscious forces within—which we do not comprehend and which are beyond our control. We will soon be formed more knowingly and more precisely by a scientific technology which will replace the crude way in which we have been molded by partially fortuitous natural events.

CARL ROGERS

The main path to health and self-fulfillment for the masses is via basic need gratification rather than via frustration. This contrasts with the suppressive regime, the mistrust, the control, the policing that is necessarily implied by basic evil in human depths.

ABRAHAM MASLOW

to create an inner world that is less threatening. It is never a freely chosen alternative, but rather a condition that takes over when we have lost our freedom of choice.

The majority of us, however, follow the easiest path; we try halfheartedly to conform to many noncoherent patterns of culture at the same time—wearing various masks, playing various roles—whatever the cost to our mental health. Even at the risk of a mild schizophrenia, the expediency is not too costly, we think. The possibility of developing autonomy will be lost, but then, nobody's perfect . . .

after 50,000 years
rapturous in sky
I find you
     Living
        in a box

12 I left the woods for as good a reason as I went there. Perhaps it seemed to me that I had several more lives to live, and could not spare any more time for that one. It is remarkable how easily and insensibly we fall into a particular route, and make a beaten track for ourselves. I had not lived there a week before my feet wore a path from my door to the pond-side; and though it is five or six years since I trod it, it is still quite distinct. It is true, I fear, that others may have fallen into it, and so helped to keep it open. The surface of the earth is soft and impressible by the feet of men; and so with the paths which the mind travels. How worn and dusty, then, must be the highways of the world, how deep the ruts of tradition and conformity! I did not wish to take a cabin passage, but rather to go before the mast and on the deck of the world, for there I could best see the moonlight amid the mountains. I do not wish to go below now.

I learned this, at least, by my experiment: that if one advances confidently in the direction of his dreams, and endeavors to live the life which he has imagined, he will meet with a success unexpected in common hours. He will put some things behind, will pass an invisible boundary; new, universal, and more liberal laws will begin to establish themselves around and within him; or the old laws be expanded, and interpreted in his favor in a more liberal sense, and he will live with the license of a higher order of beings. In proportion as he simplifies his life, the laws of the universe will appear less complex, and solitude will not be solitude, nor poverty poverty, nor weakness weakness. If you have built castles in the air, your work need not be lost; that is where they should be. Now put the foundations under them.

HENRY DAVID THOREAU

Never hope to realize Plato's republic . . . for who can change the opinions of men? And without a change of sentiments what can you make but reluctant slaves and hypocrites?

MARCUS AURELIUS

"I say it is useless to waste your life on one path, especially if that path has no heart."

"But how do you know when a path has no heart, don Juan?"

"Before you embark on it you ask the question: Does this path have a heart? If the answer is no, you will know it, and then you must choose another path."

"But how will I know for sure whether a path has a heart or not?"

"Anybody would know that. The trouble is nobody asks the question; and when a man finally realizes that he has taken a path without a heart, the path is ready to kill him. At that point very few men can stop to deliberate, and leave the path."

"How should I proceed to ask the question properly, don Juan?"

"Just ask it."

CARLOS CASTANEDA
The Teachings of Don Juan

Man is by nature a social animal; and an unsocial person who is unsocial naturally and not accidentally is either unsatisfactory or superhuman. . . Society is a natural phenomenon and is prior to the individual. . . . And any one who is unable to live a common life or who is so self-sufficient that he has no need to do so is no member of Society, which means that he is either a beast or a god.

ARISTOTLE

5-4

VALUES/
PRIORITIES

When everyone recognizes beauty as beautiful,
there is already ugliness;
When everyone recognizes goodness as good,
there is already evil.

Tao Teh Ching

1   A young couple walk along a jetty on a clear winter night. The churning surf pounds the seaward side. They had watched the red sunset, and now in the darkness the waves are laced with phosphorus and can be seen forming far out from shore; they swell gently and then move in to break on the rocks with a thunderous splash, sending a fine salt spray across the jetty. The stars of Orion glisten overhead like sparks in crystal.

This moment of time, for the young man, was beyond words and thoughts. He beheld the beauty of the sunset, felt a sense of mystery, and just a hint of eternity. Such rare moments end too soon; they should last at least forever, especially when there is someone who can share these feelings.

The depth of his feeling is shared by the girl, but differently. One wintry evening when she was twelve she and her family were fishing in a rowboat a half-mile off shore. Just at sunset the winds increased and the surf rose; the small boat took a swell broadside and capsized. In the falling darkness she could remember her father's struggle to right the boat; then she could remember shivering with cold as she clung to the deck. She looked at the stars and felt the salt spray on her face. She waited for the others to join her in the boat, but they never came.

So on this night, many years later, even beside a friend, she had a memory of consuming terror as she heard the waves pound against the jetty. Looking up at the stars and feeling the salt mist on her face brought back old fears and rekindled her feelings of loss and loneliness.

5 *Coexistence: Man's Love/Hate Condition*

They could share a sense of mystery, perhaps, but for the girl there was no beauty to be found in the sunset and no enchantment to be felt in the phosphorescent waves or shining stars.

They had come to the same scene in space and time, but each had emerged from a different world to join briefly and walk along the jetty.

2   No two people share precisely the same values; all our responses are uniquely conditioned by the endlessly changing experiences of life.

Tastes, sounds, and odors that one individual finds pleasant another dislikes. A girl may be beautiful to one man (especially if she loves and appreciates him) but unattractive to another. Music that brings pain to one can bring comfort to another. Sights and scenes which may be beautiful to one—the Pleiades, the paintings of van Gogh, the wind-waved sands of the Sahara—may leave another unmoved; and the images which might be distasteful to some—the Crucifix, Gericault's *Raft of the "Medusa",* and pop art—may be appreciated by others. Pleasure and pain are conditioned responses; what may be painful for one may be pleasurable for another.

Our emotional responses are equally personal. Our feelings about sex and sex-symbols differ. Behavior acceptable to one group or culture offends another. Our feelings about movies, TV programs, plays, and books differ, as a cross-check of critics' reviews quickly shows. Our principles and convictions differ. Playing the national anthem can send into a rage one who has been victimized by the injustice of a system less than perfect; it can bring tears of joy to the eyes of one who is returning home after years in a foreign country.

3   When we try to express the rich complexity of value-experience, we find ourselves caught (again) in the "conspiracy of language."

Sensory Experience

"I like the flavor of real Italian spaghetti." (Taste)
"I think Susan is beautiful." (Vision)
"I enjoy walking in the rain." (Touch)
"I'm turned on by the fragrance of orange blossoms." (Smell)
"I prefer the rhythms of *Bolero* to *The Rite of Spring.*" (Sound)

Emotional Experience

"I enjoy playing mathematical games."
"I hate being embarrassed in public."
"I like Susan."
"I distrust bureaucracies."
"I'm scared of love."

Rosemary's Baby *would have been a better movie if they had left out the sex.*

                A Student

A cynic is a man who knows the price of everything, and the value of nothing.

            OSCAR WILDE

     5   Coexistence: Man's Love/Hate Condition

No fact-claims are made in any of the above statements. There is no statement to which one might retort "You're wrong!" If someone states that he likes spaghetti, then (unless he's lying or doesn't know the meaning of the words) he likes spaghetti. No true/false or yes/no response is possible.

If these are not statements of fact, then what are they? Each statement is a description of one's personal experience, sensory or emotional as the case may be. If her boyfriend thinks Susan is beautiful, then—since "beauty is in the eye of the beholder"—Susan *is* beautiful *to him.* Of course, someone else can respond by saying "I don't think she's so beautiful," but he would be guilty of *changing the subject.* What is being discussed is not Susan's "beauty" (there is no such thing), but her boyfriend's sensory/emotional response *to her.* Anyone else's response is merely irrelevant. Nevertheless, we often counter such statements with our own experience ("I enjoy mathematical games." "You do? I don't"), and we fail to realize that we have in fact changed the topic of conversation.

4   To such statements we commonly respond with "Why"? For instance: "I'm scared of failing." "Why?" In the realm of sensory/ emotional experience why-questions are generally unfortunate, for we feel the necessity of producing logical reasons for our sensory/emotional responses—responses which by nature don't operate on logical principles. "I don't like to be embarrassed." "I dislike hippie-types." "I'm scared of death." If someone demands "Why?" to such questions, very few of us have sufficient self-knowledge to give correct answers; but rare is the individual who can resist giving some kind of answer to please a persistent, if misguided, questioner.

There are two appropriate responses to such personal value-statements. (1) We can acknowledge that they describe only one's subjective responses and store them away as part of our knowledge of that particular individual or of human behavior in general. (2) Further than this, and for numerous commendable reasons, we might wish to ask questions which would further clarify the nature of the experience being described; that is, we might wish to understand much more about the other person.

The important fact to note is that all such value-statements are reflexive: they describe the subject and not the object.

5   The habit of objectifying our personal value-experience insures confusion. Rather than saying "I like spaghetti" or "I'm scared of sharks" or "Susan is beautiful to me," we say "Spaghetti is good," "Sharks are scary," and "Susan is beautiful." Such objectifications are fallacies, of course; but more than that, they get us into trouble and we waste time arguing about what can't be argued about. Almost without exception, we think we are arguing about the *object* of the statement (in the above

A little knowledge of history stresses the variability of moral codes, and concludes that they are negligible because they differ in time and place, and sometimes contradict each other. A larger knowledge stresses the universality of moral codes, and concludes to their necessity.

WILL DURANT

Contentment, even in poverty, brings happiness; discontent is poverty, even in riches.

Chinese Proverb

instances, about spaghetti, sharks, and Susan, in that order) rather than our personal responses, about which there can be no argument.

It might be worth noting that, quite apart from the meaning of statements, we often argue from other motives entirely, sometimes because we like the sound of our voice, but oftener because we like the sound of another's voice. There's nothing quite as satisfying as a good argument about nothing to keep someone else within range, and the present analysis should not be construed as an attempt to put an end to such meaningful maneuvers.

6   One's sensory/emotional responses can never be validly objectified. Yet few fallacies are more common.

"Menthol 1000s have a fresher flavor." "It has a great shape" (car ad). "Economics is boring." "The beat of Japanese music is so monotonous" (from a film critic). "Sex is fun." "Sailing is great." "It has the rich aroma women go for." "It's a nauseating book" (a judge's official opinion on a popular autobiography). "It's a dirty movie" (statement by a member of a censorship board). "Baboons are ugly" (little girl at zoo). "It has a casual elegance" (carpet ad). "They have that old-fashioned comfort inside" (shoe ad). "It has a deep, pure taste" (beer ad).

To each and every such value-statement, another may reply that he doesn't experience the matter that way. The discussion can end there.

7 *No value-judgment is meaningful unless the criteria for validating the judgment are known.* Whatever the judgment is about, unless supporting facts are understood or explicitly stated, it remains unintelligible. Such a criterion may not really need clarification ("War is not healthy for children and other living things") or it may need to be stated explicitly ("India is in a more precarious situation today than it was ten years ago." "You mean more people and less food?" "No, I mean the threat from China").

Any value-judgment, or any act motivated by a value-judgment, can be shown to be either right or wrong, depending upon the criteria which are selected to evaluate it. Killing is wrong (see Exodus 20:13) or right (Deuteronomy 13:6–11). Abortion is good (it saves mothers' lives and prevents unloved babies) or bad (it's tantamount to murder). Television is good (entertaining, educational) or bad (it has created in us the "simple solution" syndrome).

The exact meaning of any value-judgment is comprehensible only in the context of the situation in which the judgment is made. (This is a specific application of a semantic axiom which contends that *no statement* can be understood apart from the context in which the statement originated.) For instance: "Kentucky blend is great tobacco." To whom? and for what? To the average smoker or to the connoisseur? In a pipe, in a cigarette, or in a hookah? For its aromatic fragrance or because it stays lit? For producing cancer-cultures? For attracting the opposite sex? Or for smoking out bees from a beehive?

8 On the basis of our values we take collective action. Any number of individuals can share similar feelings and make similar value-judgments, and group action can follow in a variety of ways: citizens' committees, lobbying, collective bargaining, picketing, passing out leaflets, protest marches, violence, legislation. Such group action is commonly designed to persuade or coerce others into adopting our values, or in some way to put our values into operation.

We might remind ourselves that no value becomes real (that is, objective) merely because it is shared by others. Two people may like spaghetti, but that hardly gives a plate of spaghetti the right to say "I'm delicious!" And what if ten, or ten thousand, or ten million share a

> It isn't just a matter
> of not knowin' what to do.
> I've known what's right and wrong
> since I been ten.
> ADO ANNIE
> *Oklahoma!*

> *The simple-minded use of the notions "right or wrong" is one of the chief obstacles to the progress of understanding.*
> ALFRED NORTH WHITEHEAD

common value? It still remains a subjective value-experience within each individual. We sometimes mistakenly assume that if a very large number of people share the value, then it is not only real, but it is also "right" and deviation from it is "wrong."

9   The social insects—bees, soldier ants, termites, etc.—probably don't suffer from the agony of moral dilemmas; they are not burdened with concerns about "value priorities," and this for a very simple reason: for them "good" and "bad" are given by instinct. Bees and ants can't *disagree* on what is right or wrong. Behavioral norms are inherent in their existence. They possess a first-rate law-and-order society *because* they all share the same values and *because* no single insect has the freedom to develop alternative notions of what is good or bad.

When instinct prevails, there is no freedom; without freedom there are no moral choices to be made. Man has moral problems because he is free. He can see alternatives and these lead to the development of conflicting values within a society.

Primitive human societies are strikingly similar to insect societies. Everyone is unconsciously conditioned to behave, think, and feel in the same way; deviation from the society's BTF -norms is simply unthinkable and therefore not possible.

No wonder numerous political philosophers (and politicians) would model human society on the insect societies. They have sensed that man's inhumanity to man is, in some way, the result of his unbridled freedom and that the solution to the problem must lie in restricting that

freedom. This is the path taken in the political theorizing of Plato (in his old age, at least), Machiavelli, Hobbes, and the apologists for almost all authoritarian institutions—religious, military, quasi-military, and so on. Countless leaders in the modern world would use all possible means to induce conformity. In the societies projected before us in Huxley's *Brave New World* and Orwell's *1984,* everyone knew right from wrong. The entire population has been conditioned to know and act upon but a single set of values.

In a word, they had become insect societies.

10   "But surely," it may be said, "people do disagree in their basic moral attitudes, and they do try to persuade other people to agree with them." Indeed they do. People seem to feel more strongly about their moral attitudes than they do about their food preferences (we do not talk, for example, about our "culinary convictions"), and few people appear willing simply to accept differences at this point and let it go at that. But the methods by which anyone can persuade anyone else to change his basic moral attitudes . . . are not those of rational argument but only the methods of non-rational persuasion: name-calling, intimidation, threats, and so on. This is probably why our language has words like "prude," "moral ignoramus," and the like.

    Does not this view lead to pessimistic conclusions about the possibility of achieving enough ethical agreement among men to make harmonious life on our planet possible? Not at all. To so conclude would be equivalent to a restauranteur's concluding that, since people's tastes differ, he might as well give up trying to develop a menu that will win the general approval of his customers. Fortunately, people by and large tend to approve and disapprove of the same sorts of things: that is why one seldom finds anyone who will disagree with statements like "The infliction of needless pain is evil," or "It is good to help others who are in need." It is not the alleged objectivity of moral judgments, but the substantial similarity of our basic moral attitudes, that renders possible a reasonably harmonious society.

WILLIAM HALVERSON

11   When pondering our axiological condition we may again feel an epistemic loneliness. But by accepting this predicament and noting our bad habit of objectifying values, perhaps we can better understand why we differ so much in our beliefs about the thoughts, feelings, and actions which we deem "good" (hence "right") or "bad" (hence "wrong").

    One of the thorniest problems in philosophy is the question of the priority of values. We asked earlier (in Chapter 3-5) if we could know what facts are true and found that there are three truth-tests which we can use to verify or falsify fact-claims. Now it is time to ask whether there are comparable value-tests for deciding what is of greater value and what less.

In civilized nations more people are hurt by the hostile use of honesty than by the direct use of dishonesty.

A visitor from Europe wandered through an American supermarket for the first time, awed by the variety of items. In one section he beheld row upon row of toilet tissue, taking up one entire aisle. It came in 2-packs and 4-packs, scented and unscented; it came in all the pastel colors of the rainbow and in floral patterns. Staring speechless for a full minute, he asked simply: "Why? Why? Why?"

C. DON MEYER

12 Claude Samuel Donatelli is forty-one years old. He never went to college. You can find him these days pumping gas at a service station in San Diego.

But Donatelli is not your average, ordinary, run-of-the-mill gas station attendant. Last year he decided to get a job as a nuclear physicist. He applied at a company in Del Mar, California, called Environmental Control Management. Naturally, they asked him about his educational background, and since he figured they wouldn't hire somebody for that sort of work who hadn't been to college, Donatelli told them he was a Ph.D. from the University of California at Berkeley. Well, the company liked the way he looked and talked, and so they hired him, and introduced him in the lab as Doctor Donatelli.

Now, if you or I tried to get away with this, the whole jig would probably have been up the first time we got into a conversation with one of our fellow nuclear physicists on the subject of nuclear physics. It's not the sort of thing you can fake very easily.

But not only did Donatelli pass muster with his co-workers, he knocked them out with his brilliance. Within four months of the time he donned his white coat, the company was so impressed with his theory on the neutralizing of atomic warheads they made him a vice-president of the firm and started considering his theory for possible submission to the government.

They're still thinking about that, even though Donatelli himself has been found out. Some federal investigator, checking up on his appli-cation, discovered that Claude Samuel Donatelli did not get a Ph.D. from Berkeley—or from any place else, for that matter—and had never even graduated from anything higher than high school. Donatelli was charged with felony violation of the California Education Code, pleaded guilty, and . . . the judge deferred sentence for a month to give the defendant a chance to think about how he could best contribute to society, working eight hours a week for some religious or charitable organization, or something. The judge will implement Donatelli's idea—if he likes it—as a condition for probation.

Offhand, coming up with a way of neutralizing atomic warheads doesn't sound like a bad contribution to society, for openers. But then we can't have pump-jockeys without degrees running around thinking about stuff like that, can we?

CHARLES OSGOOD,
"Profile," CBS News

13 Donatello's "David" was the first naked statue of the Renaissance. It's cute. Michelangelo's "David" is sixteen feet tall and carved from white marble. It's about the biggest naked thing I've ever seen, not counting some naked elephants and one naked whale. (Live ones. I've never seen a naked statue of an elephant or a whale.)

The museum in Vatican City is possibly the most fabulous place I've ever seen. Its treasures of beautiful works are without equal, and as my wife and I strolled through its corridors, we were awed by the grandeur and elegance surrounding us.

But the statues disturbed us.

Every single male statue wore a fig leaf.

Incredibly, every fig leaf looked exactly alike in shape and color—a shade lighter than the statue it adorned. As Sarah and I leafed through the museum, I felt my sense of CLEAN and DIRTY rapidly returning. The fig leafs brought back the DIRTY of nakedness.

Soon, instead of merely looking at the Sculpture, I found myself checking the fig leafs to make sure that no statue had been missed.

I stopped to look at Antonio Canova's "Perseus with the Head of Medusa." There he stood, holding the severed head in his left hand, Medusa's face graphically displaying her last anguished moment—eyes shut in death, mouth still agape for a final rending shriek. The suggestion of entrails hung from the severed neck. In Perseus' right hand was the terrible sickle with which he had beheaded the Gorgon. It was a ferocious looking weapon. One straight steel to make up the sword, with a fine point for stabbing and a honed edge for slicing. Toward the tip another blade curled outward and around, savagely awaiting a plunge into human flesh so that as the weapon was withdrawn the curled blade could hook itself into its victim's bowels, cutting and pulling them on the way out.

Besides a war helmet, a mantle on his left arm and his battle sandals, all Perseus wore was a triumphant grin—and a fig leaf.

SHELLEY BERMAN
Cleans & Dirtys

5-5

ETHICS/
CHOICES

The perfect Way [Tao] is without difficulty,
Save that it avoids picking and choosing. . . .
If you want to get the plain truth,
Be not concerned with right and wrong.
The conflict between right and wrong
Is the sickness of the mind.

SENG–TS'AN

1 Last night I invented a new pleasure, and as I was giving it the first trial, an angel and a devil came rushing toward my house. They met at my door and fought with each other over my newly created pleasure; the one crying, "It is a sin!"—the other, "It is a virtue!"

KAHLIL GIBRAN

2 It is next to impossible for most of us to accept that there is a body of fact regarding the nature of value judgments and ethical codes which might render our convictions in the area of moral behavior shaky, at least, or dead wrong, at most. In the sphere of morality, *everyone knows* what is right and what is wrong.

"We have a right to expect decent shows on television." "Killing is wrong, for the Commandment says 'Thou shalt not kill.'" "I don't care if it is fun, it is still sinful." "What we need are tighter laws against obscenity." And more—ad infinitum.

Defining our terms doesn't seem to be required in such cases.

3 A young bank employee was indicted for embezzlement, and the evidence all seemed to point to a conviction. But *he* knew he was innocent, and his wife believed him. She was soon informed by another bank employee that he knew the whereabouts of documents which would reveal the real embezzler and prove that her husband was innocent. But her informant also made it clear he would give out with the evidence only if she made herself sexually available. The couple were devout Catholics, but to clear her husband of almost certain conviction she quickly made the decision to get whatever information at whatever cost. So she spent several nights with the other bank employee. Eventually the documents were forthcoming, her husband was exonerated, and the real embezzler was indicted and convicted.

Question: Was her act moral or immoral?

4   In a World War II movie called *Manhunt,* the principal figure is a big-game hunter. For the sheer love of stalking his prey, he creeps into the forest high above Hitler's retreat at Berchtesgaden. Lying concealed in a thicket, he aligns the cross hairs of his telescopic sight on the Führer's heart as he stands on a balcony. He pulls the trigger . . . on an empty chamber. He had stalked his game, and won.

Shortly, however, the hunter is caught by the Nazis and repeatedly tortured between escapes. In the beginning it never occurred to him to *kill* Hitler; but at the end of the story, having seen the bestial cruelty of the Nazis, he parachutes by night into the German forest, this time to hunt his game with live ammunition.

(This story is not far-fetched. Many attempts were made on Hitler's life by "good and decent men who wanted to put an end to the tyranny of this maniac." One such man was Dietrich Bonhoeffer, a devout Christian leader, who was executed for attempting to do what he believed to be a Christian duty: to murder Hitler. And recently a leader of the Jewish Defense League, Meir Kahane, has stated his conviction that "if an American Nazi Party leader posed a clear and present danger to American Jews, then not to assassinate such a person would be one of the most immoral courses I could imagine.")

Question: Is it ever *right* to kill another human being deliberately and "with malice aforethought"?

The truly adequate personality has the capacity for identification with his fellows. The feeling of identification seems to produce a deep sensitivity to the feelings and attitudes of others.

One learns to identify with others, depending upon the nature of his contacts with the important people in his life.

ARTHUR W. COMBS

An intelligence that is not humane is the most dangerous thing in the world.

ASHLEY MONTAGU

5   Good morning, Mr. Phelps. Some weeks ago Ramon Prado, one of the largest narcotics dealers in Latin America, bribed a courier for the Pan-American Narcotics Agency into giving him half of a microfilm containing the names of sixteen Agency undercover men. Prado's half is useless by itself, but two weeks ago. . . .

Your mission, Jim, should you choose to accept it, is to gain possession of the microfilm before Prado and Sandoval can work out the terms of their truce, which would mean certain death to the sixteen PANA undercover agents whose names are listed on the film.

As always, should you or any of your IM force be caught or killed, the secretary will disavow any knowledge of your actions.°

This tape will self-destruct in five seconds. Good luck, Jim.

"Mission Impossible" (CBS-TV)

6   A Japanese coastal village was once threatened by a tidal wave, but the wave was sighted in advance, far out on the horizon, by a lone farmer in

°This sentence was eventually deleted from the program's taped introductions.

the rice fields on the hillside above the village. At once he set fire to the fields, and the villagers who came swarming up to save their crops were saved from the flood.

ALAN WATTS

Nature and history do not agree with our conceptions of good and bad; they define good as that which survives, and bad as that which goes under; and the universe has no prejudice in favor of Christ as against Genghis Khan.

WILL AND ARIEL DURANT

Science has proved that there exists no ethical principle which is, even theoretically, acknowledged by all human societies. Hence ethical values are nothing but functions of the societies in which they originate. The question of what is morally good or morally evil has no meaning except in reference to the moral value system of a given society. There are therefore, no "absolute" criteria by which the value system of a given society can be judged objectively. It may, of course, be judged on the basis of the value system of another society. But there is no possibility of deciding "objectively" which of the two value systems is morally better. If the two societies clash, one can only wait to see which of the two will prevail.

KURT VON FRITZ
Relativest

7 The story is told of a tragic incident that occurred when a frontier village was raided by Indians. Several members of the village hid where they could not be found. One woman had a very small baby in her arms. As some Indians drew close, she smothered the baby rather than risk giving away their hiding place and thereby insuring death for them all. Some time after the raid, she was punished by both church and community for committing murder.

8 Probably from *Playboy:* A girl was asked by a rich man if she would spend the night with him. She responded with a righteous "No!" When he asked if she would for a hundred thousand dollars, she uttered an exultant "Yes!" "Then what about ten thousand dollars?" he asked. With some hesitation: "Yes, I guess I would." "Then what about five hundred dollars?" She replied angrily, "No, what do you think I am?" To which his final words were: "We have already established that. Now we're merely haggling over the price."

9 Joseph Fletcher recounts an episode involving the ship *William Brown* which struck an iceberg off Newfoundland and sank in 1841. Seven crewmen and thirty-two passengers crowded into a lifeboat, but this was almost double the number the lifeboat could hold. Winds and heavy seas would have capsized the whole lot in a very short time. So the first mate ordered the men in the company out of the boat, but no one moved. One of the crewmen—a man named Holmes—therefore tossed the men into the ocean. The rest in the boat survived and were eventually rescued. In Philadelphia, Holmes was tried and convicted of murder, though the jury recommended clemency.

10 Near the turn of the century a young couple in a small Arkansas town were still childless after several years of marriage. When they went to their doctor to find out why, tests showed the man to be sterile. After talking over their problem, they went together to their local pastor and asked him if he would make the wife pregnant. In due time, he obliged, and she did. The child was fully accepted by the man and his wife and was loved and raised as their own. The minister, however, was forced to surrender his orders and leave the ministry.

11 Much controversy surrounded the case of the Green Beret captain in Vietnam who, under orders, executed a Vietnamese agent who had been working under his command. Strong evidence had come to light that the man was a double agent. Security-wise, he could no longer be used, nor could he be allowed to go free if he were a double agent; he carried information that could jeopardize military plans and the lives of countless men. The captain therefore carried out his orders and eliminated the agent, although they had worked together closely and had become "friends."

12   There are three questions which, if asked sincerely and explored carefully, will carry one a long way toward understanding ethical problems and deciding what moral action to take in the very human dilemmas in which we find ourselves caught. Three questions. That may sound simple; and authentic morality may indeed be simpler than our tangled intellectual analyses often indicate. However, our previous exploration of value-judgments should remind us that ethical problems can be very complex.

The three questions: (1) *Who* actually makes an ethical decision? (2) What criteria should I use in making a relevant and meaningful ethical decision? (3) To whom (or what) do my moral obligations apply?

There is a fourth question which might logically follow these three: Can I in fact *do* what I decide is right? That is, having decided what is right, can I *will* it and then *do* what I will? We need not belabor the question further at this point, since the problems of autonomy and freedom around which this question turns have been covered in previous chapters.° The more mature the self has become, the better are the chances that one will be able to will into action what he knows to be right. There is a close correlation between personal autonomy and ethical behavior.

13   The first question we must answer is: *Who is to make the ethical decision?* We can assume that only the individual can make moral choices and act them out, but determining *what* action is moral may not have been decided by him at all. On this question regarding decision, there are two schools of thought, for we can speak of (1) authoritarian decisions and (2) autonomous decisions.

In authoritarian ethics, decisions about right and wrong are given. They originate objectively and are not the product of one's personal experience. That is, the decisions of what is right and what is wrong have *already* been made, perhaps by an authority or a society—but often by a deity who subsequently revealed his decisions at some point to man. It was assumed by different peoples, for instance, that the decision had been made by Yahweh (and revealed in the Torah or the Decalogue); or by Allah (and revealed in the Quran); or by Shamash (and revealed to Hammurabi); or by Ahura Mazda (and revealed to Zoroaster). In the case of the Decalogue, an absolute decision had already been made: killing, lying, stealing, etc. are wrong, and any further debate is out of the question.

There are no ethical truths; there are just clarifications of particular ethical problems. Take advantage of these clarifications and work out your own existence. You are mistaken to think that anyone ever had the answers. There are no answers. Be brave and face up to it.

DONALD KALISH

°See pages 61–95. The material in this chapter presupposes that the problem of human freedom versus determinism (Chapter 4-3) has been resolved, to some extent at least, in favor of the conclusion that freedom is an authentic human experience. If you have concluded otherwise, then skip this chapter: the ethical problems discussed herein will necessarily be illusory and meaningless.

To have a purpose for which one will do almost anything except betray a friend,—that is the final patent of nobility, the last formula of the superman.

NIETZSCHE

What is man's task? To obey these laws. Our first responsibility is to know the rules and then to resolve the ethical problems of our daily lives by the faithful application of these laws. We also have an obligation to cultivate the moral life *so that we will be able to act morally* when forced to make moral choices.

Hence, these are authoritarian ethics. The individual takes no part in the first-order decision making on what constitutes moral/immoral behavior. The given laws are immutable and final.

14   Autonomous ethics arise from inside oneself, for the individual himself has been in on the decision making regarding what constitutes moral/immoral action. As the word *autonomy* implies, the individual is self-determined; his actions are manifestations of his own decisions.

We can contrast these two forms of ethics. The first is behavior that conforms to given codes and social customs; the second is autonomous—ethical behavior which is inner-motivated and grounded in genuine moral interest in the well-being of others. Autonomous ethics is largely the product of one's own experience; in this sense it is deeply personal, reflecting one's own sensibilities and values. Furthermore, in this perspective, "morality" is not merely *what one does;* it is rather the inevitable expression of *what one is.* It is sincere goodwill and never empty conformity to prevailing customs. In a word, it is autonomous.

15   Jean-Paul Sartre has stated his conviction, based on his belief in human freedom, that *all* ethical decisions are autonomous, that in the final analysis there are no authoritarian ethics. Sartre is saying that although we may adhere to given customs and codes—from parents, peers, society, church—when making ethical decisions each of us still decides which codes we will use in resolving our problems. If we decide to seek answers to our ethical questions by applying the Decalogue rather than our parents' values, or by appealing to our church's teaching rather than to peer values, then it is still we who make such decisions.

Ultimately, therefore, we can never escape personal responsibility for the ethical decisions that *we* make; and we are likewise responsible for the moral/immoral actions which *we* perform.

Sartre's position is a sort of half-truth. He is surely correct when speaking of persons who, to use his phrase, "have become conscious"—that is, those who have become aware of alternatives. The ethically informed individual *knows* that there are many criteria for making decisions; knowing this, his decisions rest upon his own shoulders, and he must assume responsibility for them.

But for the majority of us, such options don't exist. We are convinced that there is but a single set of rights-and-wrongs: how could it be otherwise? If one believes with all his heart that the decision of right/wrong has been wholly settled, and that this settlement is embodied in a single set of customs or codes, then he cannot justly be held responsible for *not* making ethical decisions based on other codes which (in our opinion, perhaps) would have been superior decisions. For this individual, it is not possible, as Sartre would have it, for him to say "No!" to his own given code.

Perhaps the truer half of Sartre's argument needs to be emphasized: Once we become aware that there are many criteria for making ethical decisions, then the full responsibility for our own decisions rests squarely and heavily upon our shoulders.

ABORTION AND THE COURTS

I would like to respond to Robert J. Trotter's fine article on "Abortion laws still in ferment" by saying that I think it behooves the scientific community (physicians, biologists, et al) to come forth with a viable definition of exactly what constitutes a Person whom the 14th Amendment proscribes against depriving "of life, liberty or property without due process of law." Such definition is particularly crucial insofar as the anti-abortion forces rest their case on the assumption that any human homunculus from the moment of conception onward is a "person."

It would seem to me that this involves addressing ourselves to the question of whether a fetus in utero, by virtue of its total dependency on the body of its hostmother, is closer to the status of an *internal organ* than it is to that of a separate and discrete individual.

Perhaps there is a clear-cut biological line of demarcation or threshold in utero beyond which the fetus would be capable of independent survival if born—and this may perhaps provide the much-needed distinction between surgery and murder. In any event, I believe that it is along these lines that a useful definition will one day emerge. Meanwhile I'd hate to think that a decision so vital to the human condition and to the ultimate quality of life on this planet might, by sheer apathy on the part of the scientific community, be left entirely up to the courts.

BRADFORD WILSON
New York, N.Y.
Science News, April 8, 1972

Love thy neighbor as thyself. First of all: where is my neighbor? I commute: he is not in the office, not in the elevator, not at the station, not at home. All the people I meet in those different places are looking for their neighbor as I do. Some of their children, perhaps mine, may drop a bomb, not indeed on their neighbors, but on this tired search for one.

NICCOLO TUCCI

16　　The second question we must answer is: *What criteria should I use in making a relevant and meaningful ethical decision?* Or put differently: What is the source of the data which I should take into account in making an ethical judgment? Three different answers to this question come from (1) the formalist, (2) the relativist, and (3) the contextualist.

　　The formalist believes that the criteria to be used in making ethical decisions are universal laws which apply to all men. Man's responsibility is to be informed on these rules *ahead of time*—that is, before we find ourselves caught up in life's ethical complexities. By analogy, one should know the laws in the state motor-vehicle code *before* he gets behind the wheel and takes to the streets. Likewise, we should be taught the laws of the moral life before taking to the highways. Our personal task, in both cases, is to be thoroughly acquainted with the rules so that we can apply them to concrete situations as we come to them. Whether approaching a red light or being tempted to cheat, we should know to *stop,* since we have studied the codebook. (Our first obligation, of course, is to try to avoid situations where weighty ethical decisions have to be made, but daily life rarely permits us so easy an out.)

17　　There are several kinds of formal ethical codes. One kind is represented by the Decalogue, written on Mount Sinai "by the finger of God." These are apodictic laws—absolute and incontestable. In actual practice they don't work and must be continually redefined and modified. The commandment "Thou shalt not kill" is hardly practicable if a tribe is fighting for its survival against other invading tribes. So "to kill" was understood to mean "to murder"; hence, by redefinition, it became applicable only to fellow citizens in good standing.°

　　The German philosopher Immanuel Kant (1724–1804) concluded that universal moral laws do exist, but that they are to be found within the structure of the human mind. Just as $7 + 5$ is always 12—it is a priori knowledge yet applies to the real world—there are, Kant holds, moral "rules of thought" which are a priori and therefore universal (like $7 + 5 = 12$). Kant writes that ethical rules "must not be sought in human nature or in the circumstances of the world . . . but [must be sought] *a priori* simply in the concepts of reason." Kant formulated his famous "categorical imperative" to be such an a priori rule. It categorically applies to all rational men and is imperative as an absolute "ought" that binds men to the moral law. His formula (in part) is: "Act only on that maxim whereby thou canst at the same time will it should become a universal law." This resembles our concept of natural law as described by modern physics. Kant was contending that if any kind of action can be universalized, then it is ethical. For instance, can I universalize lying? Hardly. I may think lying expediently justifiable in some particular case, but can I therefore recommend telling lies as a universal form of behavior?

°Actually, this is not a redefinition, since the Commandment was never intended to have general application. It is for this reason that the reported killing of some 3000 Israelites by Moses and the Levites in a single day (Ex 32:26–29) is not at all a violation of the Commandment against killing (Ex 20:13). To the ancient Hebrew the Sixth Commandment implicitly meant, "Thou shalt not kill a fellow Hebrew as long as he is a faithful follower of the god Yahweh." If this interpretation seems puzzling, read Deut 13:6–11.

Obviously not. Human interaction would be rendered chaotic if we couldn't depend upon one another. Therefore, telling the truth is a "categorical imperative."

A more recent attempt to develop a system of universal formal laws was undertaken by the American philosopher Edgar Brightman. For example, the Law of Autonomy: "All persons ought to recognize themselves as obligated to choose in accordance with the ideals which they acknowledge." The Law of Consequences: "All persons ought to consider and, on the whole, approve the foreseeable consequences of each of their choices." The Law of Altruism: "Each person ought to respect all other persons as ends in themselves, and, as far as possible, to co-operate with others in the production and enjoyment of shared values." These are normative laws; they state what we *ought* to do. Because of their logical and axiomatic nature, they are meant to apply universally to all ethical decisions made by man.

18   Another answer to our second question comes from the relativist. The relativist begins with the empirical fact that there are numerous systems of customs and codes to be found in various societies. The Greek Sophist Protagoras (481–411 B.C.) was one of the first philosophers to observe in his travels that different societies do in fact have different customs which are morally binding upon their respective inhabitants. Protagoras thus began to understand the function of customs and codes: they serve to regulate and give cohesion to a society. He therefore concluded that within any particular society, its own set of customs and codes is right *for it* since they perform the very pragmatic function of enabling that society to operate with a greater degree of internal harmony. What is "right" is therefore what works in a society, and whatever "works" in a society is therefore right. Notions of right and wrong are therefore relative to a particular society, and they differ from one society to another.

Protagoras also noted a corollary to his relativism. If one is to spend time in other societies (as he and his fellow-Sophists did), then one is morally obligated to obey the vital customs and codes of the societies they visit. "Who are we," he would ask, "to come as visitors to some society other than our own, bringing with us our own social customs and moral convictions which may be quite alien to that society, and then have the effrontery to claim that *our* customs and codes are the ones that are really right? Wouldn't such behavior serve to destroy the integrated system which that society has working for it? And wouldn't our actions therefore be immoral in the truest sense?" And isn't Protagoras right?

Relativists hold that one can make meaningful ethical decisions only in the social context in which an ethical problem occurs. In other words, what is right in one place or time may be wrong in another place or time. Infanticide may have been right in Caesar's time, but is not in

The great fault of all ethics hitherto has been that they believed themselves to have to deal only with the relations of man to man. In reality, however, the question is what is his attitude to the world and all life that comes within his reach. A man is ethical only when life, as such, is sacred to him, that of plants and animals as that of his fellow men, and when he devotes himself helpfully to all life that is in need of help.

ALBERT SCHWEITZER

the twentieth-century Rome. Polygamy (but with not more than four wives) may be right in Cairo, but not in Tel Aviv. Sharing one's wife with an overnight guest may be right in an Eskimo igloo, but not in Middletown, U.S.A.

Ethical relativism may mean something else: that what is right for one person may be wrong for another. This, again, is merely the recognition of the fact that different people have different convictions and follow different customs. It is wrong for Jews and Muslims to eat pork; it is wrong for Jains to eat any animal flesh at all. But such restrictions do not apply to Christians, Shintos, or others outside the faith.

19 A third answer comes from the contextualist. He believes, first, that moral laws of the kind held by the formalist don't exist. There are no rules that one can memorize ahead of time and apply meaningfully to a particular situation. Nor will the contextualist go along with the relativist. He will readily agree that societies do in fact possess different customs and codes, and that these perform the pragmatic function which the relativist claims they do. Granted: Romans practiced infanticide, Greeks practiced slavery, Cypriots practiced sacred prostitution, modern societies disenfranchise minorities, whole nations generate hate toward other nations—societies indeed do such things, but that doesn't make such practices ethically right. The fact that a practice exists doesn't make it moral. What societies actually do, therefore, is no guideline for deciding what is ethically right.

The contextualist holds that relevant criteria for making a meaningful ethical decision can be found only within the context of each concrete ethical problem. Every ethical situation is in fact unique, and a truly ethical solution to a problem can be arrived at only when *all the factors of the unique situation* can be weighed *by those involved in the problem.* Each person makes the best decision he can using the best knowledge which he possesses at that time of decision. Such a meaningful ethical judgment can be made only *after the problem situation exists,* not before.

Such ideas as "don't kill," "don't steal," etc. can be used as guidelines, but they must be abandoned if the specific situation calls for it. Dietrich Bonhoeffer phrased it eloquently: "Principles are only tools in God's hands soon to be thrown away as unserviceable." The same applies to formalistic rules which may prove irrelevant to a particular set of conditions. In fact, the contextualist contends that moral predicaments constantly make it necessary for us to kill, steal, lie, or whatever, *in order to be moral.*

20 Implied in all this is one single guideline which the contextualist uses in making all ethical decisions. That guideline is one's concern for the well-being of others. This principle can be developed in several ways. In *Situation Ethics,* Joseph Fletcher formulates it in terms of *agape,* the

Principles are only tools in God's hands, soon to be thrown away as unserviceable.

DIETRICH BONHOEFFER

5   *Coexistence: Man's Love/Hate Condition*

"ethical love" or "empathetic concern" which is the foundation of Christian ethics. Fletcher submits that only love is good, and rules are made to serve love, not the other way around. When one is truly involved in the well-being of another, he may be called upon to kill, to tell lies, or more, in order to carry through in authentic action his loving concern for that other person. Again, the *rules* serve *love*. There are no laws which the contextualist will not finally break, if forced to, to manifest his ethical love for another. Just as Thoreau could say of civil law that if it "requires you to be the agent of injustice to another," then "break the law," the contextualist would say that if so-called moral laws require you to act unlovingly toward others, then break the "moral laws."

Contextualism can also be formulated in pragmatic terms. It is only our ethical concern for the well-being of others that produces a positive environment in which all of us can more fully actualize our lives. Qualities are contagious. Compassion and concern generate compassion and concern, just as hate generates hate and distrust generates distrust. Such basically human qualities as love, concern, and trust are the only qualities upon which a fulfilling collective existence can be grounded.

To summarize, therefore, the contextualist holds the following: (1) there are no universal moral laws; (2) ethical decisions can be made only in the context of concrete situations; and (3) there is a fundamental ethical guideline for all ethical behavior—one's authentic concern for the well-being of others.

21   Contextualism has significant implications. It recognizes accurately the nature of our moral predicaments. Our most agonizing ethical decisions must be made in situations where only *bad* alternatives are open to us. If daily life always set up situations so that we had to choose between a good option and a bad option, then moral existence would be simple. But actual life-situations continually force us into predicaments in which only various degrees of bad-consequence alternatives are open to choice. We may have to kill in order to save oneself, a friend, an innocent victim; we may have to lie, to pretend, to play games in order to protect someone from serious damage.

Contextual ethics says that if, out of one's concern for the well-being of others, he makes the *best decision* he possibly can, then he is unequivocally moral. If one must tell lies to save another, he has acted morally; *not* to have lied—to have allowed irreparable harm to come to another person—would have been immoral. Since this is the way that life forces us to make decisions, there is no justification for holding a person morally guilty if he has made the best decision possible in any given predicament.

By contrast, formalism and most forms of relativism have admitted that we often have to take bad action in a situation because good alternatives don't exist, but they also contend that this doesn't make the

It must not be forgotten that although a high standard of morality gives a slight or no advantage to each individual man and his children over the other men of the same tribe, yet an advancement in the standard of morality will certainly give an immense advantage to one tribe over another.

CHARLES DARWIN

bad action right. *Having to do what is wrong doesn't make it right.* And having done wrong, we *should* feel guilt, and we may justly be subject to moral or civil recriminations. Contextualism responds that such a person is morally innocent and is, in fact, morally commendable. Having chosen the best options available, why should anyone be considered immoral?

22   Each society has its own code of ethics, including the American West of the nineteenth century. The following scene from the NBC series *High Chaparral* is an instance when that code was deliberately broken. The question is how—or if—such action can be ethically justified.

In this case a gunman, Tulsa, has extorted five thousand dollars from John Cannon by threatening to kill Cannon's brother Buck. Since Buck is hot-tempered, Tulsa knows he can needle Buck into a shootout in which he could easily outdraw him. John Cannon feels he has no choice but to pay, which he does. But Buck "steals" back the money and proceeds to the local saloon, thereby insuring a confrontation with Tulsa.

It's at this point that Buck decides to change the rules of the game. Buck is hunched over the bar when Tulsa comes to get him in the Tucson saloon.

TULSA. Turn around, Buck.
BUCK. Well, I tell you, Tulsa. If you wish to admit that *you* had made a mistake, and if *you* wish to crawl on out of here, I just might forget the whole thing.
TULSA. I don't make mistakes. Turn around.
BUCK. You sure?
TULSA. (*Kicking back the chairs and screaming at Buck.*) Turn around!
        (*Buck turns slowly . . . with a derringer in his hand.*) What are you doin'?
BUCK. Turnin' around, like you said.
TULSA. That's murder, Buck.
BARTENDER. Well, I think I'll go in the back room and check the stock. What I don't see I can't testify to.
BUCK. All right, Mr. Tulsa. It is now your play.
TULSA. It's murder, Buck. You gotta give me a chance.
BUCK. I don' have to give you anything.
TULSA. This ain't a fair fight!
BUCK. Fair. Hey, that's a good word. I bet you'd like for them to cut it on my tombstone, wouldn't you. "Here lies Buck Cannon, a *fair* man." But you know, I'd sooner end up standin' over your grave, and people whisperin' behind their hands, "That's Buck Cannon. He don' fight fair."
TULSA. Never figured you for a coward.
BUCK. Well, you live and you learn. I jus' don' want to die. That's the thing about a man like you. You're so ready to kill, you must be ready to die too. It's jus' the other side o' the coin, isn't it?
TULSA. You gotta give me an even chance.

[*When asked if he had but a single gift to bequeath to the next generation, Ray Bradbury replied:*] . . . The gift to see that not all Republicans are evil, that not all Democrats are evil, that not all Communists are evil, that not all Negroes are evil, that not all whites are evil, that not all anything is evil. The ability to see the paradox in every person.

RAY BRADBURY

BUCK. Who's gonna say it wasn't a *fair* fight. There's only you and me, and you'll be dead.

TULSA. Buck, I don't believe you'd do it.

(*A shot, from the derringer in Buck's hand. Tulsa is wounded in his right shoulder.*)

BUCK. Aim must be off. Now it's a fair fight. Draw. Whenever you're ready.

TULSA. (*His gun arm is half-paralyzed and trembling.*) No! This ain't fair!

BUCK. Tough.

TULSA. (*Throws gun down.*) You kill an unarmed man and that's murder.

JOHN CANNON. (*From background.*) He's right, Buck.

BUCK. Well, then, get out.

TULSA. It ain't over, Buck.

BUCK. Sure it is, Tulsa. For now anyways.

TULSA. We'll meet again, I promise you.

BUCK. It might happen. But jus' remember, I'm not as fast as you. I won't draw against you. So I just might have to back-shoot you next time.

TULSA. I believe you would, too.

BUCK. Try me.

(*Tulsa backs out and leaves saloon. Others crowd in.*
John comes over and leans on the bar beside Buck.)

You know what, John? I don' fight fair.

JOHN. You know what, Buck? Nobody's goin' to hold it against you. He *would* have killed you.

BUCK. C'mon, I'll ride back to Chaparral with you. All of a sudden, I feel . . . tired.

23   The third question that one must answer is: *To whom (or what) do my moral obligations apply?* We must ask ourselves how large we are obligated to draw our circle of ethical concern. Should our ethical actions apply only to ourselves and to our primary groups such as family, clan, sect, or firm? Or do they extend to all the members of our tribe, nation, religion, or race? Do they extend to one's antagonist, attacker, enemy? Do they extend to all human beings? to all higher forms of life? to all organisms that share the impulse-to-life?

Historically, men have rather universally applied their codes of ethics only to their in-groups. Since groups are forever engaged in attempts to annihilate one another, survival demands that ethical niceties be suspended during wartime. Applied to one's own group, ethical obligations produce social cohesion, predictable and orderly behavior; they reduce internecine discord of all kinds and make it possible for a united group to fight other groups with greater efficiency. Hence—as Protagoras saw so clearly—ethical codes are pragmatic necessities.

Quite simply, ethical obligations practiced in the in-group don't apply to those outside; the out-group (historically, anyway) has never been the object of serious ethical concern. This distinction between out-group and in-group, with a code governing behavior in the in-group,

There slowly grew up in me an unshakable conviction that we have no right to inflict suffering and death on another living creature unless there is some unavoidable necessity for it, and that we ought all of us to feel what a horrible thing it is to cause suffering and death out of mere thoughtlessness.

ALBERT SCHWEITZER

is merely one aspect of the whole evolutionary arrangement. From prairie dogs and baboons to man, in-group behavior is clearly prescribed, while behavior toward all out-groups is a matter of expediency: whatever aids survival is good/moral/right/just/virtuous—and necessary!

24   Since conditions on "spaceship earth" are rapidly changing, this question needs continual reexploration. Although in-group consciousness continues, and will continue, in countless forms, we need to ask whether, in a shrinking world, one's circle of obligations must be extended for purely pragmatic reasons. In the world of the seventies, traditional in-groups are being broken down and their constituents constantly rearranged.

Increasing numbers of people are thinking of the whole human species as a single in-group. If we should be attacked by extraterrestrial LGMs, the feeling of humanity's oneness would immediately surface, and for the same old reason: unite to survive. But lacking an obvious antagonist, the unity of the human species is not yet a world-fact, though sought by some and intuited by many more.

The belief that all men comprise a single *ethical* community is not new. The Stoics taught that all men are subject to the same natural and moral laws, and that they should therefore be subject to the same civil laws. All men should belong to a *cosmopolis*—a "world-city"—and should not be artificially broken up into tribes and states with different laws. Some branches of Christianity and Islam have developed similar concepts, and Jesus' mandate that we love even our enemies would, in effect, annihilate all boundaries between men.

Do our ethical obligations extend further yet? Do they extend to the higher animals? (Do they extend to our pets?) Do they extend to all animal life? The Hindus and Jains have always believed so. Do we have moral obligations to plants? to all of nature? The American Indians believe that we do.°

Exactly how does one finally decide how wide his circle of ethical concern should extend?

°See the words of the old Wintu holy woman on page 350.

25   Ethical affirmation of life is the intellectual act by which man ceases simply to live at random and begins to concern himself reverently with his own life, so that he may realize its true value. And the first step in the evolution of ethics is a sense of solidarity with other human beings.

To the primitive, this solidarity has narrow limits. It is confined, first to his blood relations, then to the members of his tribe, who represent to him the family enlarged. I have such primitives in my hospital. If I ask an ambulatory patient to undertake some small service for a patient who must stay in bed, he will do it only if the bedridden patient belongs to his tribe. If that is not the case, he will answer me with wide-eyed innocence: "This man is not brother of me." Neither rewards nor threats will induce him to perform a service for such a stranger.

REPUBLIQUE GABONAISE
200F
BACH
DOCTEUR SCHWEITZER — POSTE AERIENNE LAMBARÉNÉ

I remember on the trip home on Apollo 11 it suddenly struck me that that tiny pea, pretty and blue, was the earth. I put up my thumb and shut one eye, and my thumb blotted out the planet earth. I didn't feel like a giant. I felt very, very small.

NEIL ARMSTRONG

But as soon as man begins to reflect upon himself and his relationship to others, he becomes aware that men as such are his equals and his neighbors. Gradually he sees the circle of his responsibilities widening until it includes all human beings with whom he has dealings. . . . The idea of the brotherhood of all human beings is inherent in the metaphysics of most of the great religious systems. Moreover, since antiquity, philosophy has presented the case for humanitarianism as a concept recommended by reason.

Throughout history, however, the insight that we have a wider duty toward human beings has never attained the dominance to which it is entitled. Down to our own times it has been undermined by differences of race, religion and nationality.

Man belongs to man.

ALBERT SCHWEITZER

6

THE PROTOPLASMIC VENTURE

6-1

LIFE

1   Understanding the origin of life has been one of the two or three most ultimate problems that inquiring minds have ever probed. It is of the greatest significance that it has been only during the last few decades that any empirically sound questions-and-answers could be formulated, and this for several reasons.

    First, the problem was simply too difficult. It required the growth of our understanding in many fields of knowledge before the complexities of the problems could be analyzed. Only in our time have we been able to ask the questions which could produce viable hypotheses. (This is an excellent example of the fact that frequently we must bide our time before we know enough to ask the right questions.)

    Secondly, the field was holy ground, and empirical inquiry encountered the greatest resistance. Mythical answers had long been considered to be final.

2   Life is not one of the fundamental categories of the universe, like matter, energy, and time, but is a manifestation of certain molecular combinations. These combinations cannot have existed forever, since even the elements of which they are composed have not always existed. Therefore life must have had a beginning.

    The modern view of the origin of life differs fundamentally from that of preceding centuries in that it concerns itself with the origin of these molecular combinations, rather than of organisms endowed with certain mysterious properties. Once this viewpoint is adopted, it is seen that we have to regard the origin of life as a historical incident in the evolution of the planet—i.e., as an event limited in place and time by prevailing physical and chemical conditions.

Biology and the Future of Man

Life is not one of the fundamental categories of the universe, like matter, energy, and time, but is a manifestation of certain molecular combinations. These combinations cannot have existed forever, since even the elements of which they are composed have not always existed. Therefore life must have had a beginning.

Biology and the Future of Man

3   What is "life"? Can the word be defined? Can the reality be conceived? Long lists of defining characteristics have been proposed, yet accurate, workable definitions are still lacking.

At present, it appears that "life" can be defined with two qualities: self-replication and mutability. Any organism possessing these two qualities can be considered alive. In these two characteristics is contained the essential processes of evolution: continuity and adaptation.

An organism must be able to replicate itself (unless it's immortal—that is, deathless—and hence not a part of the process of evolution). If it can produce a likeness of itself, then it possesses the power to assure continuity of its species. But mutability—the ability to effect changes from one generation to another and adapt to a fluid environment—is essential. Without the ability to change and adapt no species could long survive. Environmental conditions are forever changing; species must be able to change along with their environments.

So far as we know, only living organisms have these two qualities, and an organism must possess both qualities to be considered alive. It has been noted that mineral crystals and flames of fire can reproduce; they both effect replication of their own kind without affecting themselves. In addition, flames display a sort of metabolism: they ingest material, digest it, and excrete wastes. However, neither crystals nor flames have adaptive mutability.

4   Several other qualities are often suggested as essential to a definition of what it means to be alive.

Motility—the ability to move about: to wiggle, crawl, run, fly, dart, bore through, swim. *Metabolism*—the ability to ingest materials, digest them (separate usable components from the unusable), and excrete wastes. *Growth*—the ability to proceed through some sort of life-cycle, beginning with seeds or embryos and moving through various stages of adulthood and beyond. *Irritability*—the ability to react to external stimuli, a first step in adaptation. *Dynamic Equilibrium*—the ability to maintain a stable internal condition within changing external conditions (such as adjusting to temperature, conserving a balance in the flow of food and liquids through the body of the organism, etc.).

5   When we say an organism possesses the ability to reproduce and mutate, we are not really defining *life* at all. In fact, we are not even thinking of life. We are only talking about the external motions ("behavioral patterns") of we-know-not-what. We are merely saying: *If* an organism can *do* these things, then we will classify it as "alive." But what is *life*? Apparently we don't know. Or, is life *nothing but* the ability *to do* certain things?

Somehow, as we continue pondering life and living things, this isn't very satisfying. Our dissatisfaction can become sharper as we subjec-

THE MURCHISON METEORITE

Just before noon on September 28, 1969, a bright flash was seen in the sky near Murchison, a small town about 85 miles north of Melbourne, Australia. An object exploded in the sky, and 180 pounds of meteorite fragments fell to the ground. Not long after, [Dr. Cyril] Ponnamperuma received a telegram from the Smithsonian's Center for Short-lived Phenomena notifying him of the meteorite's fall. He had worked with meteorites years before but had given up because of the contamination problem. Now, because of the precise and contamination-proof techniques developed by him for analyzing the moon rocks and a freshly fallen sample, Ponnamperuma was anxious to tackle meteorites again.

A number of stones were soon on their way to him at Ames Research Center near San Francisco. Analyzing a core sample from a stone having the fewest cracks and the least exterior contamination, he detected 18 amino acids. Twelve are not found in proteins made on Earth, so their presence indicates they must be of extraterrestrial origin.

The other six amino acids are commonly found on Earth—with a slight, but very important difference. Waves of natural light, which radiate in many planes, can be polarized into one plane by passing them through a prism. When polarized light is passed through amino acids, it is rotated slightly to the right or left. With extremely rare exceptions (the cell walls of certain bacteria), amino acids found in the proteins of living organisms rotate light only to the left. Outside the living world, all molecules showing optical activity consist of equal amounts of left-handed and right-handed forms, which are mirror images of each other. But life on Earth uses only one form, and that is the left-handed form. Ponnamperuma explains: "A large, sound and sturdy protein molecule just couldn't be made by using both forms—it's like trying to put a right foot into a left shoe. We don't know why nature chose left."

In contrast to the one form found in proteins, the Murchison meteorite's protein amino acids are almost equally divided between left-handed and right-handed, additional evidence that the amino acids are not the results of earthly contamination. Ponnamperuma believes that the mixture was formed in one of the steps of chemical evolution, and he terms his findings "probably the first conclusive evidence of chemical evolution occurring elsewhere in the universe."

IRENE KIEFER
The Smithsonian, May, 1972

The alphabet of life is obviously extremely simple—a handful of chemicals are responsible for the vast variety we see in the entire biosphere.

CYRIL PONNAMPERUMA

tively feel our own existence. We feel that life is not merely the ability *to do* something, but rather *is* something—a process, a flow, a flame, a special energy—something that persists through time inside us.

It is possible in theory (and likely, someday, in practice) to build a robot which would be self-replicating and adapting. In his book *I, Robot,* Isaac Asimov spins out stories of robots which, in their factory, put together other robots which put together other robots which put together other robots, ad infinitum, and which, with their sophisticated sensing equipment, can adapt to environmental change. The robots can even design adaptive changes in the robots they are manufacturing. These robots can therefore reproduce likenesses of themselves, and they can mutate.

But would they be *alive*? Something is missing. Sensitive robots, to be sure, and perhaps delightful company on a sufficiently dreary planet; but wouldn't we hesitate to call them "alive"? In the final analysis, aren't they only printed circuit-boards, metal canisters, molded plastics, wire and electricity? Can such a system be alive? Life must be something more. Or so we feel.

6   Along with the problem of defining "life" goes the vital issue of defining "death." Notice again the nature of definitions. A definition is a classification, and the primary purpose of classification is to establish a relationship with an object so that we know how to think of it and use it.° To scientists attempting to synthesize life in their laboratories, definition is of critical importance. When indeed life is synthesized, the moment will be remembered and the scientist's name will become immortal.

In order to pronounce a person "dead" and declare his body available as a source of organ transplants, we obviously need precise definitions. On what criteria does one become dead? What is death? The fact is that we know death only in terms of life: death is the condition which follows the cessation of life-processes. But this is little more than a play on words. "Death," like "life," can be defined only in arbitrary, pragmatic terms: "Life" is what an organism possesses when it can wiggle and change; when it can no longer do either, it is "dead."

7   "A man is dead when his heart stops," so we have believed. This age-old criterion is obsolete now that medical science can sustain a body's physical processes, including a beating heart, for months or years by artificial means. If the machines are shut down, the heart stops. Was the individual alive while the heart was beating?

Brainwaves are a better indicator, for to exist as a human person is to have a mind. Without the possibility of consciousness, there is no person; there exists only a physical organism which has lost its potential as a person. Therefore, when all the brainwaves are flat on the electroencephalograph, we conclude the person is dead.

Yet even this is not accurate. Cases are known in which brainwaves were nonexistent for many hours (that is, the person-potential apparently ceased to exist), but the individuals were ultimately restored to full health, physically and mentally.

Another test of life/death is the brain's utilization of oxygen. If no oxygen is being used, brain cells are dying. When sufficient cells die

°See pages 155ff.

Philosophy has not yet digested the biologist's way of looking at living nature, free of all vitalistic and finalistic ideas; but in the wake of the spectacular advances of chemical and evolutionary biology, one day there must emerge a new philosophy of science, based largely on the findings of biology rather than those of physics.

    Biology and the Future of Man

(and this occurs within minutes of the onset of oxygen deprivation), then the brain reaches a point of irreversibility. At that point in time the person can be pronounced "dead."

How arbitrary and loose are our definitions, yet how crucial! At present, we can agree upon certain working definitions of "life" and "death" without having the foggiest notion of what *life* (and its absence, *death*) really is.

8   When did life begin on the planet earth?

The solar system was born about 5 billion years ago, and about a half-billion years later our planet had become a dense, round, hot ball, still inhospitable, angry, and forbidding.

From the fossil record we know that the first hard-shelled animals emerged in late Precambrian times about 700 million years ago and continued to diversify in an explosion of species throughout the Cambrian era (beginning about 600 million years ago). Traces of these life-forms are easily found since they had reached an advanced stage of evolution when their hard shells could leave a fossil record. Soft parts dissolved, of course, and left no trace.

We can be quite sure that soft-bodied animals, including countless species of single-celled organisms, had by this time passed through a long history of evolutionary development. But they have successfully eluded fossil hunters.

The oldest known forms of life are algalike cells which lived some 3.1 billion years ago. These cells were capable of green-plant photosynthesis. Chances are that this process had been going on for some time, but no earlier record has been found.

When, then, did life begin? All we can say for sure is that life developed sometime between 4.5 billion years ago—when the earth was formed—and 3.1 billion years ago—with our earliest record of microfossil life. During that 1.4-billion-year period, some wonderful and incredible events were taking place.

We have sufficient knowledge now to make informed guesses about some of those events, and here begins one of the exciting stories in the history of human knowledge.

9   Rapid progress in the field of chemical evolution is associated with the work of three men.

In 1922 a Russian biochemist, Alexander Oparin, delivered before a group of scientists in Moscow a paper outlining his theory of biogenesis. Two years later he published his thoughts in a booklet entitled *The Origin of Life*. In 1928 the English biologist J. B. S. Haldane published a closely similar thesis in a technical paper. Both men meticulously developed highly coherent theoretical models from their knowledge of physics and

In one form or another, the concept that life entails the operation of some principle of nature which is as yet ill defined seems to be gaining ground at the present time; and there is reason to believe that it is the fear of entrenched scientific orthodoxy which stills the voice of many who believe that life involves something more subtle than the latest chemical formulae for nucleic acids.

RENÉ DUBOS

ABSTRACT (1953)

More often than not, momentous events can be sorted out only in retrospect. Here is the technical abstract of one such historical event: Dr. Stanley Miller's laboratory synthesis of organic compounds which established empirical foundations for our understanding of the origin of life on earth.

A mixture of gases, CH_4, NH_3, H_2O and H_2, which possibly made up the atmosphere of the Earth in its early stages, has been subjected to spark and silent discharges for times of the order of a week to determine which organic compounds would be synthesized. Several designs of apparatus and reasons for their construction are described. Analyses of the remaining gases were made and CO, CO_2, N_2 and the initial gases were found. A red compound that seems to be associated with the trace metals is formed, as well as yellow compounds, probably polymers, which have acidic, basic and ampholytic properties. The mixture of compounds is separated into acidic, basic and ampholytic fractions with ion exchange resins. The amino acids are chromatographed on Dowex-50 and the acids on silica. Glycine, *d, l*-alanine, β-alanine, sarcosine, *d, l*-α-amino-*n*-butyric acid and α-amino-isobutyric acid have been identified by paper chromatography and by melting points of derivatives. Substantial quantities of several unidentified amino acids and small amounts of about 25 amino acids are produced, while glycolic, *d, l*-lactic, formic, acetic and propionic acids make up most of the acid fraction. Quantitative estimates of these compounds are given. Evidence is presented that polyhydroxy compounds of unknown composition are present. HCN and aldehydes are direct products of the discharge. Although there is insufficient evidence, the synthesis of the hydroxy and amino acids may be through the hydroxy and amino nitriles in the solution. The relation of these experiments to the formation of the Earth and the origin of life is briefly discussed.

Journal of the American
Chemical Society, 77, 2351 (1955).

According to one of the most fundamental laws of physics, the universal tendency in the world of matter is for everything to run downhill, to fall to the lowest possible level of tension, with constant loss of potential energy and of organization. In contrast, life constantly creates and maintains order out of the randomness of matter. To apprehend the deep significance of this fact one need only think what happens to any living organism—the very smallest as well as the largest and most evolved—when finally it dies.

RENÉ DUBOS

biochemistry, but there was as yet no empirical evidence to support their speculations. In 1953, the American Dr. Stanley Miller performed the experiments which began to lay empirical foundations.

Oparin had theorized that in the earth's early stages a great variety of organic compounds had already developed out of inorganic materials. He showed theoretically how these compounds could develop into the first prevital organisms and then into living things. As the crust of the earth began to form and the temperature of the atmosphere dropped below $1000\,°C$, a variety of chemical reactions took place. Torrential rains poured down upon the earth, accompanied by constant discharges of lightning. Hot pools of water formed containing organic compounds that washed down from the atmosphere. Most important, Oparin thought, were the

Drs. Alexander Oparin and Cyril Ponnamperuma

carbon bonds which formed in ever-larger molecular chains. Fatty acids, sugars, and tannins could have formed this way. Eventually, amino acids were synthesized, and amino acids are the basic constituents of proteins.

Thus, during the first period of the earth's history—perhaps a billion years long—mixtures of hydrocarbons, nitrogen, hydrogen, and ammonia were continually producing an endless variety of organic compounds which formed complex molecules which became the building-blocks of living cells. At this stage the earth was covered with what Haldane appropriately called a "hot dilute soup" in which the prevital reactions were taking place. With the synthesis of proteins, the first step had been taken toward the development of life.

10   The first empirical evidence that Oparin's theory might be correct came in 1953 from Stanley Miller's experiments at the University of Chicago.

In a simple glass apparatus, Miller introduced methane, ammonia, and hydrogen. As these gases mixed with vapor from boiling water and passed through glass tubes, they flowed across two electrodes generating a continuous electric spark. All this was designed to simulate hypothetical conditions prevailing in the earth's early atmosphere. The experiment ran

We now believe with confidence, that the whole of reality is one gigantic process of evolution. This produces increased novelty and variety, and ever higher types of organization; in a few spots it has produced life; and, in a few of those spots of life, it has produced mind and consciousness.

SIR JULIAN HUXLEY

Dr. Thomas Gold of Cornell suggests that our earth may have been visited in the distant past by extraterrestrial passersby. Finding conditions inhospitable, they journeyed on, leaving their picnic trash behind. In a billion years or so, lifeforms from this debris had evolved to the point where we call them Homo sapiens.

GEOLOGIC TIME SCALE

ERA	PERIOD	EPOCH	YEARS BEFORE THE PRESENT
Cenozoic	Quaternary	Holocene (Recent)	
			11,000
		Pleistocene (Glacial)	
			500,000 to 2,000,000
	Tertiary	Pliocene	
			13,000,000
		Miocene	
			25,000,000
		Oligocene	
			36,000,000
		Eocene	
			58,000,000
		Paleocene	
			63,000,000
Mesozoic	Cretaceous		
			135,000,000
	Jurassic		
			180,000,000
	Triassic		
			230,000,000
Paleozoic	Permian		
			280,000,000
	Carboniferous — Pennsylvanian (Upper Carboniferous)		
			310,000,000
	Carboniferous — Mississippian (Lower Carboniferous)		
			345,000,000
	Devonian		
			405,000,000
	Silurian		
			425,000,000
	Ordovician		
			500,000,000
	Cambrian		
			600,000,000
Precambrian			

continuously for a week. With this simple technique, a variety of organic compounds formed, many of which turned out to be amino acids. Miller repeated and double checked his work. Since 1953 other scientists have added a vast amount of supporting data. Various gaseous mixtures have been tried, along with other forms of energy—heat, visible light, ultraviolet light, X rays, radioactivity, ultrasonic vibrations, etc.—and in every case organic compounds were formed.

One interesting fact is that in all these experiments the amino acids that have been synthesized in the laboratory are the very same amino acids that are abundant in living proteins today.

The metaphysical aura surrounding the problem of the origin of life was thus lifted; serious discussion and experimentation could be, and was, undertaken. Reports on various phases of the problem continue to come from laboratories all over the world.

It was in this glass apparatus that Dr. Stanley Miller produced the first empirical evidence supporting the theory that living organisms may have resulted from the combination of various chemical compounds.

NEW CLUES INDICATE LIFE ON EARTH
BEGAN 3.3 BILLION YEARS AGO

The beginnings of photosynthesis—and life—on earth may date back as much as 3.3 billion years, according to researchers in a joint UCLA-NASA study.

The birth of photosynthesis, a process that combines chemical compounds with radiant energy or sunlight so organisms can make their own food, had been dated at 2.8 billion years ago in previous research.

. . .

Dr. J. William Schopf and Dorothy Z. Oehler of UCLA and Dr. Keith Kvenvolden, chief of the chemical evolution branch at Ames, conducted the research in line with NASA's interest in planetary evolution and biology.

In a study of ancient rocks in the Barberton Mountain Land, southeastern Transvaal, South Africa, the team found evidence in two types of carbon that may date the inception of photosynthetic organisms.

Since all life on earth is based on carbon, Kvenvolden explained, the transition from primordial organic carbon to organic carbon produced by photosynthetic organisms should provide good evidence of life processes.

The evidence of photosynthesis, he said, comes from a change in the ratio of the two isotopes, carbon 12 and carbon 13—a widely accepted test for photosynthesis.

Rocks taken from the lowest layer of the South African site dated about 3.4 billion years old, the scientist said. These were pre-Cambrian sedimentary rocks known as cherts. They showed ancient carbon similar to that found in meteorites and thought to have been produced by non-biologic processes.

In a layer of almost identical pre-Cambrian rocks immediately above those containing the ancient carbon, however, the researchers found strong evidence of the type of carbon produced by early photosynthesis. This layer was dated about 3.3 billion years ago.

Strata at the South African site were deposited over a period of 300 to 400 million years when the area was ocean bottom, the scientists said.

The Ames–UCLA research team cautioned that other explanations of their find can be suggested and pointed out that no final conclusion can be drawn until further studies are conducted.

After about a billion years a molecule appeared that could reproduce itself and these first living molecules are thought to have rapidly exhausted the existing food supply of natural organic molecules, threatening the extinction of life.

At this point organisms that could make food by photosynthesis are believed to have appeared and established life on a stable basis.

MARVIN MILES

Los Angeles Times, April 30, 1972

11   About 3 billion years ago a momentous change occurred in the earth's atmosphere: oxygen began to be produced. Small amounts of oxygen may have been produced earlier as ultraviolet rays broke down water molecules in the atmosphere, and green-plant photosynthesis may have begun on a modest scale. As single-celled green plants multiplied, ever greater amounts of oxygen were released. This event altered the basic conditions for life on earth. It produced an ozone shield around the earth which filtered out destructive ultraviolet rays and began to produce the "greenhouse effect." As more oxygen was produced, the conditions for the beginning of animal evolution came into being. In all probability, this event triggered the explosion of the evolution of species on earth.

12   Several other theories about the origin of life have not been disproved or abandoned. Although the biogenetic model outlined above is shaping up as a sound scientific hypothesis, another theory—*pansper-*

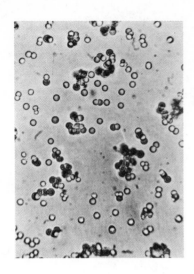

mia—may *also* be valid. This theory suggests that life may exist throughout the universe and that living substances journeyed to our planet from some other location, most likely embedded in meteorites.

This view was first held by the Greek philosopher Anaxagoras, who conjectured that fertile seeds drifted into our atmosphere from other worlds, became implanted in the warm, moist sands of the shore, and germinated. From these seeds all other forms of life have developed.

Anaxagoras' intuition may have been correct. Recent analysis has shown that biotically synthesized organisms are in fact found in certain meteorites and can remain viable for millions of years. They could indeed survive the hazardous journey through space and the plunge through the earth's atmosphere.

While panspermia may prove to be true, it is often pointed out that it doesn't solve the problem of how life began. It only pushes the problem light-years away to some unknown location.

13   The theory of *spontaneous generation* was believed for thousands of years until the experiments of Louis Pasteur proved it false. "Never will the doctrine of spontaneous generation recover from this mortal blow," Pasteur told the French Academy—and it hasn't. This theory held that fully developed species are generated out of nonliving materials: maggots from decaying meat, for example, or frogs from mud, mice from old rags, or fireflies from early morning dew. Our knowledge of microscopic life-forms renders this notion worthless.

Hylozoism is the belief that *all* matter is alive. It was held by the earliest Greek philosophers and has been championed by occasional theorists ever since. The idea that matter itself might be alive, or in some way might involve "mental" activity, has intrigued philosophers. The more dematerialized our concept of matter becomes, the more we may be tempted to consider mystical or panpsychic theories of ultimate reality.

Creationism is the belief that life can originate only by a touch of the supernatural, and *vitalism* is the hypothesis that a special "life-force" must infuse nonliving matter before it can come alive. Both theories are still widely held, but their viability depends partly upon whether it can be shown that living organisms can develop from inorganic matter. If this can be demonstrated, then hypotheses involving creationism or vitalism will be unnecessary.

14   The problem of the origin of life has not yet been solved. Much more work will be necessary to close the gaps in our knowledge.

We would like to know more about the time-scale for the origin of life during the period from the earth's beginning to those first known microscopic organisms which lived some 3.1 billion years ago. During that 1.4-billion-year gap, how long did it take for living cells to develop? Did it happen once or many times? Is the creation of life in such a manner still taking place today? We would also like to know something about the rates of evolution of these primitive organisms. How long did the blue-green algae float around in the "hot thin soup" before complex life-forms developed?

The most complex problem still facing biogenetic theorists is to reconstruct the evolution of the *genetic mechanics* by which cells replicate themselves. During the seventies, scientists will be working to show how the DNA code was synthesized from nucleic acids.

In 1957 Dr. George Wald, a Harvard biologist, stated that he was sure that we will have produced life in the laboratory within fifty years. Today most scientists would reduce such an estimate. Chances are high that such an event will take place sometime during the seventies.

15   The immediate benefits of such a breakthrough should be immense. Not only will we begin to understand the fundamental mechanisms of life, but we will be better able to know how pathological life-forms arise; breakthroughs should follow toward ending disease and malfunction, and eliminating undesirable physical characteristics.

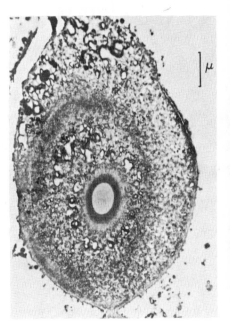

The consequences will extend much farther. We have already begun to experiment with "cloning"—producing living embryos from an enucleated egg and the DNA code of a body cell, embryos that eventually grow into healthy adults possessing precisely predetermined characteristics. Cloning will be extended to higher animals and probably to man. Someday it should be practicable to perform genetic surgery to alter and shape an organism's basic physiology; this can be done by manipulating the position of the nucleotides in the genes. Once DNA codes are precisely known, we could create in an individual any desired characteristic.

16   What will it mean philosophically when life is created in a glass tube by a scientist?

Man's creation of life is a predictable next step in his unraveling of life's secrets. It is an event in a continuing series: the use of fire, the wheel, weapons; harnessing steam power, nuclear power, and solar power for his energy needs; the control of weather; the use of chemicals to control emotions, explore psychopathological conditions, and eradicate disease. In kind, it is nothing new; but the door it will open is so momentous that in effect it will be as though a door had been opened onto a new world.

Man's entrance into the creation of life is one of the giant steps which puts man in control of his own destiny. This step, along with another momentous event—taking over his own evolution—is part of the grand transition man is now undergoing, the transition from being a *passively produced organism* to being the *active controller* of life and destiny.

With each step taken by man to control events in his two worlds, many are constrained to cry doom and declare the area off-limits. This response results both from theological conviction and from a deep distrust of man's ability to use his knowledge constructively, a distrust which can be supported with too much evidence. But historically, warnings of this sort have had little affect. Man proceeds to establish control over all that he can, and, following his deepest impulses, will undoubtedly continue to do so.

Does this not mean that man is "playing God"? Of course. Didn't man "play God" when he "invented" fire, melted iron and copper, domesticated the atom, flew at supersonic speeds, and rocketed to the moon?

And semantically, isn't "playing God" something of a play on words? Isn't the phrase merely an expression of our fear that man is gathering too much power in his hands without knowing how to use it?

Primitive man is reluctant to walk on sacred ground for fear of bringing down upon his head the wrath of an offended deity—divine revenge for his *hybris,* his arrogance. But in reality man has already left his footprints on every accessible plot of holy ground and found that he was more man for it. Hasn't he?

People used to think that the primeval elements had to sit around in the ocean for millions of years before something happened. We now know that once the right molecules accumulated at the right time and in the right arrangement, life could begin almost instantaneously. Evolution is what takes time.

CYRIL PONNAMPERUMA

17   As man's understanding advances, he will produce, at will, by rearranging nucleotides in various sequences, *new kinds* of organisms. This is genetic engineering in its ultimate form.

There is no reason, in theory, why man will not be able to design a living creature on the drawingboard, just as he now designs houses, computers, and rockets, planning down to the last detail how the organism will look and behave.

The inauguration of self-replicating, mutating organisms in a glass flask will be neither good nor evil, but the implications of power are enormous. The nightmare beings that inhabit far-out science fiction, as well as the beautiful superhumans of philosophers' utopias (for instance, the *Übermensch*—"Superman"—of Nietzsche's dreams), might actually come true.

Our fear of all this is justifiable. Can man develop the maturity rapidly enough to wield such power constructively and not for harm? Unfortunately, at present this question remains unanswerable.

6   The Protoplasmic Venture

6-2

EVOLUTION

1   When Charles Darwin finally got around to publishing the *Origin of Species* in 1859—after more than twenty years of procrastination—he had formulated a coherent theory about the development of all living things and documented his theory so massively that it swept the field. No other theory of evolution could hold its ground when compared with the concept of natural selection.

Darwin had not developed his notions out of nothing, of course. It had been noted that trait-changes take place from parent to offspring and that these variations are often inherited. Selective breeding of domestic animals and plants had long been practiced. And even the ideas of "the struggle for survival" and "natural selection" were hardly new, going back at least to the Greek philosopher Empedocles (c. 450 B.C.).

Darwin's genius was (1) his ability to bring a synoptic mind to these disparate elements and fit them all together, and (2) his meticulous gathering of scientific data to support his theory.

2   Following Darwin's development of the theory of natural selection from the struggle for survival, there were two large gaps in man's understanding of how evolution works.

First, heredity was not understood. But with the rediscovery in 1900 of Gregor Mendel's work, light began to dawn. Mendel's experiments had been forgotten since 1865; when they were recovered they fell into place in Darwin's theory. The transmission of specific characteristics from parents to offspring was by means of what Mendel called "genes" and followed predictable patterns.

The second information gap was knowledge of how trait-changes occur between parent and offspring. Understanding this process has come only during the last few years as scientists have penetrated the genetic code itself and found it to be a template determined by the arrangement of nucleotides in the helix-shaped DNA (deoxyribonucleic acid) molecule.

Today we have a general understanding of the three basic processes of evolution: (1) the laws of heredity, (2) mutations produced by changes in the DNA code, and (3) the dynamics of natural selection.

The theory of evolution has become one of man's great unifying "field theories," bringing many areas of knowledge together into a single formula and providing us with a fundamental understanding of the nature of life on our planet.

3   Since the time that living organisms first emerged from the "hot thin soup," the proliferation of species on our planet staggers the imagination. Taxonomists—those ever-patient classifiers—have so far discovered, ordered, and described about $1\frac{1}{2}$ million species of living organisms, and some ten thousand new species are added annually to the list.

To date they have recognized some eighty-six hundred species of birds and one hundred fifty thousand species of marine organisms, including nearly twenty-five thousand species of fishes. Yet at least a third of the planet's fishes are still unknown to science. Some three-quarters of a million species of insects are recorded and six to seven thousand new ones are added yearly. The higher vertebrates are mostly accounted for, but the invertebrates are relatively unknown, especially the mites, nematods, worms, and parasites which total hundreds of thousands.

About a half-million higher plants have been classified, but taxonomists estimate that a quarter-million species are still unknown, especially in the tropical climates. Lower plants, such as fungi, have hardly been touched.

It is estimated that on our planet perhaps 10 million species of organisms exist today, yet this number is less than 1 percent of all the species that have existed on earth since life began.

Almost all animal phyla with preservable hard parts are represented in the fossil record from late Precambrian times onward, but millions of soft-bodied species doubtless lived before this but left no trace. Scientists guess that perhaps one out of five thousand to ten thousand extinct species show up in the fossil record.

All told, then, how many species has evolution produced on earth since the planet's beginning? The staggering figure is in the vicinity of 10 billion.

4   More than 99 percent of all living species have become extinct. Why? What could have caused such mass annihilation? We're not yet sure. Changes in climate, perhaps, or invasion of a species' ecological niche by other species that pushed them out or ate them up.

The dynamics of natural selection dictate that whenever an ecological niche is vacated other species move in and adapt to that niche.

NAME: (Unknown)
ALIAS: Shanidar I
NICKNAME: "Nandy"
ADDRESS: Shanidar Cave, Iraq
TRIBE: Neanderthalers
CAUSE OF DEATH: Rockfall
DATE OF DEATH: 46,000 B.C.
NEXT OF KIN: Man

Creatures extremely low in the intellectual scale may have conception. All that is required is that they should recognize the same experience again. A polyp would be a conceptual thinker if a feeling of "Hello! thingumbob again!" ever flitted through its mind.

WILLIAM JAMES

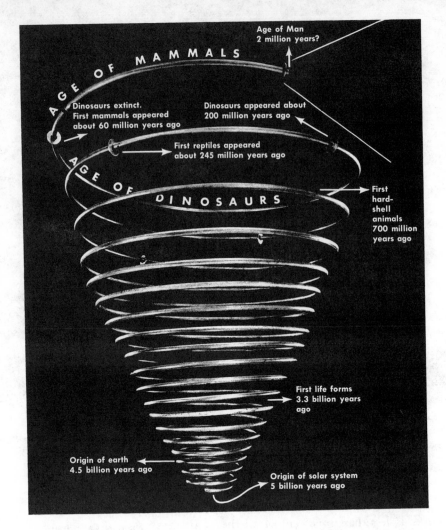

Age of Man
2 million years?

AGE OF MAMMALS

Dinosaurs extinct.
First mammals appeared
about 60 million years ago

Dinosaurs appeared about
200 million years ago

First reptiles appeared
about 245 million years ago

AGE OF DINOSAURS

First
hard-
shell
animals
700 million
years ago

First life forms
3.3 billion years
ago

Origin of earth
4.5 billion years ago

Origin of solar system
5 billion years ago

With some of the great extinctions, however, this seems not to have been the case; it was not a piecemeal process. By the close of the Cambrian period more than forty of some sixty trilobite families were extinct, and before the end of the Paleozoic era the rest vanish from the record.

By the end of the Permian period about half of all known families of the animal kingdom vanish; during the last part of the Cretaceous period a quarter more become extinct. Such vast-ranging extinction occurred in the oceans as well as on land. No life-forms were exempt.

Why? Survival seems to depend upon the species' place in the entire evolutionary ecosystem. The member species are interdependent in an extremely complex and delicate way. Whatever happens to the most dominant fauna and flora has a profound *selective effect* upon all other biota belonging to the system. Upsetting the interrelationships is relatively easy, and member species must shift their positions if they are to adapt and survive. Consequently, new species proliferate as mass extinctions take place, and new ecosystems are formed.

5 The theory of evolution has made us face numerous philosophical problems, partly because the evolutionary "field theory" is so comprehensive.

One problem is the enigma of irreversibility. We have no difficulty accepting the fact that a single organism can't move from adulthood back through adolescence into childhood, or that a butterfly can't move from its adult flying stage back through the chrysalid into its larval stage. Such notions are absurd, and we know it. But in just the same way, evolution can't move backward from complex to simpler life-forms.

The famed aphorism, *Ontogeny recapitulates phylogeny,* summarizes a well-documented fact. The long evolutionary journey of each species has left its imprint upon the embryo of the individual organism. In other words, as each embryo develops from fertilization to birth, it retraces the path of the organism's evolutionary history. For example, the human embryo at one stage exhibits a "tail" and gill-like slits which make it almost indistinguishable from the embryos of fishes or other animals which, at some point in man's dim evolutionary past, emerged from the sea.

Scientists have noted that it is not necessarily the adult stage of an ancestor which the embryo resembles. Rather the embryo mimics immature phases of its ancestors; the embryo's growth stages seem to imply that "ancestral plans of structure" may be retained in the organism's later stages of evolutionary development.

To endure life remains, when all is said, the first duty of all living beings. Illusion can have no value if it makes this more difficult for us. . . .

SIGMUND FREUD

6 Evolutionary convergence, with similar selective pressures driving unrelated and rather different genotypes into similar ecological niches, is another exciting but inadequately investigated phenomenon. The "cactus" growth form has appeared in several distinct families of plants, and some of these succulents are so similar in appearance that a non-specialist has difficulty in identifying the family. Old World tree frogs and New World tree frogs are so similar in adaptation to life in trees that it is necessary to examine the skeleton to determine which is which, yet they have originated as independent radiations within separate families. In Australia, where ordinary frogs (ranids) are virtually absent, a tree frog has evolved habits, body size, and even shape and appearance of our common leopard frog (a ranid). These and many other examples of convergence imply that there is a finite number of ways in which an organism of a given basic genotype can "make a living."

Biology and the Future of Man

This secret spoke Life herself unto me: "Behold," said she, "I am that which must ever surpass itself."

NIETZSCHE

7 The relative roles of competition and cooperation in natural selection pose another problem. Which, we wonder, has played the dominant role in the game of survival?

Competition between species seems most obvious. Species prey upon species. We watch the bloody food-chain—the "deadly feast of life"—as it operates among both animals and plants. But with a close

In a typical ocean food-chain, tuna eats mackerel, mackerel eats smelt, smelt eats copepods, and copepods eat diatoms. "Or, stated in the reverse, 10,000 lb. of diatoms will make 1,000 lb. of copepods; 1,000 lb. of copepods will make 100 lb. of smelt; 100 lb. of smelt will make 10 lb. of mackerel; 10 lb. of mackerel will make 1 lb. of tuna; 1 lb. of tuna will make 0.1 lb. of man. It takes 10 lb. of food to make 1 lb. of the animal that feeds upon it. . . ."

MAC GINITIE AND MAC GINITIE

EVOLVE OR PERISH

The value for the rate of evolution obtained by Palmer was 1 per cent per 10,000 years, corresponding to the value of a unit suggested by Haldane as an appropriate one for measuring evolutionary rates. The unit is a "darwin." . . . This is the same rate as 1 per cent in 10,000 years, which seems to be about the value for man. The rate is extremely rapid compared with that for most animals which have existed on the earth for a much longer time than the million years during which man has been developing. Specifically, using the figures for *Pithecanthropus erectus* and modern man, with a time interval of 400,000 years, the evolutionary rate works out to be 1.2 darwins. This indicates that, according to measurements of his skulls and jaws, man is evolving physically at an extremely rapid rate. Such a rapid evolutionary rate is characteristic of a new species. The rate begins to slow up after 50 million years, as judged from ancestral lines of fossils, and then dies down gradually as the species tends toward extinction. Whether or not this process applies to man is a matter for speculation. A genus can cease to be, either because all its members have died without issue, or because all its surviving descendents have changed so much as to be classified as members of one or more new genera. Simpson concludes that all mammalian genera are relatively short-lived; the average life of a genus of carnivores is about 6.8 million years. Thus, in Haldane's words, "A mammal must evolve or perish."

ROLAND FISCHER, "Biological Time,"
J. T. Fraser (ed.), *Voices of Time*

---

look, we also find countless cases of cooperation, from simple symbiosis to a higher altruism in which a single individual voluntarily suffers self-deprivation or death for the welfare of its group.

Evolution clearly employs both of these seemingly contradictory mechanisms. Evolution appears to be opportunistic, caring nothing about technique. Perhaps ideas like "cooperation" and "competition" are mere human valuations which we misapply to a system that operates outside the boundaries of such anthropomorphic notions. Evolution is seemingly pragmatic—cooperating or competing, protecting or destroying, aiding or eating—whatever will increase chances of survival. The only success *is* survival, and the only criterion is whatever helps each species survive.

The long-term problem is not merely which pattern has been dominant. Once man has taken over this planet's evolution and must deal with the complex interrelationships of all living things—*the* Ecosystem—the problem man must face is whether competition and interspecific destruction can be replaced—or *should* be replaced—by patterns of mutual cooperation.

8   MRS. VENABLE. One long-ago summer—now, why am I thinking of this?—my son, Sebastian, said, "Mother?—Listen to this!"—He read me Herman Melville's description of the Encantadas, the Galápagos Islands. . . . He read me that description and said that we had to go there. And so we did go there that summer on a chartered boat, a four-masted schooner, as close as possible to the sort of boat that Melville must have sailed on. . . . We saw the Encantadas, but on the Encantadas we saw something Melville *hadn't* written about. We saw great sea-turtles crawl up out of the sea for their annual egg-laying. . . . Once a year the female of the sea-turtle crawls up out of the equatorial sea onto the blazing sand-beach of a volcanic island to dig a pit in the sand and deposit her eggs there. It's a long and dreadful thing, the depositing of the eggs in the sand-pits, and when it's finished the exhausted female turtle crawls back to the sea half-dead. She never sees her offspring, but we did. Sebastian knew exactly when the sea-turtle eggs would be hatched out and we returned in time for it. . . .

  DOCTOR. You went back to the—?

Nature is not made in the image of man's compassion.

TENNESSEE WILLIAMS
Suddenly Last Summer

MRS. VENABLE. Terrible Encantadas, those heaps of extinct volcanoes, in time to witness the hatching of the sea-turtles and their desperate flight to the sea!

(*There is a sound of harsh bird cries in the air. She looks up.*)

—The narrow beach, the color of caviar, was all in motion! But the sky was in motion, too. . . .

DOCTOR. The sky was in motion, too?

MRS. VENABLE. —Full of flesh-eating birds and the noise of the birds, the horrible savage cries of the—

DOCTOR. Carnivorous birds?

MRS. VENABLE. Over the narrow black beach of the Encantadas as the just hatched sea-turtles scrambled out of the sand-pits and started their race to the sea. . . .

DOCTOR. Race to the sea?

MRS. VENABLE. To escape the flesh-eating birds that made the sky almost as black as the beach!

(*She gazes up again: we hear the wild, ravenous, harsh cries of the birds. The sound comes in rhythmic waves like a savage chant.*)

And the sand all alive, all alive, as the hatched sea-turtles made their dash for the sea, while the birds hovered and—swooped to attack! They were diving down on the hatched sea-turtles, turning them over to expose their soft undersides, tearing the undersides open and rending and eating their flesh. Sebastian guessed that possibly only a hundredth of one per cent of their number would escape to the sea. . . .

DOCTOR. What was it about this spectacle on the beach that fascinated your son?

MRS. VENABLE. My son was looking for—

(*Stops short: continues evasively—*)

Let's just say he was interested in sea-turtles.

DOCTOR. You started to say that your son was looking for something.

MRS. VENABLE. (*Defiantly*) All right, I started to say that my son was looking for God and I stopped myself because I was afraid that if I said he was looking for God, you'd say to yourself, "Oh, a pretentious young crackpot!"—which Sebastian was not. All poets look for God, all good poets do, and they have to look harder for Him than priests do since they don't have the help of such famous guide-books and well-organized expeditions as priests have with their scriptures and churches. All right! Well, now I've said it, my son was looking for God. I mean for a clear image of Him. He spent that whole blazing equatorial day in the crow's nest of the schooner watching that thing on the beach of the Encantadas till it was too dark to see it, and when he came back down the rigging, he said, Well, now I've seen Him!—and he meant God. . . .

TENNESSEE WILLIAMS
Suddenly Last Summer

9 One finds in the Bahamas the highly organized relationship between the Pederson shrimp (*Periclimenes pedersoni*) and its numerous clients. The transparent body of this tiny animal is striped with white and spotted with violet, and its conspicuous antennae are considerably longer than its body.

Both competition and cooperation are observed in nature. Natural selection is neither egotistic nor altruistic. It is, rather, opportunistic.

THEODOSIUS DOBZHANSKY

It establishes its station in quiet water where fishes congregate or frequently pass, always in association with the sea anemone *Bartholomea annulata,* usually clinging to it or occupying the same hole.

When a fish approaches, the shrimp will whip its long antennae and sway its body back and forth. If the fish is interested, it will swim directly to the shrimp and stop an inch or two away. The fish usually presents its head or gill cover for cleaning, but if it is bothered by something out of the ordinary such as an injury near its tail, it presents itself tail first. The shrimp swims or crawls forward, climbs aboard and walks rapidly over the fish, checking irregularities, tugging at parasites with its claws and cleaning injured areas. The fish remains almost motionless during this inspection and allows the shrimp to make minor incisions in order to get at subcutaneous parasites. As the shrimp approaches the gill covers, the fish opens each one in turn and allows the shrimp to enter and forage among the gills. The shrimp is even permitted to enter and leave the fish's mouth cavity. Local fishes quickly learn the location of these shrimp. They line up or crowd around for their turn and often wait to be cleaned when the shrimp has retired into the hole beside the anemone.

For the first time since the beginning of its history, humanity has become master of its destiny. . . . In order to grow afresh, it is forced to make itself anew. And it cannot make itself anew without pain, for it is both the marble and the sculptor. Out of its own substance it must send the splinters flying with great hammer-strokes, in order to recover its true face.

ALEXIS CARREL

Organisms are not the result of any planned, goal-directed, or predetermined course of creation. Instead, they are the result of a cumulative, opportunistic process of piece-by-piece building, based on existing organisms and governed entirely by natural selection acting on random variations.

PAUL B. WEISZ

Scientists wondered what would happen if all the cleaner-shrimp were removed. The results were striking:

> Within a few days the number of fish was drastically reduced; within two weeks almost all except the territorial fishes had disappeared. Many of the fish remaining developed fuzzy white blotches, swelling, ulcerated sores and frayed fins.

10   Perhaps the most difficult issue in evolution has been the problem of teleology. Is the evolutionary process one of sheer chance and opportunism, or in some way is it guided teleologically by some force, extrinsic or intrinsic, so that evolution is, in fact, "going somewhere"? Does it unfold according to a plan? Is it directed? Does it have a goal? Is its purpose to develop new and ever-more-complex forms of life? That it moves inexorably from simpler to more complex life-forms is undeniable; but does it do so "purposefully," or "opportunistically"? And even if its mode of operations is opportunistic, we still wonder *why* it moves toward ever-increased complexity.

Despite the tone of many biologists, the problem is not settled, and it is a very complicated one. It's helpful to remember that science

EVOLUTION AND ALTRUISM

On the matter of the survival of altruism during evolution, I believe we should note Darwin's group theory. In *The Descent of Man,* he wrote:

> "When two tribes of primeval man, living in the same country came into competition, if (other circumstances being equal) the one tribe included a great number of courageous, sympathetic and faithful members, who were always ready to warn each other of danger, to aid and defend each other, this tribe would succeed better and conquer the others."

And again:

> "Obscure as is the problem of the advance of civilization, we can at least see that the nation which produced, during a lengthened period, the greatest number of highly intellectual, energetic, brave, patriotic, and benevolent men, would generally prevail over less favored nations."

As to the survival of the altruistic individuals within the group, Darwin's theory is that devoted people propagate their own kind of personalities, not through their physical children, but through their ethical children, those who imitate the actions of the altruistic ones. The disciples that an altruistic person can create, even in a short lifetime, are a much larger number, Darwin says, than the children that a selfish man can father. (References: Charles Darwin, *The Origin of Species* and *The Descent of Man.* The Modern Library. pp. 490, 498–500.)

Spencer D. Pollard
University of Southern California
Los Angeles, Calif.

Science News, April 8, 1972

fought its way free of religious establishments which employed harsh measures to enforce belief in ideas which were shown to be false by empirical facts. Western theology pronounced that history *is* a divine teleological plan, the plot of which is the unfolding story of God's cosmic struggle with the forces of evil for the salvation of the souls of men.

Since science freed itself from this teleocosmic myth, the word *teleology* has left a bitter taste in the mouths of scientists. Furthermore, when the theory of evolution became widely known after 1859, those inclined toward teleological thinking were quick to see in the idea of the "survival of the fittest" positive proof of a natural (as opposed to supernatural) teleological movement: if only the fitter survive, then we can conclude, on purely scientific grounds, that life will climb forever toward unimaginable heights. The superior organism will always win over the inferior. Eternal progress is assured. Thus "social Darwinism" colored much late nineteenth- and early twentieth-century thought.

The myth of "inevitable progress" became a religious tenet to those wanting to believe that history has meaning. It ceased to be a scientific hypothesis and was transformed into dogma. It is against such doctrinaire teleology that biologists have struggled; it is but natural that occasional hostilities linger on.

11   Two positions have been taken on the questions of purpose and direction in evolution.

Some thinkers have explicitly affirmed the teleological concept of evolution. Writing in the 1880s, Friedrich Nietzsche was one of the first philosophers to develop the deeper implications of the idea of natural selection. In several brilliant books—most notably *Thus Spake Zarathustra*—Nietzsche envisioned evolutionary history as a grand surge of life upward toward a superior being (Nietzsche called him *Übermensch*—"Overman" or "Superman"). History's intrinsic goal, argued Nietzsche, is to produce a man who has such greatness that he would be, in essence, a new species. He would possess new qualities only dimly presaged by the greatest now living among us. While he would be nothing less than ruthless in his mission of aiding evolution in its purpose, he would also display magnanimity and compassion, even gentleness, when called for.

Nietzsche's teleological interpretation of evolution also implied an ethic (which was immediately perverted by unscrupulous followers). The criterion for deciding between virtue and evil is whether any given human activity supports or thwarts evolution's fundamental purpose of producing the superior race of men. Any human act that improves man's genetic stock is moral in the fullest sense; any act that preserves inferior qualities is immoral in the same final sense. Evolution's sublime destiny is to produce superior man. Nothing must be allowed to stand in its way.

12   One of the most influential evolutionary thinkers of the twentieth century was the French philosopher Henri Bergson, whose masterpiece, *Creative Evolution,* was published in 1907. It was Bergson's conviction that what we observe in evolution cannot be explained adequately by the mechanics of natural selection. Something more profound is taking place in evolution, and natural selection has missed it. Some further insight must be added to the idea of natural selection before it can answer the question of why higher forms of life continue to emerge. Bergson postulated the existence of an *élan vital,* a "vital life-force" or "impulse-to-life." He reflected that if adaptation and change were all that was required, then the ants had it made millions of years ago. They have been able to survive, almost unchanged, since long before the beginning of "the ascent of man." This being the case, why should evolution have bothered to evolve more complex forms of life? Something else, Bergson insisted, is at work in the forces of evolvement.

The élan vital is unpredictable and opportunistic, pushing ahead in every species of animal and plant in order to create greater complexity and higher life-forms. It has no goal as such; its only purpose is to exploit every opportunity in the struggle of an organism with its environment to advance the quality of life.

13   In contrast to such teleologies, the majority of biologists hold an opportunist interpretation of evolution. They adhere to the principle that everything can be explained solely by physical, chemical, biological, or ecological principles; there is no need to introduce mysterious factors such as an élan vital or some far-off goal toward which evolution is laboriously winding its way.

At first sight the biological sector seems full of purpose. Organisms are built as if purposefully designed, and work as if in purposeful pursuit of a conscious aim. But the truth lies in those two words "as if." As the genius of Darwin showed, the purpose is only an apparent one. However, this at least implies prospective significance. Natural selection operates in

---

SOONER OR LATER

Long before our populations reach the levels envisaged above [in which case human population growth will crowd out all other forms of life on our planet] we shall have broken so many of the rules that govern our biological nature that we shall have collapsed as a dominant species. We tend to suffer from a strange complacency that this can never happen, that there is something special about us, that we are somehow above biological control. But we are not. Many exciting species have become extinct in the past and we are no exception. Sooner or later we shall go, and make way for something else. If it is to be later rather than sooner, then we must take a long, hard look at ourselves as biological specimens and gain some understanding of our limitations.

DESMOND MORRIS
The Naked Ape

relation to the future—the future survival of the individual and the species. And its products, in the shape of actual animals and plants, are correspondingly oriented toward the future, in their structure, their mode of working, and their behavior. A few of the later products of evolution, notably the higher mammals, do show true purpose, in the sense of the awareness of a goal. But the purpose is confined to individuals and their actions. It does not enter into the basic machinery of the evolutionary process, although it helps the realization of its results. Evolution in the biological phase is still impelled from behind; but the process is now structured so as to be directed forward.

SIR JULIAN HUXLEY

14   A similar position—but with a fine distinction—is held by the microbiologist René Dubos. Dubos agrees that chance and opportunism undoubtedly operate in the adaptation of a species to a specific environment. But he observes that while most biologists disown the notion of teleology, they nonetheless *operate* on the tacit assumption that evolution does involve a kind of "purpose" or movement toward a functional complexity. Teleology, he writes, "is like an attractive woman of easy virtue, without whom a biologist cannot function happily, but with whom he does not want to be seen in public."

As we know it today, life operates as if most of its structures and functions were designed to fulfill some ultimate end, for the good of the individual and of the progeny. Life has its roots in the past, and its activities are projected into the future. Furthermore, it is a creative process, elaborating and maintaining order out of the randomness of matter, endlessly generating new and unexpected structures and properties by undergoing spontaneous changes, and by building up associations which qualitatively transcend their constituent parts. Clearly then, living things cannot be differentiated from the inanimate world only in terms of structures and properties. Their unique characteristic resides in the fact that their behavior is determined by their past and conditioned by the future, a property as yet mysterious but real nevertheless.

RENÉ DUBOS

Organisms diversify into literally millions of species, then the vast majority of those species perish and other millions take their place for an aeon until they, too, are replaced. Species evolve exactly as if they were adapting as best they could to a changing world, and not at all as if they were moving toward a set goal.

GEORGE GAYLORD SIMPSON

15   The question, "Where is evolution going?" remains unresolved. Without the assumption of any life-essence, divine plan, or evolutionary goal, the very fact that evolution is future-oriented and that it does indeed advance toward increasing complexity and qualitatively higher levels of life means that *we can still wonder what evolution might eventually produce.*

Such a question also applies to branches of evolution other than man. Let's remind ourselves that it might not be through the humanoid line that evolution may actualize such wonderful possibilities. I seem to remember a story—supposedly science fiction—in which a colony of ants on a south Pacific island have just arrived at a higher stage of intelligence and, from their anthill, are carefully watching a busy group of scientists—and planning their next move.

Could there possibly be some validity to Nietzsche's vision that higher forms of humanity will develop if evolution has its way? Dr. Harry Overstreet of Harvard has proposed the idea that man is evolving a new form of consciousness, and that "we have every reason to believe that a further form of our conscious life is already observable among us—a high degree among certain rare individuals, in lesser degree among most of us." Overstreet has in mind the sort of "cosmic consciousness" found in some of the world's religious leaders (Gautama, Jesus), mystics (Plotinus, Swedenborg, William Blake), ecstatic intellectuals (Socrates, Descartes, Shakespeare, Einstein), and visionaries (Dante, Whitman, Fuller). Overstreet adds that such manifestations of a high order of consciousness are regarded by most of us "as signs either of supernatural power or of psychic disorder. Is it not possible, on the other hand, to regard these occurrences as signs simply of a higher stage of the very same typical development through which all of us are passing?"

What indeed is evolution's potential? Are there inherent limitations in evolution, or is it unlimited? What undreamed-of life-qualities are possible and, with a little luck, might become realities?

An unlearned carpenter of my acquaintance once said in my hearing: "there is very little difference between one man and another; but what little there is, is very important." This seems to me to go to the root of the matter.

WILLIAM JAMES

17   A fantastical and fascinating notion is being entertained more and more—with how much credibility it is impossible to say: that at an advanced stage of evolution existence will consist solely of mind. We will no longer be subject to the physical encumbrance of a material body and the limitations and malfunctions of living substance. This concept of existence has long been congenial to Eastern thought—Hinduism and Buddhism, for instance—where a discarnate state of pure consciousness is accepted as the ultimate goal of human striving.

On the Western scene, Stanley Kubrick's motion picture *2001: A Space Odyssey,* developed from Arthur C. Clarke's science-fiction novel *Childhood's End,* makes a clear statement: the universe is filled with life (our universe is a true biocosmos), but that life is in the form of discarnate intelligence. The final goal of the *2001* story is to allow the earthly astronaut time to live out his mortal existence so that he might join the community of advanced life-forms in their immaterial state of mental (and apparently immortal) existence.

18   It seems to me that the greatest lesson of adult life is that one's own consciousness is not enough. What one of us would not like to share the consciousness of half a dozen chosen individuals? What writer would not like to share the consciousness of Shakespeare? What musician that of Beethoven or Mozart? What mathematician that of Gauss? What I would choose would be an evolution of life whereby the essence of each of us becomes welded together into some vastly larger and more potent structure.

FRED HOYLE

6-3

MAN

1   The Maoris of New Zealand say that a certain god, variously named Tu, Tiki, and Tane, took red riverside clay, kneaded it with his own blood into a likeness or image of himself, with eyes, legs, arms, and all complete, in fact, an exact copy of the deity ; and having perfected the model, he animated it by breathing into its mouth and nostrils, whereupon the clay effigy at once came to life and sneezed. So like himself was the man whom the Maori Creator Tiki fashioned that he called him *Tiki-ahua,* that is, Tiki's likeness.

2   Until modern times man lived close to the soil. One thing he knew how to do well—a skill universally found at a specific stage of culture—was to scoop clay from the river bank and shape it into vessels—cooking pots, water jars, urns, amphorae, lamps. Shards of pottery have been found wherever men have lit their fires and lived together.

Kingdom	*Animalia* (*Animals*)
Phylum	*Chordata* (*Chordates*)
Class	*Mammalia* (*Mammals*)
Order	*Primates* (*Primates*)
Superfamily	*Hominoidea* (*Hominoids*)
Family	*Hominidae* (*Hominids*)
Subfamily	*Homininae* (*Hominines*)
Genus	Homo (*Man*)
Species	sapiens (*Modern Man*)

    Besides practical items, man also made figurines, miniatures molded from imagination and clay—images of men and earth mothers, of barques and scarabs, of animals and gods. Some of the earthen images he used to lure bear into his trap, to placate the gods, to grow green stalks heavy with corn, to weaken his enemies.

    Some of the clay figurines he made just for fun. He molded them in his own likeness. He toyed with them, pondered them, and doubtless joked and laughed at them as he sculpted head and torso and limbs from the damp clay.

    This universal experience becomes the archetypal pattern for mankind's creation stories. What was more natural and more obvious than to know, deep in his blood and bones, that he had been shaped by an unknown Sculptor from the clay of the earth? After all, was he not a clay figurine brought to life?

3 The Ewe-speaking tribes of Togo-land, in West Africa, think that God still makes men out of clay. When a little of the water with which he moistens the clay remains over, he pours it on the ground, and out of that he makes the bad and disobedient people. When he wishes to make a good man he makes him out of good clay ; but when he wishes to make a bad man, he employs only bad clay for the purpose. In the beginning God fashioned a man and set him on the earth ; after that he fashioned a woman. The two looked at each other and began to laugh, whereupon God sent them into the world.

4 Thus, creation myths explain to man's satisfaction far more than mere physical origins. They also tell us why he must die and return to the earth, why he is only partly immortal, and why his soul can sometimes return to heaven; they explain why there are many colors of men and many languages, why some men are good and some bad, and why there are two sexes. Almost every fact of life that puzzled early man eventually called forth some sort of mythical explanation.

The Toradjas of the Celebes tell how

> "i Lai, the god of the upper world, and i Ndara, the goddess of the under world, resolved to make men. They committed the task to i Kombengi, who made two models, one of a man and the other of a woman, out of stone or, according to others, out of wood. When he had done his work, he set up his models by the side of the road which leads from the upper to the under world, so that all spirits passing by might see and criticize his workmanship. In the evening the gods talked it over, and agreed that the calves of the legs of the two figures were not round enough. So Kombengi went to work again, and constructed another pair of models which he again submitted to the divine criticism. This time the gods observed that the figures were too pot-bellied, so Kombengi produced a third pair of models, which the gods approved of, after the maker had made a slight change in the anatomy of the figures, transferring a portion of the male to the female figure. It now only remained to make the figures live. So the god Lai returned to his celestial mansion to fetch eternal breath for the man and woman ; but in the meantime the Creator himself, whether from thoughtlessness or haste, had allowed the common wind to blow on the figures, and they drew their breath and life from it. That is why the breath returns to the wind when a man dies.

5 In the earliest Hebrew account of creation, it is said that the god Yahweh moulded the first man out of clay, just as a potter might do, or as a child moulds a doll out of mud ; and that having kneaded and patted the clay into the proper shape, the deity animated it by breathing into the mouth and nostrils of the figure, exactly as the prophet Elisha is said to have restored to life the dead child of the Shunammite by lying on him, and putting his eyes to the child's eyes and his mouth to the child's mouth, no doubt to impart his breath to the corpse ; after which the child sneezed seven times and opened its eyes. To the Hebrews this derivation of our

It is the large brain capacity which allows man to live as a human being, enjoying taxes, canned salmon, television, and the atomic bomb.

G. H. R. VON KOENIGSWALD

Hockett and Ascher remind us that our ancestral proto-hominids "were not striving to become human; they were . . . trying to stay alive."

PHILIP VAN DOREN STERN

6 *The Protoplasmic Venture*

> **EXPERIMENTAL MODEL**   •
>
> So there he stands, our vertical, hunting, weapon-toting, territorial, neotenous, brainy, Naked Ape, a primate by ancestry and a carnivore by adoption, ready to conquer the world. But he is a very new and experimental departure, and new models frequently have imperfections. For him the main troubles will stem from the fact that his culturally operated advances will race ahead of any further genetic ones. His genes will lag behind, and he will be constantly reminded that, for all his environment-moulding achievements, he is still at heart a very naked ape.
>
> DESMOND MORRIS
> *The Naked Ape*

species from the dust of the ground suggested itself all the more naturally because, in their language, the word for "ground" (*adamah*) is in form the feminine of the word for "man" (*adam*).

Thus, both in language and myth, *ha-adam,* "the Man" (masculine), is created from *ha-adamah,* "the Earth" (feminine). And divine spirit/breath (in Hebrew *ruaḥ* means "spirit," "breath," "wind," and "soul") is breathed by Yahweh himself into the Man's nostrils and pumped into his lungs. The Man's body is from the earth, but his spirit/breath is from Yahweh.

6   The Shilluks of the White Nile

ingeniously explain the different complexions of the various races by the differently coloured clays out of which they were fashioned. They say that the creator Juok moulded all men out of earth, and that while he was engaged in the work of creation he wandered about the world. In the land of the whites he found a pure white earth or sand, and out of it he shaped white men. Then he came to the land of Egypt and out of the mud of the Nile he made red or brown men. Lastly, he came to the land of the Shilluks, and finding there black earth he created men out of it.

Neglect of an effective birth control policy is a never-failing source of poverty which, in turn, is the parent of revolution and crime.

ARISTOTLE [sic!]

Before man possessed an evolutionary context in which to see himself, he observed that lions produce lions, turtles produce turtles, bluejays produce bluejays—and man produces man. The logic of this was overwhelming! But a piece of the puzzle is obviously missing. There had to be a beginning: something had to create man in his full sapient form so he could stand tall in his flesh and be half-god, half-clay. And logically the first creator of man had to be like man. Doesn't man produce man?

7   An adequate understanding of man must begin—but not end—with man's place in the program of evolution. He belongs to the animal kingdom, but he is something more than an animal.

Defining man so that he knows that he differs from his animal kin has been a bothersome problem. Men have passionately and religiously guarded their lists of distinctions.

Man's origins, it was supposed, could be discerned in the fossil records by his use of fire or weapons; or it was held that only a fully human creature could make or use tools. "Man alone is a toolmaker," wrote early anthropologists.

Special physical characteristics clearly mark man as a superior being. His upright posture allows mobility, agility, and better chances of survival. His larger brain capacity (averaging about 1300 cc, at least double the volume of the closest living primate) implies greater intelligence, as does the weight ratio of the brain to body. His complex nervous system permits subtle operations. Furthermore, he is free from the instincts that so bind the lower animals within predetermined behavioral limits. Man is said to be the only animal with true freedom of choice, perhaps the only creature ever to have lived on our planet that must make agonizing decisions because of that freedom.

Man's greatly expanded "new brain" provides him with the capacity for abstract thought and reason. Greek thinkers pointed out that it is man's faculty for reason—the ability to use known facts to arrive at new facts—that makes him human and gives him a clue to his reason-for-being: to cultivate his rational mind. This faculty alone, they believed, distinguishes man from the animals. Apart from reason, they reasoned, man *is* an animal.

Along with abstract thought goes self-consciousness, man's power to reflect upon his self, his nature, his knowledge, and the meaning of his existence. Man is surely the only animal that can philosophize.

8   Three rather more ethereal qualities—man's ethical, esthetic, and religious feelings—are frequently considered to be distinctive features separating man from other animals. Only man, it is held, has a moral sense, feelings of justice and injustice, and only man develops behavioral codes to live by. Only man responds to beauty and creates objects for no other reason than to enjoy them. Only man can conceive a supernatural order of reality, believe in deities, develop a soteriology of history, and feel "ultimate concern" about the meaning of his own existence.

There is an obvious omission from all these lists: *soul*. This singular quality finally distinguishes man from all other animals. Man's soul-essence (Greek *psyche*) survives death, and no other animal is supposed to have a psyche. Considerable debate has taken place as men have tried to decide at what point along the evolutionary line prepsychic man developed (or was given) a soul.

9   Recent scientific discoveries have initiated a redefinition of man. The Naked Ape is presently undergoing agonizing reappraisal of himself vis-à-vis the animal world.

Jane Goodall's discovery that chimps not only use but manufacture tools, significantly changed the scientific definition of man. He could no longer be classified as the only maker of tools. Their achievement is a simple one by human standards, but it elevates them far above all other animals save one. *This one girl has forced the scientists and psychologists of the world to redefine man.* Her chimps have helped remove man from some remote pedestal and return him to the natural world of the animal kingdom. She sees in her chimpanzees basic recognizable emotions and a need to communicate their feelings. Though physically incapable of forming the sounds of human speech, there is an unmistakable natural language that any human being can understand, signs of recognition, affection, and reassurance. . . .

Three generations of chimpanzees are now part of Jane Goodall's life. It took years to do what no one else had done: win their trust and confidence. From her understanding of these animals has come unexpected insight and increased appreciation of mankind. These chimpanzees are a source of growing wonder, a reminder of how far humanity has really come in the evolution of man's intellect and language, his ability to love unselfishly, to appreciate and create beauty. Perhaps the narrowing chasm between man and apes will not be spanned by science alone, but by understanding and compassion.

Monkeys, Apes and Men, A National Geographic–CBS-TV program

There are 180 billion cells in the human body. Each of these little factories is carrying out hundreds of chemical processes at a speed that astounds the mind.

JOAN AREHART-TREICHEL

10   In the process of redefining man a controversy has arisen. It appears that man's propensity for violence far exceeds any possible evolutionary demands; man's intense cruelty toward members of his own species is unique in the animal kingdom. He kills not merely for food but is vicious for ideological and symbolic reasons: he will kill "on principle." In the name of mental abstractions he kills other men, whereas other animals battle members of their own species only into submission. Together, all man's religious constraints, moral codes, legal systems, and rationality seem barely able, under ideal conditions, to keep his viciousness within bounds.

The question is whether man's aggressive behavior is inherited or learned. Is it possible that man is a killer because he descended directly from a line of "killer-apes"? This is the position held by the zoologists Konrad Lorenz (*On Aggression*) and Desmond Morris (*The Naked Ape*), and the playwright Robert Ardrey (*African Genesis, Territorial Imperative*).

The suggestion has been made by Dr. L. S. B. Leakey and other paleontologists that different branches of African australopithecines pursued different evolutionary paths of development. While some remained peaceful vegetarians, at least one branch became aggressive carnivores; and it is quite possible that it is from this latter line that modern man has developed. Man's killer instinct is set deep in his genes.

A self-balancing, 28-jointed adapter-base biped; an electrochemical reduction plant, integral with segregated stowages of special energy extracts in storage batteries for subsequent actuation of thousands of hydraulic and pneumatic pumps with motors attached; 62,000 miles of capillaries. . . . The whole, extraordinary complex mechanism guided with exquisite precision from a turret in which are located telescopic and microscopic self-registering and recording range finders, a spectroscope, etc.; the turret control being closely allied with an air-conditioning intake–and–exhaust, and a main fuel intake. . . .''

BUCKMINSTER FULLER

MAN   A biodegradable but non-recyclable animal blessed with opposable thumbs capable of grasping at straws.

BERNARD ROSENBERG

Man is a biped without feathers.

PLATO

DELL
6266

95c

THE SENSATIONAL WORLDWIDE BESTSELLER BY
DESMOND MORRIS
THE NAKED APE

Man's trouble, Lorenz believes,

arises from his being a basically harmless omnivorous creature, lacking in natural weapons with which to kill big prey, and, therefore, also devoid of the built-in safety devices which prevent "professional" carnivores from abusing their killing power to destroy fellow members of their own species. A lion or a wolf may, on extremely rare occasions, kill another by one angry stroke, but. . . all heavily armed carnivores possess sufficiently reliable inhibitions which prevent the self-destruction of the species.

11　It is a curious paradox that the greatest gifts of man, the unique faculties of conceptual thought and verbal speech which have raised him to a level high above all other creatures and given him mastery over the globe, are not altogether blessings, or at least are blessings that have to be paid for very dearly indeed. All the great dangers threatening humanity with extinction are direct consequences of conceptual thought and verbal speech. They drove man out of the paradise in which he could follow his instincts with impunity and do or not do whatever he pleased. There is much truth in the parable of the tree of knowledge and its fruit, though I want to make an addition to it to make it fit into my own picture of Adam: that apple was thoroughly unripe! Knowledge springing from conceptual thought robbed man of the security provided by his well-adapted instincts long, long before it was sufficient to provide him with an equally safe adaptation. Man is, as Arnold Gehlen has so truly said, by nature a jeopardized creature.

KONRAD LORENZ

Just as we do not know what life is, yet can distinguish between an inanimate object and a living animal or plant, similarly we cannot give a scientific definition of man, yet we have no difficulty in differentiating him from even the most manlike monkey. One of the gross deficiencies of science is that it has not yet defined what sets man apart from other animals.

RENÉ DUBOS

12　The killer-ape notion has brought angry rebuttal from other life-scientists and from psychologists. They all counter that there is no significant evidence that man's aggression is inherited, but there is strong evidence that it is learned. Man's entire range of bitter emotions and cruel behavior can be causally explained by early conditioning within a hostile environment. If cruel and violent actions are "programmed" into us as acceptable forms of behavior, and if we ourselves are treated cruelly and violently so that we store up an explosive reservoir of bitterness, then we have become, in the very core of our being, killer-apes. But all this is learned, and easily learned. We don't have to look far—only as far as the nearest TV set—to discover how acceptable "man's inhumanity to man" can become.

　Dr. Ashley Montagu considers the killer-ape theory absurd and takes an opposing stand: any human being's aggressive cruelty results from the frustration of his more basic need to love and be loved. "His combativeness and competitiveness arise primarily from the frustration of his need to cooperate." The most basic drive of human nature—strictly from the standpoint of evolutionary survival—is love and cooperation.

"I made this."

The organism is born with an innate need for love, with a need to respond to love, to be good, cooperative. This is, I believe, now established beyond any shadow of doubt. Whatever is opposed to love, to goodness, and to cooperation is disharmonic, unviable, unstable, and malfunctional—evil. . . . All of man's natural inclinations are toward the development of goodness, toward the continuance of states of goodness and the discontinuance of unpleasant states. . . . Where hatreds exist in any persons within any society we may be sure that they, too, are due to love, for hatred is love frustrated. Aggression is but a technique or mode of seeking love.

Contrary to popular belief, man has long since ceased to evolve. . . .

JEAN ROSTAND

13   The question is perpetually raised: "Is man *inherently* evil or good?" "Is man *genetically* a killer-ape or fallen angel?"

Something is probably wrong with the question. The problem is whether man has the capacity to be good and love, or whether he is innately aggressive to the point of lacking such a capacity. Surely, man is *inherently* neither good nor bad. He develops his stance toward life out of life's stance toward him. It depends, for each individual, on conditioning—on whether, for him, "things go right" or "things go wrong."

A better question might be: How does man differ from his animal kin in his feelings of aggression? Probably in no significant way *except in his complexity*. With man's advanced cerebral cortex and his faculty for abstract thought, he possesses a capacity for infinitely complex re-

6   *The Protoplasmic Venture*

sponses. He has almost unlimited choice. It is his complex perception of threat and the variety of his responses to it that makes man different.

In the rest of the animal kingdom, response tends to be simple and direct: flight, fight, or submission. In human beings the basic emotional response patterns are the same, but they are obscured by endless maneuvers of each individual according to his potential for indirect response.

But where there is no threat, man is no more hostile than any of his animal relatives. To those who have lived with animals and trained and loved them, it is clear that when you take away threat, you eliminate violence; but when the environment threatens, violence results. It is more than likely that the same simple principle applies as well to man.

14   What, then, distinguishes man from the other animals? At the present time, we cannot with any certainty point to a single *human* quality which cannot be found, *to some degree,* in other animals.

The deep chasm that separates man from his animal kin reflects differences in degree. No one questions the fact that man possesses mental

There is no doubt that human survival will continue to depend more and more on human intellect and technology. It is idle to argue whether this is good or bad. The point of no return was passed long ago, before anyone knew it was happening.

THEODOSIUS DOBZHANSKY

PRIMUS INTER PARES

Man's view of himself has undergone many changes. From a unique position in the universe, the Copernican revolution reduced him to an inhabitant of one of many planets. From a unique position among organisms, the Darwinian revolution assigned him a place among the millions of other species which evolved from one another. Yet, *Homo sapiens* has overcome the limitations of his origin. He controls the vast energies of the atomic nucleus, moves across his planet at speeds barely below escape velocity, and can escape when he so wills. He communicates with his fellows at the speed of light, extends the powers of his brain with those of the digital computer, and influences the numbers and genetic constitution of virtually all other living species. Now he can guide his own evolution. In him, Nature has reached beyond the hard regularities of physical phenomena. *Homo sapiens,* the creation of Nature, has transcended her. From a product of circumstances, he has risen to responsibility. At last, he is Man. May he behave so!

PHILIP HANDLER (ed.)
Biology and the Future of Man

To regard man, the most ephemeral and rapidly evolving of all species, as the final and unsurpassable achievement of creation, especially at his present-day particularly dangerous and disagreeable stage of development, is certainly the most arrogant and dangerous of all untenable doctrines.

KONRAD LORENZ

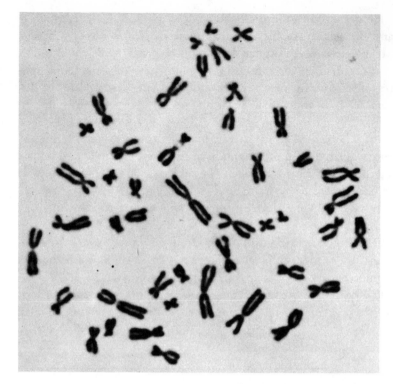

Out of the dreaming past, with its legends of steaming seas and gleaming glaciers, mountains that moved and suns that glared, emerges this creature, man—the latest phase in a continuing process that stretches back to the beginning of life. His is the heritage of all that has lived; he still carries the vestiges of snout and fangs and claws of species long since vanished; he is the ancestor of all that is yet to come.

Do not regard him lightly—he is you.

DON FABUN

Far from seeing in man the irrevocable and unsurpassable image of God, I assert—more modestly and, I believe, in greater awe of the Creation and its infinite possibilities—that the long-sought missing link between animals and the really humane being is ourselves!

KONRAD LORENZ

powers that dramatically outdistance his closest primate kin: logical reason, creative imagination, self-consciousness. It is also a fact, however, that numerous animals possess abilities that far outdistance man: highly developed sensing organs, for instance, and the ability to "intuit" subtle relationships that are missed by man.

It is probably true that every empirically observable characteristic hypothesized to distinguish man from other fauna can be found, in some degree, somewhere in the animal kingdom.

15 Science has two functions: control and comprehension. The comprehension may be of the universe in which we live; or of ourselves; or of the relations between ourselves and our world. Evolutionary science has only been in existence, as a special branch of scientific knowledge, for less than a century. During that time its primary contribution has been to comprehension—first to that of the world around us, and then to that of our own nature. The last few decades have added an increasing comprehension of our position in the universe and our relations with it; and with this evolutionary science is certainly destined to make an important and increasing contribution to control; its practical application in the affairs of human life is about to begin. (1952)

SIR JULIAN HUXLEY

16   This stage in "the immense journey" has already begun. Man is now in process of taking control of his own evolutionary destiny and, by default, the destiny of all other living creatures on his planet. While man was produced by processes of which he had no understanding and no control, it looks as though he is moving rapidly to a point of no return when there is but one choice left to him: to take on his shoulders the full burden of his future.

An average human life/time has a duration of about 10^9 seconds.

Two events have made this inevitable. First, man has made such rapid progress in science/technology that the selective function of the environment has been radically altered. Many detrimental or lethal inheritable characteristics are now being preserved; under natural conditions they would die out. Among such genetic disorders are hemophilia, retinal blastoma, sickle-cell anemia, and susceptibility to a host of physical and emotional dysfunctions. Many of these defects are now being corrected or rendered tolerable through surgery, chemistry, and psychiatry. Carriers of such genes produce offspring, and the defective genes multiply. This has now happened in the case of so many genetic traits that the "fittest" are not the individuals who survive. Natural selectivity is no longer the primary mechanism in evolution.

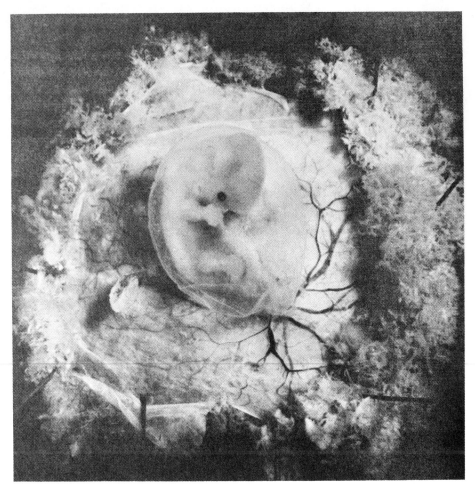

who can say
I am Japanese
american
african
when in the next day
he may be a butterfly

17   The second event forcing man to take over his own evolution is the destruction of his natural environment. Man developed through selective competition with and in a natural environment: *it* produced *him* according to *its* criteria. Man, not the environment, did the adapting. Environment is the creator; man is the creature. The ever-changing ecosystem "decided" which traits this evolving organism would possess.

But this trait-selecting environment no longer exists. Man's scientific/technological applications, along with the proliferation of his species, has altered the environment so much that it has lost the power to select specific adaptive traits. No known forces are presently operating to determine that "fitter" traits survive and weaker traits perish.

Symbolically, the offspring has annihilated the parent that produced it.

18   It is humbling to realize that man is, in this sense, only one part of nature, just as a consideration of the size of the universe makes him realize his own relative smallness. But evolutionary biology has also shown us the central role that man is destined to play in evolution from now on—unless, of course, he engineers his own extinction. Although man arose out of an evolutionary process that he didn't understand and over which he had no control, he must now realize that he is unique in the living world in the realization that the responsibility for continuance of this process is his. . . .

The capacity of biologists to develop ways by which man can determine his future evolution is undoubted. The more difficult question is whether he will choose to make such decisions, *and with what wisdom.*

Biology and the Future of Man

Man differs from the animal only by a little; most men throw that little away.

CONFUCIUS

6-4

EARTH

Greek Epitaph—for a dog.

*Stranger by the roadside, do not
   smile
When you see this grave, though
   it is only a dog's.
My master wept when I died,
   and his own hand
Laid me in earth and wrote these
   lines on my tomb.*

ANONYMOUS

1   The idea of Reverence for Life offers itself as the realistic answer to the realistic question of how man and the world are related to each other. Of the world man knows only that everything which exists is, like himself, a manifestation of the Will-to-Live. . . .

   Let a man once begin to think about the mystery of his life and the links which connect him with the life that fills the world, and he cannot but bring to bear upon his own life and all other life that comes within his reach the principle of Reverence for Life. . . . Existence will thereby become harder for him in every respect than it would be if he lived for himself, but at the same time it will be richer, more beautiful, and happier. It will become, instead of mere living, a real experience of life.

ALBERT SCHWEITZER

2   Man has never sought knowledge of his world merely to understand it with his intellect. His driving concern has been his relationship to it and his place in it. All our rational inquiries are merely a prelude to the establishment of a more meaningful relationship. The implicit question for man has always been, "What is my place in the scheme of things?"

   Man evolved in a world that is at once friendly and hostile. With one hand it gives him life, while with the other it inflicts pain and death. He has always felt like a stranger in a strange land. But he had to make it his home even while it felt to him like enemy territory.

   The story of *general evolution* is an account of how species search for a suitable niche in their environment. The story of *man's evolution* is the account of his transcendence of that evolutionary niche. And the story of *man's civilization* is the account of his gradual conquest and control of his environment.

3   Man's relationship to his natural environment seems to have moved through three stages.

Man first experienced nature in a parent-child relationship. Nature produced him; he was its offspring. He was never sure how to conceptualize the forces that generated life, but he could not doubt that they were everywhere—in his crops, his herds and flocks, in his human family. So his myths helped him conceive the inconceivable. Nature's life-giving forces were, naturally, male and female. The prime source of life was Mother Earth personified as Magna Mater, or Gaia, or Demeter—each was in some way the Earth-Mother. (We still habitually think of "her" as Mother Nature, and the very idea of "Father Nature" *feels* wrong even to us!) There must be masculine forces too, of course, so there was Jupiter (Dyaus Pitar or Zeus Pater, "Father Zeus"); and the Semitic tribal gods—Yahweh, Chemosh, Milcom, Allah—are all male figures. Generally the dynamic forces of nature such as storms, earthquakes, thunder, and lightning were conceived as masculine in potency; while the more passive aspects of nature—the quiet earth which absorbs the rain and brings forth new sprouts of corn—were thought of as feminine potencies.

These personified forces are man's parents. The characteristic response on man's part in this state is fear and awe, acceptance and obedience. He has no control over nature's forces; *they* condition *his* behavior. Like authoritarian parents, they nurture him; but they also

And the wind shall say: "Here
  were decent godless people
Their only monument the asphalt
  road
And a thousand lost golf balls."
                                    T. S. ELIOT

cut some humans from their stems
tie them in a bunch
pull a few out
stick them in a vase
look at them

throw
the
rest
away

Human arrangement
by flowers

THE EARTH IS SORE

The white people never cared for land or deer or bear. When we Indians kill meat, we eat it all up. When we dig roots we make little holes. When we build houses, we make little holes. When we burn grass for grasshoppers, we don't ruin things. We shake down acorns and pinenuts. We don't chop down the trees. We only use dead wood. But the White people plow up the ground, pull down the trees, kill everything. The tree says, "Don't. I am sore. Don't hurt me." But they chop it down and cut it up. The spirit of the land hates them. They blast out trees and stir it up to its depths. They saw up the trees. That hurts them. The Indians never hurt anything, but the White people destroy all. They blast rocks and scatter them on the ground. The rock says, "Don't. You are hurting me." But the White people pay no attention. When the Indians use rocks, they take little round ones for their cooking. . . . How can the spirit of the earth like the White man? . . . Everywhere the White man has touched it, it is sore.

(The words of an old holy woman of the Wintu Indians of California.)

DOROTHY LEE
Freedom and Culture

You can always tell when it's autumn in Hollywood. They put away the green plastic plants and bring out the brown plastic plants.
JOHNNY CARSON
NBC-TV

punish him. His dependence is almost absolute. He stands helpless before the storm, the flood, the drought, the mortal pain. He is a child who knows nothing of the motives of the forces which rule him. They possess secrets he cannot understand. Yet he does his best to relate to them and please them, to discover the "desires" of these personified forces and accede to their wills. Thus, he makes every attempt—as he would with human parents—to keep them as favorably inclined as he can.

4   The second stage—man as conqueror—is found in a rudimentary way in all man's cultures, but its successful development belongs to the West. It began with the discovery by Pythagoras of nature's greatest secret: that she speaks the language of mathematics. Foundations were thus laid for scientific control, but time dallied for two more millennia before this knowledge was used. Physics and mechanics were finally born in the seventeenth century, followed shortly by chemistry and biology and, belatedly, by the social and behavioral sciences. Communication and transportation technologies belong to our own century. Controls have now spread to almost every area of human experience. Lagging behind, of course, is control of man himself, but this appears to be the arena wherein the next giant steps will be taken.

This rapid conquest and control of our dynamic environment is sapient man's greatest success story, and it is basically a story of a love/hate relationship. Man has loved his earth; it nourished him. But he has also hated it for its relentless attempt to annihilate him. It was a life/death struggle between man and nature; and as in any love/hate relationship, the question has been *which* would win out: love or hate. *Who* would win: Man or Nature?

Man has won—or is winning. Thus love has also won, for love is possible only between equals; and love can exist only in the absence of fear. Man is on the threshold of setting controls over ever-larger forces of nature—climate and earthquakes, for instance. The control of life and evolution is near. There are repeated hints in futuristic literature that man may eventually establish control on a cosmological scale. We might alter the orbit or the tilt of the earth, for example, or capture small asteroids to serve as scientific stations or to provide transportation to remote outposts. Such comprehensive controlling power would be merely a large-scale extension of man's present capacities, and we are moving rapidly in this direction. On the condition that man doesn't destroy himself first, such controls are probably inevitable.

5 A third stage, beginning in our time, is a protective feeling toward nature. If man no longer fears nature because he understands her ways, and if he has established control over the more threatening elements of his environment, then fear can give way to other feelings: kinship, appreciation, protection. Man will become nature's advocate; then—if he is a wise landlord—he might justly be called Lord of the Earth. Man is only beginning to feel a new awareness of an environment from which, until now, he has had to wrest a living in frustration and pain.

This has been the Western experience. Other branches of the human story exhibit different responses toward nature. Western man's achievements bring mixed feelings, of course. We wonder whether his compassionate concerns have surfaced in time to salvage his spaceship. It is Western man's problem not merely because it is his controls that have caused our environmental problems; it is probably the case that only Western man has the techniques for solving the problems he has created.

6 Man has had deep, ambivalent feelings about his kinship with the other animals. He has grudgingly accepted coexistence with them.

On the one hand, man is aware of striking similarities. Skeletal systems are structurally similar, even down to single bone-shapes. The

If our numbers continue to increase at the present frightening rate, it will eventually become a matter of choosing between us and them [other animal species]. No matter how valuable they are to us symbolically, scientifically or aesthetically, the economics of the situation will shift against them. The blunt fact is that when our own species density reaches a certain pitch, there will be no space left for other animals.

DESMOND MORRIS

flesh that we carry is too much alike, and when cut we bleed red whether we be bird, beast, or man. Facial configurations are alike and sometimes appear like parodies on one another. We look into the eyes of animals and feel that we recognize. We know their inner worlds in the same way we know the inner worlds of other men. We empathize with their behavior, from the pain of a wounded deer to the playfulness of bear cubs and sea otters. We identify with the hunting instinct of a mother lioness as well as the fear-flight of the hunted antelope. We feel guilt when we have hurt an animal, just as we do if we have hurt another human being. All this gives us a queasy feeling. We do what we can to suppress it, yet the feeling of kinship remains.

It is precisely because the kinship was so obvious that we have protested so loudly that there is no kinship. Man resents it, feeling that he is endowed with vastly superior qualities which make him unique and special. As evolutionary man advanced he has felt the distance increasing between himself and the other animals.

So, our kinship with animals has been an uncomfortable one. On the one hand we intuit the kinship and confess our commonality; on the other, we deny it vehemently and demean the animal world.

7   An awareness is just dawning in our brains of the *physical*/ecological relationships with the animals of our planet, but the *psychological*/ecological relationships are probably of equal importance, though to date they have been but little explored.

From the standpoint of other animals, man is a killer to be feared. Early in his hominid evolution man learned to use weapons to kill for food. Although he is basically omnivorous, his appetites place him in a class with other killer-carnivores. But man has one behavioral pattern rarely found in the animal world: he kills for pleasure—for "sport"—even when his stomach is full. For this reason the animals of the world are realistic in their fear-response to man. This combination of pleasure-killing and advanced killing technique renders man extremely dangerous.

But all this goes without saying; today we are all aware of it. But the question persists as to *why* man kills *for pleasure*. What is meant by "pleasure" in this context? How can one experience pleasure from the act of killing something? It's a question that needs an answer, and no trite appeal to "sportsmanship" or "stalking instinct" is quite sufficient.

Man kills because there is something ultimate in what he is doing. When man kills he has in his hands the essence of life and death. Much of man's killing is done to affirm his own existence; it is a confirmation of his own still-being-alive. Man is the only animal that can reflect upon his own life *and death;* he alone can philosophize about it, question its meaning, and fear it ahead of time. Life and death are both mysteries, but while we have life it is death that haunts our living.

When one holds in his hand a pheasant, or kneels beside a bear

Don't take man too seriously, even when orienting him among the animals and plants on this local planet; and certainly not when comparing him with possibilities elsewhere in the richly endowed Metagalaxy.

HARLOW SHAPLEY

or antelope, each of which, a few moments before, shared the impulse-to-live which is the essence of existence, he can feel for a moment that he has conquered life and in so doing has also conquered death. At that moment one becomes God: although he didn't give life, he has been able to take it away—as though "it" existed as an item of personal property—like a cherished memento or trinket—which the creature "owned." Indeed, to hold a dead animal *from which* one has taken life is to *possess* life. Primitive men often believed that they could accumulate more life by collecting life from those creatures they killed. Perhaps some of this feeling lingers in us; for by contrast, as a hunter stands holding a no-longer-living animal, he often uses the phrase that he "feels alive."

Our climb to the top has been a get-rich-quick story, and, like all nouveaux riches, *we are very sensitive about our background.*

DESMOND MORRIS

Harlow and friend

8   Not too long ago, human sacrifice was practiced in most of man's religions, great and small. Sometimes members of other tribes, especially captured warriors, were sacrificed ritually to the god of the conquering tribe. Often this was a contractual obligation: the deity had helped them win in battle, so they offered a gift in return. Many tribes, however, sacrificed their own members. Instances of ritual killing are the Babylonian sacrifice of a surrogate king; the Canaanite primitial sacrifice of one's firstborn by bloodletting or "passing through fire"; the Egyptian, Assyrian, and Chinese practice of killing scores of attendants to serve the spirits of their royal masters in the next life. Abraham's near-sacrifice of his son Isaac presupposes the existence of the institution of ritual sacrifice. In one form or another, human sacrifice has been practiced in almost every ancient culture known to man.

At some point, however, sensitivity to suffering deepens, and ways are devised to avoid human sacrifice. Historically, the story of the sacrifice of Isaac by Abraham was understood by ancient Hebrews to be the origin of the ransom system. Make no mistake, one's firstborn belonged to the god Yahweh, but henceforth he could be "ransomed" with an ox, a ram, or perhaps a pair of doves. Similar animal substitutes are found elsewhere.

Eventually, in almost every tradition, ritual killing comes to an end, accompanied by appropriate theological rationale. In the Christian tradition, the sacrifice of God's only son was interpreted to be the final, complete sacrifice which replaced the Judaic sacrificial system; and the sacrifice of God's only son—which is parallel to the sacrifice of Abraham's only son—recurs eternally in the "Sacrifice of the Mass." In other religions, live sacrifices were replaced by figurines which were ritually broken, or by wood or paper substitutes bearing names which were buried or burned.

Few places in the world today still witness bloody sacrifices carried on for religious reasons.

9　Ordinary ethics seeks to find limits within the sphere of human life and relationships. But the absolute ethics of the will-to-live must reverence every form of life, seeking so far as possible to refrain from destroying any life, regardless of its particular type. It says of no instance of life, "This has no value." It cannot make any such exceptions, for it is built upon reverence for life as such. It knows that the mystery of life is always too profound for us, and that its value is beyond our capacity to estimate. . . . True, in practice we are forced to choose. At times we have to decide arbitrarily which forms of life, and even which particular individuals, we shall save, and which we shall destroy. But the principle of reverence for life is none the less universal.

ALBERT SCHWEITZER

10　Dostoevsky's psychology rests on a fundamental belief in the deep, ineradicable humanity of men. A logical, officially sanctioned decision to spill blood is reversible and remedial, if deep in a person's heart there is still a small spark of compassion. Sometimes a man is driven to things; he finds that he has to be inflexible. But it is important that he should keep the feeling that the circumstances that forced him to cruelty are themselves unnatural.

Permission to kill with the approval of one's conscience destroys the humanity of man.

PAVEL SIMONOV

11　One of the most interesting things we humans do is to anthropomorphize all our animal kin, and we did this long before Walt Disney institutionalized the technique. We project our human qualities into the lives of nonhuman creatures; we think of them as though they have the

Of the domestic animals man has attempted to corrupt with his bribes for affection and his anthropomorphic entreaties, the cat retains its magnificent autonomy. In the presence of such authenticity our facades become transparent. The cat assumes a peer relationship. If you do not, the problem's yours.

BARBARA CHRISTIAN

It was quite incomprehensible to me—this was before I began going to school—why in my evening prayers I should pray for human beings only. So when my mother had prayed with me and had kissed me good night, I used to add silently a prayer that I had composed myself for all living creatures. It ran thus: "O, heavenly Father, protect and bless all things that have breath; guard them from all evil, and let them sleep in peace."

ALBERT SCHWEITZER

same experiences we do. We endow them with our fears, angers, jealousies. In animated cartoons every animal we know—from mice to roadrunners, from dumb dogs to stammering pigs and elephants with outsized ears—feels human feelings.

We anthropomorphize (the word means "to make into human form," from the Greek *anthropos,* "man," and *morphos,* "form") for at least two reasons. (1) We can't help it. Since we experience only human experiences, it is inevitable that we would project our experience onto other creatures. (2) We want other creatures to be like us. The more humanoid they are the better we feel about them and can relate to them.

Look at the matter in another way: How could we *not* project our experiences into our fellow creatures? If we look into the eyes of a baby seal or hear the cry of a dog in pain—even though we can't know for sure what the animal is experiencing—it's difficult not to respond as though the animals feel what we would be feeling were we in their place. We empathize through our own experience to theirs, and in fact it may be that our intuition here is closer to the truth than our solipsistic skepticism.

12   In our response to our fellow creatures, Desmond Morris observes that we seem to pass through seven stages of reaction.

The first age is the *infantile phase,* when we are completely dependent on our parents and react strongly to very big animals, employing them as parent symbols. The second is the *infantile-parental phase,* when we are beginning to compete with our parents and react strongly to small animals that we can use as child-substitutes. This is the age of pet-keeping. The third age is the *objective pre-adult phase,* the stage where the exploratory interests, both scientific and aesthetic, come to dominate the symbolic. It is the time for bug-hunting, microscopes, butterfly-collecting and aquaria. The fourth is the *young adult phase.* At this point the most important animals are members of the opposite sex of our own species. Other species lose ground here, except in a purely commercial or economic context. The fifth is the *adult parental phase.* Here symbolic animals enter our lives again, but this time as pets for our children. A sixth age is the *post-parental phase,* when we lose our children and may turn once more to animals as child-substitutes to replace them. (In the case of childless adults, the use of animals as child-substitutes may, of course, begin earlier.) Finally, we come to the seventh age, the *senile phase,* which is characterized by a heightened interest in animal preservation and conservation. At this point the interest is focused on those species which are in danger of extermination. It makes little difference whether, from other points of view, they are attractive or repulsive, useful or useless, providing their numbers are few and becoming fewer. The increasingly rare rhinoceros and gorilla, for example, that are so disliked by children, become the centre of attention at this stage. They have to be "saved." The symbolic equation involved here is obvious enough: the senile individual is about to become personally extinct and so employs rare animals as symbols of his own impending doom. His emotional concern to save them from extinction reflects his desire to extend his own survival.

When I'm near that animal, I know I'm in the presence of an intelligence. Namu, I wish I could understand your language, and your mind. I don't know, maybe one day we'll find a way. Maybe . . . maybe it'll be something more direct than words, maybe something as simple as touch—language of mutual trust."
Namu, the Killer Whale
NBC-TV

"You'll be glad to know that according to our timetable, the bugs will take over the world before the Communists."

13 Man used to regard himself as somehow apart from the animals and plants, following a set of rules that were different from those followed by the rest of nature. Then the study of comparative anatomy made him realize that he is similar in many structural ways to the other animals. The study of physiology showed similar mechanisms of blood circulation, of muscle contraction, of digestion, and of other body functions. Comparative biochemistry demonstrated the basic similarity of chemical mechanisms, reaction sequences, and metabolic patterns in all living organisms. The study of evolution revealed that all these similarities were the consequences of a common origin.

The interrelatedness of all life is now regarded as a part of the beauty and excitement of nature.

Biology and the Future of Man

14 Man has always been a part—but only a part—of the evolutionary/ecological system. Man may soon be the controller of all our planet's life and the determiner of its destiny, but what he will control will be a complex system of interrelationships, and man will remain a part of the system.

It is easy for one to feel lonely in the midst of a crowd; it is easy to feel alienated in a world to which one is deeply related. We may never realize the existence of the multitudinous tie-lines that connect us to the world we live in.

Reverence for life, therefore, is applied to natural life and spiritual life alike. In the parable of Jesus, the shepherd saves not merely the soul of the lost sheep but the whole animal.

ALBERT SCHWEITZER

"No man is an Iland, intire of itself," wrote John Donne. Each man is a part of the whole. He is subject to the same physical forces that move the atoms and the planets. He is composed of the same five-score elements that make up the seas and rocks, trees and stars. He is subject to the same protoplasmic processes found throughout the animal kingdom. The same neural events explode in all our brains and our physical being is determined by a DNA code system identical to that which guides the replication of all animals and plants. Most profoundly, we share the will-to-live with every living creature.

We are a part of a magnificent, awesome, unbelievable protoplasmic venture.

Death also provides a challenge and a test, particularly to men who must prove to themselves that they can face death and not run or flinch—the essence of bravery. Perhaps a person feels that he must conquer death through flaunting it, or at least through looking straight into its hollow eye sockets before he can feel man enough to live.

THEODORE LIDZ

15   The ecological crisis provides more than an alarming opportunity for social survival responses, however necessary these may be. The crisis calls into question our whole way of experiencing ourselves, one another, cities, trees, the heavens. It has within it the impetus for straightening out our relations with all these and harmonizing our personal existence. The fully developed ecological psyche would be connected to all life's processes—feeling, eating, growing, dying; the self would be experienced as incorporating the rest of life forms as well. We are ultimately not simply man or woman, but man and woman and fish, glacier, mountain and shorebird. Our life history is the life history of the planet.

ESALEN

7

MICROCOSM/ MACROCOSM/ COSMOS

7-1

NATURE

1   Philosophy and science were born together in 585 B.C.—on May 28 at 6:13 p.m. (Milesian Standard Time); for at that instant an eclipse began in the Ionian city of Miletus, a solar eclipse which had been *predicted* by a philosopher named Thales. We have no evidence that Thales established the exact time of the event. This precise date has been calculated by modern astronomers, and if Thales had even come close—within a day or a week—he would have done well. But the significant point is that he had become aware of the regularities of nature on the basis of which he had made a prediction. However elementary this may seem, it is the dim recognition of what we now know as "natural law."

2   Our knowledge of nature and her "laws" derive from two distinct kinds of epistemic operations: empirical observation and rational system-building. Thus we have empirical knowledge and rational (or "a priori") knowledge. Both present problems not yet solved.

     Suppose you took a Jovian philosopher to a baseball game. He is a handsome humanoid with shining eyes. Having recently arrived from Jupiter, and being ever-alert to adventures of the mind, he watches the game with eager awareness. Since he has never seen a baseball game, you begin to explain the rules to him. He declines the offer and tells you he would prefer to figure out the rules for himself. And so, through all nine innings, you let him watch the action.

     As he observes the players, he notes their patterns of movement; they perform the same motions over and over again. A player walks up to a particular spot and tries to hit a small round object which another man throws at him (no, it's always thrown past him). If the man with the stick swings and misses three times, the hand of the man dressed in black goes up and the man with the stick walks away looking either sad

Philosophy is written in that vast book which stands open before our eyes, I mean the universe; but it cannot be read until we have learnt the language and become familiar with the characters in which it is written.

GALILEO

or angry. But if he hits the round object with the stick, he starts running, always in the same direction, toward another man.

And so, little by little, the "rules of the game" are inferred and reconstructed as he watches the players' consistent, repeated patterns of behavior.

The "rules of the game" exist in the players' heads, and they play by them. The players know the rules because they have read them or have grown up with them, but our extraterrestrial epistemologist must *infer* the rules by watching behavior—that is, by watching matter-in-motion.

By the end of the second inning, he has some rough ideas of a few rules. By the fifth, he has added several more consistencies to his mental list and refined some previous observations. By the end of the game—Jovian genius that he is—he has been able to understand and jot down a set of rules which describes much of the players' actions.

After the game, the Jovian checks his list of inferred rules with you, and you find that he has indeed discovered most of the rules which you know about baseball.

Now, he never *saw* the rules; he *created* the rules *in his mind* because they seemed to describe consistently the behavior of the players. All that he actually observed, of course, were players-in-motion.

3   Our minds operate in similar fashion to formulate "scientific laws." They are the "rules of the game" which we have inferred. We often deceive ourselves by thinking that we have observed the rules, whereas the fact is that we created them to account for consistencies *which we remembered* while watching matter-in-motion. We never observe the "law of gravity" or the "inverse-square law" which describes the propagation of light or the "laws" of mass-energy transformation. All the "laws" of physics are created in our minds; all this is *empirical* knowledge.

Scientists who work with submicroscopic entities are at a special disadvantage since they never even get to see matter-in-motion. They must create the "rules of the game" by observing only secondary traces (streaks on photographic plates, for example) left by particles of matter. In other words, particle physicists must create in their minds pictures of the matter as well as the principles of motion which describe the behavior of such matter.

4   All empirical knowledge is hypothetical and merely probable. That is, it consists of operational hypotheses which we continue to use as long as they are consistent with our observations.

Plants need sunlight to grow. Gray whales migrate in March. Robins lay blue eggs. Norwegians have blond hair. Water will conduct electricity if salt is dissolved in it. Light travels at 186,000 miles per second. Water cannot flow uphill. A lunar month is 27 days, 7 hours,

Does the harmony which human intelligence thinks it discovers in Nature exist apart from such intelligence? Assuredly no. A reality completely independent of the spirit that conceives it, sees it or feels it, is an impossibility. A world so external as that, even if it existed, would be for ever inaccessible to us. What we call "objective reality" is, strictly speaking, that which is common to several thinking beings and might be common to all; this common part . . . can only be the harmony expressed by mathematical laws.

POINCARÉ

Metaphysicians are musicians without musical talent.

RUDOLF CARNAP

43 minutes. Tornadoes never occur in December. A fire will not burn without oxygen. Whale sharks are harmless to man.

All these things we know from repeated experience. But do we know them for sure? *All* robins' eggs are blue, someone might argue; he has investigated countless nests and noted thousands of robins' eggs—all pale blue. That seems to settle the matter. Still, can one be absolutely positive that some berserk robin hasn't laid a bright purple egg in a nest somewhere?

No empirical knowledge is ever certain. *To every statement one can imagine an exception.* One can easily imagine a gray whale deciding

The laws of mathematics and logic are true simply by virtue of our conceptual scheme.

W. V. QUINE

Through the work of Dalton the conception of matter as a continuum was definitely displaced by the conception of discrete quanta of matter, and we are now beginning to see that this was but the first stage in a great revolution against the theory of the continuum. Step by step we are being forced to "quantize" physico-chemical phenomena. How far this revolution will go, and how much of our former belief in the continuity of nature will remain, we cannot now predict; but it is already evident that many of our best established principles of science are under fire, and we may be sure that the theory of atoms is but one of many phases of the coming theory of discontinuity in nature.

GILBERT NEWTON LEWIS
Valence and the Structure of Atoms and Molecules (1966)

It is generally recognized that present-day physical theory is no longer adequate to meet the growing demands upon it. Those theoretical concepts which only a few years ago were hailed as the keys to the innermost mysteries of nature are now totally unable to cope with the flood of new discoveries emanating from our laboratories and it has become obvious that some very different approach to the problem is essential. As one observer, Ernest Hutten, sums up the situation in a recently published book, "Most physicists feel that the time is ripe, again, for a radical change in our ideas, and for a new theory."

DEWEY B. LARSON
The Structure of the Physical Universe (1959)

Sense-perception, for all its practical importance, is very superficial in its disclosure of the nature of things. . . . My quarrel with modern epistemology concerns its exclusive stress upon sense-perception for the provision of data respecting Nature. Sense-perception does not provide the data in terms of which we interpret it.

ALFRED NORTH WHITEHEAD

not to migrate in March, or a tornado tearing across Kansas in December, or a whale shark mistaking a man for a rather large tidbit of plankton. If one can imagine an exception to the statement, then it is obviously not *necessary* knowledge; it is only *contingent* knowledge with a probability of being correct. This is true of all the "natural laws" of physics which we have formulated to describe matter-in-motion.

This is also why, in the social sciences, we must employ statistics to establish the "coefficient of correlation," that is, so we can figure the probability of correctness of an hypothesis. What we determine is the number of cases out of 100 in which the hypothesis would hold true.

5   A second kind of knowledge about the natural world is rational or "a priori" knowledge. It has baffled philosophers from the beginning and still puzzles us to the point of irritation.

We know certain *necessary* truths, it seems, to which *we cannot imagine exceptions*. Seven plus five equals twelve—now, always, and everywhere. Parallel lines in the same plane will never intersect. The area of a circle can be determined with the formula πr^2. The angles of a triangle always add up to 180°.

Now, are these truly universal truths? The rationalist answers yes. Can one conceive, in his wildest imagination, any exception to these statements? Can we imagine two parallel lines intersecting? or $7 + 5 \neq 12$? or a triangle's angles not totaling 180°? No, we can't.

Here, then, lie the foundations of the "exact sciences": all known systems of mathematics, geometry, and logic.

6   How many robins' eggs would we have to examine to be sure that *all* robins' eggs are blue? Obviously, all of them: every egg ever laid. How many triangles do we have to investigate to be sure that they all contain angles totaling 180°? One or two, or just a few. The rationalist argues that once we understand the nature of the knowledge we are dealing with, then we don't have to ponder any more triangles at all. We know a priori (that is, without further empirical observation) that the angles of *all* triangles will total 180°. And what about $7 + 5 = 12$? Is this true for this and all imaginable universes? It would seem to be.

If an ornithologist reported the discovery of a clutch of bright purple robins' eggs, we might believe him. We would have no *logical* reason to disbelieve him. But if a geometrician reported that he had spotted a circle somewhere in Antarctica whose diameter was greater than its circumference, we might think he had stayed out in the snow too long. We would disbelieve him on *logical* grounds.

Therefore, it is clear that we are dealing with two distinctly different kinds of knowledge about nature, and the way they apply to the external world is different.

Consider the way in which a great deal of mathematical thinking is actually done. The mathematician does not ask whether his constructions are applicable, whether they correspond to any constructions in the natural world. He simply goes ahead and <u>invents</u> mathematical forms, asking only that they be consistent with themselves, with their own postulates. But every now and then it subsequently turns out that these forms can be correlated, like clocks, with other natural processes.

ALAN WATTS

7   Nature's modus operandi—her most prized secret—was discovered
by a single man, one of the giants in the history of human thought.
Pythagoras (fl. 500 B.C.) laid the foundations of mathematics and geometry
and therefore made possible the development of physics. Russell comments
that Pythagoras was "intellectually one of the most important men that
ever lived, both when he was wise and when he was unwise."

Pythagoras was both mathematician and mystic, and in a strange
way this combination of qualities may have been responsible for his insight
into nature. According to Aristotle, Pythagoras recognized that in a
particular mathematical or geometrical construct, when it is clearly
understood, one knows a universal truth. The famous "Pythagorean
theorem" is a perfect example: the sum of the squares of the sides of a
right triangle is *always* equal to the square of the hypotenuse.

From this realization that absolute truths are not actual but merely
mental, he was led to the position that the realities of the universe are
nonmaterial. They are abstract mathematical principles, or, in his words,
"the whole heaven or visible universe is a musical scale or number."

8   There is a story (though probably a legend) that Pythagoras was
passing by a blacksmith shop when he heard the rings of the hammers
pounding on the anvils inside. He listened to the varied pitches of sound

which the hammers made, and when he went in to watch them he discovered that the lower notes were being made by heavier hammers and higher notes by lighter hammers. Since Pythagoras had already experimented with measurements of weights, he quickly saw that there is a relationship between weight and sound, that is, a relationship between mathematical measurement and musical intervals. He had already studied the vibration of strings and knew that the harmonic intervals were determined precisely by the length of the vibrating string.

Through observations such as these, Pythagoras discovered (as Galileo later phrased it) that "the book of nature is written in the language of mathematics." All the operations of nature can be thus described. This momentous discovery gave Western man his first great insight into the natural world.

9 Mathematics is, I believe, the chief source of the belief in eternal and exact truth, as well as in a super-sensible intelligible world. Geometry deals with exact circles, but no sensible object is *exactly* circular; however carefully we may use our compasses, there will be some imperfections and irregularities. This suggests the view that all exact reasoning applies to ideal as opposed to sensible objects; it is natural to go further, and to argue that thought is nobler than sense, and the objects of thought more real than those of sense-perception. Mystical doctrines as to the relation of time to eternity are also reinforced by pure mathematics, for mathematical objects, such as numbers, if real at all, are eternal and not in time. Such eternal objects can be conceived as God's thoughts. Hence Plato's doctrine that God is a geometer, and Sir James Jeans' belief that He is addicted to arithmetic. Rationalistic as opposed to apocalyptic religion has been, ever since Pythagoras, and notably ever since Plato, very completely dominated by mathematics and mathematical method.

The combination of mathematics and theology, which began with Pythagoras, characterized religious philosophy in Greece, in the Middle Ages, and in modern times down to Kant. . . . I do not know of any other man who has been as influential as he was in the sphere of thought. . . . The whole conception of an eternal world, revealed to the intellect but not to the senses, is derived from him. . . .

BERTRAND RUSSELL

10 And so, we have two kinds of knowledge about nature. Both of them continue to bother us.

The problem with empirical knowledge is that we can never be absolutely sure of anything. Sometimes we can't even be sure how uncertain we should be! We must always ask: Do we have sufficient experience of an event to be reasonably (operationally) sure? Most of our "scientific laws" continue to work, but then we are reminded of some "laws" which have recently become extinct.

The more theoretical problem of a priori knowledge haunts our intellects. Why is it that mathematical knowledge describes so accurately

At the basis of the whole modern view of the world lies the illusion that the so-called laws of nature are the explanations of natural phenomena.

WITTGENSTEIN

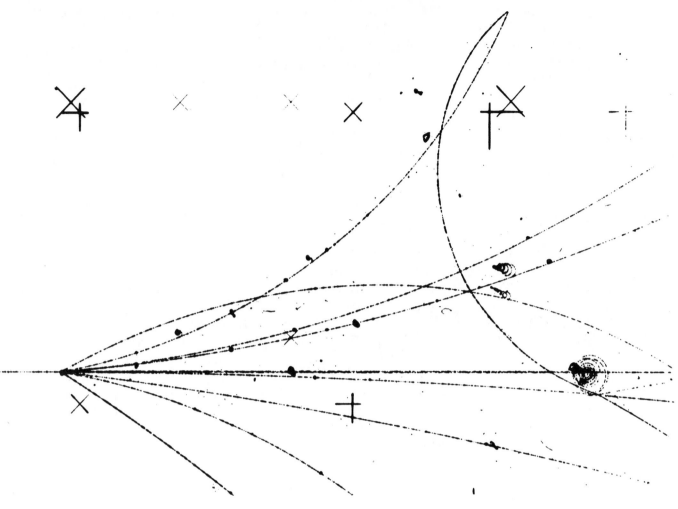

the operations of nature? Why does $7 + 5 = 12$? Could it be that we can develop a coherent mathematical system in our minds which, by some sort of coincidence, applies to the natural world? Or does nature really operate on inherently perfect mathematical principles? How do we know there are not exceptions to nature's mathematical system?

We are still mystified at the relationship between our magnificent mental system and the equally magnificent natural system—both of which are perfect mathematical systems in harmony with one another.

Or is our problem defined incorrectly? Why does two plus two equal four? Is it because we say so? Is this formula—$2 + 2 = 4$—an eternal truth because we have constructed a logical system which is internally coherent? Or is it because this operation describes real operations in nature? The pragmatist contends that we keep on using the formula only because it keeps on working; but the rationalist is not satisfied with such an answer. He argues that two plus two *must* equal four, anywhere in the universe; it is a cosmic truth, not a pragmatic model.

11   One of the most interesting philosophical twists regarding mathematics is that it never deals with anything. Russell says it best when he writes that "mathematics may be defined as the subject in which we never know what we are talking about, nor whether what we are saying is true."

Two oranges plus two oranges equals four tangible oranges; but the abstraction "$2 + 2 = 4$" is not tied to any tangible realities, and such abstract operations, cut loose from the world of things, can be deliriously free and uninhibited.

Now, a fascinating corollary of this freedom is the predictive capability of such abstract systems. There are numerous cases of mathematicians developing coherent abstract systems which predict how realities must behave, but there are no realities around to apply the system to. The mathematician is so far ahead of his time that no relevant realities are yet accessible. The mind, as it were, can soar freely ahead in time and describe what is not even known to exist; and scientists may have to wait for decades or generations before they can find anything in the real world to apply the predictions to.

The classical example of such intellectual projection "into the future" was Einstein's publication in 1916 of his general theory of relativity. His system predicted, among other things, that a beam of light would be deflected as it passed through a strong gravitational field. This was confirmed in 1919. He also predicted that time would slow down for any object moving at very high speeds approaching the speed of light. Confirmation of this prediction came more than forty years later when the disintegration rate of pions was noticed to have slowed down greatly when they were accelerated to relativistic speeds.

12   A current example of such an abstract predictive system is the astrophysicist's model of the dynamics of an imploding star. During its last stages of life, a massive star undergoes such extreme contraction that, while it may still weigh as much as our sun, it is but a few miles in diameter; its actual mass would weigh several billion tons per cubic inch. Such a massive object would generate a gravitational field so great that no light could escape from it. It would therefore be invisible. It would look like a "black hole" in space.

Such a "black hole" is unstable. Under its enormous gravitational force the star would collapse inward, and no known physical forces could hold up the outer layers of the star. Thus it would continue to implode. Calculations based upon the Einstein-Rosen field equations predict that the star would pass an "event horizon" and disappear from the universe. As it gets smaller and smaller, it finally attains infinite pressure and infinite density; it reaches a "point of singularity" and passes through the "Einstein-Rosen bridge" connecting one area of space to another. What this really means is that matter would contract through a "black hole" in space and then emerge in some other universe (or perhaps in a different space in our own universe) as a "white hole," a concentrated, glowing mass emitting fantastic amounts of energy.°

Here, then, is an abstract mathematical model which predicts events none of which are presently observable. It has the familiar ring of science fiction. But then this could have been said (and was) about Einstein's relativity theory in 1905.

°For the discovery of quasars and the development of the black hole theory, see pages 392f.

13   When it is said that there are two ways of knowing the natural world, this claim has a decidedly Western sound. It is a Western assumption that the subject is the knower and that nature is the object known. If the relationship is *defined* this way, then the foregoing elucidation of the problems involved between subject and object should be fairly accurate and not without meaning.

But we might wonder whether there are other ways of knowing. Is it a true and final fact that man is the experiencing subject and the real world is the experienced object, and that the two are distinct, separate entities? Or might there be a "field interaction" that would render false the subject-object dichotomy? Perhaps man's knowing is more immersed in the "object" than he thinks and his separateness is merely an illusion. Perhaps the processes of knowing are but part of a larger process. Or perhaps there are other *ways* of knowing realities.

A Western philosopher who was convinced there is a better way was Henri Bergson. He contended that the only true method of "doing metaphysics"—knowing the real world as it actually is—is through "intuition," a kind of "intellectual empathy." The rational mind is far too occupied with static concepts and mental filing systems to be able to perceive the ever-changing *process* we call "nature." Nature is pure duration, with no stops and starts, absolutes, or quantification. Man can only know nature by putting aside the intellect and intuiting directly the flowing reality of which he is a part.

Those familiar with Eastern modes of experience are aware that this is a meaningful way of knowing reality. Buddhism, for instance, explicitly rejects the subject-object dichotomy as dangerously false. The goal of Zen meditation is satori, a sort of "flash of realization" that man is one with reality and not separate from it. It is a sensitive, totalic awareness of being a part of nature. Subject and object merge into one, or better, they are at last perceived as always having been one.

REPUBLIQUE FRANCAISE

POSTES

50F

HENRI
BERGSON
PHILOSOPHE FRANCAIS
1859 — 1941

7-2

MATTER/MOTION

1 Man has been disturbed by the natural world into which he is born and has to live. It is clear to him that things are not quite what they seem.

There are life-giving forces that make things grow, and all living things are in a condition of constant change. There are forces which shake the ground and belch up cinders and ash from mountaintops. There are forces which rumble in a rainstorm and crackle across the sky in streaks of light. There are insidious forces which make one hurt inside and burn with heat and die. There are roots and insects and animals and seeds which give off juices which can kill.

Ancient man wondered about these things. Obviously there were all sorts of *realities beyond appearances.* They could be felt. They could be benevolent, but more often they were hostile and harmful. What were these forces—these invisible, capricious powers?

Today, of course, we know that the ancient intuition was correct: There are indeed forces beyond appearances. We must admire ancient men for making as much sense of their world as they did.

2 Sir Arthur Eddington illustrates the difference between macrocosmic reality as we experience it and some of the "realities beyond appearances."

The learned physicist and the man in the street were standing together on the threshold about to enter a room.

The man in the street moved forward without trouble, planted his foot on a solid unyielding plank at rest before him, and entered.

The physicist was faced with an intricate problem. To make any movement he must shove against the atmosphere, which presses with a force of fourteen pounds on every square inch of his body. He must land on a plank travelling at twenty miles a second round the sun—a fraction of a second earlier or later the plank would be miles away from the chosen spot. He must do this whilst hanging from a round planet head outward into space, and with a wind of ether blowing at no one knows how many miles a second through every interstice of his body. He reflects too that the plank is not what it appears to be—a continuous support for his weight. The plank is mostly emptiness; very sparsely scattered in that emptiness are myriads of electric charges dashing about at great speeds but occupying at any moment less than a billionth part of the volume which the plank seems to fill continuously. It is like stepping on a swarm of flies. . . .

Happily even a learned physicist has usually some sense of proportion; and it is probable that for this occasion he put out of mind scientific truths about astronomical motions, the constitution of planks and the laws of probability, and was content to follow the same crude conception of his task that presented itself to the mind of his unscientific colleague.

Sir Arthur Eddington has calculated that the number of particles in the universe is 2.36216 × 10⁷⁹, or, in round numbers, 2²⁶⁴.

3   The very first Greek philosophers asked questions, not about man, but about the world in which they lived. They knew nothing of the basic elements (hydrogen, oxygen, etc.) or natural law ("physics"—the science of matter-in-motion) as we do. But sensing man's perilous (mis)understanding of his world, they asked questions, and asked them in a new way.

What is this "matter" of which everything is made? Is everything made of some single substance which we know (like water, air, or fire)? Or is it made of some unknown substance which under certain conditions, turns into the water, air, and fire of experience?

And what are the forces which activate matter into motion? The winds blow, lightning fells the giant pine, crops grow and die. What are the forces behind all this? Is it a single force or many? Could the force be "divine" or "mental"? Could it be alive? Is it *outside* matter (Zeus doesn't really hurl the thunderbolt of lightning) or *inside* matter? (Thales pondered magnets and decided their forces were internal; he concluded that they must have "souls.")

These first philosopher-scientists phrased such questions as best they could. In all, they were asking but two fundamental questions: (1) What is everything made of? (2) What are the forces that cause motion? There must be a lesson in all this. Our present accumulation of scientific knowledge about the natural world is nothing less than staggering, yet what are the fundamental questions we are asking today? (1) *What is everything made of?* (2) *What are the forces that cause motion?*

The deeper science probes toward reality, the more clearly it appears that the universe is not like a machine at all.

LINCOLN BARNETT

So far as quantum theory can say at present, atoms might as well be possessed of free will, limited, however, to one of several possible choices.

BERTRAND RUSSELL

4   Take an ordinary piece of matter of any sort—a car key, a piece of chalk, a piece of candy, or a piece of paper—and suppose we were somehow able to divide it into finer and finer and even finer pieces. What would we eventually find? What, in short, are the ultimate constituents of matter?

All matter is made up of *molecules,* a specific molecule in a specific arrangement for each specific substance. Thus there are an enormous, almost incomprehensibly large, number of physically (and chemically) distinct molecules corresponding to the enormous variety of substances we see about us. The first great simplification in the description of nature came with the realization that every one of these vast assortment of molecules is composed of relatively few more elementary objects called *atoms*. About one hundred different atoms are known, ranging from the lightest and simplest, hydrogen, to the highly complex and unstable atoms that have only recently been synthesized and observed.

It was long believed that atoms were absolutely indivisible and immutable. Atoms were thought to be the basic and fundamental building blocks, mysteriously presented to us by nature, describable but intrinsically unexplainable. The next great step came when it was learned, at the turn of the century, that atoms are made up of still more fundamental objects. How many different kinds of such objects or, as the physicist calls them, *elementary particles,* are required to make up the one hundred or so different atomic species and therefore all of matter? The staggeringly simple answer is three. In short, the ultimate constituents of all ordinary matter are just three distinct and different elementary particles called the *electron,* the *proton,* and the *neutron.* . . . Reflect for a moment on the fact that all matter, everywhere in the universe, no matter its appearance, form, or properties, is made up of electrons, protons and neutrons appropriately arranged. . . .

[This] description is adequate as far as it goes. However, as the physicist began to study the elementary particles more closely, he rather quickly began to discover that the universe, at its most fundamental level, cannot be characterized by these three constituents of ordinary matter alone. Indeed, he now realizes that there are at least thirty entities (some would say as many as two hundred or more), which can be thought of as elementary particles. It is almost as if a new kind of periodic table has appeared at this subatomic level, a table that no one understands very well. It has been suggested that each of the elementary particles in this uncomfortably large array is some combination of three still more elementary objects called *quarks.* However, such objects have not yet been discovered. . . ."

SAXON AND FRETTER

At the moment man's investigation of the ultra-small ends in mystery and his investigation of the ultra-large ends in mystery. It is not a very far-fetched hope that the two mysteries will turn out to be closely connected.

FRED HOYLE

5   The present particle picture remains confused; no semblance of order has yet emerged from studies of the atomic nucleus. The search for "quarks"—is continuing. But a simple description of "ultimate reality" has yet to be found.°

A nuclear physicist, Walter Scott Houston, observes that

in many respects the physics of elementary particles today is at a very real crossroads. . . . Curiously, although many people call physics an "exact science," there is more confusion than certainty in the nuclear particle field today.

About all that we can say is that all the elementary particles discovered in the atom are forces of energy. As they interact with one

°It appears that we are at the point of moving one step deeper into the nature of matter. Recent experiments at the CERN laboratory in Geneva have added evidence that the proton is not at all a distinct particle, but is composed of "subentities." Furthermore, there is a hint that these subentities are held together by a new and very intense force of some sort hitherto unknown to us.

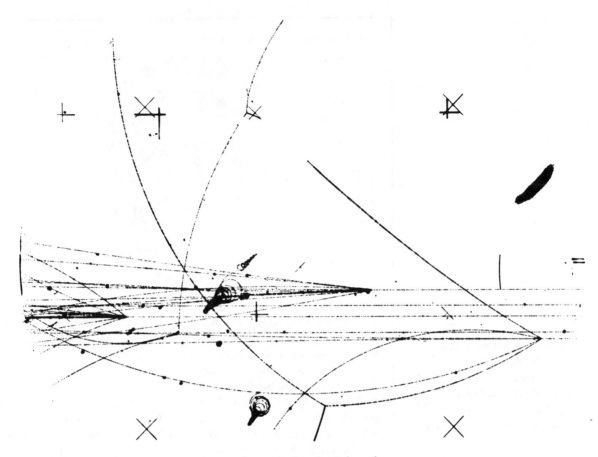

another according to what appears to be mathematical principles, they produce (or become) "matter." It is questionable whether the particles themselves are matter in any proper sense of the word; but matter as we know it is in some way dependent upon the combinations or configurations which the particles assume.

But what is "energy"? The honest fact is that we don't know, but we are beginning to suspect that it is not matter. "Energy" is *something* in motion which exerts force, but we don't know yet what that something is, and it looks more and more as though "ultimate reality," which we in the West have always assumed to be "substance" or "matter," may turn out to be nonmaterial, perhaps not unlike a set of mathematical principles in action.

6   "What is everything made of?"
     Werner Heisenberg has written that, to such a question,

the final answer will more closely approximate the views expressed in Plato's *Timaeus* than those of the ancient materialists. . . . The elemental particles of present-day physics are more closely related to the Platonic bodies than they are to the atoms of Democritus.

ZENO'S PARADOXES OF MOTION

Zeno of Elea (fl. c. 450 B.C.) left a legacy of logical paradoxes that philosophers have wrestled with for some 2400 years, often in vain. Zeno's contribution was to show that many of our common assumptions about motion and time lead to hopeless contradictions.

His most famous argument is the story of a handicap race between Achilles and a tortoise. If the tortoise begins the race some distance ahead of Achilles, then by the time Achilles reaches the point where the tortoise *was,* the tortoise, however pokey, will have moved ahead a ways. Again, when Achilles reaches the point where the tortoise *was,* the tortoise will still be ahead, though the distance between them is closing. And so on, ad infinitum. Therefore, since the distance between them is forever closing, Achilles can never overtake the tortoise.

Another paradox involves the racetrack. A runner cannot reach the end of the raceway until he has reached the half-way mark; but he can't reach the half-way mark until he has first reached the half-way mark to the half-way mark (the "quarter-way" mark), and so on, ad infinitum. Conclusion: the runner can never even begin the race, and motion is an illusion.

A similar point is made with the paradox of the arrow. At any instant, argued Zeno, the arrow in flight occupies a space equal to itself, and, therefore, is at rest. And the same holds true of the arrow at any instant of its alleged flight through the air. At *every* instant it is at rest, and therefore motion doesn't exist.

Zeno was one of the truly great Greek minds. He invented arguments, notes Russell, "all immeasurably subtle and profound, to prove that motion is impossible. . . . From him to our own day, the finest intellects of each generation in turn attacked the problems, but achieved, broadly speaking, nothing." Although his paradoxes have now been solved, mathematically and logically, they remain so intriguing that new volumes about them appear almost annually.

Relativity demands the abandonment of the old conception of "matter," which is infected by the metaphysics associated with "substance," and represents a point of view not really necessary in dealing with phenomena.

BERTRAND RUSSELL

The elemental particles of modern physics, like the regular bodies
of Plato's philosophy, are defined by the requirements of mathematical
symmetry. They are not eternal and unchanging, and they can hardly,
therefore, strictly be termed real. Rather, they are simple expressions of
fundamental mathematical constructions which one comes upon in striving
to break down matter ever further, and which provide the content for
the underlying laws of nature. In the beginning, therefore, for modern
science, was the form, the mathematical pattern, not the material thing.
And since the mathematical pattern is, in the final analysis, an intellectual
concept, one can say in the words of Faust, *"Am Anfang war der Sinn"*—"In
the beginning was the meaning."

*The notion that matter is some-
thing inert and uninteresting is
surely the veriest nonsense. If there
is anything more wonderful than
matter in the sheer versatility of its
behaviour, I have yet to hear tell
of it.*

FRED HOYLE

7 Matter has been dematerialized, not just as a concept of the philosophically real, but now as an idea of modern physics. Matter can be analyzed down to the level of fundamental particles. But at that depth the direction of the analysis changes, and this constitutes a major conceptual surprise in the history of science. The things which for Newton typified matter—e.g., an exactly determinable state, a point shape, absolute solidity—these are now the properties electrons do not, because theoretically they cannot, have. . . .

The dematerialization of matter encountered in this century . . . has rocked mechanics at its foundations. . . . The 20th century's dematerialization of matter has made it conceptually impossible to accept a Newtonian picture of the properties of matter and still do consistent physics.

NORWOOD RUSSELL HANSON

The knowledge of science fails in the face of all ultimate questions.

KARL JASPERS

8 If ultimate reality turns out to be a series of waves or vibrations, then we can turn to our other fundamental question: "What are the forces that cause motion?" We have traveled far since Thales first asked the question, but we are not yet at the end of the journey. Today there are four known forces which cause motion.

One is gravity. When we lift an arm, walk, or stumble and fall, we discover our conditioning to the earth's gravity field. Enough is known about its operation to enable us to orbit satellites, calculate the trajectory of lunar missions, and describe the orbits of the planets. In fact, gravitational interaction is the best understood of the known forces. It seems to be simply described by the inverse-square law.

However, the nature of gravity remains a mystery. Current experiments are beginning to indicate that gravity takes wave form, and strong sources of gravity waves appear to be coming from the center of our galaxy. Also it is of interest to note that gravity seems to be the only known force that is irreversible: it always attracts and never repels. Once gravity waves are better understood, it will be interesting to know whether our notions about anti-gravity forces are science or fiction.

9 A second force is the electromagnetic, and this, like gravity, is familiar at the experiential level of reality. The interaction of magnets and iron, the combining of atoms into molecules, and the transmission of signals along a neural pathway to the brain, through the air to a TV set, or along a wire to a videophone—all these are electromagnetic interactions. Because it manifests itself in so many forms at the macrocosmic level, and because of its great versatility, this is the force we have been able to put to practical use serving man's needs.

Two other forces are found at the subatomic level, and little is known about either of them. One force—the so-called "strong interaction—holds together the nucleus of the atom. Since the nuclear protons are positively charged (while neutrons are uncharged), they would strongly repel each other electrically. Despite this, the nucleus holds

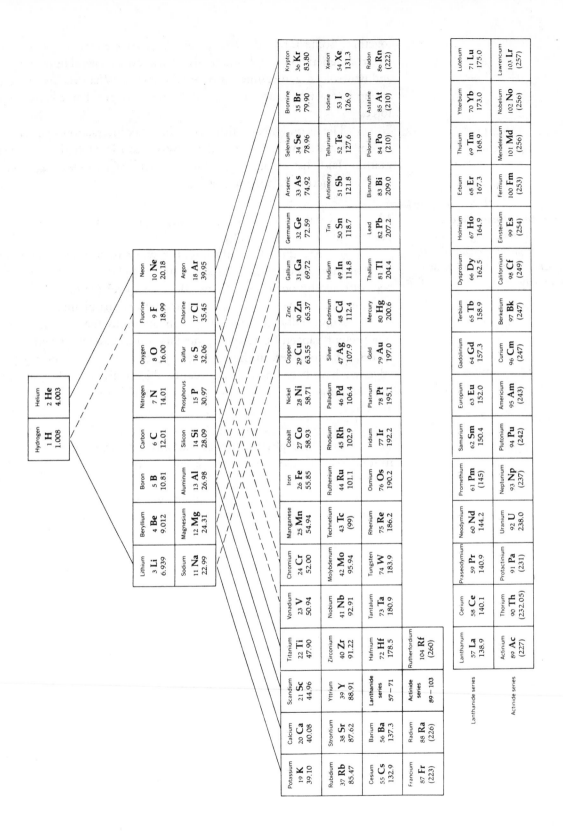

together. Some force, therefore, incredibly strong, acts to overcome the electromagnetic repulsion and binds from a few to several hundred protons and neutrons together into an ordered nucleus. Whatever its nature, this strong interaction is about a hundred times stronger than electromagnetic forces.

The second subatomic force—the weak interaction—operates only on specific atomic particles and is always associated with their disintegration. Its behavior in relation to a variety of particles is known, but its basic function is not understood.

The true lover of knowledge is always striving after <u>being</u>. . . . He will not rest at those multitudinous phenomena whose existence is appearance only.

PLATO

10   Several philosophical problems come to mind in relation to our present understanding of physics.

(1) Are these the only forces at work in our universe or might there be more, perhaps of a different kind? (2) Have our notions of reality been affected by our deeper knowledge of nature? (3) Can we make any meaningful inquiries at this point into the origins of matter/motion?

Admittedly, dealing with such questions may be quite beyond our present capacities. Our fragmentary understanding leaves much to be desired. However, in the larger perspective of man's quest for knowledge, we have been approaching reality objectively for only a short time. Our questions are really just beginning, and we may have to wait for answers.

11   Are these physical forces the only activating principles at work in our world? Do these four known sources, interacting with energy/matter, account for all of the objects/events in the cosmos? Or must we postulate other forces? What about the order and "design" of nature? or the aggregates of matter which constitute living cells? or complex life systems? or the delicate operations of mind and consciousness? Can *all* these things be accounted for by the four known physical interactions?

As one scans the panorama of human experience, it appears that there are at least three other forces which men have believed existed. In order to think of them as causative forces parallel to the physical forces, we might call them (1) mind-force, (2) spirit-force, and (3) god-force.

Many would contend that there is sufficient evidence in experience to warrant the hypothesis of some sort of mind-force. Evidence might come from telepathy, psychokinesis, or clairvoyance. If such events are actual—and present evidence is highly inconclusive—all attempts to reduce such events to known physical forces (for example, very short electromagnetic wavelengths) have failed. Of course, this might be the result of inadequate scientific technique. Those who have had experiences which they have interpreted as ESP events are convinced that mind-force is real.

Spirit-force has been postulated by men from the beginning to account for a multitude of experiences, from the blowing wind (*pneuma* in Greek and *ruaḥ* in Hebrew mean both "wind" and "spirit") to emotional disturbances. We are convinced now that most of these events experienced by prescientific man can be accounted for on physical or psychological principles. Still, when one hears reports of poltergeists that bang on doors and knock vases off shelves, one may be tempted to give second thought to the idea of a spirit-force.

Apart from religious belief derived from authority, is there any evidence for the existence of a god-force? In all of man's religions there have been mystics who claim that their lives have been touched by a god-force; they have seen the supernatural in visions or had their bodies healed by the divine. A large number of these experiences can be explained psychologically, so the problem would be to determine whether there are events which cannot be so explained and which necessitate the hypothesis of a god-force.

In man's experience, these forces—if they exist—have never been neatly separated, nor can they be now. (It has only been in our century, of course, that the four physical interactions have been distinguished as separate forces.) Whether such metaphysical forces exist remains an open question. Care must be used to apply "Occam's razor": the principle which calls for the simplest explanation and precludes hypothesizing any force which the evidence does not demand.

12 How have our notions of reality been affected by current concepts of matter/motion?

There has been a strong temptation on the part of some philosophers—especially those inclined to make their philosophy a religion—to think of reality in degrees. That is, they considered some objects/events to be "more real" than others. Precisely what the terms "more real" or "less real" could mean is not always made clear. Generally, this world—the macrocosmic world of experience—was considered unreal; therefore, it was not to be valued. Plato was convinced that this world of particular things is an imperfect reflection of the perfect abstract "forms"; qualitatively it is not up to standard and therefore should not be taken too seriously. This world is made of matter, and matter is always imperfect. It resists shaping, like thick clay resists sculpturing. Only the eternal verities of mathematics or the "forms" of Goodness, Truth, and Beauty are truly real.

Similar concepts are to be found in the philosophies of the Gnostics, Neoplatonists, and Thomas Aquinas. The Hindu system of Shankara is even less equivocal: *everything* in this world is maya ("illusion"); it is merely a mirage and only Brahman is real.

13 Unless—for religious reasons—one has a need to declare this world "unreal," current thought tends to accept all levels of existence

There is a famous anecdote about Laplace's submitting to the Emperor Napoleon a copy of his System of the World. Napoleon asked him what was the place of God in the system. Laplace answered: "Sir, I do not need this hypothesis." It is interesting to note that Laplace, who did not need the hypothesis of God in his book on astronomy, needed a Superior Intelligence in his formulation of the principle of causality. . . .

PHILIPP FRANK

What has been thought of as a particle will have to be thought of as a series of events. The series of events that replaces the particle has certain important physical properties, and therefore demands our attention; but it has no more substantiality than any other series of events that we might arbitrarily single out. Thus "matter" is not a part of the ultimate material of the world, but merely a convenient way of collecting events into bundles. . . .

BERTRAND RUSSELL

as equally real. We are gradually moving away from two extremes which have prevailed in the past: the idealism which considered macrocosmic experience as more real than, say, atomic interactions; and the over-reaction of a scientism that held that physics provides the only true picture of reality.

There seems to be no good reason not to accept all objects/events in the external world as equally real, and this must include the full range from "point-events" of energy—whatever they are—to the grandest cosmological operations involving billions of galaxies.

There may be one qualification to all this. As indicated earlier, it is too soon to tell for sure what "matter" is. When physicists write that particles cannot "strictly be termed real" and may turn out to be something like "mathematical principles," then we may have to rethink the nature of ultimate reality at this particle or subparticle level.

Or is the problem merely semantic? "Ultimate reality" may eventually turn out to be nonmaterial, but would that necessarily mean that it is "less real"?

Physical things are those series of appearances whose matter obeys the laws of physics.

BERTRAND RUSSELL

14   In the history of ideas, certain questions have to wait before they can be asked. One such question (the most obvious of all) was so over-whelming that it was asked and immediately tucked away, never to be taken seriously again. There is, however, a strong likelihood that during the seventies the question is going to be reopened and treated empirically. The question: What is the origin of matter?

The problem has been ignored because it seemed insoluble; a simple creationist answer appeared the only one possible. When did the universe begin? What created matter? Or from what was matter created? "God created the universe and set matter in motion." And the little girl who persisted—"Then who made God?"—we brushed aside.

Her question is legitimate. Philosophers have long pointed out that the creationist answer is no answer at all. It was merely a deus ex machina like that employed by Greek tragedians to unravel a tangled plot. The deity dropped in from above the stage and, by divine fiat, set every-thing right. To say that X created Y—or G created M—*ex nihilo,* "out of nothing," is merely to *define* the question as being off-limits to serious inquiry.

15   At this early stage of inquiry into the origin of matter only a few promising lines of thought have been developed. In his "steady-state" theory of the universe, Dr. Fred Hoyle assumed that matter is being created continually in space out of nothing, but he never attempted a serious explanation of how this might happen. Hoyle did little more than pose the problem.

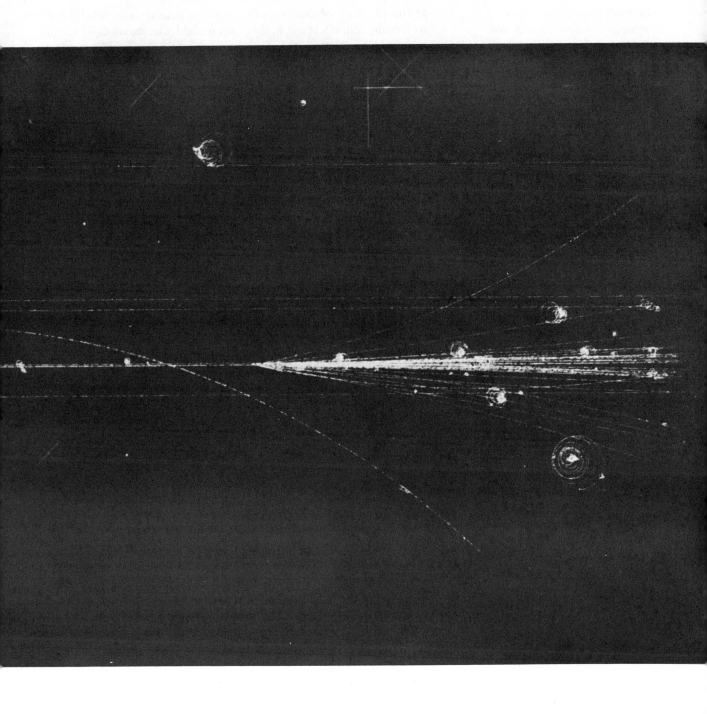

Scientists have narrowed down the mystery of creation. All that seems to be necessary is some hydrogen gas at the beginning. We understand how the hydrogen condenses into a first generation of stars, how these stars cook heavier elements in their interiors, how these heavy elements are spewed out in supernova and other explosions to enrich the interstellar medium, and how subsequent generations of stars and planets form from the hydrogen and heavier elements. . . . And yet there's the beguiling problem: Where did the original hydrogen come from?

CARL SAGAN
"The Violent Universe"
PBS-TV

Matter is capable of exerting several types of influence—or fields as they are usually called. There is the nuclear field that binds together the atomic nuclei. There is the electro-magnetic field that enables atoms to absorb light. There is the gravitational field that holds the stars and galaxies together. And according to the new theory there is also a creation field that causes matter to originate."

To this last statement, Hoyle adds: "Matter originates in response to the influence of other matter."

Matter-in-motion can create other matter; for matter-in-motion is energy, and energy can be transformed into more matter. Therefore, in theory, if we can imagine the universe beginning with even a very small amount of matter—perhaps just a few atoms—in a state of acceleration, then we can logically describe how all the matter in the universe might have come into existence. Each bit of matter traveling at high speeds can be transformed into more matter.

16   Today we can (almost) create matter in our laboratories. In a phenomenon known as "pair-creation," physicists can create electrons in the vacuum of the accelerator, that is, out of nothing. They have also succeeded in creating pairs of positive and negative protons out of nothing. Weisskopf states that, in his opinion, this represents the actual creation of matter.

Electrons can also be created from photons of light. The interesting point is that light does not have mass, while electrons have. Photons (with a rest mass of zero) are massless energy; at the speed of light the photons can be transformed into mass according to the mass-energy transformation equation: $E = mc^2$.

What does all this mean? One implication seems to be that questions about the origin of matter are not wholly out of order. Nevertheless, at the present time really convincing answers are lacking. In all cases physicists began their experiments with something (not "nothing"), and they had at their disposal sophisticated scientific equipment with which they could accelerate particles into higher energy states. Theoretically, we can imagine a universe empty of all mass but a single, lonely electron; some force can push that electron into relativistic speeds, then we can logically account for all the rest of the matter in the entire universe. But what that "prime mover" might be still bothers us.°

The best we can do at present is to hold on to the question and not be lured into thinking it has been answered. We will probably have to rephrase the question numerous times before an answer begins to come. Indeed, it might be found in some different frame of reference altogether.

°This is the problem which generated the "cosmological argument" for the existence of God as Prime Mover. See pages 454f.

7-3

TIME/SPACE

1 We live in a relativistic universe. The Newtonian universe which existed till the beginning of the twentieth century was one in which conventional physics adequately described matter-in-motion. But a relativistic universe is one in which matter is in motion at very great speeds. When velocities are sharply increased some strange things begin to happen. Such high velocities, we now know, are the general rule at both the microscopic and cosmological scales of physical reality. It is only at the macroscopic level of experience that Newtonian theories still operate.

Since Albert Einstein published his three papers on special relativity in 1905, our understanding of our universe and our place in it has undergone continual revision. It may not seem at first glance that relativistic notions affect our routine behavior, but the fact is that we are immersed in relativistic events. For instance, light photons striking our retinas can be described only in relativistic terms, and the very atoms that compose our bodies are themselves in motion at these high velocities.

Beyond all this, the significant fact is that a new world-view was born with special relativity. It has gradually become part of our consciousness.

2 Relativistic phenomena astound the layman, excite the physicist, and boggle the mind of the philosopher. In fact, the physicists don't even pretend to understand much of what they describe; they go their way developing pragmatic equations without worrying very much whether their formulas describe realities presently accessible to experience.

At the microscopic level, common sense is offended. "Almost all the 'great principles' of traditional physics turn out to be like the 'great law' that there are always three feet to a yard; others turn out to be downright false."

If space is, it will be in something; for everything that is is in something; and to be in something is to be in space. Space then will be in space, and so on (ad infinitum). Therefore space does not exist.
ZENO THE ELEATIC
(As recorded by Aristotle)

I cannot believe that God plays dice with the cosmos.
ALBERT EINSTEIN

Particles can be accelerated so as to increase their energy and when "smashed" each resulting particle will weigh as much as the original particle. Also there is discontinuity: a particle observed at one place will be subsequently observed at another place without having moved through any point to get there. Even the concept of time-reversal is used by some physicists to explain particle behavior.

There are more things in heaven and earth, Horatio,
Than are dreamt of in your philosophy.

SHAKESPEARE
Hamlet

3 Equally strange events are occurring at the cosmological level. Einstein's equations predict that as objects move at very high speeds (near the speed of light), time slows down, mass increases, and length decreases (at least, that's the way we would observe and measure them). Also the universe may be curved (positively or negatively, but as yet we don't know which), and Einstein thought in terms of "curved space."

If time is real, there may indeed be time anomalies; and if space is real, there could be space anomalies. That is, events have been observed for which hypotheses of time/space anomalies would be workable explanations.

Other unbelievable goings-on have been observed for some time. Quasars, for instance, generate far more energy than present physical theory can explain, and pulsars are probably the long-predicted neutron stars—stars in the throes of death—whose matter weighs billions of tons per cubic inch. Now astronomers are developing models of "black holes" where the gravitational attraction of a collapsing neutron star would be so great that no light could escape from it.

Another incredible fact is that our relativistic world-view was developed within the mind of one man.

I maintain . . . that the transient now with respect to which the distinction between the past and the future of common sense and psychological time acquires meaning has no relevance at all apart from the egocentric perspectives of a conscious (human) organism and from the immediate experiences of that organism.

ADOLF GRÜNBAUM

4 What Einstein did was not a formal accomplishment. He did not approach the problem from the standpoint of finding some mathematical equation which will describe a certain group of phenomena. Something much more fundamental was at stake, namely, the critical evaluation of the cultural foundation of theoretical physics. Certain things which were always taken for granted, were put under scrutiny and their falseness proved. This was no longer mere physics and mathematics. . . . Here started that dogged uphill fight of Einstein which lasted for ten years and which is perhaps unparalleled in the entire history of the human mind; a fight which did not arise from any experimental puzzle of the mind.

CORNELIUS LANCZOS

5 According to Einstein's theory, no material object can travel faster than the speed of light (which is about 186,000 miles per second). Relativistic phenomena begin to occur around 10 percent of the speed of light.

At these velocities, three significant things begin to happen to all objects in motion, including human beings: (1) time slows down; (2) the mass of objects increases; and (3) the length of objects (measured parallel to the plane of motion) decreases.

Take, for instance, the phenomenon known as "time dilation." The measurement of time—and perhaps the actual "flow" of time—is strictly relative—relative, that is, to the standpoint of the observer. Two travelers moving in different reference systems at high speeds relative to each other would *measure* time differently, and both would be right.

The "twin paradox" apparently illustrates actual realities. Imagine twin brothers twenty years old, one of whom becomes an astronaut. He takes a journey through space to a planet orbiting the star Rigil Kent (which is also known as alpha-Centauri, the nearest star to us after the sun), which is about 4 light-years distance. His spaceship travels at 148,000 mps (miles per second). At that speed (which is $\frac{4}{5}$ the speed of light), according to all the clocks on his spaceship—calendars, wristwatches,

The idea that time can vary from place to place is a difficult one, but it is the idea Einstein used, and it is correct—believe it or not.

RICHARD FEYNMAN

THE MESSAGE FROM PLANET X

There is no absolute time throughout the universe by which absolute simultaneity can be measured. Absolute simultaneity of distant events is a meaningless concept.

How radical this notion is can be seen by a thought experiment in which vast distances and enormous speeds are involved. Suppose that someone on Planet X, in another part of our galaxy, is trying to communicate with the earth. He sends out a radio message. This is, of course, an electromagnetic wave that travels through space with the speed of light. Assume that the earth and Planet X are 10 light-years apart, which means that it takes 10 years for the message to travel to the earth. Twelve years before a radio astronomer on earth receives the message, the astronomer had received a Nobel Prize. The special theory permits us to say, without qualification, that he received this prize *before* the message was sent from Planet X.

Ten minutes after receiving the message, the astronomer sneezes. The special theory also permits us to say, without qualification, and for all observers in any frame of reference, that the astronomer sneezed *after* the message was sent from Planet X.

Now suppose that sometime during the 10-year period, while the radio message was on its way to the earth (say, 3 years before the message was received), the astronomer fell off his radio telescope and broke a leg. The special theory does *not* permit us to say without qualification that he broke his leg before or after the sending of the message from Planet X.

The reason is this. One observer, leaving Planet X at the time the message is sent and traveling to the earth with a speed judged from the earth to be slow, will find (according to his measurements of the passing of time) that the astronomer broke his leg *after* the message was sent. Of course he will arrive on earth long after the message is received, perhaps centuries after. But when he calculates the date on which the message was sent, according to his clock, it will be earlier than the date on which the astronomer broke his leg. On the other hand, another observer, who also leaves Planet X at the time the message is sent, but who travels very close to the speed of light, will find that the astronomer broke his leg *before* the message was sent. Instead of taking centuries to make the trip, he will make it in, say, only a trifle more than 10 years as calculated on the earth. But because of the slowing down of time on the fast-moving spaceship, it will seem to the ship's astronaut that he made the trip in only a few months. He will be told on the earth that the astronomer broke his leg a little more than 3 years ago. According to the astronaut's clock, the message was sent a few months ago. He will conclude that the leg was broken years before the message left Planet X.

If the astronaut traveled as fast as light (of course this is purely hypothetical; not possible in fact), his clock would stop completely. It would seem to him that he made the trip in zero time. From his point of view the two events, the sending of the message and its reception, would be simultaneous. *All* events on earth during the 10-year period would appear to him to have occurred before the message was sent. Now, according to the special theory there is no "preferred" frame of reference: no reason to prefer the point of view of one observer rather than another. The calculations made by the fast-moving astronaut are just as legitimate, just as "true," as the calculations made by the slow-moving astronaut. There is no universal, absolute time that can be appealed to for settling the differences between them.

MARTIN GARDNER
Relativity for the Million

atomic clocks, heartbeats—his experience of time would slow to $\frac{3}{5}$ its normal rate *as observed and measured by his twin brother on earth.* He would therefore make the journey to Rigil Kent in 3 years and the return trip in 3 years, the entire roundtrip taking 6 years. But while he was on the 6-year journey his twin brother on earth would age 10 years. From his earthbound viewpoint, he would measure his space-traveling brother's journey taking 5 years out and 5 years back—10 years according to his calendars and clocks.

And both measurements are correct. There is no suggestion that one measurement is the real one and the other is distorted or illusory. Both are true. The astronaut would experience the passing of only 6 years and he would age only 6 years. But according to his stay-at-home brother, the space journey would have taken 10 years and he himself would have aged a full 10 years.

The search for ultimate reality, then, is a natural and necessary part of man's being. We need to realize that this kind of concern is part of what it means to be human. We also need to realize, however, that while some kind of commitment is inevitable, a final answer to this question can never be given, for man is limited, he is finite; he can never be expected to know all. In short, he is encapsulated, and for him to know the infinite is impossible by definition.

JOSEPH ROYCE

Time, therefore, is relative. It looks as though it's not merely a matter of the way we observe objects in motion. It appears that these phenomena are real. They take place within the objects themselves.

6   The relativity of time-measurement was a cornerstone of Einstein's system. In 1905 it was only theory, but we now have evidence to support it. According to predictions, all physical, chemical, and biological processes would begin to slow down when achieving relativistic speeds, and this is exactly what we find. In the accelerators, atomic particles (pions and others) have been pushed to high speeds and then subjected to high-energy collisions with other particles. When thus "smashed" these particles disintegrate at known rates. At high velocities, however, these particles disintegrate considerably more slowly, and the rate of disintegration is in exact agreement with Einstein's predictions. This means the "time experience" of the particle has slowed down to a fraction of what it was at rest.

> This direct confirmation came more than 40 years after Einstein formulated the theory in 1905, but physicists believed it implicitly from the outset because of its internal consistency and because a very substantial body of indirect evidence was gradually amassed.

A good deal of popular science fiction involving space travel (*Planet of the Apes,* for example, in which the astronauts jump ahead in time some seven hundred years) is not fiction, but plausible science. According to present understanding it is quite possible to move forward in time. How far forward one might travel depends solely on the speed he can attain.

7   Special relativity also predicts that mass will increase and length will decrease. These two ideas have also been accepted from the beginning by most physicists, and the former has been empirically verified. Again, in the accelerators, the mass of high-speed particles increases so much that adjustments must be made in the magnetic fields which drive and guide the particles. The increase in mass would otherwise fling them outside the magnetic holding field.

To date no empirical evidence has been found to substantiate the prediction about decrease in length, yet there seems to be no reason to doubt it as part of the relativistic package.

8   There is disagreement among physicists as to the philosophic implications of such relative measurements. The problem is whether these phenomena are real—that is, whether the object actually undergoes these changes—or whether the changes are merely observational phenomena.

One school of thought holds that these phenomena take place only from the standpoint of an observer in one reference system who is watch-

Hitherto people have looked upon the Principle of Causality as a proposition which would in the course of years admit of experimental proof with an ever-increasing exactitude. . . .

Now Heisenberg has discovered a flaw in the proposition. . . . The principle of causality loses its significance as an empirical proposition.

Causality is thus only conceivable as a Form *of the theoretical system.*

ALBERT EINSTEIN

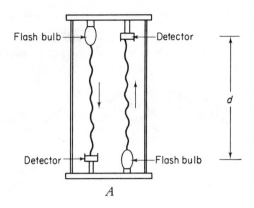

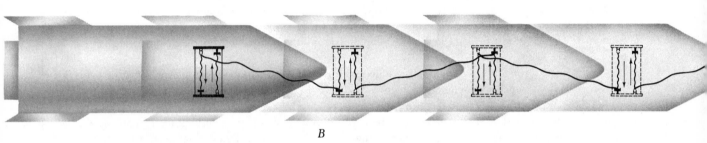

ing objects in another system moving at high speeds. In other words, they are observational, and the thought-experiment involving the light-clock appears to imply that they are perceptual only.

In the diagram, the light-clocks are on two spaceships moving at high speeds relative to one another, speeds not far short of the speed of light. What would a passenger on each spaceship see if he could observe the light-clock on the other spacecraft?

Light-clock *A*, on your ship, just sits there, blinking. The top bulb sends a beam of light down to the photoelectric cell which in turn triggers the bottom bulb which sends a beam of light to the cell at the top; so down and up the light-beams go.

There is an identical light-clock (*B*) on the other spaceship. As it passes, what would you see? You would perceive a much longer beam of light than is emitted by your own clock which (to you) is at rest. So the light-beam on the other spaceship travels farther *in the same period of time* as your light-beam. This could have two explanations: either the light of the other light-clock is moving faster or time has slowed down. The former is impossible, according to relativity, since the speed of light is a constant; it always travels at 186,000 mps. Therefore, what you are witnessing is a slower movement of time on the other spaceship compared with the movement of time according to your clock.

But ask: What would the passengers on the other spaceship see

Perhaps the most majestic feature of our whole existence is that while our intelligences are powerful enough to penetrate deeply into the evolution of this quite incredible Universe, we still have not the smallest clue to our own fate.

FRED HOYLE

The exciting discovery of quasars by astronomer Maarten Schmidt, and the subsequent development of the black hole theory, was the subject of a TV documentary on the Public Broadcasting System. The event was narrated by Robert MacNeil, PBS host, and Carl Sagan, an astronomer from Cornell University.

MAC NEIL. Six years ago such a spectrum [as in the photograph above] was a turning point in astronomy. Schmidt obtained it from a quasar. . . . Schmidt puzzled over the spectrum for six weeks. It made no sense. Then on February 5, 1963, he understood. He recognized a group of lines, but they were completely shifted to the red end of the spectrum.

SCHMIDT. That night I went home in a state of disbelief. I said to my wife, "It's horrible! Something incredible happened today!"

SAGAN. Let's see, roughly, why Schmidt was so shocked and what his spectrum meant. Imagine a bright source of light which is moving away from you. The light waves that it emits are "stretched out"—they are moved toward longer (and therefore redder) wave lengths. The faster the thing is moving away from you the more red-shifted its spectral lines become. Astronomers are by now used to the conclusion that galaxies with the biggest red-shifts—that is, those which are moving fastest away from us—are also the most distant galaxies. . . .

Schmidt recognized a pattern of three lines due to atomic hydrogen, but these three lines were not in their usual place in the spectrum. . . . They had been red-shifted by this very large distance. The amount of the red shift corresponds to a velocity of about 30,000 miles per second, and such an enormous velocity means that the quasar must be very far away, in fact that it must be about a billion light years from the earth.

Now, how is it possible that an object which appears to us so bright could be so far away? A huge mass of gas or stars falling together might conceivably produce such a large amount of energy, enough to drive a quasar. But there's a problem with this idea: it's that gravity is, in a sense, too strong. There's nothing to stop the collapse of such a mass of gas or stars. It would continue to collapse. It would pass through the neutron star stage . . . and eventually its gravity would become so intense that even light would be unable to escape from the object.

Therefore the object would "turn off"—it would disappear. It would vanish from the universe, leaving behind only a sort of "black hole" of gravity, a little like the grin on the Cheshire cat. The universe may in fact be riddled with such black holes.

Imagine a spaceship wandering around, minding its own business, encountering such a black hole. What happens to it? Well, it must vanish. It must disappear from the universe.

There are some who believe that matter which disappears down such a black hole must reemerge at some other point in space, at some other epoch in time. This may be just a sort of highbrow science fiction, or it may really be true.

The quasars are such a puzzling phenomenon that they may really lead us to revise our notions of the laws of nature.

"The Violent Universe"
PBS-TV, April 1969

H.K.WIMMER

as they watch your clock pass by? They would see precisely what you see, only reversed. To you, *his* time has slowed down; to him, *your* time has slowed down.

This sort of thought-experiment seems to indicate that the whole matter of relativity is merely perceptual. Einstein's equations describe nothing more than the way we would measure things that move very fast relative to our point of observation.

But other physicists are not so sure. Some are convinced such phenomena are not perceptual, but real, that they really happen to objects. It would seem that the increase in particle mass in the accelerators and the slowdown of decay time in the disintegration of pions is not merely a matter of measurement, but is an event which the particle actually undergoes. If this is not the case, then why the adjustments which are necessary in the magnetic fields?

The same dilemma applies to time. Saxon and Fretter candidly write that to understand relativistic phenomena, "we must realize that time dilation is a property of time itself, not of any particular clock."

At present the puzzle does not appear to be soluble.

The objective world simply is, it does not happen. Only to the gaze of consciousness, crawling upward along the life-line of my body, does a section of this world come to life as a fleeting image in space which continuously changes in time.

HERMANN WEYL

9   Is time real? Does time exist in the real world, or is time merely an experience? The majority of philosophers and psychologists (as opposed to physicists) have held that time is an experience only. It is our experiencing of the continuum of our flow of consciousness. If there were no consciousness there would be no experience of time, and therefore there would be no time. Time, they have contended, is in no sense a property of the real world.

To be sure, there are sequences of events in the real world, and it appears that certain events must happen before other events. The concept of causality has meaning as these events take place in sequence. There is a "before" and "after" which is real. But these are merely events, and events are matter-in motion; and there is no ingredient called "time" involved in such processes.

If this is the case, then before consciousness came into being, events took place over the billions of years. Atoms interacted and the forces of the universe moved matter about, but no time was involved in these events.

On the other hand, physicists are almost equally split on the reality of time. There are many who hold—and Einstein himself held—that time is in some sense a feature of the real world. Clocks and relativistic physics do not merely measure the flow of our conscious experience; they measure time itself.

10   Will man ever be able to move back and forth in time? Any answer to this depends in part on the reality of time. Our popular notions of "time travel" have been derived largely from science fiction and TV programs, and a recent book entitled *Psychic Visits to the Past* states:

Commonly we think of ourselves as captives of time, caged in the present, moving toward the future at a set speed, with the past forever behind us. But this illusion swiftly fades as we begin to investigate the experiences of those with the psychic ability to move back and forth through time with seeming ease.

What exactly a dematerialized psyche can do cannot at present be described by a scientist, but if we remain in the realm of matter-in-motion, we can get some tentative answers. Our best knowledge at present indicates that we can move forward in time, but never backward in time. If we could travel just short of the speed of light—say, at a speed of 185,000 mps—it would be quite possible in one lifetime to move millions of years ahead in time. But moving backward in time appears to be an impossibility. The heros of science fiction can move up and down the corridors of time, with or without a time-machine, tampering with historic events along the way; but it looks at present as though any "journey into the past" will be confined to fantasy.

11   Is space real? Does space exist in the real world or is space only in our heads? Immanuel Kant was one of the first epistemologists to make the unequivocal statement that both time and space are aspects of the mind. They are "modes of perception," that is, structures of consciousness through which we experience the real world. They are a priori and develop in our minds through experience, but they are not derived from any experience of real time or space. Kant contended that it is impossible for us to do any thinking about real objects without the *concepts* of time and space. We can think of nothing in the real world without the idea of a space in which we can relate objects; mentally, objects "occupy" space: they are so many feet apart or they move at a certain speed through space. But space exists only in our concepts.

The same view can be taken of time. We cannot experience an object without having it "endure" in our consciousness. As we watch an object its existence persists "in time"; that is, it endures in our consciousness. Obviously, we could not perceive an object if this experience of duration were not so structured. Therefore, time and space are both in our minds as perceptual necessities. They are in no way a part of the external world.°

°They are not a part of the real world, that is, unless we choose to define them as such. See page 190.

12   How far does space extend? For hundreds of years man has puzzled over this question. We want to know how big the universe really is. If our universe curves back on itself and is therefore a finite universe, we want to know what lies "beyond" or "outside" this universe. How far *can* space extend?

If "space" is defined as the absence of everything, then it is "nothing." We are therefore asking how far "nothing" extends, and this turns out to be a false question. Our thinking about the "extension of

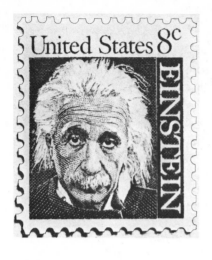

the universe" becomes a conceptual problem and not a problem about anything real.

Can we use such expressions as "empty space" or "objects in space"? According to Einstein himself (and he seems to be agreeing with Kant) such concepts are essential to our thinking. Mathematicians are aware that they must use symbolic concepts even though they refer to nothing real: irrational numbers, imaginary numbers, the square root of minus one, etc. The idea of "empty space" is such a necessary concept.

We can think of an "empty box" which means that "nothing" is in the box. But how can *nothing* be *in* a box? If we are interested in knowing how much matter (e.g., three bushels of grain) we might place in the box, then the question is meaningful. Space is a potential. Similarly, we can think of the universe as a large box and ask how much matter could be placed in this hypothetical "empty space." How much space is there between the universes and is it empty? Such concepts, Einstein has written, are mental tools, but necessities nevertheless.

It would appear at present that space is indeed "nothing." If we say there is space between any two objects, then we are saying that there is "nothing" between them. It is doubtful that space has any real status. The question, however, is not closed.

13   Is it possible for anything to exist "outside" space and time? Apart from theological assumptions, it is difficult to give meaning to such a question. Since we exist *in* space and time (or space and time exist *in* us), it is questionable whether we could know if anything exists "beyond" space and time. It is conceivable that there might be space anomalies—"holes in space"—or time anomalies—"time warps." Such ideas, however, are meaningless unless one assumes that time and space are real.

To conclude that anything, including deity, could exist outside of time would be a problematic concept. If time is merely an experience (which it most likely is), then to state that something can exist outside time is to say that it can exist outside of consciousness. This, of course, is a truism (except for Bishop Berkeley). To say that God existed before time is to say he existed before consciousness which, again, is quite possible. So we arrive at a theological statement which cannot be proved or disproved: that God alone existed and therefore (providing he is conscious) time existed only in the consciousness of God. This is a standard orthodox concept of Western theology. It is not an empirical statement and rests upon numerous unexaminable presuppositions.

7-4

COSMOS

1   Ancient man lived very close under the stars. His life was much affected by them, especially by the steady points of light that wandered through the star-fields as though they were alive. They might in fact be the bright bodies of the gods themselves playing beneath the blue-black firmament, gods such as Jupiter, Venus, and Mars.

Men felt themselves enclosed in a finite container of some sort: a box, or a valley with an inverted clay bowl arching overhead, or a flat disk under a giant crystalline dome. When men tried to make sense of their cosmos they saw different things.

Egyptians thought of their flat earth as the floor of a rectangular box. Some saw also a flat sky that extended away to the distant corners of the box; but others saw a bowl-shaped sky supported around the rim by a range of mountains surrounding the world like a great wall. The stars were burning lamps suspended high above from the roof or dome.

2   Babylonians knew their flat earth to be a round disk of land floating in a vast sea. Beyond this sea mountains rose to support the dome holding aloft the heavens. These heavens were the dwelling place of the gods and were strictly off-limits to mortals; man's sole domain was his circular disk of earth. He could neither visit the outer corners of earth nor gaze upon the abode of the immortal gods.

The ancient Hebrews saw above them a gigantic bowl of beaten metal (like the "brazen heaven" of Homer's *Iliad*) which separated the lower from the upper waters. This "firmament" was everywhere pitted with small holes through which the light of Heaven could be seen. The sun and moon were attached to the vaulted firmament and appeared to roll across it each day. The firmament was held up around the edge by a great range of mountains ("pillars of the sky"). An ocean of water

The Universe is not only queerer than we imagine—it is queerer than we can imagine.

J. B. S. HALDANE

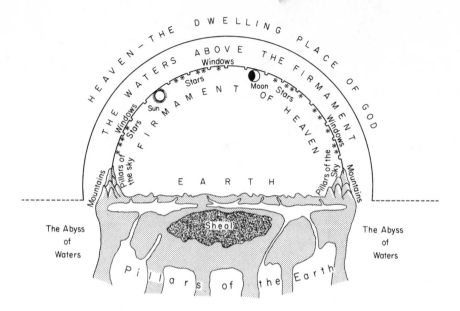

extended around the sides of the inverted bowl and down under the earth. High above the water dwelt God and the Host of Heaven. Beneath the flat surface on which man lived "roots of earth" plunged deep into the abysmal waters. Also under the earth, near its center, there existed an enormous cavern called *sheol* where (some said) the ghost-shades of men slept after death.

3 The night could be quiet, but it was the raging, blinding fireball by day which dominated the lives of men.

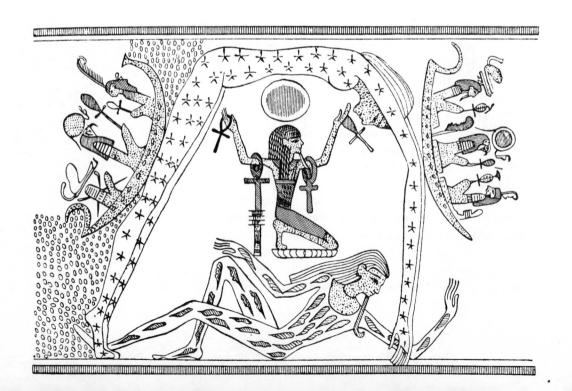

To Egyptians the sundisk which scorched the desert and brought green life to the meandering Nile was the god Amon-Ra, floating across the liquid sky in a barge. He passed into the Valley of the Gods at sunset and emerged from the valley at dawn.

Mesopotamians saw the eastern gates opening each morning and Shamash the sun god racing out in a great chariot drawn by wild asses. The sun was one of the chariot's burning orange-bright wheels. At sunset Shamash exited through the western gates and all through the night drove his chariot along a dark tunnel under the mountainous edge of the universe, emerging again from the eastern gates at dawn.

To early Greeks Helios arose daily out of the eastern sea in a quadriga drawn by four white stallions. As he lifted his fiery chariot into the sky the stars were scattered and dove into the sea. In late afternoon he approached the western boundaries of the earth, and faraway peoples living too near the edge would be singed by the heat of his chariot.

To ancient men the universe was closed, and they felt a kind of security in knowing that. There was continuous interaction among the gods, the evil spirits, and men who wandered the flat earth. Generally, good things went on above, bad things went on below, and man knew that his place was somewhere in the middle.

In the thousands of years for which men have wondered about the meaning of what goes on in the sky, there has never before been such a dramatic period as this. . . . All over the world astronomers have spotted events of breathtaking violence, scarcely explicable in the known forces of nature. They are also on the brink of establishing for the first time the history and fate of the universe we live in.

"The Violent Universe"
PBS–TV

4   As the twentieth century wanes, what do you and I see when we look up at the stars?

We know, first and last, that we are looking *out into space* and *back in time*. Whenever we look at any object in space we are also looking into the past: about $1\frac{1}{4}$ seconds into the past when looking at the nearest natural object (our moon); about 9 minutes back in time to the nearest star (our sun); about 4 years back in time to the second nearest star (alpha-Centauri); about 2 million years into the past when gazing at our nearest neighbor galaxy (Andromeda). And with the aid of telescopes we can peer into time past some 10 billion years. The farther we look out in space, the farther we are looking back in time.

Astronomers today share a unique kind of excitement because there exists a real possibility that we may be looking far enough into the past to see events which took place near the time of origins—the creation of our universe. Evidence indicates that such a beginning occurred about 20 billion years ago, and some of the objects we are now seeing (notably the quasars) are probably phenomena which happened shortly after that beginning.

5 Conceptualizing the size of the universe as we know it today strains our imaginations. Indeed, one may have to live with incredible concepts for a time before they can become believable.

Our solar system is composed of our star/sun and nine orbiting planets, plus assorted planetoids, asteroids, and comets. If we take the orbit of the planet Pluto as the outside limit of our solar system, then it is about 7½ billion miles (or 11 light-hours) in diameter. This local system is our home, our "front yard," incredibly small on a cosmic scale. The nearest star to our sun is a little more than 4 light-years away (about 26 trillion miles). Our Milky Way galaxy is about a hundred thousand light-years across, and our solar system moves within one spiral arm of our galaxy, some thirty thousand light years from its center. We are really quite far out and not even in the central plane.

Furthermore, our Galaxy is a part of a larger system. Some two dozen galaxies move together in what is known as the "local group." These include the Andromeda galaxies and the Magellanic clouds.

Photographs taken with very long exposures through giant telescopes reveal billions of galaxies extending in all directions. Many are spiral-shaped like our Milky Way, but they also come in many other shapes and sizes. Sometimes as many as several hundred galaxies appear together on a single photographic plate spanning but a few minutes of arc across the sky. The largest radiotelescopes now reach out more than 10 billion light-years—and the galaxies keep on going.

It is not impossible that we may be part of a "metagalaxy," a cluster of hundreds or thousands of galaxies spiraling together in what might look like our own Milky Way magnified a million times.

Now what is history? It is the centuries of systematic explorations of the riddle of death, with a view to overcoming death. That's why people discover mathematical infinity and electromagnetic waves, that's why they write symphonies.

BORIS PASTERNAK
Doctor Zhivago

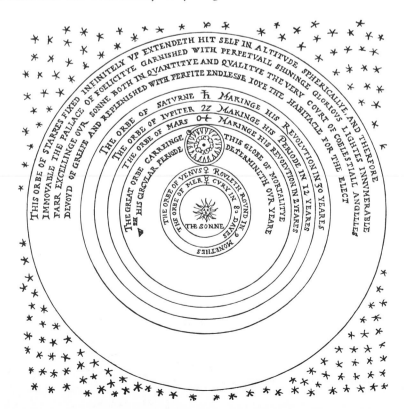

6   Modern cosmology is based on a single discovery made by Dr. Edwin Hubble in 1929. That discovery was that the universe is "expanding." With refined photographic equipment we can see literally billions of galaxies—"island universes"—and judging from the "red shift" (the Doppler effect) in their spectra, they all appear to be moving away from us at constant speeds. This expansion is the fundamental fact which any and all cosmological theories are obliged to explain.

In your mind's eye draw an imaginary sphere 1 mile in diameter and fill it with quarters and half-dollars floating about a foot apart. These coin-disks are the galaxies of our perceptual universe. If we locate ourselves at the center of this imaginary sphere, then what we observe is that all of these coin-galaxies are receding from us. Those nearer to us are moving slower; the farther away they are the greater their speed of recession from us. Out near the edge of the sphere their velocities are nearing the speed of light. When, all around the inside surface of the sphere, the galaxies reach that speed, they become invisible. Each galaxy emitting light in our direction at 186,000 miles per second, but moving away from us at 186,000 mps, would cross over the threshold of perception. Light would require infinite time to reach us; hence, it becomes invisible. This is the edge of our "perceptual universe." All galaxies reaching the speed of light would vanish from sight.

These perceptual limits we must accept, but we can't avoid wondering what lies beyond perception. If we exist in a pulsating universe, then we wonder how far the galaxies continue beyond that perceptual threshold before they begin their long journey back to the center. How much of the pulsating bubble can we actually see? Are there other bubble-universes? If so, how many? Could they possibly extend to infinity? How much space exists between the bubble-universes?

At present we can do little more than develop models which are coherent extensions of our theories about the closer parts of the universe which lie within our range of perception.

7   There are three cosmologies widely held at present: (1) the "big-bang" theory, (2) the "steady-state" theory, and (3) the "pulsating-cosmos" theory.

The big-bang theory holds that all of the matter in the universe was pulled together by gravity into one huge, hot ball—a "primordial atom"—several hundreds of light-years in diameter. As gravitational forces increased, the ball became ever more condensed. Pressure and temperature reached enormous levels. As contraction continued, there occurred a gravitational collapse amounting to an implosion. The outer layers rushed inward until they reached a critical point at which the massive cosmic ball exploded. This is the "big bang."

Matter was flung outward in all directions. Great clouds of gases and dust formed. Stars condensed from the dust clouds and pulled one

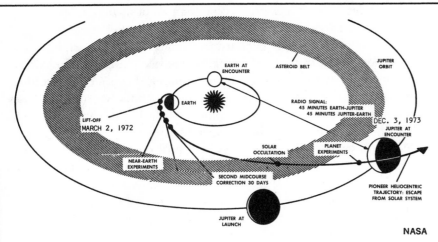

NASA

Pioneer 10 begins journey through the asteroids to Jupiter and beyond.

PIONEER 10 BEGINS JOURNEY TO JUPITER

Pioneer F (renamed Pioneer 10 after launch) finally got off on its 22-month journey to Jupiter March 2 after a four-day delay. The launch was delayed three nights by shear winds above Cape Kennedy and one night by an Air Force launch.

Other planetary payloads have been launched, but Pioneer 10 has a special ring to it. It will be the first craft to navigate through the asteroid belt (beginning in early July), and on to a rendezvous with Jupiter Dec. 3, 1973. It will then cross the orbit of Uranus in 1980 and at some point beyond the orbit of Pluto (about 5.8 billion kilometers from the sun) leave the solar system. Carl Sagan and Frank Drake of Cornell University estimate that with a residual interstellar velocity of 11.5 kilometers per second, it will take Pioneer 10 some 80,000 years to travel one parsec—about the distance to the nearest star. After mid-course correction burns early this week, Charles F. Hall, project manager of Pioneer, said the craft would exit the trailing edge of the solar system (in relation to the solar system's direction of rotation within the Milky Way galaxy). It is thought now that the craft will be headed in the general direction of the star Aldebaran. Should Pioneer 10 head for that star, it would take an estimated 1.7 million years to get there.

The spacecraft carries a plaque designed to show any intelligent civilization from another system that might intercept Pioneer 10 from what part of the galaxy and from which planet in the solar system it came and when it was launched.

The Jupiter probe left earth at a speed of 51,800 kilometers per hour—the fastest that any manmade object has ever flown. It passed the moon in 11 hours.

As a result of this week's midcourse corrections, Pioneer 10 is expected to pass within 135,000 kilometers of the surface of Jupiter and within 400,000 kilometers of Io, 300,000 kilometers of Europa and 500,000 kilometers of Ganymede, all moons of Jupiter. Three instruments aboard recorded data as the craft went through the earth's radiation belts and crossed the boundary of the earth's magnetic field.

Science News, March 11, 1972

another closer into clusters; great accumulations of matter began swirling as galaxies. This vast hodge-podge of exploded matter continued—and still continues—to journey outward from the scene of the explosion.

According to this picture, there was but a single explosion and since that time the universe has been "running down." From the time of the explosion the second law of thermodynamics (entropy) operates to dissipate energy. Living things exist only during this interim period while the fires are still burning. After that all the galaxies, stars, and planets will grow cold and die; they will float outward forever into the distant reaches of space. There will be no more heat and no more light.

8   The steady-state theory was developed by Fred Hoyle of Cambridge University. Hoyle attempted to account for the expanding universe by suggesting that matter is continually being created out of nothing in interstellar and intergalactic space. Hoyle couldn't accept the theory of a "big-bang" beginning; a one-time explosion seemed too arbitrary, too "accidental"; *unique* occurrences feel not-quite-right to scientists since they develop theories from repeated observations of regularities.

Hoyle reasoned that if matter is being continually created in space, then the "expanding universe" can be explained. The expansion is merely displacement by newly created matter.

Hoyle calculated that if one hydrogen atom is created in each cubic mile of space every hundred years, then sufficient matter is coming into existence to account for the displacement of existing matter. The creation of all other elements can also be accounted for as the hydrogen atoms combine into ever-larger accumulations of matter and develop high temperatures and pressures within star systems.

One problem with Hoyle's theory is explaining how matter can be created (create itself?) *out of nothing*. Hoyle himself neatly avoided the problem. He wrote:

> There is an impulse to ask where originated matter comes from. But such a question is entirely meaningless within the terms of reference of science. Why is there gravitation? Why do electric fields exist? Why is the universe? These queries are on a par with asking where newly created matter comes from, and they are just as meaningless and unprofitable.

Hoyle reiterates that science asks *how* things operate the way they do, but not *why*. "We must not go on to ask why, " he says. (This is a fallacious argument, incidentally, and Hoyle, like the rest of us, wants very much to ask "Why?" for elsewhere he writes: "For myself there is a great deal more about the Universe that I should like to know. Why is the universe as it is and not something else? Why is the universe here at all? . . . Throughout the history of science, people have been asserting that such and such an issue is inherently beyond the scope of reasoned inquiry, and time after time they have been proved wrong.")

When the pulsars turned up [in 1968] the Cambridge radioastronomers who discovered them were so astonished that they labelled their first records of these regular pulsars "LGM." That stood for "Little Green Men." It seemed at first less incredible to think that intelligent beings elsewhere in the universe were trying to get in touch with us, than to imagine that a star could produce this jazzy rhythm.
"The Violent Universe"
PBS–TV .

In any case, Hoyle abandoned his steady-state cosmology a few years ago. He concluded that new evidence (especially from quasars) lent strong support to some sort of explosion theory. But in admitting that his own theory was probably wrong, Hoyle proved his adherence to the highest principles of scientific objectivity.°

°Hoyle's theoretical models keep changing as new data come in, which is as it should be; but it makes it difficult to keep up with him. He has again given his support to the steady-state theory, feeling somewhat vindicated that all the new evidence has failed "to drive the nail into the coffin of the theory." So today, he says, "I'm more confident that the theory is right than I've ever been at any time in the past."

9 A third theory—the "pulsating cosmos"—is increasingly accepted as the most coherent hypothesis.

 This theory concurs with the big-bang theory that matter was shot outward in every direction by a cosmic explosion. However, the total gravitational attraction of all the mass in the universe is so great that the universe cannot "escape from itself." That is, the gravitational pull of the universe's mass is greater than the force of the explosion.

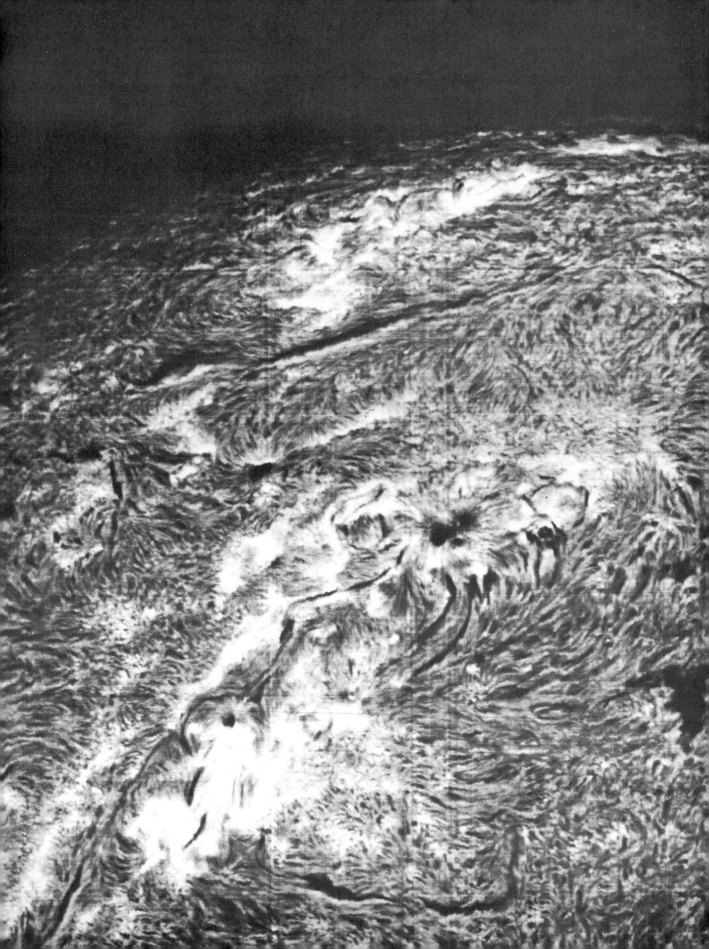

7 *Microcosm/Macrocosm/Cosmos*

Galaxies traveling outward will gradually slow down—as though there were an elastic net around the entire universe—and reverse their direction, moving back toward the center from which they were exploded. As all mass converges, it becomes again a primordial hot ball. The dynamics repeat themselves and another big bang sends matter on its way through space. Calculations indicate that explosions occur at intervals of about 80 billion years. After each explosion galaxies, stars, and planets are born and life emerges, perhaps throughout the universe. But ultimately the stars grow cold, life dies, and all matter contracts again into a hot ball.

Thus, the universe "pulsates," from explosion to explosion. A pulsating universe is anything but dead; it is a live, eternal universe, building up energy and dissipating it randomly only to build up energy again, losing nothing. Its perpetual processes are inherent and irrevocable.

We are now at a point in time about 20 billion years after the last big bang. The universe is still rapidly expanding. Some 20 billion years from now most of the galaxies will have stopped receding and begun their return journey. In 60 billion years another explosion will start the cycle again, and, perhaps, some 80 billion years hence, countless living beings will look up at the stars at night and wonder what it's all about.

10   It is interesting how closely the pulsating-cosmos theory resembles the teleocosmologies of some of man's religions. According to Hindu mythology, the god Shiva spins out the universe while he dances; when the Lord of the Dance tires, his creative activity wanes, the universe runs down, all life vanishes, and there is quiescence until Shiva revives and begins dancing again. This cosmic cycle, billions of years long, eternally repeats itself.

Similar also is the Norse cycle which ends in the Doom of the Gods (the *Götterdämmerung*), when the forces of chaos will inaugurate the final battle. In stunning contrast to most of man's religious teleocosmologies, the battle will be fought in vain. The valiant warriors of Valhalla, and even the gods themselves, will be crushed, and all life will be extinguished. Earth and cosmos will be consumed by fire. Then, after a long while, a new earth will be born, and order will be restored by the sons of Odin and Thor. Mankind too will be generated again from a human couple who will have survived the conflagration. Thus, after a fiery end, the cycle of life begins again.

11   Recent cosmologists are beginning to envision the possibility that the universe may consist not merely of a single pulsating bubble, but several bubbles or perhaps an infinite number. All that we can perceive is a portion of our own bubble-universe, but if there is one pulsating bubble, then why not more? If matter should extend infinitely, then the dynamics of pulsation must operate everywhere in similar fashion.

I think the universe is slowing down. In fact, it is slowing down so fast that sometime in the future the expansion of the galaxies will cease and contraction begin. . . . The galaxies will coalesce with one another and finally merge once again into a primeval fireball.

ALLEN SANDAGE

This multibubble universe is more gigantic than anything the human mind has heretofore tried to comprehend. Yet the more knowledge we obtain the more credible a multibubble cosmology becomes. The fact of the matter is that there is a feeling of aristocentrism about the notion that there is but a single bubble-universe—namely *ours*.

12   One aspect of the theory of relativity is that space is "curved" and that therefore we live in a "curved universe." Einstein suggested that the total gravitational force of all mass produces a universe which must be understood in terms of "curved space geometry." All objects moving in such a universe—from massive pulsars to massless photons—would follow curved trajectories. Whether the universe is curved positively or negatively (or not curved at all) has not yet been established. If negatively curved, it is an "open" universe; mass moving along gravitational lines of force would exit from our universe and vanish. But if positively curved—and there seems to be increasing indirect evidence that it is—then it is a "closed" universe curving back on itself. Mass (and photons of light) would curve in great circles through the gestalt gravitational fields.

If positive curvature is real, then visual displacement of distant objects may be far greater than we have thought. Nothing in the heavens would be where we presently "see" it. Light emitted by objects will have been bent in its journey to us. Out near the edge of our perceptual universe where galaxies are receding from us at great speeds, the objects we observe may now exist in some other part of the universe altogether; indeed, they may not now exist at all. Moreover, the speeds we observe may represent their velocities billions of years ago. Where such objects are located now, and what their velocities are, we cannot be sure. We find ourselves caught in a frustrating but exciting quandary.

We are beginning to get an idea of man's place in the cosmic picture, but undoubtedly some shattering discoveries—always the unexpected—are still in store for us.

We feel as though we've been displaced. Again. How absurd! Why must man continue to insist upon positioning himself? We are precisely where we have always been. Here.

BARBARA CHRISTIAN

I always felt that man is a stranger on this planet, a total stranger. I always played with the fancy: maybe a contagion from outer space is the seed of man. Hence, our prior occupation with heaven—with the sky, with the stars, the gods—somewhere out there in outer space. It is a kind of homing impulse. We are drawn to where we come from.

ERIC HOFFER

AND THEN WHAT HAPPENED?

There is an amusing short tale by the Irish writer Lord Dunsany (in his book *The Man Who Ate the Phoenix*) in which Atlas explains to Dunsany what happened on the day when science made it no longer possible for mortals to believe in the old Greek model of the universe. Atlas admits that he had found his task rather dull and unpleasant. He was cold, because he had the earth's South Pole on the back of his neck, and his hands were always wet from the two oceans. But he remained at his task as long as people believed in him.

Then the world, Atlas says sadly, began to get "too scientific." He decided he was no longer needed. So he just put down the world and walked away.

"Yes," Atlas says. "Not without reflection, not without considerable reflection. But when I did it, I must say I was profoundly astonished; utterly astonished at what happened."

"And what did happen?"

"Simply nothing. Simply nothing at all."

Martin Gardner
Relativity for the Million

7-5

BIOCOSMOS

1   In 1934 the British scientist Sir Arthur Eddington could write:

> Within our galaxy alone there are perhaps a thousand million stars as large and as luminous as the sun; and this galaxy is one of many millions which formed part of the same creation but are now scattering apart. Amid this profusion of worlds there are perhaps other globes that are or have been inhabited by beings as highly developed as Man; but we do not think they are at all common. The present indications seem to be that it is very long odds against a particular star undergoing the kind of accident which gave birth to the solar system.

Scientific thought has done a remarkable about-face on the possibility of the existence of extraterrestrial life. Eddington's conclusion rings to us like an outdated ethnocentrism.

The astronomer Harlow Shapley represents current thinking about the matter. He is convinced that

> sentient organisms, the product of biochemical evolution, must be a common occurrence in the universe. From general considerations of planetary origins and the evolution of chemical compounds on a cooling planet's surface, we concluded first that not less than a hundred million "high life" locations exist, and that the number is probably more like a hundred trillion. Secondly, that there is no reason not to believe that the biochemical evolution on, let us say, one half of the suitable planets has equalled or attained much greater development than here. Thus, in answer to an earlier question, we have decided that *we are not alone* in this universe. . . .

2   There are good grounds for believing that the development of life-forms through an evolutionary process is a universal operation.

In our time this search [for extra-terrestrial life] will eventually change our laws, our religions, our philosophies, our arts, our recreations, as well as our sciences. Space, the mirror, waits for life to come look for itself there.

RAY BRADBURY

The universe is old, the race of man young. There may be . . . must be . . . other races out there—or even closer to home. . . .

ROGER ZELAZNY

Assuming this to be so, Shapley and others have attempted to calculate the probabilities of evolvement of intelligent life.

Within our perceived universe we can get a fairly accurate star count. The number is in the vicinity of 10^{20} (about 100 billion billion stars). Life *on* stars seems to be out of the question because of their high temperatures, so life would most likely arise in planetary systems associated with stars. Such planets would have to move in stable, near-circular orbits which would avoid great temperature extremes. Some sort of atmosphere, the presence of some free water, and somewhat constant radiation levels might also be requisites. Within these broad parameters for tolerable conditions, it appears likely that some form of life—possibly quite alien to earth forms—will inevitably develop.

3   Shapley makes the conservative guess that perhaps one star in a thousand has a planetary system; and that perhaps one in a thousand systems has a planet with just the right temperature tolerances for life; then of these planets only one in a thousand has sufficient quantities of air and water to transform organic molecules into protoplasm.

If approached this way, Shapley writes,

we come to the estimate that only one star out of 10^{12} meets all tests; that is, one star out of a million million. Where does that high improbability of proper planets leave us? Dividing the million million into the total number of stars, $10^{20} \div 10^{12}$, we get 10^8—that is, a hundred million planetary systems suitable for organic life. This number is a minimum, and personally I would recommend . . . its multiplication by at least a thousand times, possibly by a million.

While Shapley's estimates would be considered optimistic by some theorists, it is a general concensus among the scientific community at this time that life is a common feature of our universe, and that "high life" complexes are probably fairly common. We very likely live in a biocosmos—a universe in which life is an integral part of the cosmic process itself.

4   "The only life that might be detected beyond the solar system in the foreseeable future is intelligent life." So writes a contemporary scientist.

Because of vast distances, the detection of nonintelligent life from the vantage point of our solar system is unlikely in the extreme. The probabilities are great that what we will encounter first will be *very advanced* forms of life. Any planet within a thousand light-years of the earth with an advanced culture producing great amounts of electromagnetic power we would be able to observe. There are about 10 million stars within such a radius. We could tune in any discrete interstellar or interplanetary radio emissions. Beyond these possibilities, it may be that extraterrestrials have entered the vicinity of the earth with manned craft or information probes.

5 In 1960 the National Radio Astronomy Observatory initiated Project Ozma to detect radio signals from any intelligence that might be attempting to communicate. Another attempt is being conducted at the Shternberg Observatory in Moscow. Such explorations will undoubtedly continue.

If other forms of intelligent life exist in this biocosmos, what would they look like? If we begin with a few reasonable assumptions, then we might make some plausible generalizations about appearances.

Let's make three assumptions. (1) The home planet of any "high life" would have a substantial gravity field. (2) The creature is a part of an evolutionary process and had to wrest its existence from the environment in competition with other life-forms. (3) The creature is a "protoplasmic experiment" (like us) with metabolic processes.

These would appear to be basic conditions which would apply to any life-forms we might encounter. What do these assumptions imply?

First, in any nominal gravity field the creature (if it is land-based) will have a supporting structure—an endoskeletal lattice like ours or a thick exoskeleton. It must be able to support and maintain the creature's basic shape while permitting free movement. If it should be water-based (like the octopus), then it might not have a supporting structure; it may simply float. However, we *think* that land-based life has a far better chance of developing culture and communication.

Secondly, if its heritage rests upon competitive survival techniques, then we can probably infer the following. (*a*) Its vital organs will be protected. Any sort of pumping system or gaseous cycling system would be inside some sort of protective casing where it would be less vulnerable. To have a heart located in an appendage where it could easily be lopped off would hardly be a workable arrangement. (*b*) It would have a "head." This seems believable when we note that almost every living species on earth (of a total of some $1\frac{1}{2}$ million species) has a head. The head is a center for a "guidance system" around which are clustered sensors which pick up signals from the environment. The sensors and guidance system must be positioned close to one another to permit rapid action-reaction. By contrast, think of a creature with light-sensors ("eyes") located at the ends of long appendages. If some enemy aimed a rock at the creature, by the time the distant "eye" had signaled the "brain" and the "brain" sent back a message to the appendage-eye ("Better duck!"), it could well be too late. Electrochemical messages are not that fast, so if they have to travel only short distances their efficiency is greatly increased. Also the guidance system will probably be located at some distance from the ground where it is less vulnerable and can observe more. (*c*) The creature will likely have efficient techniques for defense and attack.

HELLO, EARTH, DO YOU READ ME?

How might the first intelligence from an extraterrestrial civilization be transmitted to earth? Basing his answer on a concept originally proposed in 1961 by Cornell Astronomer Frank Drake, Electrical Engineer Bernard Oliver composed a sample universal message that could conceivably have been sent from some distant planet. The information would be contained in a series of irregularly spaced pulses picked up by radio telescopes tuned to a wave length of 21 cm. (the natural frequency of radiation from a hydrogen atom and an obvious choice of an advanced civilization). Translated into print, the message would consist of an apparently meaningless sequence of 1,271 ones (for pulses) and zeros (for gaps between the pulses).

After pondering the number 1,271, scientists of any technological society would soon recognize that it was the product of two prime numbers, 31 and 41. That would suggest that the ones and zeros might make sense if they were laid out either as 31 lines containing 41 digits each, or 41 lines of 31 digits: Breaking the message into 41 lines produces only a confusing clutter of zeros and ones, but in 31 lines (*shown above*), an organized pattern emerges. When that pattern is clarified by substituting dark spots for the ones and blank spaces for the zeros, it speaks volumes to scientific cryptographers.

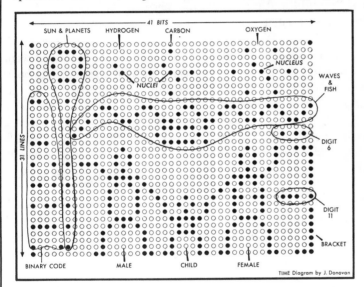

The most obvious information is that the transmitting race consists of two-legged, two-armed creatures who exist as two different sexes and care for their young. The male figure is pointing to the fourth in a line of eight dots extending directly down from a sunlike circle in the upper left portion of the diagram. Thus it can be assumed that the intelligent race lives on the fourth planet circling the distant star.

The message also makes it evident that the transmitting race has learned spaceflight. How else would it know that there is water on the third planet (as shown by the waves extending from the third dot) with aquatic life flourishing beneath it? To the left of each of the planets are dots that can easily be identified as binary numbers. By assuming that the number opposite the first planet is one, the second planet two, and so on, scientists can spot the alien binary code. Giving their imaginations free rein, they can also recognize that the three groups of dots to the right of the star represent atomic diagrams: hydrogen (with one electron circling a central nucleus), carbon (six electrons and a nucleus) and oxygen (eight electrons and a nucleus). The atoms chosen suggest that life on the distant planet is based on a carbohydrate chemistry.

Using the binary number system represented by the dots opposite the planets, it can be concluded that the three dots above the female's raised arm represent the number six and probably indicate that the alien race has six-fingered hands. Finally, the bracket at the lower right seems to measure the height of the adults and is labeled at mid-point by the binary number eleven. Because the only length that the senders and receivers know in common is the 21-cm. wave length of the transmitted signal, it can be assumed that the adults are eleven of those wave lengths, or 7½ ft. tall.

Since Drake and Oliver developed their universal code in the early 1960s, the Russians have programmed computers to recognize such binary messages, convert them into two-dimensional arrays and then perform a statistical analysis of each resulting pattern to determine if it conveys enough information to be a message from an intelligent race. Their effort should pay off in the speedy deciphering of the first extraterrestrial message—if it ever comes.

Time, December 13, 1971

Thirdly, if it metabolates, it will possess bodily openings for the ingestion of some kind of fuel. (There appears to be no good reason why any fuel-intake opening should be located near the guidance-system, except that, for some reason, in earth creatures, they generally are.) It will possess a chemical system for processing food-materials to maintain stable energy levels. Furthermore, it will undoubtedly be able to replicate, but reproduction takes such a variety of forms on earth that we can't hazard any guesses whatever about extraterrestrial sex life, if any.

Within the framework of these gross parameters, all refinements seem to depend upon variables and especially environmental niches. Creatures meeting these basic requirements could be humanoid or they could be unimaginably different. Ray Bradbury has reasoned that beings living in very thick atmospheres would probably have extremely small bodily openings to cut down on intake; but in very thin atmosphere, they would need "mouths and nose vents like barn doors."

Bradbury speculates:

> To the lonely space man, an alien woman with the above features would hardly be attractive. Right here, the entire field of esthetics looms before us. Astronautical history may depend on those concepts of beauty and utility our men take along as unacknowledged cargo to the stars. Countless books will have to be written under the general title: *Esthetics and Etiquette for Other Worlds*. Otherwise, we are in danger of mistaking a rough skin for a rough mind, a third eye for an evil eye, a cold hand for a cold and hostile heart.

6   What is man's place in the cosmos? At all points in history he has asked the question and, of course, he has received varied answers. As a better understanding of our universe has been growing, old answers have become obsolete. New answers are more realistic, but they are sometimes more painful.

Man has undergone (or is undergoing) three agonizing decentralizations. Admittedly, he has waged a perpetual struggle *against* decentralization, but our accumulating knowledge has gradually forced man to abandon his illusions about his centrality.

These three decentralizations are by nature (1) cosmological, (2) biological, and (3) psychological.

7   The *cosmological decentralization* was man's first painful reassessment of his place in the scheme of things. The evidence began to mount that the geocentric picture of our solar system was in error and that the earth is not the center of all Creation as men had hoped and religion had held. Early in the seventeenth century the Copernican theory gained ground with the observations of Galileo and the mathematical calculations of Kepler and Brahe. The battle raged between those who would defend

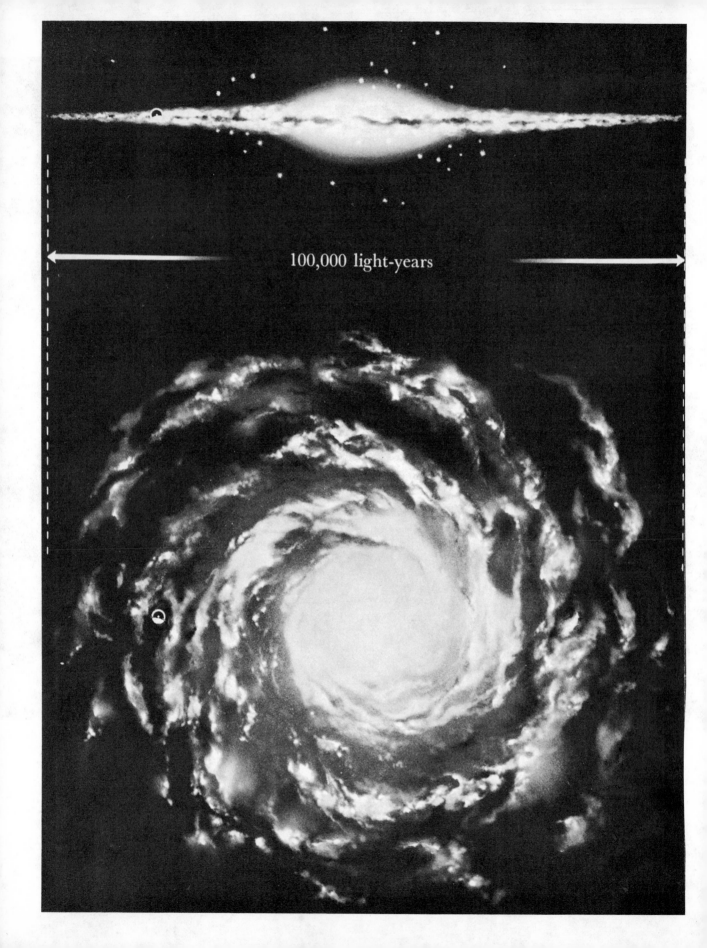

100,000 light-years

man's right to be the center of the cosmos and those who, consenting to fact, were beginning to consider the heliocentric theory. The latter theory— that the earth orbits around the sun—had been known since ancient times, and when Copernicus (1473–1543) reintroduced it there was little stir. But as evidence in support of it mounted, bitterness increased.

It was Galileo Galilei (1564–1642), a teacher of geometry and astronomy at the University of Padua, who suffered the wounds of battle. With a naive optimism, Galileo published his theories and invited scholars and churchmen to check his evidence supporting the heliocentric theory. He did not foresee the hostile reaction he received. When he invited a certain professor of philosophy at the university to look through his telescope and see for himself the moons of Jupiter, the professor merely laughed and declined. He knew, from logic alone, that Jupiter could not have moons, and he knew on theological grounds that the earth was the center of the universe and that God had assigned such significance to the number seven that there could be only seven heavenly bodies. As the professor put it,

> There are seven windows given to animals in the domicile of the head. . . . From this and many other similarities in nature, such as the seven metals, . . . we gather that the number of planets is necessarily seven. Moreover these [alleged] satellites of Jupiter are invisible to the naked eye, and therefore can exercise no influence on the earth, and therefore would be useless, and therefore do not exist. Besides [from the earliest times men] have adopted the division of the week into seven days, and named them after the seven planets. Now if we increase the number of planets, this whole and beautiful system falls to the ground.

8   Following this first cosmological displacement, three others have taken place, all minor by comparison.

The second occurred early in this century when it was discovered by astronomers that our solar system is not central in our Milky Way galaxy. Rather, it is located in a spiral arm, and this is indeed the periphery—the "south forty"—of our island universe.

The third displacement took place during the thirties when it was established that the Milky Way galaxy is only one of many island universes. We are but one of a local cluster of some two dozen galaxies; and we are an infinitessimal part of a universe composed of billions of galaxies. Our Milky Way is not central in any way that we can see, except to us.

In theory, there could be a fourth displacement: the discovery that our bubble-universe is only one of many. While much can be said for the theory, whether other pulsating universes exist is quite beyond our knowing. However, there seems to be no good reason *not* to believe that there are pulsating bubbles scattered in all directions through the Universe. To cling to the belief that there is but a single bubble-universe

I have declared infinite worlds to exist beside this our earth. It would not be worthy of God to manifest Himself in less than an infinite universe.

GIORDANO BRUNO (1548–1600)

[*Bruno was an ex-Dominican friar who became a professor of philosophy at Toulouse. For his heretical views—such as the one stated above—he was imprisoned by the Inquisition in 1593 and spent the rest of his life in prison. When ordered to recant, he refused and told his persecutors, "You're more afraid of all this than I am!" They burned him at the stake in 1600.*]

7   *Microcosm/Macrocosm/Cosmos*

rings now like another aristocentric claim. Cosmologically, we are part of the universe, which undoubtedly extends farther than we can ever know.

9   Man has also undergone a *biological decentralization.* We have considered ourselves superior to all other living creatures and believed we possessed a divine mandate to conquer, domesticate, or kill the "lower" animals. Moreover, there was a qualitative difference between man and the animals: the former had a soul, while the latter did not.

Charles Darwin brought the simmer to a boil. Shortly after his publication in 1859 of *Origin of Species,* the battlelines were drawn. The notion that man was not created as man—in distinctive Homo sapient form—and placed in the Garden by God himself; the idea that he might have developed over great spans of time from primitive animal creatures that were distinctly unhuman—this was an insult comparable to the cosmological decentralization.

The climax of the battle might be thought of as the "monkey trial" in Dayton, Tennessee, in 1925. The young science teacher, John Scopes was indicted in a test case for teaching evolution in the local high school. By the time defense attorney Clarence Darrow had shown the fallacy of the arguments against evolution and had placed William Jennings Bryan, the prosecuting attorney, on the stand, the trial had become a worldwide spectacle. Darrow lost the case, legally; but time has shown that the principle of intellectual freedom was the real victor. Since the Scopes trial we have been less disturbed that our ancestors might have been something less than totally human.

We are now undergoing another phase of the biological decentralization: it is a reassessment of our ecological status. Although our pride seems less involved in this process, we are realizing that man is but part of a system. By some criteria, we can claim to be a "superior" part of the system. We are having to admit, however, that we can't exist without the system, nor can we proceed to do whatever we wish to the fauna and flora around us. To survive we must bow to the balancing mechanisms at work within the ecosystem. Man is *not* the system; he did not *make* the system. He *belongs* to it.

10   Man is also undergoing a *psychological decentralization.* It is probably just beginning.

Until the present time nothing has challenged man's *intellectual* superiority: his capacities for abstract reasoning, communicating, knowledge-storage, and culture. These were clearly supreme. But if man must confront other intelligent forms of life, this could turn out to be the most painful "rite of passage" he will ever face. (The only greater ego-pain I can imagine would be the utterly shattering realization that the human race is irrevocably bound for extinction.)

It is enough for me to contemplate the mystery of conscious life perpetuating itself through all eternity, to reflect upon the marvelous structure of the universe which we can dimly perceive, and to try humbly to comprehend even an infinitessimal part of the intelligence manifested in nature.

ALBERT EINSTEIN

Consider the question of whether earth is the only haven for intelligent life in the universe. It is very unlikely that such is the case. On the contrary, the number of planets in the universe capable of sustaining life is believed to be enormous, perhaps as many as 10^{22}, which is about a million times greater than the total number of individual cells in the human body.

SAXON AND FRETTER

There is some likelihood that we are nearing such a confrontation. We are beginning to consider the possibility that other forms of intelligent life may exist on earth. Many of the higher primates have greater intellectual skills than we thought. Dolphins, of course, come to mind. They may possess an intelligence as great as man's but so different that we underestimate it because we don't understand it. It may turn out to be a complex intelligence deserving our sincere respect.

Man's most severe reassessment of himself will come if and when we confront extraterrestrial intelligence. Almost inevitably, *they* will contact *us,* which means that they will be far advanced compared to us. Their intelligence may be superior to man's—perhaps an I.Q. of 250 is merely bright normal to them. By comparison—however much it may hurt—the only appropriate stance for man may be one of humility.

It is often noted that science-fiction writers have prepared us, for more than a half-century now, for "future shock." Perhaps they have extended our horizons in preparation for a confrontation with intelligence so it might be less of a shock. One cannot but wonder when/if this rather ultimate "decentralization" will occur and how severe its affects may be upon man's opinions of himself.

It is most significant that the *Pioneer 10* outer-planet probe carries a plaque indicating the planet of its origin and bearing a picture of the beings that created it. The striking fact is *the explicit assumption* that other intelligent creatures might someday intercept the probe and wonder who sent it hurtling through space.

11   All these decentralizing crises which man has experienced are religious in nature, for they deal with the ultimate question of man's place in the universe and his relationships within it.

It has heretofore been a role of Western religion to affirm man's worth. Man feels inferior enough as it is. The preservation by religious institutions of the convictions that man is only just lower than the angels and that he is, in fact, a child of God has undoubtedly been both comforting and healing. Man might not have survived the struggle without the sense of worth and purpose such beliefs have given him.

Nevertheless, as a child grows he realizes that he must compromise his ego-centered nature if he is to live in the world of men. Man's decentralizations are part of his growth as a cultured species; it is a part of his humanization. To face realistically one's place in the scheme of existence offers us yet another chance to adjust to "what is." For some, accepting realities is more fulfilling than defending therapeutic beliefs. We can feel better about ourselves and others when we no longer have a need for aristocentric myth.

8

OF ULTIMATE CONCERN

8-1

OF ULTIMATE CONCERN

1   Religion is man's involvement in the meaning of existence, and the depth of one's involvement is the depth of his religion. It is participation in life in a special way for a special purpose. Religion is our attempt to find a meaningful relatedness to all the significant events of human experience. It is, as Paul Tillich phrased it, "our ultimate concern for the Ultimate."

Sometimes one finds definitions of religion which take into account only a particular set of answers to man's ultimate questions. Accordingly, religion is defined as belief in the supernatural, belief in spirits, or belief in One God; or an anthropologist might define religion as man's ritualistic expression of socially accepted beliefs and values.

But such definitions of religion miss the point. Religion is not to be defined in terms of the *answers* which men give—for they are legion—but rather in terms of the *questions* men ask. The particular local and cultural answers to which a single religious society commits itself tells us much about that group; but it is in our agonized questioning that we discover the universal religious condition of all men.

Indeed, the atheist who feels no necessity to hypothesize an Omnipotent Deity to account for the machinations of the universe is making an observation fully as ultimate, and fully as religious, as the theist who protests that the universe cannot be understood apart from belief in God.

2   Religion is not to be confused with the various forms of intellectualization which follow religious experience.

There are many paths to God, my son. I hope yours will not be too difficult.

> Words to JUDAH BEN HUR
> Ben Hur

All phases of becoming are subject to arrest. . . . Infantilism in religion results in an arrest due to the immediate needs for comfort and security or self-esteem. . . . We find many personalities who deal zealously and effectively with all phases of becoming except the final task of relating themselves meaningfully to creation. For some reason their curiosity stops at this point.

GORDON ALLPORT

As time passes and people find that they share similar convictions, doctrines develop. A *doctrine* is a formal interpretation of religious experience. Its purpose is to crystallize and preserve the fundamental elements of an experience, and to make it possible for those within the group to communicate concerning the nature of the experience. A doctrine is a social phenomenon. Those with similar beliefs are saying they belong together as part of the believing group; more than that, they are attempting to participate in the religious experience which the doctrine refers to.

As a religious institution develops, leaders emerge who are empowered to distinguish between true and false doctrines. Thus, they proclaim dogmas. A *dogma* is a doctrine which is supposed to have universal acceptance by all believers. It is a closed issue. It must be accepted as true if the particular benefits offered by the religion are to be attained.

A *creed* also is a formalization arising from religious experience. The term *creed* is from the Latin *credo*, "I believe," and a creed thus functions to distinguish believers from nonbelievers. Creeds in the form of short, capsule statements of essential beliefs are often used as membership cards and passwords.

Lastly, *theology* is the intellectualization of the totality of one's religion. Traditionally, the theologian belongs to a particular religion. He is not a "philosopher of religion" who studies, with an eye to objectivity, the religious experience of all mankind; rather he is a believer who stands within the "circle of faith," attempting to update and reinterpret the meaning of the faith for the people of his own time. Thus a Muslim theologian speaks to Muslims, a Catholic theologian speaks to Catholics, and so on.

This traditional role, however, is presently being broken and broadened. Many of today's theologians are making statements of ultimate concern which apply to all men and not merely to the members of a particular group. This change contains profound implications for the future of parochial religion.

3   Primitive man lived out his life in a world of aggressive natural forces: rainstorms, floods, forest and veld fires, locusts and famine, illness, pain and death. Most of these forces were hostile—they were "evil." But there were friendly forces, too: rain for crops, life-generating energies which brought new lambs to his flocks and new children to his family and clan, sun to make his corn grow, good winds to sail his outrigger, good conditions which filled his nets with fish. These forces were aggressive; they took the initiative; the storms, floods, and forest fires came whether he liked it or not.

These are impersonal, illusive, inconceivable forces. What caused them? What are the causal energies behind the raging hurricane or the silent, burning disease?

As we have seen, all that man can know is his own experience. He experiences his consciousness, his feelings, his will, his ideas. He also experiences a self which he does not identify with his body, so he concludes that his essence is not body but "soul."

Therefore, of necessity, the universe about him is conceived within the limits of his own experience. He cannot negotiate with unseen

We have seen the highest circle of spiraling powers. We have named this circle God. We might have given it any other name we wished: Abyss, Mystery, Absolute Darkness, Absolute Light, Matter, Spirit, Ultimate Hope, Ultimate Despair, Silence.

NIKOS KAZANTZAKIS

In a maritime community depending on the products of the sea there is never magic connected with the collecting of shellfish or with fishing by poison, weirs, and fish traps, so long as these are completely reliable. On the other hand, any dangerous, hazardous, and uncertain type of fishing is surrounded by ritual. . . . Coastal sailing as long as it is perfectly safe and easy commands no magic. Overseas expeditions are invariably bound up with ceremonies and ritual.

E. B. TYLOR

forces; he cannot even think about the inconceivable. Yet conceive them he must, for he cannot escape negotiating with them.

Therefore, in order to understand and negotiate with the forces that be, he thinks of them as consciousnesses with minds, wills, appetites, and emotions. Through a complex linguistic history, we have come to call them "spirits," and they come in many forms: demons, evil spirits, ancestral ghosts, angels, gods and goddesses, kami, jinn, and so on.

These spirits are like man, enough like him so that he can talk with them. He can cajole, threaten, complain, and bargain with them. He can understand why at times they behave with consistency (for he does) or become capricious and unpredictable (he is occasionally that way with members of his family). He can bribe them into doing him favors; he can offer them gifts of varying worth. More sophisticated spirits are believed to respond to higher, subtler forms of sacrifice: the sacrifice of one's will in obedience, or of earthly pleasures, or of one's ego.

4   These are profound processes, developed over long periods of time. They arise from man's deepest needs to survive the onslaught of the aggressive forces of nature and society. During more peaceful times, though, these personified forces can help man achieve fulfilling goals; they enable him to "grow in spirit" and become more stable, confident, and loving—a man at peace with himself.

What motivates man to colonize his universe with spirits like himself? *Survival*. The whole purpose of religion is to work out a "saving" relationship. In Judeo-Christian terms this relationship is known as "justification"—getting into a "right relationship with God." But it can be universalized: The goal of religion is to get into a right relationship with Shiva, with Allah, with Isis, with Christ, with Mithras, with Amitabha Buddha—all so that the desired end might be attained. And that end is to survive—that is, to find "salvation."

5   An interesting phenomenon often overtakes the spirits if they live a long while. They frequently become a part of a "theological complex," a system so grandiose that they are no longer accessible to the masses of men and cannot meet their daily needs. In the Greek and Roman religions the gods became so engrossed with the affairs of state that they were no longer meaningful to the common man. During the empire the great gods of the Roman pantheon were functionaries of state ceremonies, to be worshiped by emperors and other dignitaries. So distant had they become that the farmer and merchant had long since forgotten them.

The priest smiled. "What man who has lived for more than a score of years desires justice, warrior? For my part, I find mercy infinitely more attractive. Give me a forgiving deity any day."

ROGER ZELAZNY
Lord of Light

πνεῦμα, ατος, τό, (πνέω) *a blowing*, πνεύματα ἀνέμων Hdt., Aesch.: alone, *a wind, blast*, Trag., etc.   **2.** metaph., θαλερωτέρῳ πν. with more genial *breeze* or *influence*, Aesch.; λύσσης πν. μάργῳ Id.; πν. ταὐτὸν οὔποτ' ἐν ἀνδράσιν φίλοις βέβηκεν *the wind* is constantly changing even among friends, Soph.   **II.** like Lat. *spiritus* or *anima*, *breathed air, breath*, Aesch.; πν. βίου *the breath* of life, Id.; πν. ἀθροίζειν to collect *breath*, Eur.; πν. ἀφιέναι, ἀνιέναι, μεθιέναι to give up *the ghost*, Id.; πνεύματος διαρροαί *the wind-pipe*, Id.   **2.** *that is breathed forth, odour, scent*, Id.   **III.** *spirit*, Lat. *afflatus*, Anth.: *inspiration*, N.T.   **IV.** *the spirit* of man, Ib.   **V.** *a spirit*; in N.T. of *the Holy Spirit*, τὸ Πνεῦμα, Πν. ἅγιον:— also of *angels*, Ib.:—of *evil spirits*, Ib.   Hence
πνευμᾰτικός, ή, όν, *of spirit, spiritual*, N.T.
πνεύμων, in later Att. πλεύμων, ονος, ὁ, (πνέω) *the organ of* breathing, *the lungs*, Lat. *pulmo*, Il., Plat.: mostly in pl., Trag.; πνεῦμ' ἀνεὶς ἐκ πλευμόνων Eur.
πνεῦν, Dor. poët. for ἔπνεον, impf. of πνέω.
πνευστιάω, *to breathe hard, pant*, Arist.; Ep. part. πνευστιόων, Anth.
ΠΝΕ'Ω, Ep. πνείω, Ion. impf. πνείεσκον: f. πνεύσομαι, Dor. πνευσοῦμαι: aor. 1 ἔπνευσα: pf. πέπνευκα:— Like other dissyll. Verbs in -έω, this Verb only contracts εε, εει:—*to blow*, of wind and air, Od., Hdt., Att.; ἡ πνέουσα (sc. αὔρα) *the breeze*, N.T.   **II.** *to breathe, send forth an odour*, Od.:—c. gen. *to breathe* or *smell of* a thing, Anth.   **III.** of animals, *to breathe hard, pant, gasp*, Il., Aesch.   **IV.** generally, *to draw breath, breathe*, and so *to live*, Hom.; οἱ πνέοντες = οἱ ζῶντες, Soph.   **V.** metaph., c. acc. cogn. *to breathe forth, breathe*, μένεα πνείοντες *breathing* spirit, of warriors, Il.; so, πῦρ πν. Hes.; φόνον, κότον Ἄρη Aesch.; so, πνέοντας δόρυ καὶ λόγχας Ar.; Ἀλφειὸν πνέων, of a swift runner, Id.   **2.** μέγα πνεῖν *to be of* a high *spirit, give oneself airs*, Eur.; τόσονδ' ἔπνευσας Id.:—also, with a nom., as if it were the wind, μέγας πνέων Id.; πολὺς ἔπνει καὶ λαμπρὸς ἦν Dem.

If God did not exist it would be necessary to invent him.

VOLTAIRE

If there were not a Devil, we would have to invent him.

OSCAR WILDE

And so, the great gods were replaced by godlets, by the lares and penates who still had plenty of time to take care of man's mundane affairs. Pomona would look after his fruit trees, Mellona his beehives, Epona his horses, Juventa his children; and two-faced Janus still had time to act as sentinel over his door, looking after all who went in or came out of the house.

This is a common development. Whenever the deities become too great, too important—too distant in their transcendent glory—to take care of man's immediate concerns, then lesser spirits inevitably replace them and carry on their ministrations. They may be called angels, guardian spirits, genii, lares and penates, saints, bodhisattvas, or avatars of Vishnu or Shiva. But in all cases, they are concerned, responsive, and available in time of need.

News item: *This is the first step in the investigation into the bridge disaster. A public hearing will be held . . . next week. The cause may never be learned, but as Assemblyman ["Smith"] put it, "This bridge collapse was not an act of God. Someone is responsible."*

KNBC News

6   Spirits "possess" or "inhabit" people. Man has always been quite sure of this since he intuits himself to be a "spirit inside a body." If his own being is a dualism of essence and matter—soul and body—then it is only reasonable that other spirits, too, might inhabit his body.

This phenomenon—"spirit possession"—has been the universal means of accounting for the complexities of human behavior. Not only does possession explain the various forms of "insanity" and certain symptoms of illness (epileptic attacks, for instance) which we observe in others; it also accounts for the strange feelings we find inside ourselves: dizzyness, fevers, pains, convulsions. And almost all states of religious consciousness can be thus explained: ecstatic trances, visions, "conversions," "speaking in tongues," oracular phophecies, and so on. Negatively, if possessed by a bad spirit (by a demon, a witch, a jinn, or by "sin"), we can point to the cause of the evil things we do. On the other hand, when possessed by helpful spirits (Vohu Manah, the Holy Spirit, the Spirit of Allah), then we can do good things and even accomplish feats which otherwise would have been quite beyond our capability.

From earliest times special techniques have been known for exorcizing demons—for depossessing one of a bad spirit. Likewise, techniques have been used for inducing possession by good spirits. To be possessed by the "Holy Spirit" is the most valued of human experiences according to Zoroastrians, Christians, and Muslims. In some groups such a blessing would be proven by intense emotion (the "strange warming of the heart" described by John Wesley), "speaking in tongues" (among Pentecostals), or an egoless consciousness (among Catholic mystics).

Iroquois Indian Prayer

Spirit of this place, we give thee tobacco; so help us, save us from the enemy, bring us wealth, bring us back safely.

7   Men have always had experiences which they invest with ultimate significance, and often such events—from acts of courage and moments of love to visions and esthetic "highs"—effect drastic change in our lives.

We preserve the essence of an experience by reflecting on it, conceptualizing and labeling it. As time passes, the mind "processes" the

8 Of Ultimate Concern

In the year 204 B.C. Scipio Africanus sailed from Sicily to attack Hannibal's forces at Carthage. Just before the great expedition sailed, Scipio stood on his flagship at dawn and, after the herald had ordered silence, offered this prayer.

> Ye gods and goddesses, who inhabit the seas and the lands, I supplicate and beseech you that whatever has been done under my command, or is being done, or will later be done, may turn out to my advantage and to the advantage of the people and the commons of Rome, the allies, and the Latins who by land or sea or on rivers follow me, [accepting] the leadership, the authority, and the auspices of the Roman people; that you will support them and aid them with your help; that you will grant that, preserved in safety and victorious over the enemy, arrayed in booty and laden with spoils, you will bring them back with me in triumph to our homes; that you will grant us the power to take revenge upon our enemies and foes; and that you will grant to me and the Roman people the power to enforce upon the Carthaginians what they have planned to do against our city, as an example of [divine] punishment.°

Young children often attribute life to anything that is active, useful or moves of its own accord. Thus clouds, pencils, bicycles or automobiles may be considered to have life. Piaget's theory of animism states that most children outgrow these beliefs in four stages by the age of 11 or 12. . . . Alice Karmer of St. John's University in New York . . . found the correlation between age and abandonment of animistic beliefs to be less clear-cut than Piaget had predicted. Seventy of 80 subjects between the ages of 11 and 15 still held animistic beliefs.

Science News, 9–16–72

°Was Scipio's prayer answered? He shortly destroyed two great armies of Carthaginians and Numidians and went on to a decisive defeat of Hannibal in a battle near Zama on October 19, 202 B.C. There was a tradition that Scipio was a favorite of the Gods and was therefore in intimate communication with them. How does one determine whether prayers are answered if not in terms of results?

experience; it interprets it. Interpretations necessarily make use of available theological ideas and linguistic tools. What the experience "means" is therefore culturally relative, though we are not usually aware of this fact.

When attempting to understand a religious experience, there are two *kinds* of interpretations to be taken into account. One is given to the event by the experiencer himself. It will develop within the framework of his personal religious beliefs, and it is this interpretation which gives the experience meaning and affects his life.

Another interpretation, equally valid, must be made by a knowledgeable analyst or scientist. The experience may be explained in terms of motivations, emotional needs, or altered physiological states and body chemistry. Although the objective account does not pretend to include the meaning which the experience holds for the experiencer, it provides a valuable perspective for understanding one aspect of the event.

8 The word *myth* is a technical term in religious anthropology and carries none of the popular implication that it is historically false or mere imagination. By definition a "myth" is a story circulated and accepted

Ainu Prayer

O millet, thou hast grown well for us; we thank thee, we eat thee.

It seems as though the conception of a human soul . . . served as a type or model on which [man] framed not only his ideas of other souls of lower grade, but also his ideas of spiritual beings in general, from the tiniest elf that sports in the long grass up to the heavenly Creator and Ruler of the world, the Great Spirit.

E. B. TYLOR

"Out here it doesn't matter whether you're Catholic, Protestant or Jewish. I'll decide when I get home."

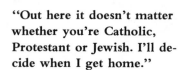

°In the history of religions a myth is a social phenomenon. However, if a story *performs the same functions* for a single individual, then the word "myth" is quite in order; and here, too, it does not carry any implication of being false or "merely imagination."

within some social group (a clan, religious community, a tribe, a nation) which gives ultimate significance and meaning to an event or explains some ultimate problem.° For example, the "Four Passing Sights" (during which Siddhartha discovered the true nature of existence by witnessing old age, disease, death, and a monk's search for the secret of life) is a myth. It "explains" to Buddhists how it happened that the man Siddhartha was drawn into the profound depths of human suffering from which he was to emerge triumphant as the "Enlightened One" (that is, as the Buddha) who had found the secret. Similarly, the Genesis account of the

8   Of Ultimate Concern

Tower of Babel explains in simple fashion the multiplicity of languages which the Amorites (later to be the Hebrews) encountered in their travels.

A "myth" is no more and no less than that: an explanatory account (which may or may not be historically accurate) which gives ultimate significance to some event. Myths are the product of man's unceasing effort to interpret meaningfully the world around him. This is further evidence for the contention that man cannot live for very long without meaning.

9   Viktor Frankl recounts a conversation between himself and a rabbi.

> He had lost his first wife and their six children in the concentration camp of Auschwitz where they were gassed, and now it turned out that his second wife was sterile. I observed that procreation is not the only meaning of life, for then life in itself would become meaningless, and something that in itself is meaningless cannot be rendered meaningful merely by its perpetuation. However, the rabbi evaluated his plight as an orthodox Jew in terms of despair that there was no son of his own who would ever say *Kaddish* [prayer for the dead] for him after his death.

Wapokomo Prayer

Let the one who put a jinx on the village die. Let him die, he who thought evil thoughts against us. Also give us fish.

"O, Great Motage, Protector of humble men, Descendant of the Great Fish, Father of the Most Terrible Volcano and Devourer of All Enemies, we humbly beg your leave to join with the Methodists."

Great Quahootze! Let me live, not be sick, find the enemy, not be afraid of him, find him asleep, and kill many of him.

But I would not give up. I made a last attempt to help him by inquiring whether he did not hope to see his children again in Heaven. However, my question was followed by an outburst of tears, and now the true reason of his despair came to the fore: he explained that his children, since they died as innocent martyrs, were found worthy of the highest place in Heaven, but as for himself he could not expect, as an old sinful man, to be assigned the same place. I did not give up but retorted, "Is it not conceivable, Rabbi, that precisely this was the meaning of your surviving your children; that you may be purified through these years of suffering, so that finally you, too, though not innocent like your children, may *become* worthy of joining them in Heaven? Is it not written in the Psalms that God preserves all your tears? So, perhaps none of your sufferings were in vain." For the first time in many years he found relief from his suffering, through the new point of view that I was able to open up to him.

10   When the *Apollo XIII* spacecraft was some fifty-six hours into its flight to the moon, an explosion in an oxygen tank blew open quad 4 of the service module.

APOLLO. OK, Houston, we've had a problem here. . . . We've had a main-B buss interval.

HOUSTON. Roger, main-B interval. OK, stand by Thirteen. We're looking at it.

APOLLO. OK, right now, Houston, the voltage is looking good. And we had a pretty large bang associated with the caution and warning there. . . . And we've got a main buss-A interval, too, showing. . . .

HOUSTON. Stand by, Jim. . . . Thirteen, Houston, We'd like you to attempt to reconnect fuel cell one to main-A and fuel cell three to main-B. Verify that quad-delta is open.

APOLLO. OK, Houston. . . . I tried to reset, and fuel cells one and three are both showing gray flags. But they're both showing zip on the flows.

HOUSTON. We copy. Thirteen, Houston, we'd like you to open circuit [to] fuel cell one. Leave two and three as is.

APOLLO. OK, I'll get to work on that.

A day later, after the spacecraft had looped around the moon and was limping homeward to earth, a course correction was necessary.

HOUSTON. Apollo Thirteen now 5,426 nautical miles out from the moon, traveling at a speed of 4,552 feet per second. . . . Less than thirty seconds away. . . . The engine is on. Stand by. . . . Ground confirms ignition.

APOLLO. We're burning. Forty percent.

HOUSTON. Houston copies. Attitude looks good at this point. . . . One minute now into the burn. . . . We've gained 451 feet per second at this time. . . . All systems are looking good. Coming up on three minutes. . . . The on-board display shows less than a minute to go in the burn now. . . . Coming up on four minutes into the burn. . . . Ten seconds to go.

APOLLO. Shut-down.

HOUSTON. Roger, shut down. . . . The engine is off. We are at 79 hours 32 minutes into the flight. . . . 5,707 nautical miles out from the moon at this time.

APOLLO. I'd say that was a good burn.

The president proclaimed Sunday, April 19, a national Day of Thanksgiving for the safe return of the astronauts. Earlier in the week the California State Senate had swiftly passed a resolution urging citizens to join in praying for the safe return of the *Apollo XIII* crew. Senator Murphy said he had learned that when you're in trouble it is wise not only to look around but to look up as well.

Frank Reynolds reported on ABC television: "In Rome the pope prayed, for which we are grateful; and in South Africa a witchdoctor did the same thing, and we are grateful for that too."

The dean of a major metropolitan cathedral prayed: "We give thanks to Almightly God for the safe return of our astronauts. . . . We

The religion of Ted Serios: *His relationship with God, which has always sustained him in the rough spots, is both intensely intimate and rather original. "God," he says, "understands me; he knows I'm human." Atheism is absolutely incomprehensible to him. "What do them guys do when they're in a tight spot," he asks, "like when the cops are layin' for them?"*

DR. JULE EISENBUD

praise Thy Holy Name that Thou hast conducted in safety through the vast vistas of space, Thy servants James, Frederick, and John, and to return them to this good Earth, our home, where Thy children dwell."

Much later a newsman asked the astronauts if they were aware of the Infinite which was looking over them. Jack Swigert replied: "If you're asking me if I prayed, I certainly did. And I have no doubt that perhaps my prayers and the prayers of the rest of the people contributed an awful lot to us getting back."

11   There is a minority report within man's religions that contends that all religions are one. Most have said this because they wanted it to be so, but some of these claims are the result of personal experience with many religious faiths.

We are not today at the point of knowing whether "all religions are one." Certainly the various Gods are thought to possess different characteristics. They behave differently and demand different responses from their worshipers.

Yet when men have experienced a religious odyssey, they commonly emerge with a feeling of oneness. It could be that our ultimate experiences are similar but become distorted in the process of interpretation. It might also be that certain universal psychophysical processes operate to produce similar experiences. Among these may be alpha rhythms and methods of self-hypnosis.

It may also be that one finds what he looks for. If he wishes to find the differences in the many religions of man, they can be found; but if one searches for the similarities which underlie man's religious approaches to the Riddle of Life, they too are there and can be found.

12   The Hindu saint Ramakrishna was born a Brahmin in Bengal and became a priest of the goddess Kali. While meditating upon her image he experienced samadhi, a trance-state he entered into repeatedly with ever-greater depth and meaning. From the beginning Ramakrishna knew that samadhi was but one of many ways of knowing God. His hunger for experience of the Divine led him to try various religions. As a Hindu he practiced yoga and worshiped in the spirit of a bhakta (that is, he sought God through faith and devotion); he in turn became a Jain, a Buddhist, a Muslim, and a Christian. As a Shakta he experienced Brahman; as a Muslim he experienced God as Allah; as a Christian he knew God in Christ.

13   There was a man who worshiped Shiva but hated all other deities. One day Shiva appeared to him and said, "I shall not be pleased with thee so long as thou hatest the other gods." The man was inexorable. After a few days Shiva again appeared to him and said, "I shall never be pleased with thee so long as thou hatest." The man kept silent. After a few days Shiva

One who has experienced this will understand something of it; it cannot be more clearly expressed, since all that comes to pass in this state is so obscure. I can only say that the soul feels close to God and that there abides within it such a certainty that it cannot possibly do other than believe.

ST. THERESA OF AVILA

again appeared to him. This time he appeared as Hari-har, namely, one side of his body was that of Shiva, and the other side that of Vishnu. The man was half pleased and half displeased. He laid his offerings on the side representing Shiva, and did not offer anything to the side representing Vishnu. Then Shiva said, "Thy bigotry is unconquerable. I, by assuming this dual aspect, tried to convince thee that all gods and goddesses are but various aspects of the one Absolute Brahman."

RAMAKRISHNA

14   The Muslim mystic Ibn Arabi is quoted as saying:

There was a time when I took it amiss in my companion if his religion was not like mine, but now my heart admits every form. It is a pasture for gazelles, a cloister for monks, a temple for idols, a Ka'aba for the pilgrim, the tables of the Law, and the sacred book of the Quran. Love alone is my religion, and whithersoever man's camels turn, it is *my* religion and *my* faith.

8-2

TELEOCOSMOS

1   Finding Dr. Faustus in his study, Mephistopheles recounted to him the story of creation.

The endless praises of the choirs of angels had begun to grow wearisome; for, after all, did he not deserve their praise? Had he not given them endless joy? Would it not be more amusing to obtain undeserved praise, to be worshipped by beings whom he tortured? He smiled inwardly, and resolved that the great drama should be performed.

For countless ages the hot nebula whirled aimlessly through space. At length it began to take shape, the central mass threw off planets, the planets cooled, boiling seas and burning mountains heaved and tossed, from black masses of cloud hot sheets of rain deluged the barely solid crust. And now the first germ of life grew in the depths of the ocean, and developed rapidly in the fructifying warmth into vast forest trees, huge ferns springing from the damp mould, sea monsters breeding, fighting, devouring, and passing away. And from the monsters, as the play unfolded itself, Man was born, with the power of thought, the knowledge of good and evil, and the cruel thirst for worship. And Man saw that all is passing in this mad, monstrous world, that all is struggling to snatch, at any cost, a few brief moments of life before Death's inexorable decree. And man said: "There is a hidden purpose, could we but fathom it, and the purpose is good; for we must reverence something, and in the visible world there is nothing worthy of reverence." And Man stood aside from the struggle, resolving that God intended harmony to come out of chaos by human efforts. And when he followed the instincts which God had transmitted to him from his ancestry of beasts of prey, he called it Sin, and asked God to forgive him. But he doubted whether he could be justly forgiven, until he invented a divine Plan by which God's wrath was to have been appeased. And seeing the present was bad, he made it yet worse, that thereby the future might be better. And he gave God thanks for the strength that

People are going to look for answers in their spiritual questing even if it means going off the beaten path to do it.

MARCUS BACH

A one-planet deity has for me little appeal.

HARLOW SHAPLEY

enabled him to forgo even the joys that were possible. And God smiled; and when he saw that Man had become perfect in renunciation and worship, he sent another sun through the sky, which crashed into Man's sun; and all returned again to nebula.

"Yes," he murmured, "it was a good play; I will have it performed again."

2   Men have rarely been able to shake the feeling that they are participants in a sweeping drama, and that their lives are a vital part of its plot. After all, man's macrocosmic existence has a sort of story line: he is born, and then proceeds physically through childhood, adolescence, and stages of adulthood. All living things around him seem to share this developmental sequence, and even "nature" goes through a birth-life-death cycle: spring-summer-winter, dawn-day-night, the lunar phases. "Everything has a pattern"; it must have meaning.

Of even greater significance is the fact that man is not alone. He exists in a universe filled with supernatural spirits with perhaps a Supreme Spirit, and these beings have a human characteristic: they play—and they fight, and play tricks, and scheme (note the Greek Olympians). They interact with human beings (note the love life of the shepherd god Krishna), and we humans become a part of their plans; we may even become the central concern or the principal characters in the cosmic drama.

Man's own search for meaning is so intense that he is more than willing to be cast in whatever cosmic dramas there be.

3   Man intuits and knows that he belongs to a teleocosmos. Teleo-cosmic programs have existed in all of man's religions, from the simplest to the most sophisticated; and they have developed with mighty effort in the Riddle-challenging minds of theologians and philosophers. Since man's need to interpret just about everything is irrepressible, his selective interpretation of the events of life take on dramatic structure. Somewhere he will find a basis for a story line, a plot, a plan, an apocalyptic drama, a goal-directed scheme, even a conspiracy (see the Book of Job, for instance).

By merely being born he was cast in the play, and his role is to be taken seriously, for how well he performs his given role affects the quality of his life and determines his destiny. There is no wonder that he attempts again and again to clarify the teleocosmic plot so that he can be a better performer. There appear to be some real and natural teleocosmic patterns that we are inherently part of, such as the evolutionary, ecological, and individual physical and psychic developmental sequences. But the teleocosmic dramas most familiar to us are theological and have their origins in the Western family of religions: Zoroastrianism, Judaism, Christianity, and Islam. They are *linear* and *historical*.

The current wave of interest in the occult is partly a way of saying that there is more to the world than the gods of science have let us know about. This isn't to say that the old gods are being restored; the new spirituality is as anti-institutional church as it is anti- or post-scientific. It is to say that we now know that there are more things in heaven and earth than are dreamt of in your philosophies, Aristotle, Thomas, and Newton.

EDWARD B. FISKE

4   The Judaic teleocosmos began (for man) in the Garden of Eden. This was paradise and the tenants were perfect, companions and children of God. This is the opening scene of the drama, and the final scene is a return to Eden—to paradise and perfection. By the time the concept had been filled out with details the Hebrews had ceased to be a wandering tribe and had become a nation. The final scene of the plot was therefore envisioned as a "messianic age" in which the nation Israel, or at least a faithful Remnant, would reign supreme over all the earth. Truly it would be a paradise, for peace would be forever and prosperity would surpass belief. As one fragment of late Jewish literature put it, every grapevine would bear a thousand clusters, and every cluster would bear a thousand grapes, and every grape would yield a gallon of wine.

Between these opening and closing scenes lies human existence as we know it, with suffering and death. It is only too likely that this is the only condition evolutionary man has ever known; but we find profound satisfaction in the conviction that there was a time when everything was all right and that we can anticipate a future setting in which all will be made right again.

5   Being an offspring of Judaism, Christianity adopted about the same beginning to the drama—the garden paradise of Eden. Christians, however, added a new element. Along the time-line of human existence, there came a moment when life was suddenly given meaning by the intervention of the Creator deity himself. Until the advent of the redeemer god, the Christ, human suffering had been pointless; it counted for nothing. But after his appearance, human suffering became a "trial by fire" to create spiritually worthy souls who, collectively, would compose a "communion of saints" to bear witness until they could join together in the Kingdom of God. Nevertheless, human suffering will continue until the final act of the drama, when the Reign of God begins with the Parousia, the Return of the Messiah. "For the Lord himself, at the summons, when the archangel calls and God's trumpet sounds, will come down from heaven, and first those who died in union with Christ will rise; then those of us who are still living will be caught up with them on clouds into the air to meet the Lord, and so we shall be with the Lord forever" (I Thess. 4:16f.).

For early Christians (and adventist groups of any century) this is the joyous fulfillment of God's plan. With a climactic crescendo—full orchestra and chorus—it closes out the tragic drama and opens the Reign of God.

6   The cosmology of the New Testament is essentially mythical in character. The world is viewed as a three-storied structure, with the earth in the centre, the heaven above, and the underworld beneath. Heaven is the abode of God and of celestial beings—the angels. The underworld is hell, the

We would be a lot safer if the Government would take its money out of science and put it into astrology and the reading of palms. I used to think that science would save us. But only in superstition is there hope. I beg you to believe in the most ridiculous superstition of all: that humanity is at the center of the universe, the fulfiller or the frustrater of the grandest dreams of God Almighty. If you can believe that and make others believe it, human beings might stop treating each other like garbage.

KURT VONNEGUT JR.

In the long run men give their supreme loyalties to overall patterns of life, to those ideas and attitudes concerning the nature of the world and of life, which provide them with incentive and direction for living. These patterns of thought and action commonly have gone by the name of religion. Their importance is evidenced by the fact that no human society of any size is long without them, and by the fact that they outlive nations and governments.

ARTHUR E. MORGAN

place of torment. Even the earth is more than the scene of natural, everyday events, of the trivial round and common task. It is the scene of the supernatural activity of God and his angels on the one hand, and of Satan and his daemons on the other. These supernatural forces intervene in the course of nature and in all that men think and will and do. Miracles are by no means rare. Man is not in control of his own life. Evil spirits may take possession of him. Satan may inspire him with evil thoughts. Alternatively, God may inspire his thought and guide his purposes. He may grant him heavenly visions. He may allow him to hear his word of succour or demand. He may give him the supernatural power of his Spirit. History does not follow a smooth unbroken course; it is set in motion and controlled by these supernatural powers. This aeon is held in bondage by Satan, sin, and death (for "power" is precisely what they are), and hastens towards its end. That end will come very soon, and will take the form of a cosmic

catastrophe. It will be inaugurated by the "woes" of the last time. Then the Judge will come from heaven, the dead will rise, the last judgement will take place, and men will enter into eternal salvation or damnation.

This then is the mythical view of the world which the New Testament presupposes.

RUDOLF BULTMANN

7 The Indian teleocosmos is cyclical. All creatures alike are bound to the Wheel of Karma, which symbolizes the transmigration of souls (*samsara*) from one painful existence to another. Both Hindus and Buddhists believe that to exist is to suffer: existence *is* suffering. Therefore, one endures each incarnation as a temporary state during which he is to follow prescribed rules on how to gain merit (good karma) so that

Imagine how the Christian conscience would react to the idea that, behind the scenes, God and the Devil were the closest friends but had taken opposite sides in order to stage a great cosmic game. Yet this is rather much how things stood when the Book of Job was written, for here Satan is simply the counsel for the prosecution in the court of Heaven, as faithful a servant of the court as the advocatus diaboli at the Vatican.

ALAN WATTS

his subsequent reincarnation will be higher in the scale of being. All creatures will be reborn a sufficient number of times until good karma has been accumulated and he can reach liberation (*moksha*) from the Wheel of Karma and enter into the blissful state of nirvana.

Thus, as the Wheel of Karma turns, all creatures, from the lowest demons and animals to the castes of men, are moving up through the levels of incarnation.

This has long been a most meaningful world-scheme. However tragic a single life might be there is always hope, for one will become incarnate repeatedly until release from the Wheel is achieved. As one practices *dharma* ("duty") or *bhakti* ("faith" or "devotion"), he has a hand in determining his status in the cosmic drama. His freedom is real: even for the lowliest creature, there is hope that the round of rebirths can be broken and the Wheel will cease its turning.

8   Platonic idealism is an example of a vertical teleocosmic philosophy. It contrasts with the linear and cyclical systems of Western and Indian religion.

The development of Plato's philosophy is the story of one man's search for Absolute Truth, and Plato discovered (or received the insight from Pythagoras) that only mathematical and geometrical statements are absolutely true. Empirical observations give us only "a likely story"—that is, probable knowledge—and Plato wanted more than this. Furthermore, he was aware that mathematical/geometrical truths exist only in thought. While these mathematical/geometrical systems must *assume* the existence of *perfect* circles, triangles, and straight lines, the "circles," "triangles," and "straight lines" we draw on wax tablets or paper are anything but perfect. Absolute Truth, therefore, exists only in thought.

But whence such perfect knowledge? Surely it cannot originate from our finite human minds. Such Truths, Plato concluded, must exist as real *idein* ("ideas," "thoughts," or "forms") quite apart from our minds.

Plato's philosophy now becomes *vertically teleological*. One who seeks Truth is obliged to move away from the "unreal" objects of sense and seek a companionship with the absolutes of philosophical thought. Only in Truth can man actualize his rational potential. This is his destiny and his fulfillment.

This teleocosmic philosophy was transformed into a mystical religion by Neoplatonists in the third century A.D. The Alexandrian scholar Plotinus made Plato's philosophy a way of salvation. By practicing meditation and asceticism, man can move out of the world of gross and evil matter—Plotinus himself was frightfully embarrassed at having to dwell in a human body at all—and find a mystical oneness with the Triune Godhead. So the Absolute Truth of Plato's philosophy becomes, in Plotinus' system, the *idein* or thoughts of God. Therefore, as one lives more with Platonic abstractions, he also becomes one with God. Our task is to think God's thoughts.

The implication is the same for Plato's philosophy and Plotinus' mystification of Plato's philosophy: Man is "called" to move out of the (unreal) real world and dwell in the world of Absolute Truth/Mind of God.

9   After the maddening chaos of the first half of the twentieth century, there has been a renewed interest in the philosophy of history. The turn of world events has sent men back to reexamining their experience in an attempt to make sense out of what, in the wake of a series of world tragedies, has seemed senseless. All too clearly, contemporary history sounds like "a tale told by an idiot, full of sound and fury, signifying nothing." Is this assessment realistic? Or does human history have a deeper meaning which man in his frenzied state has overlooked? Perhaps there are significant patterns, repetitive cycles, or dialectical movements indicating purpose and direction. In our attempt to find meaning on a cosmic scale, we may have reached too far. Perhaps *human history* is teleological, and we missed it.

10   The first great Western philosopher of history was Saint Augustine. He was prompted to write *The City of God* after the fall of the city of Rome to Alaric and his Goths in A.D. 410. This incredible event so shook the Roman world that it had to be interpreted. It was a meaningful event; there had to be meaning behind it. While the pagan Romans were complaining that the tragedy was divine punishment for the abandonment of the old Roman gods, Augustine took up his pen to show that Rome had fallen as a part of a long-range divine plan. God had not merely tolerated the degenerate city, but had used the City of Earth to accomplish his ends; for out of that City of Earth there had developed the Church to represent the Kingdom of God on Earth. When that city's task of giving birth to the Church was accomplished, then the City of Earth (Rome) would be replaced by the City of God (the Roman Church).

Therefore, in the fullness of time, the plan of God was manifesting itself on the historical plane. The City of Earth had fallen to give way to the City of God.

11   Two influential teleological philosophies of history have dominated modern times: Hegel's dialectical idealism and Marx's dialectical materialism.

Friedrich Hegel was convinced that he had discovered the nature of thought and that he had made a unique discovery. The thought process moves in a three-beat rhythm, which he called the "dialectic." It begins with an idea, a thesis, then proceeds to develop its opposite, the antithesis; after that the mind sees the relatedness of thesis and antithesis and weaves them together into a synthesis. This synthesis, in turn, becomes a thesis, and the dialectic continues. Thus the dialectic effects an ever-expanding comprehension of the connections of the contents of thought.

Hegel was quite sure that this is the way God's mind works. God is pure thought, or, in Hegel's words, the Absolute Mind. Here is no love or compassion (no emotion), just pure thought. The Absolute Mind of God manifests reason through the mind of man and therefore in human history. Whenever men think and act more rationally they are actualizing God's will, and this progressive manifestation of logic is the teleological purpose underlying human history.

Man is a crucial part of this program, and there was reason to believe, Hegel thought, that man was becoming more reasonable, especially in nineteenth-century Germany. All of this would end in a state which Hegel described as "pure thought thinking about pure thought"—Absolute Mind contemplating itself.

12   Hegel's novel way of interpreting history caught the minds of students in the German universities; but while the idea of the dialectic excited them, the notion of an Absolute Mind behaving like an Analog Computer left them cold.

Karl Marx was one of these students. Following the lead of another young philosopher named Feuerbach, Marx developed a philosophy of history, around the idea of a dialectical movement, operating in terms of the basic material essentials of life. Marx's dialectic is indeed real, but it is a dialectic of social struggle determined by man's economic needs. Class struggle creates the three-beat rhythm. Marx's interpretation is a "materialistic dialectic" in contrast to Hegel's theistic dialectic.

Thus Marx laid the foundations for a teleological interpretation of history which has come to dominate half the world. All Marxians know that history has purpose; it follows "inexorable law" toward a goal—the Classless Society where justice and plenty will prevail (which is a down-to-earth version of the Kingdom of God). Each individual is a part of history's drama. As in other teleocosmic dramas, each person must decide whether he will fight on the side of the Righteous (the revolutionaries who actively hasten history toward its appointed end) or on the side of the Wicked (the bourgeois reactionaries who resist change and progress).

13   Man is a creature of hope, and his teleocosmic dreams almost always foresee a future time when life will be good again and there will be no more fear, pain, loneliness, and death. It is here that man reveals his deepest pessimism. He intuits that he cannot bring about such conditions by himself, so he envisions supernatural beings who will appear on earth at their appointed times to call a drumroll for the last act of the teleocosmic drama.

Judaism looks forward to the coming of the *Messiah* (the "Anointed One"). According to one interpretation, the nation Israel will be established by God as the Chosen Light to the gentiles to rule over

them forever. According to another interpretation, the Son of Man will appear to usher in a spiritual Messianic Age.

Christians came to believe that *Jesus the Christ* (again, the specially "Anointed One") will return and supervise the Last Judgment, the separation of the righteous from the wicked. He will represent God himself when the Reign of God begins.

In Buddhism, *Maitreya* is at present a Buddha-in-the-making, waiting to come to earth in due time to inaugurate the final age and bring peace. In Hinduism, a messiah named *Kalki* will make his appearance riding a white horse and brandishing a flaming sword. This savior, the tenth avatar of Vishnu, will save the righteous and destroy the wicked at the end of the fourth (hopelessly depraved) world period.

In Zoroastrianism, a messiah called *Soshyans* will appear in the final days and preside over a general resurrection. A flood of molten metal will pour across the earth, purging the wicked of their evil but bathing the righteous in soothing balm. Ahura Mazda will hurl the Evil One, Ahriman, into a lake of fire, and the saved will then dwell together in a new heaven and a new earth, enjoying eternal peace. (Incidentally, in this particular drama, adults will remain forever at the age of forty and children at fifteen.)

In Islam, the Shi'ites await a messianic figure entitled the *Mahdi* to complete the task, begun by Muhammad, of carrying the message of salvation to all mankind. This "Divinely Guided One" will usher in a period of peace before the end of the world and the onset of the Last Judgment.

The Mahayana and Christianity have two intuitions in common. . . . They both accept Suffering as an opportunity for acting on the promptings of Love and Pity. And they both believe that this ideal is practicable for Man because the trail has been blazed for Man by a Supreme Being who has demonstrated his own devotion to the ideal by subjecting himself to the Suffering that is the necessary price of acting on it.

ARNOLD TOYNBEE

14   In linear/historical plots, we find that those who believe in a climax to the drama rather universally believe that they are living near the end of the play. Their undying hope is that the dramatic last scene will be acted out during their lifetime.

> Periods of unusual stress, attended by wars and other calamities, always bred a swarm of apocalyptic ideas and prophecies of the impending end of time; this was true of the Reformation, the Peasants' Revolt, the English, French, and American Revolutions, the American Civil War, and the two World Wars.

There is an old story that John Knox was interrupted by his wife in a midnight prayer for Scotland. The wife pleaded with her husband to seek rest from a terrible agony of intercession. Knox rebuked her with the reply that through his prayer he already had won half of Scotland and that, if she had not broken in upon him, he would have won it all by daybreak.

FRANCIS J. MC CONNELL

15   Many interpreters have so deciphered the symbols of Daniel and Revelation as to fix definite dates for the second advent. . . . Militz of Kromeriz, a precursor of Huss, set the end between 1365 and 1367; during the Hussite Wars the Bohemians expected the parousia (return of Christ) to occur immediately. The Bohemian Taborites selected five cities to be spared from the general conflagration, multitudes flocking thither and establishing communistic orders. The Anabaptists expected the event to occur in connection with the Peasants' War of 1525; following this revolt Melchoir Hofmann announced himself as one of the two witnesses of Rev. 11:3, took possession of Münster, at the head of a band of fanatics, and set up "New Zion" therein until the movement was suppressed by force. Alsted, in Germany, named 1694, and the French theologian Jurieu chose 1689. The Fifth Monarchy Men attempted in 1657 and 1661 to set up the throne of "King Jesus" by arms. A girl of the German Ronsdorf sect experienced a series of visions and announced that the event would occur in 1730; she was the mother of Zion and woman clothed with the sun of Rev. 12:1; she and her husband were the two slain witnesses, and one of their children was to be the savior of the world.

APOCALYPTIC TIME

In 1881 Claas Epp, a leader of the Mennonite Brethern (Bruedergemeinde) in Russia, announced himself as one of the two witnesses, and prepared to meet Elijah in the skies and with him proceed to heaven. Christ was to appear on March 8, 1889, the date being fixed by an old wallclock on which the hands pointed to 89. When 1889 passed without any cosmic happening, Epp was informed in a vision that the clock leaned slightly, and when stood erect the hands pointed to 91; hence the correct advent date was 1891. Epp finally claimed to be a son of Christ, a fourth person of the Godhead, and adopted a baptismal formula of Father, Sons, and Holy Ghost.

ELMER T. CLARK
The Small Sects in America

Date-setting continued through the nineteenth century. The German theologian Bengel fixed upon 1836. The theosophist Schönherr was certain that Napoleon was the antichrist and Königsberg the doomed city of Rev. 17:9ff. In 1826 Christoph Hoffmann undertook to rebuild the temple in Jerusalem for Christ's occupancy. The Irvingites of England and Scotland announced 1835, 1838, 1864, and 1866. Mother Ann Lee and her Shakers were so sure the end was at hand that they abolished matrimony, following Paul's advice to the Corinthians. The Plymouth Brethren specified no exact date, but their historian declared that "if anyone had told the first Brethren that three quarters of a century might elapse and the Church be still on earth, the answer would probably have been a smile, partly of pity, partly of disapproval, wholly of incredulity." William Miller, founder of the modern Adventist sects, declared in 1844 that he had the names and addresses of three thousand preachers who were proclaiming the imminence of the end. . . .

It has been said that more than a hundred speculators predicted that the advent would occur within the decade following the end of the American Civil War. The Mormons went to Utah to await the return of Christ. Cunninghame named 1839 or a period near that date. The famous William Miller named 1843 and then 1844. Elliott and Cumming looked for the end in 1866. Brewer and Decker predicted 1867, an anonymous pamphlet published in 1871 argued for 1873, and Seiss favored 1870. "Pastor" Russell taught that the millennium began in 1873, the apostles were raised in 1878, and the end would come in 1914. Guinness was certain that earthly affairs could not endure beyond 1923.

ELMER T. CLARK

And when you hear of wars and rumors of wars, do not be disturbed . . . the end is not yet.

MARK 13:7

"Yes," he murmured, "it was a good play; I will have it performed again."

8-3

ULTIMATE REALITY

1   The Ethiopians make their gods black-skinned and snub-nosed; the Thracians say theirs have blue eyes and red hair. If oxen and horses had hands and could draw with their hands and make works of art just as men do, then horses would draw their gods to look like horses, and oxen like oxen—each would make their bodies in the image of their own.

XENOPHANES

2   The questions which we ask about Ultimate Reality are always phrased in terms of our own particular world-view, of course; and the questions which have meaning to a Hindu or Buddhist may be meaningless to a Christian or Muslim. Problems about Ultimate Reality cannot be made intelligible apart from the thought-framework within which they are posed.

The questions which we in the West ask are deceptively simple: Does God exist? What is he like? How can we know what he wants of us?

In Eastern religion, the Hindu might ask: What is the true nature of the Ultimate Reality that lies beyond the gods? Is the world of physical matter merely illusion? How can I attain liberation from the round of rebirths? The Buddhist might ask: Is it really true, as the Buddha claimed, that to exist is to suffer? If so, how can I escape suffering and attain enlightenment?

Other, Far Eastern worshipers might ask: What is the true way of life—the Tao? How can I best seek the Tao so that my life may be peaceful and full? What does Heaven want of me?

We are all children in a vast kindergarten trying to spell God's name with the wrong alphabet blocks.

TENNESSEE WILLIAMS
Suddenly Last Summer

Most intellectual people do not believe in God, but they fear him just the same.

WILHELM REICH

3 Philosophy is neither theology—which attempts to make religion intellectually meaningful—nor evangelism—which attempts to persuade others to believe. Rather, philosophy's concerns are primarily metaphysical and epistemological. *Metaphysical:* What is Ultimate Reality? How many orders of reality exist? Is there a supernatural order of reality? Do deities and spirits exist? Does God exist? In fact, what exactly is meant by such terms? *Epistemological:* Can we humans who belong to the natural order know that which belongs to the supernatural order? If so, how? Does God (or do the gods) "reveal"? Does he reveal a person (as some Christian theologians claim) or a data content? How can we be sure about the source of supernatural fact-claims mediated through human beings?

4 The images of deity which men hold are largely the product of particular circumstances of time and place. Western religions of Near Eastern origin conceive deity as male. We ask if *he* exists and we speak of a *father*-god. The majority of men, however, have imagined their deities to be feminine, and to these goddesses they have prayed for intercession, tender care, love, and life-generating energies.

The Judeo-Christian God is necessarily masculine since our god-concepts originated in the bedouin sheikdoms that wandered out of

The most beautiful and most profound emotion we can experience is the sensation of the mystical. It is the sower of all true science. He to whom this emotion is a stranger, who can no longer stand rapt in awe, is as good as dead. That deeply emotional conviction of the presence of a superior reasoning power, which is revealed in the incomprehensible universe, forms my idea of God.

ALBERT EINSTEIN

the Arabian desert into the Fertile Crescent. The gods of these nomadic clans were modeled after the sheik chieftain. They were strongly masculine deities, associated with the aggressive forces of nature—volcanoes, earthquakes, storms—and with intertribal battles. Rarely, if ever, does the concept of a female deity evolve in a bedouin society with patriarchal dominance. The early Hebrew god Yahweh exhibits the characteristics of the sheik chieftain. He is authoritarian in monitoring the loyalty pledged to him by his followers. He is stern, demanding, and quick to punish backsliding. He is a "jealous God" who will tolerate no competition from other gods. This early Hebraic world was patriarchal and the survival qualities necessary in a deity were authority and firmness; he must be quick to anger and of mighty power in battle. The blood-covenant binding the deity to his tribe (Exodus 24:4–8) is basically bedouin: he will be their leader and protector as long as they obey and "keep the covenant."

By contrast, where sprawling vineyards cover the hillsides and the valleys shelter fields of grain and fruit trees, here we are more likely to find the goddesses and their consorts. In gentler climes and social settings, the qualities associated with feminine roles—love, fertility, nurturance—are more valued than the fearsome, bellicose qualities of the desert deities. These female deities are at once Earth-mothers, fertility-goddesses, and sacred virgins. As Earth-mothers they generate the life-giving forces that underlie the birth and growth of all living things. As fertility goddesses they symbolize conception, and by means of mystery rites, temple prostitution, and spring festivals, they can be persuaded to stimulate fertility in man's clans, flocks, and crops. As eternal virgin-goddesses their primary purpose is to symbolize purity and to merit the devotion of mortal men.

5   When deities are considered to be male, then they frequently mate with mortal women. Zeus was forever entangled in amorous affairs, and the shepherd-god Krishna spent much of his time in the company of beautiful milkmaids. In Zoroastrian myth, the seed of Zoroaster, preserved for thousands of years in a crystal-pure lake, will impregnate three virgins who are to appear at intervals of three thousand years; they will give birth to the savior-gods for each period of human history, the last being Soshyans, who will inaugurate the Last Judgment.

In Buddhist myth, a male Bodhisattva (savior-being) placed his reflection in the womb of Queen Maya. In her tenth month of pregnancy she gave birth to the Buddha from her right side. Her case was both a virgin-conception and a virgin-birth. We can follow the sequence of historical development by inverting this order of thinking: Buddhist apologists began with the undeniable facts of the Buddha's existence and his birth from a mortal mother. Since the Buddha's paternity was known (from doctrinal tradition) to have been divine, the supernatural parent must, of course, be male. This is a rather obvious line of logic. In similar fashion, the Holy Spirit which impregnated the Virgin Mary must be conceived in human minds as an aspect of the masculine Father-God.°

This enigma—the virgin-conception by Mary—has produced more doctrines and convened more councils than any other event in Western history. The idea of a male deity mating with a mortal maiden to produce what would logically be a God-man—half-God, half-man—is a common enough motif in man's religions, but the soteriological complexities of the Christian version required centuries of analysis and debate. Is this "son of God" himself man or God or both? Throughout the first four centuries of Christianity there were churchmen who held that he was *solely* God or *solely* man, but the doctrine that he was both God and man finally prevailed. This conclusion, however, merely posed further problems. If he was both, then how did his divine nature relate to his human nature? And what was the relationship of the divine nature in Jesus to the divine nature in the Father? (The Council of Nicea settled these questions in A.D. 325: the churchmen reaffirmed his dual nature and concluded that the divine nature in the Son and the Father were "in essence" the same.) What about will? If he was both God and man, did he have two distinct wills? (This problem—the "monothelite" controversy—was settled at a council in Constantinople in A.D. 681: Jesus has two wills, the divine and the human, but the human will was subservient in all things to his divine will.) And what of Mary? If Jesus was wholly God as well as wholly man, does this not mean that Mary was the mother of God? (The Council of Ephesus in A.D. 431 answered yes. She is properly designated *Theotokos,* "the bearer of God."°)

6   When we find ourselves theologically entangled in mundane human relationships such as these, it is easy to lose our philosophical perspective. But if we can survive the subtleties of such debates, we may

°I have heard it argued that the Holy Spirit is not masculine, but neuter (the Greek word for "spirit," *pneuma,* is neuter); but such rationales only emphasize the uneasiness we feel about the problem of anthropomorphism and the difficulty we humans have in conceiving our deities in any way other than as male and female. (I choose to ignore for the present Aristophanes' famous eulogy of the hermophroditic condition in Plato's *Symposium.*)

°St. Jerome, who is best known for his translation of the Scriptures into Latin (the *Vulgate*), had a friend named Paula whose daughter Eustochium took the vows of a nun and thus became "a bride of Christ." Jerome considered Mary to be the Mother of God, and he habitually addressed Paula as the mother-in-law of God. This is not the only case, however, where a god had a mother-in-law. Demeter, for instance, was Pluto's mother-in-law after Persephone became the bride of the king of Hades.

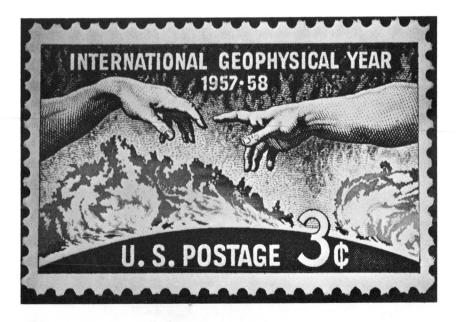

INTERNATIONAL GEOPHYSICAL YEAR 1957·58

U. S. POSTAGE 3¢

feel that our anthropomorphizing has gone too far. Xenophanes observed very early that "mortals suppose that the gods have been born, that they have voices and bodies and wear clothing like men"; he complained that "Homer and Hesiod attributed to the gods all sorts of actions which when done by men are disreputable and deserving of blame—such lawless deeds as theft, adultery, and mutual deception."

The supernatural figures of our great living religions may be ethically and spiritually nobler, but their anthropomorphic qualities are just as human as those shared by the Olympian gods and goddesses.°

°Note also our habit of anthropo-morphizing our animal friends. See pages 355ff.

7 Much thought has been given to the problem of divine knowledge by other Western philosophers who were aware of our anthropomorphic manner of thinking.

Philo of Alexandria (fl. c. A.D. 40) contended that *no* qualities conceivable by the human mind can be attributed to God. God, that is, cannot be *thought* about. Whenever we think we are thinking about God, we are merely "deifying" human qualities. All we can do, Philo concluded, is to say what God is not.

Around the year A.D. 500 an anonymous writer called Pseudo-Dionysius (his writings were for a time attributed to a certain Dionysius mentioned by Saint Paul) decided that there are two ways of knowing God. Following the positive way, we can collect the qualitative concepts which we apply to man—man is good, wise, loving, alive, etc.—and attribute these qualities in their ultimate form to the divine nature. That is, God is perfect goodness, wisdom, love, being, and so on. Since God is perfect, we can be sure that we are correct in attributing perfect qualities to God even though we cannot ourselves *conceive* these perfect qualities. (What exactly is "perfect wisdom" or "perfect being"?) But there is a second way of knowing—the negative way. We can collect in our minds all the qualities which we are sure God cannot possess: God is not corporeal matter; he is not evil; he cannot hate, cheat, deceive, etc. By a process of "remotion" all these qualities are removed from our thinking about God. Thus, as we proceed to subtract all qualities which God cannot possess, we are left with an increasingly accurate nonconcept of God. By the "darkness of unknowing" we can arrive at a mystical notion of what God in fact is.

In the multiplicity of his gods man does not merely behold the outward divinity of natural objects and forces but also perceives himself in the concrete diversity and distinction of his functions. . . . Over and over again we thus find confirmation of the fact that man can apprehend his own being only insofar as he can make it visible in the image of his gods. . . .

ERNST CASSIRER

8 In our Western philosophical tradition, there have been several attempts to prove, rationally or empirically, that God exists. At least three are noteworthy. These are the cosmological, ontological, and teleological arguments for the existence of God.

The *cosmological argument* was first stated by Aristotle and further developed by Thomas Aquinas (1225–1274). The argument attempts to prove logically that there must be an "unmoved mover" and that such a force is in fact what we have thought of as God.

8   Of Ultimate Concern

We live in a world of matter-in-motion. This is an obvious empirical fact. Aquinas observed that if an object is at rest, then it is not in motion; but any object at rest is potentially in motion. Motion is the actualized potential of a particular object. All objects at rest are potentially in motion, but no object will be activated into motion unless it is caused to move by something that is actually moving. No object at rest can be activated by another object at rest, nor can an object at rest set itself in motion. This means simply that every object in motion was set in motion by something else; but that something else must have been set in motion by something before it, and so on. Therefore we are confronted with an infinite series of objects, each of which actualizes the potential motion of the next in the series. But if we attempt to account for motion by going back in our minds in an infinite regression, we find ourselves in a logical contradiction—a dead end. Something *must* start the series, and this something, from a purely logical standpoint, must be something without an antecedent activator. Such an activator must necessarily be pure actuality and not potential. Whatever this pure actuality is, it is the "unmoved mover" which, writes Thomas, "everyone understands to be God."

9   The *ontological argument* was developed by Anselm of Canterbury (1033–1109). Anselm is sometimes called the father of Scholastic philosophy, that movement of the twelfth and thirteenth centuries which rekindled intellectual activity in the West after the Dark Ages. Saint Anselm was a devoutly religious Benedictine monk whose writings, debates, and pastoral leadership greatly influenced his time.

While Thomas's cosmological argument for God is founded upon an empirical observation of matter-in-motion, Anselm's argument has no such empirical referent. It attempts to prove God's existence from the nature of thought alone. For several weeks Anselm had been convinced that such a proof might be possible. He devoted much thought and prayer to it and finally, late one night during vigils, his proof of God's existence stood clearly before his mind. Anselm was sure that he knew, by thought alone, that God exists—indeed, that God *has* to exist. Here is his argument.

The mind has a concept of a Being than which nothing greater can be conceived. This Being, than which nothing greater can be conceived, must exist in reality as well as in thought. For if it existed only in thought (subjectively), then it would be possible for the mind to conceive of an even greater being who exists in reality (objectively) as well as in thought, and this being would be greater. But this is impossible. Therefore, this Being, than which nothing greater can be conceived, must exist in reality as well as in thought. And this Being is God.

Anselm was elated that he could prove rationally what he already knew to be true. He appends a thankful prayer to God "because through your divine illumination I now so understand that which, through your

THE ONTOLOGICAL ARGUMENT

I. Anything that can be coherently conceived is either actual or an unactualized potentiality.

  A. Meaningful statements are statements with a referent.

  B. A referent is either actual or an unactualized potentiality.

  C. Hence meaningful statements are statements referring to an actuality or an unactualized potentiality.

  D. That which is meaningful is coherently conceivable; it refers to an actuality or an unactualized potentiality.

II. God is coherently conceivable.

III. Therefore God is either actual or an unactualized potentiality.

IV. God is not an unactualized potentiality.

  A. Nothing unactualized can be actualized unless an adequate cause exists.

  B. Hence, God or Unsurpassable Being cannot be actualized unless an adequate cause exists.

  C. An adequate cause must surpass that which it causes.

  D. God as unsurpassable Being is unsurpassable.

  E. Therefore, God can have no adequate cause.

  F. Hence, God is not an unactualized potentiality.

V. Therefore God is Actual.

JAMES L. CATANZARO, Ph.D.
California State University
Fullerton, California

generous gift, I formerly believed. . . ." He continues: "So truly dost thou exist, O Lord God, both in thought and in fact, that it is impossible for the minds of Thy creatures not to know of Thine existence."

10   The *teleological argument* for the existence of God is based on the apparent order and design of nature and cosmos, and on the purposive nature of evolution.

From earliest times man has wondered about the cyclical motions of the stars and planets, the endless rounds of days and seasons, the consistency of nature's operations, and the rhythmic patterns of order in the world about him. Greek thinkers used the word *logos* (literally "word") to account for this order. This logos might be thought of as a kind of "world reason," an organizing force, possibly emanating from a divine mind, which binds all the dynamic elements of nature into a working order.

Today, of course, we know that the cosmos has more order than the ancients could have imagined, an order that can be described in terms of mathematical equations, physical and chemical formulas, and psycho-biological processes. Living organisms have distinctive metabolic and life-cycle rhythms, largely determined for each by an incredibly compli-cated DNA code. Subatomic studies have revealed the complex configu-rations of energy patterns. We also know that cosmic processes—involving suns, galaxies, and perhaps even the pulsating universe itself—run through ordered sequences resembling birth, life, and death.

The question: Can all this beautiful harmony exist apart from an ordering intelligence, a mind which would be the creator and sustainer of this order? The Stoics, among others, drew a simple analogy. The human mind is fundamentally an organizer: it orders, systematizes, labels, and stores bits of experience for later use. Our minds order our experiences of reality. Likewise, there must be a Cosmic Mind pervading reality itself

457

APRIL 8, 1966

TIME

THE WEEKLY NEWSMAGAZINE

Is God Dead?

VOL. 87 NO. 14

°For the teleological argument as it applies to evolution, see pages 328ff.

The God-complex is the focus around which other symbols gather, and from it comes the energic force with which they may be vitalized into a "lived" religion. . . . No constellation of symbols can function as a religion in the psyche unless its particular symbol for God is "alive."

IRA PROGOFF

and operating toward similar ends. The ordered world as we know it cannot be accounted for apart from the ordering of a Cosmic Intelligence.

The teleological argument—as the word "teleology" indicates—has to do with direction or destiny; and it was the development of life and the movement of evolution that seemed to demonstrate most clearly the possibility of a directive intelligence.

This argument was given careful scrutiny by the biologist Lecomte du Noüy in his book *Human Destiny*. Du Noüy calculated that according to the laws of probability the emergence of living organisms from inorganic molecules would have been less than one in a hundred billion. He concludes that life could only begin through an act of a purposive intelligence, and that the movement of evolution is, in his words, "telefinalistic."

Telefinality orients the march of evolution as a whole and has acted, ever since the appearance of life on earth, as a distant directing force tending to develop a being endowed with a conscience, a spiritually and morally perfect being. To attain its goal, this force acts on the laws of the inorganized world in such a way that the normal play of the second law of thermodynamics is always deflected in the same direction, a direction forbidden to inert matter and leading to ever greater dissymmetries, ever more "improbable" states.°

11   *Is God dead?* Friedrich Nietzsche believed so.

Have you not heard of that madman who lit a lantern in the bright morning hours, ran to the market place, and cried incessantly, "I seek God! I seek God!" As many of those who do not believe in God were standing around just then, he provoked much laughter. Why, did he get lost? said one. Did he lose his way like a child? said another. Or is he hiding? Is he afraid of us? Has he gone on a voyage? or emigrated? Thus they yelled and laughed. The madman jumped into their midst and pierced them with his glances.

"Whither is God" he cried. "I shall tell you. *We have killed him*—you and I. All of us are his murderers. . . . God is dead. God remains dead. And we have killed him. How shall we, the murderers of all murderers, comfort ourselves? What was holiest and most powerful of all that the world has yet owned has bled to death under our knives. Who will wipe this blood off us? What water is there for us to clean ourselves? What festivals of atonement, what sacred games shall we have to invent? Is not the greatness of this deed too great for us? Must not we ourselves become gods simply to seem worthy of it? There has never been a greater deed; and whoever will be born after us—for the sake of this deed he will be part of a higher history than all history hitherto."

Here the madman fell silent and looked again at his listeners; and they too were silent and stared at him in astonishment. At last he threw his lantern on the ground, and it broke and went out. "I come too early,"

he said then; "my time has not come yet. This tremendous event is still on its way, still wandering—it has not yet reached the ears of man. . . ."

It has been related further that on that same day the madman entered divers churches and there sang his *requiem aeternam deo*. Led out and called to account, he is said to have replied each time, "What are these churches now if they are not the tombs and sepulchers of God?"

12   Nietzsche and others have presaged the death of God. But what does such a statement mean? A modern death-of-God theologian, William Hamilton, rhetorically asks, "Is there really an event properly called 'the death of God'? Or is the current chatter enveloping the phrase simply another of the many non-events afflicting our time?" He answers: "No. The death of God has happened. To those of us with gods, and to those without. To the indifferent, the cynical and the fanatical. God is dead, whatever that means."

To Nietzsche it meant that the very concept of God as traditionally conceived in Western thought no longer has the power, as it once did, to transform human life. Belief in a God is still held by individuals, and countless others pay lip service to god-doctrines. But these beliefs no longer do what beliefs are supposed to do: to grip one's very existence with ultimate truths; to establish one firmly in a meaningful teleocosmic plan; to transform character and hence the quality of one's whole life; to make one feel special and of infinite worth; to provide secure and final answers to questions about living and dying.

World-views have changed. Spirits and demons have died: we now account for human behavior in terms of operant conditioning and motivation. The Devil has died: a "devil" is nothing more than a mental abstraction which we have personified and objectified. And a capricious, all-too-human deity can no longer command our devotion. We have seen too many gods; our anthropomorphic habits are too obvious to be brushed aside. God, too, is dead.

13   If we scan the pantheon of man's divinities, we discover deicides without end. Sooner or later, it seems, all the gods of men die.

There was a time when Egyptian fellahin knew that King Osiris weighed the hearts of men before they could enter into his kingdom, and Isis the Queen was a benefactress to all—revealing laws, rendering justice, calming the sea, timing the harvests, and persuading men and women to love each other.

The sky-god Varuna was able to see into the hearts of his Aryan worshipers and cast away their sins. The redeemer-god Balder returned each spring to the snow-laden northland and brought with him light and warmth. The mystery-gods Dionysus, Orpheus, and Mithras promised immortality to all who pledged their loyalty and performed the proper rites. From his temple on the slopes of Mount Parnassus the bright sun-god Apollo offered divine wisdom and worldly counsel to faithful pilgrims.

The beautiful virgin-goddess Artemis protected wandering children and assuaged the pain of women in childbirth. Persephone brought health and prosperity to her devotees, and then led them down to the nether realm where she was queen. The virgin Athena, proud and protective, was close to the hearts of her Athenian worshipers.

The virgin born Quetzalcoatl who, in Nahuatl mysteries, was a man become god, presented himself as an example of man's purest aspiration, having burned himself in a fire to purge away his sin. Lord Mazda proffered aid and eternal life to righteous Zoroastrians who believed in Spenta Mainyu (the Holy Spirit) and in the Amesha Spentas (the Immortal Ones—angel-like beings and divine messengers).

As long as there were followers who believed in them, all these gods and goddesses could transform lives. But when, with the passing of the centuries, there were no longer any believers, then no more lives were transformed, no more guilt forgiven, no more souls saved.

In the pantheon of deceased gods and goddesses are enshrined the most awesome names ever uttered by the suppliant voices of mortal men

Even for a god there is a point of no return. . . .

"Star Trek"
NBC-TV

THE DEATH OF GOD

What does the phrase "the death of God" mean to the theologians who use it? One such theologian is the Rev. William Hamilton who notes that there are at least ten ways in which the phrase is used today.

1. It might mean that there is no God and that there never has been. This position is traditional atheism of the old-fashioned kind, and it does seem hard to see how it could be combined, except very unstably, with Christianity or any of the Western religions.

2. It might mean that there once was a God to whom adoration, praise and trust were appropriate, possible and even necessary, but that there is now no such God. This is the position of the death-of-God or radical theology. It is an atheist position, but with a difference. If there was a God, and if there now isn't, it should be possible to indicate why this change took place, when it took place and who was responsible for it.

3. It might mean that the idea of God and the word God itself both are in need of radical reformulation. Perhaps totally new words are needed: perhaps a decent silence about God should be observed; but ultimately, a new treatment of the idea and the word can be expected, however unexpected and surprising it may turn out to be.

4. It might mean that our traditional liturgical and theological language needs a thorough overhaul: the reality abides, but classical modes of thought and forms of language may well have had it.

5. It might mean that the Christian story is no longer a saving or a healing story. It may manage to stay on as merely illuminating or instructing or guiding, but it no longer performs its classical functions of salvation or redemption. In this new form, it might help us cope with the demons, but it cannot abolish them.

6. It might mean that certain concepts of God, often in the past confused with the classical Christian doctrine of God, must be destroyed: for example, God as problem solver, absolute power, necessary being, the object of ultimate concern.

7. It might mean that men do not today experience God except as hidden, absent, silent. We live, so to speak, in the time of the death of God, though that time will doubtless pass.

8. It might mean that the gods men make, in their thought and action (false gods or idols, in other words), must always die so that the true object of thought and action, the true God, might emerge, come to life, be born anew.

9. It might have a mystical meaning: God must die in the world so that he can be born in us. In many forms of mysticism the death of Jesus on the cross is the time of that worldly death. This is a medieval idea that influenced Martin Luther, and it is probably this complex of ideas that lies behind the German chorale *God Himself Is Dead* that may well be the historical source for our modern use of "death of God."

10. Finally, it might mean that our language about God is always inadequate and imperfect.

WILLIAM HAMILTON
Playboy, August, 1966

and women: Adonis, Aphrodite, Apollo, Aton, Bacchus, Balder, Cybele, Demeter, Diana, Dionysus, El, Fortuna, Gaia, Hel, Hercules, Indra, Ishtar, Isis, Janus, Jupiter, Marduk, Mars, Nanna, Orpheus, Osiris, Persephone, Quetzalcoatl, Rudra, Saturnus, Shamash, Tammuz, Thor, Uranus, Varuna, Venus, Wotan, Xochipilli, Zagreus, Zeus . . .

14   One of the tasks of a theologian is to update the faith and make it intelligible to his contemporaries. Numerous attempts have been made

to deal with the problem of God-knowledge in modern terms. A notable example is that of Dr. Paul Tillich.

Tillich contended that we cannot *know* anything about God, but this limitation does not prevent God's working in our lives. Knowing about him and experiencing him are hardly the same. God is "the ground of our being." We exist, and objects exist; but "existence" is a human category of thought, and God is beyond existence. He is pure being itself.

But, Tillich notes, we are caught in a human predicament which it were best we accept. It is true that we cannot conceive the inconceivable or speak the unspeakable. But if we think or speak at all, then we must think in concepts and speak with language symbols. Therefore, we must continue to do just this, but with the full understanding that our thoughts and words refer to nothing whatever that is real. There is nothing to be gained by fighting our predicament, says Tillich. Rather, we must accept it and live within its confines. Let's continue to speak of God as "he" (or in other traditions as "she" or "it"); we can continue to think of God as "knowing," "seeing," "hearing," "loving," and so on. These are pragmatic modes of thinking and feeling. Man is a symbolic creature, and we can live with our condition providing we don't confuse symbol and reality. Such words as "God" and "he" are indispensable as symbols, but we must never mistake them for realities.

The only "God" that "exists" is beyond the gods of man. Since all our thinking ultimately is symbolic, Christians can continue to think of the Christ as the "new man" described by Paul, the whole man whose existence and essence have become one. He symbolizes the ultimate possibilities for each of us. It is only by accepting these symbols for what they truly are—as ontological aspects of the human condition—that we can come to terms with our existence and express our "ultimate concern for the Ultimate."

Almost all philosophers have confused ideas of things. They speak of material things in spiritual terms, and of spiritual things in material terms.

PASCAL

15   December is the darkest month. The sun is lowest in the sky. The nights are longest. Yet in its midst—perhaps in their hunger for warmth and light in the nadir of seasons—believers of the Western world have immemorially celebrated hope. In recent years, God has seemed to many as dim as the winter-solstice sun on the horizon. It has been a December of religion. Now, as the days grow longer into the new decade, believers and those who would like to believe are hoping that the long, bleak month is over.

Is God coming back to life? Was he ever really "dead"? Perhaps he was eclipsed during a period of dizzying social change. And if he returns, will it be to the familiar life of church and synagogue or to another locale? The marketplace? The slum? The commune? The barricade?

The most notable fact in religion today is that ministers of all denominations are trying, somewhat desperately but with immense energy and imagination, to find new ways to carry God back into the everyday life of society and to make him, in the prevailing cliché of the day, "relevant." This is not primarily a theological movement. Still, important

8   Of Ultimate Concern

new trends in theology suggest that God may best be met in the co-creation of a more humane society or, internally, in the deepest structures of our own psyches. As so often in the history of faith, this new effort to build a new ministry is a reaction against past failures.

Whatever new or old doors theology enters, for many men the reality of God in the future may well remain as elusive as it has been in the past. For all of the hoping, God will still seem painfully far ahead; for all of the evidence at hand, the rumors of angels will often be too faint to hear. What then? In secular society, as in earlier eras, the question mark will remain. But so will the glimmers of answers.

Time, December 26, 1969

16 Religious experience is absolute. It is indisputable. You can only say that you have never had such an experience and your opponent will say: "Sorry, I have." And there your discussion will come to an end. No matter what the world thinks about religious experience, the one who has it possesses the great treasure of a thing that has provided him with a source of life, meaning and beauty and that has given a new splendor to the world and to mankind. He has pistis [faith] and peace. Where is the criterium by which you could say that such a life is not legitimate, that such experience is not valid and that such pistis is mere illusion? Is there, as a matter of fact, any better truth about ultimate things than the one that helps you to live?

CARL G. JUNG

What color is God's skin?
I said it's black, brown, yellow,
It is red and it's white.
Every man's the same
In the good Lord's sight.

Up With People!

8-4

DEATH/

IMMORTALITY

1   "You been up to the grave yet?" asked the hunter, as if he knew I
would answer yes.

"No," I said.

That really surprised him. He tried not to show it.

"They all go up to the grave," he said.

"Not this one."

He explored around in his mind for a polite way of asking. "I
mean . . ." he said. "Why *not?*"

"Because it's the wrong grave," I said.

"All graves are wrong graves when you come down to it," he
said.

"No," I said. "There are right graves and wrong ones, just as there
are good times to die and bad times."

He nodded at this. I had come back to something he knew, or
at least smelled was right.

"Sure, I knew men," he said, "died just perfect. You always felt,
yes, that was good. One man I knew, sitting at the table waiting for supper,
his wife in the kitchen, when she came in with a big bowl of soup there
he was sitting dead and neat at the table. Bad for her, but, I mean, wasn't
that a good way for him? No sickness. No nothing but sitting there waiting
for supper to come and never knowing if it came or not. Like another
friend. Had an old dog. Fourteen years old. Dog was going blind and tired.
Decided at last to take the dog to the pound and have him put to sleep.
Loaded the old blind tired dog on the front seat of his car. The dog licked
his hand, once. The man felt awful. He drove toward the pound. On the
way there, with not one sound, the dog passed away, died on the front
seat, as if he knew and, knowing, picked the better way, just handed over
his ghost, and there you are. That's what you're talking about, right?"

I nodded.

"So you think that grave up on the hill is a wrong grave for a right man, do you?"

"That's about it," I said.

"You think there are all kinds of graves along the road for all of us?"

"Could be," I said.

"And if we could see all our life one way or another, we'd choose better? At the end, looking back," said the hunter, "we'd say, hell, *that* was the year and the place, not the *other* year and the other place, but that one year, that one place. Would we say that?"

"Since we have to choose or be pushed finally," I said, "yes."

"That's a nice idea," said the hunter. "But how many of us have that much sense? Most of us don't have brains enough to leave a party when the gin runs out. We hang around."

"We hang around," I said, "and what a shame."

We ordered some more beer.

RAY BRADBURY
"The Kilimanjaro Device"

2   Our feelings about death are the sublest of all motivators, but also the strongest. No problem in the human condition has been subject to man's creative imagination more than the prospect of his own cessation.

There is significant variation in how far each of us will go to avoid facing the fact that we must die. The evidence for postmortem consciousness is ambiguous, which only adds to our need to relieve anxiety about nonexistence and to mitigate the agony we associate with dying. Our minds create elaborate myths to allay our anguish over this event. Yet it is a universal event and a basic function of the teleocosmos.

3   We cannot experience death, although in our fear and confusion we may not know this to be so. Death can never be experienced because death is the *cessation* of experience. We may be able to experience dying to some degree. If one believes he is dying and indeed he is, he may be able to experience a progression of dying-events. But if one is convinced he is dying, but in fact he is not (he recovers), then he has not actually experienced dying. One can be sure he is experiencing dying only if he dies; hence no one can ever be sure that he is having such an experience.

4   Dr. Edwin Schneidman makes a helpful distinction between the unique inner experience—the cessation of consciousness—and the outer experience—the termination of physiological processes. The latter we obtain through observation of the death-events of others. We can watch the gradual deterioration of life-processes and then their actual termination, and we say *this* is the end of life: *this* is death.

Within ourselves, all we experience is the onset of the cessation of consciousness. This is often a gradual process, beginning long before the termination of our physiological processes. Most individuals subside into an unconscious state or coma at some point before death occurs, so they don't experience the later (and possibly eventful) stages leading to the death-event.

Which of these events do we fear and so desperately try to avoid? Or do we fear both? Would we really care about the termination of our physiological processes if we could be assured that the cessation of our consciousness would *not* follow?

5   We do not fear death itself, and death—the cessation of consciousness—is nothing to be feared. Each night when we enter sleep we experience the cessation of consciousness; this is an experience which probably resembles the final cessation followed by death. Each night we die, literally. (But we awaken again. There is no wonder that sleep has become a synonym for death and that we universally picture ourselves waking from it.)

Three distinct kinds of fear are associated with death, and one of them—fear of suffering—is realistic. One does not live for very long before learning that pain and grief are companions of death. As children we see animals in pain before they die; throughout life we witness the

We come from a dark abyss, we end in a dark abyss, and we call the luminous interval life.

NIKOS KAZANTZAKIS

MINER'S REQUEST: FIND PROOF OF MAN'S SOUL

PHOENIX (UPI)—An obscure Arizona miner named James Kidd was a man concerned with the human soul.

In a handwritten will dated in 1946 he said:

"After my funeral expenses have been paid and $100 (given) to some preacher of the Gospel to say farewell at my grave, sell all my property, which is all in cash and stocks and have this balance money go into a research or some scientific proof of a soul of the human body which leaves at death."

Monday a Phoenix court begins hearings to determine how to dispose of Kidd's estate, now valued at $200,000. There are many claimants to the money, including some who assert they can fulfill Kidd's strange last request.

Kidd was last seen in 1949 when he apparently left to work on two mining claims. He was 70 and a year after his disappearance he was declared legally dead. His will was filed for probate in 1964.

Little was known about the old miner. He reportedly told friends he was born in Ogdensburg, N.Y., on July 18, 1879, lived for a time in Pennsylvania, then came West. He is thought to have worked at a mill in Montana and with a mining firm in Idaho before going to Nevada and getting a job with the Kennecott Copper Co. He left Kennecott in 1916 and then there is a blank in his record until 1920 when he took a job with the Miami (Ariz.) Copper Co.

It was known that Kidd had filed mining claims on two properties in the Pinto Creek or Superstition Mountain area—possibly near the famed "Lost Dutchman" gold mine—in 1933. Their exact locations were never recorded but Gila County records show Kidd filed claims on two mines in the Miami mining district, named Scorpion No. 1 and Scorpion No. 2.

One old prospector in Globe speculated that Kidd may have found gold on his claims because there have been traces of gold found in the Pinto Creek area in the past.

He left a checking account of $4,100.66 at the time of his disappearance, and he owned stocks worth more than $100,000 which have nearly doubled because of dividends and other earnings.

A Miami man who knew Kidd said the miner had always talked about the supernatural and, despite the fact he never went to church, believed in the existence of a human soul which could be photographed as it left the body.

The court hearings on the will begin here before Maricopa County Superior Court Judge Robert L. Myers.

So far, some 19 individuals, religious and educational organizations have filed petitions with the court to receive the estate. In addition more than 1,000 persons have written Myers asserting various claims to Kidd's money.

In a certain sense the whole of mythical thought may be interpreted as a constant and obstinate negation of the phenomenon of death. By virtue of this conviction of the unbroken unity and continuity of life myth has to clear away this phenomenon. Primitive religion is perhaps the strongest and most energetic affirmation of life that we find in human culture.

ERNST CASSIRER

Phoenix Arizona
Jan 2.nd 1946

this is my first and only will
and is dated the second day in
January 1946. I have no. heir's
have not been married in my life,
an after all my funeral expenses
have been paid and $100. one hundred
dollars to some preacher of the
gospital to say fare well at my
grave sell all my property which
is all in cash and stocks with
E F Hutton Co Phoenix some in
safety box, and have this balance
money to go in a research or some
scientific proof of a soul of the
human body which leaves at death
I think in time their can be a
Photograph of soul leaving the
human at death,

James Kidd

(dated 2nd
January 1946)

some cash in Valley
bank some in Bank America LA Cal

agony of individuals caught in war, accidents, and disease. The constant association of pain and death never ceases. It becomes difficult for us to *think* of death without *feeling* the fears we have been conditioned to associate with it.

Another kind of fear, less common, results from confusion. For instance, a young girl awoke repeatedly with nightmares about death, and her terror became so intense it dominated her waking hours as well. When her ideas of death were explored with a therapist, it was discovered that what she really feared was being buried alive. That is, the body in her dreams would in fact be dead, but she was unable to separate the idea of consciousness from the buried corpse. Well-known stories by Edgar Allen Poe and others supply ideas which can grow into such nightmares. When the fallacy of identification was recognized, the girl's "fear of death" gradually diminished.

A third fear is all-pervasive. This is the universal fear: the fear of nonexistence. It is not fear of possible punishment in some hell or purgatory; nor is it merely a fear of the unknown. Rather, we experience a relentless anguish about nonexistence itself. We fear the *experience* of *nonbeing,* not recognizing that this is a contradiction in terms. However, a rational response to a nonrational fear is no solution.

Consider how that past ages of eternal time before our birth were no concern of ours. This is a mirror which nature holds up to us of future time after our death.

LUCRETIUS

We can remind ourselves that we already know "the experience of nonexistence." Most of us were not alive, say, two hundred years ago, but it didn't bother us then, nor does it concern us now. And, barring a scientific breakthrough, most of us will not be alive two hundred years hence. But *this* bothers us. The possibility of nonexistence in the future can disturb us, while nonexistence in the past doesn't.

Why?

6   *Valhalla* (Norse): the great hall of immortality where warriors await the call of Odin to join in the final battle (the Götterdämmerung). *Elysium* (Greek): a place at the end of the earth on the banks of the river Oceanus where perfect happiness rewards those favored by the gods. *Paradise* (Persian): a lush, green park which serves as a temporary resting place for righteous souls awaiting the final resurrection. *Gardens of Delight* (Islamic): a place of reward for the faithful of Allah where, robed in silk and brocade, they are given all earthly delights imaginable. *Heaven* (Christian): the abode of God where the righteous dead will dwell together in perfect happiness in God's presence after the Last Judgment. *Isatpragbhara* (Jain): the heaven at the very top of the universe whither the pure consciousnesses of the righteous will rise and enjoy perfect bliss. *Isles of the Blest* (Orphic): the mystic Greek isles where the purified, now free from rebirth, will be rewarded with eternal happiness. *Kingdom of Osiris* (Egyptian): an oasis in the western desert with lush vegetation where the souls of the blessed will forever rest under spreading shade trees. *House of Song* (Zoroastrian): a place somewhere among the stars beyond the Chinvat Bridge where the righteous will enjoy perfect happiness in their companionship with one another.

> Belief in immortality secures a bond of union between the living and the dead, which is a fact of immense importance for the continuity of culture and for the safe keeping of tradition.
>
> ASHLEY MONTAGU

7   Our endless contemplation of various heavens and hells reflects the conviction that we do not really die. Deep within we intuit that we are immortal. Actually, we are split by an ambivalence about the mystery of death. On the one hand, we know we will die, and as a social convention we confess this to others; but on the other hand, each of us has an instinctlike resistance: "It can't actually happen *to me*."

Generally, man does not identify his self/essence with his physical body. When we look at others, we see bodies, of course; we perceive physical organisms. But when we look into another's eyes, we see not merely the working parts of a transducer (cornea, iris, etc.); we "see" a person. As we watch facial expressions, we "see" in others what we feel in ourselves: a self or soul which dwells in the body but which is not part of it. Our experience of consciousness feels like a "spirit" which dwells inside a "house," and in various religious traditions man speaks of the coming and going of his "spirit" into and out of his body. It "inhabits" his body. Indeed, several spirits may inhabit his body, simultaneously or in turn.

8   Of Ultimate Concern

8   The Greeks developed the belief that the spirit of man is free and of great value, while the body, quite a separate entity, is of little importance. The spirit can leave the body and wander where it wills. Some of the Greek philosophers held that the soul can be truly free only when the body-prison dies and releases it. The Greeks, therefore, had no strong feelings about mutilation or cremation. They felt concern if the corpse could not be given proper rites without which the soul could not find release; and it was especially tragic when Greek sailors were lost at sea and could never be given proper burial. Nevertheless, the body as such was of little worth.

Our Judeo-Christian psyche-ology ("soul-ology") has been less dualistic. Jews and Christians distinguished between spirit and body, but they could never think of them as separable entities; therefore, after death reassembly of bodily materials is necessary for survival. The Hebrew could not imagine spirit wandering about without a body. For him, as for the Egyptians, Sumerians, and others, mutilation of the body is a tragic misfortune, for we must carry into the next life whatever scars we acquire in this life.

Jesus uttered words to the effect that if your eye or hand causes you to sin, then destroy it, for "it is better for you to get into the Kingdom of God with but one eye than to be thrown into Gehenna with both eyes. . ." (Mark 9:47). These words were not meant symbolically; they

When one has lived as long as I have, it's a serious matter to die. Every year one puts out new roots.
DAVID LINDSAY
Voyage to Arcturus

reflect the late Judaic notion that we take into the next life whatever scars we sustain in this one. When Jesus reappeared to his disciples after the discovery of the empty tomb, he was seen to bear on his spirit-body the wounds of the crucifixion.

In the Egyptian tomb of Menena, some culprit regained entrance to the burial chamber of this nobleman and mutilated the freshly painted frescoes. The faces of Menena and his family were chiseled away in order to insure they would go faceless into the next life.

9   In Western thought we have strong religious reassurance that we will survive physical death. Orthodox doctrine denies that we die. The recorded fact-claim that Jesus awakened after physical death and promised us that we shall do the same is a part of our Western theology of history. We have inherited a specific interpretation of the death-event: there is no death of the self, and physical death is merely an event in a continuing drama.

Since these various antideath concepts are part of our own teleo-cosmic world-view, it is easy to avoid the feeling of certainty that death, in fact, awaits each of us. The idea of total oblivion has not been widely held or seriously faced.

The bullfight is a miniature of life. Death is a part of life, and it is an integral part of the bullfight. As in life, death hovers; it is inevitable, if not for the man, certainly for the bull. And in life, each of us must eventually die. One of the things the matador is saying when he fights bravely is that the way we die is important, or, that what is really important is how we live.

JOSEPH ROYCE

10   Television has become "the great immortalizer." Each day we watch innumerable figures who, we have been told, are no longer alive. Yet obviously they live. They are alive before our eyes. The (alleged) fact that some physical organism no longer exists in space/time seems to make little difference.

From the time we enter formal education the great men of history live on in our books and our minds. They are as alive as others we read about who may or may not be alive. We don't (and can't) make any clear distinction between the living and the no-longer-living. Is George Washington dead? Not to millions of schoolchildren. Is Martin Luther King dead? John Kennedy? Dwight Eisenhower? Spencer Tracy? Marilyn Monroe? Clark Gable? Nikita Khrushchev? We see them all on TV occasionally.

We see Robert Kennedy's victory speech at the Ambassador Hotel, over and over again. . . .

11   For those who can't believe in the true survival of consciousness, the human mind has rationalized a variety of comforting alternatives. They allow us to retain the feeling that *something of us* is left after we cease to exist.

Biological immortality stresses the continuity of germ-plasm from parent to offspring. *Social immortality* reminds us that we will linger in the memories of others for the good we do. *Moral immortality* holds that while we may be forgotten, we can add our small contribution to the

I sent my Soul through the Invisible,
Some letter of that After-life to spell:
And by and by my Soul return'd
to me,
And answer'd "I Myself am Heav'n
and Hell."

OMAR KHAYYAM
The Rubaiyat

LAST FLIGHT

The following letter is by Flying Petty Officer First Class Isao Matsuo of the 701st Air Group. It was written just before he sortied for a kamikaze attack. His home was in Nagasaki Prefecture.

28 October 1944

Dear Parents:

Please congratulate me. I have been given a splendid opportunity to die. This is my last day. The destiny of our homeland hinges on the decisive battle in the seas to the south where I shall fall like a blossom from a radiant cherry tree.

I shall be a shield for His Majesty and die cleanly along with my squadron leader and other friends. I wish that I could be born seven times, each time to smite the enemy.

How I appreciate this chance to die like a man! I am grateful from the depths of my heart to the parents who have reared me with their constant prayers and tender love. And I am grateful as well to my squadron leader and superior officers who have looked after me as if I were their own son and given me such careful training.

Thank you, my parents, for the 23 years during which you have cared for me and inspired me. I hope that my present deed will in some small way repay what you have done for me. Think well of me and know that your Isao died for our country. This is my last wish, and there is nothing else that I desire.

I shall return in spirit and look forward to your visit at the Yasukuni Shrine. Please take good care of yourselves.

How glorious is the Special Attack Corps' Giretsu Unit whose *Suisei* bombers will attack the enemy. Movie cameramen have been here to take our pictures. It is possible that you may see us in news-reels at the theater.

We are 16 warriors manning the bombers. May our death be as sudden and clean as the shattering of crystal.

Written at Manila on the eve of our sortie.

Isao

Soaring into the sky of the southern seas, it is our glorious mission to die as the shields of His Majesty. Cherry blossoms glisten as they open and fall.

INOGUCHI AND NAKAJIMA
The Divine Wind

---

continuing moral development of the human species. *Life-cycle immortality* suggests that energy is never lost but is conserved in other living things: from life to dust and to life again.

In the genre of science fiction, we can comfort ourselves with quasi-immortal states such as *cryonic suspension* ("freeze now, thaw later")

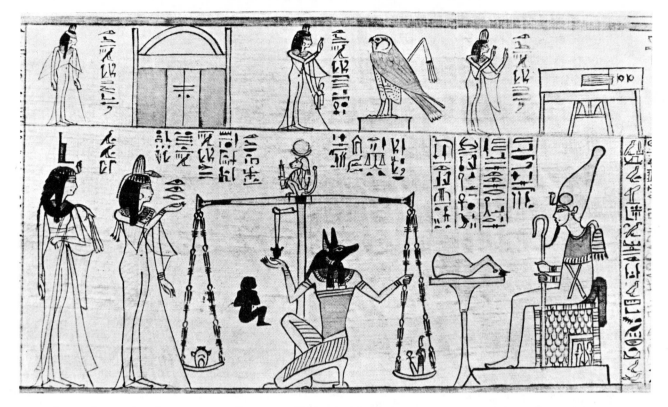

or *total transplants* whereby a continually renewed physical organism can sustain indefinitely an individual consciousness. Scientists are also researching the mechanics of *regeneration* which operate so well for some lower creatures such as starfish and lobsters.

But all such notions are consolation prizes rather than immortalities. They are designed to ease the pain of loss—the loss of conviction that consciousness survives death.

Does true immortality—the survival of a conscious self—really exist? Is there any conceivable way that there could be a continuity of conscious experience after the termination of our physical processes? What arguments—rational or empirical—might convince us that such continuity does indeed take place?

12　　The strongest *rational argument for immortality* is based on belief in the goodness of God. This is an "if . . . then" kind of argument: *If* God exists and *if* he is good, *then* immortality must necessarily exist.

According to this reasoning, it is unthinkable that God would create purposive beings who dream dreams and have the capacity for unlimited growth, only to let all this come to nothing. Could a good God *not* make provision for the fulfillment of these dreams and the actualization of this potential? The fact is that man barely begins to understand life and grow during his short lifetime. Most of us just begin

If I were given the choice of how long I should like to live with my present physical and mental equipment, I should decide on a good deal more than 70 years. But I doubt whether I should be wise to decide on more than 300 years. Already I am very much aware of my own limitations, and I think that 300 years is as long as I should like to put up with them.

FRED HOYLE

> Death plays an important part in each day of my life. I have worked half in shadow, half in sun all of my life. When I put my new book *The Halloween Tree* (a history of Death in the world, really) in the mail 8 weeks ago, I cried half-aloud: "There you are, Death, one up on you again!" My books are victories against darkness, if only for a small while. Each story I write is a candle lit for my own burial plot which it may take some few years to blow out. More than many writers, I have known this fact about myself since I was a child. It puts me to work each day with a special sad-sweet-happy urgency.
>
> RAY BRADBURY

With respect to immortality many men in the western world today are in the position of the church-warden who, when buttonholed by F. W. H. Myers . . . and asked what he thought would happen to him after death, after vainly trying to evade the question, burst out with "Well, I suppose I shall enter into everlasting bliss, but I do wish you would not talk about such depressing subjects."

ASHLEY MONTAGU

Je m'en vay chercher un grand Peut-être.
(*I am going to seek a great Perhaps.*)
RABELAIS
(*from his deathbed*)

to touch our dreams and solve some problems—and it's over. This would surely be an agonizing joke for a compassionate God to play on his children.

Therefore, there must exist an afterlife where man's self/essence can continue to grow. How great such a growth potential would be, especially if released from the impediments of the physical body, we can only imagine.

The American Personalist philosopher, Edgar Brightman, considered this to be the strongest argument for immortality. To his way of thinking there is no strong argument for immortality apart from the existence of God; but granting God's existence, then there exists no weighty argument *against* immortality.

13 The strongest *empirical evidence for immortality*—and it may seem strange to some—is from seances during which contact is allegedly established with discarnate spirits.

It would not be far wrong to say that "special effects" and/or hypnosis is involved in 95 percent of all mediumistic activity; and therefore perhaps 5 percent of seances are free of fraud and demonstrate authentic phenomena. Now, within this 5 percent, the great majority of happenings can be accounted for with known psychological principles or telepathic hypotheses. This leaves only a small part of 1 percent which necessitate hypotheses assuming something like discarnate spirits. Within this very small percentage of cases, interesting but problematic events occur. For instance, the "discarnate spirits" frequently reveal information which no one present could possibly know. It has been suggested that there is a "collective subconscious" or a "superconsciousness" which is tapped by the mind of the medium; and while such a theory is not beyond the realm of possibility, the hypothesis of the existence of discarnate spirits seems at present a simpler and better explanation.

It is somewhere within this small percentage of spiritualistic phenomena that empirical data might be found to support the idea of a continued consciousness after physical death. At present we have no verified data in this area, and much more research is needed.

14   The strongest *rational argument against immortality* derives from empirical observations that man has a profound "instinct" to stay alive. He is terrorized by this final unknown, this "great Perhaps," as Rabelais put it; and along with this ultimate fear goes man's incredible power of imagination. He can create an endless variety of concepts to meet his emotional needs. Therefore, with a simple formula—man's intense need plus his ever-fertile imagination—we may be able to explain to our satisfaction all of man's dreams of immortality: subtle imagery of blissful spirits, teleocosmic schemes of reincarnation, myths without end about heavens and hells and how we can get there, or stay out. As one surveys the range of man's fantasies about postmortem life, it seems that they just might be man's most lavish creative productions. Man dreams of a paradise, but this life is anything but a paradise. There must be a paradise somewhere . . .

This is a rational argument, but it is founded upon empirical observation and possesses considerable coherence; while it *proves* nothing, as an inductive hypothesis it is formidable.

15   The strongest *empirical evidence against immortality* is the observation—apparently without exception—that the termination of physical processes is soon followed by the cessation of consciousness as measured on EEGs and other instruments. That is, our bodies die and we have no evidence—unless the "discarnate spirits" are real—that consciousness continues in any form. We have no scientific knowledge at present which would be compatible with the continuation of consciousness; just the reverse, in fact: our best scientific knowledge is only compatible with the cessation of consciousness.

We could argue that, from the cessation of brainwaves on an electroencephalograph, we cannot validly infer that consciousness ceases. This is strictly true. Yet no alternative inference seems better. We can *think of* such things as "organized electromagnetic fields" or "vibration patterns" that somehow sustain themselves without underlying physical systems, but do we have any dependable evidence at present which would lead us to believe such concepts refer to anything real? Since there appears to be a one-to-one causal relationship between brainwaves and consciousness, there is logical justification for inferring the end of experience from the termination of the brain's electrical activity.

16   Apparently, *how* one dies is important—*while one is still alive.* We want assurance that our death will be dignified; that the conditions of termination will be surrounded by respect and honor; that it will not

Much as I love truth in the abstract I love my sense of immortality still more; and if the final outcome of all the boasted discoveries of modern science is to disclose to men that they are more evanescent than the shadow of the swallow's wing upon the lake . . . if this, after all, is the best that science can give one, give me then, I pray, no more science. I will live on in my simple ignorance, as my father did before me; and when I shall at length be sent to my final repose, let me . . . lie down to pleasant, even though they may be deceitful, dreams.

FREDERICK BARNARD (*1809–1889*)

My death does not belong to me—it is the outer limit of my consciousness, the last of my possibles. The meaninglessness of death for me is summed up in the phrase that "my death is the one moment of my life which I do not have to live." My death is not for me but for others; it is not my concern, but the concern of others who will notice it and need to deal with it. . . .

JOSEPH MIHALICH

Don Quixote's Epitaph

Que acredito su ventura,
Morir querdo y vivir loco.
(For if he like a madman lived,
At least he like a wise one died.)
CERVANTES

THE HEART OF HELLAS: EPITAPHS

My name is—What does it matter?—*My*
Country was—Why speak of it?—*I*
Was of noble birth—Indeed? And if
You had been the lowest?—*Moreover, my life*
Was decorous—And if it had not been so,
What then?
        —and I lie here now beneath you—
Who are you that speak?
To whom do you speak?

PAULUS SILENTIARIUS

Epitaph of an Abstainer

Remember Euboulos the sober, you who pass by,
And drink: there is one Hadês for all men.

LEONIDAS OF TARENTUM

Epitaph of a Slave

Alive, this man was Manês the slave: but dead,
He is the peer of Dareios, that great King.

ANYTE

Epitaph of a Young Man

Hail me Diogenês underground, O stranger, and pass by:
Go where you will, and fairest fortune go with you.
In my nineteenth year the darkness drew me down—
And ah, the sweet sun!

ANONYMOUS

Epitaph of a Sailor

Tomorrow the wind will have fallen
Tomorrow I shall be safe in harbor
Tomorrow
        I said:
           and Death
Spoke in that little word:
The sea was Death.
           O Stranger
This is the Némesis of the spoken word:
Bite back the daring tongue that would say
  Tomorrow!

ANTIPHILOS OF BYZANTIUM

Dudley Fitts (translator)
Poems from the Greek Anthology

be degrading to ourselves or loved ones; that it will not be an unplanned, messy kind of death. We want to feel sure that it will not result from ignominious causes; from cowardice, foolish anger, or stupidity. And certainly not least, we want the assurance that our last experience of consciousness will not be dominated by physical pain or emotional anguish.

17   There are two central questions involved in facing our own death: the questions of what we can leave behind and what we can take with us. It has been written that we must develop convictions and feelings about each of these questions if we are to face our own cessation with any sense of peace.

But some say that the better question is: What can I do with the days I have left to make life really worthwhile?

Whoe'er can know,
As the long days go,
That to live is happy
Hath found his heaven.
EURIPIDES

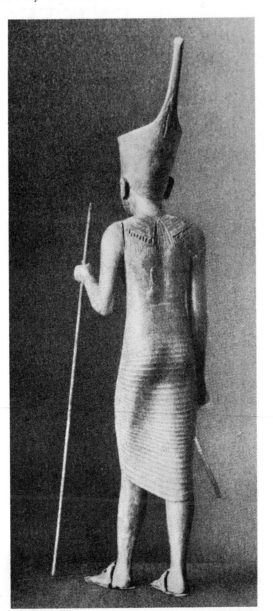

When my time comes, I hope no one drains my veins of their sustaining fluid and fills them with formaldehyde, then wastes me by putting me in a concrete box in the ground for eternity.

Rather, just a simple pine box with an acorn on top of it. Find a place where a tree is needed and return me to nature. When the acorn grows, I can nourish it and give back in some measure what I've taken. Maybe someday kids can crawl in my branches or a raccoon might curl up in my trunk or the larks can sing out from my leaves. At any rate, I would rather let an oak tree be my epitaph than a marble slab be my tombstone.
MIKE ROYKO

479

8-5

MEANING/
EXISTENCE

Ever look at a male lion in a zoo? Fresh meat on time, females supplied, no hunter to worry about—he's got it made, hasn't he? Then why does he look bored?

ROBERT HEINLEIN
The Glory Road

It is extremely important to grasp the notion that man does not yet exist.

COLIN WILSON

Does the grass bend when the wind blows upon it?

CONFUCIUS

1   Once there lived in the ancient city of Afkar two learned men who hated and belittled each other's learning. For one of them denied the existence of the gods and the other was a believer.

One day the two met in the market-place, and amidst their followers they began to dispute and to argue about the existence or the non-existence of the gods. And after hours of contention they parted.

That evening the unbeliever went to the temple and prostrated himself before the altar and prayed the gods to forgive his wayward past.

And the same hour the other learned man, he who had upheld the gods, burned his sacred books. For he had become an unbeliever.

KAHLIL GIBRAN

2   The Don Juan of the Mind: no philosopher or poet has yet discovered him. What he lacks is the love of the things he knows, what he possesses is *esprit,* the itch and delight in the chase and intrigue of knowledge—knowledge as far and high as the most distant stars. Until in the end there is nothing left for him to chase except the knowledge which hurts most, just as a drunkard in the end drinks absinthe and methylated spirits. And in the very end he craves for Hell—it is the only knowledge which can still seduce him. Perhaps it too will disappoint, as everything that he knows. And if so, he will have to stand transfixed through all eternity, nailed to disillusion, having himself become the Guest of Stone, longing for a last supper of knowledge which he will never receive. For in the whole world of things there is nothing left to feed his hunger.

FRIEDRICH NIETZSCHE

3   New Zealand, maybe. The *Herald-Trib* had had the usual headlines, only more so. It looked as if the boys (just big playful boys!) who run this planet were about to hold that major war, the one with ICBMs and H-bombs, any time now.

    If a man went as far south as New Zealand there might be something left after the fallout fell out.

    New Zealand is supposed to be very pretty and they say that a fisherman there regards a five-pound trout as too small to take home.

    I had caught a two-pound trout once.

    About then I made a horrible discovery. I didn't want to go back to school, win, lose, or draw. I no longer gave a damn about three-car garages and swimming pools, nor any other status symbol or "security." There was *no* security in this world and only damn fools and mice thought there could be.

    Somewhere back in the jungle I had shucked off all ambition of that sort. I had been shot at too many times and had lost interest in supermarkets and exurban sub-divisions and tonight is the PTA supper don't forget dear you promised.

    Oh, I wasn't about to hole up in a monastery. I still wanted— What *did* I want?

    I wanted a Roc's egg. I wanted a harem loaded with lovely odalisques less than the dust beneath my chariot wheels, the rust that never stained my sword. I wanted raw red gold in nuggets the size of your fist and feed that lousy claim jumper to the huskies! I wanted to get up feeling brisk and go out and break some lances, then pick a likely wench for my *droit du seigneur*—I wanted to stand up to the Baron and *dare* him to touch my wench. I wanted to hear the purple water chuckling against the skin

". . . in New Orleans. On Bourbon Street."
"No, that's your dream. It's not mine."
"Well, then, what is yours?"
"I have no dream."
"How terrible for you!"

TENNESSEE WILLIAMS
This Property Is Condemned

"You missed life."

of the *Nancy Lee* in the cool of the morning watch and not another sound, nor any movement save the slow tilting of the wings of the albatross that had been pacing us the last thousand miles.

I wanted the hurtling moons of Barsoom. I wanted Storisende and Poictesme, and Holmes shaking me awake to tell me, "The game's afoot!" I wanted to float down the Mississippi on a raft and elude a mob in company with the Duke of Bilgewater and the Lost Dauphin.

I wanted Prester John, and Excalibur held by a moon-white arm out of a silent lake. I wanted to sail with Ulysses and with Tros of Samothrace and eat the lotus in a land that seemèd always afternoon. I wanted the feeling of romance and the sense of wonder I had known as a kid. I wanted the world to be what they had promised me it was going to be—instead of the tawdry, lousy, fouled-up mess it is. . . .

Maybe one chance is all you ever get.

ROBERT HEINLEIN
The Glory Road

4 Who has not asked, "What am I doing here?" But what is the answer?

Socrates believed we are here to be happy, and the path of happiness is through knowledge which leads to virtue which leads to happiness. *Epicurus* taught that we are here to cultivate the pleasures of the mind— wisdom and understanding—but the Cyrenaic philosopher *Aristippus* became famous for teaching that we are here to cultivate pleasures, and the more the merrier (and those of the mind only as a last resort). A prophet from Nazareth, *Yeshua bar Yoseph,* suggested we are here to learn the qualities of faith and love toward one another so that we will merit membership in the Reign of God when it begins. Shortly after that, *Paul of Tarsus* preached that we are here to have faith in the Messiah so that our original sin could be washed away and we would be ready for the return of the Christ.

Lao-tzu apparently believed that we are here to seek the Tao and know the inner harmony of Nature's Way; but *Confucius* disagreed, declaring that we are here to discover the proper way to behave in our relationships with others. *The Buddha* taught that we are here to transcend tanha—the selfish craving which is the cause of human suffering—and enter the state of nirvana. *Shankara,* a Hindu mystic, was convinced that we are here to discover that this world is only maya ("illusion") and to realize that each of us is already one with Ultimate Reality.

Muhammad believed that we are here to render faithful obedience to Allah as revealed in the Quran. *John Calvin* told the Genevans that we are here solely to love God and so live a life of faith and discipline that we will "enjoy Him forever." But *Hegel,* being a philosopher on the rational side, wrote to persuade us that we are here to develop our capacity for reason and, in so doing, manifest the logic of the Absolute Mind in the movement of human (especially German) history.

If I had my life to live over again, I would have made it a rule to read some poetry and listen to some music at least every week. . . .
The loss of these tastes is a loss of happiness, and may possibly be injurious to the intellect, and more probably to the moral character, by enfeebling the emotional part of our nature.

CHARLES DARWIN

Man is by nature a purposive creature, who develops neuroses when purpose is denied him.

COLIN WILSON

If a patient [should ask] Frankl, "What is the meaning of life for me?" he is likely to get a Socratic answer: "What is the best chess move?"

AARON UNGERSMA

5   It is impossible to define the purpose of life in a general way. "Life" does not mean something vague, but something very real and concrete, just as life's tasks are very real and concrete. They form man's destiny, which is different and unique for each individual. No situation repeats itself and each situation calls for a different response. Sometimes the situation in which a man finds himself may require him to shape his own destiny by action. Sometimes a man may be required simply to accept fate, to bear his cross.

When a man finds that it is his destiny to suffer, he will have to accept suffering as his task; his single and unique task. He will have to struggle for the realization that even in suffering he is unique and alone in the universe. No man can relieve him of his suffering, or suffer in his place. His unique opportunity lies in the way in which he bears his burden.

VIKTOR FRANKL

How terrifying and glorious the role of man if, indeed, without guidance and without consolation he must create from his own vitals the meaning for his existence and write the rules whereby he lives.
THORNTON WILDER
Julius Caesar

6   The central character of *Nausea,* Antoine Roquentin, enunciates Jean-Paul Sartre's reflections on the meaning of human existence.

Prior to these past few days, I had really never felt what it means "to exist." . . . Ordinarily, existence hides itself. It is here, round about us, within us: we are it, and we cannot speak two words without speaking of it, but in the end we never grasp it. . . . Existence is not something which can be thought from a distance: it overwhelms you brusquely. . . .

[Existence means nothing more than] to be here; existents appear, they are encountered, but they can never be inferentially deduced. I believe

The sweetest optimism springs from an inability to face despair.
TODD GITLIN

NOTHINGS

Even as a child I could never understand why certain things that were important to me appeared to older people to be nothing. My dreams were nothing. What I "made up" to delight or terrify myself was nothing. Certain queer feelings, coming out of the blue, were nothing. I can remember, though it must be all of 65 years ago, sitting in the sun on a tiny hillock at the back of our house, and feeling, not lightly but to the very depths of my being, that I was close to some secret about a wonderful treasure, which had no size, no shape, no substance, but all the same was somewhere just behind the sunlight and the buttercups and daisies and the grass and the warm earth. And this too, it seemed, was nothing. I was surrounded and often enchanted, it appeared, by nothings.

J. B. PRIESTLEY
Man and Time

---

there are people who have understood this, but they have been trying to overcome this contingency by inventing a Necessary Being who causes himself (a *causa sui*). No Necessary Being, however, can explain existence. . . . There is not the least reason for our "being-there." . . . And I, too, am *"de trop"* [superfluous, unnecessary, absurd]. And yet people are trying to hide themselves behind the idea of law and necessity. In vain: every existent is born without reason, prolongs its existence owing to the weakness of inertia, and dies fortuitously.

7   That Man is the product of causes which had no prevision of the end they were achieving; that his origin, his growth, his hopes and fears, his loves and his beliefs, are but the outcome of accidental collocations of atoms; that no fire, no heroism, no intensity of thought and feeling, can preserve an individual life beyond the grave; that all the labours of the ages, all the devotion, all the inspiration, all the noonday brightness of human genius, are destined to extinction in the vast death of the solar system, and that the whole temple of Man's achievement must inevitably be buried beneath the debris of a universe in ruins—all these things, if not quite beyond dispute, are yet so nearly certain, that no philosophy which rejects them can hope to stand. Only within the scaffolding of these truths, only on the firm foundation of unyielding despair, can the soul's habitation henceforth be safely built.

BERTRAND RUSSELL

8   But wherein do such pronouncements about the absurdity of existence become statements about the real world? Are they not more on the order of reflexive value-judgments which betray the inner world of the individuals who make them? After all, to say the world is meaningless is merely to say, "I find no meaning in it." Value-judgments are personal responses, not scientific descriptions.

Much modern Western philosophy has contended that there are no real values and that, by a sort of hopeless *tour de force,* we each must inject meaning into his own life. Existentialists such as Heidegger and Sartre have held that only a personal confrontation with death itself puts our lives in perspective but that this "flash of authenticity" cannot be made a part of our everyday consciousness. But this is questionable, for "there are states of consciousness that are not 'everyday consciousness' and which are not 'transcendental' either. These produce a definite sense of values and purpose." In saying this, perhaps Colin Wilson is closer to the truth, and he goes on:

"Peak experiences" all seem to have the same "content": that the chief mistake of human beings is to pay too much attention to everyday trivialities. We are strangely inefficient machines, utilizing only a fraction of our powers, and the reason for this is our short sightedness. Koestler's "mystical" insight made him feel that even the threat of death was a triviality that should be ignored; "So what? . . . Have you nothing more serious

Those who have suffered much become very bitter or very gentle.

WILL DURANT

When the universe has crushed him man will still be nobler than that which kills him, because he knows that he is dying, and of its victory the universe knows nothing.

PASCAL

I have the key to happiness: remember to be profoundly, totally conscious that you are.
I myself, sorry to say, hardly ever use this key. I keep losing it.

EUGENE IONESCO

Man can will nothing unless he has first understood that he must count on no one but himself; that he is alone, abandoned on earth in the midst of his infinite responsibilities; without help, with no other aim than the one he sets himself, with no other destiny than the one he forces for himself on this earth.

JEAN-PAUL SARTRE

paper flower
paper bird
paper moon

who walks
the wild earth
any more?

to worry about?" Greene's whisky priest: "It seemed to him, at that moment, that it would have been quite easy to be a saint." Death reveals to us that our lives have been one long miscalculation, based on a triviality.

9 A painter who is painting a large canvas has to work with his nose to the canvas; but periodically he stands back to see the effect of the whole. These over-all glimpses renew his sense of purpose.

Man's evolution depends upon a renewal of the sense of over-all purpose. For several centuries now, the direction of our culture has been a concentration upon the minute, the particular. In the field of science, this has produced our present high level of technological achievement. In the field of culture, we have less reason for self-congratulation, for the concentration upon the particular—to the exclusion of wider meanings—has led us into a *cul de sac.* Yeats described the result as "fish gasping on the strand"—a minute realism that has lost all drive and purpose.

COLIN WILSON

A man who shouts "Your house is on fire" may not be able to define exactly what he means by your and house and is and on and fire, but he might still be saying something quite important.

J. B. PRIESTLEY

"My dear Rikki," Karellen retorted, "it's only by not taking the human race seriously that I retain what fragments of my once considerable mental powers I still possess."

ARTHUR C. CLARKE
Childhood's End

It is the greatest joy of the man of thought to have explored the explorable and then calmly to revere the inexplorable.

GOETHE

Authenticity is a kind of honesty or a kind of courage; the authentic individual faces something which the unauthentic individual is afraid to face.

JEAN-PAUL SARTRE

Telling a story "realistically" is such a slowpoke and ponderous way to proceed, and it doesn't fulfill the psychic needs that people have. We sense that there's more to life and to the universe than realism can possibly deal with."

STANLEY KUBRICK
Newsweek, January 3, 1972

10   In subjecting these views to the critical questioning that constitutes one important side of the philosophical task, we are, therefore, engaging in an experiment that is both very personal and at the same time "vicarious." We are not only taking the personal risk of having our views exposed as inadequate, but, since most of our views are also those of the vast majority of the rest of the people in our culture, it is the intellectual outlook of our whole culture that is here being put to the test. If we should suffer the collapse of some of our cherished beliefs (and the loss of a cherished belief does involve a very painful sort of suffering), then it is not only for ourselves that we suffer, but for those many others in our culture who share those beliefs. It is only through such suffering, however, that human thought progresses.

But human thought does progress, and this is what makes the enterprise worthwhile. Many people must have suffered the kind of intellectual agony of which we have been speaking, during the long interval of time that separates us from our primitive ancestors; but there can be little doubt that our way of looking at the world—our world-view—is closer to the truth than the superstitious, animistic, magical views that they are known to have held. If our view is not the whole truth—and it would surely be presumptuous to say that it is—then let us press on toward that elusive goal as best we can. It is the lure of beliefs that are closer to the truth that beckons us on and leaves us dissatisfied with beliefs that are obviously short of that goal.

WILLIAM HALVERSON

11   Just when a human-like consciousness—in the form of self-awareness—began, we cannot at present tell. Perhaps two million years ago, perhaps fourteen, perhaps more. But the question is academic. The significant thing is that we are giving birth to, developing, flowering, a seed planted ages ago; and that this is a glorious flowering, whatever the pain we must pay for the seeds of such flowering. After flowering, most flowers die, though most plants do not die but continue to live and grow. This inevitable flowering of man's awareness is totally unavoidable, and like a flower which has gradually, slowly, grown from bud to its moment of opening to the world, there is no turning back; it is flower, or die.

12   Now the cello has stopped. All that can be heard is the ironic funeral march from the first symphony of Mahler. The girl is walking across the desert towards a hill, the only feature in the otherwise gently sloping terrain, apart from a black plume of smoke which is rising distantly in the air. As she gets nearer to this oily cloud of smoke, scurrying human activity can be seen on the ground beneath. Occasionally a gout of bright flame bursts along the ground, and more smoke is added to the cloud rising swiftly in the air. Now the camera, in a tracking shot, reveals a close-up of the girl's face as she walks along. At first lines of concentration furrow her forehead as she tries to make out what is going on, then the concentration is replaced by bewilderment, and then, a little later, by anger. Now the camera is static, and we see the whole scene as the girl walks up.

Out yonder there was this huge
world, which exists independently
of us human beings and which
stands before us like a great, eternal
riddle, at least partially accessible to
our inspection and thinking. The
contemplation of this world beck-
oned like a liberation.

ALBERT EINSTEIN

Sartre and Heidegger are mistaken; it is not true that there is "no exit" from the "human dilemma." There is a very clearly marked exit. Any man who can see this, and is capable of making the choice that the insight demands, has already taken the first step in a new phase of human evolution.

COLIN WILSON

They talked about their troubles in a way that would embarrass any middle-class observer. I've no doubt that they were often boring, but still life had meaning for them. Even if they did get drunk and fight, they were responding; they were not defeated.

JOHN OSBORNE

Men in shirt sleeves are rushing about, their faces grimy and shining with sweat. They look bewildered and panic-stricken, but this is obviously their normal state of mind. On their backs they carry the large chemical tanks of flamethrowers, and the straps have rubbed into their shoulders for so long that they are obviously in great pain. All around the ground is seared and black. It appears that nothing could possibly grow in such a devastated place, but straggly vegetation is visibly thrusting itself up through the soil. Every moment one of the strange plants is beginning to bloom. . . . A bud appears, almost instantaneously, and begins to open. Lush, coloured petals are visible, promising future beauty. But as soon as one of the men sees this he moves up and immerses the plant in a bath of flame from the nozzle of the weapon he is carrying. All that is left when the fire dies away is charred black soil. But after only a few seconds, pushing up through this inhospitable earth, can be seen a new plant.

The girl clearly doesn't like this place, but when one of the men comes close to her, a fevered expression on his face, she lightly touches his arm.

GIRL. What is this? What are you doing?
MAN. Killing them.
GIRL. But—why?
MAN. To stop them from growing. (*The man turns away to spread a carpet*

of flame, and then turns back to the girl.) The only way is to kill them. If we weren't doing this good work they'd be spreading all over the desert.

GIRL. But why do you want to stop them?

MAN. We don't want these—these filthy blossoms all over the desert. For one thing they'd encourage laxness—all our men would be too lazy to do any useful work, like they're doing now.

GIRL. But the only reason they're working is to kill the flowers.

MAN. And besides which, we're used to the desert. When I see those disgusting petals coming out I feel a strange—tension inside me. What would happen if I gave way to that, and watched them evolving all the way? And anyway, why are you so interested? I don't like the kind of talk you're giving me.

GIRL. It's just that I can't understand you. You're killing something that's beautiful and alive, something that can grow and give you pleasure. . . .

The man looks at the girl with a disgusted expression on his face, and quite deliberately spits at the ground by her feet. Then he turns back to his work. But just before his face goes out of frame his expression can be seen to change from one of disgust to an infinite sadness. The music fades.

LANGDON JONES
"The Eye of the Lens"

13 Each man tries in his personal, and perhaps desperate, way to make this short life/time meaningful. We identify with the things of our universe which are comparatively timeless—with the rock-ribbed mountains, the washing oceans, the stars, with evolution, with life itself—in order to appropriate a little part of their time-spans, their seeming immortality. Or we alleviate nonbeing by losing our selves within great causes and great principles and great people; or by becoming a part of the teleocosmic drama of our society or our religion.

Wer immer strebens sich bemüht,
Den können wir erlösen.
(*Who strives always to the utmost, him can we save.*)

GOETHE

The true biologist deals with life, with teaming boisterous life, and learns something from it, learns that the first rule of life is living. The dryballs cannot possibly know a thing every starfish knows in the core of his soul and in the vesicles between his rays.

JOHN STEINBECK

Behind all this is the burden of our consciousness of death. We must attempt to be immortal, to be God, and to ease the dread of non-existence.

But to strive to feel one with the stars—what is this but to die? Stars die. Earth's light will go out; life may dim and vanish, here. No matter: *we are* a part, an eversotiny part, of the infinite program of the universe. I do not deceive myself into thinking I am buying time by longing for the suns or immersing myself in life. *I am* one with the stars. *I am* one with life. I identify, rightly, with all birth and all death of all time. And when I die, I shall not need to feel as though I never was at all; but rather that I was, and that is enough. I was a part of it all. I remain a part of all past and all future. I am a moment within the energy-systems of motion and life and purpose.

Does this ease my loneliness? Yes. All this follows naturally from the constantly expanding boundaries of my conscious relatedness: the finite self within the context of the infinite.

14 *What is the meaning of existence?*

For an answer which cannot be expressed the question too cannot be expressed. *The riddle* does not exist. If a question can be put at all, then it *can* also be answered. . . . For doubt can only exist where there is a question; a question only where there is an answer, and this only where something can be *said*. We feel that even if *all possible* scientific questions be answered, the problems of life have still not been touched at all. Of course there is then no question left, and just this is the answer. The solution of the problem of life is seen in the vanishing of this problem. (Is not this the reason why men to whom after long doubting the sense of life became clear, could not then say wherein this sense consisted?)

LUDWIG WITTGENSTEIN

15 The whole world is a circus if you look at it the right way. Every time you watch a rainbow and feel wonder in your heart. Every time you pick up a handful of dust and see not the dust but a mystery, a marvel there in your hand. Every time you stop to think "I'm alive! and being alive is fantastic!" Every time such a thing happens, you're a part of the circus of Dr. Lao.

The Seven Faces of Dr. Lao

"What is the Way [Tao]?" Nansen answered, "Your everyday mind is the Way." "How, then, does one get into accord with it?" "If you try to accord, you deviate." Life, he is saying, is not a problem, so why are you asking for a solution?

ALAN WATTS

*We shall not cease from exploration
And the end of all our exploring
Will be to arrive where we started
And know the place for the first time.*

T. S. ELIOT
Four Quartets

Omnes Sancti Angeli et Archangeli, intercedite pro nobis.

All ye devoted bodhisattvas, who for us your fellow living beings and for our release have forborne, aeon after aeon, to enter into your rest, tarry with us, we beseech you, yet a little while longer.

ARNOLD TOYNBEE

Postlude

The Mahayanas tell the story of a sage
who once stood on a riverbank
looking across at the opposite shore.
Although the far side
was but dimly visible
through the river mists,
he could see that it was
unspeakably beautiful.
The hills were green
and the trees were all in blossom.

So he said to himself,
"I want to go there."
There was a raft tied
at the river's edge.
He untied the raft
and began to paddle
toward the distant shore.

The journey was long and hazardous
for the currents in midstream were swift.
The raging rapids tossed and turned the raft,
and he had to work with all his strength
to maintain his balance.
From the center of the river
both shores were lost from view,
and there were times when he was not sure
which way he was drifting.
But he continued paddling,
and in due time
he reached the far shore.

He got out of the raft and said,
"Ah, at last I am here.
It was a perilous journey,
but now I have reached nirvana."
He looked about him.
The hills were green
and the trees were all in blossom.

Then he turned around and looked back.
He could not see the opposite shore
whence he came.
Nor was there any river to be seen.
And there was no raft.

GLOSSARY

When making use of the following brief definitions of terms, note again what a definition is (see p. 228). Definitions are only *predictions of possible meanings* which words may be given in living contexts. Exact meanings can never be known apart from the concrete situation in which they are used. Therefore, think of the following definitions merely as openers. For further clarification, refer to the Index and note specific contexts in which any particular term is used.

ABSOLUTE   A concept of something which is assumed to be free of all qualifications. Whatever is absolute would be underived, complete, perfect, and unconditioned; as such, it could not be modified or changed in any way.

ABSTRACTION   A concept, developed in the mind, taking into account only selected characteristics of a set of objects which are thought of as belonging to the same class. Once the mind has created a generalized abstraction (not *this* painting by Gauguin but painting-in-general), the mind is freed from having to deal with particular objects. See pp. 152f.

AGNOSTICISM   In epistemology, a term (coined by Thomas Huxley) referring to the deliberate suspension of speculation and judgment about things which cannot be known (e.g., the afterlife or the supernatural). The word can be used to mean "I don't know" or "It cannot be known."

AMBIGUOUS   Refers to a word or other symbol which is given different meanings in different contexts. To say that a word is ambiguous often means that one is at a loss to interpret it correctly because he doesn't know the original context in which it was used.

ANALYTIC   (1) A twentieth-century philosophic movement whose main concerns are the logical analysis of language and the process of reasoning. (2) In epistemology, a particular kind of statement in which the predicate merely spells out what the subject implies (e.g., "A triangle has three angles"). An analytic statement says nothing about the real world.

ANTHROPOMORPHIC   Literally, "in the form of man." The projection of human qualities onto nonhuman objects (e.g., nature, animals, deities). For instance, the Greek gods and goddesses were anthropomorphic, possessing all the physical, mental, and emotional characteristics of mortals.

ANTINOMIAN Literally, "against the law." In the widest sense, refers to those who deliberately choose to exist outside the accepted BTF-patterns of their society. (See pp. 38–41.) In Western religion, the word is often used to refer to religious groups which, considering themselves saved by their faith or special knowledge, hold that they are then above all laws and restrictions.

APOCALYPTIC A specific movement in Western religious thought and literature purporting to reveal the (heretofore hidden) divine plan of history. In the four great Western religions (Zoroastrianism, Judaism, Christianity, and Islam), apocalyptic literature moves within the framework of a cosmic battle taking place between the forces of Good and the forces of Evil, detailing dramatic events in the struggle, and revealing the future progress of the conflict to the eschaton or end-time. See TELEOCOSMOS.

A PRIORI In epistemology, a kind of knowledge not derived from, or dependent upon, experience. Rather, it is a universal and necessary knowledge, such as $7 + 5 = 12$. Kant held that time, too, is a priori; the mind *brings time to* its experience of objects/events and does not derive its notion of time from experience of anything in the real world. Time, that is to say, is *prior to* experience. (Don't confuse a priori knowledge with the notion of "innate ideas" which we are supposedly born with.)

ARGUMENT, PHILOSOPHICAL A sort of dialectical conversation, carried on with others or oneself, by which one attempts to clarify his thinking, especially to clarify the validity of the fact-claims used to support particular ideas or statements. A philosophical argument is not an ego-argument.

ARISTOCENTRIC Refers to an inordinate claim to a position of superiority, for oneself or one's group. From the Greek *aristos* (superlative of *agathos,* "good") meaning "the best of its kind" or "the most to be valued." Aristocentric claims are most often made in behalf of one's ethnic group or "race," one's tribe or nation, or one's religion. See pp. 51ff.

ATHEISM A denial of theism (a-theism); the explicit conclusion that God or gods do not exist. Often a positive statement that the hypothesis of supernatural beings is not required to account for anything observed in human experience.

AUTHORITARIANISM The claim on the part of an individual or institution to be a special source of trustworthy knowledge. In epistemology, the position that our most dependable information derives from, or is validated by, some particular authority. Contrasts with the position that knowledge is best validated by personal experience.

AUTHORITY In epistemology, one of the four basic sources of knowledge. Knowledge which we accept on the authority of others. See pp. 12ff.

AUTONOMY The capacity for self-determination; the freedom to operate in terms of one's own volition. Also, functioning harmoniously as an integrated self rather than merely responding inconsistently to disparate enviromental stimuli. "Autonomy means the capacity of the individual to make valid choices of his behavior in the light of his needs" (Gail and Snell Putney, *The Adjusted American*).

AXIOLOGY   A branch of philosophy concerned with the study of values, their origin and nature.

BIOCOSMOS   The conception of a universe which would include life as inherent and natural; that is, a cosmos in which life-forms are an integral factor in the overall process of cosmic evolution.

BIOGENESIS   The general term for the study of the origin of life. There have been numerous biogenetic theories. ARCHEBIOSIS (chemical evolution) is the theory that life develops from inorganic compounds whenever conditions permit it, both on the earth and (probably) throughout the cosmos. PANSPERMIA (or transmission) suggests that life drifted to earth from some other world, perhaps in meteorites. SPONTANEOUS GENERATION suggests that fully developed species are produced from nonliving matter. HYLOZOISM is the theory that all matter is alive. CREATIONISM is the theory that life originates only through an act of the supernatural. See pp. 307, 315f.

BRAHMAN   A Hindu doctrine of absolute and supreme Reality, as compared with the unreal and illusory nature of this world; Ultimate Reality itself; pure being.

BTF-PATTERNS   An abbreviation for Behavior, Thought, and Feeling patterns, the basic elements which together constitute selves and societies. See p. 91.

CAUSALITY   An assumption that certain events cause or produce subsequent events. This is an axiomatic assumption of naturalism and a working assumption of science: that nothing happens without prior cause and that the cause-effect principle applies universally.

COHERENCE-TEST   A truth-test which states that any fact–claim which coheres with previously accepted facts can be considered to be true.

CONCEPT   A mental construct containing all the objects/events which one has classed together according to selected common properties; an abstraction. Contrast with PERCEPT: we have percepts of particular objects/events (*this* seashell, *this* panda, *this* orbit), while a concept is a generalized notion to which the singular object/events belong (seashell, panda, orbit). Most common nouns are concepts.

CONTEXTUALISM   In ethics, the school of thought which holds that relevant ethical decisions can be made only within the context of a particular ethical problem where the unique factors of the situation can be taken into account. Contrast with ethical FORMALISM.

CONTINGENT   In epistemology, a hypothesis or conclusion which is not *necessarily* true. A conclusion which, being derived from empirical observation, is only probably true. All robins' eggs are *probably* blue, but they are not *necessarily* blue. Contrast with necessary knowledge. See DEDUCTION.

CORRESPONDENCE-TEST   A truth-test (developed primarily by Bertrand Russell) which can be used whenever empirical observation is possible. It states that if there is a high degree of correspondence between a (subjective) idea or statement and an (objective) object/event, then the concept can be considered true.

COSMOLOGICAL ARGUMENT An argument for the existence of God, first proposed by Aristotle and further developed by Aquinas. The argument is based on the assumption that causality is absolute and real. Every event must be preceded by another event which is its cause. But it is impossible to think of an infinite regress of causal events. Therefore, there must have been a first cause, an Uncaused Cause which started off this domino-chain of events; this First Cause is defined as God. See pp. 454f.

COSMOLOGY The study of the nature and structure of the universe. Sometimes used to refer to the study of the origin of the universe, though more correctly this is termed *cosmogony*.

COSMOS From the Greek *kosmos,* "the world" or "the ordered universe." Refers to the entire universe considered as a single, harmonious order; a Gestalt world-system.

CREATIONISM The theory that life originated through an act of the supernatural; carries the implication that life cannot originate through other means. (Theory is not limited to any particular account of life-origins.) For various creationist theories see pp. 335ff.

DEDUCTION In logic, the process of drawing out (explicating, making explicit) the implications of one or more premises or statements. Deductive conclusions necessarily follow from the premises. (All bitter fruit is poisonous. Manzanillas are bitter fruit. Therefore, manzanillas are necessarily poisonous.) In deductive logic, the conclusion can be valid (if it has been correctly inferred) and yet be false because the starting premises were false. But if the premises are true and the conclusion is correctly inferred, then the conclusion *must* be both valid and true.

DETERMINISM The assumption or doctrine that every event in the universe has a prior cause and that all effects are at least theoretically predictable if all the causes are known.

DIALECTIC From the Greek *dialektike,* "to converse." The attempt to clarify thought and arrive at facts through a back-and-forth sort of conversation. See ARGUMENT. Also, a thought-process (associated with and propounded by Hegel) wherein ideas attempt to grow and complete themselves through a three-beat rhythm of thesis, antithesis, and synthesis; a back-and-forth progressive movement of thought.

DOUBT, METHODICAL A philosophical method of deliberately disbelieving any idea in order to force it to prove its truth-value with empirical facts and/or rational argument. A way of making fact-claims prove their credentials and of preventing them from being accepted uncritically. Methodical doubt is a helpful corrective to our tendency to take ideas for granted.

DUALISM The view that there exist two related entities, neither of which can be reduced to or identified with the other. In psychology, dualism implies that mind and body are separate entities, different in kind, and that neither can be explained in terms of the other. Metaphysical dualism is the position that there are two orders of reality (usually assumed to be the natural and supernatural), each of which is a distinct and irreducible order.

ECSTASY   Greek *ek-stasis,* "standing outside" (of oneself). A mystical mode of consciousness found in almost every religion in which the self is considered to have been displaced by a possessing spirit (usually a good spirit) which brings about a trance or frenzied condition considered to have ultimate religious significance.

EGOCENTRIC ILLUSION   An epistemological condition: the fact that each of us perceives himself to be the hub and center of the cosmos, though in reality none of us is such a center. From a perceptual standpoint, the universe would appear to revolve around every perceiving creature, human and nonhuman alike. See pp. 50f.

EGOCENTRIC PREDICAMENT   A term coined by the American philosopher Ralph Barton Perry to describe the epistemological fact that each of us is limited to our own perceptual world and cannot move beyond perception to know what the real world is like as it exists apart from perception. Some extreme idealists (e.g., Berkeley) assess this predicament and proceed to the conclusion that the inexperiencible world doesn't exist. Realists usually accept the predicament as a nuisance but proceed to develop a structure of probable facts about the real world which (they assume) lies beyond direct perception.

ÉLAN VITAL   Literally, "vital impulse." Term used by Henri Bergson to refer to the impulse-to-life, which, he theorized, directs evolution upward toward the development of higher, more complex forms of life.

EMPATHY   The capacity on the part of any creature—man or animal—to assess correctly what another creature is experiencing but without itself sharing the experience. Empathy implies understanding of, but not participation in, another's inner world.

EMPIRICAL   In philosophy, the word *empirical* is used in at least two distinct ways. (1) It refers to knowledge acquired by our senses only. Any other knowledge (facts derived by reason, for instance) is not empirical. An "empiricist" would be one who tends to trust the senses (over reason) as our basic source of trustworthy information. In science, there is frequently the added implication that the sense data must be "public facts," that is, subject to repeated experiment and verification. (2) "Empirical" is often used to refer to *any* knowledge gained by *any* human experience (not merely sense experience). This wider definition would include dreams, emotions, religious experiences, and so on; any knowledge derived from these experiences would be called empirical.

EPISTEMIC NAIVETY   The condition of one who accepts uncritically his own vast accumulation of data, not yet having come to terms with the contradictions, fictions, and fallacies which are to be found in any large accumulation of disparate fact-claims.

EPISTEMIC   Shortened form of epistemological.

EPISTEMOLOGY   Branch of philosophy which studies human knowledge. It analyzes the sources of knowledge, processes of thought, truth-tests, fact-claims, value-judgments, etc. A study of what we truly know and don't know.

ESCHATOLOGY   Literally, the doctrine of "last things." One's ideas regarding the final events at the "end of time." The Western Zoroastrian-Judaic family of religions holds that history will end through the intervention of supernatural forces. See TELEOCOSMOS and APOCALYPTIC.

ESP   Extrasensory perception. See PSI.

ESSENCE   The qualities without which any particular object/event would not exist or would be a distinctly different kind of object/event. The qualities necessary for anything to be what it is. (Existentialists are especially concerned to point out that objects may have essences, but that man does not. See p. 197.)

ETHNOCENTRISM   A sociological term referring to the universal tendency of social groups—tribes, nations, races, cultures, religions—to take their own superiority for granted. See ARISTOCENTRISM.

ETHICS   Branch of philosophy which analyzes notions of right and wrong in human relationships. Normative ethics attempts to establish ideals for intent and behavior. The field of ethics is theoretical, in contrast to morality, which refers to one's actual behavior relative to standards by which such behavior is judged to be right and wrong.

EXISTENCE   In existentialism, the word *existence* refers to one's experience of vivid, concrete reality in the living present. Often it carries the connotation of being profoundly aware that one is; that to exist is living in, emphasizing, experiencing fully, being intensely involved in the conscious present.

EXISTENTIALISM   School of philosophy emerging from the dehumanizing conditions of World War II, but having deep historical roots, especially in the writings of Søren Kierkegaard (1813–1855). Existentialism emphasizes the uniqueness and freedom of the individual person and argues that each person must take full responsibility for his own existence and to "create himself." Most existentialists hold that existence can have meaning only as one participates fully in life. A central motif in existential thought is "the individual versus the crowd."

FACT   An idea or statement about which one can feel a high degree of certainty *because,* having been doubted and then subjected to logical and empirical analysis, it still stands. A true idea or statement.

FACT-CLAIM   Any idea submitted as a candidate for consideration as an item of human knowledge. In epistemology, a fact-claim becomes a fact only after it has been carefully checked with the truth-tests and logical analysis and has passed muster; only then does it deserve to be called a "fact."

FAITH   In philosophical usage, the capacity which enables one to act upon the best facts that he possesses, although they are incomplete and there is no signed guarantee of satisfactory results. In a general sense, faith is the courage to proceed to live—to exist as fully as possible—in terms of possibilities and probabilities rather than absolutes and certainties. Contrast with *belief.* See pp. 27, 28f.

FALLACY   An error in reasoning. In logic, a conclusion arrived at by means of inaccurate reasoning. A logical mistake.

FATALISM   The doctrine that every event of our lives is *pre*determined and that no amount of effort on our part can change anything or make any difference. The source of the predetermination is usually attributed to some vaguely conceived notion of natural causation, though it can be attributed to divine causes. (Originally "fatalism" was inflicted by the three Greek Fates or goddesses of destiny.) Fatalism can be both a mood and a rationalization for submission to conditions over which one feels he has no control.

FINITE   Limited. In theology, a limited deity; one that is not omnipotent.

FORMALISM   In ethics, the position that there are universal ethical standards that apply to all men; such "laws" are often believed to have been revealed by a deity. Formalistic ethics contrasts with both RELATIVISM and CONTEXTU-ALISM, which hold that no such universal laws exist.

FREE WILL   The theory that man's will is free to make authentic choices that are not predetermined; an affirmation that man's feeling of freedom is accurate and that our choices made between options are genuine decisions. Free will is the doctrine that, somehow, the human consciousness is not subject to the same causal principles which the scientist assumes to operate in the rest of the physical world. Some solution to the controversy over free will versus determinism is a precondition to any discussion of ethics and responsibility. See pp. 201ff.

GOD   Roughly synonymous with Ultimate Reality or Ultimate Being. In philosophy the existence of a deity would be a hypothesis developed to account for empirical data or to be supported by rational arguments. It would not be, as in religious systems, the object of uncritical belief.

HEDONISM   In ethics, the doctrine that pleasure is the ultimate goal of life which does and should determine our behavior. Philosophical hedonists (e.g., Bentham and Mill) held that man labors under "two sovereign masters": pleasure and pain. Life should be devoted to the avoidance of pain and the augmentation of pleasure, for self and others.

HYLOZOISM   Theory held by the earliest Greek philosophers that all matter is alive or in some way possesses life.

IDEALISM   Idealism is the theory that reality is primarily mental rather than material; it consists of mind (or Mind), minds, ideas, or selves. There are numerous brands of idealism, no two quite alike. Plato was an idealist since he believed that "ideas" exist in the cosmos quite apart from brains. Christians are similarly idealistic if they believe that "ideas" or "eternal verities" exist in the mind of God. Berkeley was an idealist since he believed that only minds (God's and ours) exist. Hegel was an idealist because he believed the Absolute Mind (a superlogical God of sorts) permeates human activity and that we can "think God's thoughts." Mary Baker Eddy, the founder of Christian Science, was an idealist because she believed that we all exist within the Mind of God, the only Reality. Eastern religions such as Hinduism and Buddhism are idealisms since they hold that life's true purpose (for instance, Zen *satori*, "awareness," or the trance-state of *nirvana*) is achieved only through an odyssey of the mind. Shankara's teaching that this world is maya ("illusion"), "comparable to foam, a mirage, a dream," makes this interpretation of Vedanta the Eastern world's most extreme philosophical idealism.

IMPLY To make statements from which logical inferences can be drawn, but without explicitly stating them. The process of drawing out implications is termed INFERENCE. In everyday usage there is much confusion between *infer* and *imply*. See LOGIC.

INDUCTION In logic, the process of developing generalized explanations, hypotheses, or laws from a collection of facts. Induction is the commonest of our daily procedures for gathering knowledge. It includes the hasty generalizations we are prone to make based upon very limited experience (that is, an inadequate collection of related facts). Inductive conclusions are never necessary (as are deductive conclusions), but only probable. See DEDUCTION, CONTINGENT, and p. 123.

INFERENCE An idea which the mind is forced to create after having seen the implications of certain propositions. One infers—draws out, makes explicit—what is implied in a set of premises. The branch of philosophy called logic studies the rules by which we can infer ideas correctly from given premises.

INTUITION (1) A source of knowledge—ideas, remembered facts, hypotheses, solutions to problems—which seem to emerge from the subconscious mind, apparently produced through activity of the subconscious before appearing in the light of consciousness. See pp. 124f. (2) Term used by Bergson to describe the only method he believed could give us an accurate understanding of reality; a process of "intellectual empathy" through which we can understand the duration or unbroken continuum which in fact constitutes physical reality. See pp. 158ff.

INVALID (in·val′id, not in′va·lid!) Refers to an idea which has not been inferred correctly; a fallacious conclusion produced by faulty reasoning.

LOGIC Branch of philosophy defined as the study of valid inference; systematic analysis of the correct and incorrect processes of reasoning.

MACROCOSM Refers to man's particular vantage point as he views, and attempts to comprehend, the universe. The macrocosm is man's experiential level of reality as he looks up and down, so to speak: up at cosmic realities (cosmos) and down at microscopic realities (microcosm). Without the aid of instruments man is caught at the macrocosmic level since neither cosmos nor microcosm is directly perceivable.

MATERIALISM The doctrine that everything in the universe is nothing other than various manifestations of matter-in-motion, and, in theory, can be reduced to, and explained by, principles of causality. All the objects/events for which we have such diverse labels—matter, mind, energy, life, and perhaps spirit—are only variant forms of matter-in-motion.

MAYA   The Hindu doctrine that this world is unreal; it is mere illusion. All we know are the illusory surface appearances of things. If the material world is unreal, only Brahman or Ultimate Reality is truly real.

METAPHYSICS   A branch of philosophy concerned with what actually exists, that is, with what the true nature of things really is. Traditionally, metaphysics has been divided into two subbranches: ONTOLOGY, the study of being, and COSMOLOGY, the study of the cosmos (cosmology is now generally thought of as a branch of astronomy). See ONTOLOGY.

MONISM   Any world-view which purports to reduce all existence to a single order of reality; the doctrine that there is but one order of reality, whether it be mind (which would be called "psychical monism") or matter-in-motion ("naturalistic monism"), or some other kind of reality.

MORAL   Refers to the way one overtly behaves in his relationships with others. In the most general sense, moral behavior is intended to produce, somewhere, somehow, constructive results; immoral behavior is intended to produce destructive results. Contrast with ETHICS, which is the theoretical study of ideal (normative) relationships.

MYSTIC   One who seeks or one who experiences dissolution of ego-self and separateness and feels that his being has merged or become united with Deity, Ultimate Reality, or Nature.

MYSTICISM   The school of religion which values the mode of consciousness in which the ego-self is lost and an experience of oneness with Ultimate Reality is attained. Epistemologically, the mystic commonly claims that only through a mystical experience—as opposed to rational or empirical inquiry—can reality be known.

MYTH   A story or account, by definition involving some element of the supernatural, which is accepted by a community as a satisfactory answer to, or explanation of, some meaningful question or experience. Historically, myths are held collectively by religious communities, tribes, nations, or the like; but a story can perform the same function for an individual, in which case use of the term *myth* is justifiable. See pp. 431ff.

NAIVE REALISM   The uncritical acceptance of one's sense data as representing accurately the nature of the real world; a sort of "blind faith" in what one's senses seem to tell him.

NATURALISM   The world-view which holds that there is but a single order of reality, that of matter-in-motion. Naturalism, by definition, excludes the existence of a "supernatural" order of reality.

NIHILISM   In epistemology, the doctrine that nothing is knowable, or is worth knowing; the contention that all knowledge is illusory, relative, and meaningless. Similarly, in ethics, nihilism is the doctrine that all moral judgments are irrational, relative, and, finally, meaningless. In a word, nihilism is the belief that there is no knowledge, no value, and no meaning that is of any real worth to man.

NIRVANA   A mode of consciousness valued by the Buddhist and Hindu as the supreme goal of human existence. Literally, "extinction of consciousness," but better conceived as a state of consciousness described as an experience of wholeness, peace, and joy. In Hindu and Buddhist doctrine this mode of consciousness will continue after death for one who has reached the point of liberation (*moksha*) from the Wheel of Karma—the "round of rebirths."

OBJECTIVE   Refers to whatever exists in the real world apart from our perception of it. Having to do with the perceived object as opposed to the perceiving subject. See SUBJECTIVE.

OCCAM'S RAZOR   (Also called the Principle of Parsimony.) One of the fundamental principles of scientific method. It states that, all else being equal, the simplest explanation is the best. That is, in developing inductive hypotheses, the simplest hypothesis which accounts for all relevant data is more likely to be true. Named after the scholastic philosopher William of Occam, who phrased it: "The number of entities should not be needlessly increased."

ONTOLOGICAL ARGUMENT   A logical argument for the existence of God developed by St. Anselm of Canterbury (1033–1109). Anselm attempted to prove the existence of God from the nature of thought alone. See pp. 455f.

ONTOLOGY   From the Greek *ontos*, "being," and *logos*, "study of." Branch of philosophy which studies the nature of reality or being, especially as applied to living things. The term ontological is commonly used to emphasize the fact that some specific quality is an inescapable aspect of life itself. The fear of death, for instance, is said to be ontological since there is no way—short of the extinction of consciousness—to escape the fear. We could repress it, but the fear would remain a part of our being, buried precariously in the unconscious, where it can become a powerful but unrecognized cause of puzzling behavior.

PANPSYCHISM   The doctrine that everything is composed of, or contains, mind or "soul" (*psyche*). Some Western thinkers have speculated that the binding forces within atoms might be, in some way, the operations of mind.

PANSPERMIA   The biogenetic theory that life may have developed on earth after having been transferred from other worlds, perhaps by meteorites. See BIOGENESIS, pp. 307, 315f.

PANTHEISM   The doctrine that God is All. Pantheists usually hold that God is in all matter or that the totality of all matter is "the body of God."

PARADOX   A condition where two mutually exclusive ideas or statements appear to be true; and until the arrival of further data or some sort of resolution, both ideas or statements must be accepted and acted upon.

PARSIMONY, PRINCIPLE OF.   See OCCAM'S RAZOR.

PERCEPT   The first-stage result of the mind's organization of sense data. The mind perceives a concrete object—*this* coin or *this* car—which remains in consciousness as an unnamed, singular object. A percept (or perception) is what is given in consciousness, the object of cognition. Contrast with CONCEPT, in which objects are mentally classed with other objects, and the mind henceforth thinks of the class rather than the object. Contrast also with SENSE DATUM, a raw, unorganized sense-response.

PHILOSOPHY   The love of wisdom. From Greek *philein* ("to love") and *sophia* ("wisdom"). Philosophy comprises several distinct disciplines or methods which have in common the goal of improving upon the condition of human knowledge and our knowledge of the human condition.

PLURALISM   The world-view holding that there exist more than two orders of reality, each of which is distinct and irreducible. For instance, if one believes that the universe is composed of matter, mind, spirit, and divine-essence, then he would be a pluralist. Compare with MONISM and DUALISM.

PRAGMATIC-TEST   The truth-test (developed primarily by William James) which states that if an idea or statement "works"—that is, brings about desirable results—then the idea or statement can be considered true. James held that the truth-value of any idea is to be judged in terms of the results it can produce. See pp. 36f., 164ff.

PRAGMATIC PARADOX   A human condition in which an idea must be believed to be true in terms of correspondence—that is, one must be convinced that some object/event exists as a real entity—before the idea can be considered to be true on the pragmatic-test. For example, one must believe that immortality exists as a real event (which, one must believe, could be empirically checked, under the right conditions, with the correspondence-test) before the belief in immortality can produce positive results in his life. If he believed it to be true solely on the pragmatic-test, it would in fact *not* be true because it wouldn't "work." See pp. 167ff.

PRAGMATISM   An American school of philosophy associated mainly with William James and John Dewey. One of its central themes is that philosophy should be put to work solving the more pressing human problems instead of preoccupying itself in metaphysical speculations. See pp. 36f. According to the pragmatists, truth is tentative and forever changing; truth is the quality of whatever ideas "work" at the present time. See pp. 164ff.

PRECOGNITION   Having knowledge of an event supposedly before it happens. See PSI.

PREDESTINATION   A theological term referring to divine predeterminism. The doctrine that God has already determined (at least) whether each human soul will be saved or lost, or (at most) that every singular event of existence will occur as planned. A "hard" predestination logically excludes the possibility of free will. See pp. 202ff.

PREDICAMENT   A problem condition to which, by definition, there is no solution; a situation which must be accepted. One may be able to deal productively with problems arising from a predicament (e.g., *fear* of non-being), but not with the predicament itself (that each of us faces nonbeing).

PREMISE   In logic, an idea or statement which, along with other ideas or statements, can lead to a conclusion. In reasoning, a premise is a starting statement, an opener.

PRIMAL FREEDOM   Freedom from subjective limitations, thereby enabling one to make authentic choices; freedom from primal limitations. See pp. 204f.

PRIMARY QUALITIES   In epistemology, the qualities, according to John Locke, which inhere in real objects: e.g., weight, motion, shape. Compare with SECONDARY QUALITIES. See pp. 141f.

PSI   Refers to all parapsychological or "paranormal" experiences. Among them: TELEPATHY, the sending of messages (ideas and/or feelings) from one mind to another; CLAIRVOYANCE, the mind's "seeing" an object/event at a distance; PSYCHOKINESIS (PK), "mind over matter," the power of the mind to influence the behavior of objects; PRECOGNITION, knowledge of an event (supposedly) before it takes place. ESP (Extrasensory Perception) is a rough synonym for PSI, though we do not know at present whether such experiences (if they do in fact occur) are truly *extra*sensory.

PSYCHE   Greek word meaning "soul"; usually thought of as a substantialized, objectified form of the self, though in earlier times and other places the word has been given a bewildering variety of meanings.

PSYCHOKINESIS   The power of the mind to influence directly the behavior of objects/events. See PSI.

RATIONAL   Roughly synonymous with "reasonable"; the capacity to engage in reasoned inquiry.

RATIONALISM   In epistemology, a philosophical tradition that holds that our most dependable information derives from reason rather than from empirical observation. A rationalist is one who trusts reason more than the deceptive "rabble of the senses."

RATIONALIZE   The process of developing reasons ("rationales") for holding certain beliefs or performing certain actions—reasons which are not the true reasons but which are more acceptable than the true reasons. One who is subjectively naive will thus delude himself as well as others; one who is subjectively aware may reserve his rationales only for others. By definition, a rationalization is a fallacy engaged in out of need to defend one's thoughts, feelings, or actions. (Don't confuse with RATIONALISM.)

REAL, REALISM   Among the most important terms in philosophy. To be real is to exist apart from perception. If I state that the teakwood figurine of the Buddha on my desk is "real," then I am stating the belief that the figurine exists as a "thing-in-itself" quite apart from my perception of it; if I were not perceiving it in any way whatsoever, it would still exist. (This position is *material realism,* and modern use of the term is often restricted to this meaning; *real* therefore refers to material objects or to the physical world in general.) If I should go further and claim that the Cosmic Buddha exists, quite apart from my perception of him (or It), then this is a *theological realism.* If I claim that beauty exists in the orchid or rainbow, apart from my perception (that is, I close my eyes but I am convinced that "beauty" still remains in the rainbow), then I am an *esthetic realist.* Lastly, if I claim that right and wrong (or Good and Evil) actually exist in the real world, then I am a *value realist* or an *ethical realist.*

In common parlance we speak of dreams, headaches, fears, bad vibrations, etc. as "real." "They are *my* realities," we contend. "Don't tell me my head doesn't hurt. My headache is real!" But the headache is not real, as the term is used in philosophy: the headache certainly does not exist apart from your perception of it!

REALITY   In epistemology, the totality of all things that exist apart from perception. The real world. See REAL, REALISM. In social science, a fabric of BTF-patterns shared by members of a particular society; all that is *considered* to be real by that social group.

REASON   One of many kinds of thinking (others being remembering, day-dreaming, intuiting, dreaming, etc.). The mental process of using known facts to arrive at new facts. In logic, the activity of inferring conclusions from premises.

RELATIVISM   In ethics, the belief, based on empirical observation, that what is considered to be right and wrong differs from one society to another and from one person to another. The term usually implies that there are no universal codes of right and wrong. Contrast with FORMALISM. (Don't confuse with Einstein's RELATIVITY.)

RELATIVITY   In physics, Einstein's theories of special (1905) and general (1916) relativity. Roughly, a system of mathematics and physics which predicts the behavior of matter-in-motion at high speeds. (Don't confuse with ethical RELATIVISM.)

SAMADHI   Literally, "concentration"; a form of meditation. In Hinduism and Buddhism, a trancelike mode of consciousness wherein the mind achieves a blissful, contentless, transpersonal state; the attainment of *atman,* or authentic self-essence.

SATORI   In Zen Buddhism, the "moment of awakening" when a meditator realizes the illusory nature of self and separateness; a holistic feeling of mystical oneness. See p. 179.

SCHOLASTICISM   A movement in Western ecclesiastical history beginning c. A.D. 1100 and flowering during the thirteenth century, resulting from the recovery of the Greek classics and the revitalized use of rational inquiry following the Dark Ages. A period of renewed intellectual activity within the framework of the accepted truths of medieval Catholic religion. Among the great scholastic philosophers (the "schoolmen") were Anselm of Canterbury, Bernard of Clairvaux, Peter Abelard, Albertus Magnus, and Thomas Aquinas.

SCHOLASTIC METHOD   Specifically, the use of reason by the scholastic philosophers, not to discover truth but to explore, explicate, and defend *known* (i.e., revealed) truths. The truths themselves were not subject to doubt or inquiry. See pp. 26f.

SECONDARY FREEDOM   The capacity to make genuine choices without being limited by external restrictions (e.g., economic, social, political). Contrast secondary limitations (which are objective) with primal limitations (which are subjective). See PRIMAL FREEDOM, pp. 204f.

SECONDARY QUALITIES   According to John Locke, qualities which do not inhere in objects/events but are subjective sensations (e.g., color, sound, taste). Compare with PRIMARY QUALITIES. See pp. 141f.

SELF   The conscious subject which experiences, designated by "I" or "ego." The word has frequently been used to refer to some unknown entity which unifies the data of consciousness into a coherent, operational system. Self, however, may be better conceived as the coherent system rather than some hypothetical unifying entity. An ambiguous and problematic concept.

SELF-DETERMINATION   In psychology and ethics, the position that one's personal BTF-patterns have antecedent causes, but that such causes may reside within oneself and not in the environment. We can become "self-caused." Self-determination is a middle position between an extreme free will position which denies determinism and a behavioristic position which denies free will.

SEMANTICS   Broadly, the study of meaning. A study of the total response of the human organism to symbols of all sorts (words, signs, gestures, etc.). In a narrow sense, the study of words and their meanings.

SENSATION   The immediate response of the senses to stimuli. A synonym for SENSE DATUM. (*Sensation* does not refer to emotional responses.)

SENSE DATA   Immediate sensory responses as registered in consciousness—patches of color, bits of sound—which are synthesized by the mind into the perception of an object. Sense data (singular, *datum*) are the first raw materials of experience which make their way from our sense receptors to the interpretive areas of the brain, where they are organized into perceptions of particular objects.

SKEPTICISM   In epistemology, an attitude of doubt; either a deliberate methodical doubt to force fact-claims to prove themselves or a general doctrine of philosophical agnosticism, a sincere doubt that accurate knowledge is possible.

SOLIPSISM   The doctrine that only "I" (the solipsist, of course) exist. A logical (but quite illogical) inference from the conclusion that all we can truly know are our own experiences. See p. 148.

SOUL   Roughly, a substantialized, objectified notion of the self. See PSYCHE.

SUBJECTIVE   Refers to the subject which experiences, as opposed to the object which is experienced. The term refers to the location of events which constitute the experiencing process (subjective), as opposed to the events which belong to the real world (objective).

SUBSTANCE   The ultimate "stuff" (Greek *physis*) of which any object is made; the underlying reality to which primary qualities adhere. The word *substance* is a label applied to the *assumption* that there is a continuing essence in any object which remains immutable through all ephemeral changes in its "perceivable" qualities. See pp. 141ff.

SUMMUM BONUM   In ethics, the Ultimate Good of human existence; that is, the final goal toward which all our endeavors should be directed. Various such goals have been proposed: happiness, pleasure, self-actualization, ethical love, soul-salvation, etc.

SUPERNATURAL   An order of reality above and outside the natural order. In philosophy, the supernatural is not the object of religious belief; supernaturalists would contend that it is necessary to postulate such an order to account for the complex data of experience. Contrast with NATURALISM; See also MONISM, DUALISM.

SYMPATHY   Literally, "to suffer with" another. The capacity not merely to understand what another is experiencing (which is EMPATHY), but the actual duplication, so to speak, in one's own experience of what another is experiencing. See p. 230.

SYNOPTIC   From the Greek *sun-optikos,* "seeing the whole together" or "taking a comprehensive view." The attempt to achieve an all-inclusive overview of one's subject matter and to see all its parts in relationship to one another.

TAO   In Chinese religion, "The Way"; a sort of cosmic pathway that lies between or within the interactions of the energy-modes Yang and Yin. To discover the Tao is to begin to live in perfect harmony with self and cosmos.

TELEOCOSMOS   From the Greek *teleos,* "finished" or "complete," implying purposive design and goal-directed movement; and *kosmos,* "an ordered universe." A world-view with a program which moves with direction and purpose, and in which man plays a major role. The most noteworthy teleocosmic world-views belong to man's religions and resemble cosmic dramas in structure, including a full cast of characters—protagonists and antagonists, gods and demons, supporting roles and bit players—and carefully designed plots leading to a dramatic climax and a dénouement. Man's role is the central element of teleocosmic dramas, though this fact may be obscured by large-scale cosmic events which occur as the drama unfolds. See pp. 438ff.

TELEOLOGICAL ARGUMENT   An argument for the existence of God based on the apparent purposive nature of evolutionary movement and/or the design and order of the universe. Order implies an orderer; design implies a designer. The American Personalists considered this to be the strongest empirical argument for the existence of God. See pp. 456ff.

TELEOLOGY   From the Greek *teleos,* "finished" or "complete." The theory that deliberate purposive activity, rather than mere chance, is involved in some process. The interpretation of any series of events—such as an organism's growth, evolution, or human history—as expressions of purposeful movement; goal-directed, as though planned out and guided toward a preset end or ideal. See pp. 328ff., 445ff.

TELEPATHY   Communication of mind with mind via supposedly extrasensory media. See PSI.

THEISM   Belief in gods or God. Often used to mean belief in a specific Western doctrine of an omnipotent, omniscient, and personal Deity. Contrast with atheism, the denial that gods or God exist.

THEOLOGY   The rational organization of religious beliefs and practices in order to render them logically coherent and meaningful. Theology is an intellectual discipline in contrast to religion which involves one's whole being.

TIME DILATION   A phenomenon predicted by Einstein's special theory of relativity: for any object moving at great velocities (relative to the speed of light) time would slow down. See pp. 386ff.

TRUTH   "Truth is the approximation of thought to reality" (Brand Blanshard). Truth is a quality possessed by ideas and statements, a quality which is of value to a philosopher only after having been carefully checked with one or more of the truth-tests. The notion of an ethereal, nonspecific (and untestable) truth is meaningless.

VALID   In logic, a technical term referring to a conclusion which has been correctly inferred from specific premises. Validity is the property of an idea or statement which has been correctly derived by logical inference.

VITALISM   The doctrine that a "life principle" must suffuse itself (or be injected) into inorganic matter before life-processes can begin. What this "vital" element might be is usually unspecified, but it is often associated with the supernatural.

WORLD-VIEW   In a broad sense, one's philosophy of life; an all-inclusive, coherent way of looking at life and the cosmos. From the German *Weltan-schauung,* a sort of unconscious, totalic fabric into which one incorporates all his experiences and through which he sees the world.

CREDITS

I. REFERENCES

Whenever possible, paperback editions have been used since they will usually be more accessible and convenient.

We have attempted to honor the precise wording of credit lines requested by publishers or persons granting permission to reprint materials.

Grateful acknowledgment is hereby made to all who have responded so graciously to our permission requests.

B = box; Q = quotation.

xviii From *A Concise Introduction to Philosophy*, by William Halverson, pp. 18f. Copyright © 1967 by Random House, Inc. Reprinted by permission of the publisher.

1-1

5 Alexei Panshin, *Rite of Passage* (Ace SF, 1968), p. 252.

6f. From *The Little Prince* by Antoine de Saint-Exupéry, translated by Katherine Woods, pp. 72f., copyright 1943, 1971, by Harcourt Brace Jovanovich, Inc., and reprinted with their permission.

8f. Viktor E. Frankl, *Man's Search for Meaning* (Washington Square, 1963), pp. 167f. Copyright © 1959, 1962 by Viktor E. Frankl. Reprinted by permission of Beacon Press.

9f. From *Out of My Life and Thought* by Albert Schweitzer. Translated by C. P. Campion. Copyright 1933, 1949, © 1961 by Holt, Rinehart and Winston, Inc. Reprinted by permission of Holt, Rinehart and Winston, Inc.

10f. Reprinted from *Psychology Today* Magazine, August 1970, p. 16. Copyright © Communications/Research/Machines, Inc.

11 Gordon Allport. Frankl, *Man's Search for Meaning*, pp. ix–xiii. Reprinted by permission of Beacon Press.

14 Desmond Morris, *The Naked Ape* (McGraw-Hill, 1967), pp. 187, 189, 156, 159.
Konrad Lorenz, *On Aggression* (Bantam, 1967), p. 233. Reprinted by permission of Harcourt Brace Jovanovich, Inc.

15 From "The Undersea World of Jacques Cousteau: The Night of the Squid," ABC-TV, telecast April 12, 1970.

16 Abraham Maslow, *New Knowledge in Human Values* (Harper, 1959), pp. 123, 126.

16-B René Dubos, *The Torch of Life* (Pocket Books, 1962), p. 15. Reprinted by permission of Trident Press, a division of Simon & Schuster, Inc.

17f. Program notes by E. C. Stone for the London recording of Richard Strauss' *Also Sprach Zarathustra*, by the Vienna Philharmonic Orchestra, conducted by Herbert von Karajan. (Final italics added.)

18-Q From *Kismet*. Lyrics by Robert Wright and George Forrest. Reprinted by permission of Frank Music Corporation.

1-2

19f. Socrates. Plato, *The Apology*, in *The Last Days of Socrates*, trans. Hugh Tredennick (Penguin Classics, 1954), pp. 49–52. Copyright © Hugh Tredennick 1954, 1959, 1969. Reprinted by permission of Penguin Books Ltd. (The opening line of Socrates' defense is from the Jowett translation. See reference for p. 25 below.)

25 Socrates. Plato, *The Apology*, in *The Dialogues of Plato*, trans. Benjamin Jowett (Oxford, 1924).

26 Thomas: John 20:24–29. Paul: 1 Corinthians 1:20; Colossians 2:8; Galations 3:28.
St. Augustine. Philip Schaff, *History of the Christian Church*, Vol. III, *Nicene and Post-Nicene Christianity* (Eerdmans, 1950 [1910]), pp. 998, 1004.
St. Anselm. Schaff, *History*, Vol. V, *The Middle Ages* (1949 [1907]), pp. 600f.
Peter Abelard. Schaff, *History*, Vol. V, pp. 622–624.

27 Arnold J. Toynbee, *A Study of History* (Oxford, 1954), Vol. VII, pp. 729f. Reprinted by permission of Oxford University Press.

28 Socrates. Plato, *The Meno*, in *The Dialogues of Plato*, trans. Benjamin Jowett, Vol. II, p. 47.

29 Paul Tillich, *Dynamics of Faith* (Harper, 1957), pp. 31f.
Abraham Maslow, *Motivation and Personality* (Harper, 1954). Copyright Harper & Row, Publishers, Inc., and reprinted by their permission.

29f. Bert C. Williams, "On Losing One's Faith," *The Scroll* (Winter 1957), p. 4. Reprinted by permission of the author.

1-3

32f. Aristotle. Quotation from B. A. G. Fuller and Sterling McMurrin, *History of Philosophy* (Holt, 1955), p. 172.

35 Erich Fromm, *Marx's Concept of Man* (Frederick Ungar, 1961), p. 3.

Louis Untermeyer, *Makers of the Modern World* (Simon and Schuster, 1955), p. 26.

36-B Machiavelli. Pasquale Villari, *Life and Times of Niccolò Machiavelli* (Scribner's, N.D.), Vol. II, pp. 158f.

41 Thomas Merton, *The Way of Chuang Tzu* (New Directions, 1965), p. 10. Copyright © 1965 by the Abbey of Gethsemany. Reprinted by permission of New Directions Publishing Corporation.

41f. Justus Hartnack, *Wittgenstein and Modern Philosophy* (Doubleday Anchor, 1965), p. 8. Translation copyright © by Methuen and Co, Ltd. Reprinted by permission of Doubleday and Co., Inc.

44 Ibid., pp. 4f., 8.

2-1

In Part 2 my indebtedness to others is especially great. The concept of the egocentric illusion is to be found, in various contexts, throughout Toynbee's writings. While the origins of the idea must be credited to him, he is obviously in no way responsible for my elaboration of it.

A substantial amount of material throughout this book, and especially in these chapters, was developed with my wife, Barbara Taylor Christian. I have incorporated many of her observations dealing with personality and growth. Particularly helpful were her concepts on the interaction of intellectual awareness and experience in the making of growth choices and the conditions fostering development of autonomy versus alienation.

51-Q "The Prayer of the Little Ducks." From *Prayers from the Ark,* by Carmen Bernos de Gasztold, trans. Rumer Godden (Viking, 1962), p. 59. Copyright © 1962 by Rumer Godden. Reprinted by permission of The Viking Press, Inc.

Paul Horton and Chester Hunt, *Sociology* (McGraw-Hill, 1964), p. 91. Copyright 1964 by McGraw-Hill. Used with permission of McGraw-Hill Book Company.

52ff. Milton Rokeach, *The Three Christs of Ypsilanti* (Knopf, 1964), pp. 4ff., 315, 313f. Reprinted by permission of Alfred A. Knopf, Inc.

58 Horton and Hunt, *Sociology,* p. 86. Used with permission of McGraw-Hill Book Company.

2-2

62-B David Hume, *Treatise of Human Nature,* Book I, Part ii, Sec. 5.

64 Arthur W. Combs (Chairman, 1962 Yearbook Committee), *Perceiving, Behaving, Becoming: A New Focus for Education* (Association for Supervision and Curriculum Development, 1962), p. 84. Reprinted by permission of ASCD Publications.

Erich Fromm, *The Art of Loving* (Bantam, 1963), pp. 49ff. Copyright © Harper & Row, Publishers, Inc., and reprinted with their permission.

66-B Bertrand Russell, *The Analysis of Mind* (Allen & Unwin, 1921), p. 18.

72ff. S. I. Hayakawa, "The Fully Functioning Personality," in *Symbol, Status, and Personality* (Harcourt, Brace & World, N.D.), pp. 51ff.

2-3

75ff. Excerpted from "The Young Monkeys" by Harry and Margaret Harlow in *Psychology Today* Magazine, September 1967. Copyright © Communications/Research/Machines, Inc.

78-B *Science News,* April 8, 1972, p. 233.

2-4

85 Rollo May, *Love and Will* (Norton, 1969), pp. 165ff.

86ff. Desmond Morris, *The Naked Ape* (McGraw-Hill, 1967). See Chapter IV, "Exploration."

87-B Rogers and Combs. Arthur W. Combs (Chairman, 1962 Yearbook Committee), *Perceiving, Behaving, Becoming: A New Focus for Education* (Association for Supervision and Curriculum Development, 1962), p. 84.

89 S. I. Hayakawa, "The Fully Functioning Personality," in *Symbol, Status, and Personality* (Harcourt, Brace & World, N.D.), pp. 51ff. (Italics added.)

Combs, *Perceiving, Behaving, Becoming,* pp. 141f. Reprinted by permission of ASCD Publications.

90 Alexei Panshin, *Rite of Passage* (Ace SF, 1968), pp. 241ff. Copyright © 1968 by Alexei Panshin. Used by permission of the author and Henry Morrison Inc., his agents.

92-B Gregory Bateson, "Language and Psychotherapy." Quoted from Alan Watts, *Psychotherapy East and West* (Mentor, 1961), p. 105.

93-Q From *Stop the World—I Want to Get Off.* Words and music by Leslie Bricusse and Anthony Newley. Copyright © 1961 TRO Essex Music Limited, London, England. Used by permission.

94f. From *The Madman,* by Kahlil Gibran. Copyright 1918 by Kahlil Gibran and renewed 1946 by Administrators C.T.A. of Kahlil Gibran Estate and Mary G. Gibran. Reprinted by permission of Alfred A. Knopf, Inc.

2-5

96 William Shakespeare, *As You Like It,* Act II, Sc. 7, ll. 144ff.

100-B Erich Fromm, *The Heart of Man* (Harper Colophon, 1968), p. 23.

102-B Hudson Hoagland, "Some Biochemical Considerations of Time," and Roland Fischer, "Biological Time," in J. T. Fraser (ed.), *Voices of Time* (George Braziller, 1966), pp. 325 and 360, respectively. Copyright © 1966 by J. T. Fraser. Reprinted by permission of George Braziller, Inc.

104 *Developmental Psychology Today: An Introduction* (CRM Books, 1971), p. 383. From *Psychology Today: An Introduction* (Del Mar, Calif.: CRM Books), © 1970, CRM, Inc.

107-B Sheldon Harnick, *Fiddler on the Roof.* Copyright © 1964 by Sunbeam Music Inc., 1700 Broadway, N.Y., N.Y. 10019. International copyright secured. All rights reserved.

110 Ray Bradbury, "If I Were Epitaph." Copyright 1967 by Ray Bradbury. Copyright 1971 by Rotarian Magazine. Reprinted by permission of Harold W. Matson Co., Inc.

111 Erik H. Erikson, "A Healthy Personality for Every Child," in Robert H. Anderson and Harold G. Shane (eds.), *As the Twig Is Bent* (Houghton Mifflin, 1971), pp. 136f.

112f. Leo Tolstoy, *The Death of Ivan Ilytch,* trans. Aylmer Maude

(Oxford). Quoted from Joseph Royce, *The Encapsulated Man* (Van Nostrand, 1964), pp. 108f.

113-B   *Newsweek*, January 3, 1972, p. 56.

3-1

121-B   Fernando Arrabal, *La Cimetière des Voitures* (*The Automobile Graveyard*).

3-2

135-B   Buckminster Fuller, "This Is the New Invisible World," *TV Guide*, February 6–12, 1970, p. 9.

137-B   Sir Arthur Eddington, *New Pathways in Science* (University of Michigan Press, 1959), p. 11.

3-3

142   George Berkeley, *Principles of Human Knowledge*, No. 92 in *A New Theory of Vision, and Other Writings* (Everyman's Library, 1963), p. 159.

144   Will Durant, *The Story of Civilization*, Vol. VIII, *The Age of Louis XIV* (Simon and Schuster, 1963), p. 597.

144f.   James Boswell, *Life of Samuel Johnson* (Modern Library, 1965), p. 159.

148   Will Durant, *The Story of Civilization*, Vol. VIII, p. 597.

150   David Hume, *A Treatise of Human Nature*, Book I, Part iv, Sec. 1.

3-4

153ff.   S. I. Hayakawa, *Language in Thought and Action* (Harcourt, 1963). Sections 2–9 on abstracting and classifying are heavily indebted to Chapters 10, 11, and 12 of Dr. Hayakawa's book. The story of the animals is a close paraphrase of the account found on pages 214f.

154-B   Lincoln Barnett, *The Universe and Dr. Einstein* (Mentor, 1952), pp. 123f.

155   Hayakawa, *Language in Thought and Action*, p. 216. (Original italics removed.)

157   See Ashley Montagu, *Man's Most Dangerous Myth: The Fallacy of Race* (Harper, 1952).

158ff.   Henri Bergson, *A Study in Metaphysics: The Creative Mind* (Littlefield, Adams, 1965), pp. 159ff.

158-B   Ibid., p. 175.

3-5

165   For C. S. Peirce's original article "How to Make Our Ideas Clear," see Walter G. Muelder and Laurence Sears, *The Development of American Philosophy* (Houghton Mifflin, 1940), pp. 341ff.

166f.   John J. McDermott (ed.), *The Writings of William James* (Modern Library, 1968), p. xxi. The introduction to this anthology contains an excellent brief biography of James.

169-B   William S. and Mabel Lewis Sahakian, *Realms of Philosophy* (Schenkman, 1965), p. 41.

"My World and Welcome to It," NBC-TV, February 23, 1970.

4-1

173   R. D. Laing, *The Politics of Experience* (Ballantine, 1967), p. 26.

175f.   Edward B. Fiske, "New Worldview." Reprinted, with permission, from the November/December 1971 issue of *The Center Magazine*, a publication of the Center for the Study of Democratic Institutions in Santa Barbara, California, p. 20.

175-B   Roland Fischer, "Biological Time," in J. T. Fraser (ed.), *Voices of Time* (George Braziller, 1966), p. 372. Copyright © 1966 by J. T. Fraser. Reprinted by permission of George Braziller, Inc.

176   William James. Quoted from Charles T. Tart (ed.), *Altered States of Consciousness* (John Wiley, 1969), p. 21.

176ff.   Milton H. Erickson, "A Special Inquiry with Aldous Huxley into the Nature and Characteristics of Various States of Consciousness," in Tart, *Altered States of Consciousness*, pp. 45–71.

179   Erich Fromm, D. Suzuki, and di Martino, *Zen Buddhism and Psychoanalysis* (Allen & Unwin, 1960). Quoted from Tart, *Altered States of Consciousness*, p. 490.

181f.   From a lecture by Terry Allen and used with his permission. Requested credit line: "Our Oneness—Mother the Earth . . . Father the Universe."

4-2

184   R. M. MacIver, *The Challenge of the Passing Years: My Encounter with Time* (Simon and Schuster, 1962), p. xxiii. (Italics added.)

184f.   A. Cornelius Benjamin, "Ideas of Time in the History of Philosophy," in J. T. Fraser (ed.), *Voices of Time* (George Braziller, 1966), p. 4. Copyright © 1966 by J. T. Fraser. Reprinted by permission of George Braziller, Inc.

185-B   Eric Berne, *Games People Play* (Grove, 1964), p. 178.

186   Friedrich Waismann, "Analytic-Synthetic," in Richard M. Gale (ed.), *The Philosophy of Time* (Doubleday Anchor, 1967), pp. 55f.

187-B   MacIver, *The Challenge of the Passing Years*, p. 132.

189-B   John Cohen, "Subjective Time," in Fraser, *Voices of Time*, p. 275. Copyright © 1966 by J. T. Fraser. Reprinted by permission of George Braziller, Inc.

190   St. Augustine, *Confessions*, Book XI. (Any edition.)

191   *Sir Isaac Newton's Mathematical Principles of Natural Philosophy and His System of the World*, trans. Andrew Motte (University of California Press, 1947), p. 6. Quoted from Fraser, *Voices of Time*, p. 18.

Immanuel Kant, *Critique of Pure Reason*, trans. F. Max Müller (Doubleday Anchor, 1966), pp. 29ff.

191f.   Benjamin, in Fraser, *Voices of Time*, p. 22. Copyright © 1966 by J. T. Fraser. Reprinted by permission of George Braziller, Inc.

192f.   Arthur C. Clarke, *Profiles of the Future* (Bantam, 1964), p. 138.

193f.   J. B. Priestley, *Man and Time* (Dell, 1968), pp. 205, 288.

194   Louise Robinson Heath, *The Concept of Time* (University of Chicago Press, 1936), p. 199.

195   William James, *Psychology; Briefer Course* (Holt, 1892), p. 280.

Paul Fraisse, *The Psychology of Time*, trans. Jennifer Leith (Harper, 1963), pp. 84f.

199   Carl Rogers, "Toward a Theory of Creativity." (From a typescript of an address by Dr. Rogers.)

4-3

201 Carl R. Rogers and Barry Stevens, *Person to Person: The Problem of Being Human* (Real People Press, 1967), p. 47.
202 Paul: see Romans 7:15–24.
206f. Bruno Bettelheim, "Joey: A 'Mechanical Boy,'" in *Frontiers of Psychological Research* (Freeman), pp. 223–229. Reprinted from *Scientific American*. Original article dated March 1959.
207ff. B. F. Skinner, *Beyond Freedom and Dignity* (Knopf, 1971). For similar ideas presented in fiction form, see Skinner's *Walden Two* (Macmillan, 1948).
208-B Peter L. Berger, *Invitation to Sociology: A Humanistic Perspective* (Doubleday Anchor, 1963), p. 176.
209 Rogers and Stevens, *Person to Person*, p. 50.
211 Jean-Paul Sartre, *The Republic of Silence* (Harcourt, 1947). Quoted from William Barrett, *Irrational Man* (Doubleday Anchor, 1962), pp. 239f.
211f. Barrett, *Irrational Man*, pp. 241f.

4-4

213 From *The Madman*, by Kahlil Gibran. See 94f. above.
215-B *Time*, September 27, 1971, pp. 44f. Reprinted by permission from *Time*, The Weekly Newsmagazine; copyright Time Inc.
218-B Norman O. Brown, *Life against Death* (Vintage, 1959), pp. 6–10.
219f. Peter L. Berger and Thomas Luckmann, *The Social Construction of Reality* (Doubleday Anchor, 1967), pp. 175f. (Italics added.)
220 Erich Fromm, *The Revolution of Hope* (Bantam, 1968), pp. 43f. Reprinted by permission of Harper & Row, Publishers, Inc.
221-B *Register*, Santa Ana, California, UPI report, February 20, 1971. Reprinted by permission of United Press International.

4-5

222f. Charles J. McDermott, "Inside Story," *Saturday Review*, May 30, 1970, p. 4. From Martin Levin's "Phoenix Nest," *Saturday Review*. Reprinted by permission of Martin Levin.
226-B *Newsweek*, May 24, 1965. Copyright © Newsweek 1965, and reprinted by permission.
227f. Hayakawa, S. I. "The Use and Misuse of Language: Some Thoughts on Communication with One's Children." In R. E. Farson (Ed.), *Science and Human Affairs*. Palo Alto, California: Science and Behavior Books, 1965.
228 J. Samuel Bois, *The Art of Awareness*. From an unpublished typescript of programs broadcast on Station KPFK, Los Angeles, 1961, Chapter III, p. 5. Copyright © by J. Samuel Bois.
230f. J. B. Priestley, *Man and Time* (Dell, 1968), p. 227f. From the book *Man and Time* by J. B. Priestley © 1964 Aldus Books London. Used by permission.
230-B Leland E. Hinsie and Robert Jean Campbell, *Psychiatric Dictionary* (Oxford, 1960).
231f. From the book *Psychic Discoveries behind the Iron Curtain* by

Ostrander and Schroeder (Bantam, 1971), pp. 33ff. Copyright © 1970 by Sheila Ostrander and Lynn Schroeder. Published by Prentice-Hall, Inc., Englewood Cliffs, New Jersey. Reprinted by permission of the publisher.

5-1

235ff. Arnold J. Toynbee, *A Study of History*, 12 vols. (Oxford, 1934–1961).
239-B *Time*, December 27, 1971. Reprinted by permission from *Time*, The Weekly Newsmagazine; copyright Time Inc.
240 Granville Hicks, "Arnold Toynbee: The Boldest Historian," *Harper's*, February 1947, p. 121.
   Time, November 17, 1952, p. 32.
   Arnold J. Toynbee, *An Historian's Approach to Religion* (Oxford, 1957), p. 243.
   Time, November 17, 1952, p. 32.
241 Ibid. See also *An Historian's Approach*, pp. 243ff. Toynbee, *An Historian's Approach*, p. 249.
241-B Will Durant, *The Story of Civilization*, Vol. IV, *The Age of Faith* (Simon and Schuster, 1950), pp. 343f.
242-B Jonathan Swift, *Gulliver's Travels* (Bantam, 1962), pp. 62f.
245f. Durant, *The Story of Civilization*, Vol. IV, pp. 343f. The quotations are from Will and Ariel Durant, *The Lessons of History* (Simon and Schuster, 1968), p. 100.
245-B Percy Bysshe Shelley, "Ozymandias."
247f. Fred Hoyle, *Encounter with the Future* (Trident, 1965), Chapter II, "The Anatomy of Doom." Copyright © 1965, by Fred Hoyle. Reprinted by permission of Trident Press, a division of Simon & Schuster, Inc.
248f. Ibid., pp. 36f.
249-B "The Uganda Flag." Hans Kohn, *Nationalism: Its Meaning and History* (Van Nostrand Anvil, 1955), p. 183.
250f. Stewart Robb, *Prophecies on World Events by Nostradamus* (Liveright, 1961), pp. 135–141.

5-2

255 Martin Luther King, Jr. Quoted from Milton Mayer, *On Liberty: Man v. the State* (Center for the Study of Democratic Institutions, 1969), p. 5.
   Thoreau. Paul Kurtz (ed.), *American Thought before 1900* (Macmillan, 1966), p. 312.
   Martin Luther. Quoted from Joseph Fletcher, *Situation Ethics* (Westminster, 1966), p. 62.
   Lewis F. Powell, Jr. Quoted from Milton Mayer, *On Liberty*, p. 5.
256 Immanuel Kant. Ibid., p. 78.
   Thoreau. Paul Kurtz, *American Thought before 1900*, p. 312.
258-B Henry David Thoreau, "On Civil Disobedience," in Paul Kurtz, *American Thought before 1900*, p. 316.
260f. *Unam sanctam*, in Henry Bettenson (ed.), *Documents of the Christian Church* (Oxford, 1947), pp. 161ff.
261ff. Quoted from "Another Mother for Peace" (Beverly Hills, California), December 1971. Reprinted by permission of Barbara Avedon and Dorothy B. Jones, Editors.
261-B Fred Hoyle, *Encounter with the Future* (Trident, 1965), p. 11. See 247f. above.
262-B Bettenson, *Documents of the Christian Church*, pp. 157f.
263f. Socrates. Plato, *Crito*, in *The Last Days of Socrates*, trans. Hugh Tredennick (Penguin, 1959), pp. 89ff. Copyright ©

Hugh Tredennick 1954, 1959, 1969. Reprinted by permission of Penguin Books, Ltd.

265 Joseph Klausner, *Jesus of Nazareth* (Beacon, 1964), pp. 371, 376, 226, 376.

266 Plato, *The Phaedo,* in *The Great Dialogues of Plato,* trans. W. H. D. Rouse (Mentor, 1956), p. 521.

5-3

267 Ruth Benedict, *Patterns of Culture* (Mentor, 1948), p. 2.

272 Paul Horton and Chester Hunt, *Sociology* (McGraw-Hill, 1964), p. 88.

273f. Paul Kurtz (ed.), *American Thought before 1900* (Macmillan, 1966), pp. 15f.

277 Thoreau. Peyton E. Richter (ed.), *Utopias: Social Ideals and Communal Experiments* (Holbrook, 1971), p. 65.

277-B Carlos Castaneda, *The Teachings of Don Juan: A Yaqui Way of Knowledge* (Ballantine, 1969). Originally published by the University of California Press; reprinted by permission of The Regents of the University of California.

5-4

285 From *A Concise Introduction to Philosophy* by William Halverson, pp. 254ff. See xviii above.

286 Charles Osgood, "Profile," CBS News, broadcast on the CBS Radio Network, June 8, 1972. Reprinted by permission.

286f. Shelley Berman's *Cleans & Dirtys* (Price/Stern/Sloan, 1966), pp. 43f. Copyright © 1966 by Shelley Berman. Reprinted by permission of the publishers.

5-5

288 Kahlil Gibran, *The Madman* (Knopf, 1918), p. 31 ("The New Pleasure"). Reprinted by permission of Alfred A. Knopf, Inc.

289 Bonhoeffer. Quoted from Joseph Fletcher, *Situation Ethics* (Westminster, 1966), p. 33. Also note Bonhoeffer's *Letters and Papers from Prison* (Macmillan, 1953).

Kahane. Quoted in *Playboy,* October 1972, p. 69.

289f. Alan Watts, *Psychotherapy East and West* (Mentor, 1961), p. 52.

290 This account (§8) is paraphrased from Fletcher, *Situation Ethics,* p. 17.

Ibid., p. 136.

293-B *Science News,* April 8, 1972, p. 228. Used by permission of *Science News.*

294f. For a readable account of the "Categorical Imperative," see Lewis White Beck's translation of Kant's *Critique of Practical Reason* (Bobbs-Merrill Library of Liberal Arts, 1956). For a modern formulation of ethical formalism, see Walter G. Muelder, *Moral Law in Christian Social Ethics* (John Knox, 1966).

296ff. For discussions of contextualism, see Joseph Fletcher's books *Situation Ethics* (Westminster, 1966) and *Moral Responsibility* (Westminster, 1967); and for a critical debate of contextualism and formalism, see Harvey Cox (ed.), *The Situation Ethics Debate* (Westminster, 1968).

298f. "High Chaparral," NBC–TV. David Dortort, Executive Producer, in association with the National Broadcasting Company, Inc.

300ff. Albert Schweitzer, *The Teaching of Reverence for Life* (Holt, 1965).

6-1

305 Philip Handler (ed.), *Biology and the Future of Man* (Oxford, 1970), p. 165. Reprinted by permission of Oxford University Press, Inc.

307-B Irene Kiefer, "Proving we are the stuff of which stars are made." *The Smithsonian* Magazine, May 1972, pp. 50f. Copyright © 1972 The Smithsonian Institution. Reprinted by permission of *The Smithsonian.*

313 John Keosian, *The Origin of Life* (Reinhold, 1964), p. 47.

314-B Byline: Marvin Miles, Times Aerospace Writer. *Los Angeles Times,* April 30, 1972. Copyright, 1972, Los Angeles Times.

315-B Keosian, *The Origin of Life,* pp. 7f.

6-2

323 Philip Handler (ed.), *Biology and the Future of Man* (Oxford, 1970), p. 504. Reprinted by permission of Oxford University Press, Inc.

324-B Roland Fischer, "Biological Time," in J. T. Fraser (ed.), *Voices of Time* (George Braziller, 1966), pp. 375f. Copyright © 1966 by J. T. Fraser. Reprinted by permission of George Braziller, Inc.

325f. Tennessee Williams, *Suddenly Last Summer* (New Directions, 1958), pp. 18–21. Copyright © by Tennessee Williams. Reprinted by permission of New Directions Publishing Corporation.

326ff. René Dubos, *The Torch of Life* (Pocket Books, 1962), pp. 68f. Copyright © 1962, by Pocket Books, Inc. Reprinted by permission of Trident Press, a division of Simon & Schuster, Inc.

327-B *Science News,* November 6, 1971, p. 313. Reprinted by permission of *Science News.*

329-B *Science News,* April 8, 1972, p. 228. Reprinted by permission of *Science News* and the correspondent.

331f. Sir Julian Huxley, *Evolution in Action* (Mentor, 1957), p. 13. Reprinted by permission of Harper & Row, Publishers, Inc.

331-B Desmond Morris, *The Naked Ape* (McGraw-Hill, 1967), p. 240.

332 Dubos, *The Torch of Life,* pp. 50f. See 326ff. above.

333 Harry Overstreet, *The Enduring Quest* (Norton, 1931), pp. 234f.

333-B Handler, *Biology and the Future of Man,* pp. 488f.

334 Fred Hoyle, *The Nature of the Universe* (Signet, 1955), p. 123. Reprinted by permission of Harper & Row, Publishers, Inc.

6-3

335ff. Sir James G. Frazer, *Folklore of the Old Testament* (Macmillan, 1923), pp. 3ff. Reprinted by permission of Trinity College, Cambridge.

337-B Desmond Morris, *The Naked Ape* (McGraw-Hill, 1967), p. 48.

339   From "Monkeys, Apes and Man," a National Geographic Program, CBS-TV, telecast October 12, 1971. (Italics added.) Printed by permission of The National Geographic Society.

341   Konrad Lorenz, *On Aggression* (Bantam, 1967), pp. 233, 230. Reprinted by permission of Harcourt Brace Jovanovich, Inc.

341f.   Ashley Montagu, *On Being Human* (Hawthorn, 1966), pp. 101, 97, 96.

343-B   Philip Handler (ed.), *Biology and the Future of Man* (Oxford, 1970), p. 928.

344   Sir Julian Huxley, *Evolution in Action* (Mentor, 1953), p. 9 Reprinted by permission of Harper & Row, Publishers, Inc.

347   Handler, *Biology and the Future of Man,* p. 492. Reprinted by permission of Oxford University Press, Inc. (Final italics added.)

6-4

348   From *Out of My Life and Thought* by Albert Schweitzer. Translated by C. P. Campion. Copyright 1933, 1949, © 1961 by Holt, Rinehart and Winston, Inc. Reprinted by permission of Holt, Rinehart and Winston, Inc.

348-Q   *Poems from the Greek Anthology,* translated by Dudley Fitts, p. 114. Copyright 1938, 1941 by New Directions Publishing Corporation. Reprinted by permission of New Directions Publishing Corporation.

350-B   Dorothy Lee, *Freedom and Culture* (Prentice-Hall, 1959), pp. 163f.

355   Albert Schweitzer, "The Ethics of Reverence for Life," *Christendom,* Vol. 1, No. 2 (Winter 1936). Quoted from Charles R. Joy (ed.), *Albert Schweitzer: An Anthology* (Harper, 1947), p. 270.
       Pavel Simonov, "Dostoevsky as a Social Scientist," *Psychology Today,* December 1971, p. 104.

356f.   From *The Naked Ape* by Desmond Morris, pp. 237f. Copyright © 1967 McGraw-Hill. Used with permission of McGraw-Hill Book Company.

358   Philip Handler (ed.), *Biology and the Future of Man* (Oxford, 1970), p. 491. Reprinted by permission of Oxford University Press, Inc.

359   "The Ecological Psyche," *Esalen Programs* (Winter 1971), p. 7.

7-1

363f.   Account of the baseball game taken from *The Memoirs of Professor R. Kulashto* (Ganymede, 2068), pp. 291ff.

365-B   Gilbert Newton Lewis, *Valence and the Structure of Atoms and Molecules* (Dover, 1966), p. 18.
       Dewey B. Larson, *The Structure of the Physical Universe* (North Pacific Publishers, 1959), p. 1.

367   Bertrand Russell, *A History of Western Philosophy* (Allen & Unwin, 1946), p. 48.

368   Ibid., pp. 55f.

370   Bertrand Russell, *Mysticism and Logic* (Doubleday Anchor, 1957), p. 71.

7-2

372f.   Sir Arthur Eddington. Quoted from Harry Overstreet, *The Enduring Quest* (Norton, 1931), pp. 27ff.

373f.   David S. Saxon and William B. Fretter, *Physics for the Liberal Arts Student* (Holt, 1971), pp. 13–15. Reprinted by permission of Holt, Rinehart and Winston, Inc.

374   Walter Scott Houston, *Frontiers of Nuclear Physics* (Wesleyan University Press, 1964), pp. 4f.

375f.   Werner Heisenberg, "From Plato to Max Planck," *The Atlantic Monthly,* November 1959, p. 113. Copyright © 1959, by The Atlantic Monthly Company, Boston, Mass. Reprinted by permission of the publisher and Dr. Heisenberg.

376-B   Bertrand Russell, *Mysticism and Logic* (Doubleday Anchor, 1957), pp. 79f.

377   Norwood Russell Hanson, "The Dematerialization of Matter." Quoted from Paul R. Durbin, O.P., *Philosophy of Science: An Introduction* (McGraw-Hill, 1968), p. 103.

381ff.   Fred Hoyle, *Frontiers of Astronomy* (Mentor, 1957), p. 303.

384   Victor Weisskopf, "Elementary Particles," in Samuel Rapport and Helen Wright (eds.), *Physics* (Washington Square, 1965), p. 215n.

7-3

386   Cornelius Lanczos, "Einstein and the Role of Theory in Contemporary Physics," *American Scientist, 1959.* Quoted from Joseph Royce, *The Encapsulated Man* (Van Nostrand, 1964), p. 64.

388-B   Martin Gardner, *Relativity for the Million* (Pocket Books, 1965), pp. 43ff. Reprinted with permission of Macmillan Publishing Co., Inc. © Martin Gardner 1962.

390ff.   David S. Saxon and William B. Fretter, *Physics for the Liberal Arts Student* (Holt, 1971), pp. 164f. (See p. 164n.)

392-B   "The Violent Universe," Public Broadcasting System-TV, April 1969. Produced for British Broadcasting Corporation by Philip Daly and written by Nigel Calder.

394f.   Gracia Fay Ellwood, *Psychic Visits to the Past* (Signet, 1971). Quotation from back cover.

7-4

403-B   *Science News,* March 11, 1972, p. 167. Reprinted by permission of *Science News.* Photo courtesy of NASA.

404   Fred Hoyle, *Frontiers of Astronomy* (Mentor, 1957). See especially Chapters 19 and 20. On asking how matter might originate, see p. 302. For Hoyle's own counterargument, see *The Nature of the Universe* (Signet, 1955), p. 120.

411-B   Martin Gardner, *Relativity for the Million* (Pocket Books, 1965), p. 178. See 388-B above.

7-5

412   Sir Arthur Eddington, *New Pathways in Science* (University of Michigan Press, 1959), p. 309.

412f.   Harlow Shapley, *Of Stars and Men* (Washington Square, 1960), pp. 133f., 67. Copyright © 1958 by Harlow Shapley. Reprinted by permission of Beacon Press.

413   Philip Handler (ed.), *Biology and the Future of Man* (Oxford, 1970), p. 196.

414ff.   Many of the speculations in Sections 4 and 5 are to be credited to Ray Bradbury in his article "The Search for Extraterrestrial Life," in *Life* Magazine, October 24, 1960. Page 416, quotation is from Bradbury.

415-B *Time,* December 13, 1971. Reprinted by permission from *Time,* The Weekly Newsmagazine; copyright Time Inc.

416-Q *Poems from the Greek Anthology,* translated by Dudley Fitts, p. 130. See 348-Q above.

419 Professor of the University of Padua. Quoted from W. T. Jones, *A History of Western Philosophy* (Harcourt, 1952), p. 622.

8-1

431-B Frederick C. Grant (ed.), *Ancient Roman Religion* (Bobbs-Merrill Library of Liberal Arts, 1957), p. 159.

433f. Viktor Frankl, *Man's Search for Meaning* (Washington Square, 1963), pp. 189f. Copyright © 1959, 1962 by Viktor E. Frankl. Reprinted by permission of Beacon Press.

436f. Swami Abhedananda (comp.), *The Sayings of Ramakrishna* (Vedanta Society, 1903), p. 54. Quoted from John B. Noss, *Man's Religions* (Macmillan, 4th ed., 1969), pp. 226f.

437 G. F. Moore, *The History of Religions* (Scribner's, 1919), Vol. II, p. 450.

437-B Arnold J. Toynbee, *An Historian's Approach to Religion* (Oxford, 1957), pp. 138f.

8-2

438f. Quoted from Bertrand Russell, *Mysticism and Logic* (Doubleday Anchor, 1957), pp. 44f.

441ff. Rudolf Bultmann, "New Testament and Mythology," in Hans Werner Bartsch (ed.), *Kerygma and Myth* (Harper Torchbook, 1961), pp. 1f. Reprinted by permission of Harper & Row, Publishers, Inc.

448f. From *The Small Sects in America* by Elmer T. Clark. Copyright 1949 by Pierce and Smith.

8-3

451-B Barbara Jurgensen, *The Lord Is My Shepherd, But . . .* (Zondervan, 1969), p. 20. Copyright © 1969, by Zondervan Publishing House and is used by permission.

455f. This wording of Anselm's "Ontological Argument" follows closely the text of Philip Schaff, *History of the Christian Church,* Vol. V, *The Middle Ages* (Eerdmans, 1949 [1907]), p.

456-B "The Ontological Argument." Reprinted by permission of the author, James L. Catanzaro, Ph.D., California State University, Fullerton.

458 Lecomte du Noüy, *Human Destiny* (Longmans, Green, 1947), p. 87.

458f. From *The Portable Nietzsche,* translated by Walter Kaufman. Copyright 1954 by The Viking Press, Inc. Reprinted by permission of The Viking Press, Inc.

459 William Hamilton, "The Death of God," *Playboy,* August 1966, p. 79f. Originally appeared in *Playboy* Magazine; copyright © 1966 by Playboy. Reprinted by permission of *Playboy* and the Reverend William Hamilton.

461-B Ibid., p. 84. Reprinted by permission. See p. 459 above.

462f. *Time,* December 26, 1969, pp. 40, 43. Reprinted by permission from *Time,* The Weekly Newsmagazine; copyright Time Inc.

463 Carl G. Jung, *Psychology and Religion* (Yale University Press, 1938), pp. 113f.

463-B Ernest Hemingway, *For Whom the Bell Tolls* (Scribner's, 1940), p. 41.

8-4

464f. Ray Bradbury, "The Kilimanjaro Device," from *I Sing the Body Electric!* (Bantam, 1971), pp. 3ff. Reprinted by permission of Harold W. Matson Co., Inc., New York, and the author.

466 Edwin S. Schneidman, "The Enemy," *Psychology Today,* August 1970, pp. 37ff.

468-B *Poems from the Greek Anthology,* translated by Dudley Fitts, pp. 126, 116, 106, 108, 107. See 348-Q above.

474-B Rikihei Inoguchi and Tadashi Nakajima with Roger Pineau, *The Divine Wind* (Bantam, 1960), pp. 178f. Reprinted by permission of Roger Pineau and the United States Naval Institute.

476-B Ray Bradbury in a letter to the author, April 22, 1972.

478-B "Miner's Request: Find Proof of Man's Soul," UPI report.

8-5

480 Kahlil Gibran, *The Madman* (Knopf, 1918), p. 64.
Friedrich Nietzsche. Quoted from Erich Heller, "The Modern German Mind: The Legacy of Nietzsche," in Thomas J. J. Altizer (ed.), *Toward a New Christianity: Readings in the Death of God Theology* (Harcourt, 1967), p. 103.

481f. Robert Heinlein, *The Glory Road* (Berkley Medallion, 1970), pp. 34ff. Reprinted by permission of G. P. Putnam's Sons. Copyright © 1963 by Robert Heinlein.

483 Viktor Frankl, *Man's Search for Meaning* (Washington Square, 1963), pp. 122ff.

483-B J. B. Priestley, *Man and Time* (Dell, 1968), p. 323.

483f. Jean-Paul Sartre, *La Nausée* (Gallimard, 1938), pp. 162f. The English translation used here is by Kurt F. Reinhardt in his *Existentialist Revolt* (Frederick Ungar, 1952), p. 157.

484 Bertrand Russell, *Mysticism and Logic* (Doubleday Anchor, 1957), pp. 45f.

484f. Colin Wilson, *Introduction to the New Existentialism* (Houghton Mifflin, 1966), pp. 151, 154.

486 William Halverson, *A Concise Introduction to Philosophy* (Random House, 1967), pp. 215f.

486ff. Langdon Jones, "The Eye of the Lens," in Michael Moorcock (ed.), *The Best SF Stories from New Worlds, No. 6* (Berkley Medallion, 1971), pp. 69f. Reprinted by permission.

488-B These extracts from William Thompson and Saint-Exupéry are quoted from W. Lambert Gardiner, *Psychology: The Story of a Search* (Brooks/Cole, 1970), p. 189, and the flash of genius which juxtaposed these two quotations must be credited to Professor Gardiner.

490 Ludwig Wittgenstein, *Tractatus Logico-Philosophicus* (Routledge & Kegan Paul, 1960), 6.5, 6.51, 6.52, 6.521.
From the motion picture, *The 7 Faces of Dr. Lao* (1964).

II. ILLUSTRATIONS

2-3

2-4

2-5

3-1

3-2

3-3

3-4

3-5

4-1

175   Gianlorenzo Bernini, *The Ecstasy of St. Theresa* (1645–52). Cornaro Chapel, Church of Sta. Maria della Vittoria. Bernini's sculpture depicts the moment of sublime consciousness for one of the Western world's renowned mystics, St. Theresa of Avila (1515–1582). At this moment, as she describes it, an angel pierced her heart with a flaming, golden arrow: "The pain was so great that I screamed aloud; but at the same time I felt such infinite sweetness that I wished the pain to last forever. It was not physical but psychic pain, although it affected the body as well to some degree. It was the sweetest caressing of the soul by God."

176   Aldous Huxley (1894–1963).

176ff.   Electroencephalograms showing alpha waves (pp. 176f.) and theta waves (pp. 178f.). Printouts courtesy Jay W. Klug, Department of Experiential Physiology, Veterans' Administration Hospital, Sepulveda, California.

177   Last letter of the Tibetan alphabet symbolizes the ideal state of a fully awakened consciousness.

180   Statue of Amida Buddha, Kamakura, Japan. This giant bronze, nearly fifty feet high, was cast in A.D. 1252.

4-2

188   Salvador Dali, *The Persistence of Memory* (1931). Collection, The Museum of Modern Art, New York. Reproduced by permission.

191   Sir Isaac Newton (1642–1727).

193   Pieter Brueghel, *The Triumph of Time*. Brueghel has managed to squeeze into a single picture a bewildering array of our notions, myths, and symbols about time. Father Time, depicted as Chronos devouring his own child, rides a chariot which never ceases to move. The chariot carrying the Tree of Life is drawn along by the sun and moon, the two heavenly bodies by which men measure time. The chariot wheels are mandalas. The new growth of spring brightens the background at right; the death of summer and autumn leave a pall over the landscape (at left) as Time passes by. All the precious works of man are crushed under the chariot wheels. Close behind Father Time rides Death, followed in turn by a cherub trumpeting the beginning of the Last Judgment. Photograph courtesy The Metropolitan Museum of Art, Harris Brisbane Dick Fund, 1939.

198f.   Monument Valley. *Arizona Highways,* June 1972, pp. 18f. Reproduced courtesy of the photographer, Dick Dietrich.

4-3

202   St. Paul. Greek stamp commemorating Paul's visit to Athens c. A.D. 50 (Acts 17:16–34).

203   St. Thomas Aquinas (1225–1274).

207   B. F. Skinner. Photo courtesy Dr. Skinner.

209   Carl R. Rogers. Photo courtesy Dr. Rogers.

210   Jean-Paul Sartre.

4-4

214   Paul Klee, *Senecio,* 1922. Kunstmuseum, Basel.

217   From *Cave Drawings for the Future.* Copyright © by Abner Dean - 1954. Reproduced by permission of the artist.

220f.   Four paintings by Louis Wain showing a gradual withdrawal from reality into psychosis. Wain became famed in England for his gentle and beautiful (and realistic) portrayal of cats. At the age of 57 strong signs of paranoid schizophrenia appeared in his behavior and his art; his last fifteen years were spent in mental institutions. These paintings dramatically depict one person's withdrawal from reality and escape into fantasy. © Guttman Maclay Collection, Institute of Psychiatry, London.

4-5

228   S. I. Hayakawa, by Barry McDowell. Reproduced courtesy Dr. Hayakawa and the International Society of General Semantics.

5-1

235   Acropolis in Athens, the Parthenon in the center.

236   The Egyptian pharaoh Amenhotep III and Queen Tiye. Colossi from the royal funerary temple west of Thebes. Cairo Museum.

240   Arnold J. Toynbee. Photo courtesy Oxford University Press.

244   Japanese Evacuation Order. Photo from the California State Library, Broadside Collection. Courtesy of David N. Hartman, Santa Ana College.

246   Pablo Picasso, *Guernica* (1937). Collection, The Museum of Modern Art, New York (on indefinite loan from the Artist). Reproduced by permission.

248   From *And on the Eighth Day.* Copyright © by Abner Dean - 1949. Reproduced by permission of the artist.

249   Redrawn from Fred Hoyle, *Encounter with the Future* (Trident, 1965), p. 32. Redrawn by permission of Simon and Schuster, Inc.

250   Redrawn from Philip Handler (ed.), *Biology and the Future of Man* (Oxford, 1970), p. 855. Source: "Resources in America's Future," Landsborg, Fishman & Fisher. Resources for the Future, Inc., Washington, D.C., 1963.

251   Redrawn from Handler, *Biology and the Future of Man,* p. 898. Source: *World Population: A Challenge to the United Nations and Its System of Agencies,* UNA-USA National Policy Panel on World Population, May 1969.

5-2

256   Immanuel Kant (1724–1804).
Silver denarius of the Roman Emperor Tiberius (A.D. 14–37). This is the type of the tribute coin shown to Jesus.

257   Henry David Thoreau (1817–1862). Concord Free Public Library.

263   Socrates (469–399 B.C.). Fourth century B.C. carving.

5-3

268   From *What Am I Doing Here?* Copyright by Abner Dean - 1947. Reproduced by permission of the artist.

270   Photo by Bob Fitch. Reproduced by permission of the Black Star Publishing Co.

273   From the book *What's Funny about That?* Compiled by the Editors of *This Week* Magazine. Copyright © 1954 by E. P. Dutton & Co., Inc., and used with their permission.

274   *Saturday Review,* March 25, 1961, p. 15. Reproduced by permission of *Saturday Review.*

276   Paul Reps, *Zen Telegrams* (Charles E. Tuttle, 1959), p. 38. Reproduced by permission of Charles E. Tuttle, Tokyo.

5-4

279   Marcel Duchamp, *Nude Descending a Staircase, No. 2* (1912). Collection, The Philadelphia Museum of Art (The Louise and Walter Arensberg Collection). Reproduced by permission.

282   Henry Moore, *Two Forms* (1934). Collection, The Museum of Modern Art, New York (gift of Sir Michael Sadler). Reproduced by permission.

284   Television transmission of man's first visit to another planet: Neil Armstrong stepping onto the lunar surface, July 20, 1969.

287   Antonio Canova, *Perseus with the Head of Medusa.* Vatican Museum.

5-5

295   Immanuel Kant (1724–1804).

301   Photo by Astronaut Thomas K. Mattingly II on April 16, 1972, shortly after *Apollo XVI* headed for the moon. Photo courtesy of NASA.

302   Albert Schweitzer (1875–1965), with Lambaréné Hospital in background.

6-1

311   Drs. Alexander Oparin and Cyril Ponnamperuma, pioneers in the field of chemical evolution. Photo taken by Mrs. Oparin. Reproduced courtesy Dr. Ponnamperuma.

313   Dr. Stanley Miller and the spark–discharge apparatus in which the first amino acids were synthesized in 1953. Photographs courtesy of Dr. Miller.

316f.   Microspheres produced from proteinoid (i.e., synthesized molecules closely resembling natural proteins) after treatment with hot water; these cell-like globules, capable of osmosis and permeability, separated out in the cooling process. From the experiments of S. W. Fox, Institute for Space Bioscience, Florida State University.

6-2

319   Charles Darwin (1809–1882). Etching reproduced courtesy of the New York Public Library, Picture Collection.

320   Trilobites—marine fossil invertebrates—from the Precambrian era, more than 500 million years old. Courtesy of the Smithsonian Institution.

321   Neanderthal skull, named Shanidar I. Excavated by anthropologist Ralph Solecki in a large cave near the village of Shanidar in the high mountains of northern Iraq. This ancestor of modern man, belonging to the species *Homo neanderthalensis,* called "Nandy" by his excavators, was killed some 48,000 years ago by a rock fall. Dr. Solecki's discoveries in this cave have forced a revision of our picture of Neanderthal man. Rather than the dumb brute traditionally pictured, Neanderthals may have been far more sensitive and skilled than previously imagined. One adult man, Shanidar IV, who died about 60,000 years ago, was laid to rest in a tomb in this cave with flowers gathered from the hillsides nearby. Photo courtesy Dr. Solecki.

325   Adaptation and survival: Is this the basic mechanism of evolution? On each tree in these photographs is a peppered moth and a dark moth. On the dark tree trunk, the light-colored moth would be easy prey, but on the lichen-covered trunk, it has become invisible. Photographs from the experiments of Dr. H. B. D. Kettlewell.

328   An Alaskan brown bear with his freshly caught meal, a twenty-eight-inch salmon—"the deadly feast of life." Photograph by Leonard Lee Rue III. Reproduced courtesy of the National Audubon Society.

330   Friedrich Nietzsche (1844–1900). Photo by Hans Olde.

331   Henri Bergson (1859–1941).

6-3

340   Cover of *The Naked Ape,* by Desmond Morris (Dell, 1969). Illustration by BAMA. Reproduced by permission of Dell Publishing Co., Inc.

342   From *What Am I Doing Here?* Copyright by Abner Dean - 1947. Reproduced by permission of the artist.

344   A normal set of human chromosomes (46), in this case for a human female, enlarged 15,000 times. Photo Michael A. Bender. Reproduced from Philip Handler (ed.), *Biology and the Future of Man* (Oxford, 1970), p. 135.

345   A thirty-nine-day-old human embryo surrounded by protective membranes. Reproduced from Handler, *Biology and the Future of Man,* p. 223. Reproduced courtesy the Carnegie Institute of Washington.

346   Paul Reps, *Zen Telegrams* (Charles E. Tuttle, 1959), p. 39. Reproduced by permission of Charles E. Tuttle, Tokyo.

6-4

349   Paul Reps, *Zen Telegrams* (Charles E. Tuttle, 1959), p. 97. Reproduced by permission of Charles E. Tuttle, Tokyo.

350   Reproduced by permission of Portal Publications Ltd., Sausalito, California.

354   Dr. Harry Harlow and rhesus monkey. Reproduced courtesy of Dr. Harlow and the University of Wisconsin Primate Laboratory.

356   Drawing by Charles W. Schwartz. From *A Sand County Almanac,* by Aldo Leopold. Copyright © 1949 by Oxford University Press, Inc. Reproduced by permission.

357   Reprinted from *Audubon,* the Magazine of the National Audubon Society, November 1970, p. 133. Copyright © 1970. Reprinted by permission.

7-1

363 Thales (c. 625–545 B.C.).

363ff. Snowflakes: a delicate tracery providing spectacular proof that mathematics is indeed "the language of nature." These are actual photomicrographs taken with the utmost care and in bitter cold, in the latter part of the nineteenth century, by W. A. Bentley, called "the snowflake man." For a fascinating account of how he performed this work of science, see *Audubon* Magazine, January 1971. Photographs reproduced courtesy Mr. John Buechler and the University of Vermont Library, Burlington, Vermont.

367 Pythagoras (c. 580–c. 500 B.C.). Bust from the Capitoline Museum, Rome.

Greek stamp depicting the Pythagorean Theorem: The sum of the squares of the sides of a right triangle is equal to the square of the hypotenuse. *But WHY?*

369 Particle streaks. One of the first photographs taken in the thirty-inch bubble chamber at the National Accelerator Laboratory, Batavia, Illinois, June 15, 1972. A proton with an energy of 200 billion electronvolts (GeV) enters the chamber and is propelled through liquid hydrogen. The result is this spectacular collision releasing a variety of nuclear particles. Some of the swirls are spinning electrons and other light particles. Photo courtesy of NAL.

371 Henri Bergson (1859–1941).

7-2

375 Particle streaks resulting from a proton-proton collision at 200 GeV in the thirty-inch bubble chamber at the National Accelerator Laboratory; June, 1972, Photo courtesy of NAL.

376 Zeno of Elea (fl. c. 450 B.C.).

379 The Periodic Table of Elements: a relatively simple arrangement with incredibly far-reaching implications; it shows the simplicity and orderliness of atomic arrangements. Everything in the universe is composed of these few basic elements.

Tortoise (still ahead of Achilles). Drawing by Shannon Christian.

383 Particle streaks resulting from a proton-proton collision at 300 GeV; August 1972. Photo courtesy of NAL.

7-3

387 Albert Einstein (1879–1955). Woodcut by Hal McIntosh. *Saturday Review,* January 16, 1963. Reproduced by permission of *Saturday Review.*

389 A galaxy in the constellation Centaurus (NGC 5128), a source of intense radio noise and—perhaps—the actual collision of two galaxies. Reproduced courtesy the Hale Observatories.

391 Light-clocks redrawn from David S. Saxon and William B. Fretter, *Physics for the Liberal Arts Student* (Holt, 1971), p. 165. Redrawn by permission of Holt, Rinehart and Winston, Inc.

392 The original spectrogram referred to in the dialogue from "The Violent Universe" which Maarten Schmidt puzzled over in 1963. "Spectrum of the quasar 3C 273. The lower spectrum consists of hydrogen and helium lines and serves to establish the scale of wavelengths. The upper part is the spectrum of the quasar, a star-like object of magnitude 13. The Balmer lines Hβ, Hγ and Hδ in the quasar spectrum are at longer wavelengths than in the comparison spectrum. The redshift of 16 per cent corresponds to a distance of two billion light years in the expanding universe." Photo and description courtesy of Dr. Schmidt.

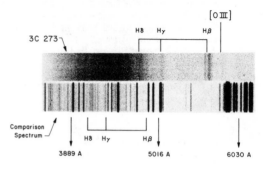

393 Representational painting by Helmut Wimmer of the theory of a black hole. Current models suggest that a star of 3 + solar masses would, after consuming its fuel, contract and collapse into infinity, the matter vanishing from the universe "down" a black hole in space, then subsequently emerging as a "white hole" (represented in the painting as a red-hot energy ball at lower right). Present speculation is that quasars might be white holes. Painting reproduced courtesy of the artist.

7-4

398 Hebrew cosmos. Noteworthy in this cosmology is *sheol,* a dank cavern beneath the surface of the flat earth where the ghost-shades of the dead will spend eternity in sleep. While this indicates the concept of an afterlife, sheol is not at this stage of Hebrew thought a place of punishment; but in later Judaic cosmology, under Zoroastrian influences, sheol was transmuted into the familiar hell of burning fires. Redrawn from S. H. Hooke, *In the Beginning,* Vol. VI of *The Clarendon Bible* (Oxford, 1947), p. 20.

Egyptian cosmos, showing the goddess Nut, her body dotted with stars, bending in a giant arch over the earth, represented by a reclining figure wearing a skin of leaves. The sun moves across the sky above the goddess in a heavenly barge. From O. Lodge, *Pioneers of Science* (Dover, 1960).

399 This woodcut dramatically depicts man's restless curiosity to know what "the heavens" are really like. Here a man has traveled to the edge of the universe and poked his head through the firmament; he beholds the machinery that moves the heavenly bodies. From John C. Brandt and Stephen P. Maran, *New Horizons in Astronomy* (Freeman, 1972), p. 82.

400 A medieval diagram of the geocentric (Ptolemaic) universe. With earth at the center, the other members of the solar system move in concentric orbits. Diagram from Peter Appian's *Cosmographia* (1539).

401 The heliocentric (Copernican) cosmos as drawn by Thomas Digges in 1576. In the center of the system is "the sonne," and the other heavenly bodies—though, strangely, not the

stars—revolve in circular orbits around the sun. Notice, however, that the moon revolves around the earth. From John C. Brandt and Stephen P. Maran, *New Horizons in Astronomy* (Freeman, 1972), p. 85.

403 Launch of *Pioneer X* aboard an *Atlas-Centaur* rocket. Photo courtesy of NASA.

404 Professor Fred Hoyle. Drawing by R. Tollast. Courtesy of Mrs. Barbara Hoyle.

405 The Whirlpool galaxy (NGC 5194) in the constellation Canes Venatici, with a smaller satellite galaxy attached to the end of one of the larger galaxy's two arms. Photo courtesy the Hale Observatories.

406 A cluster of scores of galaxies—"island universes"—in the constellation Hercules. Each of the galaxies is perhaps a hundred thousand light-years in diameter. Photo courtesy the Hale Observatories.

407 Spectroheliogram of a portion of our sun, showing the intense, large-scale activity which takes place at the outer surface of this (and all such) nuclear furnaces. Photo courtesy the Hale Observatories.

408 The Cone nebula (NGC 2264) in the constellation Monoceros, a gigantic cloud of dust and gas, photographed in red light with the 200-inch telescope on Mt. Palomar. Photo courtesy the Hale Observatories.

410 The impressive Hercules globular cluster (M13) containing some 10,000 stars. Photo courtesy the Hale Observatories.

7-5

413 Harlow Shapley (1885–1972). Photo courtesy Harvard College Observatory.

416 Ray Bradbury, author and playwright.

417 A large galaxy (NGC 4594) in the constellation Virgo, as we see it edge-on. Photo courtesy the Hale Observatories.

418 Painting by Helmut Wimmer of our own Milky Way galaxy (edge-on and top views, above and below). The circles indicate the position of our solar system, located in one of our galaxy's two spiral arms some 30,000 light-years from the galaxy's center. Our Milky Way galaxy is considered to be about average size, as galaxies run. Painting reproduced by permission of the artist.

419 Galileo Galilei (1564–1642).
Giordano Bruno (1548–1600).

420 A portion of the Rosette nebula (NGC 2237) in the constellation Monoceros. The small, dark globules in the photograph are dense masses of gas and dust which are contracting into stars; that is, *new stars* are continually being born out of such interstellar and intergalactic matter. Photo courtesy the Hale Observatories.

8-1

428 Paper currency of the Portuguese colony of Angola (Portuguese West Africa).

429 Note the variety of different, but *associated,* meanings attached to the Greek word *pneuma* and its related forms. From Liddell and Scott's *Greek-English Lexicon* (Oxford, 1889).

432 Sgt. John Cameron in Vietnam. Photo by Richard A. Swanson. *Life* Magazine, August 8, 1969, p. 53. Copyright © 1969 Time Inc. Reproduced by permission.

433 Cartoon by Clayton D. Powers, *Esquire,* December 1965, p. 213. Copyright © 1965 by Esquire, Inc. Reproduced by permission of *Esquire* Magazine.

434 The damaged service module of *Apollo XIII,* April 17, 1970. The explosion in an oxygen tank in Section 4 of the SM forced the crewmen to use the lunar lander as a lifeboat to return home to earth. Photo courtesy of NASA.

8-2

440 Detail of Michelangelo's Last Judgment from the wall of the Sistine Chapel in the Vatican.

442 Detail of painting of Adam and Eve by Lucas Cranach the Elder. Lee Collection, Courtauld Institute Galleries, London. Adam looks rather puzzled by the offer, doesn't he?

443 The incredulous horror of a lost soul, having just realized that he has been relegated to hell *for all eternity.* Detail of Michelangelo's Last Judgment in the Sistine Chapel.

444 Plato (428–348 B.C.).

445 Georg Wilhelm Friedrich Hegel (1770–1831).

446 Karl Marx (1818–1883).

447 Drawing by Ted Sallee for the Clementine Publishing Co. Diagram attempts to depict in orderly fashion the apocalyptic concepts found in the Zoroastrian-Judaic-Christian teleocosmos.

8-3

453 IGY postage stamp, detail of hands from Michelangelo's Creation of Adam, from the ceiling of the Sistine Chapel. Solar flares in the background. HANDS: Adam at left, God at right.

457 Reproduced by special permission of *Playboy* Magazine; copyright © 1968 by Playboy.

458 Cover of *Time,* April 8, 1966. Reprinted by permission from *Time,* The Weekly Newsmagazine; Copyright Time, Inc.

459 Picture "Jesus and the Children" from *Ecce Homo* by Joseph Jobé. (Harper & Row, 1962, P. 89.)

460 Statuette of the Egyptian god Osiris.

462 Cover of *Time,* December 26, 1969. Reprinted by permission from *Time,* The Weekly Newsmagazine; Copyright Time, Inc.

463 Carl G. Jung (1875–1961).

8-4

465 "The Grim Reaper" in Ingmar Bergman's motion picture *The Seventh Seal.* Copyright © 1960 by Ingmar Bergman. From *Four Screenplays by Ingmar Bergman* (Simon and Schuster, 1960). Reprinted by permission of Simon and Schuster, Inc.

467 King David weeping after having been told of the death of his son (2 Samuel 19:1). In background: Joab, the general of David's army who killed him. Painting by Guy Rowe. From *In Our Image,* by Houston Harte (Oxford, 1949). Reproduced courtesy of Houston Harte.

470 James Kidd will. Reproduced courtesy Clerk of the Superior Court, Phoenix.

471 Fresco on wall of the tomb of a nobleman, Menena, at Royal Thebes. The fresco retains its vivid colors after 3,500 years. Note that the faces and parts of the bodies of Menena and his family have been chiseled away, thus insuring that the "soul" of each would enter the next life faceless and maimed.

473 "I cannot see what lies ahead. Won't you walk with me." Photo courtesy of John Reseck.

475 Judgment scene before King Osiris. The dog-headed god Anubis is weighing the heart of the deceased—Princess Entiu-ny—against a symbol for Truth; if judged worthy, her spirit can pass on into the western paradise, the Kingdom of Osiris. The goddess Isis, sister of Osiris and compassionate interceder, stands behind the princess.

479 Funeral statuette of the Pharaoh Tutankhamon—exiting into the next life. Photograph, Griffith Institute, Ashmolean Museum, Oxford. Reproduced by permission.

8-5

481 From *What Am I Doing Here?* Copyright by Abner Dean - 1947. Reproduced by permission of the artist.

485 Paul Reps, *Zen Telegrams* (Charles E. Tuttle, 1959), p. 81. Reproduced by permission of Charles E. Tuttle, Tokyo.

487 *Earthrise.* Photo of the blue and white planet, Earth, by the first terran space travelers, December 1968. Taken by crew of *Apollo VIII* when they were 240,000 miles from home. Photo courtesy of NASA.

489 Stonehenge, showing the sunrise trilithon at center left and the moonrise trilithon at center right. Photo by Stephen Perrin.

INDEX